THE INTERNATIONAL MONETARY FUND

1972–1978

Volume II: Narrative and Analysis

THE INTERNATIONAL MONETARY FUND
1972–1978

Cooperation on Trial

VOLUME II: Narrative and Analysis

Margaret Garritsen de Vries

INTERNATIONAL MONETARY FUND
WASHINGTON, D. C.
1985

Library of Congress Cataloging in Publication Data

De Vries, Margaret Garritsen, 1922–
    The International Monetary Fund, 1972–1978.

    Includes indexes.
    Contents: v. 1–2. Narrative and analysis —
v. 3. Documents.
    1. International Monetary Fund—History. I. Title.
HG3881.5.I58D42   1985   332.1'52   85-2352
ISBN 0-939934-41-8 (v. 2)
ISBN 0-939934-43-4 (set)

The paper used in this publication meets the minimum requirements of American National Standard for Information Sciences—
Permanence of Paper for Printed Library Materials, ANSI Z39.48-
1984.   ∞™

Contents

Volume II: Narrative and Analysis

PART NINE *Analyzing the World Economy (1972–1978)*

PART TEN *Living with Floating Rates (1973–1978)*

PART ELEVEN *Resurgence of the SDR in 1978*

PART TWELVE *Continued Evolution of the Fund as an International Institution (1972–1978)*

Appendices

CONTENTS

Tables

Illustrations

▫ ▫ ▫ ▫ ▫ ▫

THE INTERNATIONAL MONETARY FUND

1972–1978

Volume II: Narrative and Analysis

PART SEVEN

Resolution of the Gold Problem (1973–1978)

"This task [collaboration among countries] inevitably requires that substantial concessions be made by all of the nations, and, I venture to say that each one will in the future respect to a larger extent than before the legitimate interests of other nations."

—PIERRE MENDÈS-FRANCE, Chairman of French Delegation, at Bretton Woods, July 20, 1944

CHAPTER
31

A Solution for Gold Agreed

*E*VEN WITH THE CREATION of the Fund and a new international
monetary system based on agreed par values, gold, long used as money,
remained at the heart of the system. The Fund's Articles of Agreement called for the
expression of par values directly or indirectly in terms of gold, for the application of
an official price to all gold transactions, and for members to pay a portion of their
subscriptions, charges, and repurchases in gold. In the international monetary
system as embodied in the Fund's Articles gold was the ultimate asset: convertible
currencies were convertible into U.S. dollars, but U.S. dollars were in turn
convertible into gold. While the Bretton Woods system involved the use of both gold
and foreign exchange, gold still received more emphasis.[1]

In the 1950s and 1960s, as noted in Chapter 5, while gold remained de jure the
base of the Fund's operations and transactions, its actual use among countries in
their financial settlements was minimal, and de facto the dollar standard emerged.
Consequently, when officials in the 1970s began planning a reformed system, they
had to decide what to do about gold. Discussions about gold in the Committee of
Twenty evoked controversy and emotion, and agreement proved exceptionally
difficult. While members of the Committee of Twenty were able to agree quickly
that, in general, the SDR rather than gold should be the ultimate reserve asset of the
reformed system, they left undecided the precise legal arrangements to be made for
gold and what to do about the large existing stocks of officially held gold. However,
not even a nonreformed international monetary system could evolve without
deciding how to phase gold out of the existing system.

Deciding what provisions about gold to include in the amendments to the
Fund's Articles of Agreement and what to do about the existing large stocks of gold

---

[1]For a brief discussion of the provisions of the original Articles of Agreement with regard to
gold and the meaning of these provisions, see *History, 1945–65*, Vol. I, pp. 39–40 and Vol. II,
pp. 174 and 559–64. For a fuller discussion see Joseph Gold, "Gold in International Monetary Law:
Change, Uncertainty, and Ambiguity," *Journal of International Law and Economics* (Washington),
Vol. 15, No. 2 (1981), pp. 323–36. For a discussion of the Fund's policies of discouraging sales of gold
at premium prices and of discouraging the payment of subsidies to gold producers in the first
20 years of the Bretton Woods system, see *History, 1945–65*, Vol. II, pp. 174–214.

held by official entities constituted "the gold problem" of the mid-1970s. The problem was resolved—at least for the next few years—by a sequence of actions taken from late 1973 to early 1976.

TERMINATION OF THE 1968 AGREEMENT
TO DEAL ONLY AT THE OFFICIAL PRICE

In November 1973, while the discussions in the Committee of Twenty were going on, the first action was taken to give the authorities of central banks of the large industrial countries some freedom to deal in gold with each other at prices other than the official price and to sell gold in nonofficial markets in which gold was traded by private dealers. In these nonofficial or private markets, prices had reached $85 an ounce, double the official price of $42.22 established after the second devaluation of the dollar formally effective in October 1973. The governors of the central banks of Belgium, the Federal Republic of Germany, Italy, the Netherlands, Switzerland, the United Kingdom, and the United States decided to terminate the agreement of March 1968, under which their central banks had applied the official price for gold only to transactions between themselves and had let nonofficial transactions take place in private markets at whatever prices might emerge.[2] In accordance with the agreement, the central banks of these countries had refrained from supplying any officially held gold to private markets.

Termination of the 1968 agreement came after European monetary authorities proposed that they no longer be obliged to hold to it. Guido Carli urged its termination at the 1973 Annual Meeting.[3] He noted that the Italian authorities had the firm support of Belgium, France, and the Netherlands in demanding the abolition of restrictions on the operations of central banks in private gold markets. They feared that prices in private gold markets might drop below the official price, a development that U.S. monetary authorities had favored for years. In that event, their official stocks of gold would decline in value. They believed that purchases by central banks could help support the price of gold in private markets. At the time, the Italian authorities especially wanted to keep up the prices for gold because, as seen in Chapter 23, Italy was experiencing balance of payments deficits and the Italian authorities were using Italy's gold reserves as collateral in borrowing abroad. The higher the valuation for Italy's gold reserves, the larger Italy's capacity to borrow.

In calling for greater freedom for central banks to deal in gold at prices other than the official price, Mr. Carli was also backing up a position long advanced by French officials. French authorities had been arguing for years for a big increase in the official price of gold. They did so partly because they wanted to return to the gold

---

[2]This agreement led to the two-tier market for gold. The circumstances precipitating it were described in *History, 1966–71,* Vol. I, pp. 403–405.

[3]Statement by the Governor of the World Bank and Alternate Governor of the Fund for Italy, *Summary Proceedings, 1973,* p. 69.

standard and partly because large stocks of gold had been accumulated both by the French Government and by private parties in France. A higher price for gold meant an upward revaluation of these gold stocks. In technical terms, the French authorities favored a uniform proportionate devaluation of all currencies in terms of gold. Consequently, the French monetary authorities had refused to help support an official price for gold. After 1967 they had not participated actively in the Gold Pool formed in 1961 for this purpose and they had not been a party to the 1968 decision.

Also speaking at the 1973 Annual Meeting, John N. Turner took a less extreme position than did Mr. Carli. He suggested that transactions in gold between monetary authorities and official purchases of gold in private markets at prices above the existing official price continue to be prohibited, but that central bank authorities be permitted to *sell* gold in private markets.[4] Such sales were valid under Article IV, Section 2 of the Articles, provided that they were not sales at a discount compared with the official price.

When the central bank governors of the large industrial countries met for their regular monthly meeting at the Bank for International Settlements (BIS) in Basle in November 1973, Jelle Zijlstra, chairman of these meetings, suggested rescinding the agreement of March 1968. To his surprise, since in the discussions of the Committee of Twenty U.S. officials had been resisting such proposals, Arthur F. Burns, Chairman of the Board of Governors of the Federal Reserve System, readily consented. On November 13, 1973, Mr. Burns notified the Managing Director to this effect. Hereafter, the central banks of Belgium, the Federal Republic of Germany, Italy, the Netherlands, Switzerland, the United Kingdom, and the United States were free to sell gold from their official reserves in private markets.

No action by the Fund was necessary. Although the Managing Director had participated in the meeting in which the original decision of 1968 had been taken, the Fund, as an institution, had not been part of the decision, which was solely that of the governors of the seven central banks participating in the Gold Pool. The central banks of Fund members (which included six of the seven countries involved, all except Switzerland) were still obliged by the Articles of Agreement not to buy gold at any price other than the official price.

The Executive Directors regarded the termination of the 1968 agreement as unimportant. With prices for gold in private markets twice as high as the official price, the desire of the authorities of central banks to be released from their commitment not to sell gold in private markets was understandable. It was unlikely, however, that the authorities of those central banks, particularly the Bank of France, that most wanted to be able to sell gold at private market prices would in practice sell much gold. Since they had large alternative reserves, central bankers did not need to sell gold held by their governments to finance balance of payments deficits. Moreover, hoping that prices for gold in private markets would go up further, they

---

[4]Statement by the Governor of the Fund and the World Bank for Canada, *Summary Proceedings, 1973*, p. 110.

wanted to retain gold to enjoy the benefits of its further appreciation. Also they feared criticism by the political opposition and others, if they were to sell official gold holdings in private markets and prices subsequently rose.

While the substance of the agreement taken in Basle in November 1973 posed no problem for the Executive Directors, the method by which the decision was taken did. Mr. Kafka, then a Vice-Chairman of the Committee of Twenty as well as an Executive Director, and some of the other Executive Directors elected by developing members all complained that the governors of the central banks of seven industrial countries, meeting in a restricted group, had taken a decision with far-reaching consequences for the international monetary system, ignoring negotiations for a reformed system in the broadly based Committee of Twenty. The thrust of this complaint was that developing countries were once again being excluded from vital decisions on international monetary topics.

Mr. Kafka elaborated in the Executive Board the feelings that officials of many developing members in the meetings of the Committee of Twenty had expressed about gold. Most developing members had been colonies when the Fund was created in 1944. Hence, their officials had little part in the decisions giving gold a central position in the Bretton Woods system. In fact, members that had then been colonies did not even hold gold. This was particularly true of the many countries in the sterling area, whose gold reserves were centralized in the Bank of England. Even in 1972, developing members, including Latin American countries that had been present at Bretton Woods, held virtually no official stocks of gold. When Latin American countries had surpluses in 1970 and 1971, they had accumulated dollars instead of gold in their reserves, a policy their monetary authorities claimed was due mainly to the insistence of U.S. authorities. Mr. Kafka elaborated other complaints. Developing members were supposed to be, at least nominally, full participants in discussions for a reformed system. It was, therefore, "blatantly wrong" for monetary officials of the large industrial countries that held most of the world's official gold to take independent decisions in this matter.

The complaint that industrial countries were making separate decisions was voiced in the Executive Board on several occasions in 1974 and 1975, particularly when gold was discussed. In originally making this complaint, authorities of developing members were undoubtedly thinking about the impact that any decision about gold might have on a decision to allocate SDRs. If gold reserves were revalued upward, international liquidity would be increased, and authorities of the industrial countries would consequently be much less inclined to favor additional allocations of SDRs, a point that officials of developing members stressed more often, as will be seen below.

DECISIONS OF THE FUND ON GOLD IN 1973

The decision of central bank governors in November 1973 to terminate their agreement of March 1968 led to an almost immediate end to the policy, initiated by the Fund at the end of 1969, of buying gold from South Africa. That policy was an outgrowth of the emergence of the two-tier gold market in 1968. Under the policy, South Africa, the largest producer by far of the Western world's newly mined gold, was permitted to sell gold to the Fund at the official price in certain quantities to finance balance of payments deficits when prices of gold in private markets were below the official price.[5] The arrangement made the official price the floor for South Africa's sales of newly mined gold. South Africa had sold gold to the Fund under this policy in 1970 and 1971, but since prices in private markets in 1972 and 1973 were well above the official price, South Africa had made no further sales to the Fund. In November 1973, Nicolaas Diederichs, South Africa's Minister of Finance, requested the Fund to end the arrangement, and the Fund agreed to do so.

In accordance with the provisions of the Articles, members usually paid 25 percent of their subscriptions and some of their repurchases in gold, but a problem arose both about the payment of subscriptions by new members and about repurchases. Developing members joining the Fund in the early 1970s held no gold. Were they to acquire it in private markets in order to pay their subscriptions to the Fund and pay prices above the official price, as French monetary authorities were intimating might be the solution, they would lose money on the transaction since the Fund valued gold at the official price.

The Bahamas demonstrated graphically in 1973 the problem for new members. The Bahamas wanted to become a member of the Fund and the World Bank on its Independence Day, July 10, 1973. After considerable discussion in the Executive Board, the Bahamas was permitted to become the first member of the Fund not required under the terms of its membership resolution to pay a portion of its subscription in gold. The membership resolution provided for a quota of SDR 20 million to be paid in Bahamian dollars, with the provision that SDR 5 million would be repurchased in gold, SDRs, or convertible currencies within 60 days after the currency subscription had been paid, but even this repurchase could be postponed. Implicitly the repurchase could be postponed until the Second Amendment took effect, permitting a member to pay its subscription in its own currency.

Even this seemingly minor decision on gold, in effect indefinitely postponing payment by the Bahamas of the gold portion of its subscription, was not reached without debate. When the issue came up in the Executive Board, although Turkey had already received permission to postpone some of its repurchases due in gold, Tom de Vries (Netherlands) objected to the concessions granted to the Bahamas. His position was that the Fund's policy on gold payments was evolving through a series of ad hoc decisions, as "shots in the dark," rather than on the basis of a general consensus on all outstanding gold problems. Mr. Viénot argued for a strict application of the Articles of Agreement. Mr. Schweitzer, Managing Director at the time, however, recalled for the Executive Board the difficulties experienced some months previously in finding members willing to sell gold to prospective members at

---

[5]The arrangement of 1969 between the Fund and South Africa was described in *History, 1966–71*, Vol. I, pp. 409–15.

the official price to cover the gold subscription stipulated in their membership resolutions. He stressed that there was nothing that Bahamian authorities could do to resolve the situation. They were innocent bystanders who held no gold of their own. As Messrs. Bryce, Bull, Harley, Monday, and Schleiminger all agreed with the management and staff's recommendation that the Bahamas be permitted to become a member without paying gold, the Executive Board approved the draft membership resolution for submission to the Board of Governors, which subsequently adopted it. Mr. de Vries and Mr. Viénot, however, dissented from the provisions of paragraph 4 on the payment of the subscription.

In addition to Turkey, beginning in 1973, Chile, Colombia, Ecuador, El Salvador, Iraq, Jordan, and the Philippines also requested and received permission to postpone repurchases payable in gold, subject to later review. For the time being these members repurchased in SDRs. Further requests for postponements of repurchases payable in gold were expected.

POSITIONS ON GOLD ENTRENCHED FOR MOST OF 1974

Although Mr. Witteveen centered most of his efforts at the beginning of 1974 on setting up an oil facility, he also moved to see if the gold problem might be resolved. Mobilization of the large gold component of the official reserves of several industrial members would give them a sizable asset with which to finance their enlarged balance of payments deficits. Also, prices for gold in private markets continued to rise. In early 1974 the price of gold was again approaching the previous record of nearly $130 an ounce, more than three times the official price. Mr. Witteveen was, therefore, also concerned that members might become increasingly hesitant to use any of the gold reserves held by their central banks. The gold component of official reserves would thus be even less available than before for international payments. In the absence of decisions about what to do with existing officially held gold stocks, Mr. Witteveen was worried, too, that the international monetary system would not evolve as it was supposed to. Gold was becoming so valuable that financial officials would soon be unwilling to hold any other asset, including the SDR, in its place, and the SDR, which under the *Outline of Reform* was eventually to overtake gold as the prime reserve asset, would be unable to compete.

For these reasons, Mr. Witteveen tried to persuade the Committee of Twenty before it finished its work in June 1974 to reach some understanding about the disposition of current gold stocks. In early 1974, he held informal talks with the finance ministers of several European members, especially with W.F. Duisenberg, Minister of Finance of the Netherlands and then Chairman of the finance ministers of the EC countries, with William E. Simon, Secretary of the U.S. Treasury, and with finance ministers of several developing members.

In these talks, Mr. Witteveen stressed the need for solutions that were fully in accord with the Fund's Articles of Agreement. Under international law, other solutions were illegal. At the time, some European monetary authorities were taking the view that since the U.S. dollar was no longer convertible into gold, U.S. authorities were already violating the Articles, and therefore European authorities need not be excessively concerned about adhering to the Fund's Articles, especially since they were soon to be amended. In fact, European authorities were arguing that their actions would not be illegal. Mr. Witteveen pointed out that the breach of the Articles by the United States would not necessarily make the actions of European members legal. He emphasized that it was unwise for them to set a precedent of violating the Fund's Articles.

As had occurred so often since 1965, officials of France held extreme positions on one side and officials of the United States on the other. French officials continued to insist on solutions that would, in one way or another, bring about higher prices for gold. They wanted freedom for monetary authorities to revalue official gold reserves at prices similar to those prevailing in private markets. They wanted monetary authorities to be free to buy and sell gold in private markets and among themselves at whatever price they could mutually agree upon. They wanted monetary authorities free to acquire more gold in their official holdings. U.S. officials, in contrast, insisted that the role of gold in the international monetary system be reduced and distrusted any step that increased the value of officially held gold or enabled central banks to acquire more gold. They believed that any such steps ran the risk of giving gold more, rather than less, importance in future international monetary relationships.

Officials of other members also held strong and conflicting views on any solution for gold. Officials of the EC countries other than France were on the whole amenable to compromise. But at a meeting of the finance ministers of the EC countries in April 1974 in Zeist, the Netherlands, they came close to the French position. They agreed that central banks ought to be free to buy and sell gold among themselves at prices close to those in the private markets and ought to be free to purchase "limited amounts" of gold in those markets at prices above the official price. Officials of developing members regarded it as "grossly unfair" if central banks that had been accumulating gold were "rewarded" by a great increase in the value of their gold stocks. They were convinced, moreover, that any new creation of reserves for financing the large oil-related balance of payments deficits ought to take the form of further allocations of SDRs rather than revalued gold reserves. They were also concerned that revaluation of gold would so augment the reserves of the industrial members that officials of these members would be loath to agree to additional allocations of SDRs. Even if officials of developing members were at long last able to obtain agreement on establishing a link between allocations of SDRs and development finance, such a link would be virtually meaningless if no further allocations of SDRs were likely to be undertaken soon.

Because of these sharp differences in view, the Committee of Twenty was unable to agree on any solution to the gold problem. Hence, when the Committee finished its work in June 1974, gold was the prime subject the Executive Directors were asked to study. Meanwhile, the Group of Ten, gathered in Washington in June 1974 for the last meeting of the Committee of Twenty, agreed that gold used as collateral for loans between the ten large industrial countries could be valued at prices higher than the official price. This understanding came about primarily to enhance the value of Italy's gold holdings by valuing them at market-related prices, since Italy was at the time using its gold reserves as collateral for a large loan from the Federal Republic of Germany. The Managing Director went along with this action of the Group of Ten, but he noted that under the Fund's Articles, if the pledged gold reserves were used to satisfy debts, they would have to be transferred at the official price.

Further Dimensions to the Gold Problem

Discussions on resolving the gold problem initiated by Mr. Witteveen within the Fund early in 1974 disclosed still another dimension to the problem. A note by the Economic Counsellor, J.J. Polak, entitled "Paper on Gold," of May 15, 1974, took up the question of how to dispose of the gold held by the Fund.[6] The Fund's holdings of gold, 150 million ounces, were about 10 percent of total official gold holdings, making the Fund the second largest official holder of gold (after the U.S. Government). One possibility for disposing of the Fund's gold was to distribute it to members in proportion to their quotas. Another, and perhaps more interesting possibility, was for the Fund to sell its gold in the market, invest the proceeds, and in one way or another give the benefit of the proceeds to developing members. The question of what should be done about the Fund's large holdings of gold was thus added to those to be answered about the gold held by central banks and about the draft amendments on gold.

When the Governors assembled in Washington in September 1974 for their Twenty-Ninth Annual Meeting, yet another question about gold was raised. The Sixth General Review of Quotas had begun, as noted in Chapter 27, and, as Mr. Simon stated, U.S. officials were eager to develop arrangements so that Fund members would not have to pay the usual 25 percent of their subscriptions in gold for quota increases under the Sixth General Review.[7] For members not to pay gold subscriptions to the Fund for the upcoming increases in quotas was, of course, consistent with the position of U.S. officials that gold should no longer be used in international transactions. Since the Articles of Agreement did not permit members to use SDRs or their own currencies in lieu of gold to fulfill their obligations to the Fund, the Articles would have to be amended first. The French and U.S. positions were again opposed. Jean-Pierre Fourcade was of the opinion that the question of payment of the gold portion of subscriptions under the larger quotas of the Sixth

---

[6]See Vol. III below, pp. 125–26.
[7]Statement by the Governor of the Fund and the World Bank for the United States, *Summary Proceedings, 1974*, pp. 88–89.

General Review should not be "the object of a piecemeal approach." Rather, all the outstanding questions about gold ought to be resolved together.[8]

The need to complete the Sixth General Review by February 1975, as required by the Articles of Agreement, gave an added urgency to the need for an agreement about gold and for amending the Articles.

Executive Board Discussions in November–December 1974

Cognizant of the urgency of settling the gold problem and trying to fulfill their mandate from the Committee of Twenty on this subject, the Executive Directors explored their various positions in an informal seminar in November 1974. They hoped to have some view to transmit to the first substantive meeting of the Interim Committee in January 1975. Because of prevailing differences of opinion, they had not considered it worthwhile to hold even an informal seminar earlier. Their discussion now had an additional dimension, since about this time U.S. officials, following up on the Fund staff's idea of selling the Fund's gold to benefit developing members, proposed a Trust Fund for this purpose.

The Executive Directors' seminar in November 1974, was followed by several formal meetings in December to consider draft amendments to the Articles of Agreement concerning gold as a prelude to the meeting of the Interim Committee in January 1975. These meetings disclosed the range of views of officials of member governments and the entrenchment of their positions. Messrs. Wahl and de Margerie continued to express the French view that gold held by official entities should be valued on the basis of prices in private markets rather than on an official price, that any official price ought to be abolished, that central banks should have unlimited freedom to deal in gold, that when the Fund's Articles of Agreement were amended, payments to the Fund in gold should not be eliminated altogether, but should be optional so that gold should have some place in the system, and that the various elements of "the gold problem" should all be decided as a package.

With regard to Mr. Simon's proposal that the Fund's gold be sold to finance a Trust Fund for the benefit of developing members, French officials advanced the counterproposal that the Fund return the gold to members in proportion to their quotas at the official price. They argued that since members had originally been obliged to "deposit" gold with the Fund at the official price, the gold held "in" the Fund—not "by" the Fund—belonged to members and not to the Fund. Therefore the Fund should not be authorized to sell this gold on the market at market-related prices. The word "restitute" came to describe the return to members of gold by the Fund at the official price, since the Articles of Agreement did not provide for the Fund to distribute or dispose of its gold in this way.

Messrs. Cross and Harley continued to express the U.S. position that all measures taken with respect to gold, including disposal of the Fund's holdings,

---

[8]Statement by the Governor of the Fund and the World Bank for France, *Summary Proceedings, 1974*, p. 96.

should reduce the use of gold among central banks and the amount of gold held by central banks. At a minimum, central banks should not acquire more gold. The Fund, moreover, should not oblige its members or the Fund to use gold for any payments between them.

Messrs. de Groote and Schneider put forward the view of the Belgian authorities that members dispose of at least some of their gold by selling it to the Fund in exchange for SDRs through a "gold substitution account." Mr. Schleiminger and Miss Fuenfgelt expressed the German view that whatever was done about gold should not translate *potential* additional liquidity into *actual* liquidity, since additional liquidity would aggravate world inflation. German officials were particularly opposed to a substitution account for gold on the grounds that since the SDR was still a much less desirable asset than gold, no officials would want to exchange gold for SDRs. Apart from these considerations, German officials expressed a readiness for some kind of compromise.

Executive Directors from other EC members held that some immediate operational problems involving gold, such as the payment of the 25 percent subscription of quota increases under the Sixth General Review, could be resolved prior to producing full-scale draft amendments on gold for the Second Amendment. Messrs. Rawlinson and Bull pointed out that the U.K. authorities were also ready to amend the Articles to abolish the official price of gold and to eliminate all payments in gold between the Fund and its members. On other issues, Messrs. Lieftinck and de Vries explained that Dutch officials, like German officials, retained more confidence in gold than in SDRs and had reservations about a gold substitution account.

Mr. Kawaguchi and Mikio Wakatsuki were worried that the international community might lose control over transactions in gold between central banks and therefore wanted some internationally agreed and coordinated rules to be established to oversee such transactions. Japanese officials were influenced by the fact that Japan held relatively little gold and did not want other central banks to acquire more official gold. They insisted that the aggregate volume of officially held gold should not be allowed to increase.

Messrs. Deif, Kafka, Kharmawan, Monday, Prasad, and Yaméogo all espoused the position of officials of developing members other than the oil producing members. Revaluation of gold would accentuate the already inequitable distribution of reserves, and if the gold-holding countries provided themselves with a reasonably ample liquidity by revaluing and using their official gold holdings at market-related prices for gold, developing members would not be able to get agreement on future allocations of SDRs. The position of officials of the oil producing members as expressed most often by Mr. Amuzegar was that a gold substitution account in the Fund could be disadvantageous because it might reinstitute an official (or exchange) price for gold and put the Fund in a position of being a broker for the major gold-holding countries. Sales of the Fund's gold for the benefit of developing members might be considered, with any profit from the disposal of the Fund's gold going exclusively to developing members.

As of November 1974, five main questions about gold remained unanswered. How free should central banks be to conduct transactions in gold among themselves or in the private market at prices other than the official price or to revalue their gold stocks? What should be done about the Fund's holdings of gold? Should the official price of gold be abolished? What provisions should govern the media of payments by members to the Fund for repurchases and charges and for payments of subscriptions on the occasion of quota increases? Should the Fund acquire gold from its members through a gold substitution account? As these questions were discussed, it was implicitly assumed within the Fund (certainly for the last four of these questions) that what was being considered were provisions to be incorporated into an amended version of the Articles of Agreement. It was not yet assumed, as would later be the case, that some action vis-à-vis gold might take place prior to amendment of the Articles.

Agreement on these questions came hard. Gold had been at the base of international finance for centuries, and financial officials were not accustomed to thinking in terms of international monetary arrangements that did not involve gold. At the same time, several members did have gold reserves and the Fund held gold, and some disposition had to be made of these holdings. In effect, arrangements now had to be devised that would simultaneously (1) ensure a gradual reduction in the role of gold in monetary reserves and in the international monetary system, the objective implicit in the Committee of Twenty's agreement that the SDR should become the principal reserve asset; (2) preserve the usefulness of gold as a reserve asset during the phase-out period; (3) avoid the danger of pushing up the price of gold held by monetary authorities; and (4) achieve equitability between countries that held gold and those that did not. Devising such arrangements was an unusually challenging task, especially since monetary authorities of different countries held sharply conflicting views.

ATTEMPTS TO RECONCILE POSITIONS, DECEMBER 1974–MAY 1975

A small but meaningful breakthrough came in December 1974, when President Ford met with President Giscard d'Estaing in Martinique. President Ford had taken office only in August 1974, and President Giscard d'Estaing, previously Minister of Finance and Economy of France, had been elected to the presidency after the death of President Pompidou in April 1974. The two Presidents seized this singular opportunity to close the economic breach between their two countries. Although the major topic was the world energy problem, the two heads of state and their finance ministers—Messrs. Simon and Fourcade—also discussed gold. They agreed that central bank authorities could, if they so wished, revalue their official holdings of gold higher than the official price. While this agreement resolved only one of the many disputed issues on gold, it signaled the beginning of the end of the impasse. U.S. officials were willing to let officials of the Bank of France show on their books much larger holdings of gold than before. For the first time in years, French officials seemed to moderate the rhetoric of Presidents de Gaulle and Pompidou that the gold standard ought to be reinstituted and that gold ought again to be the basis of international financial transactions. It was only the beginning of the end of the impasse, however, because there was still no agreement to carry out transactions in gold between central banks at prices above the official price. This bilateral economic summit was, incidentally, the start of a series of economic summit conferences.

A month after the Martinique agreement, French officials revalued their official holdings of gold at market-related prices. They planned to revalue every six months to reflect changing market prices. U.S. officials went in the opposite direction, taking steps to reduce U.S. gold holdings. In December 1974, U.S. citizens were permitted to buy, sell, and own gold without a license from the U.S. Treasury for the first time since 1933, and the U.S. Treasury announced a plan to dispose of some of its holdings of gold through a series of auctions starting in January 1975. These sales of gold in the market at premium prices were permitted under the Articles of Agreement provided that the gold was not sold to the monetary authorities of members of the Fund.

Progress at the Interim Committee Meeting in January 1975

Agreement between Presidents Ford and Giscard d'Estaing smoothed the way for further agreement when the Interim Committee met in January 1975 in Washington. All officials seemed to be trying to find a way to give central banks more freedom to engage in gold trading in private markets and trying to find solutions for draft amendments to the Articles of Agreement with regard to gold.

Mr. Simon's position illustrated the new trend toward conciliation. The world was in a deep recession. Confidence that the world's leaders could resolve difficult economic issues was shaken. Agreement among them on gold could help restore confidence and make exchange rates and prices of gold in world markets more stable. Members of the Interim Committee should agree immediately to draft amendments for the Articles of Agreement that would do away with the official price for gold and would eliminate both the obligation of members to pay gold to the Fund and the authority of the Fund to accept gold.

Mr. Simon reflected the changing views of several U.S. officials on gold trading by central banks. They were coming around to the view that central banks might be permitted to buy and sell gold in private markets, provided some limits were set to their acquisition of additional gold. While U.S. officials, wanting to limit the purchase of more gold, especially by the Bank of France, initially wanted limits on each country's individual gold holdings, they gradually accepted the Japanese position that a limit on gold held by all central banks and the Fund collectively would be sufficient. There should be some kind of internationally coordinated supervision to make sure that there were no increases in the total amount of officially held gold.

Although they thought that the Fund ought to be the agent of such supervision, U.S. officials recognized that officials of France and of other EC countries were opposed to the Fund acting as a policeman and strongly preferred that the Group of Ten implement any international arrangements to oversee gold trading. Reflecting these evolving views of the Administration of President Ford, Mr. Simon stated at the Interim Committee meeting that it should be possible for officials to agree on amendments to the Articles of Agreement in which there would be no restraints on the buying and selling of gold by governments. Moreover, it should be possible to reach agreement on some kind of supervisory arrangements for transactions in gold among the authorities of the large industrial countries. Possibly such arrangements could be supervised by the Group of Ten.

Mr. Simon stressed to the other members of the Interim Committee that while officials of the United States were ready to compromise on gold, it would be politically difficult for them to agree to amendments to the Fund's Articles of Agreement limited to gold. Congressional approval necessary for such amendments would be easier to obtain if agreement was also reached on draft amendments on exchange rates. In order to facilitate agreement on exchange rates and on his proposal for establishment of a Trust Fund, Mr. Simon was willing to discuss what some viewed as the extreme position of French officials that at least some of the gold held by the Fund be returned to members.

When it seemed possible that the positions of the United States and of France might be reconciled, officials of developing members, who had been discussing the gold problem in the Group of Twenty-Four, reiterated their stance against accepting any part of the French position. C. Subramaniam, Minister of Finance of India, for example, took issue with the argument of Mr. Fourcade that the "Fund's gold" legally belonged to its members and insisted that the gold held by the Fund had been paid to the Fund as subscriptions and definitely belonged to the Fund. In taking this stance, Mr. Subramaniam was picking up the position advanced by the Managing Director. He also stressed that any attempt to take gold away from the Fund would weaken the Fund's whole financial fabric. He and other Governors from developing members were opposed to permitting central banks to buy gold either in private markets or from other central banks. Additional acquisitions of officially held gold would surely mean a continued role for gold in the international monetary system. Officials of developing members also repeated their concern that revaluation of gold reserves would seriously affect "the creation, control, and rational distribution of international liquidity." To emphasize the point, Mr. Subramaniam calculated that if all the European countries revalued their gold holdings as French officials had done, the addition to world liquidity from Europe alone would amount to nine times the total allocation of SDRs until then.

In addition to his other anxieties about gold, Mr. Witteveen was deeply concerned that, without agreement about how central banks should handle their official holdings of gold, the monetary authorities of some European members, wanting to take advantage of the continuing rise in gold prices in private markets to add to official stocks of gold, might decide to go ahead and buy gold at prices above the official price. In his talks with European monetary authorities, Mr. Witteveen therefore repeated his view that such action was contrary to the Articles of Agreement and that central bank authorities had to respect international rules. He reiterated that it was "bad precedent" to violate agreed rules.

Without agreement on how to treat gold, it was also difficult for the staff and the Executive Board to proceed with amending the Articles. As is described in Chapter 35, the staff had begun in July 1974 to circulate to the Executive Board drafts of proposed amendments and of related explanatory memoranda, and several of these had begun to be considered by the Executive Board. Draft amendments or memoranda on gold or a gold substitution account had not been distributed, however, because of disagreements on these topics. On a number of occasions, Executive Directors had pointed out that various draft amendments on other topics, such as members' repurchase obligations, the payment to the Fund by members of subscriptions as a result of changes in quotas, the payment by members of charges on use of the Fund, and the payment by the Fund to members of remuneration, were incomplete unless the existing provisions of the Articles with regard to gold were modified. Thus, the treatment of gold in the Articles needed to be settled before other amendments could be completed.

Meanwhile, Mr. Witteveen tried to develop a solution for gold that would be best for the international community as a whole and that would not particularly favor any one member or group of members. At the Interim Committee of January 1975, he proposed that gold be taken out of the Articles of Agreement when they were amended and be removed gradually from use in international payments. To achieve the latter, the gold stocks of central banks ought to be reduced. In this way too the SDR would not only be the ultimate reserve asset in the amended Articles but would also assume an expanding role in actual transactions between central banks. Central banks should use any newly acquired freedom to deal in gold at prices other than the official price in such a way as to decrease monetary gold stocks over time. With regard to policing central banks' transactions, there would be certain advantages if central banks could supervise their own transactions in gold rather than be subject to provisions in the amended Articles under which the Fund would ensure that they abided by whatever rules were agreed among them. The Fund, however, should be kept informed about the results of trading in gold between central banks.

There were, Mr. Witteveen noted, several adverse consequences for the international community of returning gold held by the Fund to members at the official price. Because such restitution would result in profits accruing to central banks that bought gold from the Fund at the official price and then revalued it at market-related prices, the reserves of these central banks would increase, which in turn would cause international liquidity to rise. Restitution would also take away from the Fund a very important asset that the Fund could otherwise use as guarantee or collateral against any borrowing in which it might engage. The Fund needed the increase in value gained on its holdings of gold to offset the losses it suffered on gold tranche drawings that were free of charges. Also, the interests of developing members had to be adequately taken into account; increases in the value of the Fund's gold could be used to help them. Since it was difficult in the circumstances of January 1975 to determine the best disposition of the Fund's gold, Mr. Witteveen suggested that the Articles of Agreement be amended to enable the Fund to pursue various options, including the right to sell gold in the market.

By the end of the meeting, the members of the Interim Committee could take positions on some issues. They reaffirmed that steps should be taken as soon as possible to give the SDR the central place in the international monetary system, with a view to gradually reducing the role of gold in the system. They agreed, too, that, when the Fund's Articles of Agreement were amended, the official price for gold should be abolished and obligatory payments of gold by members to the Fund should be eliminated. The possibility that members might make optional payments of gold to the Fund remained open.

These results were said to represent "much progress ... in moving toward a complete set of agreed amendments on gold." But officials were not yet ready for decisions on transactions in gold among central banks and on disposition of the Fund's gold, and the Executive Directors were asked to continue with their study so that "full agreement" could be reached "in the near future."[9]

More Attempts to Secure Agreement: Mr. Witteveen Makes a Proposal

By May 1975 the Executive Directors had agreed on draft amendments to the Articles that eliminated an official price for gold and any obligations of members to pay or receive gold in operations and transactions with the Fund, while the SDR became the means of all payments vis-à-vis the Fund. Dispute continued, however, about whether the Fund's gold should be restituted, as suggested by French officials, sold at the higher prices related to those in private markets and the profits placed in a Trust Fund for use by developing members, as suggested by U.S. officials, or retained in the Fund as expressed or implied security against borrowing by the Fund or retained merely as a valuable asset for the future, as suggested by officials of oil exporting members, of Australia, and of other members. Nor was agreement reached on whether the amended Articles should contain a provision authorizing the Fund with an appropriately high majority of the voting power, such as 85 percent, to engage in a variety of operations with regard to its gold, including sale in the market. Neither was agreement reached on gold trading by national monetary authorities.

By this time, market prices for gold had soared to nearly four times the official price, and Mr. Witteveen was more concerned than ever that without an agreement on gold, making the SDR the central reserve asset of the international monetary

---

[9]Communiqué of Interim Committee, January 15–16, 1975, par. 8; Vol. III below, pp. 219–20.

system would be seriously jeopardized. He therefore proposed that, as soon as possible, the authorities of central banks be free to conduct transactions in gold at market-related prices under arrangements worked out among the Group of Ten for controlling such transactions. Central banks, however, could not engage in such transactions until the Articles of Agreement were amended. Mr. Witteveen remained adamant that the authorities of central banks had to act in accordance with the Articles until they were amended. He also came up with a proposal for disposing of the Fund's gold that put together elements of the various positions that had been advanced. Only 25 percent of the Fund's gold would be disposed of. Some would be restituted to all members; some would be sold at market prices and the profits used for developing members; the major portion would remain in the Fund. The Articles of Agreement would be amended to authorize these actions and to permit the Fund to take a number of options with respect to the rest of its gold.

When the deputies of the Group of Ten met in Paris on May 15, 1975 under the chairmanship of Mr. Ossola, prior to the next meeting of the Interim Committee scheduled for June 10 and 11, also in Paris, they discussed these matters and the Managing Director's suggestions. All agreed that national central banks should be free to enter into gold transactions between themselves at mutually agreed prices. While nearly all also agreed that such freedom should be exercised to achieve a gradual reduction in the role of gold in the international monetary system, two points of view existed about the best arrangements for supervising transactions among central banks so that these transactions would be consistent with this goal. The majority view was that the central banks of the large industrial countries should collectively supervise themselves, with the essential limitation that transactions in gold should not result in an increase of the total monetary gold stock of the countries participating in the arrangements. The U.S. view was that while mutual supervision by the central banks themselves was satisfactory, participating countries should undertake not only to ensure that official gold holdings did not increase but also to agree not to use gold as a regular medium for international financial settlements and not to purchase gold from other countries, except when the seller had an "emergency need" for liquidity.

There was general consensus that the arrangements for overseeing central banks' gold transactions should exist for about two years and be outside the Fund's jurisdiction. These arrangements were likely to be satisfactory to nearly all officials. European officials wanted to be sure that central banks were fairly free to deal in gold without any regulation by the Fund. U.S. officials, wanting gold removed from the international monetary system, did not want the Fund to be involved with any new arrangements for gold. Officials of other members, including developing members, wanted to be sure that the Fund would not be a party in any way to establishing a new official price for gold.

When the deputies of the Group of Ten discussed the disposition of the Fund's gold, they considered the three possible ways of dealing with it: distributing it to members, selling it on the market for the benefit of developing members, and amending the Articles of Agreement to enable the Fund, if agreed to by an appropriate majority of the voting power, to use its gold in a variety of ways. Many deputies were becoming more amenable to the three-way arrangement proposed by Mr. Witteveen, involving some direct return to members, possible sale of some of the Fund's gold in free markets, and retention by the Fund of the rest of its gold. In addition, they supported an enabling clause in the amended Articles of Agreement.

For the first time the deputies of the Group of Ten avoided adopting their past positions on gold and instead tried to reconcile their differences. They were also willing to concentrate on the draft amendments to the Articles of Agreement on exchange rates and to consider the compromise on gold suggested by the Managing Director. However, agreement on any of these issues was not yet attained.

When the Group of Twenty-Four held their customary meeting just before the third meeting of the Interim Committee on June 8 and 9, officials from developing members again objected to the solution to the gold problem that seemed to be emerging among the officials of the industrial members. Having examined the various proposals under discussion for the disposal of the gold held by the Fund, the Group of Twenty-Four found "that none of these proposals in their present form was acceptable to the developing nations." The Group noted, moreover, that no arrangements about gold would be acceptable to developing members that were not designed to raise substantially the flow of financial resources to them, without imposing a loss on any individual developing member. The Group of Twenty-Four insisted, too, that no decision on gold should accentuate the already inequitable distribution of international liquidity.[10]

ISSUES STILL UNRESOLVED IN JUNE 1975

Against this background, although a consensus on some topics was now beginning to take shape among monetary authorities, agreement on arrangements for gold at the June meeting of the Interim Committee was not to be expected. Mr. Witteveen looked at all possible ways to help developing members finance what were becoming extraordinarily large deficits in 1975. Encouraged by the repeated proposals of U.S. officials for the Fund to sell gold to finance a Trust Fund and by the willingness of U.S. officials to agree, as a way to obtain agreement, to some restitution of the Fund's gold as French officials desired, he pushed as an interim measure his three-pronged plan for disposition of the Fund's gold: some restitution, some sale for a Trust Fund, and some retention in the Fund. Agreement on this much of the arrangements for gold would at least help solve some immediate financing problems of developing members. But, as Mr. Witteveen well knew from the earlier meetings of the deputies of the Group of Ten and of the Group of Twenty-Four, while his compromise proposal was becoming more acceptable to officials of France and of the United States, many other officials were not yet ready to agree to it. Messrs. Wardhana and Subramaniam, for example, continued to oppose any

---

[10]Communiqué of Group of Twenty-Four, June 9, 1975, par. 6; Vol. III below, p. 639.

restitution of the Fund's gold. Mr. Simonsen, reiterating the position taken by the Group of Twenty-Four a few days earlier, insisted that the "ideal solution" was establishing in the Fund a substitution account for gold. Under such an account, whenever those members that held gold needed to use their gold holdings, they could sell gold to the Fund at market-related prices in exchange for SDRs. A gold substitution account, initially advocated by Mr. De Clercq and other Belgian officials, was supported also by Mr. Shagari.

Mr. De Clercq took the position that any agreement on disposition of the Fund's gold was premature. Decisions on this could wait. Agreement on gold held by members' central banks was urgent. As soon as possible the authorities of central banks ought to be permitted a bit more freedom to conduct transactions in gold. Eventually a gold substitution account in the Fund should be established into which members could deposit their gold in exchange for SDRs. According to Mr. Apel, the authorities of the Federal Republic of Germany could accept any reasonable agreement that would tend over time to eliminate gold from the international monetary system and that would meanwhile keep an important portion of the Fund's gold in the Fund. Per Kleppe, Minister of Finance of Norway, and Richie Ryan, Minister of Finance of Ireland, were concerned that if the Fund sold gold in private markets, it might develop a vested interest in keeping up gold prices and thus create a sort of official gold price "through the back door." Along with many other Governors, they were not willing to agree to any restitution of the Fund's gold. Officials of oil producing countries, which had been lending to the Fund for the two oil facilities, took the position that the Fund's gold should neither be sold by the Fund directly in the market nor restituted to members; the Fund should retain its gold because these holdings made the Fund all the more creditworthy.

This diversity notwithstanding, Mr. Witteveen, summarizing the discussion at the Interim Committee meeting, tried to find common ground. The solution to the gold problem would, he believed, have to be based on the following principles. The objective should be an enhancement in the role of the SDR as the central asset in the international monetary system and consequently a reduction of the role of gold. The official price of gold should be abolished. Obligations to use gold in payments between the Fund and members should be abrogated. A portion of the Fund's gold should be sold at the approximate market price for the benefit of developing members in general, and particularly those with low incomes, and another portion should be sold to members at the existing official price. With respect to the rest of the Fund's gold, the Fund should be given a range of broad enabling powers, exercisable with a high majority. A reasonable formula should be found for transactions by national monetary authorities with each other and in the market that would include understandings designed to avoid the re-establishment of an official price and limiting the volume of gold held by monetary authorities. An appropriate formula should be found for monetary authorities to collaborate with the Fund in connection with their gold transactions.

This consensus became the basis for the communiqué. The Committee then asked the Executive Directors to study further the question of gold in order to reach some final settlement on the basis of these principles and to study the possible establishment of a gold substitution account.[11]

ACCORD REACHED IN AUGUST 1975

The Chairman of the Interim Committee and the Managing Director usually held press conferences after meetings of the Interim Committee. At the press conference after the meeting in June 1975, Mr. Turner, Chairman of the Committee, and Mr. Witteveen both spoke of the lack of progress on settling the toughest issues. Mr. Turner reported, for example, that much work still had to be done at "the technical and political level on many of the issues," and Mr. Witteveen reported that despite substantial progress on the arrangements between central banks on the use of their gold reserves, it was not yet possible to reach agreement.

The gold problem was unexpectedly resolved two months later. On August 24, 1975, about a week before the next meeting of the Interim Committee and the 1975 Annual Meeting scheduled to begin in Washington, the ministers of finance of the EC countries met in Venice and endorsed the proposal of the Managing Director for disposition of the Fund's gold. Under this proposal, the approximately 150 million ounces of gold held by the Fund would be dealt with broadly by leaving two thirds (100 million ounces) with the Fund, with its disposal to be decided by an 85 percent majority of the voting power after the Articles of Agreement were amended; one sixth (25 million ounces) would be restituted to existing members in proportion to their quotas on July 1, 1975, at the official price for gold; and another one sixth (25 million ounces) would be sold by the Fund so as to maximize its yield, and any "surplus" (EC officials carefully avoided the use of the term "profits") was to be used for the benefit of developing countries, particularly those with low incomes.

The finance ministers of the EC countries also agreed that all their countries would be prepared to enter into arrangements on gold transactions by national monetary authorities, provided that such arrangements adhered to the "Zeist consensus" and did not include limitations on transactions by individual countries. Transactions would not be undertaken with the objective of establishing a fixed price for gold. No purchase of gold would be made when the effect would be to increase the combined volume of gold holdings of national governments and of the International Monetary Fund above the aggregate level held on May 1, 1975. The arrangement would become effective as soon as the Fund received authorization to sell gold. It would run for two years, subject to consultation and possible review within that period if it appeared that transactions in gold were in fact leading to the establishment of a fixed gold price. The arrangements would not be supervised by the Fund but there would be scope for review by the Fund to which countries would

---

[11]Communiqué of Interim Committee, June 11, 1975, par. 4; Vol. III below, pp. 220–21.

have to report their gold holdings. The amended Articles of Agreement would include a clause binding each member to collaborate with the Fund and with other members to promote the establishment of the SDR as the principal reserve asset in the international monetary system, in effect obliging them to reduce the role of gold and of reserve currencies. This clause was referred to as the "cooperation clause."

On August 30, 1975 just before the 1975 Annual Meeting was to open, the Group of Ten, under the chairmanship of Masayoshi Ohira, Finance Minister of Japan, came to an agreement on arrangements for the countries of the Group of Ten to supervise their transactions in gold. The arrangements were similar to those agreed in Venice the week before by the finance ministers of the EC countries. There was to be no action to peg the price of gold. The total stock of gold held by the Fund and the monetary authorities of the countries in the Group of Ten was not to be increased. The parties to these arrangements agreed that they would respect any further condition governing gold trading agreed to by their central bank representatives at regular meetings. Each party to these arrangements was to report semiannually to the Fund and to the BIS the total amount of gold that had been bought or sold. Each party agreed that these arrangements were to be reviewed by the participants at the end of two years and then continued, modified, or terminated. Any party to these arrangements might terminate adherence to them after the initial two-year period.

The communiqué issued after this fourth meeting of the Interim Committee described the consensus reached. To implement the decision of the Interim Committee of January 1975 to move "toward a complete set of agreed amendments on gold, including the abolition of the official price and freedom for national monetary authorities to enter into gold transactions under certain specific arrangements, outside the Articles of the Fund, entered into between national monetary authorities in order to ensure that the role of gold in the international monetary system would be gradually reduced," provision was to be made for the following. (i) Abolition of an official price for gold. (ii) Elimination of the obligation to use gold in transactions with the Fund and elimination of the Fund's authority to accept gold in transactions unless the Fund so decided by an 85 percent majority. This understanding would, however, allow study of a gold substitution account to be undertaken. (iii) Sale of one sixth of the Fund's gold (25 million ounces) for the benefit of developing countries, without resulting in a reduction of other resources for their benefit, and restitution of one sixth of the Fund's gold to members. The proportion of any surplus value of the gold sold for the benefit of developing countries corresponding to the share of quotas of those countries would be transferred directly to each developing country in proportion to its quota. The rest of the Fund's gold would be subject to provisions in an amendment to the Articles of Agreement that would create enabling powers exercisable by an 85 percent majority of the total voting power. The Interim Committee noted that, in order to give effect to these understandings, the countries in the Group of Ten had agreed to observe for two years certain arrangements that could be subscribed to by any other member of the Fund wishing to do so.

The communiqué recorded the concerns voiced by officials of developing members that "the proposed arrangements for gold would give rise to a highly arbitrary distribution of new liquidity, with the bulk of gains accruing to developed countries. This would greatly reduce the chances of further allocations of SDRs, thereby detracting from the agreed objective of making the SDR the principal reserve asset and phasing out the monetary role of gold." Because members of the Interim Committee who were not from developing countries did not necessarily accept this argument, however, the communiqué, referring to the arguments of the members from developing countries about the adverse effect of the solution agreed for gold, stated that "this aspect should be studied, and measures explored to avoid these distortions."[12] This study was to include examination of a gold substitution account. The Ministers of the Group of Twenty-Four, meeting as usual just ahead of the Interim Committee, had explicitly mentioned the need to expedite study of such an account.[13]

Accord Welcomed

The accord on arrangements for gold at long last reached was immediately hailed. Addressing the Board of Governors a few days later, on September 2, 1975, President Ford referred to the "major breakthrough" on "the technically complex and politically sensitive questions of a major increase in quotas [the Sixth General Review of Quotas] and on phasing gold out of the monetary system."[14] Mr. Witteveen referred to the Interim Committee's having made "much progress."[15] Mr. Turner, as Chairman of the Interim Committee, reported "agreement of great importance."[16] Although Mr. Fourcade did not comment on the arrangements for gold when he addressed the Governors, when he called on the Managing Director, mainly to talk about exchange rates, he emphasized that the settlements on gold and quotas would add to the pressure on U.S. and French officials to mend their differences on arrangements for exchange rates and so facilitate these arrangements. (Arrangements on exchange rates remained to be resolved before the program of international monetary reform and of amending the Fund's Articles of Agreement could be finished.) Mr. Simon expressed in a letter to Mr. Witteveen appreciation for his efforts over an extended period of time which made possible the achievement of a major advance toward assuring that the international monetary system remained responsive to the needs of a rapidly changing world economy. Like Mr. Fourcade, Mr. Simon was confident that the cooperative spirit manifested on the gold and quota issues would enable officials to reach agreement on exchange rates by the next Interim Committee meeting scheduled for January 1976.

---

[12]Communiqué of Interim Committee, August 31, 1975, par. 6; Vol. III below, pp. 224–25.

[13]Communiqué of Group of Twenty-Four, August 30, 1975, par. 12; Vol. III below, pp. 643–44.

[14]Address by the President of the United States, *Summary Proceedings, 1975*, p. 3.

[15]Opening Address by the Managing Director, *Summary Proceedings, 1975*, p. 29.

[16]Report to the Board of Governors by the Chairman of the Interim Committee, *Summary Proceedings, 1975*, p. 32.

CHAPTER

32

Implementing the
Arrangements for Gold

*I*SSUES CONCERNING GOLD were by no means settled. Ways now had to be found to implement the agreed arrangements. How was the Fund to bring about an across-the-board "restitution," transferring gold it currently owned to members on the basis of the existing quotas in exchange for currency at the official price of SDR 35 an ounce? The Articles of Agreement contained no provision authorizing the return of gold to members, except on the withdrawal of a member from the Fund or in case of liquidation of the Fund. In fact, under the Articles, the Fund could sell gold only to members with creditor positions or in exchange for currencies to be used in the Fund's operations and transactions. Moreover, under the Articles, the Fund could not sell gold at any price other than the official price. How precisely was the Fund to sell gold at market-related prices in order to put the resulting profits into a Trust Fund for the benefit of developing members? The only obvious and uncontroversial legal technique by which the Fund could restitute gold to members would be to make provision for restitution in the forthcoming amendment of the Articles. The amended Articles could include a specific "enabling clause" empowering the Fund to dispose of gold in ways other than to replenish its supply of currencies.

A further problem was that the Articles prohibited members from buying gold at a price above par value plus a prescribed margin. Therefore, even if the Fund should somehow find a way under the Articles to sell gold at prices other than the official price, the central banks of Fund members could not legally buy it. While all these operations and transactions might be made feasible by appropriate amendments, it would take at least two years to get amendments approved and in force. In the meantime, the monetary authorities of most members were impatient to get on with one part or another of the newly agreed arrangements. This chapter describes how these problems were resolved.

DROP IN GOLD PRICES AND MEETINGS OF THE BIS

Adding to the unsettled atmosphere after the Interim Committee's agreement on August 31, 1975, a precipitous drop in prices for gold in private markets took place immediately after the agreement was announced. Even before the Interim Committee's agreement, which included provision for the Fund to sell some gold, gold markets were already apprehensive over the possible channeling of official supplies into gold markets. Operators in gold markets were concerned, for instance, that the U.S. Treasury might conduct another gold auction later in 1975 and that the U.S.S.R. might sell additional gold to finance grain imports. Given these speculations, the announcement that the Fund was now also to sell gold upset private gold markets further. The price of gold thus dropped from $160 an ounce at the end of August to $128.75 an ounce at the London fixing on September 23. This was then considered to be a very large drop. Moreover, the price of $128 an ounce was the lowest that had prevailed in private markets in more than 20 months, since January 1974, just after the rise in oil prices.

In this unsettled atmosphere about gold governors of central banks assembled at the BIS in Basle on October 13, 1975 for their regular monthly meeting. At the top of their agenda was how to implement the new arrangements for trading in gold. The BIS had long been associated with positions favoring gold as the center of the international monetary system. In the 1960s Milton Gilbert, chief economist of the BIS, was among the staunchest advocates of solving the then-perceived shortage of international liquidity by sharply increasing the official price of gold. Mr. Gilbert persistently argued for doubling or even tripling the official price. Most other officials associated with the BIS were also regarded as "gold bugs," the strongest supporters of making gold the most important monetary instrument in the system. Jelle Zijlstra, Chairman of the governors' meetings at the BIS, also favored retaining, or even increasing, the use of gold in international financial settlements.

At the meeting in October 1975, the President of the Swiss National Bank, Fritz Leutwiler, participated as usual, as did the Managing Director, accompanied by the Fund's Treasurer, Walter O. Habermeier. In his subsequent report on the meeting to the Executive Board, Mr. Habermeier explained that the discussion in Basle centered on whether the main features of the agreement reached by the Interim Committee in August—gold sales by the Fund for the benefit of developing members, restitution of gold by the Fund to all its members, and transactions in gold between central banks and by central banks in the market—could be implemented simultaneously. The question of "simultaneity" was of prime concern. French officials, especially concerned that the sales of gold by the Fund at market-related prices would depress prices in private markets, wanted to be sure that the Fund would not start selling gold for the Trust Fund before it restituted gold to members at the official price or before central banks were permitted to buy gold at prices above the official price.

The question of simultaneity was related mainly to the Fund's authority to act under its Articles of Agreement and to the obligations of members under the Articles not to buy gold at premium prices. In the view of European authorities, if execution of some features of the three-part program, such as purchases by central banks, had to await amendment of the Articles, execution of other features of the program, such as sales of gold by the Fund, would also have to be postponed.

Most central bank governors attending the meeting in Basle, particularly those of the United States and of the Federal Republic of Germany, considered establishment of a Trust Fund as urgent and wanted the Fund to start selling gold soon. They did not want to wait the two years involved in getting the Articles amended before the Trust Fund was started. But most governors also felt that if the Fund was to find practical ways prior to amending its Articles to set up a Trust Fund, sell gold for the benefit of developing members, and restitute gold, a way should be found also for central banks to buy gold at premium prices in the market, if they so desired, within, of course, the confines of the understandings reached in the Interim Committee. Except for one, governors considered it most unlikely that central banks would actually buy gold at the high prices prevailing in private markets, but they considered the possibility of central banks making purchases essential for giving confidence to the markets. These monetary authorities wanted to be able to buy gold at a premium, as part of the program for simultaneity, so as to prevent the price of gold in private markets from falling if the Fund's gold went into private markets.

At their meeting in October, the governors of the central banks of the ten large industrial countries also started to devise the details needed to supervise their transactions in gold so as to ensure that they adhered to the understandings agreed in August. They began on the basis of a paper prepared by Mr. Zijlstra. To study the matter further a technical group of senior central bank officials, including some deputy governors of central banks, was set up under the chairmanship of A. Szasz, Director of the Netherlands Bank. The technical group was to propose specific arrangements whereby pegging the price of gold was to be avoided, observing the ceiling on aggregate official gold holdings was to be enforced, and reporting to the BIS and the Fund on gold holdings was to be implemented. The technical group was also to devise arrangements to allow other countries, if they so wished, to join the gold trading arrangements of the countries of the Group of Ten and Switzerland. The Fund was invited to send staff to meetings of the technical group. The Fund Treasurer, Mr. Habermeier, and the Director of the European Office in Paris, Leo Van Houtven, attended these technical group meetings.

At the next meeting of central bank governors at the BIS, in November 1975, which Mr. Dale, Deputy Managing Director, attended on behalf of the Fund, the governors continued on the basis of a report by Mr. Szasz's technical group their discussion of the "technical modalities" for supervising their gold trading. No decisions were taken. Any limitations that might be placed on the freedom of central banks to deal in gold were considered of concern to the highest financial officials. The final decision on the arrangements, therefore, had to be left to the ministerial level of the Group of Ten. Meanwhile the technical group continued to meet.

MEETINGS OF THE GROUP OF TEN

When the Group of Ten met in December 1975, they had one of the fullest agendas ever. Not only did they have to take difficult decisions on how to work out arrangements for gold, but they also had to decide on the new proposed Article IV on exchange rate arrangements just worked out by French and U.S. officials and agreed at the summit meeting in Rambouillet (discussed in Chapter 37).

The deputies of the Group of Ten met in Paris on December 11 and 12, 1975, as usual ahead of the ministerial meeting of the Group of Ten. One of the deputies proposed that the Executive Board might take a decision specifying that because Article IV of the Articles of Agreement could not currently be fully implemented and because the Articles were to be amended, the Fund would note that members could "reserve their right to buy gold that had been paid to the Fund." This decision would prevent any legal objection if it turned out that a central bank of a Fund member was the highest bidder in a possible gold auction by the Fund. Such a decision, however, might not be legal, since what was being proposed was in essence that the Articles be considered in abeyance. In any event, there was a strong feeling among the deputies of the Group of Ten that all outstanding questions concerning the Fund's sales of gold for the Trust Fund, including clarification as to who would be eligible to participate in those sales and how the Fund would restitute gold, ought to be settled at the next Interim Committee meeting, in Jamaica. That meeting was scheduled for early January 1976, only three weeks later.

It appeared that the governors wanted to obtain as much leeway as possible for gold transactions under the agreed ceiling, to keep the Fund at arm's length in the surveillance of the arrangements, and to discourage countries outside the Group of Ten from joining the arrangements.

In the meanwhile, beginning in October 1975, the Executive Board had also been engaged in discussing arrangements by which restitution of gold and sales of gold by the Fund for the Trust Fund might take place. Attention focused on the possibility that sales of gold by the Fund could be conducted in accordance with the Articles by making use of the provision by which the Fund could sell gold to replenish its supply of currencies. Under arrangements suggested by the staff, supported by the Managing Director, and considered in the Executive Board, the Fund would sell gold to members with creditor positions when it needed to replenish its supplies of their currencies. Arrangements would then have to be worked out for these members in turn to sell the gold bought from the Fund either to other members or to the Trust Fund. These currency replenishment operations would enable the Fund to restitute gold and to sell gold to the Trust Fund prior to amendment of the Articles. The Fund could then sell gold on behalf of the Trust Fund above the official price, also prior to amendment of the Articles. Nevertheless, purchases of gold from the Fund by members at prices above the official price could definitely *not* occur under the Articles.

When the Group of Ten met in Paris at ministerial level on December 19, 1975 under the chairmanship of Mr. Duisenberg, they agreed that the amended Articles of Agreement should include a cooperation clause (eventually Article VIII, Section 7) that would require a Fund member "to collaborate with the Fund and with other members in order to ensure that the policies of the member with respect to reserve assets shall be consistent with the objectives of promoting better international surveillance of international liquidity and making the special drawing right the principal reserve asset in the international monetary system."

The Managing Director and staff had been urging that such a clause be incorporated in the draft amendments to give the Fund more influence, if not actual authority, in reducing the roles of gold and of reserve currencies in the international monetary system and in managing international liquidity. Officials had debated this clause for some time and many still hoped to preserve a role for gold. Hence, they did not want explicit mention in the amended Articles of Agreement of a reduction in the role of gold. Others, such as officials of the United States, did not want explicit mention of reducing the role of reserve currencies or of the Fund's "management" of international liquidity. They hoped to preserve as large a role for the dollar as possible. In order to get agreement, the final wording of the cooperation clause seemed cumbersome and vague. It was a wording that the General Counsel referred to as "Stressperanto, the language of laborious international compromise." Cumbersome and vague as it was, agreement on this clause, nevertheless, represented a giant step along the road to amending the Articles.

Much more trouble attended the December 1975 discussions of the Group of Ten pertaining to the forthcoming sales of gold by the Fund. At the meeting, Mr. Witteveen made it clear that restitution and sales of gold by the Trust Fund could be carried out in advance of amending the Articles by means of currency replenishment operations, but that purchases by members of the gold sold by the Fund at prices above the official price could not be permitted. He evoked immediate indignation and extreme irritation. The finance ministers and central bank governors, fully expecting that they would be permitted to participate in the Fund's sales of gold and to offer bids at prices above the official price, were furious at the prospect of being excluded. The Managing Director stood his ground, however, under this bitter attack. He, the Fund staff, and many finance ministers and central bank governors feared that if central banks could not participate in the Fund's gold auctions, the whole agreement about disposal of the Fund's gold would break down because of the absence of simultaneity in implementing the arrangements. Certainly it seemed unlikely that the issue could be settled by the time the Interim Committee met in Jamaica only two weeks later. The meeting broke up in disarray.

The problem could be resolved, however. As the General Counsel suggested during the luncheon interval, the Fund could sell gold to members at the official price for replenishment of their currencies. These members would, in turn, sell the gold to the Trust Fund, also at the official price, and the Fund would then conduct gold auctions at market-related prices on behalf of the Trust Fund. While members could not participate in these gold auctions, the BIS *could* be permitted to participate. The BIS could not, however, act as an agent for the central banks of any Fund members. Nevertheless, the Fund would not try to "police" the actions of the BIS, since it was "a sister organization." This solution was accepted, especially since there seemed to be no other way out of the difficulty.

The finance ministers and central bank governors of the Group of Ten also agreed to specific arrangements to ensure that gold transactions conducted among their central banks were in accord with the understandings agreed in August 1975. To avoid pegging the price of gold, central banks were not to engage in any transactions with the objective of establishing a fixed price for gold. There was to be regular surveillance of developments in gold prices to ensure that the spirit of the agreement on this point was observed. The ceiling on the combined gold holdings of central banks and the Fund was to be set at their holdings as of August 31, 1975, minus any intervening sales of gold. There was agreement in principle that the ceiling should not be exceeded under any circumstances.

Twelve countries were to participate, that is, the ten countries belonging to the Group of Ten, plus Switzerland and Portugal, the latter being the only country outside the founding group to adhere to the arrangements. Each participant was to report to the BIS every transaction it undertook in gold and the price at which the transaction occurred. The BIS was to be entrusted with the task of recording the transactions in gold carried out by the central banks of the 12 countries and by the International Monetary Fund, with the General Manager, René Larre, serving as Registrar of the Arrangements. Semiannual meetings were to be held, alternately under the auspices of the BIS and of the Fund, when these institutions would review the transactions. No criteria were to be laid down in advance for the adherence of additional members to the arrangements, except that they were to be prepared to undertake the same obligations that the countries of the Group of Ten had accepted and there would be an appropriate modification of the total amount of gold subject to the ceiling. The arrangements were to go into effect on February 1, 1976. This date was a compromise between the position of French officials who favored the retroactive date of August 31, 1975 and U.S. officials who favored the date of the Fund's first gold auction, which was still in the future.

Some of the Fund staff viewed the arrangements as having been devised to leave the Fund as much as possible out of any supervising or overseeing role.

IMPLEMENTATION AND EXPIRATION OF THE ARRANGEMENTS FOR CENTRAL BANKS' TRANSACTIONS

At the next meeting of the Interim Committee in Jamaica in January 1976, the agreed solution was finalized. It was agreed that "action should be taken to start without delay the simultaneous implementation" of the various arrangements for gold, in other words, before the Articles of Agreement were amended. The currency replenishment techniques would be used, and the Managing Director would reach understandings with the members to which the Fund sold gold for replenishing their currencies to the effect that they would in turn sell this gold at the official price either to other members (for restitution) or to the Trust Fund (for auctioning by the Fund). The Fund's gold auctions were to take place over a four-year period.[1] It was understood that the BIS would be able to bid in these auctions, but the central banks of Fund members would not. The auctions are described in Chapter 33.

In July 1976, the Managing Director attended the first semiannual review by the BIS of gold transactions by central banks, along with the governors of the central banks of the 12 countries adhering to the arrangements. The second semiannual meeting was to be held at the Fund in early 1977, in conjunction with the Interim Committee meeting. However, when the Interim Committee meeting was postponed until April, the second semiannual review was held at the BIS. There were two further such semiannual meetings, in July 1977, which the Deputy Managing Director attended, and in January 1978.

The arrangements were unpopular with the members of the Fund other than the 11 members involved. One objection was that the initial period was too brief. Another was that a fixed period implied that when the arrangements came to an end members would be free of all restraint in their gold transactions and might then take steps to elevate the status of gold. Developing members objected to the Group of Ten's arrangements for trading in gold among themselves as they did for all other arrangements for gold. They feared that these arrangements could result in a large increase in the liquidity of the industrial members that held gold, which could detract from the status of the SDR.

The arrangements of the Group of Ten for trading in gold among themselves were allowed to expire on January 31, 1978, two years after they went into effect. By that time there was not much pressure from the major participants to extend the life of the arrangements, and with the amended Articles of Agreement expected to come into force in a short time, there was no need for extension. France, in fact, opposed a prolongation. Thus on January 23, 1978, Gösta Bohman, the Minister for Economic Affairs of Sweden, in his capacity as Chairman of the Group of Ten, formally announced that there was no need to extend the arrangements.

The United States, through Anthony M. Solomon, Under Secretary of the Treasury for Monetary Affairs, issued a statement of its own, an unusual occurrence after meetings of the Group of Ten. The statement indicated that the United States supported the statement of the Group of Ten and believed that the gold arrangements had "served a useful role." The United States also concluded that the experience of the past two years—including the absence of actions to peg the price of gold or to increase the monetary role of gold in other ways—and the expectation that this situation would continue indicated that these transitional arrangements need not be formally extended. The statement went on, however, to say that if this situation was to change and U.S. authorities saw a need for resumption of these or similar arrangements, they would not hesitate to seek them.[2]

---

[1]Communiqué of Interim Committee, January 8, 1976, par. 3; Vol. III below, p. 226.
[2]U.S. Treasury Department, *News* (B-654), January 23, 1978.

The separate statement of the United States put the monetary authorities of the other large industrial countries on notice that should they take measures again to give gold a central place in international monetary relations, the U.S. authorities would again seek international arrangements to prevent it. Thus, as late as January 1978, the U.S. monetary authorities were still concerned that European monetary authorities might again try to resurrect gold as a major monetary asset.

At the expiration of the gold trading arrangements of the Group of Ten, Mr. Witteveen sent a note to the Executive Directors emphasizing his view that expiration of the arrangements did not mean any change in the agreed objective of aiming at the gradual reduction of the role of gold in the international monetary system. He believed that the Fund would have sufficient authority under its amended Articles to maintain surveillance. He also pointed out that developments in market prices of gold, in official transactions in gold, and in the price at which such transactions were effected were of continuing interest to the international community and that he was asking the staff in the light of the Fund's responsibilities under the amended Articles to examine whether the Fund received sufficient information on the changes in the composition of reserves of members.

A SUBSTITUTION ACCOUNT FOR GOLD: SEEKING TO MANAGE INTERNATIONAL LIQUIDITY

Remaining to be examined was the possibility of establishing in the Fund a substitution account for gold by which members might turn some of their gold reserves into the Fund in exchange for a special issue of SDRs. This subject was examined at some length in 1975.

A substitution account for gold was part of the management of international liquidity, a subject of great personal concern to Mr. Witteveen, who regarded controlling liquidity as essential to containing world inflation. Even in the midst of the 1975 recession, he stressed the need for greater management of international liquidity to help check inflation. In an address in Washington on May 14, 1975, for example, he identified the most important problem left unresolved by the Committee of Twenty as the means by which international liquidity should be controlled and the related question of the role of different reserve assets in the settlement of payments imbalances. He reminded financial officials that lack of control over international liquidity had complicated management of the Bretton Woods system and had eventually contributed to its breakdown.

In his speech Mr. Witteveen pointed out that he was well aware that in the wake of the oil crisis the problem of the "dollar overhang," which had for years so exercised European monetary authorities, suddenly seemed less urgent. With enormous and widespread payments deficits by oil importing countries and with the related dangers of recession in the world economy, large and expanding international reserves, including reserves in dollars, had been seen as providing useful flexibility in financing balance of payments disequilibria. Since a substantial proportion of newly created international liquidity accrued to the oil exporting countries, which were not expected to use all of it, increases in liquidity were not regarded as unduly inflationary. He warned, however, that there would come a time when accretion of reserves by oil producing countries would diminish and perhaps even be reversed and when inflation rather than recession would again be of uppermost concern. At that time, problems of creating a satisfactory mechanism to control international liquidity "will . . . come back to our agenda as a vital issue."[3]

Turning to the subject of gold, he explained the economic reasons why he was trying so hard to bring about agreed arrangements for gold. (He wanted, for legal reasons, to get in place agreed arrangements consistent with the Articles of Agreement before monetary authorities took illegal steps under the Fund's existing Articles, as explained earlier in this chapter.) While there was understandable pressure to free central banks to mobilize their gold reserves by enabling them to engage in transactions at market prices, this freedom, if effectively usable, would imply recognition and acceptance of a very large increase in international liquidity. The total monetary gold stock of about $50 billion would be revalued at anything up to the $200 billion implied by existing market prices. This fourfold increase in the value of gold reserves was an important consequence in itself, but complete freedom for central banks to buy and sell gold could also open the door to additional uncontrolled increases in international liquidity through a further rise in the market price of gold. If central banks became net buyers of gold, this could have a strong upward impact on prices, given the relatively narrow base of the gold market. Turning next to the role of reserve currencies, Mr. Witteveen explained that the critical question was how their growth should be controlled.

He was especially concerned about the potential expansion of international liquidity because of three developments on the horizon by 1975. First, in addition to U.S. dollars and pounds sterling, many countries were holding French francs, deutsche mark, Swiss francs, Japanese yen, and other currencies as reserves. Second, and perhaps even more important, an increasing number of countries with balance of payments surpluses were keeping their increases in reserves in short-term balances either in national money markets or in the Eurocurrency market, and a larger number of countries with balance of payments deficits were borrowing the funds thus made available rather than running down their reserves. In this situation almost any balance of payments disequilibria could lead to increases in international liquidity whereas previously liquidity creation had been confined to financing disequilibria between reserve-center and other countries. Third, recycling operations of private commercial banks had resulted in a spectacular growth in international private credit.

---

[3]Mr. Witteveen's address, given at a seminar on U.S.-European policies sponsored jointly by the Atlantic Council, the School of Advanced International Studies of the Johns Hopkins University, and the International Management and Development Institute, was published in *IMF Survey* (Washington), Vol. 4 (May 26, 1975), pp. 145 and 148–51. The portion quoted is on p. 149.

In Mr. Witteveen's view, potential growth of international liquidity and credit made for a serious gap in the world's anti-inflationary defenses. He regarded the increase in reserves of surplus countries and the relative ease with which deficit countries could borrow as unusually worrisome, especially since inflationary pressures were likely to resurge after the current recession ended.

On October 28, 1975, in a speech in Frankfurt, Mr. Witteveen again addressed himself forcefully to the topic of the management of international liquidity. He was concerned that the agreement on gold of August 1975 could increase international liquidity and create an inflationary potential. In light of intensified concern in the early 1980s with how to prevent the spread of excessive liquidity, especially liquidity by private banks, Mr. Witteveen's speech of October 1975 seems prophetic.

Addressing himself to the expansion of liquidity, he concluded that "we will have to find ways and means to manage the growth of international liquidity—both in its private and its official form. The current system, which allows a predominantly demand-determined growth of these international means of payment, may turn out to be a potential source of inflation in the next cyclical expansion, and might well hamper the efforts of the monetary authorities of the various countries to bring inflation under control." Since these problems were international in scope, they required international solutions and it was time to place the dual problem of controlling the growth of private and official international liquidity on the international agenda.[4]

Mr. Witteveen had two immediate suggestions—establishment in the Fund of a gold substitution account, then being discussed in the Executive Board in connection with the Second Amendment, and greater regulation of the Eurocurrency market. Control over international liquidity meant taking steps to base the international monetary system on the SDR, reducing the role of gold in the system, and regulating the volume of national currencies used as reserves. These objectives had already been agreed in principle in the *Outline of Reform*. Establishment of a gold substitution account would work toward these objectives by simultaneously reducing members' reserves of gold, thereby reducing the danger of greater liquidity from this source, and injecting into the system more SDRs, over which the Fund had control. It would also make possible avoiding the sudden creation of potentially large additional international liquidity by stretching the payment of SDRs for the gold sold by members to the Fund over a considerable number of years.

Mr. Witteveen realized that the question of the substitution of SDRs for reserve currencies considered by the Committee of Twenty was not then "being actively discussed," but stressed that eventual replacement of gold and currency reserves with SDRs was the way to bring official international liquidity more closely under effective international control. He also suggested steps to achieve better control over the creation of reserves in the form of national currencies. Countries might, for

---

[4]His speech, "The Control of International Liquidity," given before the Conference Board in Frankfurt, is published in *IMF Survey* (Washington), Vol. 4 (October 28, 1975), pp. 313–16. The quoted portion is on p. 316.

example, agree to hold a certain minimum proportion of their international reserves in the form of SDRs. Adjustments in the aggregate volume of SDRs in the reserve ratio would then bring about some degree of international management of the global amount of reserves without making the SDR the exclusive or even the main reserve asset. The problem was that such a step would involve a certain measure of compulsory asset settlement and would thus raise all the issues in that regard that had been discussed in the Committee of Twenty.

Turning to developments in the private international banking sector, Mr. Witteveen graphically illustrated the size of the increase in the Eurocurrency market, which had been growing at an average annual rate of 30–40 percent. Its aggregate volume was larger than the money supply of the United States as narrowly defined. While he recognized that the absence of supervision or regulation had aided the development of the Eurocurrency market and permitted its efficient performance, he stressed that officials had to recognize that the Eurocurrency market as presently constituted might well make effective monetary control more difficult. Therefore, "one might want to investigate more closely whether steps designed to control the aggregate amount of private liquidity in international financial markets would be appropriate."

EXECUTIVE BOARD'S CONSIDERATION OF A GOLD SUBSTITUTION ACCOUNT

Against this background the Executive Directors, taking up the request of the Interim Committee of August 1975, explored the possibility of a gold substitution account at some length at the end of 1975. Discussing the details of the account would help the Executive Board decide whether provision should be made in the Second Amendment empowering the Fund to establish such an account.

The Executive Board's discussion was based on two staff papers that suggested how the account might operate. In addition, Mr. de Groote circulated his own detailed proposal for an alternative gold substitution account. Although Executive Directors did at times circulate their own proposals, this practice was rare. Mr. de Groote's separate paper reflected the persistent interest of the Belgian authorities in a gold substitution account and was given a great deal of attention by the Executive Board.

Mr. de Groote's proposal took into account the gold that the Fund held and would later hold as a consequence of substitutions, while the staff scheme considered only the latter. An essential element of Mr. de Groote's plan was, in fact, the transfer of the Fund's own gold or some part of it, as well as that of members, to a gold consolidation account. As the Fund relinquished gold to the gold account, it would correspondingly allocate SDRs to its General Account on the basis of SDR 35 an ounce of gold to preserve the liquidity of the General Account. An additional amount of SDRs, calculated on the basis of a formula related to the market price of gold, would be issued by the Fund to a Trust Fund for the benefit of developing members or would be distributed to these members directly. In this way the increase in the value of the Fund's gold would assist developing members and enable members that did not hold substantial amounts of gold, primarily developing members, to benefit along with members that did hold gold.

Under Mr. de Groote's proposal no distinct type of SDR would be issued to members in exchange for gold, as suggested by the staff. Moreover, under Mr. de Groote's gold consolidation account the Fund would from time to time enable members to substitute SDRs for gold, rather than have a fixed once-for-all exchange.[5]

Mr. Kafka came out strongly in favor of a gold substitution account. He had been privately criticial and skeptical of the arrangements for gold made in August 1975 and took the occasion of the Executive Board's discussion on the gold substitution account in November 1975 to express his views more formally to his colleagues. In his view, the agreement of August 1975 would not phase gold out of the international monetary system, the presumed objective of the U.S. Government. On the contrary, central banks could not only revalue their gold reserves at very high prices but could acquire more gold and might well do so. French officials had achieved everything they wanted with respect to gold and at some later date would inevitably push for use of their augmented gold reserves in international financial transactions, or even for return to a gold standard. Gold was, therefore, more likely than ever to be used in future international settlements.

Mr. Kafka pointed out that it was precisely to counter the prospect of gold again becoming in practice the prime reserve asset that officials of developing members wanted to have a gold substitution account introduced. Such an account would remove gold from central banks and put it under the control of the Fund. It would also inject SDRs into the monetary system so that their total supply would increase just when the supply of gold in the hands of national monetary authorities was reduced.

Mr. Kafka's position was supported by Messrs. Gavaldá, Guarnieri, Jagannathan, Kharmawan, and Monday. Executive Directors appointed or elected by the industrial and more developed members, however, were nearly all opposed to a gold substitution account. Mr. Cross, again citing the objectives of U.S. officials to have gold phased out of the international monetary system and to have an orderly disposal of the Fund's gold, questioned whether a gold substitution account would, in fact, achieve these objectives. Might not such an account merely ratify a particular price for gold, since the Fund would have to make exchanges between gold and SDRs at some price? U.S. officials, moreover, doubted that the major holders of gold, Belgium, France, Italy, and the Netherlands, were prepared to turn over to the Fund in exchange for SDRs all, or even a sizable portion, of their holdings. Yet, to be successful, a gold substitution account needed to encompass all the major holders.

---

[5]The two papers on the objectives and possible provisions of a gold substitution account prepared by the staff in April and July 1975 and Mr. de Groote's alternative proposal are in Vol. III below, pp. 305–16.

Otherwise, central banks that continued to hold gold could be a potential lobby against later sales by the Fund of the gold received in the gold substitution account.

As rarely happened, Mr. Wahl agreed with Mr. Cross, although their motives differed. While Mr. Cross wanted gold phased out of the system, Mr. Wahl wanted members to own and control gold. Mr. Wahl opposed the establishment of a gold substitution account which would allow the Fund to control more gold and would decrease the holdings of central banks. In this way the Fund would have greater control over disposition of gold and central banks would have less. Mr. Wahl questioned what would happen later to the gold acquired by the Fund and wondered about the price at which substitutions of gold for SDRs would be made. Would a fixed or official price for gold again emerge?

Mr. Pieske was also against a gold substitution account. As the authorities of the Federal Republic of Germany had always feared, allocating SDRs for currently inactive stocks of gold would make actual additional liquidity out of what was now only potential liquidity. A gold substitution account would also reinstitute a price for which gold was exchanged and possibly also an official price. This would hardly phase gold out of the international monetary system. Gold would be merely shifted around between members and the Fund, transferred first from central banks to the Fund, and then, when the Fund sold or disposed of the gold, back to central banks. Finally, Mr. Pieske argued, a gold substitution account was unnecessary. Members did not, at least then, need to mobilize their gold reserves into some usable form.

Mr. Whitelaw agreed with Mr. Pieske that a gold substitution account in the Fund did not really remove gold from the international monetary system and did not address the basic problem of how to abolish use of gold. Mr. Drabble raised a number of technical questions as to precisely how a gold substitution account would operate and whether it would be mandatory or voluntary for members to surrender gold to the account.

Mr. Lieftinck brought up the most basic question of all. Why was a gold substitution account needed, but not an account in which holdings of reserve currencies were at least partly removed from the system? Mr. Lieftinck's question brought out a difficulty inherent in the whole discussion in 1975 about a substitution account. While the staff draft on a gold substitution account also discussed the possibility of a substitution account for reserve currencies, no monetary authorities were yet prepared to talk seriously about the latter. All members, including developing members, wanted to keep their currency holdings.

This inconclusive discussion reflected conflicting governmental positions. Hence, when the members of the Interim Committee met in January 1976, they took similarly conflicting positions. In addition, many members of the Committee, including Mr. Fourcade and Mr. Simon, took the position that it was difficult enough to agree on all the other draft amendments to the Articles without getting into an amendment setting up a gold substitution account that had not yet been adequately examined. Moreover, they believed that, when it came time to have the proposed Second Amendment approved by their legislative bodies, their respective legislatures might object to surrendering their countries' gold to the Fund. Provision in the Second Amendment for a gold substitution account might therefore make it more difficult to get the Second Amendment approved.

It was abundantly clear from this discussion that officials of the industrial and relatively more developed members were far from agreeing to provisions in the Second Amendment that would give the Fund an enabling power to establish a gold substitution account. The idea was dropped.[6]

In his suggestion in 1975 that a substitution account be created, at least for gold if not for reserve currencies, and that measures to check the expansion of private liquidity be considered, Mr. Witteveen and those favoring such measures were ahead of their time. Monetary authorities were not yet ready to take such action, even though it had been over 30 years since Keynes had suggested, in his Clearing Union, that Fund members deposit gold with the Fund and nearly 16 years since Professor Robert Triffin had again suggested a similar account for reserves.

The year 1975 was especially inopportune for monetary authorities to agree to give up any of their familiar gold or currency reserves or to agree to regulations on private lending and borrowing. Mr. Witteveen's main concern in 1975, which motivated him to suggest greater management of international liquidity, was with potential inflation, although 1975 witnessed the deepest recession in 40 years. He had to stress at the time that inflation *could* again be a problem. Although price levels were not falling, unemployment was high and monetary authorities were more concerned about coping with the current recession than they were with prospects of future inflation. In the year 1975, moreover, following the oil price rise, the balance of payments deficits of most oil importing members, including some industrial members, were at their largest. These deficits were, in fact, the justification for the Fund's 1975 oil facility (Chapter 18). Monetary authorities of industrial countries were not, in these circumstances, about to exchange any of their traditional reserves for the less tried SDR. As developing members encountered massive deficits, they were seeking funds everywhere. They feared that private banks would not lend enough; and if officials of developing members or commercial banks had fears about the rapidly accumulating debts of developing members, these fears were well suppressed. Emphasis of developing members was almost entirely on finding financing at the moment in order to stave off cuts in imports that would curtail consumption and investment. Private banks were regarded as part of the solution, not as part of the problem, as would become the case in 1982 and 1983. The monetary authorities of developing members certainly did not, at the time, want any discussion of controls on lending by banks or on their operations in the Eurocurrency market.

---

[6]Additional information on the Executive Board's consideration of a gold substitution account in 1975 can be found in Sir Joseph Gold, "Substitution in the International Monetary System," *Case Western Reserve Journal of International Law* (Cleveland), Vol. 12 (Spring 1980), pp. 265–326. See particularly pp. 295–302.

Mr. Witteveen recognized that the circumstances of 1975 were anything but propitious for considering a gold substitution account or controls on the Eurocurrency market. He was rather using the occasion of the drafting of the Second Amendment to get these "radical ideas" accepted. He was to try both ideas again in 1978, as will be described in Chapter 46.

Control of Reserves Considered in a Special Conference

Control of international liquidity was addressed again, together with exchange rates, at a conference on the new international monetary system, held at the Fund's headquarters, on November 11–12, 1976. With regard to control over international liquidity, the following questions were considered. Is such control feasible and desirable under a system of widespread floating exchange rates, including the exchange rates of reserve currencies? What will be the role of the various reserve assets, such as gold, foreign currencies, and Fund-related assets, as the international monetary system evolves? What is the impact of public and private international credit facilities? And, finally, what avenues would be open to the international community to control international liquidity if such control should be deemed desirable? All these were regarded as important policy questions needing answers if informed choices were to be made.

The 29 participants in the conference were well-known monetary economists and experts from universities and governments. The results of this conference, like consideration of the gold substitution account in 1975, suggested that monetary authorities and economists needed more experience with the new floating rate regime before they could agree on features needed to restore a smoothly functioning international monetary system. Opinions differed on virtually every question about exchange rates and reserves, and in spite of the wisdom and experience of the participants, the discussions brought to light complexities and even confusions rather than agreement. There seemed to be little doubt among the participants, however, that the Fund would eventually need more authority. Professor Mundell concluded the conference with the following statement:

> The IMF in 1944 was given a certain set of functions and responsibilities. It has grown mightily since then. But it is still too small to cope with increasing responsibilities. In the new setting of managed flexible exchange rates it will, sooner or later, have to embark on the new career of Supreme Monetary Authority.[7]

---

[7] The papers presented at the conference and the related discussion were published as Robert A. Mundell and Jacques J. Polak, eds., *The New International Monetary System* (New York: Columbia University Press, 1977). The portion quoted is on p. 244. A summary of this conference was given in Malcolm Knight and Joanne Salop, "The New International Monetary System: Some Issues," *Finance & Development*, Vol. 14 (June 1977), pp. 19–22.

EXAMPLE OF INTERNATIONAL DECISION MAKING

The sequence of events by which the gold problem was resolved from 1973 to 1976 demonstrates unusually well how decisions on international monetary topics were taken in those years. A schism existed between financial officials, reflecting divergent economic philosophies as well as vested interests. To move forward on needed international monetary action, the schism had to be healed. To this end the highest-ranking financial officials of the largest industrial countries took the occasion of their frequent meetings to hold private talks among themselves. As a beginning step, they often reached bilateral understandings. Limited groups of countries with more or less common interests, such as the EC, the Group of Ten, the Group of Twenty-Four, and the governors of the central banks of those countries which met regularly at the BIS, then held meetings to work out mutually agreed positions. At the international level, the Managing Director met informally with many financial officials to ascertain common ground. He saw his role as enunciating emerging consensus and stating general principles around which agreement might be achieved. In so doing, he often helped forge agreement.

Gradually, in the interest of political expediency officials of the large industrial countries, especially the United States and France, tried to close the gaps between their positions. U.S. officials, for example, conceded to the French position on gold, while French officials conceded to the U.S. position on exchange rates. Taking advantage of this situation, the Managing Director worked with Fund staff to come up with compromise suggestions and with draft language that seemed to reflect the evolving agreement. Public officials welcomed this initiative by international civil servants which formed the basis for final agreement.

The solution eventually reached had "something for everybody." Industrial countries played the major role in the decision-making process, but believed that they were making concessions to developing countries. Yet developing countries remained convinced that their interests were only marginally taken into account and the decisions taken primarily benefited industrial countries. The agreement reached, moreover, and the language in which it was couched were often left deliberately ambiguous so that officials on either side could view the final compromise as a victory. Furthermore, many decisions reached even after much effort, except those about the provisions of the Second Amendment, were intended only for an interim period. The arrangements for transactions among the Group of Ten, for example, were to last only for three years. In other words, despite all the debate, many of the hardest decisions about what to do about gold in the longer term were left for the future.

The arrangements agreed for gold in the mid-1970s must be construed as straight pragmatic compromise. Officials of some industrial members were satisfied that the arrangements, especially the provisions of the amended Articles of Agreement, worked toward reducing the use of gold in the international monetary system. Officials of other industrial members were satisfied that monetary agencies, including the Fund, could retain the bulk of their gold, with any future dispositions to be determined later. Officials of industrial members were also satisfied that the arrangements gave all developing members of the Fund some of the Fund's gold by direct restitution and gave a further restitution to the great majority of developing members so that most developing members received a double restitution of gold. Many developing members that had never had gold before thus received gold from the Fund. Officials of developing members, nonetheless, remained unhappy about the arrangements. At its meeting in January 1976, the Group of Twenty-Four continued to express "strong dissatisfaction" with the arrangements.[8]

A WORD IN RETROSPECT

As noted, despite the above long-debated and complicated solution to the gold problem, many arrangements for gold, except provisions of the Second Amendment, were temporary. It remained to be seen how the rest of the Fund's gold would be disposed of and what would happen to officially held stocks of gold. Officials of many members still regarded gold as a desirable asset despite the change in its legal status and its lack of use in international payments.

The interim character of many arrangements agreed in 1975 was to become apparent almost immediately after the period described in this History. Beginning in 1979 prices for gold in private markets went to levels that few observers would have ever expected. At times gold prices were to reach $800 an ounce or higher as panic buying of gold took place and "gold fever" resurged.

The gold story never really seems to be ended. By 1980, oddly, the "gold bugs" had changed their habitat. In the United States, where the government had long aimed at abolishing the use of gold, many old questions, such as whether gold should be revalued by all countries at the new higher prices, were coming up again. Some individuals with increasing political clout believed that the United States had made a mistake by not revaluing its gold stocks at the high prices prevailing in private markets, as France had done, and by selling off some of its gold. Bankers, businessmen, and public officials in the United States increasingly joined their counterparts in France as advocates of a return to a gold standard. They believed that restoration of the gold standard was the only way in which worsening inflation might be halted. A larger number of monetary authorities throughout the world increasingly looked on the Fund's remaining gold holdings as its most useful asset, a sizable and valuable collateral against the Fund's ever larger borrowings.

The influence of those who wanted to strengthen the role of gold in the monetary system gradually became greater in the United States, and in 1980 when the quota increase under the Seventh General Review was considered in the U.S. Congress, that body required the President to appoint a commission to "conduct a study to assess and make recommendations with regard to the policy of the U.S.

---

[8]Communiqué of Group of Twenty-Four, January 6, 1976, par. 6; Vol. III below, p. 645.

Government concerning the role of gold in domestic and international monetary systems."[9] Shortly after his inauguration in January 1981, President Ronald Reagan appointed a Gold Commission, but the Commission subsequently recommended against restoration of any formal monetary role for gold.[10] Thereafter, there was much less talk about increasing the status of gold in the international monetary system.

One could, in retrospect, reach two contradictory conclusions from the history of gold in the 1970s. On the one hand, it could be concluded that, by early in 1983, the gold issue was virtually dead. When one considers the passions with which gold was viewed as late as 1976 and the frequent and strongly voiced arguments for resurrecting gold as the center of the international monetary system, it is surprising that by 1982 only a very few economists, and virtually no monetary authorities, argued any longer that gold receive a key role in international monetary arrangements. Only the monetary authorities of South Africa, whose economy depends heavily on gold production, were inclined to mention gold at international financial meetings.

On the other hand, longer-run history confirms the persistence of traditional attitudes toward gold. Myths about "the precious metal" persist. From time to time, well-known specialists again seek solutions to economic problems through the use of gold. As of 1982, the topic was still sufficiently alive to be re-examined.[11] Moreover, early in 1983, in the gloom of global recession brightened by new prospects for recovery, a prominent specialist, Robert Mundell, was again advocating stabilizing the price of gold as the principal way to stabilize exchange rates and to contain inflation.[12]

---

[9]Sec. 10 of Public Law 389, 96th Cong., October 7, 1980, 94 Stat. 1555, *An Act to Amend the Bretton Woods Agreements Act to Authorize Consent to an Increase in the United States Quota in the International Monetary Fund, and for Other Purposes.*

[10]For a discussion of the report of the U.S. Gold Commission, see Joseph Gold, *SDRs, Currencies, and Gold: Sixth Survey of New Legal Developments,* IMF Pamphlet Series, No. 40 (Washington, 1983), pp. 75–83.

[11]Richard N. Cooper, "The Gold Standard: Historical Facts and Future Prospects," in William C. Brainard and George L. Perry, eds., *Brookings Papers on Economic Activity: 1* (1982), The Brookings Institution (Washington), pp. 1–45.

[12]See, for example, Robert Mundell, "Floating Rates Lead to Monetary Chaos," in Jack Kemp and Robert Mundell, *A Monetary Agenda for World Growth* (Boston, Mass.: Quantum, 1983), pp. 20–28.

CHAPTER

33

Selling the Fund's Gold

S *ELLING ITS HOLDINGS OF GOLD* in the sense agreed in 1975–76 was another first for the Fund. In the past, the Fund had often used its authority under the Articles of Agreement to sell gold to replenish its holdings of particular currencies when the Fund's supplies of these currencies were being depleted. It was also the Fund's practice to sell gold to replenish its currency holdings when it activated the General Arrangements to Borrow (GAB). By selling gold on these occasions, an extraordinarily large drawing by an industrial member did not excessively draw down the Fund's existing balances of usable currencies. The Fund also sold gold on these occasions to placate GAB participants and induce them to lend by providing them an opportunity to add to their gold stocks. To help implement the Fourth Quinquennial Review of Quotas in 1964 and the Fifth General Review of Quotas in 1970, the Fund also sold gold to a few members with creditor positions in the Fund (implying that the Fund's holdings of their currencies were low). These members had sold gold to other members to enable them to pay the Fund the 25 percent of their increased subscriptions due in gold. In this way the Fund alleviated the indirect, or secondary, impact on the gold reserves of members who sold gold to help other members make gold payments to the Fund.[1]

The sales of the Fund's gold planned to begin in 1976 were of a new kind, however. Though all previous sales were undertaken to help the Fund execute its traditional operations and transactions, beginning in 1976 sales of gold were unrelated to the Fund's regular financial operations. In fact, the Fund was actually to *dispose* of some of its gold, permanently reducing its holdings. In these circumstances entirely new procedures for sales of gold had to be devised. Adding to the complexity of devising such procedures was the need to make them consistent with

---

[1]Each of these reasons for sales of gold by the Fund was described in earlier volumes of the Fund's History. Sales to replenish the Fund's holdings of particular currencies in short supply were described in *History, 1945–65*, Vol. I, pp. 433–34 and 487 and Vol. II, pp. 454–55; and in *History, 1966–71*, Vol. I, pp. 236 and 417–20. Sales at the time of activations of the General Arrangements to Borrow were described in *History, 1945–65*, Vol. I, pp. 568–69 and Vol. II, pp. 455–59; and in *History, 1966–71*, Vol. I, pp. 375 and 417. Sales to alleviate the impact of gold subscriptions being paid to the Fund on the occasion of the general quota increases agreed in 1964 and 1970 were described in *History, 1966–71*, Vol. I, pp. 254, 297–98, 301, and 416–17.

the Articles, which had never provided for the Fund to sell off its basic holdings of gold. Need for this consistency arose from the agreement of officials that the Fund's sales of gold were to start as soon as possible and not await amendment of the Articles, which was expected to take some time.

DECISION TO HOLD AUCTIONS

How the Fund should best dispose of its gold was a question that the Managing Director and the staff, especially Mr. Habermeier, the Treasurer, considered with great care throughout 1975. Procedures were needed both for selling 25 million ounces at market-related prices and for distributing another 25 million ounces to members at the official price over a four-year period. The greatest difficulty was the disposal of gold at market prices; working out procedures for distribution to members at the official price was easy. Since the Fund had had no experience with selling gold, one option was to turn the sales over to an agent, such as a major bank accustomed to buying and selling gold. Members of the banking community, fearful that the Fund's gold sales would be unduly influenced by political considerations, that the Fund would prove incapable of carrying out such a specialized task, or that the Fund's sales would flood and upset the sensitive private market for gold, strongly preferred that the Fund use one of their number as agent. Another option was to let the BIS, which had some experience in gold dealing, undertake sales on behalf of the Fund. Finally, the Fund, despite its inexperience, could conduct its own gold sales.

The Fund was in a "no-win" position regardless of which method of selling gold it decided upon. By turning its gold over to a private bank or to the BIS for sale the Fund would be criticized for giving away control over the handling of its gold. Furthermore, since the Fund would turn over its gold to an agent at a prearranged price, the agent rather than the Fund would be the beneficiary if the market price for gold subsequently rose. The Fund would therefore be criticized for not maximizing its profit from the sale. Conducting its own sales of gold subjected the Fund to criticism for whatever developments took place in gold markets once the sales began. The Fund might also be blamed for upsetting the market.

Given these considerations, the Treasurer's Department, supported by the Managing Director, decided to propose to the Executive Directors that the Fund conduct its own gold auctions. In this way the Fund would at least retain control over the disposition of its gold holdings. Given that no official agency had had much experience in selling gold, the Fund was as likely as was the BIS to be competent in handling gold sales. This proposal was accepted by the Executive Directors and by the Interim Committee in the course of 1975. By January 1976, it was agreed that the Fund would conduct gold auctions and to give the Fund legal authority to do so, a Trust Fund would be established on whose behalf the International Monetary Fund would sell the gold. The Fund would sell gold to members with net creditor positions in the Fund, that is, members with super gold tranche positions, at the official price (SDR 35 an ounce), consonant with the idea that the Fund was replenishing its holdings of their currencies. These members would in turn transfer the gold to the Trust Fund at the same official price against the payment of currency. As Trustee for the Trust Fund, the International Monetary Fund could then sell the gold at public auctions at market-related prices. The Managing Director had already reached an understanding with central banks of members in creditor positions that they would cooperate in this currency replenishment operation.

The Interim Committee also agreed in January 1976 (as described in the previous chapter) that the BIS could bid in the Fund's auctions but could not do so on behalf of the central bank of any Fund member. Central banks of members were obliged by the Articles not to buy gold at any other than the official price and hence were precluded from participating directly in the auctions until after the Articles were amended.

ARRANGING AUCTIONS

Beyond these general principles no procedures had been agreed. Establishing procedures involved answering many vexing questions. How frequently should gold auctions be held and how much gold should be offered at each auction? Should the Fund limit bidders to large gold dealers, bankers, and financial institutions, and exclude industrial users of gold, or should they and possibly even private citizens be permitted to bid? What should be the size of a minimum appropriate bid? Could the Executive Directors reject a bid and if so, by what criteria? How should the Executive Directors determine the prices at which to accept bids? Should gold be awarded to successful bidders at the prices which they actually bid or at a common price to all? (Under the bid-price method, all bidders paid the actual price which they had bid. Under the common-price method, all bidders paid the same price, which was the highest price bid at which all the gold that was offered was actually sold.)

In addition, related topics had to be settled. Before distribution (or restitution) of gold directly to members at the official price could begin, how to execute sales at the official price had to be decided. Decisions also had to be taken about how to distribute the profits from the Trust Fund to developing members.

As these questions were considered in February 1976, there was considerable anxiety among Executive Directors about the possible effects of the Fund's sales on prices of gold in private markets. Because the amount of gold exchanged in private markets was small compared with the 50 million ounces that the Fund was planning to sell, they were apprehensive that the sale could sharply depress prices in private markets. Declines in gold prices would mean lower profits for gold producers, a special concern for officials of Canada and South Africa. Lower prices for gold could also mean potentially lower valuations for official gold reserves, should countries decide to value their gold reserves at market-related prices. This concern was of importance not only to France, which already valued its gold reserves at market-related prices, but also to several other European countries that held relatively large amounts of gold reserves. Lower profits from the Fund's gold sales were also of grave concern to officials of the developing members that were to receive those profits.

The Executive Directors were also concerned about the impact of the Fund's gold sales on the distribution of ownership of the world's officially held gold. Financial officials might scramble to acquire gold as the Fund disposed of its holdings. Although central banks of members were forbidden to bid in the Fund's auctions until after the Articles of Agreement were amended, the eagerness of some central banks, especially in Europe, to acquire more official holdings of gold occasioned concern that they might try to participate secretly or indirectly in the Fund's auctions.

Since the amended Articles of Agreement, which would alter the rules for sales of gold by the Fund, were expected to come into effect in about two years, it was quickly agreed that the four-year program of gold auctions and gold distribution should be divided into two two-year periods, the second one to occur after the Articles were amended. But resolution of all other questions was to take months of debate. The Executive Directors, like the staff, were especially worried that the prices bid and the names of bidders at the auctions would be leaked to the press or to other prospective bidders. The Executive Board's general discussion of gold auctions had already been leaked to the press. What would happen in the case of a specific gold auction? The Executive Directors therefore considered it essential that the names of bidders, the prices offered, and how the Fund determined successful bids were all to be kept absolutely secret. Since their individual votes on whether to accept or reject bids necessarily reflected their views on "appropriate" prices for gold, they were concerned to keep their voting confidential even from each other. They were also worried that while individual bids were being considered, the prices being accepted by the Fund might be leaked. If there were a great number of bids to decide on, accepting bids could go on for hours, increasing the risk of leaks. Hence, the Executive Directors even contemplated installing electronic devices in the Board Room to speed up deciding on bids.

Other questions also had to be considered before gold auctions could begin. How often should the auctions be conducted? Using the recent experience of the U.S. Treasury with two gold auctions in 1975, Mr. Cross recommended a definite program of gold sales so as not to unsettle private markets. The Fund should announce in advance the frequency of auctions and the amounts to be sold over the whole four-year period. Mr. Pieske, however, preferred that the Fund's program not be too fixed in advance so as to allow the Fund flexibility after it had gained experience with the auctions.

Another disputed point was how to ensure effectively that central banks did not participate. Mr. Wahl was so insistent that the BIS be able to bid in the Fund's auctions that other Executive Directors became skeptical that the BIS might serve as agent for the Bank of France or for the central banks of other members. Mr. Kawaguchi, wanting to be assured that this was not the case, proposed that bidders state in writing that they were not serving as agent of the central bank of any member, but such a statement seemed to reflect on the integrity of those bidding in the auctions. Messrs. Jagannathan, Monday, and Suárez argued that developing members eligible to receive profits from the gold sales be given the option of receiving gold in the form of specie instead of in currency. They could add this gold bullion to their reserves and sell it later, thereby benefiting directly from subsequent higher prices for gold.

Members of the Executive Board who were concerned that the Fund's sales might depress prices for gold in private markets did not speak directly about this point. They rather spoke about the consequences of lower gold prices on the profits that the Fund would realize on its gold sales and hence on the amounts available for developing members. In this way they hoped to gain the support of Executive Directors from developing members for their suggestions on procedures for gold auctions. Mr. Wahl, for example, argued that the Fund ought to maximize its profits from gold auctions and suggested that the Executive Directors determine, just before the opening of bids, a minimum profit that the Fund would regard as acceptable. If bids were too low to achieve the minimum acceptable profit, the Fund would refuse to sell. But Mr. Wahl recognized the dilemma posed by his suggestion. The Fund could not fix a floor on the profits from its gold sales without at the same time establishing a new semiofficial, or quasi-official, price for gold.

Because of their unique sensitivity, all sessions of the Executive Board relating to gold auctions were restricted, that is, they were not open even to members of the Fund staff, except for a very limited few, a relatively uncommon situation in the Fund.

PROCEDURES AGREED

It was not until May 1976 that the Executive Directors agreed on arrangements for the sale at auction of 12.5 million ounces of gold (half of the 25 million ounces to be sold) during the next two years and for the restitution to members of 12.5 million ounces of gold in the same two years, before the Articles were amended. Arrangements for the auction of the second 12.5 million ounces and for the restitution of another 12.5 million ounces after the Second Amendment came into force were to be announced sometime in 1978.

There were to be 16 public auctions at the Fund's headquarters in Washington, D.C., at intervals of six weeks, except during the main holiday seasons. About 780,000 ounces of gold were to be offered at each auction. Procedures such as the method of pricing, the minimum acceptable bid, or the place of delivery could be changed from time to time. For at least the first two, but no more than the first three auctions, the common-price method was to be used, and for at least the two following auctions the bid-price method was to be used. An announcement of the terms and conditions for each auction would be made some weeks in advance. No bid could be submitted by the government of a member of the Fund or by an agent acting on behalf of a member government at a price inconsistent with the Articles of Agreement, but the BIS might submit bids. Each bidder was regarded as bidding on its own behalf. The Fund reserved the right to reject any or all bids.

Developing members eligible to receive profits from gold sales would have an option to receive their share of these profits in gold rather than in currency. Any member electing this option was to inform the Fund of its choice not later than 60 days after agreement was reached on the list of developing members eligible to receive profits from gold sales.

Gold restitution was to be carried out once a year during each of the four years of the gold sales program, with the first operation taking place around the middle of the 12-month period following the first auction. The technique to be used before the Articles of Agreement were amended was complicated, involving replenishment of the Fund's holdings of needed currencies, the only legal way for the Fund to sell gold under its Articles. Gold was to be sold directly to all members whose currency was usable in the Fund's transactions and whose creditor positions were large enough by an agreed minimum amount to permit the Fund to sell gold against those members' own currencies, that is, the sale of gold by the Fund in exchange for their currency would not raise the Fund's holdings of the member's currency above 75 percent of its quota. Distribution of gold to other members, not in a creditor position in the Fund, was to be carried out indirectly. Their share of the gold to be distributed was to be sold to the creditor members whose super gold tranche positions were large enough to accommodate the additional replenishment with the understanding that the creditor members would resell the gold at the official price to the other noncreditor members against convertible currency acceptable to the creditor members. A noncreditor member with a balance of payments need could postpone its participation in gold restitution until after the amended Articles of Agreement came into effect, when it could buy gold from the Fund directly with its own currency.

Internal Procedures for Auctions

The procedure for deciding within the Fund on the bids to be accepted was spelled out precisely. A procedure was emphasized in which the Executive Directors could vote on accepting bids in strict secrecy. Sealed bids from the public were to be submitted to the Managing Director. These bids had to follow certain prescribed rules and were to be carefully checked by the staff. The Managing Director was then to formulate a proposal as to how much gold to award to which bidders at which prices. He was then to call the Executive Directors to the Executive Board Room, supply them with information on the quantities and prices of the bids but not the names of bidders, and advise them of his proposal. If the Managing Director's proposal was to sell the full amount of gold offered in the auction, he was to proceed with the acceptance of individual bids. An Executive Director could register his disagreement on an individual bid and this disagreement would immediately convert the assembly of Executive Directors into an Executive Board meeting. At that meeting, a vote on whether the Executive Directors would or would not support the Managing Director's proposal was to be taken without discussion. The vote was to be secret even from each other.

To ensure that the gold prices being bid were not leaked, all persons present in the Executive Board Room were to remain there and were not to communicate with anyone outside the Executive Board Room until the course of action was decided upon.

If the Managing Director's proposal to sell the full amount of gold being auctioned at the time was not acceptable, the Executive Directors were to vote on successively higher bids beginning with the bids at the lowest price that would allow the awarding of the full amount of gold subject to auction. If bids had not been received for the full amount subject to auction or if the Managing Director was to propose a course of action different from the sale of the full amount, he was to call a meeting of the Executive Board for a secret vote on his proposal. If the proposal was not accepted, the Executive Directors would then vote according to the procedure described above.

Even the term "Executive Board Room" was defined. It was interpreted to include the anteroom and all the adjacent space lying inside the doors between the corridor and the anteroom. When gold auctions were taking place, these doors were to be guarded and could be passed through only by maintenance or other support personnel or by persons specifically authorized by the Managing Director or the Deputy Managing Director. The telephones inside this area were to be disconnected. No messages were to be sent by persons inside the area to persons outside the area, or vice versa. Although he usually attended Executive Board meetings, a Technical Assistant to an Executive Director could attend the auction only if the Executive Director or his Alternate was absent. The Managing Director was to determine which staff members he wished to have present; all other staff members were to be excluded from the Board Room.

After an auction, the following minimum information was to be made available to the public immediately: the quantity of gold offered, the quantity bid, the quantity sold, the average or common price, and the maximum, average, and minimum prices of successful bids. If he considered it useful, the Managing Director could at his discretion supplement this information with more details about the quantities bid in suitably arranged price brackets. For a short while after the auction, the Managing Director would have available in his office a list of the names of the successful bidders for scrutiny only by the Executive Directors.

Never had the Fund gone to such lengths to ensure secrecy, and not for many years had the Fund spelled out its internal procedures in such detail. In this respect, the exercise was reminiscent of debates 25 years earlier when the Fund was inaugurating procedures for conducting Article XIV consultations with members. Then there had been considerable concern among Executive Directors that the Fund might extend its jurisdiction excessively or that the Fund management and staff might pursue topics of great sensitivity to members. Accordingly, the Fund's procedures for consultations were carefully defined in advance.[2]

THE AUCTIONS

The first auction took place on June 2, 1976. The Fund awarded 780,000 ounces of gold, the total amount for which bids were invited, to successful bidders at a common price of $126.00 an ounce. At the second auction, six weeks later, on July 14, the Fund again awarded 780,000 ounces of gold to successful bidders, this time at a common price of $122.05 an ounce. On September 15, at the third auction, 780,000 ounces of gold were awarded to successful bidders according to the bid-price method. By this time prices in free markets for gold were falling and prices in the Fund's auction were lower than those of earlier auctions; they ranged from $108.76 to $114.00 an ounce.

When the Governors gathered in Manila in October for their Annual Meeting, some expressed satisfaction with the results of the Fund's gold auctions. Per Kleppe noted that the Fund's gold sales had taken place without any attempt at pegging a price for gold.[3] A number of other Governors, however, were disturbed by the declining prices for gold in private markets and queried whether the Fund should continue its program. Emphasizing that the benefits to developing members from sales of the Fund's gold declined when gold prices were lower, Donald S. Macdonald was concerned that the Fund's sales program might be having adverse effects on the gold market.[4] Bernard Clappier likewise argued that the decline in the price of gold since the Fund's gold sales got under way would reduce the resources of the Trust Fund. It was important, he stated, that the Fund's gold sales take place in the best possible "technical conditions, so as to maximize the profits derived from the sale of the metal."[5] Bernal Jiménez M., speaking on behalf of the Latin American countries, also noted that holders and producers of gold as well as beneficiaries of the Trust Fund had been hurt by the fall in the price of gold to which the Fund's auctions "may have contributed" and requested the Fund to reconsider its mandate to sell gold over a four-year period.[6]

These concerns led the Executive Directors after the Annual Meeting to discuss the possibility of changing the schedule of gold auctions. They concluded, however,

---

[2]The Executive Board's discussions in 1951–52 relating to the procedures for Article XIV consultations and the procedures agreed were described at length in *History, 1945–65*, Vol. II, pp. 229–41.

[3]Statement by the Governor of the World Bank for Norway, *Summary Proceedings, 1976*, pp. 31–32.

[4]Statement by the Governor of the Fund and the World Bank for Canada, *Summary Proceedings, 1976*, p. 37.

[5]Statement by the Governor of the World Bank for France, *Summary Proceedings, 1976*, p. 77.

[6]Statement by the Governor of the Fund for Costa Rica, *Summary Proceedings, 1976*, p. 176.

that the Fund had to carry out its mandate for selling gold over the next four-year period and that it was less unsettling to the gold market for the Fund to adhere to its agreed schedule of auctions rather than to hold auctions irregularly when prices were relatively high. Concern about declining prices for gold was lessened a few weeks later. In the fourth auction, on October 27, the range of prices bid was higher than in the third auction, and in the fifth auction, on December 8, the bids submitted were at considerably higher prices than they were in any of the previous auctions; successful bids ranged from $137.00 an ounce to $150.00 an ounce. Relatively high prices, ranging from $133.26 an ounce to $142.00 an ounce, prevailed again at the sixth auction, on January 26, 1977.[7]

Changes in Procedures in 1977

Following a review of the experience with the first six auctions, Executive Directors in November–December 1976, again in restricted session, made changes in the auctions starting in March 1977.[8] The most important change was in timing. Starting with the auction on March 2, 1977, auctions were to be held monthly, on the first Wednesday of each month. Fund officials believed that holding auctions at irregular times every six to nine weeks was creating uncertainty in the market, and that it would be preferable to hold to a preannounced schedule of monthly auctions. The amount to be offered at each sale was adjusted to this greater frequency of auctions; 525,000 ounces of gold were to be offered each time.

Some modifications were made also in the pricing method, the minimum bid, the place of delivery, and the period allowed for payments. For example, although in the first six auctions the common-price method had been used for four and the bid-price method for two, the new arrangement stipulated that the pricing method was to remain unchanged for three successive auctions. To widen the circle of potential participants, the minimum bid was lowered from 2,000 ounces (five standard bars) to 1,200 ounces (three standard bars).

By early 1977, the Executive Directors and the management and staff generally agreed that the Fund's experience with gold auctions was successful. Demand was high, all the gold offered was being sold, and the auctions were all oversubscribed. Professional gold market dealers participated regularly. The need for secrecy had also been exaggerated. After the first few auctions, the Fund even published the names of successful bidders.

---

[7]Prices in the Fund's auctions closely followed the prices prevailing in private markets for gold. Developments in private markets for gold in 1975–78 and beyond were described by Michael G. Martin, "Gold Market Developments, 1975–77," *Finance & Development* (Washington), Vol. 15 (March 1978), pp. 31–35, and "The Changing Gold Market, 1978–80," *Finance & Development*, Vol. 17 (December 1980), pp. 40–43.

[8]E.B. Decision No. 5273-(76/163) TR, December 7, 1976; Vol. III below, pp. 560.

AUCTIONS AFTER THE SECOND AMENDMENT

In May 1978, after the second year of the four-year program was completed, the Executive Board reviewed the policies and procedures relating to gold auctions and decided on the terms and conditions for the second two-year period. With three exceptions, the previous terms and conditions remained unchanged. As a result of the entry into force of the amended Articles, members could transact in gold at any price, and consequently official agencies of members were not restricted from participating in the auctions held from June 1978 onward. A further consequence of the Second Amendment coming into effect was that the Fund could no longer replenish its currency holdings by the sale of gold; instead, it could sell gold directly on the market. Third, the Fund reduced the amount to be offered in each auction to 470,000 ounces in order to accommodate noncompetitive bids from developing members.

Developing members that were eligible to receive profits from the Trust Fund and had elected to receive gold in specie rather than in currency were to be able to obtain this gold by submitting noncompetitive bids in the gold auctions.[9] A noncompetitive bid was a bid that did not indicate a price. If the Fund used the common-price method, those developing members submitting a noncompetitive bid would get gold at the common price. If the bid-price technique was used, they would get gold at the average price. In effect, developing members submitting noncompetitive bids would get that amount of gold for which they bid at the price that resulted from the auction.

Of the 104 developing members that the Executive Board decided were eligible to participate in the distribution of profits from the Trust Fund (described in the next chapter), 39 had informed the Fund that they wished to retain the option to receive gold instead. These 39 members accounted for 14.6 percent of Fund quotas as of the end of August 1975, entitling them to submit noncompetitive bids for a total of 3.5 million ounces of gold. Members that retained the option, however, were not obliged to submit noncompetitive bids. The Fund agreed that noncompetitive bids from developing members could be submitted in one or more of the auctions held after May 1978 and before the end of May 1979. The amount of gold sold to noncompetitive bidders in an auction was in addition to that awarded to competitive bidders and reduced the amount remaining to be sold in later auctions.

Otherwise, after the Second Amendment came into effect, the modalities for the auctioning of gold remained unchanged. Auctions continued to be held on the first Wednesday of each month, the minimum bid remained at 1,200 ounces, a deposit of the higher of $10 an ounce or $25,000 continued to be required, delivery was to take place at one of the Fund's gold depositories, and payment was to be completed approximately seven business days after the auction. All auctions were to be conducted on the bid-price method.

---

[9]E.B. Decision No. 5779-(78/74) TR, May 19, 1978; Vol. III below, pp. 562–63.

In the last six months of 1978, participation by competitive bidders at the Fund's monthly gold auctions was heavy and the prices bid gradually rose. In the June auction, the prices of successful bids ranged from $182.86 an ounce to $183.92 an ounce and, by the November auction, they were still higher, ranging from $223.03 an ounce to $230.00 an ounce. In the December auction, prices bid were somewhat lower. In this period, noncompetitive bids by developing members were submitted by Colombia, Cyprus, India, Kenya, Korea, Malaysia, Mauritius, Mexico, Nepal, the Philippines, and Tanzania. As had been planned when noncompetitive participation in gold auctions was begun, the Executive Directors regularly reviewed the amount of gold to be sold in each monthly auction, taking into account the purchases of gold by noncompetitive bidders. They decided to continue with the monthly sale of 470,000 ounces of gold through May 1979 when they planned another review of the gold sales program.[10]

Table 29 gives data for the dates of the Fund's auctions from June 2, 1976 to December 6, 1978, and for the pricing method used, the amounts bid, the amounts awarded to noncompetitive bidders after June 1978, the price range of successful bids, the average award price, and the resulting profits.

In summary, the Fund's gold auctions quickly became a regular feature of the world's gold market. They continued to attract the substantial participation of major international gold dealers. The sales prices in the auctions remained close to prices prevailing in private gold markets, with the Fund's average sales prices generally within a range of $1 above or below the average London fixing price on the day of the auction. In the end, just as had happened earlier in regard to consultations procedures, it was evident that the need for secrecy and worry that the new techniques would be abused had been overemphasized. There was some suspicion that a few central banks may have participated indirectly in the Fund's gold auctions through the BIS, but relatively little was made of these incidents.

Because of rapidly rising gold prices in world markets, the Fund earned a great deal more money than had been expected on its gold auctions to the satisfaction of virtually all Executive Directors and officials from member governments.

---

[10]In May 1979, when the third year of the program and the end of the period during which noncompetitive bids could be submitted was completed, the Executive Board reviewed gold sales policies and procedures and decided on the terms and conditions for the fourth and last year. The only important change was a reduction of the amount to be auctioned every month, from 470,000 ounces to 444,000 ounces, an adjustment required because of the gold that had been sold to developing members earlier in noncompetitive bidding. This adjustment permitted an equal amount of gold to be sold in each of the 12 auctions held in the last year of the program. Auctions continued through May 1980. When the last auction was finished, there had been 45 public auctions at which 23.52 million ounces of gold were sold at prices ranging from $108.76 an ounce in September 1976 to $718.01 an ounce in February 1980. The total profits that the Fund received in the four-year period amounted to $4.6 billion. Details of all 45 auctions can be found in *Annual Report, 1980*, p. 86.

Table 29. Gold Auctions, 1976–78

Date	Pricing Method	Ounces Bid (thousands)	Ounces Awarded to Noncompetitive Bidders (thousands)	Price Range of Successful Bids (US$ a fine ounce)	Average Award Price	Profits (millions of U.S. dollars)
1976						
June 2	Common	2,320	—	126.00–134.00	126.00	67.1
July 14	Common	2,114	—	122.05–126.50	122.05	64.0
Sept. 15	Bid	3,662	—	108.76–114.00	109.40	53.8
Oct. 27	Bid	4,214	—	116.77–119.05	117.71	60.2
Dec. 8	Common	4,307	—	137.00–150.00	137.00	75.4
1977						
Jan. 26	Common	2,003	—	133.26–142.00	133.26	72.5
Mar. 2	Bid	1,633	—	145.55–148.00	146.51	55.6
Apr. 6	Bid	1,278	—	148.55–151.00	149.18	57.0
May 4	Bid	1,316	—	147.33–150.26	148.02	56.4
June 1	Common	1,014	—	143.32–150.00	143.32	53.9
July 6	Common	1,358	—	140.26–145.00	140.26	52.2
Aug. 3	Common	1,439	—	146.26–150.00	146.26	55.3
Sept. 7	Bid	1,084	—	147.61–149.65	147.78	56.2
Oct. 5	Bid	971	—	154.99–157.14	155.14	60.0
Nov. 2	Bid	1,356	—	161.76–163.27	161.86	63.3
Dec. 7	Common	1,134	—	160.03–165.00	160.03	62.1
1978						
Jan. 4	Common	985	—	171.26–180.00	171.26	67.7
Feb. 1	Common	598	—	175.00–181.25	175.00	69.7
Mar. 1	Bid	1,418	—	181.13–185.76	181.95	72.9
Apr. 5	Bid	1,368	—	177.61–180.26	177.92	70.8
May 3	Bid	3,104	—	170.11–171.50	170.40	66.8
June 7	Bid	1,072	925.2	182.86–183.92	183.09	195.6
July 5	Bid	797	20.8	183.97–185.01	184.14	69.0
Aug. 2	Bid	1,468	70.0	203.03–205.11	203.28	85.8
Sept. 6	Bid	773	133.6	212.39–213.51	212.50	101.4
Oct. 4	Bid	806	134.4	223.57–224.62	223.68	107.7
Nov. 1	Bid	690	80.0	223.03–230.00	224.02	98.4
Dec. 6	Bid	1,965	20.0	195.51–196.75	196.06	74.2

RESTITUTION

The distribution, or restitution, of gold was to be carried out in four annual installments in proportion to their quotas as of August 31, 1975 to all countries that were members of the Fund on August 31, 1975 and to Papua New Guinea.[11] In December 1976, the Executive Directors made arrangements for the first phase of restitution.[12] It was to begin on January 10, 1977, a change from the previously envisaged starting time of December 1976, six months after the first gold auction on June 2, 1976. This short postponement was due to operational considerations of the

[11]A membership resolution by the Board of Governors had been adopted on August 10, 1975, but Papua New Guinea had not yet accepted membership.

[12]E.B. Decision No. 5274-(76/163), December 7, 1976; Vol. III below, pp. 561.

Fund's gold depositories during December (a holiday period for most Fund members). Direct restitution took place to members with creditor positions in the Fund by their exchanging their currencies for gold sold to them by the Fund. Indirect restitution to other members took place in two phases. The Fund sold gold to a creditor-intermediary member against its own currency and then the intermediary member immediately resold the gold to a noncreditor member against payment by the noncreditor member of a currency acceptable to the intermediary member. Twelve members with relatively large creditor positions in the Fund acted as intermediaries: Austria, Belgium, Brazil, Canada, France, the Federal Republic of Germany, Japan, the Netherlands, Norway, Sweden, the United States, and Venezuela. Just under 6 million ounces (SDR 210 million valued at the official price of SDR 35 an ounce) were sold to 112 members.

In the second of the four annual distributions, in January 1978, the Fund sold just over 6 million ounces (SDR 213.2 million at the official price) to 114 members, with the same 12 creditor members again serving as intermediaries. The Executive Board agreed to the requests of several developing members that their participation in the second gold distribution be postponed for reasons of balance of payments, just as a number of developing members had postponed the purchase of their shares of gold in the first distribution. Such postponements could continue until not later than 30 days after the entry into effect of the Second Amendment.[13] The Second Amendment was to make it possible for members to buy gold directly from the Fund in exchange for their own currencies, with no handling charges. The Fund's holdings of a member's currency in excess of quota acquired as a result of payments for gold were to be subject to charges at the rate that applied to holdings from a purchase in the credit tranches and to be repurchased not later than two years after the sale of gold to the member. After the Second Amendment came into effect on April 1, 1978, several members that had requested postponement of their participation in previous distributions of gold received gold from the Fund in exchange for their own currencies.

The bulk of the third annual distribution of gold to members occurred in December 1978, with the rest of the distribution taking place in the first three months of 1979. The Fund sold 6.1 million ounces (SDR 214.5 million) to 126 members. As in the first two distributions, arrangements were again not completed with regard to distributions to Democratic Kampuchea and China. The third annual distribution took place under the amended Articles that permitted the sale of gold to all participating members in exchange for their own currencies.[14]

---

[13]E.B. Decision No. 5314-(77/6), January 10, 1977; Vol. III below, p. 562.

[14]Two further developments took place shortly after the end of 1978. In March 1979 the Executive Board adopted a decision specifying the circumstances under which a member that had used its currency for the purchase of gold from the Fund was obliged to buy back its currency. A member whose balance of payments and reserve positions were considered sufficiently strong had to repurchase the balances of its currency acquired by the Fund as a result of the Fund's distribution of gold within 30 days after the Executive Board's decision adopting a particular operational budget or 30 days after the date of the distribution of gold, whichever date was later. Early in 1980 the fourth, and last, distribution of gold by the Fund—6.6 million ounces to 127 members—was made, bringing the total distribution over the four-year period to just under 25 million ounces.

CHAPTER
34

A Trust Fund Established

E STABLISHMENT OF A TRUST FUND in 1976 was the clearest expression of the changed character of the Fund's financial assistance after 1973. After 1973 the Fund, for the first time, started to resemble a lending institution. It was committing its resources for longer periods. It "lent" money through an expanding number of facilities rather than under a more or less monolithic policy, as had been its custom. It permitted members to draw amounts that resulted in the Fund holding their currencies in amounts substantially larger than 200 percent of quota, the previous limitation. The size of a member's quota, the traditional measure of its contribution to the pool of currencies making up the Fund's assets, consequently became less of a restriction on the amount a member might draw from the Fund. The Fund resorted more and more to borrowing to augment its own resources.

These new directions in Fund policy were reflected even in the words used to discuss the Fund's financial policies and operations. Terms like "lending by the Fund," "Fund loans" or "Fund credits," "members' borrowing from the Fund," and "interest rates," customarily used to describe the operations of banking institutions, including the World Bank, gradually crept into the vocabulary of discussions of the Fund's financial assistance. Technical terms such as "drawings," "purchases," "repurchases," and "charges" that more accurately described the revolving character of the currencies which members temporarily exchanged to tide themselves over short-term balance of payments deficits, receded into the background, appearing mainly in documents prepared by the staff.

The Trust Fund went so far in a new direction that it required the creation of a separate arrangement. The Trust Fund was sui generis. It had its own resources, separate from those of the International Monetary Fund. It extended loans in the traditional sense. The International Monetary Fund was the Trustee and administrator, receiving payment for its services. This arrangement and use of the term "Trust Fund" was in line with similar funds already created by the United Nations and its other specialized agencies. The Subsidy Account, described in Chapter 18 above, was also a kind of trust fund.[1]

This chapter describes the creation of the Trust Fund and two of its first four years.

PROPOSAL AND INITIAL REACTIONS

The proposal for a Trust Fund originated with U.S. officials in late 1974. As noted in Chapter 18, it was part of Mr. Kissinger's proposal in November 1974 that a financial support fund be created in the OECD to give the members of that organization a safety net to help finance their balance of payments deficits stemming from higher oil prices. Mr. Kissinger also considered it politically expedient to propose some comparable facility for developing countries. Mr. Kissinger's desire for a facility for developing countries coincided with that of U.S. Treasury officials, especially of Mr. Simon and Jack F. Bennett, then Under Secretary for Monetary Affairs, to phase gold out of the international monetary system. Together they came up with the idea of the Fund's selling some of its large holdings of gold at the high prices prevailing in the free market and putting the profits into a trust fund for disbursal to selected developing members. This technique was attractive because it would make extra money available to developing countries without the need for industrial countries to allocate additional funds. Thus, the proposal for a Trust Fund to help finance payments deficits of the poorest oil importing developing countries on highly concessional terms was aimed at making the proposals of industrial countries to solve their own problems more palatable to developing countries. In much the same way in the mid-1960s the Group of Ten had initiated proposals for reserve assets for developing countries so as to make more acceptable their proposals for creation of a new reserve asset for themselves.[2]

When the proposed Trust Fund was first discussed in the Executive Board in December 1974, Mr. Cross explained the essence of the U.S. proposal. The special needs of the poorest developing countries in adjusting to sharply higher prices for oil and for foodgrains had already been recognized in the discussions for a Subsidy Account to help defray the high interest costs of using the Fund's 1975 oil facility and in the emergency operation of the United Nations for the most seriously affected (MSA) countries.[3] Beyond these measures, the poorest developing members would need temporary balance of payments assistance on concessional terms even after the Fund's oil facilities ended early in 1976. Appropriate periods of grace before repayment, long repayment periods, and low interest rates would all be necessary.

---

[1]The reader interested in legal principles underlying the establishment of the Trust Fund is referred to Joseph Gold, "Trust Funds in International Law: The Contribution of the International Monetary Fund to a Code of Principles," *American Journal of International Law* (Washington), Vol. 72 (October 1978), pp. 856–66.

[2]See *History, 1966–71*, Vol. I, pp. 69–70.

[3]The Subsidy Account and the UN Emergency Operation of 1974 were described in Chap. 18, pp. 351–55.

The Fund could not provide this combination of concessional terms through its usual policies partly because the Fund followed—and rightfully so—the principle of uniform treatment for all members specified in its Articles of Agreement.

From Mr. Cross's explanation and from statements by other U.S. officials at the time, a way to get around this uniformity of treatment appears to have been the principal motivation of U.S. officials in suggesting a special Trust Fund.[4] By means of a Trust Fund to be used only by developing members, the Fund could channel resources to a specified category of its members. This arrangement was unusual for the Fund: all of its other resource arrangements were intended for use by all members.

There was a second reason why U.S. officials proposed a separate Trust Fund. As noted in Chapters 31 and 32, some special arrangement was needed to enable the International Monetary Fund to sell its holdings of gold at a profit. Under the Articles of Agreement prior to the Second Amendment, the Fund could sell its holdings of gold only at the official price of SDR 35 an ounce.[5] It could, however, replenish its holdings of currencies by selling gold (at the official price) to members whose currencies the Fund needed because its holdings of these currencies were running low. In other words, the Fund could sell gold to members with creditor positions in the Fund. The Fund could also have an understanding with these creditor members that they, in turn, would transfer any such gold, again at the official price, to the newly created Trust Fund. In this roundabout way the Fund could effectively place gold in the Trust Fund. The Fund could then, acting as Trustee for the Trust Fund, sell gold from the Trust Fund at a profit and disburse these profits to any selected group of members. To make this arrangement consistent with the Articles of Agreement, the Trust Fund would have to be an entirely separate arrangement from the International Monetary Fund but it could be administered by the staff of the International Monetary Fund. For these staff services the International Monetary Fund would receive payment.

Initial Reactions

After examining the U.S. proposal, the staff concluded that it would be possible for the Fund to administer a Trust Fund of the type proposed but that a separate affiliate organization with its own constitution and another Board of Executive Directors, as initially envisaged by U.S. officials, would not be necessary. The Trust Fund could be set up on the basis of an Instrument legally designating the

---

[4]See statement of the Secretary of the Treasury, William E. Simon, before the Joint Economic Committee, November 25, 1974, reprinted in U.S. Treasury Department, *News* (WS-164), November 25, 1974, pp. 3 and 8, and remarks of Under Secretary of the Treasury for Monetary Affairs, Jack F. Bennett, before the National Economists Club, Washington, D.C., December 17, 1974, reprinted in U.S. Treasury Department, *News* (WS-185), December 17, 1974, p. 8.

[5]The reason the official price of gold held by the Fund remained at SDR 35 an ounce, even after two devaluations of the U.S. dollar in terms of gold raised the official price of gold in terms of dollars to $42 an ounce, has been explained in Chap. 29, fn. 8, p. 582.

International Monetary Fund as Trustee. The same Board of Executive Directors and staff could serve both the International Monetary Fund and the Trust Fund.

Mr. Witteveen and the staff welcomed the U.S. proposal. In their view there would be a need to help low-income developing members finance oil-related payments deficits on concessional terms after the 1975 oil facility had expired. The latter arrangement was to last only until early 1976. Once it was finished, the problem of how to ease the adjustment to higher energy prices of low-income members unable to afford much foreign debt would become acute. The existing facilities of the Fund, based as they necessarily had to be on the principle of uniformity of treatment of members, could not be sufficiently adapted to help these members.

Officials of developing members were at first skeptical of the U.S. proposal. For two years in the Committee of Twenty, they had been insisting on a link between allocation of SDRs and development finance and did not want the proposed Trust Fund, admittedly a temporary expedient for financing oil-related balance of payments deficits for only a few developing members, to substitute for a longer-term arrangement for development assistance for all developing members, such as the long-advocated link would be. Nonetheless, looking for any and all means of financial assistance, they agreed to study the Trust Fund proposal. The Development Committee, meeting in January 1975, in addition to welcoming the 1975 oil facility in the Fund and the establishment of the Subsidy Account, invited the Executive Boards of the World Bank and the Fund "to study the desirability of creating a special trust fund that would provide, for the period immediately ahead, additional highly concessional resources to meet the requirements of the most seriously affected countries, and the possible modalities of such a fund."[6]

In the next several months of 1975, the staffs of the Fund and of the World Bank worked together to determine the desirability of setting up the Trust Fund and its "modalities," that is, the forms it might take. The Executive Boards of both organizations also considered the proposed Trust Fund. The Executive Directors of the World Bank, other than the Executive Director appointed by the United States, were not inclined to support it. The World Bank was just establishing a new "third window," and its Executive Directors were reluctant to add another facility to the growing number of schemes proposed for financing the oil-related payments deficits of the poorest developing members. They were also concerned that the Trust Fund might drain resources away from the World Bank's other financial arrangements. For the special Trust Fund to serve its intended purposes, they concluded it had to receive resources additional to those assigned to existing institutions, such as the International Development Association (IDA), or to those to be assigned to the new proposed third window of the World Bank. Since the Trust Fund was to be capitalized through the sale of gold belonging to the International Monetary Fund,

---

[6]Communiqué of Development Committee, January 17, 1975, par. 4; Vol. III below, pp. 580–81.

most Executive Directors of the World Bank also felt that further discussion should be deferred until the Fund made the crucial decisions on the sale of its gold.

When the Fund's Executive Directors discussed the proposed Trust Fund in early 1975, they also had serious reservations. While Messrs. Deif, Roberto Gavaldá (Argentina), Kharmawan, Monday, Prasad, and Yaméogo, Executive Directors from developing members that would be the main beneficiaries, urged that the Trust Fund be created, the Executive Directors from industrial members had a number of arguments against it. Mr. Wahl's arguments were the strongest. The gold held by the Fund should not be sold in private markets; it should be "given back" to all members at the official price. In any event, the debate about the future role of gold in the international monetary system had to be resolved on its own merits and not within the context of setting up a special Trust Fund to help poor developing members. No such development financing institution as the Trust Fund, with or without its own Board of Executive Directors, should be created outside the framework of the International Monetary Fund; the provision of development aid, as was envisaged for the Trust Fund, should be accomplished through the World Bank. A special Trust Fund to provide assistance for oil-related balance of payments deficits could conflict with the purposes of the 1975 oil facility just put into operation after considerable debate.

Mr. Kawaguchi also did not favor the proposed Trust Fund. Like Mr. Wahl, he believed that the disposal of the Fund's large holdings of gold should be discussed separately and not as a means of "providing additional resources for development finance." Mr. Pieske voiced the doubts of officials of the Federal Republic of Germany on the desirability of a special Trust Fund using arguments similar to those raised in the Executive Board of the World Bank. With the oil facility, the extended facility, the new proposed third window of the World Bank, and the Emergency Operation of the United Nations, all created in 1974–75, there were already enough facilities for balance of payments financing or development assistance. Moreover, additional resources could not be mobilized for the Trust Fund; potential funds would be obtained at the expense of funds that would otherwise be channeled to existing institutions. Messrs. Drabble and Rawlinson were concerned that attention to the proposed Trust Fund might jeopardize establishment of the new Subsidy Account.

An added complication to the discussions was that the Iranian authorities proposed that the special Trust Fund be financed by voluntary contributions of any members in a position to make them. In this way, the oil producing members would have an outlet for their surplus revenues under the auspices of an international organization rather than of national governments, and the Trust Fund would have available resources additional to those obtained as profits from the sale of Fund gold. This proposal complicated the discussions because it caused a debate among the Executive Directors as to whether the entire Trust Fund, or at least a substantial portion of it, might not be financed from voluntary contributions instead of from sales of the Fund's gold. Financing by voluntary contributions avoided the need for officials of industrial members to resolve the extremely controversial questions about gold. However, officials of the industrial and developed members were not immediately receptive to the alternative, because if the Trust Fund was to be wholly or mainly financed by voluntary contributions, officials of members with surplus oil revenues would surely insist on having a much larger share of the voting power in any new Trust Fund or even in the International Monetary Fund than they currently had.

Following these discussions, the Executive Directors both of the Fund and of the World Bank sent to Henri Konan Bédié, Minister of Economy and Finance of Ivory Coast, and Chairman of the Development Committee, a report on the Trust Fund in time for the Development Committee's meeting in June 1975. The report concluded that a special Trust Fund was needed and that, in view of the character of the assistance needed, it would be best administered by the International Monetary Fund, rather than by the World Bank. The major question, however, was whether sufficient financial support could be mustered to finance it. There was certainly no agreement that the International Monetary Fund might sell its gold to provide the necessary financing nor that voluntary contributions might be collected. With the basic question about financing totally unresolved, the Executive Directors of the Fund and of the World Bank suggested that the Development Committee at its meeting in June 1975 determine, in the light of the prospects for voluntary contributions and the solution of the general problems of gold, whether there would be sufficient support to justify establishment of a Trust Fund.

MOVES TOWARD AGREEMENT

At their meeting in June 1975, the Development Committee and the Interim Committee showed much more interest than they had six months earlier in the possibility of a Trust Fund. The recession of 1974–75 was at its deepest, and the aggregate payments deficit of the non-oil developing countries for 1975 was then estimated at $50 billion, much larger than anticipated and larger by far than any aggregate payments deficits of developing members financed up to that time. Many developing countries were experiencing or were expecting to experience difficulties in finding adequate financing from private commercial banks and were concerned about high interest rates and relatively short repayment schedules. In this atmosphere, the Group of Twenty-Four, meeting just before the Development Committee, stressed the need for establishment of a Trust Fund, financed from a number of sources and subscribed to universally by all countries with the capacity to contribute, to provide urgently needed additional balance of payments support for several years on concessional terms.[7] Following up on the action suggested by the Group of Twenty-Four, the Development Committee likewise concluded that a special Trust Fund administered by the International Monetary Fund ought to be created and

---

[7]Communiqué of Group of Twenty-Four, June 9, 1975, par. 16; Vol. III below, p. 641.

urged the Executive Directors of the Fund to study the possibility of establishing such a Trust Fund.

The Interim Committee took no particular note of the special Trust Fund. Its members were concentrating on finding a solution to the gold problem that had to be resolved before sales of the Fund's gold for financing a Trust Fund could be undertaken. As part of this solution, the Managing Director had made the proposals described in Chapter 31. As recounted in Chapter 31, settlement of the unresolved questions concerning gold came suddenly and unexpectedly in August 1975. Among the features of the settlement was agreement about the Fund's gold holdings: one sixth (25 million ounces) was to be restituted directly to all members and another one sixth (25 million ounces) was to be sold in world markets with the profits (or surplus value) distributed to developing members through a Trust Fund. These profits were to be distributed in two ways. A certain portion—the percentage of the profits that the quotas of developing members represented in total Fund quotas—was to be disbursed directly to all developing members. The remainder was to be available for loans on highly concessional terms for a selected group of developing members with low per capita incomes. All developing members were thus to receive gold or profits from gold sales through direct restitution at the official price and through direct disbursement of some of the profits from gold sales put into the Trust Fund, and those developing members with the lowest per capita incomes would also receive profits from gold sales in the form of loans from the Trust Fund.

Agreement in August 1975 on what to do generally about gold in the international monetary system and about the Fund's holdings of gold enabled progress to be made on the Trust Fund. A day or so after agreement was reached, in a plenary session of the 1975 Annual Meeting, Mr. Simon reminded the Governors that a year had passed since the U.S. Government initially proposed a Trust Fund and urged that a portion of the Fund's gold be sold to help finance "this worthy cause."[8]

DETERMINING THE FEATURES

By the time of the 1975 Annual Meeting most officials thus agreed on the principle of a Trust Fund as the best way to give balance of payments assistance on concessional terms to selected poor developing members for a few years after the expiration of the oil facility. They also supported a number of modalities suggested by the staff and agreed that financing should come mainly from the sale of some of the Fund's gold at market prices, with some additional voluntary contributions. Considering that enough progress had been made to allow discussion of the specific

---

[8]Statement by the Governor of the Fund and the World Bank for the United States, *Summary Proceedings, 1975*, p. 114.

features of the Trust Fund, Mr. Witteveen urged the Executive Directors in October 1975 to determine these features before the Interim Committee held its next meeting in January 1976.

Despite broad agreement, it was to take six or seven months of discussions before the details of the Trust Fund were worked out, a not unusual period for discussions of Fund lending in the 1970s. The oil facility, the extended facility, the liberalizations of the compensatory financing facility, the supplementary financing facility, and the increases in quotas had all involved months of discussions and frequent recourse by the Executive Directors to the Interim Committee to obtain the views of higher-level officials.

In discussing the Trust Fund, several issues arose. A number of Executive Directors did not want to consent to arrangements for use of the Fund's gold in the the Trust Fund until full agreement had been reached on all the amendments concerning gold in the revised Articles of Agreement. Also, still to be decided was the suggestion made by Mr. Pöhl in the Development Committee in June 1975 that financing through the Trust Fund include some compensatory financing of shortfalls in export earnings. Officials of the Federal Republic of Germany favored this idea for a variety of reasons. It augmented compensatory financing without additional use of the Fund's regular resources. It enabled compensatory financing to be channeled mainly to poor developing members, since the International Monetary Fund could, through a separate Trust Fund, differentiate between members. It increased the available facilities related to the sharp declines in commodity prices at a time when officials of developing members were clamoring for attention to commodity price problems. It kept the International Monetary Fund in its more traditional business of supplying short-term balance of payments assistance and out of the business of providing longer-term development aid. None of the officials from developing members liked the German proposal, however.

There was also considerable discussion in the Executive Board about the size of the Trust Fund. How much money would be raised by selling gold was uncertain, especially since prices for gold in world markets in late 1975 and early 1976 were declining. Mr. Pieske and Mr. Wahl, agitated by the possibility that sales of gold by the Fund might further depress the price of gold in world markets and convinced that U.S. officials would welcome such price declines, suggested that the Trust Fund rely on borrowed funds rather than on profits from sales of gold. Mr. Wahl suggested alternatively that the Fund transfer gold to members in the form of specie rather than selling gold and distributing profits from its sale. In this suggestion he was supported by Mr. Jagannathan. Indian officials favored the acquisition and retention of gold as part of India's reserves, and obtaining some of the gold held by the Fund was a way for India to acquire gold. All these suggestions were raised and refuted several times. There were differences of view, too, among the Executive Directors on whether the Fund's gold sales should proceed over a three-year or a four-year period. The period selected had direct implications for the number of years in which profits would be fed into the Trust Fund and in which loans from the Trust Fund would be available.

Considerable discussion took place among the Executive Directors also about the conditionality that would be applicable to loans from the Trust Fund. Messrs. Kafka, Kharmawan, Monday, and Yaméogo wanted the conditionality not to exceed that applicable to drawings and stand-by arrangements under the first credit tranche. To satisfy the desire of some Executive Directors for stricter conditionality, some members of the Executive Board suggested that conditionality be differentiated with various circumstances. Mr. Yaméogo, for example, advocated that the poorest developing members be subject to less conditionality than developing members with relatively higher per capita incomes. Many members of the Executive Board from industrial and developed members, arguing that it was difficult to plan conditionality because circumstances in which the Trust Fund would operate were very uncertain, considered it best to begin with first credit tranche conditionality for the initial loans, probably those made in 1976, and then to have some progression in conditionality for the loans made later, say, in 1977 and 1978. The Executive Directors all agreed that, in any event, conditionality for loans from the Trust Fund would have to be reviewed after the end of the first year of the Trust Fund's operation.

Much discussion of the interest rates that would apply to Trust Fund loans also took place. Mr. Amuzegar wanted no interest charges at all on loans from the Trust Fund and wanted to have even the service charge limited to the actual costs involved in the Trust Fund's operation. Mr. Cross suggested that the Trust Fund should give grants rather than make loans. Mr. Kafka and J.B. Zulu (Zambia) favored a two-tier interest rate structure, with a low interest rate applying to members with the lowest per capita incomes and a higher rate applying to those members with higher per capita incomes.

The nature of the concessional terms depended, of course, on how the Trust Fund was financed. Very concessional interest rates were possible if the money was obtained from profits from the sale of the Fund's gold and from voluntary contributions. If, however, the resources of the Trust Fund had to be supplemented by other means, such as borrowing, interest rates would probably have to be higher. Similarly, whether there were to be grants or loans depended on whether the Trust Fund was to be a revolving fund or not. Loans would make money available for further loans from the Trust Fund after the original amounts had been disbursed. Obviously, these questions could not be answered until the methods of financing the Trust Fund were decided.

As these issues remained unresolved, the Executive Directors asked the members of the Interim Committee, meeting in January 1976, for direction on the following questions. What should be the relative roles of profits from gold sales and of voluntary contributions in the financing of the Trust Fund? Should some part of the resources of the Trust Fund be used for stabilizing export earnings, supplementary to the compensatory financing facility? Over how many years should gold be sold? Should the main emphasis be on grants or on highly concessional loans? The Interim Committee answered these questions as follows. Resources of the Trust Fund should be derived primarily from profits of sales of the Fund's gold and only augmented by voluntary national contributions. The Trust Fund should not be used for compensatory financing. Gold should be sold over a four-year period. The Trust Fund should provide loans on concessionary terms rather than make grants.[9] On this basis, the Interim Committee urged the Executive Directors to establish the Trust Fund as quickly as possible.

As difficult as the above questions seemed to be, another question proved more difficult: which members were to be eligible to receive profits from the Trust Fund. Two lists had to be drawn up: the list of "developing members" to receive a direct distribution of profits from gold sales in proportion to their quotas in the Fund and the list of "poor developing members" eligible to receive loans from the Trust Fund. Drawing up the second list proved the easier of the two and is described immediately below. The protracted process by which the list of members for direct distribution was agreed is described later in this chapter.

It was generally accepted by Fund officials that the criteria for selecting poor developing members for purposes of the Trust Fund had to be something other than the concept of most seriously affected (MSA) countries used for the Subsidy Account. The MSA concept referred to a short-run emergency, but the Trust Fund was intended for the period after the emergency. It was readily agreed, too, that per capita income ought to be used as the criterion for poor developing members and that the figures for per capita income compiled by the World Bank were the most authoritative. The World Bank had taken the leadership among international organizations in developing the methodology for determining the national income and per capita incomes of all its members and it regularly issued a *World Bank Atlas*, giving full data on income figures. Nevertheless, despite rapid agreement to use the readily available per capita income data of the World Bank, the decision on eligible members was not easy. There was still the question of the level of per capita income that should be set as the appropriate cutoff point. Any level set necessarily contained an element of arbitrariness; none could be fully defended. At the request of the Executive Directors for a decision on the appropriate level of per capita income to use, the Interim Committee, in January 1976, determined as follows: members initially eligible for loans from the Trust Fund should be Fund members as of August 31, 1975 with per capita incomes in 1973 not in excess of SDR 300.

There were 59 such members. Of the 59 eligible members, 35 were African members and 13 were Asian.[10] Six were members in the Caribbean region or in Latin

---

[9]Communiqué of Interim Committee, January 8, 1976, par. 6(a); Vol. III below, pp. 225–28.
[10]Bangladesh, Burma, India, Indonesia, Democratic Kampuchea, Lao People's Democratic Republic, Nepal, Pakistan, the Philippines, Sri Lanka, Thailand, Viet Nam, and Western Samoa.

America[11] and 5 were Middle Eastern members.[12] In addition, Guatemala, which had a per capita income in 1973 which was slightly higher than SDR 300 was included on the argument of Mr. Suárez, supported by Messrs. Kafka, Monday, and Wahl, that Guatemala was a hardship case following a natural disaster. Papua New Guinea, which was in the process of joining the Fund as of August 31, 1975, although it did not officially become a member until October 9, 1975, was also added to the list. The list was to be reviewed for the second period.[13]

Most elements of the Trust Fund were now in place, but the Executive Board still had to decide how the sale of the Fund's gold should proceed, and, as was seen in Chapter 33, agreement on auctioning the Fund's gold was controversial. Once the gold auction program was agreed in May 1976, the Trust Fund could come into being. Thus, the gold auction program and the Trust Fund were born as twins. In May 1976 the Executive Board at long last took a decision establishing the Trust Fund.[14]

ELEMENTS OF THE DECISION

Gold sales were to be conducted over two periods of two years each, the first running from mid-1976 through mid-1978, and the second from mid-1978 through mid-1980. For each period, the amount available for disbursement through the Trust Fund both as direct distribution and as loans was to be the proceeds from the sale of one half of the gold to be sold plus any income made by investing the proceeds from the sales of gold pending disbursements.

Before approving a request for loan assistance, the Trustee (that is, the International Monetary Fund) was to be satisfied that the member had a need for balance of payments assistance and was making a reasonable effort to strengthen its balance of payments position. Need was to be assessed on the basis of the member's balance of payments position, its reserve position, and developments in its reserves. A member was to be considered as making a reasonable effort to strengthen its balance of payments position if it had presented to the Fund a program for 12 months in connection with a stand-by arrangement, an extended arrangement, or a drawing from the Fund in the credit tranches. For the first period, the program was to begin not earlier than January 1, 1976 or not later than December 1, 1977. For the second period, the program was to begin not earlier than

---

[11]Bolivia, El Salvador, Grenada, Haiti, Honduras, and Paraguay.

[12]Afghanistan, Egypt, Jordan, the Yemen Arab Republic, and the People's Democratic Republic of Yemen.

[13]The list of 61 members eligible for loans from the Trust Fund for the first period was Annex A of the decision establishing the Trust Fund (E.B. Decision No. 5069-(76/72), May 5, 1976); see Vol. III below, pp. 563–69.

[14]Ibid.

January 1, 1978 or not later than November 1, 1979. If the member wished to qualify for a loan from the Trust Fund but did not have a program in effect for the relevant periods, in making its determination, the Fund was to apply the criteria that would apply to a request for a drawing in the first credit tranche.

Loans from the Trust Fund were to bear an interest rate of ½ of 1 percent a year and were to be repaid in ten equal semiannual installments starting five years after the date of the loan. The Trustee was to review the terms of repayment before the first repayments were made.[15] The resources available for lending during each of the two periods of the Trust Fund were to be allocated to eligible members in proportion to their quotas in the Fund on December 31, 1975.

DISBURSEMENTS

The Executive Directors decided that, to the extent possible, the Trust Fund should disburse loans at half-yearly intervals, in January and July of each year. The first interim disbursements of Trust Fund loans (for the period July 1, 1976 through June 30, 1978) were made in the financial year ended April 30, 1977 to 12 of the 61 members that qualified by the end of January 1977. In October 1977, the Executive Board decided that a member could qualify for a loan in the first period if its program began not later than June 1, 1978, rather than December 1, 1977. In the financial year ended April 30, 1978, two additional interim disbursements were made. The final loan payments for the first period were made in July 1978. In total, for the first period, 43 of the 61 eligible members qualified for loans and received SDR 841 million ($1,023 million). The largest loans went, in decreasing order of magnitude, to Pakistan, Egypt, the Philippines, Thailand, Bangladesh, Morocco, Zaïre, and Sri Lanka. Loans were distributed to each qualified member in proportion as its quota was to the total quotas of qualified members with a balance of payments need. Some members, including some with relatively large quotas, such as India and Indonesia, did not have a balance of payments need and hence did not receive loans from the Trust Fund. The amounts of loans of each of the 43 members are listed in Table 30 below.

The amount of loans made available through the Trust Fund was considerably larger than had been expected when it was inaugurated. For example, for 26 of the 43 members receiving loans, the loans amounted to more than one half of the balance of payments deficits originally projected for them for the 12-month program period. For 13 members, the assistance they received was more than 80 percent of their projected balance of payments deficits. Twenty-three members received Trust Fund loans and used the Fund's regular resources. Fund-related financing covered all the assessed balance of payments need of almost all these members in the period for which they had an agreed program with the Fund.

---

[15]Since the first loans were made in 1977, the first repayments started in 1982.

Table 30. Loans from the Trust Fund for the First Period, July 1, 1976–June 30, 1978, by Member

Member	Quota on December 31, 1975 (*in millions of SDRs*)	Quota as Percent of Qualifying Members' Quotas	Amount (*in millions of SDRs*)
Bangladesh	125	6.16	51.8
Benin	13	0.64	5.4
Bolivia	37	1.82	15.3
Burma	60	2.96	24.9
Burundi	19	0.94	7.9
Cameroon	35	1.72	14.5
Central African Republic	13	0.64	5.4
Chad	13	0.64	5.4
Congo	13	0.64	5.4
Egypt	188	9.27	77.9
Ethiopia	27	1.33	11.2
Gambia, The	7	0.34	2.9
Grenada	2	0.10	0.8
Guinea	24	1.18	9.9
Haiti	19	0.94	7.9
Ivory Coast	52	2.56	21.6
Kenya	48	2.37	19.9
Lao People's Dem. Rep.	13	0.64	5.4
Lesotho	5	0.25	2.1
Liberia	29	1.43	12.0
Madagascar	26	1.28	10.8
Malawi	15	0.74	6.2
Mali	22	1.08	9.1
Mauritania	13	0.64	5.4
Mauritius	22	1.08	9.1
Morocco	113	5.57	46.8
Nepal	14[1]	0.69	5.8
Niger	13	0.64	5.4
Pakistan	235	11.58	97.4
Papua New Guinea	20	0.99	8.3
Philippines	155	7.64	64.2
Senegal	34	1.68	14.1
Sierra Leone	25	1.23	10.4
Sri Lanka	98	4.83	40.6
Sudan	72	3.55	29.8
Tanzania	42	2.07	17.4
Thailand	134	6.60	55.5
Togo	15	0.74	6.2
Upper Volta	13	0.64	5.4
Viet Nam	62	3.06	25.7
Western Samoa	2	0.10	0.8
Yemen, People's Dem. Rep. of	29	1.43	12.0
Zaïre	113	5.57	46.8
Total	2,029	100.00	841.0

[1]Amount to which Nepal had consented on December 31, 1975.

DEBATING THE LIST OF COUNTRIES TO PARTICIPATE IN DISTRIBUTION OF PROFITS FROM GOLD SALES

The amount disbursed as loans represented nearly 80 percent of the $1.3 billion in the Trust Fund in the first period. The remainder, $363 million, was to be distributed "for the benefit of developing countries," the term used in the Interim Committee's communiqué of August 31, 1975.[16] The Executive Directors agreed that these direct distributions should be made each year in July and planned the first distribution for July 1977.

The first distribution was delayed, however, for nearly a year, until April 1978, when it became urgent because the end of the first period was almost at hand. The delay was caused by the great difficulty the Executive Directors had in agreeing on a list of "developing countries," the term having been left vague by the Interim Committee. The Executive Directors started to discuss a list of developing countries in November 1975, when the Trust Fund was first considered, but were to take almost two and a half years before agreeing on the list. In April 1978, when agreement was finally reached, several Executive Directors stated that determining the list had been one of the "most unpleasant" experiences in their term on the Executive Board. Political arguments were used much more than was customary in the Executive Board's deliberations, and the Managing Director seemed powerless to bring about agreement.

What happened was simple: virtually all members insisted on being on the list of developing countries, while some industrial members could not go along with calling certain relatively high-income members developing countries. For developing members the terminology could have ramifications for their participation in the Group of 77 and in other North-South dialogues, for aid from the World Bank and other financial institutions, and for the application of the rules of the General Agreement on Tariffs and Trade (GATT), as well as for their receipt of profits from the Fund's gold sales. For industrial members, the distribution of profits from gold sales was mainly at stake.

When the issue was first discussed in November 1975, several Executive Directors wanted to start with the classification of 85 "other developing members" used in connection with the Sixth General Review of Quotas as an initial base (plus Grenada which became a member in August 1975 and Papua New Guinea which became a member in October 1975) and then add to the list the 13 major oil exporting members (Algeria, Ecuador, Indonesia, Iran, Iraq, Kuwait, Libya, Nigeria, Oman, Qatar, Saudi Arabia, the United Arab Emirates, and Venezuela), and 7 of the 13 members usually classified by the Fund for statistical purposes as "other developed and more advanced developing countries" (Greece, Malta, Portugal, Romania, Spain, Turkey, and Yugoslavia). The rationale of including these last 7 members was that in the classification used by the International Development Association (IDA) of the World Bank Group, 5 of these members (Portugal and Romania had not joined

---

[16]Par. 6(c); Vol. III below, p. 224.

IDA)—Greece, Malta, Spain, Turkey, and Yugoslavia—were Part II members of IDA (recipients) and not Part I members (donors). Such a list of developing countries came to 107 of the Fund's 128 members; only the 14 industrial members (Austria, Belgium, Canada, Denmark, France, the Federal Republic of Germany, Italy, Japan, Luxembourg, the Netherlands, Norway, Sweden, the United Kingdom, and the United States), 6 "other developed and more advanced developing countries" (Australia, Finland, Iceland, Ireland, New Zealand, and South Africa), and China were left out.[17]

Mr. Cross, in conjunction with other U.S. officials, opposed the inclusion of the more affluent of the major oil exporting countries and of some of the nonindustrial relatively developed countries. The initial U.S. proposal for a Trust Fund, he reiterated, was intended to help finance the payments deficits of poor developing countries and not to give money to virtually all countries, some with relatively high per capita incomes, substantial reserves, and no balance of payments deficits. He put forward a list prepared by the U.S. Government that excluded the following 15 countries: Argentina, the Bahamas, Greece, Iran, Iraq, Israel, Kuwait, Libya, Malta, Qatar, Saudi Arabia, Singapore, Spain, the United Arab Emirates, and Venezuela. The U.S. list brought forth immediate objections from Mr. Al-Atrash, Mr. Amuzegar, Mr. Dini, Mr. Drabble, Mr. Kharmawan, and Mr. Ruding, all of whom had in their constituencies countries that were not on this list.

In an attempt to resolve the issue, the Managing Director proposed in March 1976 that the list of 107 members be retained but made it known that he would informally request the 46 members ineligible for Trust Fund loans (members that had a per capita income above SDR 300 for 1973) to forgo part or all of their share of the profits from gold sales, either by opting out of the receipt of such profits or by donating them to the Trust Fund. This solution enabled members to continue to be classified as developing countries but not to gain from the sales of the Fund's gold. Mr. Witteveen's request induced Yugoslavia to contribute one third of its share of the profits and Romania to make available 10 percent of its share as a ten-year loan at the same rate of interest as the Trust Fund was to charge on its loans.

Since these results were not enough, the Managing Director undertook what was informally referred to in the Executive Board's discussions as the Manila agreement. On the occasion of the 1976 Annual Meeting in Manila, Mr. Witteveen suggested to officials of 12 members that they agree to give up their shares of the profits from the Fund's gold sales. The 12 members he selected met one of two criteria. Either they had per capita incomes of at least SDR 1,400 in 1973 and SDR 1,600 in 1974, as listed in the most recent *World Bank Atlas*, or they had reserves at the end of 1974 which were greater than the value of their imports in 1974. The 12 members were 8 major oil exporters—Iran, Iraq, Kuwait, Libya, Qatar, Saudi Arabia, the United Arab Emirates, and Venezuela—plus Greece, Israel, Singapore, and Spain. The Managing Director decided not to request the Bahamas and Malta to

---

[17]See fn. 6 of Chap. 2.

forgo part of their profits. Although the Bahamas met the per capita income criterion, the Bahamian officials argued that a sizable proportion of this income was received by high-income expatriates, thereby unduly raising the calculated average. This claim was substantiated by a paper that the World Bank staff prepared in connection with a loan for the Bahamas in 1976. While Malta's exchange reserves as of the end of 1974 exceeded the level of its imports in 1974, a large source of foreign exchange and of employment in Malta was to be terminated in 1979 when the United Kingdom withdrew its long-standing naval base.

By July 1977, when the first direct distribution of profits from the Trust Fund was scheduled to take place, the ministers of finance of the 8 oil exporting members had agreed that they would recommend to their governments the donation to the Trust Fund of their shares of the profits from the Fund's gold sales, and the officials of Greece had stated their country's willingness to contribute 25 percent of its share of the profits. The officials of Israel, Singapore, and Spain had not been heard from. Anxious to get a decision, the Managing Director circulated for decision by the Executive Board two alternative lists of developing countries, the initial list of 107 members and a list of 103 members, which omitted Greece, Israel, Singapore, and Spain.

An acrimonious discussion took place in the Executive Board on July 25, 1977. The Executive Directors with Israel, Singapore, and Spain in their constituencies opposed the omission of these countries from the shorter list. H.O. Ruding (Netherlands) declared as "arbitrary and not acceptable" the criteria used for determining the countries to be asked to forgo part of their shares in the profits from the Fund's gold sales. He pointed out that special factors might apply to the "four target countries" of Greece, Israel, Singapore, and Spain, just as they did to the Bahamas and Malta. Determination of the lists of eligible developing countries was, he insisted, being resolved by force. Mr. Kharmawan stressed that members were asked to contribute *voluntarily* part or all of their shares of the gold profits to the Trust Fund; voluntarily meant that they were not to be compelled to do so and were not to be struck off the list should they find it impossible to forgo these profits. He, too, considered use of per capita income data as arbitrary and explained that the per capita income figures for Singapore, like those for the Bahamas, had an upward bias. The high incomes of expatriate workers, including the foreign resident managers of large multinational companies, pulled up the average for Singapore. In reality, the country was a "city-state," poor in natural resources. Eduardo O. de Toledo (Spain) had complaints similar to those of Mr. Ruding and explained that his Spanish authorities had simply not been in a position earlier to reply to the Managing Director's request to donate a portion of Spain's share of the profits from gold.

Other Executive Directors also rejected the shorter list. Mr. Drabble believed that it treated a handful of members in a highly arbitrary way and that the kind of rigid criteria that Mr. Cross had suggested for deciding which nonindustrial countries should be obliged to forgo their share of the Fund's profits from gold sales inevitably raised questions of equity. Mr. Hollensen and Winston Temple-Seminario

(Peru) argued that it was not up to the Executive Board to determine its own list of developing countries; the list of 107 members was at least consistent with the actions of the Governors when they considered the Sixth General Review of Quotas.

There were, however, arguments for the shorter list. Mr. Cross explained that distributing the profits from the Fund's gold sales to countries with relatively strong reserve positions or relatively high per capita incomes would reduce the amount available for the poorest countries, thereby distorting the initial concept of the Trust Fund. Distribution of profits from gold sales to the newly rich oil exporting countries also exposed the Fund to criticism that it did not care about the poor and worked mainly to the advantage of the rich. In defending the criteria used to exclude countries from the direct distribution of gold profits unless they in effect returned the amounts received, he realized that some countries with which the United States had the closest and friendliest relations might be excluded.

Mr. Cross was by no means alone. Kadhim A. Al-Eyd (Iraq) repeated that six of the oil exporting members in his constituency—Iraq, Kuwait, Libya, Qatar, Saudi Arabia, and the United Arab Emirates—had agreed to contribute their shares of the direct distribution to the Trust Fund in the definite expectation that other developing countries in a position to do so would contribute their shares as well. They did not want to be the only contributors, but wanted to set an example for other relatively high-income developing countries. Mr. Amuzegar likewise argued that if relatively well-to-do countries other than the major oil exporting countries did not voluntarily contribute, the Fund would be discriminating against the major oil exporters. Adoption of the longer list could jeopardize the contributions of the oil exporting members, thereby lessening considerably the amount of assistance that poorer Fund members might receive. For this last-mentioned reason, Messrs. Kent, Matsunaga, Mung'omba, and Nana-Sinkam supported Mr. Cross's position favoring the shorter list.

To settle the matter, Mr. Ruding and Mr. de Toledo requested the Executive Directors to take a formal vote. Inasmuch as the Executive Directors nearly always took decisions by reaching a consensus, formal voting was rare, which indicated the sensitivity of this topic. The vote was close, 45.93 percent in favor of the list of 103 countries and 35.58 percent for the list of 107 countries, with four Executive Directors, Messrs. Nestor Caldera (Nicaragua), Deshmukh, Foglizzo, and Alan G. Morris, Temporary Alternate to Mr. Whitelaw, abstaining.

The controversy was still not settled, however, and the distribution of profits from gold sales could not go forward. Singapore officials were so irritated by the decision that they intimated to Fund staff that Singapore, not needing to draw from the Fund, might give up its membership. These officials argued that although virtually all countries in Africa, Asia (except Japan), Latin America, and the Middle East and even some countries in Europe were regarded as developing countries, the Fund list suggested that Singapore alone was not so regarded by the international community. They were particularly concerned about Singapore's classification for the purposes of the GATT. Through Mr. Kharmawan, they proposed to present statistical material to make a special case for Singapore to be added to the Fund's list.

Mr. Amuzegar, who had Greece in his constituency and who had assured Greek officials that he would oppose any alteration to the agreed list, refused to implement arrangements for Iran to contribute its share of gold profits to the Trust Fund until the list was finally fixed. Other oil exporting countries that had agreed to return their shares of the profits did not make the necessary formal arrangements, and the Fund's Treasurer hesitated to proceed with the distribution of profits from gold auctions when only four members—Kuwait, Qatar, Saudi Arabia, and Venezuela—had completed such arrangements. In March 1978, after informal discussions with Mr. Kharmawan and Fund staff, the Singapore officials presented to the Fund detailed statistics supporting their contention that per capita income for Singapore was not a reliable indicator of the country's state of wealth, income, or economic development and requested reconsideration of the Fund's decision. After the Managing Director had received informal assurances from the Executive Directors of Greece, Israel, and Spain that they would not use the occasion of the reconsideration of Singapore's classification to reopen the issue of the classification of their own countries, the Executive Board agreed to take up Singapore's request. Upon reconsideration, the Executive Board agreed to include Singapore in the list of developing members. Singapore officials immediately cabled the Managing Director to tell him they welcomed the new decision. The inclusion of Singapore made for a list of 104 members to receive direct distribution of profits from the Fund's gold sales through the Trust Fund.

DIRECT DISTRIBUTION OF PROFITS

Consequently it was not until June 1978 that the Executive Board decided to go ahead with the direct distribution of profits from gold sales for the first period. Profits totaling $362.6 million were distributed to 104 members, with Iraq, Kuwait, Qatar, Saudi Arabia, the United Arab Emirates, Venezuela, and Yugoslavia agreeing to transfer all or part of their shares to the Trust Fund and Romania lending some of its share. Each of the 104 members received a share of total profits from the sale of gold in proportion to its share in total Fund quotas on August 31, 1975. The quotas of the 104 members represented 27.771 percent of aggregate Fund quotas on that date and so these members received 27.771 percent of the profits as direct distribution. The amount received by each member is listed in Table 31 below. Moreover, provision was made in the Articles of Agreement after the Second Amendment was approved for members to receive their direct distributions from the Trust Fund in the form of gold if they so desired. Members that wanted to exercise the option to acquire gold instead of currency or SDRs prior to the approval of the Second Amendment were to inform the Fund to hold up their distributions until the amended Articles became effective.

Table 31. Direct Distribution of Profits from Gold Sales for the First Two-Year Period, July 1, 1976–June 30, 1978

Member	Share in Quotas (*percent*)	Amount of Profits Received (*in millions of of U.S. dollars*)
Afghanistan	0.13	1.6
Algeria	0.44	5.8
Argentina	1.51	19.7
Bahamas	0.07	0.9
Bahrain	0.03	0.4
Bangladesh	0.43	5.6
Barbados	0.04	0.6
Benin	0.04	0.6
Bolivia	0.13	1.6
Botswana	0.02	0.2
Brazil	1.51	19.7
Burma	0.21	2.7
Burundi	0.06	0.8
Cameroon	0.12	1.6
Central African Republic	0.04	0.6
Chad	0.04	0.6
Chile	0.54	7.1
Colombia	0.54	7.0
Congo	0.04	0.6
Costa Rica	0.11	1.4
Cyprus	0.09	1.2
Dominican Republic	0.15	1.9
Ecuador	0.11	1.5
Egypt	0.64	8.4
El Salvador	0.12	1.6
Equatorial Guinea	0.03	0.4
Ethiopia	0.09	1.2
Fiji	0.04	0.6
Gabon	0.05	0.7
Gambia, The	0.02	0.3
Ghana	0.30	3.9
Grenada	0.01	0.1
Guatemala	0.12	1.6
Guinea	0.08	1.1
Guyana	0.07	0.9
Haiti	0.06	0.8
Honduras	0.09	1.1
India	3.22	42.0
Indonesia	0.90	11.6
Iran	0.66	8.6
Iraq	0.37	4.9
Ivory Coast	0.18	2.3
Jamaica	0.18	2.4
Jordan	0.08	1.0
Kampuchea, Democratic	0.09	1.1

679

Table 31 (*continued*). Direct Distribution of Profits from Gold Sales
for the First Two-Year Period, July 1, 1976–June 30, 1978

Member	Share in Quotas (*percent*)	Amount of Profits Received (*in millions of of U.S. dollars*)
Kenya	0.16	2.1
Korea	0.27	3.6
Kuwait	0.22	2.9
Lao People's Dem. Rep.	0.04	0.6
Lebanon	0.03	0.4
Lesotho	0.02	0.2
Liberia	0.10	1.3
Libya	0.08	1.1
Madagascar	0.09	1.2
Malawi	0.05	0.7
Malaysia	0.64	8.3
Mali	0.08	1.0
Malta	0.06	0.7
Mauritania	0.04	0.6
Mauritius	0.08	1.0
Mexico	1.27	16.5
Morocco	0.39	5.1
Nepal	0.04	0.5
Nicaragua	0.09	1.2
Niger	0.04	0.6
Nigeria	0.46	6.0
Oman	0.02	0.3
Pakistan	0.80	10.5
Panama	0.12	1.6
Papua New Guinea	0.07	0.9
Paraguay	0.06	0.8
Peru	0.42	5.5
Philippines	0.53	6.9
Portugal	0.40	5.2
Qatar	0.07	0.9
Romania	0.65	8.5
Rwanda	0.06	0.9
Saudi Arabia	0.46	6.0
Senegal	0.12	1.5
Sierra Leone	0.09	1.1
Singapore	0.13	1.6
Somalia	0.06	0.8
Sir Lanka	0.34	4.4
Sudan	0.25	3.2
Swaziland	0.03	0.4
Syrian Arab Republic	0.17	2.2
Tanzania	0.14	1.9
Thailand	0.46	6.0
Togo	0.05	0.7
Trinidad and Tobago	0.22	2.8

Table 31 *(concluded)*. Direct Distribution of Profits from Gold Sales
for the First Two-Year Period, July 1, 1976–June 30, 1978

Member	Share in Quotas (*percent*)	Amount of Profits Received (*in millions of of U.S. dollars*)
Tunisia	0.16	2.1
Turkey	0.52	6.8
Uganda	0.14	1.8
United Arab Emirates	0.05	0.7
Upper Volta	0.04	0.6
Uruguay	0.24	3.1
Venezuela	1.13	14.8
Viet Nam	0.21	2.7
Western Samoa	0.01	0.1
Yemen Arab Republic	0.03	0.4
Yemen, People's Dem. Rep. of	0.10	1.3
Yugoslavia	0.81	9.2
Zaïre	0.39	5.1
Zambia	0.26	3.4
Total	27.77 [1]	362.6

[1]Components may not add to totals because of rounding.

INVESTMENTS BY THE TRUST FUND

After receipts from the periodic gold auctions came in to the Trust Fund and before disbursements were made, the International Monetary Fund, as Trustee, was able temporarily to invest the liquid assets of the Trust Fund. In the past, investments by the International Monetary Fund were always in U.S. Government securities, with the concurrence of the U.S. Government. Throughout the first period of the Trust Fund, from July 1976 to June 1978, this remained the case. In June 1978, however, the Executive Board decided that investments of the Trust Fund should be held in SDR-denominated assets (the value of the investments thus being guaranteed in terms of SDRs) and that the Trust Fund could place SDR-denominated deposits with the Bank for International Settlements (BIS). The decision was significant in that for the first time investments by the Fund could be in a form other than U.S. Government securities. In order to find still further investment outlets for the Trust Fund, the staff was to make arrangements with the 16 members whose currencies were included in the SDR basket as of July 1, 1978 and which issued obligations in their currencies that the Trust Fund could hold for placing investments in their obligations. The choice of investments was to depend on the yields from alternative investments.[18]

In December, in reviewing this decision, the Executive Board broadened considerably the authority of the Trust Fund to invest in alternative investments.

---

[18]E.B. Decision No. 5812-(78/90) TR, June 16, 1978; Vol. III below, pp. 570–71.

Balances of currency held by the Trust Fund could be invested in marketable obligations of international financial organizations, marketable obligations denominated in SDRs issued by members or by national official financial institutions of members, marketable obligations issued by, and denominated in the currency of, the member, or its national official financial institutions, whose currency is used to make an investment, and deposits denominated in SDRs with commercial banks.[19] If the Managing Director considered an offer by the BIS as not sufficiently attractive, he was to inform the Executive Board and make proposals for alternative investments. The International Monetary Fund, through the Trust Fund, could now invest in a variety of monetary instruments issued by both official entitites and private banks, so long as their value was protected in terms of SDRs.

THE SECOND PERIOD

The second period of the Trust Fund (July 1, 1978 through June 30, 1980) goes beyond this History. Before the end of 1978, however, it was decided that 59 members with per capita incomes in 1975 of up to $520 would be eligible for loans in the second period. The list for the second period differed from that of the first in that it included Zambia but not Guatemala, Mauritius, or Paraguay.[20]

As 1978 ended it was becoming evident that the profits in the Trust Fund were going to be much larger than expected. Gold prices had risen from an average of $126 an ounce at the time of the first gold auction in June 1976 to $196 in December 1978, and in 1978 had gone as high as $224 an ounce. High gold prices necessarily enlarged the Trust Fund. Consequently, the Trust Fund was on the way to becoming, in its second period, a major source of funds for the Fund's developing members, especially for those eligible for loans.

---

[19]E.B. Decisions Nos. 5972-(78/189) and 5973-(78/189) TR, December 4, 1978; Vol. III below, p. 571.

[20]Annex B to E.B. Decision No. 5563-(77/150) TR, October 28, 1977; Vol. III below, p. 570.

PART EIGHT

Amending the Articles of Agreement (1974–1978)

"...we would be wise to adopt an amendment of our Articles of Agreement that would allow the exchange system to develop in the manner best suited to evolving circumstances."

—H. JOHANNES WITTEVEEN, addressing the Board of Governors, in Washington, September 1, 1975

CHAPTER

35

Preparing Draft Amendments
(July 1974–January 1975)

*P*REPARING THE SECOND AMENDMENT of the Articles of Agreement, the Fund's most absorbing undertaking in the years reviewed here, began within a few weeks after the Committee of Twenty held its last meeting. On July 9, 1974 the staff of the Legal Department circulated to the Executive Directors a new series of memoranda containing draft amendments of the Articles. These drafts were followed—eventually almost daily—by a deluge of drafts, redrafts, and explanatory memoranda until the end of March 1976. The Executive Directors discussed and negotiated individual amendments during 280 hours of debate at 146 sessions. On four occasions they sought the guidance of the Interim Committee on a number of political issues that could be resolved only at the level of finance ministers and central bank governors. The amended provisions of the Articles of Agreement for gold and exchange rates were so controversial as to require separate negotiations by high-ranking officials of the few largest industrial members in forums outside the Executive Board and the Interim Committee.

Preparation of the Second Amendment was more prolonged and complicated than preparing the First Amendment, which became effective on July 28, 1969. The First Amendment, designed mainly to provide for the creation of the SDR, was relatively simple for two reasons. Most of the amendments had the unifying theme of providing for the establishment of the SDR. Second, as changes in most original Articles were not necessary, the amendments could be attached almost as a separate treaty.[1] The Second Amendment, even if less exciting intellectually, was more complex because it was an anthology of projects without a unifying theme. It encouraged further proposals and fragmented opinion. Modifications infiltrated the Articles as a whole and could not be added as a simple attachment.

The intent here is to present a chronological narrative that describes the sequence of events by which the Second Amendment came into being, the main

---

[1] A summary of the drafting and negotiation of the First Amendment in 1967–69 can be found in *History, 1966–71*, Vol. I, pp. 166–78.

issues involved, the reasons why the participating parties took certain positions on various issues, and the principal provisions of the agreed Second Amendment. This overview forms the subject of four chapters.[2]

Without overlooking the valuable contributions made also by other staff, both in the Legal Department and in other Departments, it should be emphasized that Joseph Gold, then the Fund's General Counsel and Director of the Legal Department, put his personal stamp on the Second Amendment. Building on his familiarity since the 1940s with the operation of the Fund under its original Articles and on his experience in drafting the First Amendment in 1967–69, Mr. Gold was well versed in the changes needed in the Articles if they were to serve the Fund adequately in its next period. He wanted the amended Articles to be the best that could be agreed in the circumstances of 1974–76 and at the same time to advance the international monetary law. With these objectives in mind, Mr. Gold developed a philosophy and a set of principles to guide the drafting of the amended Articles. He initiated individual amendments and supervised their drafting and redrafting. He saw the amendments through numerous debates and discussions in the Executive Board and in the Interim Committee. He kept track of the differing points of view and sought ways and arguments to advance agreement. In the end he made sure that the modifications were consistent and were couched in as eloquent and concise language as possible, given the need to compromise on words as well as on substance.

INITIAL DRAFT AMENDMENTS AND
INITIAL RESPONSES BY EXECUTIVE DIRECTORS

In July 1974, the staff started to circulate to the Executive Board draft amendments on the topics on which the Executive Board had been asked to prepare amendments by the Committee of Twenty both in their last communiqué and in the

---

[2]Among the writings to which the reader is referred are Joseph Gold, *The Second Amendment of the Fund's Articles of Agreement*, IMF Pamphlet Series, No. 25 (Washington: International Monetary Fund, 1978); *A Report on Certain Legal Developments in the International Monetary Fund* (Washington: World Association of Lawyers, 1976), pp. 1–40; "Law and Change in International Monetary Relations," *The Record*, Association of the Bar of the City of New York, Vol. 31 (April 1976), pp. 231–38; *Voting Majorities in the Fund: Effects of Second Amendment of the Articles*, IMF Pamphlet Series, No. 20 (Washington, 1977); *Use, Conversion, and Exchange of Currency Under the Second Amendment of the Fund's Articles*, IMF Pamphlet Series, No. 23 (Washington, 1978); and *Legal and Institutional Aspects*, pp. 4–73, 125–27, 236–37, 317–18, 349–51, 387–89, 408–40, 441–45, 468, and 515–19. For the implications of the Second Amendment for domestic and international law, for the practice of other international organizations, and for the contractual arrangements of private parties, see, for example, Joseph Gold, *SDRs, Gold, and Currencies: Third Survey of New Legal Developments*, IMF Pamphlet Series, No. 26 (Washington, 1979); *SDRs, Currencies, and Gold: Fourth Survey of New Legal Developments*, IMF Pamphlet Series, No. 33 (Washington, 1980); *SDRs, Currencies, and Gold: Fifth Survey of New Legal Developments*, IMF Pamphlet Series, No. 36 (Washington, 1981); and "Exchange Arrangements and International Law in an Age of Floating Currencies," *Proceedings of the Seventy-Third Annual Meeting of the American Society of International Law* (Washington, April 26–28, 1979), pp. 1–8 and 10–12.

Outline of Reform.[3] The communiqué stated that draft amendments should be prepared (i) to establish the Council referred to in paragraph 31 of the *Outline*; (ii) to enable the Fund to legalize the position of countries with floating rates during the interim period before the reformed system described in Part I of the *Outline* could be finally agreed and fully complemented; (iii) to give permanent force to the voluntary pledge described in paragraph 36 of Part II of the *Outline*, concerning trade or other current account measures for balance of payments purposes; (iv) to authorize the Fund to establish a "substitution account"; (v) to amend the existing provisions of the Articles concerning gold; (vi) to authorize the Fund to implement a link between development assistance and SDR allocations; and (vii) to introduce improvements in the General Account and in the use of the SDR. In addition, other amendments could be prepared to give effect to Part II of the *Outline*.[4]

By mid-August 1974 the Executive Board had draft amendments which covered the full range of these topics, except for gold and a substitution account. The staff had circulated draft amendments relating to the Council, to changes in the General Account, to exchange arrangements, to restrictions on trade and other current account transactions, and to changes in the SDR. Explanatory notes and memoranda accompanied some of these drafts.

The staff proceeded urgently because the *Outline of Reform* envisaged that draft amendments, if agreed, would be presented for the approval of the Board of Governors at the latest by the completion of the Sixth General Review of Quotas, then under way. That would be on February 9, 1975, five years after the Fifth General Review of Quotas, as required by the Articles. In view of the absence of the use of gold in international payments and debates over the use of gold in the future, it was not expected that Fund members would pay 25 percent of quota increases in gold as was the Fund's normal practice under the Articles. Yet in the absence of payment in gold, there was no legal alternative mode of payment. The occasion of the Sixth General Review of Quotas and the deadline of February 1975 was initially considered, at least by the Fund staff, as a good target date for prompting an agreement about gold, including amended provisions of the Articles of Agreement with respect to the payment of the "gold portion" for quota increases.

Executive Directors' Concerns

The Executive Directors started to consider the draft amendments in the third week of July 1974. They did not aim to agree on particular texts of amendments or even to express official positions but wanted only to explore the policies and technical problems involved.

During August and September many complex and technical issues were raised. By the third week of September the Executive Directors started to draft for

---

[3]Communiqué of Committee of Twenty, June 13, 1974, par. 3(l) and the attached "Detailed Statement of Immediate Steps to Assist the Functioning of the International Monetary System," par. 11; Vol. III below, pp. 201, 205.

[4]Pars. 31, 36, and 41 of the *Outline of Reform* can be found in Vol. III below, pp. 174–76.

consideration by the Board of Governors a resolution in which the new Interim Committee would urge the Executive Directors to proceed quickly with amendments. In addition, they started to be concerned about the approaching deadline of February 1975 for the quota exercise. In these circumstances, Executive Directors realized that they faced the formidable task of amending the Articles in a few months' time. Several Executive Directors from industrial members were concerned that the scope of the initial draft amendments circulated by the staff might be too sweeping. These amendments seemed to eliminate much of the structure of the existing Articles and procedures. These Executive Directors did not accept the staff argument that they were only doing what was requested in the *Outline of Reform*. It was not enough, they contended, for the staff to direct attention to paragraph 41 of the *Outline of Reform* which requested amendments on certain topics. The staff had a hand in drafting that paragraph. Some Executive Directors complained further that the staff was going beyond the topics specified in the *Outline of Reform*.

In essence, the Executive Directors in this first round of discussions were questioning the principles underlying the particular amendments, especially since a fully reformed international monetary system was not being instituted. The staff responded with two memoranda, one entitled "A General View of Proposed Amendments to the Articles," and a second entitled "Objectives of Draft Amendments Already Issued," circulated toward the end of September 1974 and explaining the general thrust of the draft amendments and the principles that had guided the staff in suggesting particular amendments.

The staff explained that while the amendments envisaged as of mid-1974 were limited and would not lead to a fully reformed system, they would do more than merely patch up the existing Articles. Five broad principles had guided the staff. The first principle was the desirability of adopting provisions to enable the Fund to deal with immediate problems, particularly those connected with the Fund's financial activities, since as matters stood the Fund and its members could not act under the existing Articles. The Fund was obviously having problems with members using gold for effecting repurchases that the existing Articles required to be made in gold and to pay for subscriptions related to quota increases under the Sixth General Review of Quotas. Clearly, amendments were needed to help the Fund deal with the inconsistencies between actual circumstances and the existing Articles.

The second principle was the desirability of improving the institutional structure of the Fund. Here the staff had reference to a permanent Council of Governors. Since 1972 the Fund had been functioning with the aid of temporary bodies with only advisory roles, such as the Committee of Twenty and the Interim Committee. It was preferable to set up a permanent decision-making organ with explicit powers.

The third principle was the desirability of strengthening the Fund's ability to function effectively as a financial, supervisory, and regulatory organization. The General Account needed to be changed, for example, to oblige a member to convert its currency when that currency was purchased from the Fund by another member.

Under the original Articles, if a member's currency was purchased from the Fund, the member had no obligation under the Articles to convert it for the benefit of the purchasing member. Although most members had been willing to convert their currencies at rates of exchange consistent with the Fund's policies, there had been problems.

The Fund might also be strengthened by empowering it to sell gold, in amounts not exceeding its reserves, and to invest the proceeds in income-producing securities of members or of development finance organizations. Furthermore, the Fund could be empowered to establish a separate Investment Account to receive such proceeds. The proceeds in the Investment Account could be used to meet the Fund's current budgetary deficits or to augment reserves against future budgetary deficits.

The Fund could also be strengthened if it had jurisdiction to approve restrictions on trade and on other current transactions imposed for balance of payments purposes. So far, the Fund's authority to approve restrictions was confined to restrictions on payments and transfers for effecting current international transactions, that is, exchange restrictions; the Fund had no jurisdiction over restrictions applied directly to the transactions themselves, that is, restrictions on trade or on services. Responsibility for the latter rested with the GATT. Draft amendments had been circulated both establishing an Investment Account and giving the Fund authority over restrictions on trade and other international transactions on current account for balance of payments reasons.

The fourth principle was the creation of more acceptable roles for gold, reserve currencies, and SDRs in the international monetary system. To make the SDR the principal reserve asset of the system, as stated in the *Outline of Reform*, amendments were needed to loosen the various restraints placed on SDRs at the time of the First Amendment and to improve the characteristics and extend the uses of the SDR.

A return to legality was a further principle underlying proposed amendments to the Articles. Floating exchange rates, such as were already used by several large members, were clearly inconsistent with the Articles. Illegality had debasing and debilitating effects, and international jurisdiction over exchange arrangements needed to be restored. Failure to do so could undermine the capacity of the Fund to contribute to an orderly and legal system in the future.[5]

How Many Amendments and for How Long?

Although these broad principles suggested many far-reaching and permanent amendments, the idea at first was to draft amendments that would be used for a limited period, as contemplated by the *Outline of Reform*. The Managing Director, the staff, and the Executive Directors felt that this project might have to be

---

[5]The dangers of illegality have been described further by Joseph Gold in his *Legal and Institutional Aspects*, pp. 8–11.

completed by a third amendment. There was little consideration of, or even reference to, undertaking a permanent, thoroughgoing revision of the Articles in 1974. The Second Amendment was thus initially thought of as an interim or stopgap measure.

Even though the Second Amendment was originally conceived as an interim measure, several Executive Directors resisted many draft amendments. Some argued that there was no mandate for these amendments, though the staff pointed out that the *Outline of Reform* mentioned a residual category of "any other consequential amendments" for some items and though the Committee of Twenty had requested the Executive Board to prepare amendments to give effect to Part II of the *Outline of Reform* "or as otherwise desired."

Some Executive Directors had other reasons, too, for resisting the draft amendments. Many Executive Directors were disappointed that Part I of the *Outline of Reform*, or something like it, was not their terms of reference. They resisted undertaking substantial modifications of the Articles of Agreement to last for the indefinite future since the major parts of the reformed system would not be incorporated. Moreover, many member governments had to present to their legislatures amendments to the Articles. Presenting a list of amendments that did not encompass a reformed system highlighted the lack of agreement on reforming the system. Japanese monetary authorities, for example, had no desire to confront their parliament with a confession of the failure to reach agreement on a reformed system. Mr. Kawaguchi therefore took the stance that it would be better to postpone amending the Articles. He argued that any amendments short of a complete reform might even deter further efforts at such a reform. In addition, the Executive Directors realized that it would be difficult for them to reach agreement on a broad range of discrete proposals.

The attitude that an interim amendment was being prepared also affected the early stages of the drafting. On occasion, particularly regarding exchange rates, Executive Directors complained that the staff draft went beyond the requirements of an interim period.

While a few Executive Directors elected by developing members took the position that there should be amendments on all the topics in paragraph 41 of the *Outline of Reform*, the majority did not support this position. The view that received most support among the Executive Directors in early discussions was that the number of amendments should be limited to those that were "absolutely necessary" for an interim period and that further amendments should be made when a complete reform of the system was agreed upon.

DISCUSSIONS OF INDIVIDUAL AMENDMENTS

When the Executive Directors began to discuss the initial draft amendments starting in July 1974, they disagreed on many topics. After all, a number of these topics had been debated for two years in the Committee of Twenty and had not been resolved. There were a number of reasons why negotiations were expected to be arduous. Several difficult questions about the basic shape of future international monetary arrangements had to be answered. What provisions would govern exchange rates? Would floating rates be permissible? What provisions would govern transactions in gold? Would the Fund continue to receive gold from its members? What disposition would be made of the Fund's holdings of gold? Topics relating to the Fund's operations and transactions and to the SDR raised complex technical questions. Furthermore, as international monetary questions are not isolated from other international problems, the solution of even the most sophisticated international monetary question can affect the distribution of world political and economic power. Though some international monetary questions may not be political in this sense, they can be employed as strategy to gain advantage in the negotiation of intrinsically political problems.

In order to expedite discussion by the Executive Directors, which some felt was proceeding too slowly, the Executive Board decided to hold more meetings and to devote more time at these meetings to consideration of proposed amendments. The staff was to prepare more explanatory memoranda. The customary format of Executive Board meetings in which Executive Directors spoke first and staff replied to questions at the end of the meeting was to be altered to permit direct, informal dialogue between Executive Directors and staff on each proposed amendment. This format began to be used after the 1974 Annual Meetings. Discussions went on until December.

The Council

One of the first draft amendments to be discussed in the Executive Board provided for the establishment of a Council. Since early in 1972 U.S. authorities had been pressing for the establishment of some high-level "political body" in the Fund, just as they had argued for a special body to negotiate the reformed system, which had resulted in the temporary Committee of Twenty. They had added to the agenda of the Committee of Twenty revamping or restructuring the Fund on a more permanent basis. While it was not clear what the U.S. authorities meant by "revamping" the Fund, they seemed to envisage finance ministers joining the Executive Directors from time to time in their deliberations on critical issues such as the exchange rate of large industrial members. By "restructuring," U.S. authorities seemed to have in mind adding a permanent high-level political body, such as a body of finance ministers or a group like the Committee of Twenty, to the Fund's machinery.

U.S. authorities pressed for these arrangements because they wanted finance ministers from time to time to take decisions, or at least to express opinions, on the exchange rates of Fund members. This could bring considerable political pressure on members to alter their exchange rates. The establishment of a high-level political body was consistent with their view that more frequent changes in exchange rates by industrial members would help the balance of payments adjustment process, especially exchange rate revaluation by members with payments surpluses. U.S. authorities were not convinced that, whatever authority the Fund might have over exchange rates, decisions by the Executive Board alone would carry sufficient weight.

When the Committee of Twenty ended its work in mid-1974, it was agreed that after the Fund's Articles of Agreement were amended, provision would be made for a Council of Fund Governors with decision-making powers. Until the Council was set up, an Interim Committee with advisory functions would serve. As a result of this understanding, U.S. authorities dropped the issue of revamping or restructuring the Fund.

When the draft amendment providing for a Council was discussed in the Executive Board, some Executive Directors were apparently skeptical of the desirability of introducing a new policymaking organ into the body of the Fund. They wanted to know how the Council would be composed and how it would work. Was it to be "a sort of committee or adjunct of the Board of Governors," or was it to be totally independent? Would each Councillor cast his votes only as a unit as did Executive Directors, or would each Councillor be authorized to cast separately the votes allotted to each member country in his constituency, as did each Governor in the Board of Governors?

Voting in the Executive Board does not take place frequently; rather, the Chairman determines the sense of the meeting. But despite the infrequency of voting in the Executive Board, a vote can be called for at any time. Furthermore, in determining the sense of an Executive Board meeting, the Chairman inevitably pays attention to the voting power of individual Executive Directors.

The issue of bloc versus split voting raised in the context of the proposed Council was especially important to developing members. Some elected Executive Directors had "mixed" constituencies, that is, they were elected by some industrial members and by some developing members. Since Executive Directors voted by bloc, an Executive Director with developing members in his constituency could not cast the votes of those members separately. This inability meant that the developing members in a mixed constituency, such as the Bahamas, Jamaica, or the Philippines, could not, if they so wished, ask their Executive Director to vote on an issue along with the nine Executive Directors elected exclusively by developing members. In the Board of Governors, however, the Governor of every member cast his vote individually. Since developing members were increasingly inclined to take common positions, many were inclined to prefer split voting to bloc voting and voting in the Board of Governors to voting in the Executive Board. On the other hand, Executive Directors from some of the larger developing members and those from industrial members strongly opposed split voting. They were concerned that if votes could be cast separately for each member in a constituency, the ability of Executive Directors to change their minds, to explain their motives, or to negotiate compromises acceptable to all the members for which they spoke would be seriously damaged. Every Executive Director would have binding instructions from each member in his constituency.

The issue of bloc versus split voting in the Executive Board had first arisen in the discussions leading to the establishment of the SDR. One of the deputies of the Group of Ten had suggested that split voting be used on proposals for allocations of SDRs, but his suggestion was vigorously opposed by Executive Directors.[6] The issue in 1975 was how voting would be conducted in the newly proposed Council of Governors.

The powers of the Council were further discussed, even though the Executive Directors had already had a preliminary discussion of the various powers of the Fund and how they were distributed under the Fund's Articles. The original Articles had been simple: all the Fund's powers except for those conferred directly on the Executive Directors or on the Managing Director were vested in the Board of Governors. The Board of Governors could, with some exceptions, delegate these powers to the Executive Directors. What was to be the distribution of powers under the amended Articles? What powers would the Council have that the Executive Directors now exercised? Would the Council take decisions on topics on which the Executive Board now took decisions? At stake was whether the Executive Board or the Council would be the effective decision-making organ.

Mr. Lieftinck, Mr. Nana-Sinkam, and Mr. Prasad feared that any powers given to the Council would be at the expense of the Executive Board. Wanting the Executive Board to be the most effective decision-making body in the Fund, they were strongly opposed to the Council. The Executive Directors from developing members also feared that establishment of the Council would diminish the role of the Board of Governors in the Fund's policymaking process. In their view, the Annual Meetings of the Board of Governors provided an unusual opportunity for the Governors of developing members to express their views publicly and privately to the Managing Director. Annual Meetings could be overshadowed by the activities of the Council.

Since it was assumed that the Council would be established as soon as the amended Articles of Agreement came into force, answers to questions about the distribution of powers among the Fund's various organs were expected to have almost immediate effect on the Executive Board and the Board of Governors. As a way to put off establishing the Council, several Executive Directors from developing members proposed that before the Council was established, the Fund should first gain more experience with the Interim Committee.

It was quickly becoming apparent that an intense struggle for control of the Fund's policymaking organs similar to what had gone on prior to the formation of the Committee of Twenty, described in Chapter 8, was now taking the form of a fight over the Council.

---

[6]*History, 1966–71*, Vol. I, pp. 123–24 and 151–52.

AMENDMENTS RELATING TO THE GENERAL ACCOUNT

In August and September 1974, the Executive Board discussed a host of draft amendments proposing changes in the General Account. Changes were proposed in the provisions of the Articles governing repurchases, the media to be used for payments to the Fund by members in connection with increases in quotas, and charges and repurchases. The staff also circulated amendments dealing with the currencies used in the Fund's operations and transactions and on other financial matters.

Objectives of Amendments Drafted by the Staff

In drafting amendments relating to the General Account, the staff had two main objectives. One was to modernize the Articles by giving expression in the Articles of Agreement to practices that had already evolved from Executive Board decisions over the previous 30 years. A second objective was to introduce improvements and possibilities for further improvements in the Fund's financial activities. Here, the intent was to give the Fund flexibility in its future operations.

The staff had drafted proposed amendments on all the topics relating to financial matters in such a way as to give the Fund flexibility and make it easier for it to operate in the future, as opposed to specifying in the Articles themselves what might be regarded as the Fund's policies. The reasoning behind the staff's approach was as follows. In the original Articles many provisions had been drafted as formulas, mainly because the original Articles represented "a bold adventure in international cooperation." Because of suspicion about how the new organization might work, the negotiators had attempted to provide considerable detail in the Articles themselves. They had thus rigidly formulated a number of rights and obligations of members. This rigidity had made it difficult for the Fund to evolve in the rapidly changing circumstances in the late 1960s. After 1971 the Fund could clearly no longer function and had to create a number of "extra-legal arrangements" not encompassed within the Articles, as has been described in earlier chapters.

Drafting the Second Amendment presented an opportunity for officials to adopt a different attitude and to give more authority to the administrators of the Fund and of its various organs. The Fund's past experience indicated the desirability of incorporating as much flexibility as possible in the amended Articles with respect to financial operations and transactions to enable it to withstand the impact of future events. Examples of this flexibility abound in the draft amendments. On the occasion of an increase in quota, a member was to pay 25 percent of the increase in SDRs but the Board of Governors might prescribe that this payment be made in whole or in part in the currencies of other members specified by the Fund or in the member's own currency, provided all members had the same option. Another provision allowed the Fund to perform financial and technical services consistent with the purposes of the Fund, including the administration of resources contributed by members. Thus, should the need for an arrangement similar to the Subsidy Account for the oil facility or to the Trust Fund arise in the future, the Fund would, under its amended Articles, have the flexibility it needed to administer such an arrangement directly.

Although "credit" and "lending" were becoming commonly used terms in connection with use of the Fund's resources, draft amendments on use of the Fund's resources avoided the impression that the Fund's transactions were a form of lending by continuing to refer to the "purchase" and "repurchase" of currencies and not to a "loan" or "repayment." There were both legal and policy reasons for the continued use of the traditional terminology. Legally the Fund could sell a member's currency. Such a sale had the effect of discharging the member's repurchase obligations. In addition, since under the original Articles there was no set period of time when repurchase was obligatory, the Fund's arrangements for "repayment" differed considerably from the customary arrangements for repayment of traditional loans. In other words, because of the revolving way in which the Fund used members' currencies, its operations were unique, and the concepts of purchases and repurchases of currencies were retained in the draft amendments. On the policy side, use of the traditional terminology avoided the impression that a member requesting use of the Fund's resources was a suppliant, coming to the Fund for a loan. The Fund made resources available to stabilize a member's economy. Stabilization benefited not only the member but the whole international monetary system. Hence, it seemed preferable to continue to regard use of the Fund's resources as involving the purchase and sale of currencies and not as an extension of credit or as loans.

Provision Relating to Currencies

One modernization proposed in the draft amendments concerned the selection of currencies used in purchases and repurchases. In practice, since 1962 the Fund had been using currency budgets that specified the currencies to be used in purchases and repurchases, as was explained in Chapter 29. There was, however, no express basis in the existing Articles for this practice. The proposed draft amendments changed the wording with regard to the entitlement of members to use the Fund's general resources. This entitlement was no longer to be formulated in terms of a member's requesting the currency of a specific member for making payments in that currency. Rather, the entitlement of a member to draw from the Fund was to be formulated in terms of a member's drawing from the Fund a parcel of currencies or even SDRs that could be used by a member, directly or indirectly, to meet its payments or build up its reserves. Thus, the proposed amendments would make it possible for a member to request a purchase without specifying a particular currency. The currency would be selected by the Fund in accordance with the Fund's policies on the use of currencies. A parallel system would exist with respect to repurchase.

A further modernization proposed in the initial draft amendments related to the availability of members' currencies for use in the Fund's operations and transactions. Although the Fund had worked out arrangements under which it could sell many of the currencies it held, the successful operation of the Fund's policies with regard to currencies depended entirely on the voluntary collaboration of members. In particular, the Fund's ability in practice to sell the currencies of individual members depended on the issuers' willingness to exchange balances of their currencies sold by the Fund for currencies that would help purchasing members solve the problems for which they had made purchases. (Not all currencies can be used to support a member's currency in interventions in exchange markets or are acceptable in settlement of international transactions.) Not all members had been willing to collaborate with the Fund in the necessary exchanges. Similarly, the Fund's policies with regard to currencies used in repurchases depended on voluntary adherence by members to these policies. The media of repurchase, which included gold and SDRs as well as currencies for mandatory repurchases, were determined by formulas.

Moreover, the absence of an established obligation to convert into another currency meant that members could exercise a de facto veto on the inclusion of their currencies in the currency budgets that the Fund regularly prepared and used to determine the particular currencies to be used in purchases and repurchases. The draft amendments proposed, therefore, that when the Fund sold a member's currency, the member should at the request of the purchasing member be obliged to convert it at exchange rates determined in accordance with agreed provisions or practices. An obligation to convert was also proposed for currencies required for repurchase.

The obligation to convert was essential if the Fund was to choose the currencies it would supply to members, as was being proposed, rather than having the member specify the currency it wanted to purchase, as was provided in the original Articles, and if the Fund was to specify the media for repurchases. In proposing these amendments, the staff had in mind that the member does not necessarily always have to effect the conversion; it might take place in the market.

Provisions Regarding Repurchases

The draft amendments also substantially revised the provisions of the original Articles governing repurchases. Under the original Articles, repurchase obligations were determined principally by formulas based on the level of, and increases in, a member's monetary reserves and the Fund's holdings of a member's currency. In essence, a member used its own reserves in the year in which it made a purchase from the Fund that increased the Fund's holdings of its currency above 75 percent of quota and pari passu shared with the Fund increases in monetary reserves until the Fund's holdings of its currency were reduced to 75 percent of quota.

These rules of the original Articles relating repurchases to a member's monetary reserve position were designed to support the concept that a member purchasing from the Fund had a balance of payments and reserve need and to support the revolving character of the Fund's resources. The drafters of the original Articles felt it was impolitic to regard the transaction involving the sale of currencies by the Fund as a loan, and this view led them to avoid a fixed date for repurchase.

In practice, however, over the years the repurchase provisions of the original Articles had come to be regarded, both by Fund officials and by member governments, as rigid and unworkable. It was difficult to apply the formulas in the Articles. Hence, to the extent permitted by the Articles, the Fund developed over time various practices, interpretations, and conventions regarding repurchase. These practices, sometimes referred to as "a secondary system of repurchase," included the rule that repurchases be effected over a three-to-five-year period and were used to ensure that the Fund's resources were available for a temporary period. The secondary system could be made mandatory only in the case of drawings for which waivers were granted. Hence, the Fund had to rely in part on a voluntary system. The coexistence of two parallel systems was excessively complex.

To help correct this situation, several amendments concerning repurchases—especially concerning the formulas for calculating repurchase obligations—were made when the proposed First Amendment went to the Board of Governors for approval in 1968. These amendments formed the lengthiest chain of the "reform" amendments of 1968. (The reform amendments had been insisted on by the monetary authorities of the six countries then belonging to the EC—Belgium, France, the Federal Republic of Germany, Italy, Luxembourg, and the Netherlands—as a condition for their acceptance of the amendments incorporating SDRs into the Articles. By 1968 the currencies of the six countries of the EC were being used in the Fund's operations and transactions in a cumulative account that exceeded use of the dollar. Hence, the monetary authorities of these countries expressed a strong interest in the provisions of the Fund's Articles relating to the use of the Fund's resources.)[7]

Despite the reform amendments, problems continued. Emphasis on incorporating SDRs into the Articles at the time of the First Amendment had diverted attention from the repurchase provisions. In addition, as time went on, the currencies of the EC countries were used even more heavily in purchases from the Fund. Hence, the monetary authorities of these countries grew more interested in changing the repurchase provisions. Also, the provisions of the Articles regarding repurchase continued to be cumbersome and troublesome and gave rise to both operating and legal problems. By 1974 they seemed to be ill-adapted to the Fund's actual operations and unnecessary from a legal point of view.

For all these reasons, the repurchase provisions were a prime contender for amendment. The staff seized the opportunity to suggest wholly new provisions for

---

[7]The provisions of the original Articles concerning repurchases, the most important decisions interpreting these provisions, several of the difficulties that arose in implementing repurchase procedures, and the solutions worked out by the Fund in its first 20 years are summarized in *History, 1945–65*, Vol. II, pp. 436–37. The provisions of the First Amendment governing repurchases are summarized in *History, 1966–71*, Vol. I, pp. 258–59. They are discussed in detail in Joseph Gold, *The Reform of the Fund*, IMF Pamphlet Series, No. 12 (Washington, 1969).

repurchase. They initially drafted very simple repurchase obligations, based mainly on fixed periods for different facilities without reference to improvement in a member's balance of payments or reserve position.

When the Executive Board discussed these draft provisions for the first time in August 1974, the General Counsel stressed that the draft amendments were rooted in the experience of the Fund. They tried to correct problems that went back to the beginning of the Fund's operations. The basic principle of the proposed draft amendment was that a member should repurchase within a temporary period but certainly when the problem for which it had used the Fund's resources had been solved.

Several Executive Directors, however, argued that the draft provisions for amending the Articles with respect to repurchase were excessively general. Agreeing that the staff had made a laudable effort to remove the "overly tight straightjacket" of the existing repurchase obligations, Mr. Lieftinck particularly objected that certain principles of the original Articles were no longer taken into account in the proposed draft amendments. That a member in balance of payments difficulty using the Fund's resources was expected to use its own reserves too had completely disappeared. In his view, the stress in the draft amendments on a period of time in which repurchase was to take place, though reasonably related to the balance of payments problem, left the impression that it was only this period that was important. What was also important was the *amount* of a member's currency held by the Fund while the purchase was outstanding. This idea had been lost. He wanted to retain the principle that repurchases should be made in the light of improvement in a member's monetary reserve position.

Mr. Kafka agreed with Mr. Lieftinck. The principle of a member's repurchasing from the Fund when its monetary reserves increased ought to be preserved for the benefit of the liquidity of the Fund. When members' external positions improved, the Fund's position should also improve. Messrs. Brand, Cross, Schleiminger, and Schneider likewise believed that the draft amendments for repurchase obligations suggested by the staff represented too extreme a reaction to the experience of the past. These Executive Directors appealed for a middle-of-the-road solution that would simplify the complicated repurchase provisions yet would retain the past principle of tying repurchase obligations to developments in a member's balance of payments and reserve position.

Some favored specifying in amended repurchase provisions a normal period for use of the Fund's resources as a safeguard against longer use. They were inclined to regard a period of five years as appropriate. Mr. Bull argued that it might be wise to inscribe the normal three-to-five-year period in the Articles of Agreement. He noted that the proposed extended facility, then being considered in the Executive Board, already went dangerously close to blurring the distinction between the Fund's normal lending and less normal "medium-term" lending. In his view, the need to preserve that distinction was great.

Obviously more discussion of the provisions on repurchase was going to be needed.

Provisions on Other Financial Subjects

The exploratory discussions of the Executive Board in August 1974 also covered draft amendments relating to other financial subjects, such as the media to be used in payments by members to the Fund and by the Fund to members. Payments took place, for instance, for increases in quotas, charges, repurchases, and remuneration on creditor positions in the Fund. In the draft amendments SDRs replaced gold as the medium of payment, irrespective of other media that might be usable. The portion of increased subscriptions payable in gold under the existing Articles, for example, could under the draft amendments be paid in SDRs or in currencies of other members prescribed by the Fund. But the provisions to be included in the amended Articles relating to gold were controversial, as seen in Chapter 31. In late 1974, when the Executive Directors discussed the media of payments to and by the Fund, their discussions were accordingly preliminary and their positions reflected the controversy described in this earlier chapter.

Only after the gold problem was resolved in late 1975 could draft amendments relating to the General Account be finalized. Meanwhile, debate among the Executive Directors centered on the extent to which members, if not required to pay in gold, should be required to pay the Fund in SDRs or in reserve currencies or permitted to pay entirely in their own currencies. The issue was whether the Fund should be deprived of its stock of primary reserve assets.

Other draft amendments proposed establishment of an Investment Account. (The Fund had maintained a small investment program from 1956 to 1972 but only under an implied power and subject to restrictive conditions.) A draft amendment would give the Fund the express power to invest a part of its gold or currency assets in the obligations or securities of its members or of international organizations to help raise revenue for its administrative or operational expenses. The proceeds in the Investment Account could be used for meeting current budgetary deficits or for augmenting reserves that could be used for meeting budgetary deficits in the future. An advantage of an Investment Account was that it need not be subject to the provisions requiring the maintenance of value of currency holdings as was required of currency holdings in the General Account. Nor would changes in the Investment Account that changed the Fund's holdings of their currencies affect the positions of members in the Fund, as was the case in the General Account.

Certain practices based on earlier Executive Board decisions of fundamental importance to the Fund's operations and transactions were also incorporated in the draft amendments to help modernize the Articles. The existing Articles contained no provision, for example, to deal expressly with stand-by arrangements even though these arrangements had become the main instrument for making the Fund's resources available to members. The draft amendments included a provision that allowed for and defined a stand-by arrangement.

In late 1974 the Executive Directors explored all these draft amendments relating to the General Account and to the Fund's operations and transactions, as well as a number of further questions related to the Fund's finances. Should the requirement of need for use of Fund resources be linked both to an unfavorable balance of payments position and to a level of reserves considered low by some appropriate criteria? In other words, should the balance of payments and reserve positions be regarded as two criteria of need or as a single joint criterion? Should the Fund have explicit authority to adopt special policies on use of its resources for particular balance of payments problems, as it did when it adopted the compensatory financing facility, the buffer stock facility, the oil facility, and the extended facility? Should the Articles be amended so as to separate the rate of interest on the SDR from the rate of remuneration? (Under the existing Articles, these two rates were connected.) How much progression should there be in the Fund's schedules of charges?

Although the Executive Directors had already had a preliminary discussion, in April 1974, of possible changes in the General Account, the draft amendments elicited further discussion. Though sympathetic to providing the Fund with flexibility, several Executive Directors expressed discomfort with the proposed elimination of detail. Their concern about the simple draft provisions relating to repurchase, for example, has already been noted. In the same way, some Executive Directors were concerned that, under the draft amendments, the schedule of charges would no longer contain a graduated progression. Some were concerned about elimination of the legally required relationship between the rate of remuneration and the rate of interest on the SDR.

LEGALIZATION OF FLOATING RATES DEBATED

The initial draft amendment on exchange rate arrangements provoked most disagreement, however. Draft amendments that would legalize the widespread use of floating rates were clearly of major significance, as they touched the nerve center of the international monetary system. Not only was the issue of exchange rates at the center of the Fund's Articles but, as the discussions in the Committee of Twenty made evident, monetary authorities held opposite views on the direction in which the exchange rate system should move. These views were tantamount to two theologies, and the schism between them was as deep as that pertaining to gold and equally fraught with emotion.

The monetary authorities of many European countries believed that an internationally agreed commitment to a fixed exchange rate system would force the pursuit of noninflationary domestic and monetary policies so as to maintain fixed rates. According to this view, fixed exchange rates—or better still fixed exchange rates combined with convertibility into gold or other primary reserve assets of any currency balances acquired by foreign monetary authorities—would provide an automatic, self-policing, and stable international monetary system. In contrast, monetary authorities of the United States and Canada, and to some extent of the United Kingdom, argued that the causation in a stable international monetary system went, not from exchange rates to domestic policies but from domestic policies to exchange rates. In other words, stabilizing domestic economic policies had to come first. Stable exchange rates would then follow.

French authorities were almost fanatic in their arguments for fixed rates, and U.S. authorities were rapidly becoming strong proponents of floating rates. These strong differences of view were evident once more at the 1974 Annual Meeting. U.S. and French monetary authorities saw in opposite ways the relation between the prevailing exchange rate arrangements and the then pressing problems of world-wide inflation, the slowdown of economic growth in most industrial members, and the massive payments imbalances after the rise in oil prices. Noting that exchange markets in 1973 and 1974 had escaped the recurrent crises that beset them earlier under the Bretton Woods system, despite the overall uncertainties and the sudden changes in the external payments prospects of most industrial members following the oil crises, Mr. Simon concluded that in these difficult times "flexible exchange rates...have served us well."[8] But Mr. Fourcade, convinced that generalized floating aggravated economic instability and inflation, wanted to reinstitute a regime of exchange parities. In the interest of "stability, modernization, equality, and solidarity," the primary aim should be to establish a new international monetary system based on par values as soon as possible.[9]

Other Governors held less extreme positions. Mr. Wardhana, who had just finished his term as Chairman of the Committee of Twenty, repeated the position that had been taken by the Committee of Twenty several months earlier. He argued that like higher oil prices, generalized floating had to be accepted as a reality. What officials had to do, therefore, was to establish as much order and stability as possible through rules or guidelines for floating rates and to work gradually toward a more permanent system along the lines envisaged in the *Outline of Reform*.[10]

Messrs. De Clercq and Duisenberg also expressed conciliatory positions. Mr. De Clercq emphasized that in the amended Articles the Committee of Twenty's principle of stable but adjustable par values was to be primary. In accepting floating rates, officials should regard them as an exception. There should also be surveillance by the Fund.[11] Mr. Duisenberg argued similarly that floating rates should be accepted but should be guided by the general principles spelled out in the *Outline of Reform* and subject to surveillance by the Fund.[12]

---

[8]Statement by the Governor of the Fund and the World Bank for the United States, *Summary Proceedings, 1974*, p. 87.

[9]Statement by the Governor of the Fund and the World Bank for France, *Summary Proceedings, 1974*, p. 98.

[10]Statement by the Governor of the Fund for Indonesia, *Summary Proceedings, 1974*, p. 71.

[11]Statement by the Governor of the World Bank for Belgium, *Summary Proceedings, 1974*, p. 142.

[12]Statement by the Governor of the World Bank for the Netherlands, *Summary Proceedings, 1974*, pp. 150–51.

These views indicated that by September 1974 most monetary authorities realized that generalized floating was likely to continue for some time, that a par value system could not be reintroduced soon, and that in these circumstances it was best to work toward some degree of management or surveillance of exchange rate policies by the international community, presumably by the Fund.

Consideration by the Executive Board

It was in the midst of these arguments about the merits of floating rates that the Fund staff began to prepare draft amendments. When the staff and the Executive Directors came to consider the redraft of Article IV, dealing with par values and constituting the heart of the original par value system, a number of basic questions arose. Should there be any amendment to the Articles before widespread recourse to floating rates came to an end? If there were to be amendments while floating rates continued, should an amended Article IV emphasize the need for members to re-establish a par value system with floating rates accepted as an exception, or should it emphasize acceptance of floating rates, with the possibility of a system of stable but adjustable par values evolving in the future? In either case, what treatment should be accorded a floating rate? Should a floating rate be viewed as an exception to be tolerated only with the approval of the international community, or should it be viewed as an entitlement as long as the member acted consistently with guidelines established by the Fund?

With an eye on paragraph 41 of the *Outline of Reform* on the preparation of draft amendments, the staff drafted an amended Article IV that would legalize floating rates. Paragraph 41 mentioned amendments "to enable the Fund to legalize the position of countries with floating rates during the interim period." In the draft amendments, the staff tried to capture the idea they felt existed among many monetary authorities that the opportunity of drafting amended Articles should be taken "to remove the sense of sin" by conferring some measure of legality on existing practices. At the same time the idea was also to provide for the longer term.

The staff argued that were the amended Articles to relate only to the longer run, with provisions for adjustable par values and for floating rates only in particular circumstances, nonobservance of those provisions would continue inasmuch as widespread floating already existed. The staff draft, therefore, tried to provide for the immediate period, legalizing the existing situation from the day the amendment took effect, as well as for the longer term when a major reform of the international monetary system could be initiated. The draft amendment would also give a specific legal basis to the guidelines for floating that the Fund had established in June 1974 (described in Chapter 16), as well as to any modified or new guidelines that might be adopted in the future.

When the draft amendment of Article IV was first discussed in the Executive Board in September 1974, sharp differences of view were expected and were expressed. Many Executive Directors vehemently opposed amending the Articles to legalize general floating. Mr. Kharmawan emphasized that he had "clear instructions" from the members that had elected him that they were universally opposed to this. They all agreed with the Committee of Twenty that there should be an adjustable par value system allowing for floating rates only in particular situations. The monetary authorities of the developing members that had elected him insisted on steps toward that objective and could agree with provisions in the Articles of Agreement that went in that direction. Draft amendments for legalizing general floating, however, had no connection at all with "a flexible par value system." Mr. Kharmawan concluded that, given this situation, the Fund should continue to operate under its existing Articles.

Miss Fuenfgelt and Mr. Kawaguchi likewise believed that the Articles ought not to be amended so as to legalize floating rates in general. Mr. de Margerie recalled for his colleagues that the French authorities were decidedly attached to the principle of fixed exchange rates and were convinced that rules for floating rates should be extremely precise and strict. The French authorities did not want to legalize floating rates even for an interim period. Mr. de Groote, too, complained that the draft amendment was "of little help in achieving an international monetary system based on stable but adjustable par values." Yet, in his view, such a system should be established. Executive Directors opposed to legalizing the existing floating rates proposed adding such words as "temporary," "exceptional," and "conditional" to the amended Article IV.

Mr. Cross, on the other hand, insisted that legalizing floating was critically important. Only through such an amendment could the international monetary system evolve toward longer-run reform. A floating exchange rate had to be an option open to members on equal terms with the option of establishing and maintaining a par value. There was to be "no onus" to a floating exchange rate. Other Executive Directors supported his position on the grounds that the Articles ought to contain provisions that would enable the Fund to do more than simply take note of a member's decision to let its exchange rate float, as did the existing Articles.

This discussion of the possible legalization of floating exchange rates was universally regarded as preliminary. The issue and its resolution would become the high drama discussed in Chapter 37.

AMENDMENT GIVING THE FUND AUTHORITY
OVER TRADE RESTRICTIONS CONSIDERED

A draft amendment dealing with members' avoidance of restrictions on trade and other current account transactions for balance of payments reasons was discussed in the Executive Board in October 1974. The draft amendment would give the Fund direct jurisdiction over restrictions on trade and on other current international transactions imposed for balance of payments reasons. The starting point for this draft amendment was the concept that the Fund was empowered to approve or disapprove "restrictions on payments and transfers for current international transactions." Although the Articles defined what was meant by "current international transactions," in practice it had often been difficult to determine whether a particular restriction by a member was imposed directly on payments and transfers for current international transactions and was thus within the Fund's jurisdiction, or whether the restriction was imposed directly on the transaction itself and was thus outside the Fund's jurisdiction. In the 1950s, when the Fund's consultations under Article XIV were started, there had been long, heated debates among the staff and in the Executive Board on how to gauge precisely the type of restrictions over which the Fund had authority. In 1959 and 1960 the Fund had considered its jurisdiction in respect of restrictions and the Executive Board had adopted certain decisions delineating the Fund's authority.[13]

As time went on, more of the staff came to view the distinction between a restriction on a transaction imposed for balance of payments purposes and a restriction on the payment for the transaction as artificial. Hence, on the occasion of the Second Amendment the staff believed that problems in making such determinations would disappear if the provisions of the Fund's Articles applied to both classes of restrictions.

The staff's consideration in drafting the precise provisions of the amendment was this. Under the GATT's charter the procedure followed was that after a country (i.e., a CONTRACTING PARTY) had imposed restrictions on trade or on other international transactions for balance of payments purposes, the GATT held a consultation to determine the need for the restrictions. As part of the consultation, the GATT asked the Fund to make a determination as to the need for the restrictions in light of the balance of payments and reserve positions of the country concerned. Under its charter, the GATT was required to accept the Fund's findings. This procedure by the GATT was a post hoc procedure. In other words, the consultation took place after the country had imposed the restrictions. The draft amendment provided for the Fund to have authority for *prior scrutiny* of restrictions on current international transactions, including trade, that a member *intended* to impose. The Fund could still collaborate with the GATT in the usual post hoc procedure. Hence, new authority for the Fund would not derogate from the jurisdiction of the GATT.[14]

The staff had worded the draft amendment to avoid the pitfalls experienced with the voluntary declaration against trade restrictions drafted earlier in 1974. (The declaration of January 1974 asking members voluntarily to pledge themselves against imposing tighter restrictions as a way to cope with the larger payments deficits brought on by the onset of the oil crisis early in 1974 has been described in Chapter 16.) For example, the phrase "trade and other current account measures" was avoided in the draft amendment and there was no reference to the jurisdiction of the GATT.

---

[13]*History, 1945–65*, Vol. II, pp. 235–40 and 280–88.

[14]The new authority for the Fund over restrictions would apply only to restrictions imposed for balance of payments reasons, not to restrictions imposed for reasons of commercial policy.

No matter how carefully the language of the amendment was drafted, the issue of whether the Fund ought to have jurisdiction over restrictions on trade and other current international transactions was bound to be troublesome. When the topic of the Fund having authority in the trade field had come up in the past, many Executive Directors had vigorously and consistently objected. The topic came up now in the form of an amendment to the Fund's Articles because U.S. authorities were strongly interested in finding ways to bolster international control over trade barriers.

Since about 1971, U.S. authorities had favored strengthening the authority of the international community over restrictions on trade. They had wanted the Committee of Twenty, whose full name was the Committee on Reform of the International Monetary System *and Related Issues,* to deal with this subject. They favored tightening the international rules on restrictions on trade since they were convinced that barriers to imports of U.S. goods and services by several industrial countries, particularly the EC countries and Japan, were the major impediment to the reduction of U.S. trade deficits.

In the Executive Board's discussion in October 1974, Mr. Cross, as was expected, fully supported the draft amendment. In fact, he argued for stronger language that would give the Fund even more authority than that proposed by the staff. He argued, for example, that the term "trade measures" rather than the term "restrictions" might be used so that measures other than restrictions, such as export subsidies, would be included under the Fund's jurisdiction. He insisted on a clear distinction between the authority of the Fund and that of the GATT. The Fund would not be "delving into commercial aspects of trade measures but would be limiting its consideration to the broader balance of payments aspects." Indeed, Mr. Cross wanted to know precisely how the provision of the draft amendment would be implemented.

Messrs. de Vries and Schleiminger were also willing to support the draft amendment. However, Messrs. Brand, Bryce, and de Margerie were very much opposed. Mr. Brand's view was expected as the Australian authorities had long been opposed to giving the Fund authority over trade. Since the Fund's inception, the Australian authorities had expressed themselves on this topic more strongly and consistently than the authorities of any other member. Moreover, they and the Canadian authorities felt that it was premature in October 1974 to discuss such an amendment when only a few members had subscribed to the voluntary trade declaration requested in January 1974. Mr. Brand also argued that if the voluntary trade declaration of January 1974 became effective, it would be advisable to observe its operation closely before seriously considering the amendment to the Fund's Articles. Mr. Bryce was concerned that the traditional distinction between the jurisdictions of the Fund and the GATT might be blurred. The French authorities were also strongly opposed "to the concept of including something like the trade pledge in the Articles of Agreement."

Messrs. Kafka, Kharmawan, Monday, and Yaméogo were concerned that the Fund might not be sufficiently strong to apply the provisions "equitably" to both large and small members, and hence the obligations would be applied mainly to developing members. Consequently, they were also reluctant to support the proposed amendment.

The preference of countries for the Fund or the GATT as the agency having authority over trade restrictions was influenced by differences in voting power. Countries holding relatively large voting power in the Fund favored giving the Fund more authority; countries holding relatively less voting power favored the GATT. Another factor was how attached their authorities were to a philosophy of free trade. Countries whose authorities were strongly committed to free trade favored giving the Fund authority over trade in the belief that action by the Fund was likely to be more effective than action by the GATT.

DISCUSSION OF CHANGES IN THE SDR

In late 1974 the Executive Directors also considered draft amendments relating to SDRs. These amendments were intended to loosen the restraints placed on the SDR at the time of its creation, to improve its characteristics, and to extend its uses to make it a more attractive reserve asset. The amendments would enable members to use SDRs for payments due to the Fund, relax the requirement of need for the use of SDRs, expand the freedom of participants to enter into transactions by agreement (that is, without designation of the transferee of SDRs by the Fund), enable the Fund to permit operations and transactions in SDRs that were not yet possible, such as the direct discharge of obligations between members or the use of SDRs as collateral, modify the provision under which participants might opt out of allocations of SDRs, increase the obligation of members to accept SDRs, enlarge the categories of other authorized holders of SDRs and the operations and transactions in which they might engage among themselves and with participants or with the Fund through the General Account, cut the tie between the rate of remuneration and the rate of interest on SDRs, and simplify the concept of "currency convertible in fact," that is, the currency to be received when SDRs were encashed in transactions in which the Fund designated the transferee.

A draft amendment would also permit the Fund to abolish the obligation of members to "reconstitute" their positions in SDRs. The concept of "reconstitution" and its rules agreed when the SDR was first negotiated in the 1960s resulted from controversies over whether a participant that used its SDRs should be bound to restore its holdings of them. These controversies reflected different views on whether the SDR should be regarded as an asset or as a credit. If it was a credit, some repayment or reconstitution ought to be required.

It was eventually agreed that a participant's net use of SDRs had to be such that the average of its daily holdings of SDRs over any five-year period would be not less than 30 percent of the average of its net cumulative allocation over the same period. If a participant used no more than 70 percent of its average net cumulative allocation at all times, it automatically fulfilled this obligation. If it used more than 70 percent for some part of a five-year period, it had to increase its holdings above 30 percent for a long enough period to bring its use for the whole five-year period to no more than 70 percent on the average. These rules for reconstitution were to be reviewed before the end of the first and of each subsequent basic period of SDRs and new rules adopted if necessary. Otherwise, the same rules would continue to apply. An 85 percent majority of the total voting power was required for decisions to adopt, modify, or abrogate the rules for reconstitution.[15]

These rules had been reviewed and retained in 1972, as is explained in a later chapter, but the review was a "hold-the-line" action until new draft amendments could be considered. In 1974, the staff was proposing an amendment that would permit the Fund to abolish reconstitution obligations.

Another draft amendment would establish a link between allocations of SDRs and development finance. The link had a history going back to the 1960s and the *Outline of Reform* had proposed an amendment authorizing the Fund to implement such a link.

INTERIM COMMITTEE'S DIRECTIVES IN JANUARY 1975

After their preliminary discussions, the Executive Directors decided on several topics on which "there ought to be amendments." They agreed on the need for amendments to establish a Council, to update the Articles regarding the use of the Fund's resources and to change the provisions for repurchase and for payments to and by the Fund through the General Account, including payments in gold on the occasion of increases in quota, to enable the Fund to invest reserves in interest-bearing obligations issued by members or by other international financial organizations to obtain revenue for its budget, and to improve the characteristics and uses of the SDR. But they were far from ready to agree on the text of particular amendments on any of these topics and had not yet agreed that there should even be amendments about gold (other than those concerning payments of gold to the Fund on the occasion of increases in quotas) or about the exchange rates to be permitted even for an interim period. The deadline of February 9, 1975 for amendments to the Articles was not going to be met.

The Executive Directors asked advice of the Interim Committee, which was scheduled to meet in January 1975. They asked for direction on a number of basic questions which seemed to be political and whose answers would facilitate drafting the amendments. Should they try to agree on proposed amendments for all the topics set forth in paragraph 41 of the *Outline of Reform*? What powers should be given to the Council? Should the Council be established soon or should the Fund first gain more experience with the operation of the Interim Committee, as several Executive Directors, especially those from developing members, were proposing?

---

[15]For background on the rules for reconstitution, see *History, 1966–71*, Vol. I, pp. 113–14, 142, 152, 156–58, and 186.

Should each Councillor be able to cast his votes only as a unit, as did Executive Directors, or should he be authorized to cast separately the votes allotted to each member country in his constituency as was done in the Board of Governors? How should the Executive Directors proceed with regard to legalizing floating rates? Should there be a transition period before amended provisions with regard to floating rates became operative? Or should existing floating rates become legal as soon as the amended Articles went into effect? Should there be an amendment allowing for a link between SDR allocations and development finance?

Another topic left for the Interim Committee at its January 1975 meeting was what to do about the failure of monetary authorities to resolve by February 1975 issues relevant to the Sixth General Review of Quotas. Not only was there no agreement on draft amendments which might excuse members from paying gold to the Fund when their quotas were increased, but there was as yet no agreement on the overall size of the quota increase. Even if quotas had been agreed, there would be difficulty in getting monetary authorities to submit requested increases in quotas to their legislative bodies. Monetary authorities of several members were embarrassed to go to their legislatures to ask for increased subscriptions to an international organization in which members were violating the most substantial obligations of the Articles of Agreement.

As noted in Chapter 27, at its January 1975 meeting, the Interim Committee opted to have the Board of Governors pass a pro forma resolution merely requesting the Executive Directors to go on with their work on the Sixth General Review of Quotas. This resolution fulfilled the necessary legal requirement that the Board of Governors review quotas at intervals of not more than five years.

Resolution of the deadline issue with regard to the Sixth General Review of Quotas was by far the easiest issue to resolve. It was apparent that many issues, especially the legalization of floating rates and arrangements for gold, were still very controversial. There was also little hope that a link between allocations of SDRs and development finance would be established, since the authorities of both the United States and the Federal Republic of Germany continued to oppose such an arrangement. At the Interim Committee meeting, Mr. Simon noted that the U.S. authorities had already supported a Trust Fund and a Subsidy Account for the 1975 oil facility as substitutes for the link. Moreover, there was so little support for an amendment giving the Fund authority over restrictions on trade and other current international transactions imposed for balance of payments purposes that it was dropped.

The Interim Committee helped resolve other issues, however. It agreed that the Executive Directors should continue their work on the amendments and as soon as possible submit draft amendments on the following subjects: (a) the transformation "at an appropriate time" of the Interim Committee into a permanent Council to which each of the then 20 constituencies of the Fund would appoint a Councillor able to cast the votes of the countries in his constituency separately and which would have decision-making authority delegated by the Board of Governors; (b) improvements in the General Account, including (i) elimination of the obligation of member countries to use gold to make such payments to the Fund as quota subscriptions and repurchases and the determination of the media of payment to be used instead, and (ii) arrangements to ensure that the Fund's holdings of all currencies would be usable in its operations under satisfactory safeguards for all members; (c) improvements in the SDR to make it the principal reserve asset of the international monetary system; and (d) provision for stable but adjustable par values and the floating of currencies subject to appropriate rules and surveillance of the Fund, in accordance with the *Outline of Reform*.[16]

These encouraging actions would enable the Executive Directors to resume their work on drafting what was eventually to become known as the Second Amendment.

---

[16]Communiqué of Interim Committee, January 16, 1975, par. 6, Vol. III below, pp. 218–20.

CHAPTER
36

Continuing Consideration
of Amendments
(January 1975–March 1976)

*F*OLLOWING THE INTERIM COMMITTEE MEETING in January 1975, the Executive Directors, often meeting twice a day in February and early March, resumed their consideration of draft amendments. Later in March the staff, encouraged by the broad scope of the decisions taken by the Interim Committee and eager to proceed more quickly, sent to the Executive Directors a comprehensive draft amendment of the Articles. It contained revisions of all the provisions of Articles requiring amendment. Few provisions did not require modification of some sort. This draft amendment, based on staff memoranda, discussions of the Executive Directors, and the communiqué of the Interim Committee of January 1975, was accompanied by a detailed commentary explaining the proposed amendments.

The Executive Directors began to discuss the comprehensive draft amendment on March 21, 1975. It advanced their discussions to a new stage as the Executive Directors could now see how all the Articles would be affected and interrelated. Furthermore, elimination of amendments on the link between SDR allocations and development finance and on restrictions on trade and on other current international transactions imposed for balance of payments reasons allowed negotiations on the amendments to center around five main topics—gold, exchange arrangements, improvements in the General Account, improvements in SDRs, and the Council.

TECHNIQUES USED TO FACILITATE AGREEMENT
AND TO GIVE THE FUND FLEXIBILITY

In proposing the comprehensive draft amendment, the staff made considerable use of techniques that they expected would facilitate agreement and would provide the Fund with flexibility in conducting its activities.

Enabling Powers

One technique was to give the Fund "an enabling power." This technique made it unnecessary to spell out fixed rules in the Articles but gave discretionary authority to take specific action later. Even though monetary authorities might agree that the Articles of Agreement might have to be further amended at a later date in order to establish a reformed system, an opportunity to amend the Articles would not occur frequently. Therefore, on the occasion of this consideration of the amendments, it was thought useful to adopt provisions that would give the Fund authority to take action later, particularly for controversial topics that would not currently be settled.

In using the technique of an enabling power, proposed amendments had to be formulated cautiously so as to specify clearly the authority to be given to the Fund and the obligations of member governments. It was imperative that any authority given to the Fund to take action in the future should not at a later date impose additional obligations on members. Amendments had to be formulated so that as new international monetary arrangements were agreed, the Fund could give content to, or implement, obligations already accepted by member governments.

This formulation of amendments to the Articles was to avoid the objection, especially by legislators in member governments, that members were being subjected to new obligations in the Fund without appropriate parliamentary approval. From the point of view of international law, the objection had to be avoided that the process of amendment was circumventing parliamentary approval. Thus, the refusal of negotiators at the Bretton Woods Conference to allow organs of the Fund (the Board of Governors and the Executive Board) to amend the Articles was repeated in the drafting of the Second Amendment.

As the drafting proceeded, the technique of enabling powers proved exceedingly useful. It gave the Fund flexibility. It also facilitated agreement when there was a prolonged difference of opinion among the Executive Directors or among members of the Interim Committee since it could be used to defer resolution of a contentious issue once it became clear that further effort was unlikely to be rewarded with agreement.

The new enabling powers given to the Fund under the Second Amendment allow for the evolution of the international monetary system without having to amend the Articles.

Voting Majorities

From its inception the Fund has had weighted voting. Each member has a number of votes reflecting the size of its quota. In the original Articles, nearly all decisions of the Board of Governors and of the Executive Board were to be taken by a majority of votes cast. A simple majority would help decisions to be taken and business to be conducted with maximum ease. The few exceptions to this rule provided for varying proportions of total votes as special majorities for a few categories of decisions thought to have unusual political or economic importance. For example, decisions relating to changes in members' quotas and an increase in the number of elective Executive Directors were made subject to the special high majority of 80 percent of total voting power.

After the First Amendment, additional categories of decision, such as those relating to SDRs, were made subject to special voting majorities. This was to give the then six EC countries a veto over important decisions relating to the SDR, and a new majority—85 percent of the total votes—was created to give effect to this intent.

Like the technique of enabling powers, the technique of special voting majorities proved extremely useful. It was a way to provide adequate safeguards so that virtually all members would have to concur before further action was taken under the Fund's enabling powers and a way to ensure that certain members might individually or collectively have a veto over proposed actions. Special voting majorities were proposed by one Executive Director or another on almost every occasion when it seemed that they could break or circumvent a stalemate. Two special voting majorities were adopted, 85 percent and 70 percent. The higher majority was chosen not only because it was already in existence after the First Amendment, but also because it gave a veto to the United States, to the members that belonged to the European Community (as a group), and to developing members (as a group).

After considerable argument, U.S. authorities had accepted 85 percent as a special voting majority in the negotiation of the First Amendment as a concession to the EC countries. Paradoxically, in the negotiation of the Second Amendment, U.S. authorities themselves became advocates of an 85 percent majority for numerous decisions. In the original Articles, the majority of 80 percent for certain decisions had been adopted because the United States had well over 20 percent of the total votes in the original Fund and, accordingly, could readily veto decisions requiring an 80 percent majority. By the time of the Sixth General Review of Quotas in 1974–75, however, as noted in Chapter 27, consideration was being given to decreasing the proportion of the U.S. quota and hence of the votes of the United States to below 20 percent, and it was possible that this proportion might diminish still further. U.S. authorities solved this problem by agreeing to reduce the U.S. proportion below 20 percent provided the majority of the total votes needed for critical decisions in the Fund was raised to 85 percent.

As the negotiations for the Second Amendment proceeded, it developed that an 85 percent majority would be required for some decisions taken under the provisions of the Articles after the Second Amendment and an 80 percent majority for some decisions taken under the original Articles. Confusion over the size of voting majorities needed for various decisions could result. Hence, in the interest of simplification, the use of an 80 percent majority in the amended Articles was eliminated altogether.

The lower majority used in drafting and negotiating the Second Amendment, 70 percent, was a compromise between 75 percent and two thirds of total votes.

Authorities who wanted 75 percent were reconciled to 70 percent to some extent by the thought that the transitional provisions of the Second Amendment would maintain the existing rules and regulations, rates, procedures, and decisions in effect when the Second Amendment went into force and that the need for a 70 percent majority would make it sufficiently difficult to change them to something less acceptable to these authorities.

More decisions and amendments in the Second Amendment were made subject to a special voting majority than in the First Amendment which, in turn, had required more special majorities than did the original Articles. The original Articles required special majorities for 9 categories of decision, the First Amendment for 21, and the Second Amendment for 53.

There are two explanations for this increase and for the selection of the particular categories. First, monetary authorities and Fund officials believed that enabling powers that give the Fund authority over its members should be exercised only with the concurrence of members having a large total voting power. The requirement of a large voting majority provides assurance that most members agree with the implementation by the Fund of a specific enabling power before the Fund implements it.

Second, members or groups of members wanted to be assured of a veto or at least wished to make it difficult for the Fund to exercise a particular enabling power. This motive applies especially to amended Articles accepted by some members as a compromise but without enthusiasm. Economic and political changes in the world have made it necessary to take fully into account the interests of more members and groups of members as the Fund exercises its powers. Moreover, their influence had become such that they could virtually insist on having their interests taken into account.

Making Implied Powers Explicit

Another technique that the staff used in the comprehensive draft amendment was to make explicit powers for the Fund that were only implicit in the original Articles. One power made explicit was especially useful in connection with the future evolution of the international monetary system. The Fund had concluded that under its original Articles it had an implied power to perform financial and technical services for members, including the administration of resources contributed by members and others, if the services were consistent with the purposes of the Fund. The Fund's administration of the Subsidy Account associated with the 1975 oil facility and of the Trust Fund and the services that the Executive Board authorized the Managing Director to perform with respect to sterling balances, all described in foregoing chapters, are examples of the Fund's exercise of this implied power. The Second Amendment makes this power of the Fund "to perform financial and technical services, including the administration of resources contributed by members, that are consistent with the purposes of the Fund" explicit. It was to become Article V, Section 2(b).

Alternative Formulations

Another device the staff used to facilitate agreement was to provide in square brackets alternative formulations of a provision. At the outset of the Executive Board's discussion of each set of square brackets, Mr. Witteveen, as Chairman, explained the issues involved and indicated his preference among the alternative formulations. After the Executive Directors expressed their views, the staff quickly redrafted the provisions to reflect these views and any consensus that seemed to be developing. Supplementary memoranda were also circulated and discussed in the Executive Board.

By use of these techniques, the Executive Directors, working intensively with the guidance of the Interim Committee, were by the end of March 1976 able to draft amended provisions for the Articles, including numerous modifications for which there was no specific mandate in Part II of the *Outline of Reform*. Gradually, the feeling that the Second Amendment was an interim measure diminished and was replaced by the desire to have permanent amended Articles.

EXECUTIVE DIRECTORS' FURTHER CONSIDERATION OF DRAFT AMENDMENTS IN EARLY 1975

From February to May 1975 the Executive Directors considered individual draft amendments in detail, trying to reconcile their differences in order to agree on specific features of amendments and on language.

Improvements in the General Account

As in 1974, the Executive Directors in early 1975 again considered a number of draft amendments with regard to the General Account, such as those relating to the conditions for members' use of the Fund's resources. As noted in Chapter 35, an important question involved the extent to which the Fund, in considering a member's need to draw on the Fund, should take its reserve position into account, as well as its current balance of payments position. Another question was the extent to which a member should be required, or expected, to use its own reserves before drawing on the Fund. The requirement that a member use part of its own reserves was part of the existing Articles, embodied in the repurchase provisions. Among the amendments was also a draft Article V, Section 3(*d*), under which the Fund would have to adopt policies with respect to the selection of currencies used in the Fund's transactions and operations that would take into account, first, the present and prospective balance of payments and reserve positions of members and, second, the desirability of promoting over time a balanced distribution of reserve positions in the Fund.

The Executive Directors also considered revised versions of draft amendments on the media to be used for payments by members to the Fund when quotas were increased. On this issue, most Executive Directors still favored requiring members to pay some portion—probably 25 percent—of the increase in their quotas in SDRs or in national currencies specified by the Fund, with the concurrence of the issuing member, that is, requiring members to use their reserve assets. In this way, the Fund would receive especially needed currencies or SDRs. Executive Directors especially from developing members favored permitting members unable to pay a portion of their increased quotas in SDRs or in other members' currencies to pay the whole of their increased quota in their own currencies.

Mr. Wahl wanted the Fund to retain the option of members paying in gold. This position reflected the continuing insistence of the French authorities in March 1975 that allowance be made for retaining some use of gold in the international monetary system. Mr. Kafka and other Executive Directors from developing members, however, in line with the views of their constituencies described in Chapter 31, strongly opposed retaining a "gold option."

The Executive Directors considered revised draft amendments on the Fund's charges. One issue was the voting majority that should be required for determining the rates of charge. Mr. Drabble, Mr. Wakatsuki, and others argued that flexibility in determining the Fund's rates of charge was essential and that Executive Directors should consequently have as much discretion as possible in determining charges. Hence, a simple voting majority should be used. But Maung Shein (Burma) and other Executive Directors from developing members wanted to retain the majority of 75 percent of total voting power currently required for decisions relating to charges. In this way, the consent of many developing members would be needed for any changes in the Fund's charges.

The Executive Directors also considered revised provisions for repurchase and a revised draft amendment empowering the Fund to invest its assets up to an amount equal to its reserves. They also considered a draft Article V, Section 3(e) that would oblige members, when their currencies were sold by the Fund, to convert them into freely usable currencies. This amendment was unusually important: it would make all members' currencies usable in the Fund's transactions. The controversial question that was debated was whether currencies were still to be "convertible" in the traditional sense into primary reserve assets. Several arguments for and against asset settlement that had come up in the negotiations of the Committee of Twenty were repeated. U.S. authorities wanted all references to convertibility eliminated. They insisted that convertibility in the traditional sense was obsolete. U.S. authorities had no intention of agreeing to language implying they would assume convertibility obligations in the future. European authorities, however, wanted to retain the idea that at some time currencies, especially the dollar, would again be convertible into primary reserve assets. The debate persisted.

At this time the Executive Directors also considered the subject of the "norm" of 75/25 percent of quota. This concerned the question of whether there should be a change in the traditional "75 percent norm," that is, a change in the understanding that the normal amount of a member's currency that the Fund would hold was

75 percent of the member's quota. Under the existing Articles, holdings by the Fund of a member's currency in excess of that member's quota were subject to repurchase. Also, remuneration was paid on the difference between 75 percent of quota and the Fund's actual holdings of a member's currency. Once the Fund no longer required 25 percent of quota to be paid in gold, or in other primary reserve assets, the question arose whether the concept of 75/25 percent of quota made sense.

Mr. Whitelaw proposed that the norm be changed from 75 percent to 100 percent of quota. He argued that use of a norm of 100 percent would make the Fund's operations and transactions simple. The complexities of distinguishing between something comparable with the gold tranche and other tranches would disappear. A member would receive remuneration when the Fund's holdings of its currency fell below 100 percent of its quota, rather than the existing 75 percent.

Mr. Whitelaw's proposal met with a favorable reception by most Executive Directors and by the Managing Director and staff. It had the attraction of operational simplicity. Repurchase would no longer be allowed if the Fund's holdings of a member's currency were less than 100 percent of quota. Reduction of the Fund's holdings of a member's currency below 100 percent would then take place when the Fund sold the currencies of those members whose balance of payments and reserve positions were sufficiently strong. The Managing Director was concerned, however, that as a practical matter, the cost to the Fund of remunerating all positions below 100 percent would be very large. This cost might be large even if the rate of remuneration was set low, which its relationship to the interest rate on the SDR might make very difficult. The adoption of the 100 percent level for remuneration would be costly because while drawings in the gold tranche yielded the Fund no income from charges, the Fund had to pay remuneration on the increased creditor positions in the Fund resulting from gold tranche drawings. The management and staff, therefore, sought a solution by finding a way to determine norms of Fund's holdings of currency that might be used for purposes of remuneration.

Among the Executive Directors who opposed Mr. Whitelaw's proposal and wanted to retain the traditional 75 percent norm were Mr. Kawaguchi and Mr. Lieftinck. Throughout the discussion, Mr. Kawaguchi expressed the Japanese view that any amendments ought to be limited to the essential minimum. He regarded the existing proportions of 75/25 percent of the Fund's holdings of a member's currency as basic to the financial structure of the Fund. There was no need to change this structure.

As he frequently did in Executive Board discussions, Mr. Lieftinck undertook to explain for newer Executive Directors his understanding of the original concepts and purposes of the Fund. That the Fund would normally hold 75 percent of a member's quota in the member's own currency was put in the original Articles so that members would have to make a contribution to the Fund, equivalent to 25 percent of their quota, in gold, the most liquid and valuable prime asset in 1944–45. The Fund could compel a member to pay up to 25 percent of its quota in gold. This contribution was to be made without financial compensation to the member in order to permit the Fund to set its charges below those demanded by private institutions. Behind this arrangement was the understanding that, even with low charges, the Fund would not operate at a loss. Indeed, Mr. Lieftinck observed, the original Articles contained no provisions covering possible losses; they contained only provisions dealing with possible distribution of profits. The repurchase provisions of the original Articles were consistent with these concepts; they were inspired by the need to preserve the Fund's liquidity and the revolving character of its resources. The proposal seemed to abrogate these fundamental concepts of the original Articles. He stressed that, in the future as in the past, members should make a contribution to the Fund in the form of reserve assets without receiving compensation. Emphatically they should not be allowed to pay their full subscriptions to the Fund in their own currency. Nor should the traditional 75/25 percent distinction be eliminated.

Some Executive Directors suggested that different norms, that is, different proportions of a member's quota, might be set for different purposes. One set of norms, for example, might apply to repurchase obligations and another to remuneration. If different norms were to be used for different purposes, another question was whether the norm for each purpose should be uniform for all members or whether there could be exceptions for individual members, depending on the proportions of currency or of reserve assets, such as gold or SDRs, in which their subscriptions had been paid.

The possible use of a separate norm for remuneration and of different norms for individual members helped the staff solve the problem of the excessive cost of remuneration if a 100 percent norm were to be used for all members. But the solution finally worked out was unusually complicated, even by the standards of the Fund where many concepts were complicated.

Improvements in SDRs

The Executive Directors' discussions of draft amendments on the features and uses of the SDR, arduously worked out as recently as 1967–68, raised many issues and debates. Most Executive Directors recognized that the SDR was no longer to be valued in terms of gold. However, because the alternative method of valuation with reference to a basket of currencies worked out in June 1974 provoked disagreement, and had been agreed to only temporarily, this issue had to be addressed in amending the Articles. Particular attention centered on the size of the voting majority to be required for decisions involving the method of valuing the SDR.

The Managing Director and the staff preferred low voting majorities so that decisions on valuing the SDR would not be too difficult to attain. But since the SDR could be an alternative reserve asset to the dollar, U.S. authorities had a strong vested interest in how the SDR was valued and wanted a high voting majority (85 percent) that would give them a veto over any intended change in the method of valuation. European authorities, on the other hand, wanted a reserve asset competitive with the dollar and favored a low voting majority.

The U.S. and European authorities thus had attitudes toward the SDR opposite to those they held at the time of the creation of the SDR. In the 1960s U.S. authorities pressed for agreement on a new reserve asset against the reluctance of European authorities. In the mid-1970s, however, these positions were reversed. The dollar was under attack and the U.S. authorities were more anxious than they had been ten years earlier to defend it. They also wanted to keep interest rates on dollar-denominated securities low in a general effort to maintain low interest rates in the United States, since low interest rates would stimulate the U.S. domestic economy. They regarded such stimulation as important because of the 1975 worldwide recession. They were therefore reluctant to agree to features of the SDR, such as higher interest rates, that would make the SDR more attractive to investors than the dollar. Investors might then shift out of dollars, weakening the U.S. balance of payments position. European authorities, on the other hand, eager to find an alternative to the dollar, wanted to improve the SDR, including raising its interest rate.

Another question was whether the reconstitution obligation should be reduced or even abolished. This issue had been examined in 1974, as described in Chapter 35. By 1975 some Executive Directors were ready to abolish the obligation to reconstitute SDR positions as a way to make the SDR a more attractive reserve asset. Others, including the U.S. Executive Director, argued that abolition of the reconstitution obligation might reduce the demand for SDRs and accordingly weaken the SDR. These Executive Directors argued that if countries were not required to hold certain amounts of SDRs, some might dispose of their SDRs altogether.

Other questions included the following. What entities other than member governments or the Fund itself should be permitted to become holders of SDRs? Should only official entities be permitted to become "other holders" or could private agencies do so? Should all international organizations be permitted to hold SDRs or only certain "international financial institutions"? By what voting majority should decisions to accept an entity as an other holder of SDRs be taken? Which organ of the Fund—the Executive Board, the Board of Governors, or the new Council—should take such decisions? Should the limits on required acceptance of SDRs by participants be raised or eliminated?

Participants in the Special Drawing Account were to be permitted to engage more freely in voluntary transactions in SDRs among themselves. Should the Fund insist that provisions continue to govern the exchange rates used when SDRs were transferred so as to ensure the principle, so carefully worked out at the time of the First Amendment, of equal value regardless of the currency received? If not, different "prices" for the SDR might develop. The SDR could even be transferred at rates of exchange different from those that the Fund used in its designation plan. In considering the possible emergence of "unofficial prices" for the SDR, the Executive Directors were being influenced by the emergence of unofficial prices for gold. Events in the gold markets seemed to be the sword of Damocles hanging over their heads.

The Council and Other Issues

With regard to the Council, the Executive Directors elected by developing members were insisting that establishment of the Council be postponed and come into being only when an 85 percent voting majority could be secured. Their position was a way to put off the event indefinitely.

There was also the question of which voting majority—85 or 70 percent—should be used for decisions for which a qualified majority was required. The Executive Directors quickly agreed in principle that decisions on matters of a predominantly operational character should be taken by a majority of 70 percent, while decisions on matters essentially political or structural in character should be taken by a majority of 85 percent. But this distinction was rough and not observed rigorously so that for several decisions there was considerable debate on which majority should be required.

The Executive Directors decided to hold off consideration of amendments relating to gold until some of the outstanding issues in this matter were resolved.

INTERIM COMMITTEE'S DECISIONS IN JUNE AND AUGUST 1975

By June 1975, when the Interim Committee next met, the Executive Directors had reached agreement on numerous provisions of amendments to the Articles and expected to settle several other issues regarded as technical, rather than political. They sought guidance from the Interim Committee on what to do not only with regard to gold and exchange rates, but also with regard to the General Account, the SDR, the Council, and the size of the voting majorities for various decisions.

The Interim Committee meeting produced agreement on some of these topics. The Committee endorsed the principles that the Executive Directors suggested to improve the General Account and the Special Drawing Account and agreed that the Executive Directors should be asked to find solutions for the few remaining issues on these topics. It attached particular importance to the inclusion of effective provisions under which the Fund's holdings of the currencies of all members would be usable, in accordance with appropriate economic criteria, in its operations and transactions. It also agreed that the Executive Directors should study and report on investing a part of currency holdings, in amounts not exceeding the Fund's reserves, to raise income to meet administrative or operational deficits.

With regard to the Council, Mr. Witteveen explained to the Interim Committee that under the amended Articles, the number of decisions requiring an 85 percent majority of the total voting power would increase and that it would be useful if the Council rather than the Board of Governors could take such decisions. Consequently, there was a practical case for establishing the Council as soon as possible. He was given powerful support by Messrs. Fourcade, Kleppe, and Simon. At its meeting two days before, however, the Group of Twenty-Four had taken a strong stand against the Council's coming into effect immediately upon amendment of the

Articles, arguing that the Council should come into effect only after further experience had been gained with the Interim Committee and a decision to establish the Council was taken by the Board of Governors, with an 85 percent voting majority.[1] Before agreeing to a Council with real powers, authorities of developing members, very much dissatisfied with the outcome of the Committee of Twenty, stated that they wanted to see how their interests were taken into account by the Interim Committee, which had only an advisory function. Some Executive Directors from developing members had also been lobbying for postponing establishment of the Council because they feared that the position of Executive Directors would be undermined. The argument of the authorities of developing members about the need to gain more experience with the Interim Committee seemed to be a facade.

Messrs. Apel and Duisenberg, nevertheless, agreed that more experience with the Interim Committee was needed before establishing the Council. Finance ministers seemed to have been strongly influenced by some Executive Directors, such as Mr. Lieftinck, who feared that establishment of the Council would weaken the position of Executive Directors. The Interim Committee, therefore, concluded that the Council should come into being when a decision was "taken for that purpose." The Interim Committee took the general position that except for a few powers of a political or structural character reserved to the Board of Governors, the Governors should in principle delegate all their powers to the Council, to the Executive Directors, or to both concurrently. It was understood that this formula was not to apply to powers conferred directly by the Articles on the Executive Board.

The Interim Committee agreed that an 85 percent voting majority should be required under the amended Articles for those decisions taken under the existing Articles by an 80 percent majority, thereby eliminating the 80 percent majority. The Committee also noted with approval the draft by which amendments to the Articles would become effective when accepted by three fifths of the members having 85 percent of the total voting power, instead of the 80 percent under the original Articles.[2]

Members of the Interim Committee were less able to come to decisions about SDRs. Although they endorsed the principle of the improvement of the Special Drawing Account and agreed that the Executive Directors should be asked to find solutions for the few outstanding issues, they could not agree on the questions raised by the Executive Directors concerning the abolition of reconstitution, the raising or elimination of acceptance limits, or the size of the voting majority for decisions on the method of valuation. Most members of the Interim Committee, especially from the developing countries, were ready to abolish the need for reconstitution of SDRs, as Mr. Witteveen suggested, but Messrs. Androsch, Apel, Duisenberg, and Simon argued that reconstitution should be maintained at least for the time being. Like some Executive Directors, they also argued that if members

---

[1]Communiqué of Group of Twenty-Four, June 9, 1975, par. 8; Vol. III below, p. 640.
[2]Communiqué of Interim Committee, June 11, 1975, pars. 6 and 7; Vol. III below, pp. 221–22.

could dispose of all their SDRs, the potential demand for SDRs and hence their marketability would be reduced. This would weaken rather than strengthen the SDR.

Because of this difference of view about abolishing reconstitution obligations, Mr. Turner, Chairman of the Interim Committee in June 1975, concluded that despite strong support for deleting reconstitution from the Articles, there was also important sentiment for retaining it. He suggested that the Executive Directors consider an intermediate solution along the following lines: the reconstitution provisions of the existing Articles would remain unchanged, but could eventually be abolished by the Board of Governors by an 85 percent majority vote. Most members of the Interim Committee also favored retaining the existing obligations of members to accept SDRs upon designation by the Fund, so that countries could not decide against holding SDRs and therefore reject proffered transfers. If this happened, the legal foundation of the SDR would be destroyed.

By the next Interim Committee meeting, on August 31, 1975, the Executive Directors had had informal exchanges among themselves and with the Managing Director but no formal meetings on the comprehensive draft amendment except for a few topics, such as reconstitution of holdings of SDRs, the voting majority needed for decisions on the method of valuation of the SDR, and possible changes in the norm of 75/25 percent. They were still not in agreement on any of these topics. On the issue of eliminating reconstitution of holdings of SDRs, Messrs. Bull, Drabble, Jagannathan, Jorn H. Kjaer (Denmark), Palamenghi-Crispi, Yaméogo, Jose Luis Zabala (Chile), and Zulu all supported the staff draft amendment abolishing reconstitution. Messrs. Cross, de Vries, Laske, Schneider, and Whitelaw opposed abolishing reconstitution.

There was much support for a voting majority of 70 percent for decisions on the method of valuation of the SDR, as suggested by the staff, on the grounds that a higher majority would be harmful to the effective use of the SDR. But there remained some support, especially by Mr. Cross, for an 85 percent voting majority for "fundamental changes in the method of valuation," but this would make it necessary to decide whether a proposed change was fundamental or not. For those decisions, it was understood that a majority of the votes cast would suffice; otherwise, there could be an impasse. The Executive Directors were still discussing possible changes in the norm of 75/25 percent both in Executive Board meetings and in the Committee of the Whole on the Sixth General Review of Quotas. No conclusions were reached.

While the Interim Committee reached major agreement at its August 1975 meeting on the problems of gold, as described in Chapter 31, so that the Executive Directors could now proceed with amendments relating to gold, the Committee did not take much action with regard to amendments on other topics. The Committee merely repeated its agreement of June on the question of majorities.[3]

---

[3]Communiqué of Interim Committee, August 31, 1975, pars. 5 and 8; Vol. III below, pp. 223–25.

COMPLETION OF THE COMPREHENSIVE
DRAFT AMENDMENT BY THE END OF 1975

After the Interim Committee meeting of August 1975, the Executive Directors resumed their discussions on the draft amendments, aiming to finish their work by the time the Interim Committee next met in January 1976 in Jamaica. By now agreement had been reached on the arrangements to be worked out for gold, and agreement on arrangements for exchange rates was anticipated soon. Hence, it seemed likely that the comprehensive draft amendment could at last be completed. Apart from gold and exchange rates, other topics on which decisions still had to be taken included reconstitution of holdings of SDRs; the voting majority needed for decisions on the method of valuation of the SDR; the obligations of members to provide what was now being called "freely usable currency" for the Fund's operations and transactions; the power of the Fund to invest its currency holdings in amounts equivalent to its reserves, including investment of the proceeds from any sales of gold the Fund might make in excess of the former official price of gold; the obligation of members to collaborate with the Fund concerning the use of reserve assets in international payments; and the question of whether a gold substitution account was to be established.

In late 1975, the Executive Directors devoted a great deal of attention to these topics. By the end of the year, they had worked out draft amendments on virtually all of the four main topics taken up in this chapter. In addition, as is described in Chapter 37, they had considered the version of Article IV on exchange rate arrangements agreed between French and U.S. officials. They had also considered a gold substitution account, described in Chapter 31, but decided that support for it was insufficient to warrant its inclusion in the draft Second Amendment.

The wide area of agreement notwithstanding, a few issues remained unsettled at the end of 1975. Hence, the Executive Directors again sought the advice of the Interim Committee, at its meeting in Jamaica in January 1976. As most of the issues still outstanding were settled at that Interim Committee meeting, the Executive Directors could proceed with their work on drafting amendments.

AMENDMENTS RELATING TO THE GENERAL ACCOUNT

The two Accounts set up after the First Amendment in 1969—the General Account and the Special Drawing Account—were renamed the General Department and the Special Drawing Rights Department. The new nomenclature permits the establishment of separate "accounts" in the General Department. Provision is made for three accounts—the General Resources Account, the Investment Account, and the Special Disbursement Account—as well as for possible additional accounts. Although the General Resources Account, in which the Fund holds the general resources previously held in the General Account, was established, the Investment Account has not yet been set up. Nevertheless, the Fund now has express authority to invest part of the currencies held in the General Resources Account and part of the profits from the sale of the Fund's gold in income-producing and marketable obligations, such as those of the World Bank, of regional development banks of members, or of other international financial organizations. Income from these investments can be used to meet administrative deficits of the Fund, but not for members' drawings from the Fund. If it is established, the Investment Account will hold the securities purchased for investment and the resulting proceeds.

The third account, the Special Disbursement Account, was also established. In it the Fund is to place proceeds from the sale of its gold, except for those proceeds that are to be transferred to the Investment Account and proceeds equivalent to the official price which are to go to the General Resources Account so as to reimburse that Account for the gold disposed of. Trust Fund assets are also placed in the Special Disbursement Account and repayment of Trust Fund loans is to be made to that Account.

Amendments were also agreed that substantially revised the provisions of the Articles dealing with the use of the Fund's general resources. The conditions under which members can use the Fund's resources are unchanged, but many specific arrangements previously laid down in the Articles were changed. For example, while the original Article V, Section 3 had provided for a member to buy the currency of another member, the amended Article V, Section 3 eliminated this bilateral exchange of currencies and provided that a member would purchase "the currencies of other members," that is, a parcel of currencies. Moreover, the provision of the previous Articles was eliminated that required a member to represent that the currency it wished to draw was presently needed for making payments in that currency. That provision was regarded as obsolete since the Fund had for some years furnished a purchasing member with a parcel of currencies. Moreover, now when a member represents to the Fund its need to draw, both its balance of payments and reserve position are considered jointly, rather than separately as before. As a result of this understanding, a member may, for example, be entitled to draw on the Fund even though it does not have a deficit in its balance of payments if it is faced with an impending discharge of liabilities which would affect its reserve position. Developments in a member's reserves as a justification for using the Fund's resources is a novel feature of the amended Articles.

The amendments also involved deletion of the provision of the original Articles limiting a member's drawing to 25 percent of its quota during any 12-month period. Contrary to the expectations of the drafters of the original Articles, this limit was frequently waived and no longer seemed useful.[4] The limit of 200 percent of quota on the Fund's total holdings of a member's currency was retained but, as in the past, the Fund could waive this limit.

---

[4]The provisions governing waivers and the frequent granting of them were described in *History, 1945–65*, Vol. I, pp. 101–102, 347, 364–66, 412, 434, and 524–25, and *History, 1966–71*, Vol. I, p. 322.

The Second Amendment also requires the Fund to adopt policies on use of its resources and permits the Fund to adopt special policies on the use of its resources for particular balance of payments problems. The Fund had been adopting such policies for many years, as exemplified by the compensatory financing facility, the buffer stock facility, and the oil facility. The new Articles make the authority explicit. They give the Fund more authority, too, to permit members to draw in the credit tranches and to engage in transactions under special policies without at the same time forgoing an equivalent amount of their reserve tranche positions.

Provisions Governing Repurchase

Chapter 35 recounted the discussion of the draft amendments relating to repurchase. The Articles as finally amended contain the provision that a member is normally expected to repurchase as its "balance of payments and reserve position" improves.

A member is entitled to repurchase at any time the Fund's holdings of its currency subject to periodic charges. But it is also expected "normally," as its balance of payments and reserve position improves, to repurchase the Fund's holdings of its currency resulting from the drawing. The repurchase is to keep pace with improvement in the member's balance of payments and reserve position and is not to await total recovery from the problem for which the drawing was made. The word "normally" indicates that exceptional circumstances may be recognized by the Fund as justification for not repurchasing. In addition, the Fund can convert an expectation of repurchase into an obligation. In other words, the Fund can compel a member to repurchase.

In any event, the member has an obligation to repurchase not later than five years from the date of a drawing. The Fund is given authority to change the three-to-five-year period and to adopt other periods for special policies on use of its resources but an 85 percent majority of the total voting power is required and the change in period is to apply to all members. Members have an absolute right to make all repurchases with SDRs, the Fund having no authority to refuse to accept them. Gold may not be used in repurchase.

The provisions regarding repurchases establish three important innovations. First, cumulative levels of the Fund's holdings of a member's currency are no longer a relevant criterion governing repurchase obligations since all facilities now float against the reserve tranche (formerly the gold tranche). Therefore, the Fund's holdings of currency from all drawings not in the reserve tranche must be repurchased. Second, all drawings subject to repurchase have a fixed maturity from the outset. Third, repurchase must be made irrespective of the member's reserve position.

The transitional arrangements of paragraphs 1 to 5 of Schedule B of the Second Amendment deal, inter alia, with the repurchase of currency acquired by the Fund under the Articles prior to the Second Amendment and held on the date of the

Second Amendment. They are designed to deal equitably with all members for repurchases of holdings acquired prior to April 1, 1978.

Provisions Governing Charges

By the end of 1975 the Executive Directors had also agreed to a number of amendments that would formally incorporate into the Articles changes that had taken place in Fund policy over the years by operational decisions with regard to charges. Since drawings in SDRs had come to make up a sizable portion of total drawings from the Fund, they agreed to an explicit provision for a service charge on drawings in SDRs as well as in currencies. The long-standing practice of applying a service charge on stand-by or similar arrangements was also incorporated into the Articles. In order to indicate the special nature of the reserve tranche, the service charge on reserve tranche drawings can be lower than that on other drawings, as in the original Articles, but is not to exceed ½ of 1 percent. These changes are relatively minor.

A more significant change is that periodic charges on the Fund's holdings of members' currency balances can vary depending on the particular policy or facility under which such balances were acquired. The original Articles gave the Fund only limited power to distinguish its holdings of members' currencies in accordance with the policy or facility under which the Fund had acquired them, and all currency balances in excess of a member's quota were subject to the same charges. The Second Amendment empowers the Fund to exclude drawings under any policies on use of its resources from depleting members' reserve tranche positions, and charges are to be levied on currency holdings obtained under a special policy, even though the Fund's holdings are not in excess of a member's quota, as well as on currency holdings in excess of a member's quota after the balances attributable to drawings under special policies are excluded. In brief, while the original Articles emphasized the size of the Fund's holdings of a member's currency in excess of quota and on the length of time that the Fund had held these currency balances, the Second Amendment emphasizes ways to effect different rates of charge for various facilities.

Under the amended Articles, a 70 percent majority of total voting power can determine rates of charge instead of the 75 percent majority required by the original Articles. All charges are to be paid in SDRs, but in exceptional circumstances the Fund can permit a member to pay in its own currency or in the currencies of other members specified by the Fund after consultation with them.

Provisions Governing Selection of Currencies

By December 1975, the Executive Directors had also agreed on certain draft amendments relating to the selection of currencies. Amendments were agreed under which the Fund is to adopt policies for the selection of currencies to be sold and to be used in repurchases and for the transfers of SDRs by the Fund. These policies are to take into account, in consultation with members, the balance of payments and reserve positions of members and developments in their exchange markets, as well as the desirability of promoting over time balanced positions in the Fund.

Amendments were agreed requiring the Fund to formulate policies regarding currencies appropriate for use in repurchase. In principle, the Fund can accept all currencies although previously it could accept in repurchase only the currencies of members that had undertaken to perform the obligations of convertibility under Article VIII, Sections 2, 3, and 4, or balances of other currencies deemed convertible by decision of the Executive Board. Under the amendments, the Fund is to apply similar criteria in the preparation both of the operational budgets for the currencies and SDRs to be used for drawings and repurchases and of the designation plans to enable participants to encash SDRs.

The amended Articles thus recognize the policies and procedures that the Fund had been using for some years in its currency budgets. Moreover, the Fund's quarterly currency budgets are now referred to as operational budgets, since they include SDRs as well as currencies and deal with all movements in the General Resources Account, that is, all operations and transactions of the Fund. The budgets for currencies for use of the Fund's general resources that had been part of the Fund's procedures since 1962 and the quarterly "designation plans" for transactions in SDRs which had been incorporated into the Articles at the time of the First Amendment in 1969 now are both given recognition in the Articles.

It was also agreed that the concept of the "freely usable currency" was to be introduced and the concept of "convertible currency" was to disappear, although what used to be called the obligations of convertibility under Article VIII was retained. Retaining an obligation of convertibility under Article VIII though dropping the concept of a convertible currency is a great oddity, but is explained by the desire of the authorities of the EC countries not to forgo the opportunity of a return to official convertibility under a future par value system or something like it. At the same time, U.S. authorities insisted on ridding the Articles of references to convertibility, except under Article VIII. The staff proposed the compromise solution of retaining a reference to convertibility in Article VIII but deleting it everywhere else in the Articles. This technique of leaving a reference to a controversial issue somewhere in the Articles but deleting it everywhere else was often used to resolve controversial issues.

An essential part of the compromise especially with respect to the convertibility provisions of Article VIII, Section 4, on "convertibility of foreign-held balances," was an understanding that there would be no obligation for members to convert balances of their currencies held abroad by official entities so long as exchange markets for the currencies serve this function. Members are, of course, free to agree to convert balances of their currencies held by other members, as they have done on occasions in the past, or can by agreement transfer SDRs to other members for this purpose. It was considered unnecessary, therefore, to modify the convertibility provision when the Second Amendment was drafted, taking into account the possible emergence of circumstances similar to those that the drafters of the original Articles had in mind, thus justifying more reliance on the provisions of Article VIII, Section 4.

Some members were initially troubled by use of the term "freely usable" because their currencies were already freely usable in the sense that these members imposed no restrictions on transactions in the currency by nonresidents. This problem was to be resolved by including a definition of a freely usable currency in the amended Articles. Even more important, compromise was made possible because it was agreed to include in the Executive Directors' report to the Board of Governors on the Proposed Second Amendment fairly lengthy explanations.[5] The requirements for a currency to be designated freely usable and the obligations of a member whose currency is not freely usable to ensure that balances of its currency purchased from the Fund can be exchanged for a freely usable currency were to be explained in the report. Similarly, the report was to explain that each member, whether or not its currency is defined as a freely usable currency, is required to collaborate with the Fund and other members to enable balances of its currency held by another member as the direct or indirect result of a purchase from the Fund to be exchanged, at the time of the purchase, for the freely usable currencies of other members. The report would explain the need for this provision and how the arrangement would be implemented, as well as the definition of a freely usable currency to be incorporated in the Articles.

On this and on other provisions of the Proposed Second Amendment, the Executive Directors' report not only provided a commentary on the provisions of the Second Amendment but was also a repository of compromises.

While the Executive Directors had agreed by the end of 1975 that the concept of a freely usable currency was to be introduced into the Articles, the techniques by which the currencies of all members would be made effectively usable in the Fund's transactions through the General Resources Account were yet to be resolved. It was generally agreed that a member purchasing another member's currency from the Fund should be able to exchange that currency for another currency to be used to make payments or intervene in the market and that a member that needed another member's currency to repay the Fund should be able to obtain the needed currency with a freely usable currency. Nevertheless, there was no agreement on how these exchanges were to be carried out or on the definition of a freely usable currency. In particular, agreement had not been reached on whether the issuer of a freely usable currency, as defined, should be obliged to ensure that its currency could be exchanged for the freely usable currency of another member at exchange rates that produced equal value in connection with such a transaction. Still another element in the freely usable controversy was the question whether a member could insist that an exchange must be made with its monetary authorities even though it had the option of sending the other member to the market.

---

[5]*Proposed Second Amendment to the Articles of Agreement of the International Monetary Fund: A Report by the Executive Directors to the Board of Governors* (Washington, 1976). (Hereafter referred to as *Report on Second Amendment*.)

At the Interim Committee meeting in January 1976, agreement was reached generally that the Fund's holdings of each member's currency should be usable in the Fund's operations and transactions and that appropriate provisions for this purpose were to be included in the draft amendments. The Interim Committee also agreed that even before the amended Articles went into force, each member was to make the necessary arrangements for the Fund to use its currency in its operations and transactions.

AMENDMENTS RELATING TO GOLD

Chapters 31 and 32 recount the complex negotiations on arrangements for gold that went on from late 1974 through most of 1975. There were conflicting views on the role to be given to gold in the international monetary system. One view, held mainly but not exclusively by European authorities, was that the use of gold as a reserve asset should be reduced but not terminated. A second view, held by U.S. authorities and by authorities of developing members, was that an evolutionary process in the monetary system should eventually end the use of gold as a reserve asset. Those holding the latter view wanted amendments to the Fund's Articles to preclude the development of any practice that permitted gold to regain its status as a principal reserve asset or possibly become even more coveted than in the past because of its being valued at a higher fixed price. These conflicting views held up agreement on amending the Articles. However, as a result of the successful negotiations concerning arrangements for gold in the last several months of 1975, the Executive Directors were able to agree on draft amendments relating to gold.

As the amendments relating to gold took shape, several provisions aimed at reducing its role as a primary reserve asset. For example, while a member may, if it wishes, maintain the value of its exchange rate in terms of a denominator, that denominator may not be gold under the Second Amendment. The SDR is no longer defined in terms of gold. If the Fund decides to reintroduce a par value system, gold is not to be used as the common denominator of the system. With only a few exceptions that are not important in the Fund's normal activities, all former obligations of members and of the Fund to pay or to receive gold are eliminated. The SDR and, in some instances, national currencies are the means of payment. The former gold portion of an increase in a member's quota is thus payable in SDRs or, if the Fund so decides, in the member's currency or in the currencies of other members.

There is no longer an official price for gold. Members are free to deal in gold in the market or among themselves at any price they wish. The Fund is obligated not to attempt to manage the price or to establish a fixed price in the market and has the authority to object if members attempt to do so. The rationale for eliminating the official price for gold is that fluctuations in the price of gold will discourage its use as a monetary asset, thereby hastening its demise in international transactions. All these provisions are the exact opposite of the original Articles.

The draft amendments agreed by the Executive Directors by the end of 1975 also empowered the Fund to sell the gold it held on the effective date of the Second Amendment. In resolving the gold problem in 1975, special techniques of currency replenishment were needed to permit the restitution of gold to members at the official price and to permit the auctioning of the Fund's gold holdings at market-related prices. These techniques were needed because under the Articles before the Second Amendment the Fund had no authority to sell its holdings of gold except to replenish its holdings of members' currencies. Mr. Witteveen had been urging monetary authorities to agree to a provision in the amended Articles that would give the Fund greater power over disposing of its gold. Still unsettled, however, at the end of 1975 was the question of the size of the voting majority that would be required for decisions on the disposition of profits from the Fund's gold sales.

Still unsettled too was the question whether the amended Articles should allow for the establishment of a gold substitution account. Nor had the "cooperation clause" referred to in Chapter 32 yet been finally approved. After several months of consideration and after compromise on the language to be used, the Group of Ten had agreed in December 1975 to the insertion of a cooperation clause. Explicitly, they agreed that a provision was to be included in the Articles by which members would "collaborate with the Fund and with other members in order to ensure that the policies of the member with respect to reserve assets shall be consistent with the objectives of promoting better international surveillance of international liquidity and making the special drawing right the principal reserve asset in the international monetary system." The Interim Committee had not, however, yet approved this cooperation clause.

These outstanding matters relating to gold were finally settled at Jamaica in January 1976. To take the last matter first, it was agreed that the Articles would contain a cooperation clause in the language cited above. This clause was to become Article VIII, Section 7.

It had not proved possible to get agreement on a stronger clause. Not only were monetary authorities who still favored some use of gold reluctant to use wording that referred explicitly to reducing the role of gold in the system, but so were the U.S. authorities. The U.S. authorities resisted use of a stronger cooperation clause that referred to reducing the role of gold in the international monetary system because the authorities of other members would also want to add a phrase about reducing the role of reserve currencies in the system. U.S. authorities wanted to avoid any reference to the role of reserve currencies. They had proposed the substitute formulation which emphasized making the SDR the principal reserve asset and which mentioned neither gold nor reserve currencies. Under pressure from the Managing Director, who had been arguing strongly for some provisions and who at one point was concerned that no provision might be possible, the monetary authorities of the other large industrial members accepted the formulation put forward by the U.S. authorities.

The Interim Committee also agreed that the amended Articles would contain an enabling provision under which the Fund could sell any part of its gold held after the distribution of gold described in Chapter 31 and use the proceeds (1) to augment the general resources of the Fund for immediate use in its ordinary operations and transactions, or (2) to make balance of payments assistance available on special terms to developing members in difficult circumstances. The Committee also agreed on the voting majorities that would be required for decisions relating to distribution of the profits from the Fund's gold sales. An 85 percent majority of voting power was to be required to distribute profits from gold sales to developing members, a 70 percent majority for their use in the Fund's regular operations and transactions, and an 85 percent majority for their use in other operations and transactions.

The Interim Committee also agreed to the simultaneous implementation of the three-way solution for current dealings in gold—restitution of some portion of the Fund's gold, sale of an additional portion and placing the profits in a Trust Fund, and gold trading, under supervision, by the Group of Ten, as described in Chapter 32.

Because of pressure from authorities of developing members, the Interim Committee did not explicitly state that consideration of an amendment to the Articles permitting the Fund to establish a gold substitution account should be dropped. Rather, the communiqué of the Interim Committee stated that the Executive Directors should continue their consideration of the subject of a substitution account "without delaying completion of the comprehensive draft amendment."[6]

AMENDMENTS RELATING TO THE SDR

The Executive Directors had also agreed by the end of 1975 on a number of amendments improving the SDR. They agreed on draft amendments, for example, under which the SDR is to be the unit in terms of which the values of currencies of members held in the General Resources Account of the Fund are to be maintained and on the basis of which computations are to be made in applying the provisions of the Articles. The value of the SDR is no longer tied to gold, and the SDR replaces gold as a means of payment by members to the Fund and by the Fund to members.

Another draft amendment gave all participants freedom to transfer SDRs among themselves without the need for the Fund's authorization. Under the previous Articles, a participant could enter into a transaction in SDRs by agreement with another participant only if it was exchanging SDRs for its own currency held by the transferee or if the Fund authorized the transaction in narrowly defined categories of transactions. Furthermore, under the Second Amendment, the participant transferring SDRs is no longer expected to observe the criterion that transfers have to be associated with a need to use reserve assets, such as the existence of a balance of payments deficit. The Fund now also has the important power to permit operations in SDRs among participants, a power it did not have under the First Amendment.

---

[6]Communiqué of Interim Committee, January 8, 1976, par. 7(f); Vol. III below, p. 227.

Amendments were agreed making the range of other holders of SDRs that the Fund can prescribe more extensive than in the past although it is still confined to official entities; private agencies are not yet allowed to hold SDRs. Other holders can also make more extensive use of their SDRs. Thus, the Fund can permit prescribed holders of SDRs to enter into operations and transactions with other prescribed holders, as well as with participants, whereas after the First Amendment other holders could enter into operations and transactions only with participants. Other amendments make it easier for the Fund to modify or abrogate rules for reconstitution.

Still outstanding as of January 1976, however, were critical questions concerning the SDR. Needing resolution were questions of the voting majority to be required for two actions, the adoption of decisions on the method of valuation and the adoption of decisions relating to reconstitution obligations.

The Interim Committee agreed in January 1976 that the majority required for the adoption of decisions on the method of valuing the SDR under the amended Articles was to be 70 percent of the total voting power, with the exception of decisions involving a change in the principle of valuation or a fundamental change in the application of the principle in effect, which were to be taken by an 85 percent majority. With respect to the obligation of participants in the Special Drawing Account to reconstitute their holdings of SDRs, the Interim Committee agreed that the amended Articles should authorize the Fund to review the rules for reconstitution at any time and adopt, modify, or abrogate these rules by a 70 percent majority of the total voting power.

AMENDMENT RELATING TO THE COUNCIL

By December 1975, the Executive Directors had also agreed that an enabling power would be introduced under which the Fund could establish a Council as an organ of the Fund. Still outstanding were the issues of whether the Council would come into being immediately after the Second Amendment came into effect and whether a high voting majority—85 percent of total voting power—would be required to establish the Council. The authorities of developing members were pressing for the need for the 85 percent voting majority. At Jamaica, in January 1976, they won. It was agreed that the Council would not be established until members having 85 percent of the voting power agreed.

OTHER ACTIONS CONCERNING AMENDMENTS

Another outstanding problem at the end of 1975 related to the number and size of special voting majorities. So much use had been made of special voting majorities in the draft amendments that it was feared that the future conduct of the Fund's business might be hampered and that the emphasis on special voting majorities would undermine the Fund's long-standing practice of taking decisions on the basis of consensus without voting. Suggestions had therefore been made in the Executive Board to have the Executive Directors review these voting majorities during the final stage of the preparation of the draft amendments and to give the Board of Governors power to reduce their number and size without going through the process of amending the Articles again. These suggestions still had to be considered by the Executive Directors.

With these agreements in place, the Interim Committee requested the Executive Directors to complete their work on the amendments in the light of the guidance it had given them and noted that it expected Executive Directors to be able to submit a comprehensive draft amendment for the approval of the Board of Governors, together with a report, within a few weeks.

The Interim Committee took special note of the report of the Executive Directors on the amendments, welcomed the progress made toward the solution of the outstanding issues, and commended the Executive Directors for the voluminous and successful work that they had done in revising the Articles.

In his opening statement to a press conference held with Willy De Clercq, Chairman of the Interim Committee, following the Interim Committee meeting, Mr. Witteveen stated that "I think we can say that we have now come to the end or almost to the end of a long process in which we have run through all the Articles very thoroughly, and I think we have achieved a complete updating of the Articles of Agreement in the present situation."[7]

---

[7]Reprinted in *IMF Survey* (Washington), Vol. 5 (January 19, 1976), pp. 22–23.

CHAPTER

37

Agreement on Exchange Rates: Rambouillet and Jamaica

*E*XCHANGE RATES remained the sharpest thorn in the flesh of monetary authorities. After abandoning their attempts to introduce a reformed international monetary system and deciding to let a system evolve, monetary authorities recognized that floating rates for the main currencies were likely to continue, possibly indefinitely. The situation was awkward. There was still a philosophical schism between authorities who argued in favor of floating rates and those who argued for par values. All were aware that a "non-system" prevailed at least in the sense that there were no agreed rules for exchange rates. Under its existing Articles of Agreement, the Fund could not legally approve unitary floating rates. Hence, the floating rates were in violation of the Articles. So too were pegged rates. It was in fact impossible for a member to maintain an effective par value as required by the Articles because the U.S. dollar was floating and no other currency was stable in relation to gold.

This situation made monetary officials uneasy. U.S. authorities were particularly eager to clear up the status of floating rates to avoid being accused of violating their international obligations. The Fund staff were concerned not only because Fund members were in violation of the Articles but also because the breakdown of the par value system, in addition to causing economic problems, was giving rise to many novel problems of international and domestic monetary law. Many treaties, statutes, contracts, and other legal instruments contained references to the provisions of the Fund's Articles of Agreement on par values and gold or to other provisions, and cases were being tried in courts because of the difficulties created since member governments were no longer adhering to these provisions.[1]

---

[1]For a discussion of these legal problems and court cases, see Joseph Gold, *Floating Currencies, Gold, and SDRs: Some Recent Legal Developments*, IMF Pamphlet Series, No. 19 (Washington, 1976); *Floating Currencies, SDRs, and Gold: Further Legal Developments*, IMF Pamphlet Series, No. 22 (Washington, 1977); and *The Fund Agreement in the Courts*, Vol. II (Washington: International Monetary Fund, 1982).

Yet, as indicated in Chapter 35, when the staff began in July 1974 to prepare draft amendments for discussion by the Executive Directors, they were stymied by what provisions to include for exchange rates. Monetary authorities were by no means agreed on what these provisions should be. The initial discussion in the Executive Board of a draft amendment that would legalize floating rates brought out sharp disagreements and heated emotions. As the Second Amendment took shape, getting agreement on amendments to the Articles with respect to exchange rates clearly proved the most difficult exercise of all.

THREE VERSIONS OF ARTICLE IV

Following their discussion in 1974, the Executive Directors turned to the Interim Committee, meeting in January 1975, for guidance on legalizing floating rates. The members of the Committee could provide at best only general guidance, however. Taking a cautious position, Mr. Turner, Chairman of the Committee, pointed out that the Committee could recommend to the Executive Directors that the Articles be amended to legalize floating rates and that such an amendment could be agreed in conjunction with a provision giving the Fund authority to adopt guidelines over floating rates. This position was not too far removed from that of the U.S. authorities. Although he noted that the countries in his constituency favored a system of fixed but adjustable par values, Mr. De Clercq seemed willing to go along with such an amendment, provided that any legalization of the existing regime of widespread floating was considered an exception to the rule of effective par values and was made subject to specific conditions that would ensure a return to that system. Other Governors were likewise ready to accept amended Articles that would legalize floating rates, subject to authorization and surveillance by the Fund.

Once again the strongest holdout was the French authorities. Mr. Fourcade considered legalization of floating rates "wrong and dangerous" and counter to the *Outline of Reform* and to the understandings reached at the 1973 and 1974 Annual Meetings. Returning to the language of the *Outline*, he stated that the French authorities insisted on a system "based on fixed but adjustable par values" and that they were willing to wait to amend the Articles until such a system was agreeable to all. They were not prepared to agree to the elimination from the Fund's Articles of obligations relating to the observance of par values. Mr. Simon also held firm to the opposite position. The U.S. authorities were equally insistent that floating rates were as acceptable as par values and that the Fund's Articles be amended accordingly. Since the U.S. authorities did not intend to re-establish a par value for the dollar soon, they adamantly refused to accept any obligation to do so.

In this situation, it was impossible for the Interim Committee in January 1975 to give the Executive Directors much guidance for their drafting of an amended Article IV. As seen in Chapter 35, their communiqué called for a draft amendment that provided for both stable but adjustable par values and the floating of currencies in particular situations subject to appropriate rules and for surveillance by the Fund, in accordance with the *Outline of Reform*.[2] The term "particular situations" was a calculated obscurity.

Against this background, the Executive Directors, together with the staff, tried in the first several months of 1975 to make some headway on a draft amendment of Article IV. By the time of the next meeting of the Interim Committee, in June 1975, three separate versions of Article IV were up for consideration. The first was submitted to the Executive Board by Mr. Wahl. The second was submitted by Mr. Cross. The third was prepared by the staff.

Mr. Wahl's draft called for an immediate restoration of a par value system, with par values expressed in terms of a common denominator yet to be determined by the Fund (since gold was no longer to be the common denominator), and for the maintenance of actual exchange rates on the basis of these par values. While the Fund could authorize members' deviations from par values, such deviations were to be permitted only in exceptional circumstances and for such periods and subject to such conditions as the Fund determined. In effect, a member could have a floating rate only with the advance permission of the Executive Directors.

Mr. Cross's draft provided for exactly the reverse. Members would be free to choose whatever exchange rate arrangements they preferred. Greater attention was to be devoted to members' domestic monetary and financial policies than to the forms of their exchange rates. Although members were generally obliged to observe guidelines for floating rates established by the Fund, there was no mention of par values. Under this version of Article IV, a member could have a floating rate for as long as it wished without Executive Board approval, provided that it acted consistently with guidelines adopted by the Fund.

The staff's draft was eclectic, containing portions that suited the U.S. position and portions that suited the French position. To suit the U.S. position, each member was to be subject to certain general obligations to collaborate with the Fund and with other members to promote exchange stability, to maintain orderly exchange arrangements, and to pursue domestic monetary and financial policies that would contribute to balance of payments adjustment. Members could float their currencies if they wished, provided that they observed these general obligations. To suit the French position, members that so wished could establish par values, and provision was made for an eventual system of par values for all members when the Fund decided conditions permitted. The rules as to how such a par value system would work were similar to those of the original Articles. There were, for example, to be margins around par values in which exchange rates were to be maintained. Also, the concept of "fundamental disequilibrium" was maintained. But there was an important departure from the original Articles. A member was not to propose a change in par value except to correct, *or to prevent the emergence of*, a fundamental disequilibrium. Some officials thus regarded the amended draft Article as stronger than the original Articles in that a member could propose an exchange rate change *in*

---

[2]Communiqué of Interim Committee, January 16, 1975, par. 6; Vol. III below, p. 219.

advance of experiencing a fundamental disequilibrium. Other officials, however, considered this feature as weakening a par value system: changes in par values would be permitted more readily than under the earlier system. The staff's intent was, indeed, to design a more flexible par value system.

Because of the difference in the French and the U.S. positions, the staff's draft contained two variants of how to get to a par value system. Authorities were to choose between these two variants. Alternative A reflected the U.S. approach. It permitted a member to propose an initial par value at any time. In other words, members had almost complete freedom with respect to the timing of establishing a par value. Alternative B reflected the French approach. It provided that a member should propose an initial par value within a reasonable time unless it presented to the Fund, and the Fund agreed, that its circumstances did not justify establishment of a par value. In other words, members were obliged to declare a par value unless the Fund excused them from doing so.

An innovation in this draft was that before the introduction of a par value system a member could opt for a central value in lieu of a par value. After the Smithsonian agreement in December 1971, the Fund had introduced the concept of a central rate as a temporary option to par values and in November 1973 had taken a decision broadening the concept of a central rate. Currencies for which rates were maintained in terms of an intervention currency could be regarded as having a central rate, even if the intervention currency was floating. Now the staff was proposing use of the concept of a central value in the amended Articles.

In effect the staff draft of an amended Article IV put par values and other exchange arrangements, including floating rates, on the same footing, gave members an opportunity to establish a par value, and opened up the option of central values rather than par values.[3]

In the Executive Board's discussions of the three drafts, Messrs. Cross and Wahl both opposed the staff draft. Mr. Cross questioned the kind of par value system that would be established and how it might operate. He also objected to the strong philosophical bent in the staff draft, which suggested that a par value system was the eventual goal. Such a philosophical bent implied that par values were preferable to floating rates, contrary to the view held by U.S. authorities.

Mr. Wahl's objections to the staff draft were, of course, different. He thought that in speaking of initial par values to be introduced at some future date, the staff was ignoring the legal status of existing par values. The underlying legal reality under the Fund's present Articles was, he insisted, that a par value system still remained in force. Governments had never announced that they had suspended their par values. How then could the amended Articles of Agreement refer to initial par values for some *new* par value system? Mr. Wahl's point highlighted the oft-repeated argument of the French authorities that by not adhering to a par value

---

[3]The complete texts of the three drafts are in Vol. III below, pp. 287–300.

system, the United States was in violation of the Fund's Articles and acting counter to a treaty.

That the United States was in violation of the Articles was also the position of the Fund. In fact, at least partly because they were embarrassed by the illegal status of the exchange arrangements maintained by the United States, U.S. monetary authorities were pressing for amendments to the Articles. Not only was the United States in violation of the existing Articles but so were all other members as no currency was maintained in value through gold transactions. Moreover, no members were maintaining parities among themselves because the U.S. dollar was the main currency used for intervention in exchange markets and the dollar was floating.

Most Executive Directors preferred the staff draft, which allowed for an eventual return to a par value system but permitted floating rates to exist in the meantime, or even the very permissive U.S. draft, to the strict French version calling for the restoration of an immediate par value system. Executive Directors elected by developing members, like the French authorities, were dedicated to a return to "stable but adjustable par values." They argued that the large fluctuations in exchange rates since March 1973 brought considerable risk and uncertainty to international transactions and made management of the exchange rates of developing members difficult. Consequently most developing members had resorted to some type of pegging of their rates but were willing to go along with the staff draft that legalized floating rates provided the stricter of the two alternatives in the draft was used. In other words, they wanted Article IV to be written in such a way that return to a par value system was the main intent of the Fund's amended Articles, with the legalization of floating permitted only for an interim period in exceptional circumstances affecting all members or in exceptional circumstances for an individual member. This position was expressed in the communiqué of the Group of Twenty-Four when that Group met on June 8–9, 1975, just prior to the next meeting of the Interim Committee.[4]

DISSENSION BETWEEN FRANCE AND THE UNITED STATES

When the Governors on the Interim Committee and their associates assembled on June 10–11, 1975 in Paris, they received the three versions of Article IV that the Executive Directors had been considering with a request to indicate their preference. Mr. Witteveen made a plea for the staff draft on the grounds that it seemed to fit prevailing circumstances and to accommodate the hopes and objectives of most authorities. At that time, it was impossible to establish a par value system, yet the majority of Executive Directors felt that it was important for members to move gradually toward greater stability of exchange rates and that the ultimate aim was to arrive at a system of stable but adjustable exchange rates. The staff draft contained

---

[4]Communiqué of Group of Twenty-Four, June 9, 1975, par. 7; Vol. III below, pp. 639–40.

two alternative ways to fit the dual circumstances of moving gradually to more stable exchange rates but meanwhile permitting floating rates.

By this time, most Governors on the Interim Committee (except for the French and U.S. Governors) were ready to go along with the staff draft, as most Executive Directors had been. They were prepared to accept as inevitable legalization of floating rates. At the same time, they wanted stability of exchange rates and an eventual return to par values to be stressed as the principal objectives. They were also concerned that the U.S. version of Article IV might give members excessive freedom in the conduct of their exchange rate policies and accordingly wanted the amended Articles to emphasize guidelines for floating rates under the surveillance of the Fund. But they were not very sympathetic to the idea introduced by the staff of central values or central rates as an added option.

By this time it was obvious that the French authorities would also have to accept legalization of floating rates and that the U.S. authorities would have to allow for a provision in the amended Articles that ultimately permitted return to a par value system, subject to a majority of the total voting power large enough to give the United States a veto over the timing of the introduction of a par value system. French authorities would have to accept legalization of floating rates because the deep recession of 1975 and countries' differing degrees of tolerance for inflation and for unemployment made it abundantly evident that giving up floating rates was unlikely for some time to come. U.S. authorities would have to accept a provision for an eventual return to a system of par values because the authorities from most European members and from all developing members continued to insist on such a system as a goal.

At the dinner meeting usually held by members of the Interim Committee and the Managing Director, agreement between French and U.S. authorities seemed to have been reached. Mr. Fourcade, working in English, came away from the dinner believing that he had reached agreement with his U.S. counterparts on a new Article IV based on a formula using the term "a system of stable exchange rates." The next morning, however, when Mr. Fourcade saw the text of the agreement, he realized that it referred instead to "a stable system of exchange rates," a more ambiguous phrase. Thereupon, the agreed formula fell apart.

The General Counsel was immediately appointed to chair an ad hoc group to redraft the formula. The group prepared a document full of variant drafts, which brought nobody around. Mr. Fourcade refused to participate in further informal negotiations in English, and, indeed, in any further negotiations on exchange rates at that particular meeting of the Interim Committee.

Hence, when the Interim Committee met, both the U.S. and the French authorities reverted to their previous positions. Mr. Fourcade tossed aside the staff's draft of Article IV as a "caricature of the par value system." In his view, only the French text was consistent with the January 1975 communiqué of the Interim Committee. He reiterated that the French authorities were in no hurry to draft new exchange rate provisions to the Fund's Articles. Amending the Articles had to be undertaken in an environment that would guarantee the long-term objective of establishing an international monetary system based on fixed and adjustable par values, as had been so carefully worked out and agreed in the Committee of Twenty. Exchange rate obligations of members ought to be strict. Any legalizing of floating rates should be temporary, limited to specifically defined circumstances agreed to by the international community, and kept under close surveillance by an international organization.

Mr. Simon also repeated his stance. He noted that the U.S. authorities, who did not want any obligation to return to a par value at any time, had already made a notable concession by agreeing to the insertion into the staff draft of Article IV of the words "with the ultimate aim of establishing a stable but adjustable exchange rate system." U.S. authorities could not, he stressed, accept an Article IV that contained any time limit or moral disapproval of floating rates. They did not accept the idea that floating rates were one of the causes of worldwide inflation or that floating rates were disrupting world trade. On the contrary, in their view, it was rampant inflation throughout the world that had made floating exchange rates necessary, and, in the existing circumstances, "floating rates had served the world well." Given these considerations, Mr. Simon regarded the staff draft as acceptable to U.S. authorities with the proviso that the softer lines of alternative A be adopted.

Because of the stand of French and U.S. authorities, the portions on exchange rates of the communiqué of the Interim Committee following the June 1975 meeting could again be only vague and general. The Committee, so read the communiqué, had discussed the exchange rate arrangements that members of the Fund should observe and there was widespread agreement that members have a basic obligation to collaborate with the Fund and with other members to promote exchange stability, to maintain orderly exchange arrangements, and to pursue exchange policies that contributed to adjustment, and that the Fund should adopt policies in order to enable members to act consistently with their basic obligations whatever their exchange arrangements might be. Provision should be made for stable but adjustable par values and the floating of currencies in particular situations, subject to appropriate rules and surveillance of the Fund, in accordance with the *Outline of Reform.*[5]

There could be no consideration as yet of the detailed points to be decided on: the majority of total voting power to be required before a par value system could be introduced, the extent to which it would be mandatory for members to enter the system once it was introduced, and whether, once members had entered into a par value system, they would be free to leave it.

Like Sisyphus, monetary authorities trying to agree on a draft of an amended Article IV were eternally damned to see their efforts undone.

---

[5]Communiqué of Interim Committee, June 11, 1975, par. 5; Vol. III below, p. 221.

From June to August 1975

Because of the apparently unbridgeable gap between the French and the U.S. authorities, the Executive Directors saw little purpose in considering redrafts of Article IV before the Interim Committee met again on August 31, 1975. Meanwhile the Managing Director continued to pursue the subject informally. He spoke with Mr. Simon and his colleagues in the U.S. Treasury about how eventually to introduce a par value system acceptable to the U.S. authorities. Mr. Simon's view, however, was that the return to a par value system was not the goal of the U.S. Government and was not acceptable as a goal. The amended Articles, therefore, should impose neither a moral nor a legal obligation on a member to establish a par value, either currently or in the future.

Mr. Witteveen visited Paris in July 1975 and took the occasion, in the absence of Mr. Fourcade, to speak about exchange rate arrangements with J. de Larosière, then Director of the Treasury of France. Mr. de Larosière explained that, in taking the strong line of advocating nothing less than a full par value system, French authorities wanted to keep pressure on U.S. authorities to recognize that a return to a par value system was the best goal for exchange rates and to get U.S. authorities to relent somewhat from their view that exchange markets should operate with relatively little or no intervention, without much interference or surveillance by the international community.

The gap between their positions was so wide that the question of the exchange rate provisions to be included in the amended Articles would clearly have to be settled at the very highest level of the U.S. and French governments, probably at the economic summit meeting planned for November 1975. In the meantime, in order to settle arrangements for gold and quotas under the Sixth General Review it seemed advisable to split the package of unsettled issues and to try to make progress on these two subjects in the Interim Committee's meeting of August 31, 1975. Agreement was reached on gold and quotas in that meeting, as noted in earlier chapters, raising hopes that agreement could soon be reached on exchange rate arrangements as well, although the latter was not discussed. The communiqué after the meeting stated merely that acceptable solutions must be found on the subject of the exchange rate system under the amended Articles and asked the Executive Directors to continue their work in order to arrive at acceptable solutions and to prepare appropriate draft amendments.[6]

When the Governors met a day later for their 1975 Annual Meetings, Mr. Fourcade and Mr. Simon, like fencing partners in a duel, again took opposing positions. Mr. Fourcade told the Governors that "a more equitable and stable monetary order also means that a return to stable but adjustable parities must be the fundamental objective we have to pursue."[7] Mr. Simon asked the Governors to

---

[6]Communiqué of Interim Committee, August 31, 1975, par. 8; Vol. III below, p. 225.
[7]Statement by the Governor of the Fund and the World Bank for France, *Summary Proceedings, 1975*, p. 101.

recall "the chaos and disorder of the closing years of the Bretton Woods system" and insisted that "the right to float must be clear and unencumbered."[8]

But other monetary authorities were impressed by the agreement reached on arrangements for gold, described in Chapter 31. Hence, the monetary authorities of the Big Five (France, the Federal Republic of Germany, Japan, the United Kingdom, and the United States), meeting in August 1975 on the U.S. presidential yacht, the *Sequoia*, on the Potomac River, broached the subject of exchange rates. They agreed that it would be absurd not to resolve the exchange rate issue by the time of the next Interim Committee meeting, scheduled for January 1976 in Jamaica. The exchange rate situation had to be settled and the package of draft amendments completed. They regarded the solution as a matter of language. The reality was that floating rates were likely to continue indefinitely and that a new system of par values would not be introduced for some years to come. Any language that expressed this reality would be satisfactory. They were also aware that, following the June meeting of the Interim Committee, Mr. Turner had urged the French and U.S. authorities to settle their differences.

As the *Sequoia* was docking, the authorities of the other three assured the monetary authorities of France and the United States that they would accept any solution to the exchange rate issue that was mutually acceptable to the United States and France. In giving *carte blanche* they probably did not really expect the U.S. and French authorities to settle their differences.

BILATERAL NEGOTIATIONS BETWEEN
FRANCE AND THE UNITED STATES

While the rhetoric between French and U.S. authorities was often contentious, it drove no permanent wedge between the basically friendly nations they represented. Moreover, France and the United States had succeeded in resolving their differences on monetary topics on several occasions in the past few years. Since the authorities of the three other largest industrial members had stated their willingness to accept "almost any reasonable compromise," Edwin H. Yeo III, who had just been confirmed as Under Secretary of the U.S. Treasury for Monetary Affairs, took the initiative to work out a bilateral understanding between the U.S. and French authorities. Shortly after the *Sequoia* agreement on gold, Mr. Yeo contacted his French counterpart, Mr. de Larosière, to arrange a talk in Paris about exchange rates. Mr. de Larosière felt circumstances for agreement were opportune. By the second half of 1975 the U.S. dollar had improved considerably. The oil crisis and the recession that had started a year earlier had diverted attention to economic problems other than international monetary reform. The negotiations of the Committee of

---

[8]Statement by the Governor of the Fund and the World Bank for the United States, *Summary Proceedings, 1975*, pp. 116 and 117.

Twenty, then over for more than a year, seemed distant and forgotten. The change in the international economic situation reduced concern among authorities abroad about "the dollar overhang," the risk of excessive dollars accumulating in the hands of authorities abroad, and about symmetry and asymmetry in the international monetary system, issues that had generated so much debate in the Committee of Twenty in 1972–73.

U.S. authorities were, of course, pleased with these developments and wanted to resolve the exchange rate issue. According to Mr. Yeo, there were three reasons for this. First, U.S. authorities were concerned by the lack of a code or agreed rules of behavior for exchange rates. Exchange rates could develop in almost any way: there could be manipulation and competitive depreciation, and given the recent experiences of the oil crisis and the 1974–75 recession, these dangers could increase in the absence of agreed rules. Rates could become even more unstable.

Second, U.S. authorities were acutely conscious of the political cost to the United States of continuing arguments about the appropriate kind of exchange rate system. Monetary authorities—particularly of the Federal Republic of Germany— were finding it difficult to choose sides between France and the United States on this issue. The U.S. authorities saw advantages in freeing their European friends from this awkward position.

Third, they believed in the need for balance of payments adjustment. They wanted exchange rates to be used as an instrument of policy and to be subject to surveillance by the Fund. These views espoused by the Administration of President Ford in 1975 were consistent with those of U.S. authorities expressed in the Committee of Twenty in 1972–73, during the Administration of President Nixon.

In addition, U.S. authorities were embarrassed at running an illegal system, contrary to the Fund's Articles. Moreover, since they expected the dollar to float indefinitely, they did not envisage a time when the United States would have an exchange rate consistent with the existing Articles. The Articles might therefore just as well be amended quickly.

As noted in earlier chapters, Mr. Simon suggested that U.S. authorities also wanted the Articles amended to expedite phasing out gold from international monetary transactions, to enable the Fund to get on with its transactions and operations without the use of gold, and to permit the increases in quotas under the Sixth General Review to go forward without the need for members to pay part of their increased subscriptions in gold.

According to Mr. de Larosière, French authorities were also willing to compromise. Like U.S. authorities, they were uncomfortable with an exchange rate system that was unregulated and contrary to the Fund's Articles of Agreement. Moreover, they realized that their long-held position in favor of immediate restoration of par values was unrealistic, particularly in the circumstances of the oil crisis and of the other world economic problems prevailing in 1975, and that they were becoming increasingly isolated from the positions of other countries. They did not want to be considered excessively uncompromising.

President Giscard d'Estaing in effect had to choose between two positions. He could continue to insist on par values and risk the accusation of being uncompromising. Or he could choose to introduce French concerns into the text of an amended Article IV. These concerns were three. First, there should be an eventual reinstatement of a par value system. Second, there should be some kind of exchange rate surveillance by the Fund. Third, there should be equal treatment of all Fund members with respect to their exchange rates. In other words, all countries should be subject to the same deliverations and scrutiny by the Fund with respect to their exchange rates.

Mr. Yeo believed that it was futile to attempt agreement with French authorities on exchange rates in some larger gathering, such as the Group of Ten, because of the past rhetoric and repetition of positions by both U.S. and French authorities. It would be embarrassing to back down from oft-repeated views in front of other authorities. It was better to work bilaterally, out of the limelight. He believed that agreement could be reached only if he and Mr. de Larosière worked alone and secretly. He was well aware of the near-agreement in June and of how it was upset by a misunderstanding in language. As it was easy to disturb any potential accord, even officials in the U.S. and French treasuries were not to be informed of the discussions between Mr. Yeo and Mr. de Larosière.

Following up on his initiative, Mr. Yeo made many trips to Paris (about 17 in less than three months) to reach an understanding with Mr. de Larosière. After comparing views on how the international monetary system should evolve, they compared their attitudes on the present reality of floating rates, on the desirability of a new par value system, on the need for stable domestic economies, and on the need for strong authority for the Fund over exchange rates. They also talked about the eventual need for a system of asset settlement. These discussions showed that their views were not as dissimilar as they had expected. Mr. Yeo then drafted language for an amended Article IV that reflected these discussions to see if Mr. de Larosière could agree.

According to Mr. de Larosière, in France any arrangement on the monetary system was political. French authorities had long believed that international monetary arrangements and political relationships between Europe and the United States were intertwined. Moreover, Mr. Giscard d'Estaing, then President of France, had been an extremely able Minister of Economy and Finance for several years and was an expert on international monetary problems. Hence, although Mr. de Larosière had his full confidence, Mr. Giscard d'Estaing wanted personally to approve the draft text of an amended Article IV, which he often discussed with Mr. de Larosière. Gradually Mr. Yeo and Mr. de Larosière, working secretly, produced a draft of the whole of Article IV and the related Schedule containing the details of how a par value system should operate if installed.

In the meantime, plans took shape for an economic summit conference to be held on November 15–17, 1975 at the Chateau de Rambouillet, outside Paris. This time the economic conference of heads of state or government was to include not only those of France and the United States, as at Martinique the year before, but also of the Federal Republic of Germany, Italy, Japan, and the United Kingdom. This conference represented the first economic summit meeting. The six leaders were to discuss possible joint action to deal with the serious world economic conditions, especially inflation and recession.

Because the Heads of Government of Belgium, Canada, and the Netherlands felt excluded from the summit conference, their monetary authorities suggested that the Group of Ten also meet. Mr. Duisenberg, its Chairman, consequently called a meeting of the Group of Ten for the middle of December. This meeting was also to be held in Paris since finance ministers from many countries would be assembling about that time for the opening of the Conference on International Economic Cooperation (CIEC), that is, the North-South dialogue.

Just before the economic summit meeting, Mr. Witteveen was again in Paris to meet with Mr. Fourcade, Mr. de Larosière, and Bernard Clappier, Governor of the Bank of France, to discuss the outlook for agreement on an amended Article IV at the next meeting of the Interim Committee in January 1976. Mr. Fourcade encouraged Mr. Witteveen to believe that some progress might be made on exchange rates at the economic summit meeting that could lead to progress at the Interim Committee meeting. Much would depend, however, on what was accomplished at the economic summit meeting. Mr. Fourcade emphasized to Mr. Witteveen that French authorities regarded as most important some moderation of the large swings in exchange rates, especially for the dollar, that had characterized 1974 and 1975. If U.S. authorities would move toward greater management of floating rates to stabilize the dollar, French authorities could become more flexible on the wording of an amended Article IV.

Breakthrough at Rambouillet

When President Valéry Giscard d'Estaing, Chancellor Helmut Schmidt, Premier Aldo Moro, Prime Minister Takeo Miki, Prime Minister Harold Wilson, and President Gerald Ford met at Rambouillet on November 14–15, 1975, the leaders of the four other nations had no idea that agreement on exchange rates had been reached by U.S. and French authorities. The latter regarded their draft for Article IV as secret, to be made public only when the Group of Ten looked at it on December 19. In agreeing on exchange rates, which lay at the heart of the international monetary system, Mr. Yeo and Mr. de Larosière realized that they had in effect quietly agreed among themselves what the future international monetary system was to be. They were conscious that other monetary authorities would be sensitive to what they had done. Many monetary authorities and specialists had been devoting their attention to the future of exchange rates for at least a decade. Now, the final negotiation had left out these experts, and yet their acceptance of what the French and U.S. authorities had agreed was imperative. The total silence following the announcement of the accord by President Giscard d'Estaing at a dinner at Rambouillet indicated how stunning the news was.

At the next day's meeting of finance ministers, the text of the draft Article IV was initialed by all five, although only Messrs. Fourcade and Simon had seen it. The three other finance ministers agreed to an unseen text because of their elation that the differences between French and U.S. authorities had at last been reconciled.

Given the predilection of U.S. authorities for floating rates, French authorities considered recognition by U.S. authorities of a possible future par value system as an achievement. They also regarded as something of a victory their obtaining provisions in Article IV for "firm surveillance" of exchange rate policies by the Fund. President Ford, moreover, acceded to the other great concern of the French authorities by agreeing that U.S. authorities would take measures "to counter erratic fluctuations in exchange rates." The U.S. authorities in return achieved legalization of floating rates for an indefinite period and emphasis on domestic economic stability as a prerequisite for exchange rate stability.

Several paragraphs of the declaration of Rambouillet contained general statements on the need to overcome high unemployment, continuing inflation, and serious energy problems and on the need for new efforts in world trade, monetary matters, and raw materials. Paragraph 11, which dealt with international monetary problems, affirmed the intention of these leaders to work for greater stability. In deference to U.S. authorities, the summit participants agreed to "efforts to restore greater stability in underlying economic and financial conditions in the world economy." In deference to French authorities, monetary authorities were also to act "to counter disorderly market conditions or erratic fluctuations in exchange rates." The heads of state or government also welcomed "the rapprochement, reached at the request of many other countries, between the views of the United States and France on the need for stability that the reform of the international monetary system must promote." This rapprochement would, so went the declaration, facilitate agreement through the Fund at the next session of the Interim Committee in Jamaica on the outstanding issues of international monetary reform.[9]

Paragraph 11 showed two parts to the understanding about exchange rates. First, there was agreement between the French and U.S. Governments on "their mutual perception of the shape of international monetary reform," that is, an agreement on a draft Article IV for the Fund's amended Articles. Second, there was agreement that treasuries and central banks would collaborate or consult regarding developments in their exchange rates and counter disorderly market conditions or erratic fluctuations.

REDRAFTING AFTER RAMBOUILLET AND APPROVAL BY THE GROUP OF TEN

It was essential, of course, that monetary authorities of other countries also approve the draft Article IV worked out by Mr. Yeo and Mr. de Larosière. The draft

---

[9]Declaration of Rambouillet, November 17, 1975, par. 11; Vol. III below, p. 302.

was submitted to both the Group of Ten and the Executive Board of the Fund, and there was an immediate flurry of activity to get them to accept it before the Interim Committee met the first week of January.

On December 8, Messrs. Cross and Wahl circulated the joint U.S.-French draft of the provisions of Article IV and the related Schedule to the Executive Directors, in English and in French. Copies were given to Mr. Witteveen and Mr. Dale. This occasion was the first time that anyone in the Fund had seen the draft on which the U.S. and French authorities had been working.

On December 12, the deputies of the Group of Ten met in Paris to consider the draft. As usual, Mr. Gold and Mr. Polak attended the meeting as representatives of the Managing Director. Mr. Yeo and Mr. de Larosière considered the meeting sensitive as they wanted the other deputies not only to agree to the draft but also to be tolerant of the sequence of events that had produced it. They also realized that their draft considerably strengthened the hand of the Fund in exchange rates and that some deputies did not necessarily welcome provisions that made the Fund stronger in this regard. The meeting was tense, but gradually the deputies seemed to go along with the draft text.

Toward the end of the meeting, Mr. Gold criticized the draft for incompatibility with the Fund's Articles and with international treaty practice. He cited an example of this inconsistency. One of the provisions made it possible for the Fund to impose new obligations on members without further amendment of the Articles. In drafting the comprehensive draft amendment, the Fund's staff had meticulously avoided such provisions and had drafted the provisions so that members' obligations were fully specified in the proposed amendment. The Fund could at a later date "give content" to these obligations. From the point of view of international law this drafting was important. Otherwise, the Fund might seem to be imposing obligations on members without members having received the required prior consent of their legislatures to these obligations.

At this meeting, Mr. Polak also criticized the economic implications of the provisions of the draft Article IV. As a result of their criticisms, Messrs. Gold and Polak were highly unpopular with the deputies of the Group of Ten at the meeting and were attacked for obstructing a long-awaited political resolution of the problem of exchange arrangements.

It was agreed that Mr. de Larosière would come to Washington as soon as possible and that he, Mr. Yeo, and Mr. Gold would attempt to reach agreement on a draft. Everyone emphasized that only revisions required for legal purposes, that is, to make the provisions of Article IV consistent with the rest of the Articles, were to be considered. The substance of the draft worked out by Mr. de Larosière and Mr. Yeo was to remain unaltered. For this reason, the deputies of the Group of Ten indicated that Mr. Polak did not need to be part of the redrafting group. As far as they were concerned, the economic issues involved in the amended Article IV had already been settled.

On December 13 and 14, Mr. Gold drew up a redraft that he considered tolerable, without departing from the basic lines of the U.S.-French draft. On December 15, a small group consisting of Mr. de Larosière, accompanied by Mr. Wahl, Mr. Yeo, accompanied by Mr. Cross and another person from the U.S. Treasury, and of Mr. Gold, accompanied by the Deputy General Counsel, George Nicoletopoulos, met at Fund headquarters. As the meeting started, Mr. Gold was invited to react to the U.S.-French draft, but replied that it would be tedious for everyone if he gave his reactions line by line and that he would prefer to present his redrafted version that would demonstrate his views.

Mr. Gold's suggestion caused Mr. Yeo and Mr. de Larosière some annoyance. They were firm that the substance of their agreement was to remain unaltered. Mr. Gold then withdrew from the room so that they could decide whether they would consider his redraft. After about an hour, he was asked to return. The principals had implicitly agreed to work on the basis of Mr. Gold's redrafted version because they believed that Mr. Gold's changes were relatively minor, of a legal nature, and affected only language, not substance. The meeting then proceeded to a lengthy and detailed examination of the redraft, on the whole, with great good humor. After a virtually all-night session, the task was finished on December 16.

The meeting of the Group of Ten at ministerial level was to be held in Paris on December 19. Because Mr. Cross suggested minor revisions on the redraft agreed on December 16, a meeting was held on the evening of December 18 at the French Ministry of Finance. At this meeting the revisions were considered by Mr. de Larosière, Mr. Yeo, Mr. Wahl, Mr. Cross, and Mr. Gold, and agreement was reached a little after midnight.

On December 19, the Group of Ten considered the full text. Mr. Fourcade and Mr. Simon called on Mr. Gold to explain the agreed draft and both thanked Mr. Gold for his work which they agreed had led to an "important improvement in the text." The monetary authorities present were well aware that the document was a political compromise. The French and U.S. representatives, anxious to protect their compromise, were reluctant to accept any changes. Nevertheless, the finance ministers and the central bank governors of the eight other countries in the Group of Ten expressed profound satisfaction that a basis for agreement by the Interim Committee to be held in Jamaica in January 1976 had at last been found. They agreed to the text with some minor amendments and discussed the possible intervention arrangements in exchange markets that might come out of the Rambouillet agreement. In fact, this intervention concerned them most. The communiqué following the December 19 meeting referred to the prospect that central banks would be deepening and broadening their consultations to help counter erratic fluctuations in exchange rates.

EXECUTIVE BOARD'S DISCUSSION OF THE PROPOSED ARTICLE IV

The Executive Board proceeded with some urgency to consider the draft of the amended Article IV before the Jamaica meeting, taking up the topic on December 22 and again on December 23. December 23 was an unusually full day with three meetings devoted totally to this topic. Mr. de Larosière came from Paris to serve as an official delegate to consider any changes in the text.

Since with only a few changes the draft amendment considered in the Executive Board became Article IV of the amended Articles, the final text of Article IV is described first at some length.

Provisions of Article IV

The draft Article IV contained five main sections. Section 1 states the general and specific obligations of members. In effect, it notes that the provisions on exchange arrangements are based on the recognition that the essential purpose of the international monetary system is to provide a framework that facilitates the exchange of goods, services, and capital among countries, and that sustains sound economic growth, and that a principal objective is the continuing development of the orderly conditions necessary for financial and economic stability. Each member of the Fund undertakes a general obligation to collaborate with the Fund and other members to assure orderly exchange arrangements and to promote a stable system of exchange rates. Members are to perform their general obligation by observing, in particular, the undertakings with respect to domestic and external economic policies set forth in Article IV, Section 1(i), (ii), (iii), and (iv). Thus, each member is to endeavor to direct its policies toward reasonable price stability, with due regard to its circumstances; to seek to promote stability by fostering orderly underlying economic and financial conditions and a monetary system that does not tend to produce erratic disruptions; to avoid manipulating exchange rates or the international monetary system in order to prevent effective balance of payments adjustment or to gain an unfair competitive advantage over other members; and to follow exchange policies compatible with the undertakings under this section.

Emphasis in this section is thus both on domestic economic stability, as U.S. authorities desired, and on an international monetary system that does not have "erratic disruptions" and in which exchange policies are compatible with all the obligations of members under this provision, as French authorities desired. The undertakings referred to are general in scope and applicability. There is recognition, however, of the relevance of the circumstances of members in the formulation of the undertakings according to which members must "endeavor" or "seek" to pursue certain courses, as well as in the clause "with due regard to its circumstances" in Article IV, Section 1(i).

Section 2 deals with general exchange arrangements. Each member is to notify the Fund, within 30 days after the Second Amendment goes into effect, of the exchange arrangements it intends to apply. Section 2(*b*) states that, under an international monetary system of the kind prevailing on January 1, 1976, exchange arrangements may include (i) maintenance by a member of a value for its currency in terms of the SDR or some other denominator, other than gold, selected by the member, or (ii) cooperative arrangements by which members maintain the value of their currencies in relation to the value of the currency or currencies of other members, or (iii) other exchange arrangements of a member's choice. Thus, Section 2(*b*) describes two of the principal types of exchange arrangements and refers in a general way to all others as arrangements that members may apply in an international monetary system like the one prevailing at the beginning of 1976. The provision refers to the system as it existed on January 1, 1976 in recognition of the fact that it may develop in new directions thereafter. In the context of a different international monetary system, members may find it necessary or convenient to apply exchange arrangements other than those referred to in Section 2(*b*)(i) or (ii).

Section 2(*c*) provides that as the international monetary system further evolves, the Fund may by an 85 percent majority of the total voting power recommend general exchange arrangements that accord with the development of the system. This action of the Fund, however, cannot limit in any way the right of members to have exchange arrangements of their choice consistent with the purposes of the Fund and the obligations of members under Section 1.

Reference to the type of international monetary system prevailing on January 1, 1976 gives legal recognition to the exchange arrangements of members at that time. There is no longer any doubt that floating rates are recognized as legal by the Fund. Moreover, this section makes explicit that members have freedom of choice with regard to their exchange arrangements under all conditions. There is no mention of par values. If it so desires, a member can fix "a value for its currency" in terms of the SDR or another denominator, other than gold, selected by the member. This value is not a par value. The denominator is not a common denominator.

Section 3 deals with surveillance over exchange arrangements. Under Section 3(*a*) the Fund is required to oversee the international monetary system to ensure its effective operation, and to oversee the observance of each member with its obligations under Section 1. Section 3(*b*) emphasizes the functions of the Fund under Section 3(*a*). The Fund is directed to exercise firm surveillance over the exchange rate policies of members and to adopt specific principles for the guidance of all members with respect to those policies whatever exchange arrangements a member may apply. Thus, the Fund has specific power for surveillance of exchange rate policies, as French authorities wished.

Each member is to provide the Fund with the information necessary for such surveillance and, when requested by the Fund, to consult with the Fund on its exchange rate policies. The principles adopted by the Fund may be adapted from time to time in the light of experience and the development of the international monetary system. The principles will have to be based on, and respect, the general obligations of members under Section 1 and must be consistent with the freedom of members to choose their exchange arrangements.

It is to be noted that in Section 3(*b*), as well as in Section 2(*b*), there is special reference to cooperative arrangements by which the values of currencies are maintained between or among members. This double reference to cooperative arrangements had a political objective. The French authorities, who from the Fund's inception have been keenly concerned with the legal aspects of the Fund's activities and policies, wanted to make it very clear that the "snake" arrangements are compatible with the amended Articles. Under Section 3 the principles that the Fund adopts for surveillance must also respect the domestic social and political policies of members. In applying these principles, the Fund is required to "pay due regard to the circumstances of members."

Section 4 deals with par values. It authorizes the Fund to make a determination, by an 85 percent majority of the total voting power, that international economic conditions permit the introduction of a par value system, that is, a widespread system of exchange arrangements based on stable but adjustable par values. The criteria that the Fund must take into account for making that determination are also set forth in Section 4. The Fund is to take into account the underlying stability of the world economy, including price movements, rates of expansion in the economies of members, the sources of international liquidity, and the ways in which adjustment is being made in payments imbalances. A separate schedule (Schedule C) explains how the par value system will work when it is introduced. If the Fund makes a determination, it must notify members that the provisions of Schedule C apply, and Schedule C is then operational.

How Schedule C would work was explained in some detail in the Commentary attached to the Proposed Second Amendment when it was sent to the Board of Governors in March 1976.[10] Application of the provisions of Schedule C requires a member to establish a par value for its currency unless it intends to apply other exchange arrangements. If it chooses the latter course, it must consult with the Fund and ensure that its exchange arrangements are consistent with the purposes of the Fund and are adequate to fulfill its obligations under Article IV, Section 1. A member wishing to establish a par value under the provisions of Schedule C can at any time propose a par value to the Fund, whether initially under Schedule C, paragraph 2, or subsequently under Schedule C, paragraph 4. The proposed par value will take effect if the Fund concurs in it. The Fund shall not object because of the domestic social or political policies of the members proposing the par value.

Under Schedule C, paragraph 5, the margin for spot exchange transactions between currencies for which par values are maintained is 4½ percent on either side of parity. Members can maintain narrower margins consistently with this provision if they wish to do so. The Fund will be able, by an 85 percent majority of the total voting power, to establish a different margin, which might be either wider or narrower than 4½ percent, for all spot exchange transactions or to permit, for example, the application of one margin for the currencies of members participating in a multicurrency intervention system and another margin for spot exchange transactions between these currencies and other currencies. The authority of the Fund under the Articles before the Second Amendment to establish specific margins for other exchange transactions, including forward exchange transactions, has been

---

[10]See *Report on Second Amendment*, Vol. III below, pp. 317–76.

eliminated. In view of the greater width of margins, it has been made clear that the Fund's jurisdiction over multiple currency practices and discriminatory currency arrangements applies to rates within or outside margins observed by members under Article IV or prescribed by or under Article IV or prescribed by or under Schedule C, paragraph 5 (Article VIII, Section 3). The Fund will be able to develop a body of principles on what practices are to be regarded as multiple currency practices or discriminatory arrangements subject to the practices authorized by the provisions of the Articles. This is the way in which these concepts were applied under the Articles before the Second Amendment.

A change in the par value of a member's currency for the purpose of the Articles of Agreement may occur only if the member proposes the change in order to correct, or prevent the emergence of, a fundamental disequilibrium and if the Fund concurs in the change. The concept of preventing the emergence of a fundamental disequilibrium which, as described earlier in this chapter, was in the staff's initial draft of an amended Article IV and which went beyond the text of the Fund's original Articles, was thus retained in the final version. If a change in par value is proposed by a member, the Fund must concur in or object to it within a reasonable period. The Fund must concur if it is satisfied that the change is necessary to correct, or prevent the emergence of, a fundamental disequilibrium. As in the Articles before the Second Amendment, it is provided, in Schedule C, paragraph 7, that the Fund shall not object because of the domestic social or political policies of the member proposing the change. It will continue to be possible, therefore, for the Fund to object because of other policies. If the Fund does object, the proposed change will not take effect for the purposes of the Articles. If nevertheless the member was to make the change, the Fund would be able to apply the measures of Article XXVI, Section 2, against the member (i.e., ineligibility to use the general resources of the Fund and compulsory withdrawal). The Fund is not required to apply these measures.

Only the member is authorized to propose a change in the par value of its currency, which was the position under the original Articles. Although the Fund is not authorized to propose a change, it is required to discourage the maintenance of an unrealistic par value by a member.

Under Schedule C, paragraph 1, the Fund will choose the common denominator of the par value system under that schedule. It may be the SDR or some other denominator except gold or a currency. If the SDR is chosen as the common denominator, the Fund might wish from time to time to make a uniform proportionate change in the par value of all currencies. For this purpose Schedule C, paragraph 11 authorizes the Fund to decide, by a 70 percent majority of the total voting power, to make a uniform proportionate change in the par value of all currencies if the change will not affect the value of the SDR. A uniform proportionate change in the par value of all currencies would not be made in order to increase or decrease global liquidity, as was the purpose of the provision in the original Articles, since changes in global liquidity can now be achieved by the allocation or cancellation of SDRs. Rather, a uniform proportionate change in the par value of all currencies might be needed to bring par values into line with the values of currencies in terms of the value of the SDR in transactions as determined under Article XV, Section 2. A member will have the right, which it had under the original Articles, to decide that the par value of its currency will not be changed, but it must give the Fund notice of this decision within seven days after the Fund's action. Thus, the amended Articles, like the original Articles, contain a provision for a uniform proportionate change in the par value of all currencies but it is for a different purpose.

Executive Board's Consideration of the Draft Article IV

When the Executive Board took up the draft Article IV in December 1975, Messrs. Cross and Wahl were reluctant to agree to changes since the text had already been initialed by Messrs. Fourcade and Simon. Other Executive Directors, including Mr. Ryrie, were incensed by their inflexibility. Despite the reluctance of the U.S. and French Executive Directors, three changes of consequence came out of the Executive Board's discussion.

First, at the urging of Messrs. Jagannathan, Kafka, and Suárez, supported by Mr. Lieftinck, the words "sustains economic growth" were added to the first sentence of Section 1. These words, included in the above description of Article IV, had not been in the draft version circulated to the Executive Board in December. The Executive Board thus changed the draft to indicate that the essential purpose of the international monetary system is to provide a framework that facilitates the exchange of goods, services, and capital among countries "and that sustains sound economic growth." The Articles thereby explicitly recognized economic growth as one of the criteria for judging the successful functioning of the international monetary system.

Second, Section 1 and Section 3 were altered to make explicit that the Fund is to pay "due regard to the circumstances of members" when it judges the extent to which they are fulfilling their obligations to the Fund and when it exercises firm surveillance over exchange rate policies. These words, included in the above description of Article IV, had not been in either Section 1 or Section 3 of the draft received by the Executive Directors in December 1975.

The provision may not have been necessary since the Fund, in applying its policies, has customarily taken into account members' individual circumstances, but the Executive Directors elected by developing members wanted these words inserted. While they did not want to upset "the one-world approach" of the Fund in which there was no distinction between the obligations undertaken by developing members and by other members, they did aim, nonetheless, to obtain statutory recognition in the Fund's Articles of Agreement of the special concerns or circumstances of developing countries. Although the developing members did not get this statutory recognition in the Fund's amended Articles of Agreement, their Executive Directors did manage to work into the amended Article IV in two places a phrase which obliges the Fund to pay heed to the particular circumstances of individual members. (When the ministers of the Group of Twenty-Four met in Jamaica in January 1976, they included in their communiqué a paragraph with similar language that "ministers agreed that, in interpreting the obligations and applying the principles under the amended Articles dealing with exchange arrangements, the International Monetary Fund should pay due regard to the special circumstances of the developing countries and to the importance of currencies for the international financial system.")[11]

Third, a phrase was added relating exchange rate policy to balance of payments adjustment. Mainly at the urging of Mr. Whitelaw, the phrase "balance of payments adjustment" was put into the draft of Section 1(iv). The staff had also favored the inclusion of this phrase but had hesitated to change the draft. This straightforward language obliges members to follow exchange policies compatible with the undertakings in the rest of Section 1. (When the Interim Committee met in Jamaica, Mr. Fourcade, however, did not want to alter Section 1(iv). He liked its existing simplicity. He therefore suggested that the phrase for balance of payments adjustment be moved to Section 1(iii). Hence, Section 1(iii) was changed to read that members would "avoid manipulating exchange rates or the international monetary system in order to prevent effective balance of payments adjustment or to gain unfair competitive advantage over other members.")

After the Executive Board's discussion, a few other small word changes remained in Section 1 on which the Executive Directors could not agree. While some Executive Directors wanted some slight alterations in language, Messrs. Cross and Wahl continued to be reluctant to change the text. The verbal changes were accordingly passed along to the Interim Committee for consideration.

BIRTH OF ARTICLE IV

At their meeting in Jamaica in January 1976, the members of the Interim Committee, under the chairmanship of Mr. De Clercq, Mr. Turner's successor, agreed to the proposed Article IV on exchange rate arrangements. Some of the verbal changes left to be decided were made, others were not.

The exchange rate provisions of the amended Articles are those most often commented upon. Because exchange rates form the crux of an international monetary system, and because a system of par values had been at the heart of the Fund's original Articles, the provisions about exchange arrangements are understandably viewed as the primary thrust of the amended Articles.

The emphasis is on freedom of choice of exchange arrangements, not on freedom of behavior. As in the original Articles, a great deal of emphasis is given to orderliness and stability in exchange arrangements. Members have certain obligations as they apply their chosen exchange arrangements. They undertake a general

---

[11]Communiqué of Group of Twenty-Four, January 6, 1976, par. 11; Vol. III below, p. 646.

obligation to collaborate with the Fund and with other members in order to assure orderly exchange arrangements and to promote a stable system of exchange rates. Each member is to endeavor to direct its economic and financial policies toward the objective of fostering orderly economic growth with reasonable price stability, with due regard to its circumstances. Each member is to seek to promote exchange rate stability by fostering orderly underlying economic and financial conditions and a monetary system that does not tend to produce erratic disruptions.

Stability of the system is emphasized rather than stability of individual exchange rates, as in the past, and the need for orderly underlying domestic economic and external conditions as a precondition for exchange rate stability is emphasized, rather than the other way around, as in the past. Under the previous system, stable exchange rates were the goal and members were expected to adjust their domestic economic and financial policies to help keep exchange rates stable; now a member is not to gear its domestic economic policies to defending its exchange rate as much as it is to pursue domestic economic policies that will help to produce a stable rate.

As a result of this provision, the Fund has much more authority over domestic policies than it had originally. The amended Article IV contains more sophisticated provisions relating to exchange rates than did the original Articles. Thus, just as the First Amendment gives the Fund the new purpose (not explicitly stated in Article I) of managing international liquidity, so the Second Amendment gives the Fund the new purpose (not stated in Article I either) of ensuring that members pursue policies consistent with the continuing development of the orderly underlying conditions necessary for financial and economic stability.

Although the par value system that can eventually be introduced under the amended Articles is similar to the par value system of the original Articles, there are some important departures designed to make any new system more flexible and to avoid some of the rigidity and other flaws that may have caused the collapse of the original par value system. Under the amended Articles, for example, the margins around the parity relationships between the currencies of members maintaining par values that will have to be observed are wider than the margins under the original Articles, 4½ percent rather than 1 percent, and, by decisions taken by a majority of 85 percent of the total voting power, the Fund can vary these margins. A member can propose a change in the par value of its currency not only to extract itself from a fundamental disequilibrium, as was provided in the original Articles, but also to forestall an emerging fundamental disequilibrium. In addition, while the principle of the original Articles is retained that only a member, and not the Fund, is entitled to propose a specific change in the par value of a currency, under the amended Articles the Fund has the duty to discourage the maintenance of an unrealistic par value. A par value is to cease to exist for the purpose of the Articles of Agreement if the member terminates it or if the Fund finds that the member is not maintaining rates for a substantial volume of exchange transactions in accordance with the par value. These provisions eliminate the embarrassing principle under the original Articles that a par value continued to exist for the purposes of the Articles even though it had been completely out of touch with actual rates for many years and there was no prospect that it would be made effective again.

THE JAMAICA AGREEMENT

With agreement reached on exchange arrangements at the Interim Committee meeting in Jamaica in January 1976, the last stages of preparing the Second Amendment were at hand. Because of agreement on this and on other controversial issues, the Jamaica agreement is considered a landmark. It had a number of elements. First, the Interim Committee agreed to the proposed Article IV on exchange rate arrangements. In addition, monetary authorities agreed that the various arrangements for gold under discussion since August 31, 1975 should be immediately implemented, thereby paving the way for the Fund's gold sales. The Interim Committee also agreed that the amended Articles should include a cooperation clause by which members would help to reduce the role of gold in the international monetary system. After considerable discussion, the Group of Ten agreed in December 1975 that a provision should be included by which members would "collaborate with the Fund and with other members in order to ensure that their policies with respect to reserve assets shall be consistent with the objectives of promoting better international surveillance of international liquidity and making the special drawing right the principal reserve asset in the international monetary system."[12] With agreement on gold and exchange rates, the most controversial of the amendments to the Articles could now be put in place.

The Interim Committee also helped settle other disputed issues in drafting the amended Articles that the Executive Directors had been unable to resolve. The amended Articles were to contain a provision enabling the Fund to sell any part of its remaining gold to augment its general resources or to make balance of payments assistance available on special terms to developing members in difficult circumstances. The Committee also agreed on the majorities of total voting power needed for decisions to distribute profits from the Fund's gold sales—85 percent of total voting power to distribute profits to developing members, 70 percent for use of profits from gold sales in regular operations and transactions, and 85 percent for the use of profits from gold sales in other operations and transactions.

The Interim Committee also agreed that the Fund's holdings of each member's currency should be usable in the Fund's operations and transactions, and appropriate provisions for this purpose were to be included in the draft amendments. The Committee agreed, moreover, that the majority required for the adoption of decisions on the principle of the method used for valuing the SDR under the amended Articles was to be 70 percent of the total voting power, with the exception of decisions involving a change in the principles of valuation or a fundamental

---

[12]Communiqué of Group of Ten, December 19, 1975, par. 6; Vol. III below, p. 633.

change in the application of the principle in effect, which were to be taken by an 85 percent majority. With respect to the obligation of participants in the Special Drawing Account to reconstitute their holdings of SDRs, the Committee agreed that the amended Articles should authorize the Fund to review the rules for reconstitution at any time and adopt, modify, or abrogate these rules by a 70 percent majority of the total voting power.

The Interim Committee took special note of the report of the Executive Directors on the amendments drafted so far, welcomed the progress made toward the solution of the outstanding issues, and commended the Executive Directors for the voluminous and successful work that they had done to achieve a major revision of the Articles. With the new decisions taken, the Interim Committee requested the Executive Directors to complete their work on amending the Articles of Agreement and expected a comprehensive draft amendment for the approval of the Board of Governors, together with a report, within the coming weeks. The attempt at reform of the international monetary system begun in 1971 was thus at an end, but with the recognition that evolution would be possible under the Fund's Articles.

At the Jamaica meeting the members of the Interim Committee also discussed the world economic situation and outlook. They characterized the "current rates of both unemployment and inflation" as "still unacceptably high," and called on the industrial countries, especially those in relatively strong balance of payments positions, to conduct their policies so as to ensure a satisfactory and sustained rate of economic expansion while they continued to combat inflation. The members of the Committee also expressed concern about the deterioration in the external position of the primary producing countries, especially the developing ones. And the Committee took a number of actions described in earlier chapters regarding the Fund's resources.[13]

Jamaica in Perspective

With this much agreement on amending the Articles and on ways to enlarge use of Fund resources to help with the critical balance of payments deficits of many members, monetary authorities and financial officials, including those in the Fund, were understandably euphoric. Immediately after the Jamaica meeting, Mr. Witteveen explained to journalists that the "very long and extensive discussions" have now yielded "complete agreement on the far-reaching amendments" of the Fund's Articles, and Mr. De Clercq told them that he credited the success of the meeting "to the political will" of all the delegations present. By reference to political will, Mr. De Clercq, although possibly not intentionally, used the same words which Mr. Morse had used in 1974 to explain the failure of the Committee of Twenty. The significance of the same words was that they called attention to the changed political environment: the inclination of authorities to compromise that was notably lacking in 1973 and 1974 existed in January 1976. Mr. Fourcade saw the meeting as marking

---

[13]Communiqué of Interim Committee, January 8, 1976, par. 4; Vol. III below, p. 226.

"the beginning of a new political and monetary era" and Mr. Simon compared the results with those achieved at Bretton Woods.

Monetary authorities were elated that after years of bitter debate and protracted negotiations, they could agree on international monetary arrangements. Several economists and monetary experts who for more than a decade had devoted their finest energies to designing a reformed international monetary system interpreted the outcome at Jamaica differently, however. Expressing their disappointment, many took the view that nothing momentous was achieved, that the agreed international monetary arrangements added up to no system at all. There had been no reform or, at best, only a partial reform.

They had specific complaints about the Jamaica agreement. The principles in the *Outline of Reform* of June 1974 had been lost or dropped. There were no rules in the amended Articles for balance of payments adjustment, either by countries in deficit or by countries in surplus; chronic payments imbalances could persist indefinitely. There were no rules or guidelines for the management of exchange rates. There were no criteria to judge when exchange rates ought to be changed. It appeared that flexible rates were to be managed so as to produce stability in much the same way as par values had been managed. Advantage was not taken of arrangements that allowed more flexibility of exchange rates than did the Bretton Woods system.

No provision was made, moreover, for convertibility or settlement in primary reserve assets of currency balances accumulated from new current account surpluses. Nor was provision made for monitoring or controlling the supply and composition of international liquidity. The gold substitution account had been neglected and no other way was instituted to reduce the volume of gold held officially by members. There was, therefore, no guarantee that use of gold in the international monetary system would be sharply reduced in favor of the SDR. Similarly, no provision was made for reducing the use of reserve currencies in the system. Yet these were the issues that economists, monetary specialists, public officials, and international civil servants had been discussing for years as they tried to devise arrangements that would overcome the defects of the Bretton Woods system.

It seemed to these observers and critics that at the Jamaica meeting monetary authorities took a 180-degree turn from the *Outline of Reform*. Far from reforming the system, monetary authorities merely codified or legalized existing international monetary arrangements. Two members of the Executive Board present at Jamaica— Mr. de Vries and Mr. Kafka—expressed these complaints in articles with titles that virtually apologized for the action taken.[14] Similar expressions of disappointment

---

[14]Tom de Vries, "Jamaica, or the Non-Reform of the International Monetary System," *Foreign Affairs* (New York), Vol. 54 (April 1976), pp. 577–605; and "Amending the Fund's Charter: Reform or Patchwork?" *Quarterly Review*, Banca Nazionale del Lavoro (Rome), Vol. 29 (September 1976), pp. 272–83; and Alexandre Kafka, *The International Monetary Fund: Reform Without Reconstruction?* Essays in International Finance, No. 118 (Princeton, New Jersey: Princeton University Press, 1976).

came from Professors George N. Halm of the Fletcher School of Law and Diplomacy of Tufts University, Fritz Machlup of Princeton University, and Robert Triffin of Yale University, who had been among the academic leaders in years of discussion about international monetary reform.[15]

Other experts intimately familiar with the issues of international monetary reform, such as Edward M. Bernstein, President of EMB Ltd. and former Director of the Fund's Research Department, and Professors Richard N. Cooper of Yale University, Gottfried Haberler of Harvard University, and Charles P. Kindleberger of the Massachusetts Institute of Technology, reflecting on the Jamaica agreement, placed less emphasis on the lack of specific rules for balance of payments adjustment and for changes in exchange rates and on the lack of control over international liquidity. They directed attention to the broader responsibility given to the Fund to oversee the international monetary system and to exercise firm surveillance over exchange rates and to the new involvement of the Fund in the world economic situation and in providing more balance of payments assistance to developing countries.[16]

Another Executive Director present at Jamaica—Mr. Amuzegar—pointed out that the Jamaica agreement could be regarded as a successful compromise between the North and the South.[17]

How should the Jamaica agreement be viewed? The agreement expressed the type of international monetary arrangements to which monetary authorities from 128 countries were willing collectively to commit themselves in the circumstances of the middle of the 1970s. It was a political compromise, exemplifying Machiavelli's dictum that "he is happy whose mode of procedure accords with the needs of the times."

French authorities got the arrangements on gold that were of paramount importance to them. While they gave up hopes of restoring an international monetary system based on gold, in which their accumulated gold reserves would be fully utilizable at a high officially guaranteed price, they would eventually be able, if they were willing to take the risks involved in fluctuating free market prices for gold, to use their gold reserves at much higher prices than before. They could, if they

---

[15]See George N. Halm, *Jamaica and the Par-Value System*, Essays in International Finance, No. 120 (Princeton, New Jersey: Princeton University Press, 1977); Fritz Machlup, "Between Outline and Outcome the Reform Was Lost," and Robert Triffin, "Jamaica: 'Major Revision' or Fiasco?" in Edward M. Bernstein et al., *Reflections on Jamaica*, Essays in International Finance, No. 115 (Princeton, New Jersey: Princeton University Press, 1976), pp. 30–38 and 45–53.

[16]Edward M. Bernstein, "The New International Monetary System," ibid., pp. 1–8; Richard N. Cooper, "Monetary Reform at Jamaica," ibid., pp. 9–14; Gottfried Haberler, "The International Monetary System after Jamaica and Manila," *Weltwirtschaftliches Archiv: Review of World Economics* (Kiel), Vol. 113 (No. 1, 1977), pp. 1–30; and Charles P. Kindleberger, "The Exchange-Stability Issue at Rambouillet and Jamaica," *Reflections on Jamaica*, (cited in fn. 15 above) pp. 25–29.

[17]Jahangir Amuzegar, "The North-South Dialogue: From Conflict to Compromise," *Foreign Affairs* (New York), Vol. 54 (April 1976), pp. 547–62. A version of this paper was orginally prepared for a conference on alternatives to growth, held in Houston, Texas, October 19–21, 1975.

wished, thereby refrain in international transactions from using dollars whose use they had been trying for years to decrease. U.S. authorities got the arrangements on exchange rates that they wanted. In return, they agreed to words about the introduction of a par value system in the future. The introduction of this system was, however, subject to their own veto. U.S. authorities committed themselves to avoiding disorderly conditions in exchange markets and erratic fluctuations in the rates for the dollar, with "firm surveillance" by the Fund, but with all the implementing arrangements undetermined. Authorities of developing members received more resources from the Fund, much of which was to be available immediately, and a larger share in the Fund's quotas, both of which were of primary concern to them. They did not get the link between SDR allocations and development finance for which they had been pushing for a decade or other features of the *Outline of Reform* that recognized the need for the transfer of real resources from developed to developing countries.

The Jamaica agreement was another step in the evolution of international monetary arrangements that started with the suspension of the convertibility of official holdings of dollars by the United States in August 1971, went on to include the introduction in March 1973 of floating rates by several large industrial members, and to the failure of the Committee of Twenty to agree on a reformed system. These developments all represented significant breaks with past acceptance of agreed rules for international monetary arrangements. The legalization of these breaks was the next logical and necessary step in an evolving system.

The Jamaica agreement must be seen, moreover, in the context of the resurgence in the mid-1970s in the United Kingdom and the United States of an economic philosophy that advocated rollbacks of government from economic life. The Jamaica agreement was an early embodiment at the international level of neoconservative thinking favoring free markets and private enterprise rather than governmental regulation, thinking that was later to become dominant in the United Kingdom and in the United States. The middle of the 1970s was an unlikely environment for the Fund to be converted into the supranational central bank or the stronger international regulatory agency as implied in a stricter international monetary system.

Although the negotiators at Bretton Woods had carefully delineated the Fund's authority, those at Jamaica agreed that the Fund was to be empowered to take a number of actions when circumstances so permitted, provided, of course, large specified majorities of the total voting power concurred. Since the political will at Jamaica was not sufficient for further action, it was understood that the Fund could take further action in the future when the needed political will did exist. Thus, while the major advance of the Bretton Woods agreement was the acceptance by nations of international scrutiny of their exchange rates, the major advance of the Jamaica agreement was recognition that the Fund was to be the forum through which further international monetary arrangements were to be negotiated. This advance reflected three decades of Fund history. For its first 20 years the Fund had worked hard to establish its authority.[18] Monetary authorities had learned that any arrangements to which they agreed on paper were workable in practice only to the extent that member governments cooperated to make them work. At Jamaica these lessons of history were institutionalized in the amended Articles of Agreement: the Fund was empowered to introduce new arrangements when member governments were ready.

Jamaica signaled a turning point in the Fund's history in yet another way. The Fund's regulatory functions and its role as custodian of international monetary arrangements were de-emphasized. Increased attention was to be devoted to the role of the Fund as a provider of financial assistance, especially to its developing members.

---

[18]A description of how the original Articles limited the areas of the Fund's jurisdiction, especially in the field of exchange restrictions, and a recounting of the Fund's efforts in its early years to establish its authority in fields, such as exchange rates, where its jurisdiction was more clearly specified, can be found in *History, 1945–65*, Vol. II, pp. 24–35, 51–83, 90–110, 126–36, and 219–25.

CHAPTER

38

Finishing the Proposed Second Amendment

(January–March 1976)

*T*HE EXECUTIVE DIRECTORS resumed their deliberations on the draft amendments in January 1976. They still had considerable work to do, as a number of post-Jamaica problems existed. Toward the end of March 1976, after more than 18 months of discussions, they finally completed their work on the comprehensive draft amendment. It then became the Proposed Second Amendment.

This chapter briefly summarizes these final stages. By way of illustration, the results of amendments on two subjects, use of members' currencies and the composition of the Executive Board, that were worked out in the final stages of the drafting are briefly described.

AMENDMENTS RELATING TO USE OF MEMBERS' CURRENCIES

Earlier chapters described the need for provisions concerning the use of members' currencies in the Fund's operations and transactions. After Jamaica, agreement was finally reached, and the outcome was as follows.

A freely usable currency is defined by the amended Articles as a member's currency that the Fund determines (i) is in fact widely used to make payments for international transactions, and (ii) is widely traded in the principal exchange markets. Freely usable currencies are to have special roles in both the General Resources Account of the General Department and the Special Drawing Rights Department. In the General Resources Account, a distinction is made for the purposes of both purchases and repurchases between currencies that are freely usable and those that are not. If a member's currency purchased from the Fund is not freely usable, the member has to exchange it, at the request of the purchasing member at the time of the purchase, for a freely usable currency at exchange rates that produce equal value.

In the Special Drawing Rights Department, the main importance of the freely usable currency is that it has to be provided by a transferee designated by the Fund to receive SDRs from a transferor. The currency has to be provided at a value in terms of the SDR that accords with equal value.[1] The obligation of interconvertibility associated with a currency convertible in fact under the First Amendment disappeared. This obligation, which applied to the French franc, the pound sterling, and the U.S. dollar, required each of the three issuers to convert its currency provided for SDRs into either of the other two currencies if requested by the recipient of the currency, at exchange rates in accord with equal value. For some years before the Second Amendment entered into effect, interconvertibility had not been in full operation. Under the convertibility system for SDRs, the issuers of five other currencies (the Belgian franc, the deutsche mark, the Italian lira, the Mexican peso, and the Netherlands guilder) also undertook to convert balances of their currencies in return for SDRs into one of the three interconvertible currencies at equal value.[2] This undertaking, too, was abolished by the Second Amendment, but according to the revised Rules and Regulations, the Fund will continue to help a transferor obtain the freely usable currency that it prefers.

AMENDMENTS RELATING TO THE EXECUTIVE BOARD

In the final stages of drafting the Second Amendment a problem arose concerning the provisions of the amended Articles relating to the appointment and election of Executive Directors. This problem had a complex history. The original Articles provided that the Fund should not have fewer than 12 Executive Directors, of whom 5 were to be appointed by the five members having the largest quotas and 7 were to be elected under Article XII, Section 3(b). Two of the elective 7 were to be elected by the American Republics not entitled to appoint Executive Directors (Article XII, Section 3(b)(iv)). Specifically, inasmuch as the United States was an "American Republic" that was to appoint an Executive Director, the Latin Americans were guaranteed the right to elect 2 Executive Directors. The original Articles also provided for an increase in the number of Executive Directors to be elected, by a four-fifths majority of the voting power, when countries that had not sent delegations to Bretton Woods joined the Fund. An increase in the number of Executive Directors could occur either by increasing the number of Executive Directors elected by the American Republics or by increasing the number of Executive Directors elected by other members, or both. The formation of constituencies for the election of Executive Directors was left to diplomatic negotiations among

---

[1] A detailed explanation of the concept "freely usable currency" and of its use both in the General Department and in the Special Drawing Rights Department can be found in Gold, *Use, Conversion, and Exchange of Currency* (cited in fn. 2 of Chap. 35 above), pp. 58–98.

[2] For a description of interconvertibility for three currencies and the convertibility obligations for five other currencies as worked out at the time the SDR system was introduced, see *History, 1966–71*, Vol. I, pp. 168–70 and 223–26. Also see Gold, *Use, Conversion, and Exchange of Currency* (cited in fn. 2 of Chap. 35 above), pp. 45–55.

members. Another provision permitted the appointment of Executive Directors by the two largest creditor members, if these members were not already entitled to appoint an Executive Director.

Starting in 1947, the number of Executive Directors to be elected was gradually increased. Executive Directors elected by the American Republics were increased to 3 when Argentina joined the Fund in 1956. The last increases came in 1963 and 1964 when two more additions were made to the number of elected Executive Directors, just after the admission to membership of a large number of African countries in the early 1960s. These additions brought the number of elective Executive Directors to 15 and the total number of Executive Directors to 20.[3] Once it had reached this size, many Executive Directors felt that 20 was as large as the Executive Board should become.

In preparing rules for the conduct of the 1970 regular election of Executive Directors, the Executive Board raised questions about its own size and structure. What was the optimal size of the Board? Should the number of Executive Directors be increased from 20 to 21 by adding to the number of elective Executive Directors? Moreover, the 2 Executive Directors from the African members requested that the rules of election be arranged so as to ensure 2 seats for the African members. Under the existing rules, it was conceivable that in an election groupings of members could be such that the African members would no longer have 2 Executive Directors.

During the discussion in the Executive Board, there was broad support for the view that, if the large number of African members—Maurice P. Omwony (Kenya) then had 15 members in his constituency and Mr. Yaméogo had 18—could elect only a single Executive Director, the burden on him would be excessive, and the efficient conduct of the business of the Executive Directors as a group, particularly when the interests of the African members were involved, would be hindered. Executive Directors widely supported the view that African members should have the opportunity to elect 2 Executive Directors. The Executive Directors also strongly preferred as a matter of principle to keep the existing number of Directors at 20.

The Executive Directors did not want to try to reach any conclusions on these questions before the 1970 election. They believed that these and other questions relating to the size and structure of the Executive Board deserved further study. Accordingly, paragraph 7 of the report of the Executive Directors to the Board of Governors on the rules for the 1970 election stated that they intended to complete such a study within two years. This study was finished and sent to the Board of Governors in July 1972, a few months before the next biennial election of Executive Directors. The study concluded that "for the time being at least, the size of the Executive Board and the procedures for electing executive directors should continue as in the past." Because of the problem of African members, however, it also concluded that the Executive Board was prepared, if necessary, to reconsider the

---

[3]The periodic increases in the size of the Executive Board were described in *History, 1945–65*, Vol. I, pp. 164–66, 195, 197, 302, 427, 443, 498, and 550.

issue of its aggregate size. The report mentioned explicitly the problem of the African members and, in language similar to that of the Executive Board's discussion in 1970, expressed concern that if there was to result from an election of Executive Directors only one Executive Director for all the African members, "this result would hinder the efficient conduct of the business of the Executive Directors, particularly when the interests of these members were involved," and stated there was "widespread support for the view that it was desirable that this large number of countries should have the opportunity to elect two executive directors under the present Articles." The Board of Governors took note of these points in August 1972.[4]

New Provisions

In January 1976, during the final discussions of the amendments to the Articles, when a draft Article XII which was virtually the same as that of the original Articles was being considered, Mr. Nana-Sinkam, at the time Alternate to Mr. Yaméogo, once again raised the concern of the African members about retaining 2 seats on the Executive Board. This time the African Executive Directors were concerned about the possible implications of Article XII, Section 3(c). That section provided that the two members that were the largest creditors to the Fund each might appoint an Executive Director if they did not already do so. At the time Saudi Arabia was becoming a large creditor to the Fund and was likely to be entitled to appoint an Executive Director. Thus there would be 6 appointed Executive Directors. In this event, should the total size of the Executive Board remain at 20 Executive Directors, there would be only 14 elective Executive Directors. Consequently, the African members would find it harder to obtain enough votes to assure them two seats on the Executive Board. Mr. Nana-Sinkam's concern gained sympathetic support from Mr. Amuzegar, Mr. Finaish, and Mr. Whitelaw, who proposed that should there be an additional appointed Executive Director, the size of the Executive Board should be increased.

After discussing an amended Article XII, Executive Directors agreed that the objectives and considerations referred to in the 1972 report should continue to guide the Fund. The size of the Executive Board should contribute to the effective dispatch of its business, a desirable balance should be maintained in the composition of the Executive Board, the size of constituencies should not place undue burdens on Executive Directors, members should be as free as possible within the provisions of the Articles and the regulations for the elections to form constituencies of their choice, and a relative equilibrium should be achieved in the voting power of the constituencies electing Executive Directors. For the future, these objectives and considerations were to be relevant not only for the composition of the Executive Board but also for the Interim Committee and for the Council on its establishment.

---

[4]*Report of the Executive Directors to the Board of Governors on the Size and Structure of the Executive Board*, July 24, 1972 and Board of Governors' Resolution No. 27-12, August 31, 1972. This report and resolution were reprinted in *Annual Report, 1973*, pp. 94–95.

The Executive Board concluded, too, that the number of elective Executive Directors—at the time, 15—gave effect to these objectives under existing circumstances and should be incorporated in an amended Article XII. The amended Article XII, Section 3(*b*) would provide, however, that all members eligible to elect Executive Directors would participate in one election of all 15 elective Executive Directors and that the distinction in the original Articles between Section 3(*b*)(iii) and (iv) would be eliminated. Two seats on the Executive Board were no longer to be guaranteed to the Latin American members. Moreover, the number of Executive Directors could exceed 20 if the Board of Governors so voted.

The provisions of the amended Articles allowing for a larger number of Executive Directors became applicable shortly after the new Articles went into effect. In 1978 Saudi Arabia, as a sufficiently large creditor member, became eligible to appoint an Executive Director, and on November 1, Mahsoun B. Jalal took a seat on the Executive Board, along with the 5 other appointed Executive Directors and 15 elected Executive Directors. The Executive Board consequently grew to 21 Executive Directors for the first time.[5]

THE SECOND AMENDMENT COMPLETED

By the end of March 1976, the Executive Directors not only completed their drafting of amendments but also worked out a report to the Board of Governors. This report included a detailed Commentary which explained Article by Article the provisions of the Proposed Second Amendment. The Executive Directors went over the Commentary with great care. The Commentary contained many phrases, as noted in Chapter 36, which made it possible to engineer agreement among the Executive Directors on many issues without encumbering the Articles themselves. The Commentary was thus legislative history that could assist in the interpretation of problems involving such numerous and diverse changes in the Articles.

The task that had taken nearly two years was thus finished. The Executive Directors had already been commended by the Interim Committee in January 1976. Now it was the staff's turn to receive recognition for its two years of arduous efforts. On behalf of his colleagues, Mr. Lieftinck, the Dean of the Executive Directors (the Executive Director currently on the Board who has the most years of service), proposed the following resolution which the Executive Directors adopted. "The Executive Directors express their high appreciation for the excellent work which the General Counsel, the Economic Counsellor and many other persons, both professional and nonprofessional, from numerous parts of the staff have done in the preparation of the proposed second amendment to the Articles of Agreement."

---

[5]Early in 1980, after the Government of the People's Republic of China took up the representation of China in the Fund, the Board of Governors decided that there would be a sixteenth elected Executive Director. In November 1980, Zhang Zicun (Tse Chun Chang) took a seat on the Executive Board.

APPROVAL BY GOVERNORS
BUT SLOW ACCEPTANCE BY MEMBERS

The Executive Directors then sent the Proposed Second Amendment to the Board of Governors with a recommendation for approval.[6] The package of papers mailed to the Governors was the most massive and complex in the Fund's experience. It contained a Part I: "Introduction," which explained the background to the Proposed Second Amendment and summarized the main themes of the modifications being proposed. It contained a lengthy Part II: "Commentary on the Proposed Amendment of the Articles of Agreement." This Commentary was nearly 80 pages of fine print explaining Article by Article the reasons for the proposed changes.

Attached to the Commentary was an Annex that set forth in tabular form the special majorities of voting power required for certain decisions under the amended Articles and which bodies, whether the Board of Governors, the Council (if it was established), or the Executive Board, that could take these decisions. Also attached to Part II was an Appendix that compared the proposed and the existing Articles of Agreement, provision by provision, side by side. The package also contained a Part III describing the procedure to be followed to enable the Proposed Second Amendment to go into effect.

The Board of Governors first had to adopt a resolution approving the proposed amendment, by a majority of the votes cast, and then ask all members if they accepted the amendment. Constitutional procedures in Australia, Belgium, Canada, the Federal Republic of Germany, India, the United Kingdom, and the United States, for example, required that the Proposed Amendment be submitted to their legislative bodies. The Proposed Amendment would enter into force only if three fifths (60 percent) of the members having four fifths (80 percent) of the total voting power accepted the amendment and so notified the Fund. The Proposed Amendment could be accepted only in its entirety; it was not possible for members to accept only some provisions as modified and reject others. In addition, a Part IV contained the draft resolution that the Executive Directors recommended to the Board of Governors for adoption. Annexed to the resolution was the proposed text of the amended Articles of Agreement, that is, an unencumbered text of the amended Articles, with a related index. These documents were sent in English, French, and Spanish, although only the English version was the authentic text for legal purposes.[7]

The Board of Governors quickly adopted the resolution without meeting, voting by mail by April 30, 1976.[8] But the acceptance by members took another two years, much longer than had initially been expected. Because the First Amendment

---

[6]E.B. Decision No. 5049-(76/51), March 24, 1976; Vol. III below, pp. 559–60.

[7]See *Report on Second Amendment* (cited in fn. 5 of Chap. 36). Except for the Appendix to Part II and the proposed text of the amended Articles with related index (Part IV), this report is reproduced in Vol. III below, pp. 317–76.

[8]Resolution No. 31-4, Vol. III below, pp. 375–76.

had gone through the constitutional procedures of governments relatively expeditiously and became effective within 14 months, the Managing Director and staff originally expected a similar period for members' acceptance of the Second Amendment. By November 1976, however, more than six months after the Proposed Second Amendment had been submitted to the membership, only Japan and the United States, among the largest members of the Fund, and 9 smaller members— Bahrain, Bangladesh, Bolivia, Chad, Indonesia, New Zealand, the Philippines, Saudi Arabia, and Senegal—had notified the Fund of their acceptance. By the middle of May 1977, only 26 members, accounting for only about a third of the total voting power, had sent their acceptance notifications to the Fund. Many members with the largest quotas, such as Australia, Brazil, Canada, France, the Federal Republic of Germany, India, Italy, the Netherlands, Sweden, and the United Kingdom, still had not accepted the amended Articles. At its meeting in September 1977, the Interim Committee expressed concern at the delay and urged all members that had not yet accepted the Amendment to do so at the earliest possible date.[9]

There were several reasons why the acceptance was so drawn out. First, the new Articles and the long Commentary had to be translated into other languages. Only after member governments had put these documents into their own languages could their processes of acceptance begin. Second, officials of administrations and of executive branches of governments, and then members of parliamentary committees and of legislatures, raised many technical questions that had to be answered. Third, national legislation had to be drafted to give effect to the Second Amendment. In many instances, the termination of existing par values necessitated amending legislation. In some instances, necessary national legislation raised constitutional issues that also had to be resolved. In France, for example, one of the opposition parties in the National Assembly raised a constitutional question concerning the legislation passed to accept the Second Amendment which had to be resolved by the Constitutional Council.[10] Finally, in many instances, other national legislation also had to be amended.

It was to take until April 1, 1978 before the Fund could inform its members that the Proposed Second Amendment had at last been accepted by the number of members having the requisite proportion of total voting power. By that date, 97 members exercising 83.97 percent of the total voting power had finally sent their notifications to the Fund, and the amended Articles entered into force for all 133 members of the Fund, whether they had accepted the Amendment or not. The effective date for the entry into force of the Proposed Second Amendment was thus two years after the Amendment was first sent to the Board of Governors for its approval and 23 months after submission of the proposal to members for their acceptance.

---

[9]Communiqué of Interim Committee, September 24, 1977, par. 6; Vol. III below, p. 234.

[10]Discussion of the constitutional issue raised in France can be found in Joseph Gold, *The Fund Agreement in the Courts*, Vol. II (cited in fn. 1 of Chap. 37 above), pp. 284–94.

SIGNIFICANCE AND SCOPE OF THE CHANGES

The entry into force of the Second Amendment of the Articles of Agreement on April 1, 1978 brought to an end the extraordinary period in the history of the Fund that began on August 15, 1971 when the United States suspended the official convertibility of the dollar. This period of nearly seven years was characterized by the illegality of international monetary arrangements; no members were performing their exchange rate obligations in accordance with the Fund's Articles. During this period officials of the Fund had continuously sought to find ad hoc solutions to enable the Fund to conduct its financial operations and transactions in its General Account and to facilitate transactions in SDRs, the Fund's new reserve asset.

As of April 1, 1978, the Fund functioned under totally revised Articles. Few provisions of the original Articles remained unchanged and fundamental changes were made in several of its concepts.

The broad principles on which the staff started to prepare draft amendments were retained throughout the drafting. The final version of the Second Amendment did indeed contain provisions that enabled the Fund to deal with immediate problems, such as managing the use of its resources and the SDR in an era characterized by floating exchange rates and the reluctance by officials to use gold in international settlements. The Second Amendment provided a better institutional structure in the Fund by making improvements concerning the Executive Board and by making room for a permanent Council of Governors if members so desired. The Second Amendment strengthened the Fund's ability to function effectively as a financial, supervisory, and regulatory organization, for example, by giving the Fund some authority over floating exchange rates. It also once again made exchange arrangements legal.

The Second Amendment did not cover all the topics for possible amendment which had been listed by the Committee of Twenty in Part II of the *Outline of Reform*. The amended Articles contained, for instance, no provisions specifically authorizing or obliging the Fund to establish a substitution account through which members might exchange their holdings of gold or reserve currencies for SDRs. Nor was express provision made for a link between the allocation of SDRs and development finance. No provision was included obliging members to consult the Fund on the introduction or intensification of restrictions on trade or on other current account transactions for balance of payments reasons. The staff prepared draft amendments on these topics and the Executive Board discussed them, but proposed draft amendments on these topics were abandoned when it became apparent that agreement was still impossible even after consideration at the ministerial level in the Interim Committee.[11]

---

[11]In addition to the description of the discussions of a gold substitution account in Chapter 32, information on a substitution account is to be found in Gold, *Use, Conversion, and Exchange of Currency* (cited in fn. 2 of Chap. 35 above), pp. 105–110; and Gold, "Substitution in the International

The final product was complicated, the outcome of an unusual exercise in international negotiation. In general, the main features of the Second Amendment allowed the Fund's members to choose their exchange arrangements, aimed at a gradual reduction of the role of gold in the international monetary system, aspired to make the SDR the principal reserve asset of the system, modernized the Fund's financial operations and transactions, and made changes and allowed for possible changes in the Fund's organizational structure, and gave the Fund the capability to adapt to further developments in the international monetary system.

Monetary System" (cited in fn. 6 of Chap. 32 above), pp. 265–326. In the absence of a specific amendment, any substitution account would come under Article V, Section 2(*b*), a general provision that authorizes the Fund to perform financial and legal services consistent with its purposes.

CHAPTER

39

Retooling the Fund to Implement the New Articles

N *UMEROUS CHANGES IN THE ARTICLES OF AGREEMENT* made
by the Second Amendment required the Executive Directors to undertake a
full-scale review of the Fund's By-Laws and Rules and Regulations. Many of the
Fund's general decisions also needed to be reviewed. In 1946, when the Fund first
began, initial By-Laws and Rules and Regulations had been written and several
general decisions had been taken to implement and interpret the Fund's original
Articles. Now a review of these was needed to ensure that they were compatible
with the new Articles of Agreement and that they provided the necessary operating
principles and procedures to enable the Fund to implement the amended Articles.
Additional general decisions were also needed to implement the amended Articles.

This process went on for about two years while the Second Amendment was
being considered by member governments. The process was tantamount to a
retooling of the Fund: it was a reshaping of the original legal and procedural
instruments needed for carrying out the Fund's transactions and operations. So that
he might assist in the retooling process, Mr. Gold, who had reached the Fund's
mandatory retirement age of 65, remained on as General Counsel and Director of the
Legal Department for another two years.

AMENDING THE BY-LAWS AND
REVISING THE RULES AND REGULATIONS

Now that the proposed amended Articles had been approved by the Board of
Governors and circulated to member governments for their acceptance, the
Executive Directors started in March 1977 to consider revisions of the By-Laws and of
the Rules and Regulations. Of the two, the By-Laws are paramount in the hierarchy
of legal provisions of the Fund since they represent determinations by the Board of
Governors. The Managing Director and staff also considered it useful to tackle the
By-Laws first because they were less detailed than some of the other material that

would have to be revised in the light of the amended Articles. The By-Laws deal with such topics as the location of the Fund's headquarters and the conduct of business by the Board of Governors—for instance, holding their Annual Meetings, authorized attendance at these meetings, the agenda, the selection of the Chairman and Vice Chairmen, keeping a summary record of the proceedings, the Executive Directors' Annual Report to the Board of Governors, and voting by the Governors. The By-Laws also deal with topics concerning the Executive Directors, such as their terms of service, their exercise of authority delegated by the Board of Governors, their adoption of regulations for the conduct of the Fund's business, and the handling of vacancies on the Executive Board or adding to its size. In addition, the By-Laws cover such matters as the Fund's budget and audits of its financial accounts, countries' applications for membership in the Fund, and procedures for amending the By-Laws.

The set of By-Laws that the Executive Board started to consider in March 1977 had never before been amended, although a few changes had been made, especially regarding salaries and expenses, the Fund's budgets and audits, and changing the unit in which the Fund's accounts were kept from U.S. dollars to SDRs.

By June 13, 1978 the Board of Governors had adopted amendments to all but 2 of the 26 sections of the By-Laws as they existed on March 20, 1972.[1] Sections 23 and 25 were deleted, reducing the By-Laws to 24 sections. Former Section 23 had since 1968 allowed for a Committee of the Board of Governors on Interpretation of the Articles which had never been established. Former Section 25 dealing with applications for "other holders" of SDRs was now to be added to the Rules and Regulations because the power to prescribe other holders was no longer conferred by the Articles on the Board of Governors, but devolved on the Executive Directors. A majority of the amendments to the By-Laws in 1978 were made merely to adjust the wording of the By-Laws to the change in usage in the amended Articles of the term "Executive Board" instead of "Executive Directors."

The Rules and Regulations supplement the Articles of Agreement and the By-Laws adopted by the Board of Governors. The Executive Board adopts the Rules and Regulations and simply notifies the Board of Governors of any changes in them.

Revising the Rules and Regulations was more complicated than amending the By-Laws. The Rules and Regulations provide numerous operating rules, regulations, definitions, and procedures by which the business of the Fund is conducted. They deal with such topics as the conduct of the meetings of the Executive Board (C-Rules); the precise method by which a country is to apply for membership in the Fund or to request a change in its quota (D-Rules); the method by which members are to pay their subscriptions to the Fund (E-Rules); how a member is to propose to change its par value (F-Rules); techniques by which the operations and transactions

---

[1]For the By-Laws as of March 20, 1972, see *History, 1966–71*, Vol. II, pp. 158–67. The amended By-Laws, as of August 1, 1979, are in Vol. III below, pp. 447–56.

of the Fund with its members are to be executed (G-Rules); and the provision by members of information to the Fund regarding their exchange controls and currency practices and the method by which a member might complain to the Fund about the exchange controls or practices of another member (H-Rules). Many of these A- through H- Rules had been approved by the Governors on September 25, 1946 at the time of the First Annual Meeting. Other A- through H- Rules had also been approved in the early years of the Fund, in 1947, 1948, and in the early 1950s. A few changes were also made in September 1969 in order to allow for activities involving SDRs.

In addition to the A- through H-Rules, the Fund's Rules and Regulations contained a lengthy section spelling out details for the payment of charges on drawings under the General Account, for effecting repurchases, for the rates of charge on drawings, and for the payment of remuneration on members' creditor positions in the Fund (I-Rules). They also spelled out how the Fund's accounts were to be kept and reported (J-Rules); the procedures to be followed if a member's access to the Fund's resources was to be limited (K-Rules); the techniques to be used to control large capital outflows from members (L-Rules); relations between the Fund's members and countries that were not Fund members (M-Rules); and regulations governing the Fund staff (N-Rules). As with the A- through H- Rules, so most of the I- through N- Rules were originally adopted in September 1946. On September 18, 1969, two months after the First Amendment had gone into effect, Rules were added relating to exchange rates in terms of the SDR and procedures regarding transactions in SDRs (O-Rules); reconstitution of SDRs (P-Rules); interest, charges, and assessments in respect of SDRs (Q-Rules); and suspension of the use of SDRs (R-Rules). On March 20, 1972, a revision was made to accommodate the changeover from use of the U.S. dollar to use of the SDR in the Fund's accounts.[2]

Because of the nature of the Rules and Regulations and because of the far-reaching scope of the Second Amendment, substantial revision of the Rules and Regulations was required. Some revisions were simple. The term Executive Directors was changed to Executive Board to conform with the amended Articles of Agreement and the amended By-Laws. The nomenclature in the Rules and Regulations was changed from General Account to the General Resources Account, and the new concepts in the Articles of Agreement of the General Department and Special Drawing Rights Department were added to the Rules and Regulations. Other revisions in the Rules and Regulations reflected the experience of the Fund since 1946. For example, the rules governing how a country applies for membership were updated. Revisions of the Rules and Regulations were needed also because of the changes in the Articles of Agreement concerning par values and gold. Substantial revisions had to be made in the I-Rules (relating to charges, repurchases, and remuneration) and in the O-Rules (on valuation of currencies in terms of the SDR)

---

[2]The Rules and Regulations as of March 20, 1972 were reproduced in *History, 1966–71*, Vol. II, pp. 168–91.

and other Rules relating to the SDR. After revision the Rules and Regulations went through to S- and T-Rules.[3]

SEVERAL NEW DECISIONS TO IMPLEMENT THE AMENDED ARTICLES

A number of general decisions, particularly with regard to the use of the Fund's resources, also had to be taken by the Executive Board in order to implement the provisions of the amended Articles. Some of these general decisions involved only small changes in wording. For instance, the decision on the Subsidy Account taken in 1975 needed only to have the phrase "in excess of its quota" deleted and replaced with the phrase "subject to charges" to make the original decision specifying how the subsidy was to be calculated conform with the amended Articles.[4] Other decisions were also relatively simple. For instance, once the amended Articles had gone into effect, decisions were needed to permit members' drawings under the oil facility and under the buffer stock facility to float alongside the reserve tranche. Hence, well ahead of April 1, 1978 the Executive Board took decisions explicitly stating that the Fund's holdings of a member's currency as a result of purchases under these two special facilities were to be excluded when the reserve tranche was calculated for that member.[5]

Because of the inclusion in the amended Articles of a requirement that members exchange their currencies for "freely usable currencies" when their currency is purchased from the Fund or is to be used in repurchase, the Executive Board had to take a decision specifying which currencies are "freely usable currencies." In March 1978, just before the Second Amendment went into effect, the Executive Board decided that the deutsche mark, the French franc, the Japanese yen, the pound sterling, and the U.S. dollar are freely usable currencies.[6] Members other than the issuers of these five currencies were to make arrangements for exchanging their currencies into one of these five. (By the end of 1978 most members had agreed on arrangements for this purpose.)

The Executive Board also had to take a decision agreeing to the revised forms that stand-by and extended arrangements would have after the Second Amendment. In September 1977 such a decision was taken, giving as attachments the new form for a stand-by arrangement and the new form for an extended arrangement.[7] In a similar manner, a decision had to be taken at about the same time for the form of

---

[3]In the first half of 1979, the N-Rules (on staff regulations) were substantially revised. The Rules and Regulations, as of August 1, 1979, following this revision of the N-Rules and agreement to the changes by the Board of Governors are in Vol. III below, pp. 471–74.

[4]E.B. Decision No. 5694-(78/35), March 17, 1978; Vol. III below, p. 503.

[5]E.B. Decisions Nos. 5371-(77/51), April 8, 1977, effective April 1, 1977 and 5591-(77/163), December 5, 1977; Vol. III below, p. 560.

[6]E.B. Decision No. 5718-(78/46) G/S, March 31, 1978; Vol. III below, pp. 556–57.

[7]E.B. Decision No. 5546-(77/138), September 14, 1977; Vol. III below, p. 515.

the stand-by arrangement and of the extended arrangement to be used in connection with supplementary financing.[8]

In December 1977 the Executive Board also took a new general decision, effective April 1, 1978, specifying the exchange rates the Fund would use in its operations and transactions and would use to compute the value of its holdings of members' currencies in the General Resources Account in order to determine their value in terms of the SDR. Some decision was needed to implement the provisions of Article V, Sections 10 and 11. The decision taken demonstrates how technical and complicated it was in a world of floating exchange rates to provide for the exchange rates to be used in the Fund's operations and transactions and to evaluate the Fund's holdings of the currencies of its members. The principle of equal value, regardless of the currency involved, that applies to the use of SDRs by participants had to be made effective. That principle was now to be implemented by use of representative exchange rates based on market rates instead of the par values used in the past.

The decision provided for two sets of rates. The exchange rate for computations by the Fund relating to the currency of a member in the General Resources Account was to be the rate as of three business days before the "value date" of an operation or transaction between the Fund and another member, and if this rate could not be used, the rate of the preceding closest day that was practicable.[9] The exchange rates at which the currency was held by the Fund were to be used for all other purposes.

The distinction between the two sets of exchange rates was based on the need to ensure that a rate of exchange close to the value date would be applied if another member was involved in an operation or transaction with the Fund, while this need did not arise if only the issuer of the currency was involved. If only the issuer was involved, a more up-to-date adjustment of the value between the member and the Fund could be made at some later date. Meanwhile, there was no prejudice to the interests of the Fund or the member. This practice moderated the need for the more frequent adjustments that might be called for by a practice that took closer cognizance of the fluctuations in the value of a currency in terms of the SDR.

The decision also provided that the Fund's holdings of currencies could be adjusted on other occasions as well, as when a computation relating to a currency was made as just described. These other occasions were at the end of the Fund's financial year, when a member requested an adjustment of the Fund's holdings of its currency, and on such other occasions as the Fund might decide. In addition,

---

[8]E.B. Decision No. 5585-(77/161), November 30, 1977; Vol. III below, pp. 518–23.

[9]"Value date" is a term commonly used in banking and business parlance. It is the date on which the value of a transaction, including the exchange rate to be used for valuing the transaction, is determined. This date usually precedes, by about three business days, the date on which the actual transaction takes place. The term became frequently used in the Fund after the end of the par value system. In the days of par values, the value of an exchange rate was simply the par value, and there was no need to refer to a special date for valuing a transaction. With the introduction of floating rates and of a changing value for the SDR, however, some date for determining the exchange value of an operation had to be selected.

because of the Fund's continuous use of U.S. dollars for administrative purposes, the Fund's holdings of U.S. dollars were to be adjusted on the last business day of each month.

Whenever it adjusted its holdings of a member's currency, the Fund was to establish an account receivable or an account payable, as the case might be, for the amount of currency payable by or to the member. In computations for the purposes of the Articles, the Fund's holdings of a member's currency were deemed to include the balance in any account receivable or to exclude the balance in an account payable. Settlement of an account receivable or an account payable was to be made by or to a member promptly after the end of the Fund's financial year and at other times when requested by the Fund or by the member. Complicated and detailed as it was, this decision brought to an end the legal and operational problems concerning the values at which the Fund had conducted its transactions and operations during the previous seven years.[10]

A decision was also needed to cover situations in which a member was unable to pay charges in SDRs either because it was not a participant in the Special Drawing Rights Department or because its holdings of SDRs were insufficient.[11]

In order to implement the new exchange arrangements, the Executive Board also had to take a decision requiring members to notify the Fund of the exchange arrangements that they intended to apply under the new Article IV. This decision clarified in some detail what notifications were to be made to the Fund when members made changes in their exchange arrangements.[12]

DECISIONS REGARDING REPURCHASES

In the course of 1978, the Executive Board took several decisions which clarified members' responsibilities with regard to their repurchase obligations under the Second Amendment. The timing of repurchases of drawings made under the various facilities was spelled out and permission was granted to members to discharge any outstanding repurchase obligations payable in gold with SDRs or, at a member's option, with the currencies of other members specified by the Fund.[13]

Moreover, inasmuch as the Second Amendment provided that a member would normally be expected to repurchase as its balance of payments and reserve position improved, the Fund had to establish guidelines for these "early repurchases" and did so by an Executive Board decision in March 1978. The criterion for an improvement in a member's balance of payments and reserve position was

---

[10]E.B. Decision No. 5590-(77/163), December 5, 1977, effective April 1, 1978; Vol. III below, pp. 526–27.

[11]E.B. Decision No. 5702-(78/39) G/S, March 22, 1978, effective April 1, 1978; Vol. III below, p. 526.

[12]E.B. Decision No. 5712-(78/41), March 23, 1978; Vol. III below, pp. 492–94.

[13]E.B. Decisions Nos. 5703-(78/39), March 22, 1978, effective April 1, 1978, and 5809-(78/88), June 12, 1978; Vol. III below, pp. 523–24, 526.

whether the Fund could justify the sale of the member's currency or the designation of the member to accept transfers of SDRs. A member would not be expected, however, to make any repurchase before a stated period after a drawing. A formula was adopted to determine the amount of the repurchase that was expected: a member was expected to repurchase holdings of its currency equivalent to 1.5 percent of its latest gross reserves plus (minus) 5 percent of the increase (decrease) in gross reserves over the latest six-month period for which data were available. Expected repurchases were limited to 4 percent of a member's latest gross reserves and to an amount that would not reduce these reserves below 250 percent of the member's quota.[14]

Despite all the efforts of the management and staff in trying to simplify repurchase obligations when the Articles were amended, as recounted in Chapter 35, repurchase obligations were in danger of again becoming complicated. Rules for repurchase previously set forth in the Articles were now being set forth in decisions of the Executive Board.

In addition, the Executive Board took a decision freeing each member to attribute a reduction in the Fund's holdings of its currency to any of its obligations to repurchase.[15] The term "obligations to repurchase" is of unusual importance, however. Members have no authority to reduce those Fund's holdings of their currencies that are not subject to charges because such holdings are not subject to repurchase obligations. Holdings of a member's currency resulting from drawings in the reserve tranche, for instance—which are not subject to charges or to repurchase obligations—cannot be repurchased by the member. Notably, a member having drawn its reserve tranche cannot of its own accord reinstitute its reserve tranche position in the Fund.

Elimination of Augmentation Rights Under Stand-By and Extended Arrangements

In taking decisions about repurchases, the Fund had yet another problem. For many years, a typical stand-by arrangement had provided that a member could augment the amount it might purchase under the stand-by arrangement by the amount of any repurchases already effected under the stand-by arrangement. This provision was included in stand-by arrangements to overcome the rigidity of the formulas for repurchase obligations under the Articles prior to the Second Amendment. Under the formulas, a repurchase obligation could accrue during the period of

---

[14]E.B. Decision No. 5704-(78/39), March 22, 1978, effective April 1, 1978; Vol. III below, pp. 525–26. In 1979, the Executive Board reviewed the Fund's experience with these guidelines and altered them somewhat. Cumulative expected repurchases during any period of four quarters were not to exceed 10 percent of a member's latest gross reserves, and a member's repurchases made in advance of maturity, or sales of its currency, in excess of the minimum reduction expected during a quarter were to be taken into account when the Fund determined expected repurchases during the following five quarters. As of late 1984, these guidelines for early repurchase had been applied only in very few instances.

[15]E.B. Decision No. 5705-(78/39), March 22, 1978; Vol. III below, p. 526.

a stand-by arrangement solely because of a purchase under that arrangement, for example, because of the increase in the Fund's holdings of the member's currency resulting from a purchase under the stand-by arrangement. A member would not necessarily have to have any increase in its reserves. Because the formulas were rigid, it was not possible to eliminate the member's obligation to repurchase. Fund officials considered it appropriate, therefore, to temper the effect of these formulas by permitting a member to augment the amount of a stand-by arrangement by the amount of a repurchase in respect to purchases under the stand-by arrangement. Thus, early in the history of stand-by arrangements, a stand-by arrangement was usually written so as to include a provision to the effect that the amounts available under the arrangement should be augmented by amounts equivalent to repurchases in respect of purchases under the stand-by arrangement, unless at the time of a repurchase the member informed the Fund that it did not wish to avail itself of the augmentation.[16]

After the extended Fund facility was introduced in 1974, a limited form of augmentation was used also in extended arrangements. Under an extended arrangement, drawings might be augmented during each year by the amounts of repurchases made during the same year in respect of purchases under the arrangement, but the augmentation could not be made as a result of repurchases made subsequently. Augmentation under either a stand-by arrangement or an extended arrangement did not give the member any more net resources than the amount initially provided for in the arrangement.

With the elimination in the Second Amendment of the repurchase formulas of the original Articles, there was no longer a clear need for the augmentation provision. In fact, under the less rigid repurchase provisions of the amended Articles and with the free attribution of repurchases, which became a matter of practice in March 1977 and a matter of official policy in April 1978 when the Second Amendment went into force, there was a risk that augmentation rights could be abused. Augmentation rights combined with the freedom to attribute repurchases would also allow a member with a current stand-by or extended arrangement which made *any* repurchase in effect to "renew" the amount of such arrangement, after it had already made drawings under the arrangement. After March 1977, when the free attribution of repurchases was begun as a practice, a number of members had, indeed, already begun to attribute repurchases incurred as a result of past drawings to purchases made under current stand-by arrangements and had subsequently redrawn the amounts thereby becoming available. Thus, an unintended consequence of the new freedom given to members to attribute reductions in the Fund's holdings of their currencies to any of their obligations to the Fund was a considerable increase in the scope of the augmentation provision typically inserted into stand-by

---

[16]A description of the history of augmentation rights, including a change in practice made in 1959, can be found in Joseph Gold, *The Stand-By Arrangements of the International Monetary Fund: A Commentary on Their Formal, Legal, and Financial Aspects* (Washington: International Monetary Fund, 1970), pp. 86–96.

and extended arrangements. In addition, since the period of time for which stand-by arrangements were granted was gradually being lengthened, the likelihood was greater that a member might experience improvements in its balance of payments and reserve position during the life of the stand-by arrangement, and the risk enhanced that a member might indeed repurchase some of the Fund's holdings of its currency during the time the stand-by arrangement was in force. For these reasons, the management and staff, early in 1978, recommended to the Executive Directors that augmentation rights in stand-by and extended arrangements be eliminated.

The case for eliminating augmentation rights was not immediately acceptable to many members of the Executive Board. Among industrial members, the United Kingdom had the most vital interest in the Fund's repurchase policies, since it had frequent recourse to the Fund and the stand-by arrangement approved in early 1977 was still in force. Mr. Kent made a strong case for retention of some limited form of augmentation rights. He was supported by other Executive Directors. The staff restudied the situation, but concluded that all ways of retaining augmentation rights were too complicated to implement in practice, especially in the context of the more liberal rules for repurchase. Upon reconsideration, the Executive Directors therefore agreed in March 1978 that the texts of stand-by and extended arrangements approved after the date of the Second Amendment, including the texts of such arrangements in connection with the supplementary financing facility, would not provide for augmentation rights to make purchases under the arrangements.

DECISIONS ON CURRENCIES USED

Once the Second Amendment went into effect, a number of issues also had to be decided in order to implement the new provisions with respect to the currencies used in the Fund's transactions and operations. The Second Amendment provided that the Fund would apply similar criteria in the preparation of both the operational budgets for drawings and repurchases and the designation plans for transferring SDRs. Hence, criteria had to be determined for selecting the members whose currencies were to be used in drawings and repurchases and for selecting the members which might be designated to provide freely usable currency in exchange for the receipt of SDRs. The principles that should determine the amounts of currencies to be used and received by the Fund and the amounts of SDRs to be used in drawings and repurchases also had to be formulated. The rules of designation and the methods of calculating amounts for which participants might be designated in the operation of the SDR system also had to be decided. The central questions at issue were these. How should the Fund apply the amended Articles of Agreement to the operations and transactions, both through the General Resources Account and the Special Drawing Rights Department, in which it could influence the distribution of Fund-related reserve assets, such as reserve positions in the Fund and holdings of SDRs, with consequential effects on the composition of members' reserves? Which members should be required to increase (or decrease) their holdings of Fund-related assets? How should the amounts be distributed? Particularly important was the definition of a "sufficiently strong combined balance of payments and gross reserve position," since the inclusion of members in operational budgets and in designation plans depended on that definition. A member whose balance of payments and reserve position was relatively strong was to be prepared, in exchange for Fund-related reserve assets, to make its currency available to a member whose position was relatively weak. From the Fund's point of view, it was important that Fund-related assets move to members that would be relatively firm holders of these assets; the Fund needed some assurance that recipients would not need to encash these claims on the Fund in the near future.

As 1978 came to a close, the Executive Board was just beginning to discuss these questions. In the meantime, the operational budgets and the designation plans for SDRs were being drawn up in much the same manner as before. For the first time, however, the operational budget and the designation plan for SDRs for each quarter were considered together. The amended Articles had been in effect for only nine months, and the Fund was still developing methods and techniques for living with them.

PART NINE

Analyzing the World Economy (1972–1978)

"*Three decades of existence of the Fund and the Bank have brought progress and a better life for the people of the world. Like you, I want to build on that record to achieve still further economic cooperation, progress, and a better life.*"

—President Jimmy Carter, addressing the Board of Governors, in Washington, September 25, 1978

CHAPTER

40

Expansion of the World Economic Outlook Project

O NE OF THE FUND'S PRINCIPAL RESPONSES to the troubles plaguing the world economy in the 1970s was an expansion of a project known internally as the "World Economic Outlook." Earlier chapters, notably Chapter 17 where the impact of the 1973 oil price increases and the origin of the Fund's oil facility were described and Chapter 20 where the shaping of the Fund's policies to the world economic problems persisting after 1974 was discussed, described the Fund's accelerating concern with continuing worldwide economic and financial problems, the attitudes toward these problems taken by Fund officials, and the explicit ways in which the Fund tried to help its members deal with these problems. What Fund officials stated publicly about the world economy, as expressed in the Annual Reports of the Executive Directors to the Board of Governors and in the speeches of the Managing Director, as well as some of the rationale for the solutions suggested and the policies proposed to a large extent derived from the world economic outlook exercise.

The world economic outlook project consisted of regular, informal discussions in the Executive Board of recent trends in world economic developments and of the short-term outlook for these developments based on comprehensive assessments prepared by the staff. Although this project was well launched by 1972, the year with which this History starts, subsequent events were to propel it into the forefront of the Fund's activities. The expansion of the project from its limited, experimental beginning in 1969 to a broadly based activity encompassing input from Fund staff in a number of departments, regularly discussed at length in the Executive Board, regularly considered by the Interim Committee, and eventually quoted on the front pages of the world's leading newspapers, exemplifies how the Fund worked in the 1970s.

ORIGIN OF THE PROJECT

Ministerial-level assessments of the economic situation and outlook of its members had been taking place within the OECD for years and were often quoted by financial officials. In 1966 and 1967 the Fund staff, believing that the Fund ought to increase its attention to broad world economic developments, circulated several papers on the world payments situation, which were discussed by the Executive Board. Several Executive Directors, Mr. Schleiminger in particular, welcomed these papers and discussions.

The first world economic outlook paper was circulated to the Executive Directors in June 1969. It was a short paper prepared in the Research Department, regarded only as giving "some notes and statistical material as a basis for discussion of the short-run outlook for the world economy." It described prospective changes in aggregate demand, output, prices, and trade balances for the rest of 1969 and the first half of 1970 in the seven largest industrial Fund members—Canada, France, the Federal Republic of Germany, Italy, Japan, the United Kingdom, and the United States. Although the staff made some independent estimates for prospective changes in macroeconomic variables, reliance was placed mainly on estimates published by member governments, as, for example, in their budget presentations, and use was made of estimates prepared by the OECD Secretariat.

With this paper as background, the Executive Board met in informal session for discussion of the outlook for the world economy. The discussion was only partially successful. In addition to Mr. Schleiminger, Mr. Kafka welcomed "this new experiment," especially since OECD reports were not available to Executive Directors elected by Fund members that did not belong to the OECD. But many of the Executive Directors queried the usefulness of such sessions, contending that the Executive Board's agenda was too full for informal academic discussions in which no decisions needed to be taken.

As the events of 1970—especially an unusually large U.S. payments deficit—began to undermine the par value system, regular appraisals by the Executive Board of the short-term outlook for the world economy and the international monetary system seemed to Mr. Schweitzer and the staff to have merit. The Fund had no multimember consultations in which several members were obliged simultaneously to consult the Fund on their policies, particularly their exchange rate policies, and Mr. Schweitzer and the staff were inclined to think that regular reviews of world economic outlook could in effect substitute for those consultations. Reviews of the world economic outlook would enable the Executive Directors to focus on the economic situation and policies of the main industrial members together rather than individually as in the usual consultations process. Mr. Schweitzer and the staff decided on a trial procedure. Staff papers to be used as the basis for appraisals of the world economic outlook would delineate trends and problems and raise questions rather than present staff views. Although comments from staff in other departments would be solicited, these papers would be the responsibility of the Research Department, a different procedure from that customarily used for staff memoranda in which a joint view of the staff of various departments was agreed upon and supported by the Managing Director before it was presented to the Executive Board.

In January 1971, a world economic outlook paper along these lines was circulated to the Executive Board. In keeping with the idea that the Executive Directors' discussions were to be in informal sessions in which the exchange of views would be unofficial and as free as possible, the paper was more speculative than the staff memoranda papers ordinarily presented to Executive Directors. Accordingly, a new series of "Informal Documents" was introduced for these papers. Because of their informal nature, the papers were considered highly confidential and distribution even within the Fund was restricted.

This initial paper, describing recent changes in demand, production, and prices in the largest industrial members and the broad character of their demand-management policies, presented projections for changes in output and prices for 1971. This time, the staff translated into its own projections estimates for gross national product published by the seven large industrial members. These staff projections were based on the assumption that existing policies, such as monetary, fiscal, and exchange rate policies, would continue; thus they did not attempt to allow for subsequent changes in policies. The staff also made estimates for flows of international trade for 1970 (for which final data were not yet available) and projections for 1971, including some estimates and projections for primary producing members. In addition, the staff gave descriptions of developments in commodity markets, general trends in the prices of products widely traded, and changes in countries' shares of export markets. In a final section of the paper, several trends warranting discussion by the Executive Board were set out, the following four of which are noteworthy. First, many of the underlying economic forces at work in industrial members were becoming universal and the national policy decisions to be made were becoming increasingly interdependent. Second, the economic projections of industrial members in the previous several years had consistently proved overly optimistic, with output overstated and price increases understated. Third, to help cope with inflationary pressure, some industrial members, most notably the United Kingdom, were beginning to use incomes policies. Fourth, as a result of the huge U.S. balance of payments deficit in 1970, developing members as a group had achieved very favorable levels of foreign exchange reserves.

In general, the Executive Directors liked the type of informal discussion that they held on the basis of this paper. Executive Directors from developing members were pleased with the inclusion of projections for the trade of their countries and urged that attention be devoted also to the short-run prospects for output, investment, and prices in developing members. They emphasized that the Fund differed from the OECD in that it contained representatives of developing countries. Therefore, the Fund's assessment of the world economic outlook ought to cover in a comprehensive way the outlook for developing countries as well as for industrial countries.

The second paper in the new Informal Document series was circulated in May 1971 for an Executive Board discussion in June. The Executive Board's discussion of this paper established holding periodic reviews of the short-term world economic outlook. By now the meaning of "short term" was also becoming established as approximately the next 6 to 18 months. But the staff continued to use different time horizons from one paper to the next, depending on the circumstances being analyzed.

The staff paper of May 1971 covered roughly the same material as that of January 1971 except for somewhat greater coverage of developing members. It updated the projections for gross national product (GNP) for 1971 for the largest industrial members, described the prospects for international trade of industrial and of primary producing members, including developing members, and presented a fairly full description of the balance of payments developments of all economic categories of members and the short-term prospects for their payments positions. Issues for discussion by the Executive Directors included factors bearing on the outlook for the international payments situation, especially the disturbing short-term capital flows in mid-1971 threatening the stability of the international monetary system and the possible coordination by national governments of policies to help control such flows. The Executive Directors were also to address the prospects in 1971–72 for increases in the external trade of primary producing members.

The Executive Directors all welcomed this stimulating paper. They were especially pleased that the paper not only highlighted the economic outlook for industrial members but also dealt extensively with the outlook for trade and payments of developing members and their related problems.

Because of the suspension of dollar convertibility three months later, in August 1971, and attention to the negotiations which led to a realignment of exchange rates at the Smithsonian Institution in December 1971, the next world economic outlook paper was not circulated until well into 1972, and the Executive Board discussion took place in May. This third paper included projections for real GNP and for prices (GNP deflators) for 1972 for ten industrial members, with Belgium, the Netherlands, and Sweden being added to the "big seven." There were also projections for merchandise exports and imports for industrial members individually and for groups of primary producing members. In addition, the paper contained an analysis of the balance of payments developments for all economic groupings of countries since 1970 and of the outlook for the global pattern of payments for the rest of 1972. The questions and issues for Executive Board discussion this time centered on the factors bearing on the international adjustment process, that is, the process of adjusting global balance of payments disequilibria, with pointed reference to the likely effects of the exchange rate realignments of December 1971. The basic paper was accompanied by two additional papers, also prepared in the Research Department, one of which assessed the impact of the December 1971 exchange rate realignments on the value of members' official reserves and the other the impact on the trade of developing members. In June 1972, a third companion paper, prepared by the Exchange and Trade Relations Department, assessed the impact of the exchange rate realignments on the external debt of developing members. This paper was also made available in French and in Spanish, an arrangement limited to papers of widespread interest.

PROJECT COMES OF AGE IN 1973

The world economic outlook project was to come fully of age in 1973. Three developments converged in that year to add to the importance of this project. First, staff in other departments began to participate with the staff of the Research Department in the preparation of papers. In the January 1973 paper, the forecasting part of the project was made a joint effort of the Research Department and of three of the five Area Departments, the Asian, European, and Western Hemisphere Departments. With the participation of Area Departments, the staff projections could be virtually independent of projections done outside the Fund, could be enlarged to cover all the countries that the Fund then classified as industrial, that is, 14 Fund members (Austria, Belgium, Canada, Denmark, France, the Federal Republic of Germany, Italy, Japan, Luxembourg, the Netherlands, Norway, Sweden, the United Kingdom, and the United States) and Switzerland, not a Fund member, and could cover not only changes in total output (real GNP) and overall prices (GNP deflators) but also in unit labor costs in manufacturing industries. With the participation of Area Departments, the projections for trade balances and external current accounts of the 15 industrial countries also could be made mutually compatible. In other words, projections for each of the industrial countries individually took into account the projections being made for the other industrial countries. In addition, much greater material was possible for what the Fund then classified, mainly for statistical purposes, as "more developed primary producing members."[1] Forecasts were thus made for exports and imports, in volume and value terms, for trade balances, for balances on services and private transfers, and for current account balances of broad groups of primary producing members; for exports (giving value, prices, and volume) of major groups of commodities, such as food, agricultural materials, petroleum, other minerals and metals, and manufactures; for changes in real GNP and GNP deflators for 12 more developed primary producing members, namely 9 European members (Finland, Greece, Iceland, Ireland, Malta, Portugal, Spain, Turkey, and Yugoslavia) and for 3 members in the Southern Hemisphere (Australia, New Zealand, and South Africa); and for the growth of exports for each of these 12 more developed primary producing members.

In a format that was to become fairly standard, a general survey set forth the principal economic problems facing members, the policies they were currently pursuing, and short-term projections for the main economic variables. Following the general survey, a separate section on industrial members indicated, country by country, the main assumptions about the monetary, fiscal, and exchange rate policies that underlay the projections. A separate section on primary producing members described both for the more developed and the less developed countries the main trends in their trade and payments and the short-term outlook for their trade and payments. At the end, an ever-growing statistical appendix supplied details, country by country, of the economic indicators used and of the principal projections being made.

---

[1]The individual members in each category are listed in Chap. 2, fn. 11, p. 42.

In the mid-year assessment in June 1973, this evolving format was divided into two papers, a general survey and a background information paper. The general survey summarized economic trends and gave for industrial members projections of real GNP and GNP deflators for 1973 and 1974, thereby extending projections somewhat further than the projections of earlier papers. Projections continued to be based on the assumption of "present policies." For a few countries, present policies have been interpreted to encompass certain policy adaptations or changes that seem likely to occur even though they have not been announced by the authorities.

As in the past, the general survey again undertook to describe developments in international trade and payments and the prospects for external trade and current account balances for both industrial and primary producing countries for 1973 and 1974, by broad groups of countries and for the main industrial countries individually. In addition, it discussed the factors bearing on the outlook for capital flows and overall adjustment of payments imbalances, and through use of the multilateral exchange rate model (MERM) analyzed the effects of the exchange rate changes in the major currencies that had taken place since 1970, including those following the introduction of floating rates earlier in 1973. The second paper containing background material was the product not only of the staff of the Research Department and of the three Area Departments previously participating but also of the staff of the Exchange and Trade Relations and the Treasurer's Departments. The latter two departments made substantial contributions to a summary of recent developments in foreign exchange and gold markets, to a review of trends in the flows of short-term capital during the previous two years, and to explanations of the disturbing capital flows in terms of changes in interest rates and in capital controls. Statistical tables contained data that went back to 1960 as well as the projections for 1974.

Mr. Witteveen's Interest and the Incorporation of Special Consultations

The second development in 1973 bringing an additional dimension to the world economic outlook project was the arrival in September of Mr. Witteveen as Managing Director. Challenged by the complexities of the severe economic problems confronting the world in the 1970s and believing that the international community should provide leadership in the analysis and solution of the problems, Mr. Witteveen, himself an economist, became deeply interested in assessments of the world economic outlook and in the policies that members might most appropriately pursue. He was to push into the forefront of his own work and public speeches consideration of the near-term prospects for world economic conditions and action that might be taken by officials in industrial countries. In January 1974 he involved the members of the Committee of Twenty in evaluating the then critical world economic situation following the steep jump in oil prices. Thereafter, he was regularly to involve members of the Interim Committee in wide-ranging discussions of short-term world economic prospects and in taking positions on proposed policies. In these respects, Mr. Witteveen can be said to have established the world economic outlook as one of the Fund's primary endeavors.

The third development in 1973 which gave momentum to the project was the decision in October to incorporate in the papers on the world economic outlook the results of the special consultations with selected members to be inaugurated in November 1973.[2] This development, too, was largely the result of Mr. Witteveen's interest both in special consultations and in the world economic outlook exercise. Special consultations were not confined to discussions of exchange rate policy, but went into other policies, such as fiscal, monetary, and trade policies, and national officials expressed their views on the short-term prospects in their countries for prices, output, budgetary phenomena, and trade and payments. Hence the results of these special consultations were ideal for incorporation into the world economic outlook assessments. The papers circulated in December had the benefit for the first time of the information obtained in special consultations. Later, as the review of the world economic outlook took place more than once a year, so were special consultations conducted as part of the project held more than once a year.

In 1973 there were also other significant developments in the project. The hazards of forecasting economic phenomena, even for the short run, were graphically demonstrated by the experiences of the staff in December 1973. Having finished writing the papers on the world economic outlook on December 19, 1973, the staff circulated the papers to the Executive Directors and looked forward to a relaxing celebration of the coming Christmas and New Year's holidays after an unusually hard-working stint. Just after the papers had been circulated the oil exporting countries decided on the first round of increases in crude oil prices, effective January 1, 1974. Immediately the staff had to hurriedly revise all its projections and analyses.

These revised projections, circulated in the first week of January 1974, relating the dire expectations of massive balance of payments disequilibria for all Fund members for 1974, laid the basis for Mr. Witteveen's proposal in mid-January for an oil facility in the Fund, as described in Chapter 17. The staff's projection of a $65 billion surplus for the major oil exporting countries in 1974 proved quite accurate. The final revised figures available some years later showed the 1974 oil exporters' surplus at $68 billion. The accuracy of their projections was a matter of some satisfaction to the staff inasmuch as these projections had been made extremely quickly, within a few days, and other forecasters at the time had missed the mark by a wide margin.

FURTHER GROWTH OF THE PROJECT

The coverage of world economic outlook papers continued to expand. As world economic problems became more intractable, the staff's analysis increasingly went beyond projecting the short-term outlook to discussion of the policies that members were pursuing and how these policies might be changed and coordinated

---

[2]The inauguration of special consultations has been described in Chap. 15.

to improve the outlook for the world economy. At each review, the Executive Directors devoted hours to informal discussions which gradually became fuller, franker, more frequent, and more focused. In this way the world economic outlook exercise became the vehicle by which Executive Directors exchanged views among themselves on the prospects for the world economy, the vehicle for reacting and responding to the views of the Managing Director on Fund policy, and the vehicle for Executive Directors to sort out their positions to be expressed in the Annual Report and in papers presented to the Interim Committee. The world economic outlook studies accordingly grew to be an integral part of the work of the Fund, contributing both to the development of the Fund's own policies and to the establishment of a global framework against which the Fund could evaluate the economic policies and performance of individual members.

Inclusion of Measures to Evaluate Fiscal Impact

Starting in 1975, work done by the Fiscal Affairs Department designed to refine the analysis of government budgets of industrial members was incorporated in the world economic outlook exercise. Financial officials and economists in national governments were finding it useful in their analyses of the impact of the budget on the economy to separate the changes taking place from one year to the next in a government's budget (that is, the changes in the aggregate levels of expenditure and revenue) that were associated in some measurable way with cyclical swings in the economy from those changes that could be attributed to other factors, including changes in fiscal policy. The Fund staff deemed it desirable to make a similar separation in the governmental accounts used in world economic outlook papers. They decided to use an adaptation of the "cyclically neutral budget" technique developed and used by the Council of Economic Experts of the Federal Republic of Germany. The staff preferred the cyclically neutral concept because they believed that, although subject to limitations, cyclically neutral budget balances were simpler to calculate than were budgetary surpluses or deficits based on the full employment budget concept used at the time in the United States. Moreover, the concept placed less emphasis on the distinction used in other countries between automatic and discretionary changes in fiscal aggregates.

According to the concept of the cyclically neutral budget, government expenditure was cyclically neutral if its growth was in proportion to the growth of *potential* output (converted to current prices by use of the GNP deflator) and was expansionary (contractionary) when it grew faster (slower) than potential output. Revenue was cyclically neutral when it changed in proportion to *actual* GNP. The cyclically neutral fiscal balance was the difference between cyclically neutral revenue and expenditure. The difference between this cyclically neutral fiscal balance and the actual fiscal balance gave an indication of the expansionary or contractionary impact of the budget (after adjustment for cyclical factors as measured by the cyclically neutral concept) compared with the budget in a base year (for which the staff selected 1972). Year-to-year changes in the impact could thus be taken to measure stimulative or restrictive fiscal "impulses" that were not oversensitive to the choice of the base year.[3] In later years, use of the concept of the cyclically neutral budget in world economic outlook papers was somewhat reduced.

More Companion Papers

Starting in 1975, separate long studies prepared by the staff on topics of general interest were also occasionally circulated to the Executive Directors as part of the world economic outlook project and discussed in the Executive Board. The general survey paper circulated at the end of 1975, for instance, was accompanied by a separate study describing developments in the non-oil primary producing countries and assessing their short-term prospects in greater depth than was feasible in the general survey, and the survey paper circulated in the middle of 1976 was accompanied by a separate study describing the payments positions and prospects of the major oil exporting countries. By this time, all five Area Departments were participating in the preparation of world economic outlook papers.

The world economic outlook project thus came to involve a general survey, a statistical summary or supplement, a background information paper, and separate papers on topics of current concern. The project had clearly evolved into an intensive staff effort describing in depth the trends in major economic phenomena for the various economic categories of members and for many members individually, presenting refined projections for the main macroeconomic variables, and analyzing broad current policy questions of special interest to financial officials in the Fund's members as a result of the outlook for the world economy.

The intensive effort by the staff of a number of departments involved in the world economic outlook exercise can be illustrated by the papers prepared in 1978. There were six lengthy papers in all. The general survey gave projections through the first half of 1979, discussed recent and prospective changes in domestic economic activity and the policies being pursued for four groups of countries, the industrial members, the major oil exporting members, the non-oil developing members, and the more developed primary producing members. It evaluated the functioning of the international adjustment process since the onset of the oil price increase in 1974. It

---

[3]A detailed study by Fund staff of the various measures used to evaluate the macroeconomic impact of a budget can be found in Sheetal K. Chand, "Summary Measures of Fiscal Influence," *Staff Papers*, International Monetary Fund (Washington), Vol. 24 (July 1977), pp. 405–49. An explanation by the staff of the concept of a cyclically neutral budget as used in the Federal Republic of Germany can be found in Thomas F. Dernburg, "Fiscal Analysis in the Federal Republic of Germany: The Cyclically Neutral Budget," *Staff Papers*, Vol. 22 (November 1975), pp. 825–57. The concept of the full employment budget used in the United States gave an estimate of what the budget surplus or deficit of a given set of expenditure and taxation policies would be if the economy were at full employment. A description and analysis of this concept by the staff is to be found in Daryl A. Dixon, "The Full Employment Budget Surplus Concept as a Tool of Fiscal Analysis in the United States," *Staff Papers*, Vol. 20 (March 1973), pp. 203–26. A discussion by the staff of a third technique, which distinguished between automatic and discretionary budget effects, can be found in Robert G. Di Calogero, "Techniques of Fiscal Analysis in Sweden," *Staff Papers*, Vol. 21 (July 1974), pp. 463–83.

presented staff views of a scenario under which coordinated policies by the industrial members could provide a sustained improvement of the world economy and a faster reduction of persistent balance of payments imbalances, as was described in Chapter 20. A second paper, "Supporting Material on the International Adjustment Process," provided analyses of the recent and prospective external positions of the four major groups of countries and of the largest industrial members individually. The background information paper presented the results of research on three problems emerging as particularly in need of attention: the weakness of private investment in the main industrial members and the reasons why private investment was lagging, including the possibly low profitability of business enterprises, the continually high levels of unemployment in the major industrial members, and the flare-up of inflation in non-oil developing members. A fourth paper brought together some 45 statistical tables used in support of the three other papers based on estimates and projections prepared by the staff in the Area Departments and the Research Department, who relied in part on the data fund compiled in the Fund's Bureau of Statistics. For industrial members, there were tables giving such variables as real output, price increases, real consumption and investment, employment and unemployment, and labor costs and productivity, as well as the usual economic projections and indicators. There were also tables giving exports and imports (volume and value), terms of trade, balance of payments positions, and financing for industrial members, major oil exporting members, and non-oil primary producing members. An appendix gave the estimated impact of fiscal balances in selected industrial members. In addition to these four papers, two studies prepared by the staff of the Exchange and Trade Relations Department under the general heading, "The Rise in Protectionism," were issued as supporting papers for the exercise, to be discussed by the Executive Board and distributed to members of the Interim Committee.[4]

INVOLVEMENT OF THE INTERIM COMMITTEE

A crucial development in the evolution of the world economic outlook project was the involvement of high-level financial officials in discussions of the world economic outlook based on these papers. In January 1974 the Committee of Twenty discussed the prospects for the world economy and endorsed the idea of an oil facility in the Fund. At its last meeting in June 1974, the Committee of Twenty took note of world economic developments, especially of governments' policies for combating inflation, which was emerging as the major problem of 1974, and for dealing with the large oil-related payments deficits.[5]

In September 1974, the timing of the Executive Directors' reviews of the world economic outlook began to be geared to the timing of the Annual Meetings and

---

[4]The Fund later published part of this study as *The Rise in Protectionism*, Trade and Payments Division, Bahram Nowzad, Chief, IMF Pamphlet Series, No. 24 (Washington, 1978).

[5]The Communiqué of Committee of Twenty, June 13, 1974, pars. 4 and 5; Vol. III below, pp. 201–02.

meetings of the newly established Interim Committee. The next full-scale review of the world economic outlook scheduled for January 1975 was thus held by the Executive Directors on January 8, just a few days ahead of the Interim Committee meeting scheduled for January 15–16. For the first time, too, the world economic outlook papers were made available to the members and associates of the Interim Committee, together with a note from the Managing Director describing the key issues. The practice thereby began of the Managing Director's submitting to the Interim Committee a "Note on the World Economic Outlook" that greatly condensed the larger papers and of having discussions of the world economic outlook regularly placed on the Interim Committee's agenda. As an illustration of the linking of the review of the world economic outlook by the Executive Directors to the meetings of the Interim Committee, in 1978 the full-scale review of the world economic outlook usually held by the Executive Directors in January of each year was postponed until April so that it would take place just ahead of the Interim Committee meeting scheduled for the end of that month.

As the members of the Interim Committee turned their attention to the world economic outlook, their discussions inevitably influenced their decisions about Fund policy. In January 1976, the projections made by the staff in the latest world economic outlook paper included greatly expanded projections for the balance of payments positions of many developing members. Based on detailed input by the staff of the five Area Departments, these projections were done country by country. The persistent large payments deficits projected for many non-oil developing members for 1976 influenced the Interim Committee to endorse the temporary enlargement of the credit tranches, pending the completion of the Sixth General Review of Quotas, recommended by the Executive Directors.[6] Because of this direct impact of the work on the world economic outlook on an agreement of the Interim Committee to go along with an important decision on use of the Fund's resources, this project was now generally recognized within the Fund as an influential force in the Fund's policymaking process. All the Fund staff now gave the world economic outlook project increasing attention.

In April 1978, moreover, the Interim Committee agreed with the "coordinated economic growth scenario" developed in the course of the staff work on the world economic outlook, as described in Chapter 20. The Committee reached consensus "on the general outlines of a coordinated strategy, containing mutually supportive and reinforcing elements, designed to promote noninflationary growth of the world economy" in the medium term, through 1980.[7] Partly because of this decision, partly because of the work of the OECD in presenting its own broad program of internationally concerted action by members to achieve more sustained economic growth, and partly because of pressure from the Group of Twenty-Four, action for a coordinated growth strategy was also taken at the summit level in July 1978.[8]

---

[6]See Chap. 27 above.

[7]Communiqué of Interim Committee, April 30, 1978, par. 3; Vol. III below, pp. 235–36.

[8]For the statements of the Group of Twenty-Four on this issue, see Communiqué of Group of Twenty-Four, April 28, 1978, pars. 3, 4, 5, and 7; Vol. III below, pp. 652–53.

When Prime Minister Pierre Trudeau, President Valéry Giscard d'Estaing, Chancellor Helmut Schmidt, Prime Minister Guilio Andreotti, Prime Minister Takeo Fukuda, Prime Minister James Callaghan, and President Jimmy Carter met in Bonn on July 16–17 for their fourth economic summit, they agreed on a "comprehensive strategy" of concerted "mutually reinforcing" action to promote world economic recovery. Each country spelled out its proposed program of action. As attention turned to the Federal Republic of Germany, German officials, heavily pressured by world opinion to take measures to stimulate their economy, altered their previous position and promised to propose to their legislative bodies "additional and quantitatively substantial measures up to 1 percent of gross national product, designed to achieve a significant strengthening of demand and a higher rate of growth."[9]

The Fund's world economic outlook exercise can thus be said to have had a role, in conjunction with the work of other bodies, in influencing policymaking at the highest levels.

INTERNAL IMPACT

The project also had an important internal impact. Faced with the need to make regular projections of the macroeconomic variables and assessments of the economic prospects for each member for world economic outlook papers, staff in all Area Departments devoted more effort to evaluating the economic outlook in the individual members on which they worked and the near-term policies that these members were likely to pursue. In addition, staff in the Research Department circulated to all Area Departments masses of information, data, and projections for members collected throughout the Fund. For instance, computer printouts were circulated giving projections for gross national product, prices, money supply, composites of interest differentials, budgetary data, and estimates for trade flows for nearly all members. In effect, the information supplied on each member enabled the economist covering an individual Fund member to take systematically into account a synthesis of statistical work and analytic views of colleagues elsewhere in the Fund bearing on the prospects for that member. Thus, the staff in one Area Department making projections for members in a given geographic region became aware of the projections made for members in other regions by staff in other Area Departments. For example, staff in the Middle Eastern Department making projections for oil exporting members and staff in other Area Departments making projections for non-oil developing members could take into account the developments being projected for the industrial members by staff in other departments. In an integrated world economy, such coordinated staff work was imperative, but before the world economic outlook project, any interdepartmental consultation had usually been informal and sporadic.

---

[9]Excerpts from the declaration issued at Bonn following this economic summit meeting can be found in *IMF Survey* (Washington), Vol. 7 (July 31, 1978), p. 237.

The world economic outlook project benefited greatly from the input of staff of the Area Departments, and the staff of Area Departments benefited greatly from the coordination of projections for all Fund members done by the staff of the Research Department.

PUBLICATION

From the beginning of the project Erik Brofoss, Executive Director from Norway, had urged that the Fund publish at least some portions of these "high-quality" papers so as to give the analysis greater public attention. The management and staff and many of the other Executive Directors were reluctant, however, to publish any substantial portion of the studies. They were concerned that publication could adversely affect the nature of the project itself. Officials of member governments supplied the staff with highly confidential information and views, especially on their exchange rate policies, in the special consultations in preparation for the world economic outlook. They were willing to have free and candid discussions with the staff because these discussions were confidential. Information obtained by the staff in these special consultations was given only in general terms even to the Executive Board. No details for individual governments were revealed.

After the April 1978 meeting of the Interim Committee in Mexico City, Mr. Witteveen made his "Note on the World Economic Outlook" available to the press on an informal basis. Subsequently, Mr. de Larosière took a direct interest in the publication of the world economic outlook papers.[10]

---

[10]In May 1980, the Fund published the first of what has become a series of comprehensive annual reports entitled *World Economic Outlook: A Survey by the Staff of the International Monetary Fund*.

PART TEN

Living with Floating Rates (1973–1978)

"In the final analysis the success of surveillance must depend on the members themselves—on the policies they follow and on their willingness to cooperate with the Fund and with each other."

—J. DE LAROSIÈRE, speaking in Chicago on November 14, 1978

CHAPTER
41

Variability of
Exchange Rates
(1973–1977)

F *LOATING RATES* were zealously examined and assessed not only by Fund
officials, but also by monetary experts, economists, bankers, and businessmen
everywhere. Some of the interest in the experiences with floating rates stemmed
purely from curiosity. After years of debate about the wisdom—or folly—of letting
exchange rates be flexible, both those favoring flexible rates and those opposed were
keen to see them tested in practice and to praise or condemn them accordingly. But
most of the interest was policy oriented. The emergence of floating rates, which left
exchange rates to market forces, did not end concern about exchange rate policy. On
the contrary, exchange rate policy continued to be of intense concern to individual
nations and to the international community. Just as they had when the par value
system existed, economic experts and policymakers fervently debated the appropriateness of alternative exchange rate policies, including policies that the Fund should
adopt.

Developments in exchange rate arrangements and in members' exchange rate
policies from the beginning of the floating rate era in March 1973 until the end of
1977 are described in this chapter. Chapter 42 presents a preliminary analysis of the
floating rate experience. Chapter 43 describes the Fund's surveillance of exchange
rates from 1975 to 1978, picking up where Chapter 16 left off. Chapter 44 contains a
discussion of the special crisis of the U.S. dollar that took place in 1978.

A VARIETY OF ARRANGEMENTS

For the first two years or so after March 1973 when floating rates were
introduced for several major currencies, the enormous debate over how the Fund
should treat these rates made it impossible for the Fund even to characterize the
nature of the overall system. Fund documents customarily termed it "widespread
floating" or "generalized floating," but Fund officials were fully aware of the

deficiency of this terminology. Members were pursuing a variety of exchange rate arrangements and the majority did not have a floating rate. Many still had some form of a fixed exchange rate. Another problem was that members frequently changed their exchange rate arrangements, and without the obligation to inform the Fund of their latest arrangements, it was difficult for the staff even to keep abreast of the arrangements being followed. Moreover, for the Fund to classify members' exchange arrangements was controversial. Given the heated debate that went on until January 1976 about the desirability of floating versus fixed rates, officials were unsure about the policies the Fund was likely to adopt toward exchange rate arrangements. In the meantime, many relatively smaller members hesitated to be stamped as having a floating rate. In addition, because officials, finding their way while the international monetary system was continuously changing, wanted to retain as much flexibility in their exchange rate policies as possible, they preferred not to have the Fund classify their arrangements.

By early in 1976, most of these difficulties had ended. The provisions of Article IV of the Second Amendment, agreed in January 1976, resolved the question of members' notifying the Fund of their exchange arrangements by obliging them to do so. The matter of having the Fund classify exchange rate arrangements also became less sensitive. By that time member governments had more or less decided how they were going to respond to the new regime of floating rates and were making changes in their exchange arrangements less frequently. Fund officials could at last, as a start in understanding and assessing the new exchange rate situation, officially classify members' arrangements. These arrangements, as of early in 1976, fell into five categories: (i) pegging to a single currency; (ii) pegging to a composite (or basket) of currencies, including the SDR; (iii) pegging to a single currency but with frequent changes being made in the peg according to a predetermined formula; (iv) joint floating under mutually agreed intervention arrangements; and (v) independent floating. The staff thereafter periodically circulated to the Executive Directors statements tabulating exchange rate arrangements of all members into these five categories. Arrangements existing on June 30 of each year were published in the Annual Report.

The vast majority of members pegged their exchange rates, that is, their exchange rate arrangements fell under the first two of the five categories listed above. Specifically, on June 30, 1978, 95 of the Fund's 135 members maintained pegged rates. Of these, 63 pegged to a single currency, that is, to the U.S. dollar, to the pound sterling, to the French franc, or to some other currency. Another 32 pegged to the SDR or to some other basket of currencies, and this group was growing in number.

The other 40 members had floating rates of one form or another, that is, their exchange rate arrangements fell under the last three of the five categories listed above. These members included most of the large industrial members. In Europe most of the countries belonging to the EC participated in the European narrow margins arrangement (the snake), in which they undertook to maintain maximum margins of 2.25 percent between their own currencies, but floated against the U.S. dollar. As of June 1978, Belgium, Denmark, the Federal Republic of Germany, Luxembourg, the Netherlands, and Norway were participating in the snake, but Sweden and France had also been participating for most of the period since 1973. The currencies of these 8 members thus all floated against the dollar, and when any of them left the snake arrangement, they, too, temporarily had floating rates against all major currencies. All other members had fully floating rates, although a few of these members periodically adjusted their rates according to a set of indicators. Table 32 lists the members in each of these five categories.

Because the great bulk of members had some form of pegging arrangements, the system resembled a pegged or fixed rate system. But since the largest members had floating rates and since much of the pegging done by other members was to currencies that were themselves floating, the system could rightfully be regarded as a floating rate system.

Rather than simply use the number of members with fixed or floating rates to characterize the system, the staff preferred use of the amount of world trade conducted at fixed and at floating rates and used two methods to measure it. The simplest measure was merely to count the value of each member's exports in accordance with the five-way exchange rate classification described above. By this measure, less than one fifth of world trade in 1978 was carried out by the more than 90 members classified as having pegged rates. The second measure, which the staff preferred, took into account the amount of trade actually conducted at pegged and at floating rates. Thus, for members whose currencies were pegged to the U.S. dollar, only their trade with the United States and with other members whose currencies were pegged to the U.S. dollar was counted as being conducted at fixed exchange rates. Their trade with other members (for example, with Canada, with the United Kingdom, and, as the U.S. dollar fluctuated vis-à-vis the snake currencies, with members of the European common margins arrangement) was regarded as being conducted at floating rates. In the same way, members of the European snake arrangement conducted trade both with countries that were inside the arrangement and with others that were outside it. The result of such a measurement for the members of the snake was that, although the proportion varied for individual countries, on average less than one third of the total exports of the members of the snake as of 1978 was conducted at pegged rates, and the rest was conducted at floating rates.

Using this second measure for all of world trade, the staff again calculated that less than one fifth of trade in 1978 was conducted at pegged rates and four fifths at floating rates. The similar results derived from the two methods arose because the trade of members classified as having pegged rates that was actually conducted at floating rates was roughly equal to the trade of members classified as having floating rates that was actually conducted at pegged rates. While any measure of the relative extent to which pegged or floating rates were used should extend beyond trade to other international transactions, including services and capital flows, and while

Table 32. Exchange Rate Arrangements,[1] June 30, 1978

Currency Pegged to					
U.S. dollar	Pound sterling	French franc	Other single Currency	SDR	Other composite[2]
Bahamas	Bangladesh	Benin	Equatorial Guinea (Spanish peseta)	Bahrain	Algeria
Barbados	Gambia, The	Cameroon	Lesotho (South African rand)	Burma	Austria
Bolivia	Ireland	Central African Republic		Guinea	Cyprus
Botswana	Seychelles	Chad		Iran	Fiji
Burundi	Sierra Leone	Comoros	Swaziland (South African rand)	Jordan	Finland
China[5]		Congo		Kenya	India
Dominican Republic		Gabon		Malawi	Kuwait
Ecuador		Ivory Coast		Mauritius	Malaysia
Egypt		Madagascar		São Tomé and Principe	Malta
El Salvador		Mali		Tanzania	Mauritania
Ethiopia		Niger		Uganda	Morocco
Ghana		Senegal		United Arab Emirates	New Zealand
Grenada		Togo		Viet Nam	Singapore
Guatemala		Upper Volta		Zaïre	Sweden
Guyana				Zambia	Thailand
Haiti					Tunisia
Honduras					Western Samoa
Indonesia					
Iraq					
Korea					
Lao People's Dem. Rep.					
Liberia					
Libya					
Maldives					
Nepal					
Nicaragua					
Oman					
Pakistan					
Panama					
Paraguay					
Romania					
Rwanda					
Somalia					
South Africa					
Sudan					
Suriname					
Syrian Arab Republic					
Trinidad and Tobago					
Venezuela					
Yemen Arab Republic					
Yemen, People's Dem. Rep. of					

Floating Jointly[3]	Floating but Rates Adjusted According to a Set of Indicators[4]	Floating Independently	
Belgium	Brazil	Afghanistan	Malawi
Denmark	Colombia	Argentina	Mexico
Germany, Federal Republic of	Peru	Australia	Nigeria
Luxembourg	Portugal	Burma	Papua New Guinea
Netherlands	Uruguay	Canada	Philippines
Norway			
		Chile	Qatar
		France	Saudi Arabia
		Greece	Spain
		Guinea-Bissau	Sri Lanka
		Iceland	Turkey
		Israel	United Kingdom
		Italy	United States
		Jamaica	Viet Nam
		Japan	Yugoslavia
		Lebanon	

[1]Excluding Democratic Kampuchea, for which information is not available. For members with dual or multiple exchange markets, the arrangement shown is that in the major market.
[2]Comprises currencies that are pegged to various baskets of currencies of the members' own choice, as distinct from the SDR basket.
[3]Refers to the cooperative arrangement maintained under the European narrow margins arrangement.
[4]Includes exchange arrangements under which the exchange rate was adjusted at relatively frequent intervals, on the basis of indicators determined by the respective member countries.
[5]See fn. 6 in Chap. 2.

supplementary information on the currencies actually used for invoicing trade or for carrying out capital transactions would provide still greater accuracy, sufficient data were not available to enable the staff to undertake these more refined measures.

FACTORS INFLUENCING THE ARRANGEMENTS USED

Why the large industrial members resorted to floating rates in the first place and why European members belonging to the EC decided to float jointly against the dollar have already been described in Chapter 4. These same reasons caused these members to continue their floating and snake arrangements through 1978, the end of the period reviewed here. By the start of 1974, policymakers had decided that inflation in industrial countries, differences in countries' rates of inflation and in their degrees of tolerance for inflation, and the large imbalances in their current account payments positions made the indefinite continuation of floating rates inevitable.

Given floating rates for the major currencies, officials of other members were influenced by many factors in choosing an exchange arrangement. Industrial members in Europe with relatively small open economies, namely, Austria, Belgium, Denmark, Finland, Luxembourg, the Netherlands, Norway, Sweden, and Switzerland, wanted some type of stable rate arrangement. Since most of their trade was within Europe, either they used the snake arrangement, wholly or partly, or pegged to some composite of currencies. European members that had more inflation or greater balance of payments problems than this group, such as Greece, Israel, Spain, Turkey, and Yugoslavia, had recourse to floating rates.

As the larger developing members in Latin America, such as Argentina, Brazil, Chile, and Colombia, had inclined toward flexible exchange rates even when the par value system was in operation, in a floating rate world, they readily turned to floating rates. Even Mexico, which had long held sacred a fixed relation between the Mexican peso and the dollar, introduced a floating rate in 1976.

Developing members in Africa and Asia had long had fixed exchange rate relationships, usually with the pound sterling or with the French franc. They tended to peg their rates mainly for administrative convenience; as a first step, for many pegging involved no more than the continuation of their existing practice. Continuing to peg to the single currency in which most of their trade was denominated also ensured that the trade with their major trading partner was conducted at a stable exchange rate. The smaller developing members, including many in Latin America, also pegged their currencies because they feared that independent floating might result in unstable exchange rates that would hamper their development planning efforts and jeopardize inflows of foreign capital and possibly even domestic investment.

As time went on, many developing members gave up use of the pound sterling as a peg and turned to the U.S. dollar. Officials of developing members became increasingly aware of the major disadvantage of pegging to any single currency:

developments in the balance of payments of the major country whose currency was used as the peg brought about exchange rate changes in the currency of the developing member and these exchange rate changes were not necessarily consistent with the needs of the developing member's own balance of payments position. Such changes could interfere with the developing members' own internal economic and monetary policies and objectives. As several developing members emerged as newly industrializing countries and evolved a more diversified pattern of trade and of trading partners, they also found that, with wide fluctuations taking place among the exchange rates for the major currencies, pegging to a single currency resulted in disruptive fluctuations in the prices of a large portion of their exports or imports.

For these reasons, an increasing number of developing members began to switch from pegging to a single currency to pegging to some composite of currencies. This composite was usually a combination of the currencies of their trading partners or the SDR. It was significant that among the members switching their pegging arrangement was India, which had for decades pegged to the pound sterling. In choosing a composite of currencies, officials of developing members especially liked to peg to the SDR, for several reasons. The composition of currencies in the SDR basket was determined by the Fund, which relieved government officials of the need to decide which group of currencies to peg to. The SDR basket of currencies, moreover, was well known and not likely to be suddenly changed. The value of the SDR, furthermore, was calculated daily, and this information was generally available.

The most appropriate criteria for a developing member to use in choosing an exchange rate policy began to emerge in the second half of the 1970s as one of several new topics concerning exchange rates to which the Fund staff turned its attention.[1]

Additional Diversity and Changeability of Arrangements

Exchange rate practices were even more diversified than the five major categories of arrangements suggested. This diversity tended to increase after the formal recognition in January 1976 that free choice of exchange arrangements was to be legal under the Fund's amended Articles. Currencies officially regarded as floating were often managed in such a way that they were little different from formal pegging arrangements. Conversely, some members that maintained a formal peg made frequent adjustments of the peg or permitted relatively wide margins around the peg, so that some pegged rates really were not fixed exchange rates.

---

[1]See, for instance, Andrew D. Crockett and Saleh M. Nsouli, "Exchange Rate Policies for Developing Countries," *Journal of Development Studies* (London), Vol. 13 (January 1977), pp. 125–43, reprinted in *Finance in Developing Countries*, P.C.I. Ayre, ed. (London: Frank Cass, 1977), pp. 125–43; Leslie Lipschitz, "Exchange Rate Policy for a Small Developing Country, and the Selection of an Appropriate Standard," *Staff Papers*, International Monetary Fund (Washington), Vol. 26 (September 1979), pp. 423–49; and Leslie Lipschitz and V. Sundararajan, "The Optimal Basket in a World of Generalized Floating," *Staff Papers*, Vol. 27 (March 1980), pp. 80–100.

Members were much more inclined than in the past to reappraise their exchange rate policies and to let such reappraisals lead to changes in their exchange rate practices or policies. For example, in the three calendar years 1968–70, only Canada, and, for a brief period, the Federal Republic of Germany, changed from a fixed peg to a floating rate. By contrast, in the three years 1973–75, most members changed their exchange rate arrangements. In 1973, in addition to the introduction of floating rates by several large industrial members and of a joint float by several large industrial European countries, Greece, Iceland, and Yugoslavia elected to float independently, and Finland, Malaysia, New Zealand, and Singapore adopted composite pegging arrangements. In 1974 there were 10 changes in members' exchange arrangements, including a temporary floating by France and South Africa and the introduction of a floating rate by Nigeria. In 1975 there were 22 changes in exchange arrangements, the great majority of which were movements from a unitary peg to pegging to a composite of currencies. (In 1976 and 1977 there were fewer changes in exchange practices since by that time many members were already operating under arrangements that they considered appropriate to the new circumstances; even so, in 1976 Mexico stopped pegging to the dollar to float independently, and in 1977 Portugal and other members made basic changes in their exchange arrangements.)

The frequency with which members changed their exchange rate arrangements, as well as the introduction of arrangements that permitted more flexibility of exchange rates, reflected a much greater inclination by financial officials of all members to reconsider their exchange rate policies as balance of payments pressures mounted. Even members that used pegging arrangements were more prepared than they had been for decades to change their intervention points as a means of responding to balance of payments disequilibria. For example, in the three years 1968–70, of the 99 members that were continuously operating under par values or unitary pegs and were members of the Fund during the entire period, only 6 proposed changes in their par values to the Fund or adjusted their pegged rates. In the three years 1974–76, by contrast, of the 73 members that continuously maintained a unitary peg (or a peg to the SDR), 19 members made one or more changes in their intervention points.

Several factors induced members to give greater attention to exchange rate policy as part of their overall economic strategy. Most important, the unstable economic conditions and high level of worldwide inflation after 1972 made any fixed exchange rate inappropriate more rapidly than in the 1950s and 1960s when economic conditions were stable and rates of inflation low. Second, the rapid changes occurring in the structure of world trade in the 1970s and uncertainty on the part of officials as to how to adapt their exchange rates to these changes necessitated greater attention to exchange rates. Third, officials of smaller members that adopted the technique of pegging to a single currency found themselves experiencing severe disadvantages when the currency used as the peg itself fluctuated widely; hence, they were forced to re-examine their exchange rate policy. Last, the breakdown of the par value system encouraged officials of all members, as they formulated their overall economic policies, to give more active consideration to the role of the exchange rate.

FLEXIBLE RATES PROVE TO BE FLUCTUATING RATES

The era that began in 1973 was quickly characterized by highly volatile floating rates of major industrial members. Exchange rates for the major currencies changed widely from day to day, from week to week, and from one calendar quarter to the next. Many of the fluctuations were abrupt and were often soon reversed. "Flexible exchange rates" in practice became "fluctuating rates."

Attention centered especially on the rates for the dollar vis-à-vis the European currencies in the snake, particularly the deutsche mark; on the rates for the dollar vis-à-vis European currencies not in the snake, particularly the pound sterling and the Italian lira; and on the rates for the dollar vis-à-vis the Japanese yen and the Canadian dollar. Vis-à-vis most of these currencies the dollar dipped sharply early in 1973 when floating rates were first introduced. Then, as the energy crisis began in late 1973, the dollar strengthened and rebounded during the first months of 1974. Frequent variations in the rates for the dollar vis-à-vis the main currencies were common again in late 1974 and throughout much of 1975. By 1975 observers detected that, in addition to the relatively large day-to-day and week-to-week changes in the dollar/deutsche mark rate, there were also cycles in the rate relationship, with each cycle lasting three to six months.

In 1976 the exchange rates for most major currencies, especially the much observed relation between the dollar and the deutsche mark, were relatively stable. Nonetheless, even in this relatively quiet year, several large movements of exchange rates occurred. The Italian lira and the pound sterling underwent sudden, deep declines after periods of stability. The Japanese yen began to appreciate as Japan once more started to move to a current account surplus after the first round of oil price increases. Frequent tension, at times extreme, erupted within the European snake arrangement, and depreciation of the franc forced France temporarily to leave the snake arrangement. Late in the year, the U.S. dollar appreciated considerably vis-à-vis the deutsche mark.

In the first six months of 1977, as in 1976, the floating rate regime seemed to be working reasonably smoothly. The Italian lira and the pound sterling made rapid recoveries, with sterling undergoing a particularly dramatic comeback after a stand-by arrangement with the Fund was approved in January 1977, while exchange rates for the other major currencies were relatively stable. But this stability again proved short lived. In the last few months of 1977 the U.S. dollar began again to depreciate, especially against the deutsche mark, the Swiss franc, and the yen. This depreciation of the dollar continued into 1978, bringing about another exchange rate crisis in October-November 1978 (described in Chapter 44). Strains in exchange markets often overflowed to the private gold markets as sudden flights from currencies into gold caused the price for gold to soar.

Early in the period of floating rates, the Fund staff decided that because of the many changes going on simultaneously in the exchange rates for the major currencies, a special technique was needed to obtain a meaningful measure of the change in the exchange rate of a particular currency. What was required was some kind of a trade-weighted exchange rate, an average "effective exchange rate."[2] At first, the staff used two types of weights to determine an average effective rate. One set of weights was derived by calculating the relative importance of 27 members in the bilateral trade for each member for which an effective exchange rate was computed. A second, and preferred, method was derived by using the weights used in the staff's multilateral exchange rate model (MERM). This model took into account the commodity composition of the member's trade and the relative importance of other members as trading partners and as competitors in third markets.[3] After a year or so of calculating effective exchange rates using both sets of weights, the staff decided to calculate effective exchange rates only on the basis of the MERM weights.

The use of effective exchange rates made it possible not only to compare the changes in the effective exchange rates for major currencies but also to examine other economic relations important in assessing exchange rate changes, such as changes in the effective exchange rates of the major currencies compared with changes in the price levels of the major industrial members, changes in effective exchange rates compared with changes in members' current account balances, and changes in effective exchange rates compared with changes in members' terms of trade. The Fund published such comparisons in its Annual Reports for 1975, 1976, and 1977.[4]

Trade-weighted exchange rates were developed by other institutions as well as by the Fund. The Morgan Guaranty Trust Company, the OECD, the U.K. Treasury, and the U.S. Federal Reserve Board, for example, all began to calculate and regularly publish figures for effective or trade-weighted exchange rates. The various indices each had somewhat different characteristics and showed somewhat different numerical measures of effective exchange rate change.[5] Nonetheless, all the

---

[2] A study by the staff done before floating rates came into being, which explained the need for the concept of an effective exchange rate and the methodology for measuring such a rate, is that of Fred Hirsch and Ilse Higgins, "An Indicator of Effective Exchange Rates," *Staff Papers*, Vol. 17 (November 1970), pp. 453–84.

[3] The MERM model was developed by the staff in the late 1960s and early 1970s to estimate the medium-term (two-year to three-year) effects of changes in the exchange rates of the large industrial members on their external trade balances. It was described in Jacques R. Artus and Rudolf R. Rhomberg, "A Multilateral Exchange Rate Model," *Staff Papers*, Vol. 20 (November 1973), pp. 591–611. Subsequently, the model was continuously used, and as time went on the staff introduced numerous changes to improve its structure, to increase its empirical content, and to modify it so as to maintain its relevance for the study of newly evolving policy alternatives. The revised model was described in Jacques R. Artus and Anne Kenny McGuirk, "A Revised Version of the Multilateral Exchange Rate Model," *Staff Papers*, Vol. 28 (June 1981), pp. 275–309.

[4] *Annual Report, 1975*, pp. 31–33; *Annual Report, 1976*, pp. 31–33; and *Annual Report, 1977*, pp. 31–35.

[5] The measures of effective exchange rates developed in the Fund were described and compared with those of other institutions by Rudolf R. Rhomberg in "Indices of Effective Exchange Rates," *Staff Papers*, Vol. 23 (March 1976), pp. 88–112.

measures showed broad similarity in the direction and general magnitude of exchange rate movements. The effective rates for the U.S. dollar, the pound sterling, the deutsche mark, the Japanese yen, the Canadian dollar, the French franc, the Italian lira, and the Swiss franc all exhibited frequent and wide fluctuations.[6]

DEVELOPMENTS IN THE SNAKE

The efforts of European countries to achieve stable exchange rates among their own currencies through the narrow margins arrangement which they set up in 1972 and changed in 1973 met with some success, although in this arrangement, too, European officials frequently experienced difficulty in keeping the agreed margins. At times countries were forced to leave the arrangement. By June 1972, when the pound sterling floated, the United Kingdom and Ireland had to suspend their participation in the snake arrangement. In February 1973, with the floating of the lira, Italy also left the arrangement.

On April 3, 1973, the European Monetary Cooperation Fund (EMCF) was established to facilitate interventions in exchange markets by the central banks of the participating countries so as to help keep exchange rates within the agreed margins. The EMCF was to administer short-term monetary support (credit of up to six months) for intra-EC settlements under the arrangement.

Then in January 1974, France, a strong advocate of the snake, had to withdraw temporarily from the arrangement because of its own balance of payments difficulties. Initially, French officials planned a withdrawal from the snake for six months, but were not able to return until July 1975, 18 months later, and then only for a short time. In 1974 only Belgium, Denmark, the Federal Republic of Germany, Luxembourg, and the Netherlands were in the arrangement.

When France returned to the snake in July 1975, the whole arrangement was working better. Belgium, Denmark, the Federal Republic of Germany, Luxembourg, the Netherlands, Norway, and Sweden, as well as France, were participating, and the Austrian schilling a. : the Swiss franc were moving closely with the rest of the snake currencies. While the effective exchange rates for the U.S. dollar and for the deutsche mark fluctuated considerably, movements in the effective rates for the other currencies in the snake were much less sharp than the dollar-deutsche mark rate because the trade of the participants in the snake other than the Federal Republic of Germany was dominated more by their relations with their trading partners within Europe than by their trade with the United States.

France's unusually good external position in mid-1975 worsened later that year, and faced again with large losses of foreign exchange reserves, France once

---

[6]The extent of the short-term variation in the effective exchange rates for these eight currencies over the period March 1973–June 1978 can readily be seen in a chart published in *Annual Report, 1978*, p. 36.

more left the snake in March 1976. As of June 30, 1976, participants in the snake were Belgium, Denmark, the Federal Republic of Germany, Luxembourg, the Netherlands, Norway, and Sweden. In March 1976 the special arrangement for narrow margins between the currencies of Belgium, Luxembourg, and the Netherlands, an arrangement referred to as the worm since it was smaller than the snake, had to be terminated.

Tensions in the snake arrangements in late 1976 led to realignments of the exchange rates for several of the participating currencies. In October the deutsche mark was appreciated by 2 percent in terms of the SDR (which was used as the numeraire for establishing intervention points under the snake arrangement), the Danish krone was depreciated by 4 percent, and the Norwegian krone and the Swedish krona were each depreciated by 1 percent. This currency realignment was needed because the difference of 4 to 5 percentage points between the rate of inflation in the Federal Republic of Germany and that in the other countries participating in the snake, especially the Nordic countries, together with the weakening of the current account balances of some of the Nordic countries, was encouraging speculative capital flows into the deutsche mark in anticipation of a realignment. Interventions in exchange markets to maintain the established currency relationships had been sizable, and several countries had been resorting to stringent domestic monetary policies in order to defend their currencies and keep their exchange rates within the agreed margins.

After the realignment of the deutsche mark and of the currencies of the Nordic countries in October 1976, tensions within the snake abated, and during the first half of 1977, rates were fairly stable. Although no speculation against their currencies had been evident, the Nordic countries made another adjustment in their intervention points in April 1977, chiefly because of the weakness of Sweden's current account and the loss in competitiveness of Sweden's exports. The Danish krone and the Norwegian krone were each depreciated by 3 percent and the Swedish krona by 6 percent. In August 1977, another realignment of the relative exchange values of the currencies participating in the snake arrangement took place. Sweden withdrew from the arrangement and devalued the krona by 10 percent vis-à-vis a basket of currencies of its main trading partners. Denmark communicated a new central rate and Norway established new intervention points in further currency realignments that represented a depreciation of 5 percent for both the Danish krone and the Norwegian krone.

In 1978 a number of realignments of the currencies of the members still participating in the arrangement again took place. In February, for example, Norway established new intervention points for the Norwegian krone which represented a depreciation of 8 percent. In October there was an adjustment of exchange rates which led to shifts, as measured by central rates, of 4 percent between the deutsche mark and the Danish krone and the Norwegian krone, and of 2 percent between the deutsche mark and the Netherlands guilder, the Belgian franc, and the Luxembourg franc. In December, Norway withdrew from the snake arrangement, leaving only

Belgium, Denmark, the Federal Republic of Germany, Luxembourg, and the Netherlands as participants. In all these years, the officials of Belgium and the Netherlands tried to keep the rates for the Belgian franc and the Netherlands guilder in line with the deutsche mark.

The snake arrangement thus continued throughout the period reviewed here, working better at some times than at others. The arrangement persisted for a number of reasons. First, adherence was flexible. When necessary, countries could withdraw from the arrangement, which some of them, such as Italy and the United Kingdom, did indefinitely. Intra-European credit was extended so as to facilitate interventions. Realignments in exchange rates were often made. Monetary policy was used to create offsetting interest rate differentials so as to influence capital flows. In addition, there was a shortage of capital funds available for speculation and there were other impediments to the movement of capital which might have upset the arrangement. European officials were also learning that if they were to maintain stable exchange rates among their currencies with less tension and greater success, they would have to integrate their economic and monetary policies more closely. To do so, they accelerated plans in 1978 for the formation of a European Monetary System (EMS).[7]

CONTRASTING VIEWS OF OFFICIALS WITH REGARD TO THE MANAGEMENT OF FLOATING RATES

Officials of the large industrial members held contrasting views about the extent to which floating rates ought to be managed or left unmanaged. In late 1971, when the exchange rates of industrial members floated for a few months for the first time, Karl Schiller characterized some floating rates as "cleaner" than others.[8] The terms "clean" and "dirty" were subsequently commonly used by economists and occasionally by public officials to distinguish a situation in which a floating rate was left wholly to market forces (a clean float) from that in which the rate was influenced by buying and selling operations (intervention) by the central bank, by the imposition of restrictions, surcharges, or advance deposit requirements as a way to restrain purchases of foreign exchange, or by other governmental actions aimed deliberately at influencing the demand for and the supply of a country's currency in exchange markets (a dirty float). Officials also differed on the extent to which they should shape their domestic monetary policies, particularly interest rate policies with a view to their external consequences. The more the exchange rates for the main currencies fluctuated, the more differing views on exchange rate policy held by officials of different countries took on the attributes of a debate.

---

[7]On December 5, 1978, the EC adopted a resolution regarding establishment of a European Monetary System, which entered into force on March 13, 1979. See also Chap. 44, pp. 866–68.

[8]Statement by the Governor of the World Bank for the Federal Republic of Germany, *Summary Proceedings, 1971*, p. 196.

In general, just as U.S. officials had argued in the Committee of Twenty for greater changes in exchange rates and just as they had favored the introduction of floating rates early in 1973, so they favored clean floating. In fact, dirty floating itself had an unfavorable connotation in the minds of U.S. officials. As a matter of philosophy, they thought that the rates for the dollar in terms of other currencies ought to be freely determined in exchange markets. As a matter of policy, they refrained from intervention in exchange markets. They resisted suggestions by officials of European members that they take action to defend the dollar. They were accused by their European counterparts of continuing to pursue a policy of benign neglect, passively letting whatever happened to the dollar take place. The preference of U.S. officials for clean floating stemmed in large part from their conviction, going back to 1969–70, that the currencies of the other industrial countries, especially the deutsche mark and the yen, needed to appreciate and that clean floating was the only way in which the dollar could be adequately realigned vis-à-vis these other currencies. They believed too that intervention would be very costly in terms of foreign exchange reserves. They also believed that so long as industrial countries were encountering different rates of inflation and payments imbalances, intervention would be futile. It was impossible to make rates for the dollar in terms of other currencies stable so long as each industrial country pursued different policies for countering inflation and had markedly different payments positions.

At his first Annual Meeting, in Nairobi in September 1973, just six months after floating exchange rates had been introduced, Mr. Witteveen spoke of the need for governments to accept responsibility for exchange rates within a context of internationally agreed rules. In his judgment, the depreciation of the U.S. dollar had been excessive and at times changes in rates were so sharp—as much as 5 percent in a few days—as to justify the view that exchange market conditions were disorderly. He advocated wider use of intervention to stabilize exchange rates and to support an appropriate and internationally agreed set of currency values. In the meantime, he believed that the Fund could play an important role in consulting with members on their intervention policies and, more generally, on monetary policies influencing exchange rates.[9] What Mr. Witteveen had in mind was some degree of management of floating rates.

The debate over management of floating rates had only just begun. At the time of the Annual Meeting in Nairobi, the negotiations in the Committee of Twenty were not completed and Mr. Shultz merely stated his "full acceptance of the idea that the center of gravity of the exchange rate system" would be a regime of "'stable but adjustable par values,' with adequately wide margins and with floating 'in particular situations.'"[10] After Mr. Simon and Mr. Bennett succeeded Mr. Shultz and Mr. Volcker in the U.S. Treasury in mid-1974, U.S. officials were even stronger advocates of free markets in general and of as little government regulation as

---

[9]Opening Address by the Managing Director, *Summary Proceedings, 1973*, pp. 19–20 and 21.

[10]Statement by the Governor of the Fund and the World Bank for the United States, *Summary Proceedings, 1973*, p. 54.

possible. Mr. Simon and Mr. Bennett were convinced that it was best for governments not to interfere with exchange rate movements. Hence, even when the rates for the dollar moved sharply downward, U.S. officials refrained from intervention.

Officials of Canada, the member with the longest experience with a floating rate, did not usually try to manage the rate for the Canadian dollar. At times when the Canadian dollar seemed to be falling too rapidly, Canadian officials engaged in active intervention, but this intervention did not result in sizable net changes in Canada's official reserves. In meetings of financial officials, they customarily supported arguments in favor of clean floating advanced by U.S. officials.

In contrast to the positions of U.S. and Canadian officials, officials of the other industrial members frequently intervened in exchange markets, often in large amounts. They also adapted their interest rates and other monetary policies at least partly with exchange rates in mind. In times of severe payments crisis, such as Italy and the United Kingdom had experienced, authorities resorted to foreign borrowing rather than let too much pressure fall on their exchange rates. The relation between the dollar and the other major currencies was thus not entirely determined by free market forces. In this sense the floating rate regime was usually termed "managed floating."

Conflicting views toward exchange rate policy were expressed at Executive Board meetings as well as at the Annual Meetings, especially beginning in 1975. By then, the earlier battle as to whether or not the Fund ought to condone or legalize floating rates was over; floating rates were recognized as inevitable for some time to come, and debate centered on how much these rates ought to be managed.

At the Executive Board discussion of the world economic outlook in June 1975, for example, there were opposing views on the management of floating rates. Mr. Cross explained the U.S. policy on intervention which was aimed only at smoothing out "violent" fluctuations in rates. It was not intended to move the exchange rate to a level different from that indicated by market forces. Taking issue with countries managing their exchange rates, Mr. Cross suggested that members with balance of payments surpluses were intervening in exchange markets, at times heavily, to support the dollar. The aim of these countries in such intervention was to prevent appreciation of their own currencies to protect their own exports.

Mr. de Vries, on the other hand, argued that there was increased unrest in European countries because the dollar exchange rate was hampering European export opportunities. The Netherlands authorities, for instance, were concerned that an exchange rate structure might develop that did not genuinely reflect the competitive positions of the industrial members. Like many European officials seeking a solution to the problem of exchange rate instability, Mr. de Vries advocated that the authorities of the industrial members coordinate their domestic monetary policies. This coordination would help to prevent large differences in interest rates and hence reduce swings in exchange rates. Officials of industrial members might go so far as to try to achieve exchange rate "targets," or "exchange rate zones," or "reference rates."

Mr. de Vries, however, realized the dilemma in coordinating domestic monetary policy. Were a country to coordinate its monetary policy with that of other countries to influence its exchange rate, the role of monetary policy for internal purposes would be reduced. Fiscal policy would have to be the mainstay of domestic economic policy. But in most industrial countries reliance mainly on fiscal policy for controlling inflation had not proved possible. Since industrial countries had not been able to cut expenditures enough or to raise taxes sufficiently to come close to budgetary balance, fiscal policy could not be the main weapon in combating inflation. It was for this reason that officials of most industrial countries had recourse to tight monetary policies, including high interest rates. The fight against inflation was often fought through use of monetary policy. Unfortunately, tight monetary policies, especially the high interest rates that usually accompanied them, induced capital inflows which, in turn, caused the country's exchange rate to appreciate. If monetary authorities then intervened in exchange markets to limit the extent of exchange rate appreciation, they undid the domestic effects of the restrictive monetary policy. It was for these economic reasons—not for any general unwillingness to cooperate—that monetary authorities could not agree to harmonize their monetary policies and interest rates to reduce movements in exchange rates.

In explaining the exchange rate policy of the Federal Republic of Germany, Mr. Pieske confirmed that German officials attempted to smooth out temporary or erratic fluctuations, going beyond merely avoiding disorderly conditions in exchange markets. They usually had in mind an approximate range for the dollar/ deutsche mark rate but ran into difficulty because there were no criteria for distinguishing day-to-day fluctuations in the dollar/deutsche mark rate from longer-term movements and for forming a judgment on an appropriate medium-term rate. Japanese authorities, according to Mr. Kawaguchi, were extremely sensitive to complaints that they were "manipulating" the yen. They insisted that they did not try to aim at a target level for the dollar/yen rate; they aimed simply at moderating the speed of exchange rate changes, intervening from time to time to moderate sharp and disruptive fluctuations. Austria, Belgium, Denmark, the Netherlands, Norway, and Sweden were following policies that enabled them to keep their currencies in line with the deutsche mark, and the Executive Directors for these members explained that their officials at times also intervened in exchange markets. They emphasized, however, that for the most part, these members relied on changes in exchange rates and on monetary policies, and not on intervention, to achieve their exchange rate objectives.

The exchange rate policies of France, Italy, and the United Kingdom were put to their severest tests in 1976 when all three of these members faced serious balance of payments deficits and rapidly depreciating currencies. They all engaged in large-scale official borrowing abroad, and Italy and the United Kingdom drew large amounts from the Fund to prevent excessive exchange depreciations. Officials of all three members also intervened in exchange markets, at times heavily.

H. Johannes Witteveen, Chairman of the Executive Board and Managing Director, September 1, 1973–June 16, 1978

Meeting of the Executive Board, December 13, 1976

Meeting of the Executive Board, January 17, 1979

J. de Larosière, Chairman of the Executive Board and Managing Director,
June 17, 1978–

President Jimmy Carter of the United States addressing
Governors, Annual Meeting, Washington, September 26, 1977

(above) H. J. Witteveen and Chairman John N. Turner, Washington, August 31, 1975
(below) J. de Larosière and Chairman Denis Healey, Washington, September 24, 1978

Interim Committee of Board of Governors, Press Conferences

William B. Dale, Deputy Managing Director, March 1, 1974–May 31, 1984

Joint Session of the Governors of the Fund and Bank, Washington, September 26, 1977

At the 1976 Annual Meeting, the year when exchange rates, at least for the dollar, were more stable than they had been earlier, not only Bernard Clappier but also the Governors of the smaller European members, such as Messrs. W.F. Duisenberg, Xenophon Zolotas, Willy De Clercq, and Jacques-François Poos, insisted that U.S. officials needed to defend the dollar in the interest of reducing exchange rate instability.[11] Governors from developing members, while not arguing explicitly for management of floating rates or even for intervention by U.S. authorities to support the dollar, cited adverse effects on developing members of the exchange rate instability that had characterized the floating rate regime. Prices for their exports and imports, denominated in the currencies of the major industrial members, usually the U.S. dollar, were undergoing excessive variations. The value of their foreign exchange reserves was continuously changing, making their portfolio management difficult and aggravating the burden of their foreign debt service.[12]

U.S. officials once more resisted suggestions that they intervene in exchange markets so as to support the dollar, as Mr. Simon reiterated the U.S. position underlying the negotiation of Article IV in November 1975. Stable exchange rates could be achieved only through responsible management by the industrial members of their underlying economic and financial policies; in the meantime, exchange rates ought to move in accordance with market forces, no matter how unstable the resulting rate movements were. In Mr. Simon's words, "market forces must not be treated as enemies to be resisted at all costs, but as the necessary and helpful reflections of changing conditions in a highly integrated world economy with wide freedom for international trade and capital flows."[13]

Donald S. Macdonald, along with Karl-Otto Pöhl, were also less concerned than other officials about instability in exchange markets. They agreed with Mr. Simon that the floating rate system had functioned well in the swiftly changing world economic environment since 1973 and that floating rates had "shielded the international community from falling back into a nightmare of trade restrictions and from a resurgence of capital controls."[14]

By the time of the 1977 Annual Meeting a year later, rates for the dollar were declining sharply and exchange rate instability received even more comment.

---

[11]Statements by the Governor of the World Bank for France, the Governor of the World Bank for the Netherlands, the Governor of the Fund for Greece, the Governor of the World Bank for Belgium, and the Governor of the Fund and the World Bank for Luxembourg, *Summary Proceedings, 1976*, pp. 73–74, 28, 53–54, 131–32, and 155.

[12]See, for example, statements by the Governor of the Fund for the Central African Republic, the Governor of the World Bank for Malaysia, the Governor of the Fund for Guinea, and the Governor of the Fund and the World Bank for Tanzania, *Summary Proceedings, 1976*, pp. 123, 135, 144, and 148–49.

[13]Statement by the Governor of the Fund and the World Bank for the United States, *Summary Proceedings, 1976*, p. 93.

[14]Statements by the Governor of the Fund and the World Bank for Canada and the Alternate Governor of the Fund and Temporary Alternate Governor of the World Bank for the Federal Republic of Germany, *Summary Proceedings, 1976*, pp. 36 and 107–108. Quoted portion is on p. 107.

Governors from the small open economies in Europe vigorously protested what was happening to exchange rates. Gaston Geens, for example, complained of excessive fluctuations and Hannes Androsch doubted whether the flexible rate system had a "better adjustment adaptability" than the former par value system.[15] Mr. Duisenberg was particularly emphatic, taking issue with the U.S. view that exchange rate developments should be left completely to market forces and that the task of the monetary authorities should be limited to smoothing out so-called erratic movements. What he called the feedback of the exchange rate to the national economy, that is, the effects of exchange rate changes on the macroeconomic variables of an economy, implied the need for internationally consistent exchange rate targets and for international coordination of domestic economic policies, especially of monetary policies.[16] French officials, too, again complained about exchange rate instability, as Robert Boulin wanted "to make it plain that the freedom of choice that IMF members are given under the new Articles must not lead to license or disorder."[17]

Although in January 1977 President Jimmy Carter had succeeded President Ford, the views of U.S. officials with regard to exchange rate policy paradoxically enough remained unchanged. Following the policy begun by President Nixon, U.S. officials continued to favor floating rates with little defense of the dollar through intervention. To reduce domestic unemployment and help foster world economic recovery after the 1974–75 recession, the United States was following relatively expansionary macroeconomic policies and, consequently, was encountering large external trade and current account deficits. Other industrial members, especially the Federal Republic of Germany and Japan, were, on the other hand, pursuing more restrained domestic policies and experiencing substantial trade and current account surpluses. In the interest of promoting world economic recovery, the members with surpluses ought to undertake more expansionary measures and let their currencies appreciate as much as market forces dictated so as to foster more imports into their countries. At the 1977 Annual Meeting, Mr. Blumenthal, like Mr. Simon before him, although less emphatically and with less free market ideology, stated simply that underlying economic and financial factors should determine exchange rates.[18] Defending Japanese policy, Hideo Boh pointed out that the Japanese authorities had been letting market forces determine the rate for the yen, intervening only to smooth out short-term disruptive movements.[19]

The era of floating rates, and even agreement on Article IV, had by no means ended debate about exchange rate policy.

---

[15]Statements by the Governors of the World Bank for Belgium and Austria, *Summary Proceedings, 1977*, pp. 24 and 36.

[16]Statement by the Governor of the World Bank for the Netherlands, *Summary Proceedings, 1977*, pp. 44–45.

[17]Statement by the Governor of the Fund for France, *Summary Proceedings, 1977*, p. 82.

[18]Statement by the Governor of the Fund and the World Bank for the United States, *Summary Proceedings, 1977*, p. 67.

[19]Statement by the Governor of the Fund and the World Bank for Japan, *Summary Proceedings, 1977*, p. 29.

RENEWED PRESSURE ON THE DOLLAR
STARTING IN SEPTEMBER 1977

In the last week of September, right after the 1977 Annual Meeting, exchange markets again became unsettled. Largely because of a growing concern about the size of U.S. trade and current account deficits, the dollar remained under heavy selling pressure during the remainder of 1977. It declined particularly against the Swiss franc, the deutsche mark and other European currencies in the snake, and the Japanese yen, depreciating 9–15 percent against these currencies in the last three months of 1977. Exchange markets were extremely disorderly and official intervention in exchange markets by the authorities of several countries abroad was heavy. To add to the confusion, there were conflicting statements of policy intentions by public officials. When U.S. officials restated the U.S. policy of letting the dollar be freely determined, they were accused of suggesting that under no circumstances would they support the dollar. Rather than instilling confidence in the dollar, these policy statements were followed by still further declines in the rates for the dollar in exchange markets. Exchange rates, a contentious issue in the last years of the par value system, continued to be a source of serious disagreement among officials of the major countries even after floating rates were introduced, and pressure from officials abroad on U.S. officials to take measures to defend the dollar was strong.

In response to this pressure and to help rebuild confidence in the dollar, President Carter issued a new broad policy statement on December 21, 1977. He explained to the public the reasons for the emergence of the large U.S. deficits on trade and current account. They were due to the high oil imports by the United States, even four years after the start of the energy crisis, and to the relatively slow economic growth of Japan, the Federal Republic of Germany, and other countries, which gave these countries large current account surpluses while the U.S. expansionary policies produced current account deficits. President Carter explained that the solution lay in getting the U.S. Congress to enact his proposed energy legislation so as to reduce U.S. dependence on imported oil and to get the authorities of countries in payments surplus to accelerate their economic growth, as the United States had done. In the meantime, he announced several more immediate measures to increase U.S. domestic oil production and to expand U.S. agricultural and other exports. In a somewhat changed policy stance about direct intervention to defend the dollar, President Carter also announced the intent of the U.S. authorities, in close consultation "with our friends abroad" to "intervene to the extent necessary to counter disorderly conditions in the exchange markets."

President Carter's assurance to the exchange markets that the United States would intervene was followed on January 4, 1978 by an explanatory joint statement of the U.S. Treasury and the Federal Reserve Board on intervention policy.[20] The Exchange Stabilization Fund of the U.S. Treasury was to be used together with the

---

[20]The text of this statement was reprinted in *IMF Survey* (Washington), Vol. 7 (January 9, 1978), pp. 1 and 8.

$20 billion swap network operated by the Federal Reserve System. The Exchange Stabilization Fund, which then amounted to $4.7 billion, had been created in 1934 to stabilize the exchange value of the dollar after the United States went off the gold standard. It had been used twice in joint exchange market operations between the U.S. Treasury and the Federal Reserve System. The swap network was a series of short-term reciprocal credit lines arranged starting early in the 1960s between the U.S. Federal Reserve System and central banks abroad, and gradually expanded, now including the BIS as well.[21]

At the end of 1977, the issue of exchange rate stability was of paramount concern for the world's economic policymakers.

---

[21]The start of these swap arrangements was described in *History, 1966–71*, Vol. I, pp. 14–15.

CHAPTER

42

Analysis of the Floating Rate Experience

*A*NALYZING ECONOMIC EVENTS has always been vital to the Fund's activities. At the Fund's beginning in 1946, international economics was in its infancy compared with domestic macroeconomic theory revamped by the Keynesian revolution. By 1960 major advances had been made in knowledge of the factors determining exchange rates, of the mechanism of balance of payments adjustment, and of the effectiveness of various policies to deal with balance of payments problems. During the 1960s, further understanding of the functioning of the international monetary system was achieved, particularly of the role of international liquidity and of the significance of the size and composition of reserve assets. "International monetary economics" really came into its own as a separate discipline.

Economists in the Fund, benefiting from interchanges with economists in universities, member governments, and other international organizations, and with policymakers in member governments, advanced international economics through, for example, their understanding of the factors determining exchange rates. Early in the 1950s, staff worked on the price and income elasticities of demand and supply and the implications of these elasticities for effective changes in exchange rates. They also worked on "absorption approaches" to the effects of exchange rate changes and on the relationship between monetary phenomena in an economy and developments in a country's balance of payments position. In the 1960s, the Fund staff developed the innovative SDR. Several theoretical and empirical studies by the staff were published in *Staff Papers*, a Fund journal published since 1950. Fund appraisals of the world economic scene and of developments in the international monetary system from 1946 onward were also presented in the Annual Reports.

After 1973 much more was learned about the dynamics of exchange rate movements. Many developments described in the previous chapter, such as wide fluctuations in floating rates, had not been anticipated on the basis of economists' earlier understanding. Just as economic theories have usually resulted from the need to explain actual events inexplicable by existing doctrines so further economic theories and analyses of exchange rates were developed in the 1970s. These new analyses formed part of the environment in which the Fund's policies with regard to exchange rates after 1973 were formed. These policies are described in Chapter 43. As a prelude to the description of the Fund's policies vis-à-vis exchange rates after 1973, the present chapter briefly summarizes the new analyses of exchange rates developed in the 1970s, particularly the work developed or written up by the Fund staff.

EXPLANATIONS FOR EXCHANGE RATE VARIABILITY

Explanations were urgently needed after 1973 for the pronounced variability in exchange rates for the main currencies. Under the theories of the previous 20 years, it was well understood that once exchange rates became flexible, there would be considerably more movement of exchange rates than had taken place under the system of agreed par values. Changes in underlying economic conditions, such as in consumers' tastes, production techniques, money supply, domestic price levels, and trade and current account positions, were bound to cause free exchange rates to move. Flexible exchange rates were also expected to move because of differences in the rates of inflation among the large industrial countries. In fact, economists who had been advocating floating rates had done so precisely on the grounds that flexible exchange rates, which could move in response to market forces without the need for administrative decisions, would permit quick and smooth adjustment to changes in underlying economic conditions in various countries and to differences in their rates of inflation. They argued that flexible rates would thereby provide greater stability of exchange rates than did the system of institutionally agreed par values, under which every change, anticipated change, or delayed change in a par value for a major currency resulted in speculative capital flows and hence in sudden jolts in the exchange rates of all the main currencies.

As economists sought explanations for the unexpectedly wide movements that characterized floating rates after 1973, they immediately turned to the differential rates of increase in the general price levels among the main industrial countries. For nearly 60 years economists had relied on the purchasing-power-parity doctrine to explain movements in exchange rates that were not deliberately pegged or to determine appropriate exchange rates. According to the purchasing-power-parity doctrine, exchange rates were determined, or should be determined, mainly by the relative domestic purchasing power of different currencies. It was understandable, therefore, that when the floating rate era of the 1970s began, the purchasing-power-parity doctrine underwent a revival.[1] However, use of the purchasing-power-parity doctrine alone was soon found deficient for explaining the wide movements in

---

[1]For example, Professor Lawrence H. Officer, of Michigan State University, did two studies of the purchasing-power-parity doctrine while on a temporary stay in the Fund. See his "The Purchasing-Power-Parity Theory of Exchange Rates: A Review Article," *Staff Papers*, International Monetary Fund (Washington), Vol. 23 (March 1976), pp. 1–60, and "The Productivity Bias in Purchasing Power Parity: An Econometric Investigation," *Staff Papers*, Vol. 23 (November 1976), pp. 545–79.

exchange rates after 1973. Many of the large swings in exchange rates among the major currencies went well beyond movements called for by differences in the industrial countries' domestic rates of inflation. In fact, movements in exchange rates even went beyond changes in the basic underlying economic conditions of the large industrial countries. In a word coined to denote large swings of exchange rates well beyond changes in general domestic price levels or in basic economic conditions, exchange rates were said to "overshoot."

Alternative explanations for large swings in exchange rates were accordingly needed. In seeking such explanations, economists recognized that the influences operating on exchange markets in the 1970s were too numerous and diverse to permit a single explanation. They also recognized that much exchange rate variability was attributable to the generally unsettled economic conditions of the times. In the span of a few years the world had witnessed several upheavals: the continuation in 1971–72 of sizable payments imbalances by the industrial countries culminating in the final collapse of the par value system early in 1973; the high and divergent rates of worldwide inflation that began in 1973; a jump in oil prices in late 1973 which greatly aggravated disequilibria in payments positions; in 1974–75, the deepest worldwide recession of the previous four decades, and the continuation in 1976–78 of both unusually high levels of unemployment and high inflation in most industrial countries. Troubled times were certainly a reasonable explanation of why flexible rates had worked differently and less well than had initially been expected. Those who had advocated flexible rates and expected them to be relatively stable had surely not anticipated the introduction of flexible rates just when the severe disequilibria most industrial countries were experiencing in their balances of payments were distorted even further by oil price rises after 1973. Nor had they expected flexible exchange rates to be introduced during the novel period of coexistence of severe unemployment and inflation, when officials of the industrial countries were unevenly tolerant of unemployment and inflation and pursued differing macroeconomic policies. It was small wonder that actual experience with floating rates differed from that expected on the basis of previous economic understanding and doctrines.

Inflation and Capital Movements as Explanations

In addition to realizing that general upheavals caused exchange rate instability, economists searched for specific reasons for the instability of exchange rates after 1973. They identified two factors: the unusual amount of inflation that characterized these years and the large flows of short-term capital across national boundaries starting in the 1960s.

In order to pinpoint inflation as a cause of exchange rate instability, the staff calculated the average rate of inflation for 14 industrial members (measured by the deflators of gross national product) and the dispersion of inflation among the 7 major industrial members (a measure of the differences in countries' rates of inflation).

They then compared these measures of inflation and its dispersion among members with exchange rate movements in the currencies of these 14 members in the years 1974–78. The same calculations (the average rate of inflation, the dispersion of inflation among countries, and exchange rate movements) were then derived for the pre-floating rate period, 1960–73. The data for the two periods, 1974–78 and 1960–73, were then compared and provided concrete evidence that high rates of inflation and a large dispersion of the rate of inflation were correlated with sizable changes in the structure of exchange rates for the 14 industrial members.

Another key general observation was that for countries with well-developed money and capital markets, conditions in the financial markets seemed more critical in determining short-run exchange rate movements than those in the goods markets. More explicitly, changes in capital accounts in countries' balances of payments had more to do with movements in the exchange rates for their currencies than did changes in their current account positions. Because disruptive short-term capital flows in the 1960s and in 1970–72 were a cause of the collapse of the par value system, economists, including those in the Fund, had already begun to study the relation between capital flows and exchange rate changes.[2] In the 1960s Fund staff also introduced into the theory of exchange rate determination the idea of mobility of capital, initiating the "asset" approach into exchange rate theory.[3]

Under floating rates, capital flows were again found to be a strong factor in exchange rate changes. Because capital flows were heavily influenced by relative yields available on assets, such as bank accounts or money instruments, issued in different countries, differences in interest rates between the main industrial countries affected short-term capital flows. Hence, interest rates affected exchange rates. It was soon apparent that just as changes in domestic monetary policy, especially in interest rates, had frequently caused disruptive short-term movements of capital under the par value system and had led to the collapse of that system, so changes in domestic monetary policies, especially in interest rates, gave rise to short-term capital flows and produced instability of exchange rates in the floating system. The stabilizing effects of short-term capital movements anticipated by many advocates of flexible exchange rates thus not only failed to materialize in practice but, even under floating rates, capital movements proved destabilizing, as they had been under the par value system.

To help explain the phenomenon of capital movements producing exchange rate changes, economists built on the theory, initiated in the Fund, of the asset

---

[2]In the 1960s and early 1970s, for instance, Fund staff surveyed the growing literature on the subject of short-term capital flows and undertook studies that explained capital flows in terms of the interest rates prevailing in the major industrial countries. See Zoran Hodjera, "International Short-Term Capital Movements: A Survey of Theory and Empirical Analysis," *Staff Papers*, Vol. 20 (November 1973), pp. 683–740; Victor Argy and Zoran Hodjera, "Financial Integration and Interest Rate Linkages in the Industrial Countries," *Staff Papers*, Vol. 20 (March 1973), pp. 1–77; and William H. White, "Interest Rate Differences, Forward Exchange Mechanism, and Scope for Short-Term Capital Movements," *Staff Papers*, Vol. 10 (November 1963), pp. 485–503.

[3]See J. Marcus Fleming, "Domestic Financial Policies Under Fixed and Under Floating Exchange Rates," *Staff Papers*, Vol. 9 (November 1962), pp. 369–80; and Robert A. Mundell, *International Economics* (New York: Macmillan, 1968).

approach to exchange rate determination. Since at that time monetary approaches to all macroeconomic policies were in the ascendency, it was understandable that much of the theoretical work in the 1970s on floating exchange rates would take the form of developing the asset approach to exchange rate determination into a full-blown monetary approach. The new econometric models of exchange rate determination and of the mechanism of exchange rate dynamics all began to use this asset approach.

Under this approach, the foreign exchange market was thought of as a market for financial assets, or money instruments. The exchange rate between two currencies was regarded as a price for assets denominated in the two currencies. Changes in an exchange rate were viewed as movements to equilibrate the international demand for and supply of money instruments (assets) needed to pay for goods and services and to finance capital transactions. The demand for and supply of foreign exchange associated with capital movements were thus incorporated into the theory of exchange rates, which up until then had centered only on the demand for and supply of foreign exchange associated with goods and services on current account.[4] Economists also made significant advances in the analysis of capital movements and examined the actual experiences of countries with floating exchange rates in an era of free capital movements.[5]

Expectations of Future Exchange Rates as a Determinant of Exchange Rate Movements

In addition to the effects of monetary policy on relative yields on money instruments in differing countries and therefore on capital flows and on exchange rates, economists singled out another prime determinant of exchange rate movements: expectations of future exchange rates. Because of the close link between actual inflation and the public's expectations of further inflation, the psychological factor of expectations had come to be a key element of contemporary macroeconomic theory. Economic theorists came to explain the dynamics of inflation primarily in terms of expectations, with the theory of "rational expectations" in particular becoming a new development in macroeconomic theory in the 1970s. The world in general had become conscious of what was likely to happen generally in the near term, and, in such a future-conscious world, expectations of future exchange rates understandably became part of the contemporary theory of exchange rate determination.

Expectations were worked into exchange rate theory on the assumption that exchange markets as they operated in the 1970s were "very efficient." Traders,

---

[4]The full-blown monetary approach to exchange rate determination was developed mainly by academic economists. A study by Fund staff testing the approach empirically is that of John F. O. Bilson, "The Monetary Approach to the Exchange Rate: Some Empirical Evidence," *Staff Papers*, Vol. 25 (March 1978), pp. 48–75.

[5]See, for example, Jacques R. Artus, "Exchange Rate Stability and Managed Floating: The Experience of the Federal Republic of Germany," *Staff Papers*, Vol. 23 (July 1976), pp. 312–33, and Zoran Hodjera, "Alternative Approaches in the Analysis of International Capital Movements: A Case Study of Austria and France," *Staff Papers*, Vol. 23 (November 1976), pp. 598–623.

businessmen, bankers, speculators, and others who needed exchange assets or who were asset holders operating in foreign exchange markets were fully cognizant of the information pertinent to exchange rates currently available. Existing exchange rates, therefore, already reflected the up-to-date assessment of participants in exchange markets of the relative yields on alternative assets and of the various factors bearing on the risk of holding these assets, such as countries' fiscal and monetary policies and their trade and current account positions. Market participants had already taken into account even a host of noneconomic factors affecting the holding of assets, such as political stability of a country. Hence, what brought about variations in exchange rates, especially the frequent wide short-term swings, were expectations about the future course of economic and political factors. More correctly, *changes in expectations* were relevant, since existing expectations were already part of the current information on which existing exchange rates were based. Only new and unexpected information would cause market participants to change their current evaluation of the future exchange rate for a currency and would influence their current demand for and supply of that currency, and thereby the existing exchange rate. In short, changes in expectations led to changes in exchange rates.

Attributing changes in exchange rates to changes in expectations about the future of that exchange rate was especially useful for explaining the volatility of exchange rates in the floating rate era. A myriad of factors, political as well as economic, influenced the expectations of market participants for the rates for various currencies. In the unstable economic environment of the 1970s, moreover, all these factors were subject to frequent change. This explanation made large and frequent changes in exchange rates easy to understand.

In sum, contemporary economic analysis explained exchange rates in terms of current rates of return on monetary assets and in terms of the expectations for the rates of return on these assets in the near future. When any of the many factors affecting current rates of return or expectations of rates of return changed, so did exchange rates. Rapidly shifting interest rate differentials, the sudden imposition or relaxation of capital and exchange controls, and any element changing exchange rate expectations were apt to cause significant swings in exchange rates, even when the relative overall price levels in the countries concerned changed only slowly. In this light, it was understandable that exchange rates were so volatile.[6]

In addition to these theoretical explanations of exchange rate variability, Fund officials recognized that short-term fluctuations in exchange rates were also affected by official intervention in exchange markets. But as noted in the previous chapter,

---

[6]Fund staff also studied the role of expectations in exchange rate determination. See, for example, John F. O. Bilson, "Rational Expectations and the Exchange Rate," in Jacob A. Frenkel and Harry G. Johnson, eds., *The Economics of Exchange Rates: Selected Studies* (Reading, Mass.: Addison-Wesley Pub. Co., 1978), pp. 75–96; and Michael G. Porter, "A Theoretical and Empirical Framework for Analyzing the Term Structure of Exchange Rate Expectations," *Staff Papers*, Vol. 18 (November 1971), pp. 613–45. A summary by the staff of the explanations of exchange rate variability can be found in Susan Schadler, "Sources of Exchange Rate Variability: Theory and Empirical Evidence," *Staff Papers*, Vol. 24 (July 1977), pp. 253–96.

financial officials disagreed about the effects of official intervention on exchange rates; European and Japanese officials argued that official intervention could help smooth an otherwise disorderly market while U.S. and Canadian officials held that intervention was of little use in stabilizing exchange rates. There was no consensus on the effects of intervention on exchange rates.

Relation of Explanations to Fund Policy

The primary aim within the Fund of finding out the reasons for exchange rate variability was to ascertain the implications for general Fund policy on exchange rates or, at least, for the policy advice that the Fund might give to officials of its individual members. Given all the causes of short-term exchange rate fluctuations, the conclusion reached within the Fund was that promising methods for controlling exchange rate fluctuations were relatively few and that, since the market was continuously confronted with new information, "some degree of short-term variability" was "probably inevitable." Fund officials concluded too that there was need for measures that reduced the frequency and duration of disorderly market conditions and that, with reservations, a "potential contribution" to greater exchange rate stability might be made if officials of the major industrial countries announced targets for monetary growth.[7]

While the Fund found it difficult to develop policies to help reduce exchange rate instability, the staff continued with its analysis of exchange rate movements, periodically assembling a series of statistical charts and tables containing data relevant to the evolution of exchange rates. These "exchange rate indicators" included current account payments imbalances, short-term interest rates, consumer prices, relative costs and prices of manufactured goods, and monetary aggregates. The type of data collected was a recognition of the need to look beyond the current account, which had traditionally been the focal point of exchange rate analysis, to factors that affected the capital account.[8]

EFFECTS, AND EFFECTIVENESS, OF EXCHANGE RATE CHANGES

Because of the Fund's responsibility for exchange rates, Fund officials devoted themselves tirelessly to examining the effects, and the effectiveness, of changes in exchange rates. Examination of the effects of the widespread devaluations of 1949 was, for instance, one of the tasks to which the Fund staff turned a few years after the Fund started. In a similar manner, the staff undertook examinations of the effects of exchange rate changes after 1973. To help explain these effects, the staff made use

---

[7] *Annual Report, 1978*, p. 37.

[8] These charts and tables of exchange rate indicators can be seen in *Finance & Development*, Vol. 17 (June 1980), pp. 40–43. An explanation of them can be found in Andrew Crockett, "Determinants of Exchange Rate Movements: A Review," *Finance & Development*, Vol. 18 (March 1981), pp. 33–37.

of two new analyses—"J-curve" effects and the "vicious circle" hypothesis—which were also being developed by economists outside the Fund.

J-Curve Effects

Early in the floating rate period of the 1970s, considerable cognizance was taken of what were known as J-curve effects. Officials and economists first became aware of J-curve effects from the experiences of the United Kingdom after the devaluation of the pound sterling in 1967. After this devaluation, the U.K. balance of payments position unexpectedly worsened, and it was only after a year or more that the benefits of the devaluation in increasing U.K. exports and reducing U.K. imports began to materialize.[9] The term J-curve was used as a shorthand way of denoting this phenomenon. Specifically, J-curve refers to the shape of the adjustment path frequently followed by the trade balance of countries after an exchange rate devaluation. Devaluation often at first produces a deterioration in the external account (the short downward shaft of the J) and later produces an improvement in the external account, that is, an improvement which is considerably in excess of the initial deterioration (the long upward shaft of the J).[10] The initial deterioration comes about because the immediate impact of devaluation is a worsening of the country's terms of trade while the effect on trade volumes occurs only after time lags of considerable duration.

Essentially what happens is this. If exporters maintain their prices in terms of local currency, the resulting lower cost to foreign customers in terms of their own currencies should stimulate buying and in time increase the volume of exports enough to produce some increase in export values in terms of foreign currencies and a considerable increase in terms of local currency. On the import side, if foreign exporters hold their export prices in their currencies unchanged, the local currency cost to the customers in the devaluing country rises; eventually the lowering of the volume of purchases will reduce aggregate local currency expenditures on imports. Thus, as current receipts are enlarged and current payments are reduced, the current account position improves.

These effects, however, take a long time to materialize, much longer than economists and officials had realized before 1967. Shifts in demand, both at home and abroad, and changes in resource allocation are required before the quantity of exports of goods and services increases and the quantity of imports of goods and services decreases. Meanwhile, the quantities of exports and imports may well remain substantially unchanged, and the increase in the aggregate local currency

---

[9]These effects of the devaluation of the pound sterling in 1967 were described briefly in *History, 1966–71*, Vol. I, pp. 444–45.

[10]A graph of the J-curve with the horizontal axis denoting time, expressed in calendar quarters, and the vertical axis denoting the trade balance, expressed in billions of units of local currency, can be seen in Morris Goldstein and John H. Young, "Exchange Rate Policy: Some Current Issues," *Finance & Development*, Vol. 16 (March 1979), p. 10.

value of imports is likely to outweigh any favorable impact on exports. Hence, the current account position often worsens immediately following a devaluation.

This phenomenon was observed in virtually all exchange depreciations of the major currencies after 1973. Often initial adverse terms of trade effects (the downward part of the J-curve) were substantial and lasted for more than a year. Exports of an industrial country were slow to respond to a change in its exchange rate because its exports were strongly influenced not only by relative prices but also by nonprice factors, such as the ties of consumers to traditional suppliers, long-term contracts already in force, marketing networks, a reputation for quality, reliable delivery schedules, good after-sales service, and the development of new products. It was consequently unrealistic to expect that an unanticipated change in relative prices, induced by an exchange rate change, would rapidly affect patterns of production and demand that reflected such structural factors. In economists' parlance, the price elasticities of demand and supply, at least in the short run, were low. The critical value for price elasticities was unity. Estimates by the Fund staff for 14 industrial countries showed that the import and export price elasticities for manufactured exports and imports were each below unity for a period of up to one year.[11]

The phenomenon of adverse terms of trade effects initially outweighing the volume effects of an exchange depreciation and the low price elasticities of demand and supply for exports and imports, discovered in the 1970s as common for industrial countries, had previously been associated mainly—or even solely—with exchange devaluation by countries exporting primary products.

The "Vicious Circle" Hypothesis

Immediately after generalized floating was introduced in 1973, officials started to disagree about whether floating rates were themselves a source of inflation. Did floating rates stimulate the inflation then accelerating throughout the world? European officials argued that they did. When an exchange rate for a major currency, such as the U.S. dollar, depreciated, domestic prices for imports in the country experiencing the depreciation rose, as did wage costs, further fueling internal inflation. Mr. Clappier, at the 1976 Annual Meeting, stated that an unmanaged exchange rate was an independent source of inflationary pressure. Exchange rate depreciation and inflation reinforced each other, setting in motion a cumulative process of exchange rate depreciation and inflation so that the exchange

---

[11]Several studies were made in the Fund in the 1970s on the effects of exchange rate changes, especially the effects on trade and on prices. Some of these studies were produced by academic specialists temporarily in the Fund, such as those by Mordechai E. Kreinin, of Michigan State University, "The Effect of Exchange Rate Changes on the Prices and Volume of Foreign Trade," *Staff Papers*, Vol. 24 (July 1977), pp. 297–329 and by Alfred Steinherr, of the Catholic University of Louvain, Belgium, "Effectiveness of Exchange Rate Policy for Trade Account Adjustment," *Staff Papers*, Vol. 28 (March 1981), pp. 199–224. Other studies were prepared by the Fund staff, such as that by Erich Spitäller, "Short-Run Effects of Exchange Rate Changes on Terms of Trade and Trade Balance," *Staff Papers*, Vol. 27 (June 1980), pp. 320–48.

value of a country's currency continued to fall.[12] U.S. officials, on the other hand, argued that the rate of domestic inflation was determined primarily by domestic monetary and fiscal policies and that the exchange rate played only a passive role in inflation.

The European position, that inflation leads to devaluation which in turn leads to more inflation, came to be known as the vicious circle view of exchange rate change. The possibility of an inflation-exchange rate depreciation spiral had been stated in the 1930s by Professor Gottfried Haberler, but in the 1970s economists turned afresh to this phenomenon.[13] The reverse thesis, called the virtuous circle hypothesis, was associated with exchange rate appreciation and price stability.

The vicious circle hypothesis simply put was that, in a world of floating rates, exchange rate changes led to offsetting movements in domestic prices and costs and therefore to further exchange rate changes. The cycle was continuously repeated. This hypothesis seemed in accord with the experiences of some of the largest industrial members with floating rates. By 1975–76 the Federal Republic of Germany and Japan were experiencing large current account surpluses, low rates of domestic inflation, and more or less continuously appreciating exchange rates. Italy and the United Kingdom, in contrast, were experiencing large current account deficits, high rates of domestic inflation, and more or less continuously depreciating exchange rates. In Italy and the United Kingdom a depreciation-inflation spiral seemed to exist, suggesting that, at least in some situations, floating exchange rates might be inherently unstable and could themselves be an independent source of inflation.

Exchange rate depreciation, in particular, led rapidly to higher domestic prices and costs because wages were increasingly geared to changes in domestic prices. High rates of inflation in the 1970s caused wage bargainers to focus on wages and prices in real rather than in nominal terms and brought about a spread of indexing wages to prices. By 1976, for example, wage contracts in more than half the industrial countries in Europe were indexed to a considerable degree, and a large number of labor contracts in Canada and the United States included cost of living clauses. Even in countries where there was no formal indexation, wages responded quickly to rises in domestic prices.

The Fund's Attitude Toward the Vicious Circle Hypothesis

Recognition of the cumulative process of depreciation and inflation caused Fund officials to stress the need for members, especially the large industrial

---

[12]Statement by the Governor of the World Bank for France, *Summary Proceedings, 1976*, p. 74.

[13]Professor Haberler's statement of an inflation-depreciation spiral was presented in his *The Theory of International Trade with Its Applications to Commercial Policy* (New York: Macmillan, 1937). A theoretical presentation of the contemporary vicious circle hypothesis by Fund staff can be found in John F. O. Bilson, "The 'Vicious Circle' Hypothesis," *Staff Papers*, Vol. 26 (March 1979), pp. 1–37; and in Marian E. Bond, "Exchange Rates, Inflation, and Vicious Circles," *Staff Papers*, Vol. 27 (December 1980), pp. 679–711. A short nontechnical explanation can be found in Marian Bond, "Exchange Rates, Inflation, and the Vicious Circle," *Finance & Development*, Vol. 17 (March 1980), pp. 27–31.

members, to coordinate their exchange rate and demand-management policies. In the Annual Report for 1977, for example, the Fund specifically explained the action needed to prevent the vicious circle phenomenon. In deficit countries, adequate restraint on the increase in nominal demand had to be instituted, coupled with efforts to minimize the feedback from the exchange rate to wages and other domestic costs so as to hold down unemployment. An incomes policy governing price and wage developments, negotiated among the government, labor unions, and industry, might be helpful in making exchange rate policy effective. Surplus countries also had to be willing to maintain an adequate level of domestic demand and to accept the appreciation of their effective exchange rates resulting from the play of market forces.[14]

These points were stressed again in 1978, first by Mr. Witteveen and then by Mr. de Larosière. Early in 1978 Mr. Witteveen publicly emphasized the importance of maintaining an appropriate relationship between exchange rates and demand-management policies. Exchange depreciation had to be accompanied by more restrictive demand-management policies so that its inflationary effects would be offset. Surplus countries, notably the Federal Republic of Germany and Japan, had to accompany the exchange rate appreciations occurring for their currencies by additional expansion of demand in their domestic economies.[15] Addressing the Governors in September at the 1978 Annual Meeting, Mr. de Larosière stressed again that for exchange rate changes to work, accompanying adequate internal measures had to be taken. Surplus countries had to take the measures necessary to counteract the deflationary effects of their exchange rate appreciations; countries incurring exchange rate depreciations, such as the United States, had to be ready to counteract the resulting expansionary effects.[16]

Just as Fund economists had discovered in the 1950s that, under the par value system, exchange rate changes had to be accompanied by changes in internal policy if exchange rate changes were to be effective, so by 1977, economists were learning that the same was true even under floating exchange rates.

ROLE OF EXCHANGE RATES IN
BALANCE OF PAYMENTS ADJUSTMENT

As was described in Chapter 20, in 1976 the Fund shifted its emphasis from members' financing the balance of payments deficits resulting from the oil price increases of 1973–74 to their taking what Fund officials called "adjustment measures" to reduce those deficits. The shift in emphasis came about because, although initially many officials believed that too rapid an adjustment to the new oil prices by

---

[14]*Annual Report, 1977,* p. 35.

[15]Address entitled "Financial Stability in the World Economy," delivered before the Conference Board, New York, February 15, 1978. Reprinted in *IMF Survey* (Washington), Vol. 7 (February 20, 1978), pp. 49 and 57–61.

[16]Opening Address by the Managing Director, *Summary Proceedings, 1978,* p. 17.

industrial countries was not desirable, by late 1976 they were concerned that adjustment was taking place too slowly. They were especially concerned about the role of exchange rates in bringing about balance of payments adjustment. It had been more than three years since the fixed rate system had collapsed and since greater exchange rate flexibility had been introduced; yet, a number of industrial countries continued to experience sizable external imbalances, either large surpluses or large deficits.

Consequently, much of the Fund's attention by late 1976 was directed toward the role of the exchange rate in the adjustment process. Indeed, Fund officials were concerned with the theoretical analysis of J-curve effects and the vicious circle hypothesis because these effects were seen as seriously limiting the usefulness of exchange rate changes for correcting balance of payments disequilibrium.

The adjustment process, including the role of exchange rates in effecting payments adjustment, was discussed by the Executive Board on several occasions when the world economic outlook was considered, as described in Chapter 40. The contribution of exchange rate movements to the reduction of existing imbalances among industrial countries was found to have been limited. From early 1973 to well into 1977, changes in exchange rates tended mainly to offset differences in the rates of inflation experienced by the major industrial countries. Since price and exchange rate developments merely offset each other, the pattern of price competitiveness among most of the major industrial countries in 1977 was similar to what it had been prior to March 1973. The greater exchange rate flexibility after March 1973 was helpful to balance of payments adjustment insofar as exchange rate movements prevented certain current account imbalances from developing or widening owing to divergent rates of inflation. But exchange rate changes seem not to have played much of a role in reducing chronic current account imbalances among the industrial countries.

Two main explanations were advanced for the limited contribution of exchange rates to balance of payments adjustment. First, officials of industrial countries did not give high priority to the need for balance of payments adjustment. They intentionally reduced the degree to which exchange rate relations between their currencies varied by resorting to intervention and other policy measures, such as official and quasi-official borrowing, aimed at curbing changes in their exchange rates. Second, the effectiveness of exchange rate changes was impaired by the absence of appropriate accompanying domestic policies. In other words, the vicious circle phenomenon was not appropriately handled.

By 1978 Fund officials began to see greater evidence that changes in the relationships between the major currencies were having beneficial effects on the current account positions of the largest industrial countries. The changes in competitiveness from 1976 to 1978 between the United States, on the one hand, and the Federal Republic of Germany and Japan, on the other, were, for instance, in the direction required for the elimination of the U.S. deficit and of the German and

Japanese surpluses. Considerable empirical evidence showed too that relative price changes have a strong influence on the volume of imports and exports, at least in the longer run after the initial J-curve effects end. For these reasons, staff estimates as of 1978 suggested that by 1980 there could be a significant improvement in the U.S. trade balance and a major reduction in the surpluses of the Federal Republic of Germany and Japan. The Fund management and staff, in fact, tried to use these estimates to help restore confidence in the dollar in 1978, the story told in Chapter 44.

PRELIMINARY CONCLUSIONS ON EXPERIENCES WITH FLOATING RATES

As of 1978, Fund officials, in common with economists and financial officials outside the Fund, were able to draw only preliminary conclusions about the experiences from 1973 onward with floating exchange rates. In general, given the relatively unstable economic and financial conditions that had prevailed since 1973, floating rates were regarded as inevitable and their volatility as understandable. Virtually all officials conceded that no system of fixed rates could have been maintained in the unsettled situation of the 1970s. The common view was that if the par value system had not collapsed in August 1971 and had not come to an end in March 1973, it certainly would have collapsed later. There simply seemed to be no alternative to floating rates. Therefore, floating rates were generally regarded as working as well as if not better than any other system that might have prevailed.[17]

At the same time, a majority of officials expressed at least some disappointment with the instability of floating rates and with their limited contribution to resolving the long-standing balance of payments disequilibria among the main industrial countries. There was disappointment, too, with the extent to which floating rates enabled authorities to pursue independent monetary policies. Initially officials of some countries, especially of the Federal Republic of Germany and of Switzerland, had believed that freedom from the obligation to adhere to any particular exchange rate would make it easier for them to cope with inflationary pressures and to preserve internal financial stability. By letting the rate for the deutsche mark appreciate when capital inflows occurred, the authorities of the Federal Republic of Germany believed, for example, that they could insulate themselves from the need to lower their domestic interest rates so as to discourage these flows. They could thereby keep their monetary policy restrictive to buffer the country against what they regarded as lax demand-management policies in other

---

[17]The assessment of floating rates as of 1980 of a number of economists and policymakers outside the Fund, including the views of several persons who were early advocates of floating rates, can be found, for example, in Jacob S. Dreyer, Gottfried Haberler, and Thomas D. Willett, eds., *The International Monetary System: A Time of Turbulence* (Washington: American Enterprise Institute for Public Policy Research, 1982). This volume contains the proceedings of a conference held by the American Enterprise Institute in 1980 to assess the performance of the flexible rate regime of the 1970s and possible policies to help correct the shortcomings of that regime.

countries, such as the United Kingdom and the United States. They could also protect themselves to some extent against an influx of reserves that would otherwise be difficult to offset. Finally floating rates provided a way to protect the country from "imported inflation." Similarly, Swiss authorities, also finding it difficult to maintain a restrictive monetary policy together with a fixed exchange rate and relatively free capital movements, found the idea of flexible rates attractive. Conversely, by letting the exchange rate for the dollar depreciate, U.S. authorities believed they would be freer to pursue more expansionary domestic policies without worrying about the consequences on the U.S. current account position and the need to defend the dollar.

The belief that officials would have greater independence of monetary policy was expressed at the time, for example, in the following words: "By depoliticizing and de-emphasizing decisions about exchange rate policy, a regime of managed floating increases the policy options of the monetary authorities and adds to the flexibility of national policy."[18]

After over five years of experience with floating rates, however, it was far from clear that floating rates, in practice, enhanced the ability of officials to pursue independent monetary policies. A high degree of interlinkage in countries' monetary policies, especially of their interest rate policies, meant that officials of the major industrial countries could not ignore the external implications of such policies. Restrictive monetary policy with high interest rates in the Federal Republic of Germany, for instance, continued to attract short-term inflows of capital, and caused the deutsche mark to appreciate to a degree that distressed German exporters. U.S. pursuit of expansionary policies that caused the dollar to depreciate sharply aggravated inflation in the United States, and encouraged excessive capital outflows. Independent monetary policy under floating rates proved illusory. The disappointment of many officials with the extent to which floating rates gave them freedom in monetary policy was reflected in their gradual shift of emphasis away from the pursuit of independent monetary policies to the need for nations to coordinate their monetary policies.

Thus, because of their instability and limited role in balance of payments adjustment, and because they did not enable officials to pursue independent monetary policies, floating rates were in many respects disappointing. The flexible rate system seemed to be more a managed rate system, not all that different from the par value system, with many of the drawbacks that had characterized the par value system. Disappointment with floating rates became intense in 1978 when the dollar underwent continuous sharp declines for many months.

On the other hand, if the advantages of floating rates fell far short of the expectations of their advocates, their drawbacks were found to be less damaging than anticipated by their detractors. The risks of total dislocation of international economic relations had been a major theme of the critics of flexible exchange rates in

---

[18]Conrad J. Oort, *Steps to International Monetary Order: The Exchange Rate Regime of the Future*, the 1974 Per Jacobsson Lecture (Tokyo, October 11, 1974), p. 28.

the 1950s and 1960s. The Fund had itself for years been especially opposed to any general system of fluctuating rates, partly on the grounds that fluctuating rates would create great uncertainty for traders and investors and discourage foreign trade and international investment.[19]

The statistical evidence on trade and investment in the 1970s, however, showed no great negative effects. On the contrary, flexible exchange rates proved compatible with a rapid expansion of international trade and capital flows. World trade had continued to grow in the 1970s and at a rate higher than world output. Surveys of the reactions of businessmen in industrial countries to exchange rate uncertainty also suggested that they had adjusted their behavior to take account of exchange rate uncertainty rather than reducing their international transactions.

On the whole, as 1978 ended, the reactions of officials, including those in the Fund, to floating rates were thus mixed. Arguments over whether floating rates aggravated inflation and whether they helped balance of payments adjustment persisted. For some, floating rates remained an evil; for others, they remained the only possible alternative and even a blessing. The experience with floating rates, the dynamics of exchange rate movements, and the factors affecting exchange rates continued to be intensively studied within the Fund.[20] As 1978 ended, the Fund was also turning increasing attention to the implications of the floating rate regime for its developing members.[21]

---

[19]The Fund's views toward fluctuating rates as expressed in the 1950s and the first half of the 1960s were described in *History, 1945–65*, Vol. II, pp. 170–73.

[20]Additional studies on the experiences with floating rates by the Fund staff that were published after the end of 1978 include those by Jacques R. Artus and John H. Young, "Fixed and Flexible Exchange Rates: A Renewal of the Debate," *Staff Papers*, Vol. 26 (December 1979), pp. 654–98; by Morris Goldstein, *Have Flexible Exchange Rates Handicapped Macroeconomic Policy?* Special Papers in International Economics, No. 14 (Princeton, New Jersey: Princeton University Press, 1980); and *The Exchange Rate System: Lessons of the Past and Options for the Future—A Study by the Research Department of the International Monetary Fund*, IMF Occasional Paper No. 30 (1984), a summary of which can be found in Morris Goldstein, "Whither the Exchange Rate System?" *Finance & Development*, Vol. 21 (June 1984), pp. 2–6. Other studies analyzing exchange rate movements made by Fund staff published after the end of 1978 include John F.O. Bilson, "Recent Developments in Monetary Models of Exchange Rate Determination," *Staff Papers*, Vol. 26 (June 1979), pp. 201–23, and Michael Dooley, "An Analysis of Exchange Market Intervention of Industrial and Developing Countries," *Staff Papers*, Vol. 29 (June 1982), pp. 233–69. A study prepared in the Fund after 1978 that analyzed the determinants of exchange rate movements and especially the reasons why exchange rates tended to overshoot is that of Jacob A. Frenkel and Carlos A. Rodriguez, "Exchange Rate Dynamics and the Overshooting Hypothesis," *Staff Papers*, Vol. 29 (March 1982), pp. 1–30. In addition, on August 31, 1982, the National Bureau of Economic Research and the Fund jointly sponsored a conference on exchange rate regimes and policy interdependence to explore the channels by which economic disturbances in one country are transmitted to other countries in the post-Bretton Woods system. The proceedings of this conference were published in *Staff Papers*, Vol. 30 (March 1983), pp. 1–222.

[21]For a paper by an Executive Director on this topic, see Alexandre Kafka, "The New Exchange Rate Regime and the Developing Countries," *Journal of Finance, Papers and Proceedings of the Thirty-Sixth Annual Meeting of the American Finance Association* (New York), Vol. 33 (June 1978), pp. 795–802.

CHAPTER

43

Planning Surveillance of Exchange Rates

*T*HE REAL ADVANCE OF BRETTON WOODS was recognition by
governments that exchange rates were a matter of international concern. As far
back as Alfred Marshall, economists had viewed an exchange rate as having
important ramifications beyond the individual economy. But in 1944 public
authorities recognized that monitoring changes in exchange rates by the international community was essential. Establishing the Fund's authority over exchange
rates was not easy, however. Sovereignty over exchange rates was a prerogative to
which countries tenaciously clung. It was to take years for the Fund to develop and
implement its policies on exchange rates under the par value system and to obtain
some degree of authority.[1]

Recognition of the vested interest of the international community in the actions
taken by Fund members with respect to their exchange rates was carried over into
the provisions of the amended Article IV. The Fund was to "oversee the
international monetary system" and to "exercise firm surveillance" over the
exchange rate policies of members. On the surface these powers were greater than
those the Fund had exercised under the par value system. But since there were no
longer specific rules governing members' actions vis-à-vis the Fund with regard to
their exchange rates as there had been for par values, Fund officials were left with
the need to decide how to implement the new powers. They turned to this task early
in 1976.

EXPLORING WAYS TO ACHIEVE SURVEILLANCE

Prior to 1976, the Fund found it awkward even to ascertain the exchange rate
policies of many members. Officials of the large industrial members were especially

---

[1]The evolution of the Fund's policies and authority with regard to the establishment and
maintenance of par values and to changes in par values formed the subject of several separate
chapters in *History, 1945–65*, Vol. II. See pp. 51–173.

secretive about how they managed their governments' exchange rates or about the intervention policies they used. Countries with deliberate policies preferred secrecy because disclosing such information could immediately affect exchange markets. The United States did not disclose this information because intervention and other exchange rate policies were not precisely formulated; rates for the dollar were left fairly much to market forces.

In this atmosphere, even casual discussions about exchange rates between Mr. Witteveen and the Executive Directors from the large industrial members did not go well. The Executive Directors insisted that information on exchange rate policy, so confidential that it was not given by administration officials to members of congresses or parliaments, could not be supplied to the Fund even on a very informal, secret basis. Some Executive Directors from the large industrial members also complained that the Fund was not treating its members uniformly, that the Fund management and staff were not making equal efforts to get information from all the large industrial members. Mr. Cross queried the excessive interest in U.S. intervention policy.

To help overcome these objections, Mr. Witteveen began in 1975 to hold discussions at small luncheon meetings. He invited the Executive Directors of the seven largest members to discuss simultaneously the exchange rate policies of Canada, France, the Federal Republic of Germany, Italy, Japan, the United Kingdom, and the United States. Because these luncheon discussions, also attended by Mr. Dale, the Deputy Managing Director, and a few staff, proved frank and informative, Mr. Witteveen continued them for several months.

Luncheons could hardly suffice for exchange rate surveillance, however. Hence, after the Jamaica accord in January 1976, Mr. Witteveen and the staff began to explore techniques by which surveillance under the proposed amended Article IV would take place. They quickly concluded that the priority was to obtain information; surveillance could not be conducted if Fund officials did not know what was going on. As a minimum, regular statistical information on intervention in exchange markets was needed. Information on intervention should cover both spot exchange markets and forward markets. Yet the staff wanted to avoid the suspicion that they were looking for ways to collect a mass of material relating to intervention or that they were merely taking a statistical approach to exchange rate surveillance. It was easy to resort to a statistical approach since members' officials were sensitive to any deep questions of exchange rate policy. But the staff recognized that information on both the recent actions of members and their intentions with regard to their exchange rates was essential. Especially useful was information about the economic priorities of members, particularly their attitudes toward their general price levels, since these attitudes affected the exchange markets.

The management and staff believed that such information was necessary at least for the major industrial members whose exchange rates had pervasive effects. For other members, it was essential to remedy the lacunae in information about the nature of their exchange rate arrangements, policies pursued, and the levels of reserves. Mr. Witteveen and the staff recognized the difficulties involved in getting from members such information and that the Fund would have to regard even information supplied to the management and staff on an informal and confidential basis as information supplied officially to the Fund.

In addition to questions about obtaining information, other questions were explored. How was the information gathered from members best used and how were members to be influenced in their exchange rate policies? How was the Executive Board to be brought into the consultative process? A technique that might be used for surveillance of the exchange rates of the major industrial members was for the Managing Director to have informal, confidential discussions with the seven Executive Directors concerned, either individually or as a group. This technique would not be acceptable, however, to the nine Executive Directors elected by developing members nor to the Executive Director elected by Australia. Since these Executive Directors did not receive from their home sources the type of information pertinent to exchange rates available to the Executive Directors from the major industrial members, they often felt left out whenever an exchange crisis occurred and were anxious to receive briefings in the Fund on what was going on. These informal procedures might not be acceptable either to the three Executive Directors elected by smaller industrial members, such as Belgium, the Netherlands, and the Nordic countries.

Still another issue was the extent to which principles and procedures for surveillance would fit the situations both of members with floating exchange rates and those with pegged rates. Here, the question was whether a member with a fixed exchange rate, either pegged to a single currency, to a basket of currencies, or to other rates in a joint relationship, such as the snake, should have to consult the Fund prior to changing its pegging arrangement, comparable to the obligation of prior consultation under the par value system. The Managing Director and staff favored continuing the requirement of prior consultation with the Fund because that requirement at least enabled them to have some informal contact with a member whenever an exchange rate was changed, even if the subsequent review of the change in rate by the Executive Board proved something of a formality. Elimination of the requirement of prior consultation would considerably reduce the role of the Fund in informal discussions with member governments of exchange rate changes. Members with floating rates could not, of course, be required to have prior consultation. Since pegged rates were used mainly by developing members, the staff of area departments handling relations with developing members expressed fears about different procedures for members with pegged rates and for members with floating rates.

To accommodate the differing views of the staff on how to proceed, the paper on exchange rate surveillance prepared in the Research Department in early 1976 underwent several redrafts. As a prelude to a discussion of exchange rate surveillance in the Executive Board, the staff also prepared a paper on the linkages between members' domestic interest rates and their exchange rates, intended to show how deep into a member's domestic economic policies exchange rate surveillance by the Fund could penetrate. Fund surveillance could involve discussion of many purely domestic policies, such as interest rates, since these policies directly influenced exchange rates. The subject of the relation between interest rates and exchange rates was considered by the Executive Directors in an informal seminar prior to the Executive Board's formal discussion of exchange rate surveillance.

The staff paper on exchange rate surveillance circulated to the Executive Directors in July 1976 suggested principles and procedures. The principles were based on the Fund's experience, which revealed two ways in which members' exchange rate policies could interfere with balance of payments adjustment and hence with the smooth functioning of the international monetary system. First, an exchange rate inconsistent with the achievement of balance of payments equilibrium at a high level of employment and output interfered with the adjustment process. Second, an exchange rate, especially for a major currency, that was continuously fluctuating and changing created disorderly market conditions and thereby hindered the adjustment process. The principles for surveillance proposed by the staff on the basis of this experience accordingly aimed at ensuring that "wrong" exchange rates were not maintained and that excessive fluctuations were prevented.

With regard to procedures for surveillance, the staff highlighted a few essential questions for the Executive Directors' consideration. Should there be annual consultations for exchange surveillance plus provision for additional consultations if a member significantly altered its exchange rate policies between annual consultations? Should there, at least occasionally, be additional discussions with two or more members simultaneously so that the Fund could discuss with all concerned officials important exchange rate developments that affected two or more currencies? Should the procedure be retained by which a member with a pegged exchange rate was obliged to consult the Fund prior to a change in its pegging arrangements?

EXECUTIVE DIRECTORS' PRELIMINARY CONSIDERATION

When they took up the subject of exchange surveillance on the basis of the staff paper in September 1976, the Executive Directors were troubled by the same issues that had bothered the Managing Director and staff. They recognized that any surveillance of members' exchange rates in the Fund had to be couched in general terms. Officials of members were extremely sensitive to any discussions of their exchange rate policy, even in limited groups, and whether they would permit the Fund to extend its surveillance of exchange rates to other economic policies, such as interest rate policies, was uncertain. At the same time the Executive Directors recognized that in judging an exchange rate Fund officials could not concentrate solely on the use a member had made of reserves or on its policies of intervention in exchange markets or even only on its domestic monetary and other macroeconomic policies. The Fund would have to review a member's entire economic situation. Due consideration would have to be given, for instance, even to developments in the member's structure of production and to the outlook for its relative position in world trade.

These topics went well beyond those on which the Fund customarily took an official position. Discussions in the Fund even of members' macroeconomic demand-management policies had been accepted only gradually in the course of the Fund's consultations under Article XIV and Article VIII and in the course of discussions with members regarding their use of the Fund's resources.[2] The Executive Board still refrained from conclusions about the implications of a member's macroeconomic policies for its exchange rate and had never commented formally on the adequacy of an exchange rate of any of the Fund's large industrial members. In fact, even the Fund staff was exceedingly cautious in their appraisal of issues concerning the member's exchange rate. The staff was particularly reluctant to comment on the implications of an exchange rate for economic phenomena not under the Fund's authority, such as the structure of a member's production. While the Fund might have further powers over exchange rates under the amended Articles, the Executive Directors believed that it would be unwise for the Fund to "advertise" those new powers for fear of arousing the suspicion of officials of members that, by way of surveillance over exchange rates, the Fund was trying to exercise control over members' internal economic policies.

With regard to procedures for surveillance, the Executive Directors agreed with the staff's recommendations that periodic, presumably annual, consultations under Article IV be merged with existing consultations under Article VIII and Article XIV. Most Executive Directors, however, were concerned about the staff's suggestion that a member with a pegged rate be required to have a prior consultation with the Fund when it changed its peg. Mr. Amuzegar, Mr. Kafka, and other Executive Directors elected by developing members regarded such a requirement as a "dual system of surveillance procedures," applying a stricter system to developing members than to industrial members.

Executive Directors appointed or elected by continental European members likewise rejected prior consultation for changes in pegging arrangements. Mr. Dini and Mr. Pieske were concerned that members might be discouraged from pegging their rates if they had to consult the Fund in advance on changes in the pegs they used. Such discouragement was unwise. Pegging rates and especially making changes in pegged rates were desirable. Indeed, the Fund should be more concerned with pegged exchange rates that remained unaltered when a change was warranted than with asking members to consult the Fund when they did change their rates. Similarly, for a member with a floating currency, the absence of a change in its policy or of any reform in its exchange arrangements might well suggest the need for surveillance more than did the usual swings in its floating rate.

---

[2]The debates that arose in the early 1950s about whether the Fund was to discuss members' macroeconomic policies with them and how these debates gradually subsided were described in *History, 1945–65*, Vol. II, pp. 25–26 and 229–47.

As the discussion continued, it was apparent that the area of agreement among the Executive Directors was small. Some Executive Directors objected to the whole approach to exchange rate surveillance suggested by the Managing Director and the staff. Mr. Leddy disagreed with Mr. Pieske and other Executive Directors appointed or elected by Western European members that the Fund's surveillance ought to aim at achieving broad policy objectives, such as greater exchange rate stability. He also could not accept the suggestion by the staff that the degree of movement in a member's exchange rate should be used to trigger a special consultation with the Fund. He disagreed with the staff's interpretation of Article IV. U.S. officials regarded the new Article IV as an injunction to avoid manipulation of rates, not as an injunction for a member to take action to keep its exchange rate within a defined range. The Fund's emphasis should be on stopping members from taking actions that manipulated their exchange rates and not on encouraging members to take actions to influence their exchange rates to some level. In contrast to this U.S. view, the staff, Mr. Leddy pointed out, was putting too much emphasis on the notion of a "proper" level for an exchange rate. The staff approach was based more on how to manage an exchange rate than on the need for watchfulness to ensure that members did not violate the basic principles of Article IV. The staff paper devoted a great deal of attention, for example, to fluctuations in short-term exchange rates as evidence of disorderly market conditions. U.S. authorities could not accept such a criterion. Large changes in exchange rates in response to major changes in underlying economic conditions might well be desirable. In any event, a number of factors had to enter into any judgment of whether or not an exchange market was disorderly. Among these factors was the willingness of market participants to deal in the market and the ability of commercial businesses to conduct transactions. If the market was continuing to function reasonably satisfactorily, it could hardly be regarded as disorderly.

Like Mr. Leddy, Mr. Whitelaw had difficulty with the suggestion by the staff that the need for special reviews by the Fund of a member's exchange rate might be triggered by movements in the rate. In his mind, a criterion expressed in terms of the degree of movement of an exchange rate resembled the kinds of objective indicators for exchange rates rejected in the discussions of the Committee of Twenty three years earlier. Mr. Kawaguchi rejected the other criterion for special consultation suggested by the staff, that of changes in reserves. Changes in reserves, the Japanese officials believed, could be a misleading indicator of whether an exchange rate was out of line. Mr. Wahl objected to the staff's approach to surveillance on another ground. In his view, it displayed a definite bias in favor of members with floating currencies as against members with pegged, stable, or fixed exchange rates. He, too, rejected the idea that the appropriateness of an exchange rate level could be inferred from changes in a member's exchange reserves.

As Mr. Lieftinck expressed it, the basic dilemma concerned the kind of exchange rate system over which the Fund was to exercise surveillance. Was it to be a system in which national authorities used management policies to help determine their exchange rates or was it to be a system in which the free play of market forces determined these rates? The two approaches to the nature of the exchange rate system raised different questions for the Fund's surveillance. Was the Fund to try to promote a pattern of exchange rates among its members that reflected underlying structural and fundamental conditions, that is, was the Fund to aim at some "correct" pattern of rates? Was the Fund, for instance, to suggest to a member that an exchange rate be altered when it did not reflect a member's fundamental economic situation? In other words, was the Fund to indicate to members when it regarded their exchange rates as overvalued or undervalued? Or, alternatively, was the Fund merely to accept the exchange rates that resulted from daily market fluctuations? The staff was suggesting, and Mr. Lieftinck, along with several Executive Directors from other industrial members, agreed that some judgment about exchange rates ought to be the object of the Fund's surveillance principles and procedures. If the Fund merely accepted exchange rates that moved with daily market fluctuations, it had little reason to exercise surveillance over those members whose currencies floated freely.

Clearly Mr. Lieftinck's position, like that of other European Executive Directors, was the opposite of that of Mr. Leddy. But Mr. Leddy's position was also supported by Mr. Drabble and Mr. Ryrie. In their view, the Fund could have no firm rules on surveillance. At best, guidelines for the adjustment of exchange rates would have to be developed over time on a case-by-case basis. The need for a member to have a special consultation with the Fund would have to be identified by judging a number of factors, including the entire balance of payments situation of a member. No automatic triggers, such as movements in an exchange rate or in reserves, could, or should, be adopted.

This preliminary discussion by the Executive Directors demonstrated that any policy on surveillance of exchange rates would require a revised approach by the management and staff and much more discussion in the Executive Board. The Managing Director and staff looked to the solution suggested by Messrs. Drabble and Ryrie that guidelines for surveillance be developed over time on a case-by-case basis.

CONSIDERATION RENEWED IN LATE 1976

A revised staff paper on surveillance was circulated to the Executive Directors in December 1976. This paper again aimed only at pinpointing the main issues that would confront the Fund in meeting its obligations under Article IV so that the Executive Directors might try again to agree on the elements of a policy. The management and staff hoped that the discussion of this paper by the Executive Directors would give them the guidance they needed to draft a set of specific principles and procedures. The staff paper began by explaining the need for international surveillance of exchange rate policies in a world in which free rates were presumed to prevail. Surveillance of exchange rates by the international community was needed because of the high rates of inflation and the domestic economic and financial instability that characterized the 1970s. In a relatively stable world economy, variations in flexible or floating exchange rates would broadly reflect the relative competitiveness of different economies and any random shocks to the world monetary system, such as those arising from cyclical fluctuations or crop failures, could be handled relatively easily by existing methods for international collaboration and financial assistance.

In the complex period of the 1970s, however, flexible rates were not always free. The floating rate system was in many respects managed. In a managed system, conflicts over the appropriateness of a particular exchange rate were inevitable since countries had divergent interests. Countries with high rates of inflation at times attempted to limit the inflationary impact of exchange rate changes on their domestic economies. They did so by restricting the degree of depreciation. Their trading partners, however, often saw such limitations on exchange rate depreciation as increasing inflationary pressure in the rest of the world, as hindering effective balance of payments adjustment, and as leading to additional instability when the depreciation that was postponed eventually took place. In the opposite situation, when the currencies of countries with low rates of inflation were under strong upward pressure, the authorities often intervened to reduce exchange rate appreciation. Yet, this intervention was often seen by competitor nations not as merely offsetting temporary factors or speculative pressures, but as attempting to maintain undervalued exchange rates to help the exports of these countries.

Because of these divergent ways of looking at exchange rate policy, the Fund had to have some guidelines for floating rates. Establishing guidelines was difficult, however. Because, under the amended Articles, a member had freedom to have a floating rate, it was hard to know where to draw any lines for surveillance. There was also a problem for pegged exchange rates. Previous experience under the Bretton Woods system had shown that it was not uncommon for pegged rates to become inappropriate even when world conditions were generally stable. Hence, in addition to guidelines for floating rates, the Fund had to have ways to suggest to members with pegged rates that they change these rates.

Going beyond stressing the need for surveillance, the staff paper again tried to present some principles by which the Fund might judge exchange rates. While accepting the conclusion that had emerged from the earlier Executive Board discussion that the principles of the Fund with respect to exchange rate surveillance should be allowed to develop on a case-by-case basis, the management and staff believed that members needed to have some idea of the kinds of exchange rate behavior that would raise questions in the Fund and the procedures that the Fund would follow to deal with these questions. Therefore, even if a case-by-case basis was to be used, some general statement of policy intentions by the Fund was still needed.

To work out such a general statement, such principles would again have to be deliberated and debated among the Executive Directors. As a first principle, in developing and applying their intervention policies, members with floating rates ought to bear in mind the interests of other members, including those that issued the currency in which they were intervening. The management and staff felt assured that the Executive Directors would easily agree with that principle and anticipated ready agreement on the desirability of avoiding disorderly market conditions. The practice of official intervention on a day-to-day basis had become widespread and was broadly accepted as long as it was restricted to smoothing out disorderly conditions. When intervention went beyond short-term smoothing, however, opinions varied as to whether there should be an active policy of exchange rate management. The staff paper suggested that intervention be measured by changes in reserves and in official net short-term indebtedness as well as by the size of transactions in exchange markets. Whether intervention was regarded as large scale was to be judged in relation to suitable magnitudes, such as the size of a member's trade, the level of its reserves, and the size of its domestic money supply. The staff made no attempt, however, to develop a formula. A definition was also needed for manipulation since each member was obliged by Article IV to avoid manipulating its exchange rate. The staff suggested that manipulation meant retaining an overvalued or undervalued rate. The next question was how to recognize overvaluation or undervaluation.

In effect, what the staff was doing in the revised paper of December 1976 was to raise a number of general issues involved in determining the duties and responsibilities of the Fund in a world of floating exchange rates.[3]

After the earlier discussion in the Executive Board, the management and staff concluded that the principles by which the Fund would exercise firm surveillance could not be very precise. In the revised paper, the staff therefore put more emphasis on the procedures for surveillance. The first required procedure would be that members should notify the Fund of their exchange arrangements and of any changes in these arrangements. The Executive Directors were expected to agree fairly quickly with this requirement. Beyond this, the staff suggested that, in lieu of a strict prior consultation requirement for changes in exchange arrangements, it would be desirable and sufficient to have members contemplating changes in their exchange arrangements or in the intervention points for their currency discuss their situation informally with the Managing Director. Later, the Fund could receive the required formal notice. In this way, the Managing Director and the staff would continue to have some input into changes in members' fixed rate arrangements.

The staff suggested that the Fund also have regular—probably annual—consultations under Article IV, integrating the consultations previously carried out under Article VIII and Article XIV. In the great majority of instances, these Article IV consultations could be expected to give the Fund adequate coverage of members' exchange rate policies. Some provision should be made, however, to deal with

---

[3]A lengthy summary of these general issues that is available to the public can be found in Jacques R. Artus and Andrew D. Crockett, *Floating Exchange Rates and the Need for Surveillance*, Essays in International Finance, No. 127, Princeton University (Princeton, New Jersey: Princeton University Press, 1978).

exchange rate developments occurring between such consultations, that is, there should be some provision for special consultations should the need arise.

Working Toward a Policy

Beginning with this revised staff paper, the Executive Directors undertook in late 1976 to work out a policy with respect to surveillance to propose to Fund Governors at the next Interim Committee meeting, scheduled for April 1977. Four months of discussions in the Executive Board ensued. The Executive Directors recognized that it was incumbent on the Fund to provide members with guidelines on the kinds of exchange rate actions in which they should or should not engage in the interest of the international community. Yet it was impossible to lay down precise rules for exchange rate policies beyond those that had been incorporated in the first two guidelines for the management of floating rates established in 1974. They also recognized that it would not be easy for them to arrive at an agreed finding of whether a particular exchange rate was overvalued or undervalued. And they were not willing to accept any of the indicators, such as the use of restrictions, the drawing down or the building up of reserves, large amounts of official borrowing or lending, abnormal capital outflows, or large-scale intervention, suggested by the staff for triggering a special consultation by the Fund. They found it hard to agree even on the definition of a disequilibrium in a member's balance of payments.

Some Executive Directors, moreover, emphasized that the Fund should adopt only a limited policy that it could fully implement. The Fund should not be too ambitious by trying to encompass the wide range of members' policies bearing on exchange rates, since it could not, in practice, exert much influence on these policies. What could the Fund do, for instance, about members' interest rate policies, now recognized as having a pivotal influence on the exchange rates of the main industrial members? Executive Directors also emphasized that the reluctance of many members to have the Fund institute firm surveillance had to be accepted. In this regard, many Executive Directors thought that the staff was moving too hastily to establish a set of principles by which the Fund was to judge members' exchange rates and to influence their policies. They advised that the Fund rather proceed slowly and realistically, at most developing generally worded principles of the style of the guidelines for the management of floating rates of 1974.

DECISION OF APRIL 1977

On April 22, 1977, the Executive Board adopted a tentative decision, pending endorsement by the Interim Committee. The Interim Committee endorsed the decision and the Fund had a policy on exchange rate surveillance to be carried out when the amended Articles went into force.

The procedure of the Executive Board in taking only a tentative decision subject to endorsement by the Interim Committee had not been used before and raised some difficulties in the Executive Board. The Executive Directors who had been longest on the Executive Board were sensitive to the risk that the Board might lose its decision-taking role and were hesitant to take action which gave the Interim Committee more than an advisory function. On the other hand, they realized that the decision on exchange rate surveillance by the Fund was important and controversial and would have a much greater impact on financial officials if it was endorsed by the Governors on the Interim Committee. They therefore consented to the procedure.

Endorsement by the Interim Committee of an Executive Board decision raised another procedural question of some consequence. Should the decision, which was a decision of the Executive Board, be released to the press at the same time that the Interim Committee issued its communiqué? Not to release the decision would leave a gap in the information available to the press and public. To release the decision, however, meant that the decision on exchange rate surveillance was being treated differently from all other Executive Board decisions. It would be announced publicly even before the Executive Board had formally adopted it, since final adoption could take place only after the Executive Directors reassembled after the Interim Committee meeting. It would also be announced publicly long before it went into effect, since it was not to go into effect until the Second Amendment was in force (which was to take another year). Moreover, many Executive Board decisions, even of a general nature, were not given to the press immediately after adoption and Executive Directors were concerned that they would subsequently be pressured by the press to release their decisions, thereby leaving them less free to be secretive, if they so desired. Because of these concerns, the Acting Chairman, Mr. Dale, explained to the Executive Board the widespread public interest in the Fund's future exchange rate surveillance activities and that there was a precedent for the suggested procedure in that in June 1974 the guidelines for the management of floating rates were formally adopted by the Executive Board on the same day as the Committee of Twenty met and that these guidelines were released to the press simultaneously with the Committee of Twenty's press communiqué. While Mr. Kafka expressed reservations about the procedure, most of the Executive Directors agreed with it, so it was followed.

Elements of the Decision

The Executive Board decision on exchange rate surveillance began with a statement making clear that while the decision dealt with the Fund's responsibilities in exercising firm surveillance over the exchange rate policies of members, it did not deal with the Fund's responsibilities to oversee the international monetary system, also contained in Article IV.[4] In other words, the decision was deliberately narrow. Three principles were then set forth for the guidance of members in applying their exchange rate policies. A member shall avoid manipulating its exchange rate or the international monetary system in ways that prevent effective balance of payments

---

[4]E.B. Decision No. 5392-(77/63), April 29, 1977; Vol. III below, pp. 487–91.

adjustment or enable the member to gain an unfair competitive advantage over the other members. This principle repeated an obligation specified in Article IV. It was mandatory for the member to follow this principle. The second principle was that a member should intervene in exchange markets if necessary to counter disorderly conditions; the latter were defined as, inter alia, disruptive short-term movements in its exchange rate. The third principle was that a member should take into account in its intervention policies the interests of other members, including those of the countries in whose currencies it intervened. The second and third principles were hortatory and not legally binding.

Three additional principles stated how the Fund would implement surveillance. Surveillance was to be geared to the needs of international adjustment of payments imbalances, which were to be kept under review by both the Executive Board and the Interim Committee. Particular developments which could suggest the need for Fund discussion with a member were specified: protracted large-scale intervention in one direction in the exchange market; an unsustainable level of official or quasi-official borrowing, or excessive and prolonged short-term official or quasi-official lending, for balance of payments purposes; the introduction, substantial intensification, or prolonged maintenance, for balance of payments purposes, of restrictions on current transactions, or of special incentives for current transactions; the introduction or substantial modification for balance of payments purposes of restrictions on capital flows, or of special incentives for capital flows; the use of monetary and other domestic financial policies that gave abnormal encouragement or discouragement to capital flows; and behavior of the exchange rate apparently unrelated to underlying economic and financial conditions.

Also stated in the decision was how the Fund would appraise any of these developments when a member was called to consult. Appraisal was to be broadly based. The member's whole balance of payments situation was to be evaluated against the background of its reserve position and its external indebtedness and within the framework of a comprehensive analysis of the member's overall economic situation and policy strategy. The appraisal was also, in effect, to recognize that the member's objective was not only to achieve balance of payments adjustment but also "sustained sound economic growth and reasonable levels of employment."

The last section of the decision described the procedures for surveillance. Each member was to notify the Fund in appropriate detail of its exchange arrangements and thereafter of any changes in these exchange arrangements. Members were also to consult with the Fund annually under Article IV, with Article IV consultations "comprehending" consultations previously held under Article VIII and Article XIV. General developments in exchange rates were to be reviewed periodically by the Executive Board mainly in the course of its discussions of the world economic outlook, and special consultations in conjunction with that exercise would continue.

The Managing Director was to maintain close contact with members in order to discuss with them, on their initiative, important contemplated changes in exchange arrangements or policies. He could informally and confidentially question any actions that seemed to be out of keeping with the principles stated, discuss these actions with any member, and then report to the Executive Board. The Executive Directors were to review annually the general implementation of the Fund's surveillance over members' exchange rate policies.

It was the procedures, rather than the principles, that provided the necessary framework for Fund surveillance of exchange rates. The procedures aimed at setting up a mechanism that would enable continuous and effective surveillance to take place on a case-by-case basis without stating precise ground rules or principles to be enforced and that allowed for the divergent interests and situations of members.

THE START OF SURVEILLANCE

Implementing this decision was the next difficult step. In late 1977, the staff undertook internal discussions to consider such implementation. To get members to notify the Fund formally of their exchange arrangements and of any changes in their arrangements took priority. As noted in Chapter 39, a week before the Second Amendment went into effect the Executive Board took a decision requiring such notification and spelling out the details. Members were told that it would be appropriate to notify the Fund of all changes in a peg, of every change in the central point around which a member was maintaining margins, and any change in the composition of a composite basket of currencies used as a peg, other than one occurring from a redistribution of currency weights on the basis of newly available trade or payments data. For members with flexible exchange arrangements, it was more difficult to specify changes that would require notification to the Fund. But here, too, some attempt was made to suggest when the Fund should be notified. Certainly notification should be made whenever a member issued a public policy statement. The Managing Director was to consult with the member if he believed that a significant change had occurred and the Fund had not been notified.

Upon receipt of notification of a change in exchange arrangements, the staff was to circulate information to the Executive Board, and, if the Executive Board so wished, the staff was to prepare a paper describing the context of the change in exchange policy and giving the staff's assessment.

A member was not obliged to consult the Fund before making changes in its policies, as it had been under the par value system. There was no obligation even to notify the Fund in advance of changes in exchange arrangements. A member was, however, to notify the Fund of changes in its exchange arrangements, which could be after the fact. A requirement of advance approval by the Fund continued in effect, however, for multiple currency practices, for discriminatory currency arrangements affecting current payments (not for those affecting capital transactions), and for restrictions on current payments.

The Executive Board later agreed to procedures for Article IV consultations. The subjects to be discussed between the member and the Fund are in most respects similar to those discussed in the consultations under Article VIII and Article XIV. At the end of an Article IV consultation, there would be a brief summing up by the Managing Director in his capacity as Chairman of the Executive Board. A statement by the Managing Director summing up the Executive Board's discussion of each topic was gradually becoming a regular feature of Executive Board meetings. Endorsement by the Executive Board of the Chairman's summing up represented conclusions adopted by the Executive Board.

The Article IV consultations, it was realized, would also have to proceed on a trial-and-error basis. Executive Directors elected by developing members, for example, wanted to be certain that "members whose exchange rates had important effects on other members" received greater attention than did developing members. Another question was whether an Article IV consultation report would contain a candid assessment by the staff of a member's exchange rate policy. In preparing Article VIII and Article XIV consultations reports, the staff usually refrained from any discussion giving its views of a member's exchange rate, since exchange rates were a highly sensitive topic and since revelation of the staff's view could severely damage the member's policies. It was decided, too, that, because sensitive material might be included in the staff papers reporting on Article IV consultations, the Fund would have to be extraordinarily cautious in making such papers available to groups outside the Fund, such as other international organizations. In the past, background papers could be requested by other groups and, with the approval of the Executive Board, were made available. Article IV consultation papers might have to be more restricted.

There was also the question of whether or not two or more members might have to be requested to have simultaneous Article IV consultations with the Fund, particularly at times of disturbances in exchange markets that inevitably involved the currencies of at least two large industrial members.

■　■　■　■　■　■

As 1978 ended, the Fund thus confronted the critical question of how to monitor exchange rates in the new floating rate era. In addition to the problems described in this chapter, the Fund was likely to have other problems. Discussions of the exchange rate policies of the principal industrial countries were often held in forums in which officials from the Fund were not present or at best present only in an observer's capacity. These forums included Working Party 3 of the OECD's Economic Policy Committee, the finance ministers' meetings of the EC, the regular meetings of central bank governors at the BIS, and the informal meetings of the Group of Five. Daily telephone exchanges took place between financial officials of the major industrial countries concerning developments in the exchange rates for their currencies but Fund officials were not, of course, privy to these conversations. Moreover, many members did not want to have their exchange rate policies reviewed by the Fund. On the other hand, if the Fund did not put some force into its surveillance process, it risked becoming a bystander, abdicating a reason for its existence. Meanwhile, the European Monetary System (EMS), then in the final stages of planning, might gradually usurp the Fund's exchange rate functions with respect to the currencies of several of the Fund's European members.

As when the Fund was first made guardian of the par value system in the 1940s, Fund officials at the end of 1978 anticipated a struggle to establish and implement its authority over exchange rates.

CHAPTER
44

The Dollar in 1978:
Anatomy of a Crisis

S *UPPORTING THE DOLLAR* became an international issue in 1978. The
declines in the rates for the dollar, beginning in late 1977 and persisting
throughout 1978, brought on the worst exchange crisis since rates first floated in
1973. As illustrative of events typical of an exchange crisis under the regime of
floating rates, this chapter presents a play-by-play description of the 1978 crisis of the
dollar.

U.S. DOLLAR CONTINUES UNDER PRESSURE

Immediately after the announcement of January 4, 1978, described at the end of
Chapter 41, that the United States would intervene in exchange markets, the Federal
Reserve Bank of New York, acting for the U.S. Treasury and the Federal Reserve
System, moved to more open and forceful intervention in the markets. Its
intervention from December 1977 to March 1978 was equivalent to $2.7 billion, a
substantial amount compared with past intervention.

The dollar recovered in January 1978, but began to lose ground again and by
March 10 had lost any gains made after January 4, especially vis-à-vis the deutsche
mark and the yen. In March 1978, U.S. officials took further actions, the most
concrete of which were with officials of the Federal Republic of Germany. The
amount of the reciprocal swap arrangement between the Deutsche Bundesbank and
the U.S. Federal Reserve System was doubled, to $4 billion, bringing the amount of
swap lines between the Federal Reserve and 14 central banks and the BIS to
$22 billion. The U.S. Treasury also arranged for the sale of SDR 600 million of its
holdings of SDRs to purchase deutsche mark. In addition, because public statements
by financial officials were vital in restoring confidence to exchange markets,
Mr. Matthöfer, Finance Minister of the Federal Republic of Germany, and
Mr. Blumenthal, U.S. Secretary of the Treasury, "pledged" their countries' support
in cooperation with other industrial nations for policies "firmly oriented toward self-
sustaining recovery, steady noninflationary growth, and stability in exchange

markets." They also pointed out that additional cooperative efforts, including more financial resources, to defend the dollar could result from forthcoming meetings of the European Community, of the OECD, and of the International Monetary Fund. Reference was made explicitly to the U.S. reserve position in the Fund of some $5 billion which the United States would "draw if and as necessary to acquire additional foreign exchange."[1]

Other actions were taken to bolster the dollar vis-à-vis the Japanese yen. The Federal Reserve Bank of New York had already been intervening since January in the New York foreign exchange markets as agent for the Bank of Japan. As the dollar continued to depreciate in terms of yen, the U.S. Treasury, in March, issued a statement noting that close and frequent consultations were taking place between the authorities of the United States and of Japan. In addition, on March 15, the Japanese authorities announced further domestic measures, including a reduction in the discount rate, in an effort to promote faster economic growth in Japan, to reduce Japan's trade and current surpluses, and to restrain speculative inflows of capital that were causing the yen to appreciate.

Despite these steps, the dollar continued to decline rapidly. By early April 1978, the effective exchange value of the dollar, as measured by the weights in the Fund's multilateral exchange rate model (MERM), which had declined only slightly in the first nine months of 1977, had fallen by 8 percent from its level of late September 1977.

DISCONTENT WITH FLOATING RATES

At the Interim Committee meeting in Mexico City at the end of April 1978, for the first time in several years exchange rates were the dominant topic. Dismay was expressed at what was happening to the dollar. Many were ready to abandon the regime of floating rates. Speaking on behalf of the European Community, Knud Heinesen, Minister of Finance of Denmark, complained that extensive depreciation of the dollar, not warranted by "fundamentals," negatively affected business confidence and private investment needed to help foster world economic recovery. ("Fundamentals" was a vogue term in government, business, and banking parlance for basic factors in an economy, such as prices, incomes, gross national product, and trade and current account positions that bore on an exchange rate, as distinct from speculative influences.) While Mr. Heinesen welcomed the recent more active intervention policies of U.S. authorities, he insisted that the time was ripe for countries to revert to a system of fixed exchange rates.

Other European officials, while not going so far as actually to expect a return to fixed rates, also took the position that exchange rate instability was a prime cause of

---

[1]The text of this statement was reprinted in *IMF Survey* (Washington), Vol. 7 (March 20, 1978), pp. 86–87.

low economic growth and that large-scale collective intervention in exchange markets could significantly reduce such instability. René Monory (France), for instance, emphasized the need also to solve the energy problem and especially for the United States to reduce its oil imports; but he also argued that the erratic fluctuations in exchange rates since September 1977 made domestic policies in other countries difficult and led to a reduction in investment. He, like other officials, used the term "erratic fluctuations," which had come to be the accepted euphemism after the Rambouillet conference for any exchange rate disorders that were to be avoided. The word "erratic" appears in Article IV, Section 1(ii). Hans Matthöfer reassured his colleagues on the Interim Committee that the Federal Republic of Germany accepted its share of responsibility to help bring about self-sustaining world economic growth, but he, like other officials from EC countries, also believed that appreciation of the deutsche mark had already put business profits in his country under further pressure and adversely affected the propensity to invest. Gösta Bohman (Sweden) welcomed all appropriate steps to stabilize exchange rates and Gaston Geens (Belgium) urged that the Fund exercise its new powers of surveillance.

By this time, since oil prices were expressed in dollars and since oil exporting countries had accumulated huge reserves in dollars, oil exporting countries also had an enormous vested interest in the exchange value of the dollar, and at the Interim Committee meeting, officials from these countries spoke up about the depreciating dollar. Khalid M. Al-Gosaibi, Vice Governor of the Saudi Arabian Monetary Agency, for example, "deplored" exchange rate instability as adversely affecting international trade, creating inequities between borrowers and lenders, and constituting a potential source of friction in international relations.

Tatsuo Murayama assured other members of the Interim Committee that Japanese officials were taking a series of measures to expand domestic demand and to reduce Japan's current account surpluses. The measures included a number of actions to stimulate imports directly: accelerating tariff reductions, opening further domestic markets, and expanding facilities for financing imports. Japan's financial assistance to developing countries was also being enlarged to offset Japan's current account surpluses with long-term capital outflows. Having stated Japanese willingness to open its economy so as to reduce its current account surpluses, Mr. Murayama was more inclined to agree with European officials than with U.S. officials about the need to prevent sharp changes in exchange rate relations. Stability of exchange rates, he stated, was a prerequisite for effective economic policy in Japan and for growth of the world economy, rather than growth being a prerequisite for stability, the position that U.S. officials were espousing. He concluded that the Executive Directors ought to review and evaluate the entire floating rate system.

In response to these complaints, Mr. Blumenthal tactfully repeated what had become the stance of both Republican and Democratic Administrations. Priority had to be given to domestic measures in the major industrial countries, which would stimulate lagging world economic growth and alleviate persistent high levels of unemployment. Insofar as international monetary stability was concerned, stability of exchange rates could not be imposed on countries through enforcement of external rules, as the par value system had tried to do, but had to be developed by countries through the application of sound underlying economic and financial policies appropriate to the individual circumstances of industrial countries. In line with that philosophy, the U.S. program for assuring a strong and healthy dollar did not call for extensive exchange market operations to hold or attain a particular exchange rate or exchange rate zone for the dollar. U.S. authorities had intervened, at times in large amounts, to counter disorderly market conditions, but the main thrust of the U.S. program was aimed at the root causes of the problems. To this end, President Carter was pushing a program to reduce the dependence of the United States on foreign oil and was mounting a comprehensive effort to counter inflation, using fiscal restraint and seeking the cooperation of business and labor to slow down price and wage advances. The U.S. Administration was also engaged in a new program of providing incentives to expand U.S. exports as another way to reduce the U.S. trade deficit. These steps were designed to enhance and underscore the fundamental competitive strength of the U.S. economy which, U.S. officials insisted, was the ultimate and only reliable guarantee of a strong and stable dollar.

Reflecting the preference of Canadian officials also for unmanaged, flexible rates, Jean Chrétien took a stand similar to that of Mr. Blumenthal. It was not always possible to achieve economic growth targets, and wide differences remained in the rates of domestic inflation in the various industrial countries. Officials could not hope to achieve genuine stability of exchange rates until they had restored greater domestic and external equilibrium in their economies. Until such time, it would be unwise to try to constrain exchange movements artificially.

Trying to suggest a compromise, Filippo Maria Pandolfi (Italy) supported the coordinated scenario for world economic growth and reduction of payments imbalances advocated by the Managing Director. Mr. Pandolfi drew attention to the implications of this scenario for stabilizing exchange markets. Agreement on targets for economic growth would improve the basic economic factors that influenced the balance of payments positions of industrial countries and thereby facilitate the management of exchange rates by individual countries. Such agreement would also provide a framework against which the Fund could carry out its new powers of surveillance; a coordinated growth scenario would stress the underlying economic and financial factors involved in improving the performance of the floating rate regime rather than mechanical rules for the management of exchange rates.

The communiqué issued at the end of the Interim Committee meeting brought in the points of view of both those who insisted on action for exchange rate stability and of the U.S. officials who resisted it. Reflecting the staff's skillful draftsmanship and the line advanced by Mr. Pandolfi, the communiqué expressed both viewpoints and stressed the need for the Managing Director's plan for concerted growth, even in the same sentence: "the improvement in basic underlying conditions" coming from a concerted growth strategy would "contribute to greater stability of exchange markets which [in turn] is extremely important for the health of the world economy." Reflecting the views of those officials who were by now so unhappy about existing exchange rate instability that they were ready to return to fixed rates, the communiqué went on at some length about the Fund's new surveillance powers. It explained the Fund's need to take action but in such language as not to be offensive to U.S. officials: "The Fund has always concerned itself with situations in which the value of a currency is not compatible with the smooth working of the adjustment process, or where disorderly conditions exist in exchange markets." The communiqué noted, too, that some members of the Interim Committee asked that the Executive Board consider bringing into existence the proposed Council under the amended Articles so as to put more force into the Fund's surveillance.[2]

U.S. Concessions at the Bonn Summit

By 1978 international gatherings of financial officials were a common occurrence. At the OECD ministerial meeting in Paris in June, at the meeting of the finance ministers of the EC countries in Bremen in July, and at the economic summit meeting in Bonn in July, officials, especially from the European countries, again expressed their heightened concern about the continued declines in the dollar. At the meeting in Bremen, officials from the EC countries, aiming at achieving greater exchange rate stability at least for their own currencies, stepped up their plans for a European Monetary System. At the Bonn meeting, officials of the Federal Republic of Germany promised, after long resistance, to take specific actions to stimulate their economy.

Against a background in which European officials were forming the European Monetary System and German and Japanese officials were finally promising to take the domestic measures that U.S. officials had been urging upon them, U.S. officials felt obliged to make some concession. The declaration issued after the Bonn summit included a section on international monetary policy in which the sharply contrasting views of both sides were spelled out publicly in more forthcoming language than in the Interim Committee's communiqué six weeks earlier. Giving the views of European officials, the Bonn declaration stated that the erratic fluctuations of the exchange markets in preceding months had a damaging effect on confidence, investment, and economic growth throughout the world and that greater exchange rate stability would improve confidence and the environment for sustained economic growth. All officials were committed to continue to intervene to the extent necessary to counter disorderly conditions in the exchange markets, to maintain extensive consultations to enhance these efforts' effectiveness, and to support surveillance by the International Monetary Fund. Giving the views of U.S. officials, the Bonn declaration stated also that exchange rate stability could be achieved only by attacking the fundamental problems that had contributed to the existing large balance of payments deficits and surpluses.[3]

---

[2]Communiqué of Interim Committee, April 30, 1978, pars. 3 and 4; Vol. III below, pp. 235–37.

[3]Excerpts from the declaration issued after the Bonn economic summit were reprinted in *IMF Survey*, Vol. 7 (July 31, 1978), p. 237.

MORE DECLINES IN THE DOLLAR
AND TENSION AMONG OFFICIALS

While U.S. officials made public declarations about intervention to counter disorderly market conditions, their actual intervention to support the dollar remained modest. By mid-August the dollar's average exchange value had declined by another 6.5 percent from the level of early April. On August 17, President Carter again stated his concern about the decline in the dollar and instructed Mr. Blumenthal and G. William Miller, Chairman of the Board of Governors of the Federal Reserve System, to consider what action might be taken. A few days later, the Federal Reserve Board announced an increase of half a percentage point in the discount rate. On August 22 the U.S. Treasury announced that beginning in November the amount of gold offered at its monthly auctions would be increased from 300,000 ounces to 750,000 ounces to help break the spiraling price for gold as flights from the dollar into gold accelerated. On August 28 the Federal Reserve Board announced the elimination of a 4 percent reserve requirement on foreign borrowing by U.S. banks. These actions helped temporarily. The effective exchange value of the dollar recovered by 2.5 percent from August 17 to September 16, although this recovery, too, was interrupted by a sharp drop in the rate for the dollar at the end of August. After a brief period of relative calm in the beginning of September, exchange markets became unsettled again later in the month.

In this environment financial officials gathered in Washington in late September for the 1978 Annual Meeting. When the Interim Committee met on Sunday, September 24, its members had behind them the initiation of the expansionary measures of the Federal Republic of Germany pledged at the Bonn summit, measures aimed at injecting an additional stimulus into the German economy of the equivalent of 1 percent of gross national product. As Mr. Matthöfer explained, these measures involved primarily a substantial reduction of income taxes and other tax reliefs intended to stimulate business activity directly. They were costly in that they were expected to increase substantially the overall public sector deficit. The Japanese Government had also declared that it was ready to take the additional measures necessary to reach a growth target of 7 percent and that it had adopted a supplementary stimulatory budget. It appeared that German and Japanese officials were responding to concerns of the international community, and that, despite continuing declines in the dollar, U.S. officials were pursuing a policy of benign neglect. Mr. Monory took the view that now the dollar might well be undervalued in exchange markets. Mr. Geens pressed strongly for U.S. authorities to defend the dollar. Mohammad Said Nabulsi, confining his comments to "the grave situation of exchange rate instability," complained that members of his constituency—which included Saudi Arabia and Kuwait—were suffering "in an unprecedented manner" from the impact of exchange rate instability on their reserves, their investments, and their trade. Mr. Pandolfi was concerned, since a substantial correction in 1979 was forecast of the current account payments imbalances of the industrial members, principally as a result of the exchange rate movements that had already taken place, but in a context of a slowdown in economic growth, that the burden of balance of payments adjustment was falling too heavily on exchange rates instead of being achieved through economic growth in surplus members. Hence, adjustment was falling excessively on the deficit members. Even Mr. Chrétien was forced to refer to exchange rate movements as being at times "erratic." He called for education of the public that would discourage irrational currency speculation.

The communiqué of the Interim Committee again took two positions. Because of adverse effects on prices, confidence, and investment, exchange rate instability had made more difficult the formulation and implementation of members' economic policies. But return to exchange market stability would require the adoption of national policies to reduce inflation and to achieve more convergent rates of growth in domestic demand.[4] The Group of Twenty-Four, meeting two days before the Interim Committee, had also referred to the instability of the exchange rates of the major currencies, which was giving rise to considerable uncertainty and having adverse effects on the rate of investment and on economic activity.[5]

At the Annual Meeting, almost all Governors spoke out more vociferously than ever against the extreme movements taking place in the rates for the major currencies. Responding to the intense concern of financial officials about the dollar, President Carter in his welcoming address to the Governors stated that he was "determined to maintain a sound dollar."[6] In his first opening address as Managing Director, Mr. de Larosière also referred to "the very marked changes in exchange rates" that had taken place in the previous year and a half. But he was inclined to see benefits in these changes in the rates for the dollar, the deutsche mark, and the yen. "These changes would lead to a substantial improvement in the pattern of current account balances among the industrial countries." Mr. de Larosière, however, also had to note concerns expressed in the Executive Board and in the Interim Committee about the disadvantages of too great a variability in exchange rate movements, and he reassured the Governors that the Fund's surveillance principles not only permitted intervention in exchange markets but also obligated members to intervene in order to counter disorderly conditions.[7]

Messrs. Matthöfer, Pandolfi, Monory, Geens, Colley, and Poos all explained why they had stepped up plans for the European Monetary System. They simply had to achieve exchange rate stability at least for their own currencies.[8] Mr. Pandolfi warned once more that the continued pursuit of economic policies that fell short of the requirements of the adjustment process, the unclear signals given to exchange

---

[4]Communiqué of Interim Committee, September 24, 1978, par. 2; Vol. III below, pp. 239–40.
[5]Communiqué of Group of Twenty-Four, September 22, 1978, par. 6; Vol. III below, p. 655.
[6]Address by the President of the United States, *Summary Proceedings, 1978*, p. 3.
[7]Opening Address by the Managing Director, *Summary Proceedings, 1978*, pp. 17 and 19.
[8]Statements by the Governor of the World Bank for the Federal Republic of Germany, the Governors of the Fund for Italy and for France, the Governor of the World Bank for Belgium, and the Governors of the Fund and the World Bank for Ireland and Luxembourg, *Summary Proceedings, 1978*, pp. 30, 36–37, 42–43, 101–102, 128, and 144.

markets by policymakers, the lack of coordination of intervention in the markets and the resulting short-run exchange rate variability all had negative effects on trade, on investment flows, and on inflation. As French officials had done so often in the past, Mr. Monory condemned the system of floating rates; on this occasion, he stated that floating rates were incapable of preventing erratic movements or of restoring balance of payments equilibrium.

Because Japanese officials continued to be acutely sensitive to criticism of Japan's large and persisting current account surplus, Mr. Murayama drew attention to the fact that the yen had appreciated by about 36 percent against a basket of currencies of Japan's major trading partners since the previous Annual Meeting and argued that such appreciation would inevitably bring about a substantial equilibrating effect on Japan's balance of payments position. He asked that the Fund help find a way to make the floating rate system more stable.[9]

Governors from more developed primary producing members were upset, too, by exchange rate instability. R.D. Muldoon, for instance, stated that the exchange rate instability of the previous 12 months, the speed with which changes occurred, and the disorder and uncertainty of the exchange markets "have had effects on us all."[10] Mauno Koivisto warned that if the major countries whose currencies had moved significantly were not willing or able to offset through internal measures the subsequent effects on domestic demand, the underlying disparities in growth and price performance were likely to get worse.[11] Commending the concerted strategy for economic growth to which the industrial members had committed themselves at the Bonn summit, Xenophon Zolotas stressed that, while the world might effectively be on a dollar standard, the burden of maintaining order in the international monetary system ought not to be considered solely the responsibility of the United States. Concerted action by all the major industrial countries was imperative. Certainly, the uncoordinated efforts of central banks to control foreign exchange markets had proved futile.[12]

Once again many Governors from developing members in Africa and Asia that had long been committed to fixed exchange rates and Governors from oil exporting members repeated their objections to the exchange rate fluctuations that the major currencies were experiencing. Yong Hwan Kim, H.M. Patel, Marcel Yondo, Ali Wardhana, Abdellatif Ghissassi, Benito Raúl Losada, and Sir Veerasamy Ringadoo, all explained that, with sharp fluctuations in the exchange rates for the major currencies, it was difficult for officials of developing members to know whether their own exchange rates were adequate. Continuously appreciating and depreciating currencies of the industrial countries, moreover, had unsettling effects on the

---

[9]Statement by the Governor of the Fund and the World Bank for Japan, *Summary Proceedings, 1978*, pp. 50 and 52–53.

[10]Statement by the Governor of the Fund for New Zealand, *Summary Proceedings, 1978*, p. 107.

[11]Statement by the Governor of the Fund for Finland, *Summary Proceedings, 1978*, p. 125.

[12]Statement by the Governor of the Fund for Greece, *Summary Proceedings, 1978*, p. 68.

growth of income and trade of developing members and caused problems for investment in these countries and for their reserve management.[13]

In the light of these criticisms of floating rates, it was revealing that while Mr. Blumenthal gave the full support of the United States to the Fund's role in surveillance and noted with great interest the actions of the European Community to move toward economic and monetary integration—a goal that the United States had long supported—he said virtually nothing about rates for the dollar. He concentrated his attention on the intensified anti-inflation efforts of the United States, on U.S. efforts to reduce its dependence on oil imports, and on a new national policy to expand exports.[14]

Seeing an opportunity to dispel fears about the dollar and to try to calm exchange markets, the Managing Director, Mr. de Larosière, and the staff took the occasion of the Annual Meeting to point out publicly and privately the favorable effects likely to result from the sharply changed dollar-deutsche mark and dollar-yen rates. The depreciation of the dollar vis-à-vis these currencies, or alternatively expressed, the appreciation of the deutsche mark and the yen vis-à-vis the dollar, would in a few years substantially reduce the chronic current account deficit of the United States and the chronic current account surpluses of the Federal Republic of Germany and of Japan. The imbalances in world payments that had persisted for a decade would finally be corrected. In making such a prediction, the Managing Director and the staff were committing themselves to a proposition not yet accepted by many economists: that changes in effective exchange rates did in the medium or long term correct current account imbalances. Also, in an analysis that was becoming prominent in the thinking of the management and staff—that there was a close link between improvement in a country's balance of payments and its internal macroeconomic policies, even under floating rates—Mr. de Larosière pointed out to the Governors that control of inflation in the United States and domestic demand expansion in the Federal Republic of Germany and in Japan were basic to improvement in their payments positions. In effect, he was saying that the comprehensive domestic measures being taken in the three countries, the anti-inflation program in the United States and the expansionary measures being taken in the Federal Republic of Germany and Japan, were more likely to produce the desired stability of exchange rates than was direct intervention in exchange markets.

The longer-term favorable effects of the changes taking place in the exchange rates for the dollar, the deutsche mark, and the yen, and the prospective improvement in balance of payments positions as a result of the internal policies being taken by the three major countries did not, however, receive sufficient attention in press reports on the Annual Meeting. Attention continued to center on

---

[13]Statements by the Governors of the Fund and the World Bank for Korea and India, the Governors of the Fund for Cameroon and Indonesia, the Governor of the World Bank for Morocco, and the Governors of the Fund for Venezuela and Mauritius, *Summary Proceedings, 1978*, pp. 47, 71–72, 85, 98, 110, 169, and 212.

[14]Statement by the Governor of the Fund and the World Bank for the United States, *Summary Proceedings, 1978*, pp. 90–93.

whether U.S. officials would intervene in large amounts in the exchange markets to defend the dollar. Meanwhile, the Fund's statistical projections of current account improvement for the industrial countries were regarded as too optimistic. The efforts of the Managing Director and the staff had little effect, therefore, in dispelling pessimism in exchange markets.

THE UNITED STATES DRAWS ON THE FUND

The dollar once again started to depreciate rapidly in the first half of October 1978. To arrest this depreciation, President Carter announced a tougher anti-inflationary program on October 24, 1978. Measures were taken in "a balanced, concerted program under which tight budgetary restraint, private wage and price moderation, and responsible monetary policy" were to support each other.

Much to Mr. Carter's disappointment and to the surprise of most observers, however, instead of resurging after such an announcement or at least stabilizing, rates for the dollar came under intensified downward pressure. This development, following a presidential announcement of a much tougher anti-inflationary program, was not only unexpected and unusual, but suggested how far confidence in U.S. economic programs had been undermined.

In the six weeks from mid-September 1978 to the end of October, the effective exchange value of the dollar fell by 7.25 percent, the depreciation being particularly large in relation to the deutsche mark. From September 1977 to the end of October 1978, the dollar had declined by about 40 percent against the Japanese yen, 35 percent against the Swiss franc, and 13 percent against the deutsche mark. On a trade-weighted basis, that is, the basis of a basket of currencies with weights for trade derived from the multilateral exchange rate model, the dollar, "in effective terms," had declined by 19 percent in these 13 months.

This sharp deterioration of the dollar convinced U.S. officials that they had to intervene in exchange markets in massive amounts. Stating that the continuing decline was unwarranted by fundamentals and threatened his recently announced anti-inflationary program, President Carter announced on November 1, 1978 a package of measures to be taken by U.S. authorities to defend the dollar directly in coordination with officials of the Federal Republic of Germany, Japan, and Switzerland. The United States mobilized the equivalent of $30 billion in deutsche mark, yen, and Swiss francs for intervention purposes. Included were transactions with the Fund for $5 billion—a $3 billion drawing by the United States of its reserve tranche and $2 billion of sales of SDRs by the United States from its SDR holdings. The swap lines of the Federal Reserve System were increased to $15 billion, from $7.4 billion, with the swap line with the Deutsche Bundesbank increased from $4 billion to $6 billion, with the Bank of Japan from $2 billion to $5 billion, and with the Swiss National Bank from $1.4 billion to $4.0 billion. These swap lines, which now came to $29.76 billion, were fully available except for about $1.8 billion utilized in earlier operations. There was also a U.S. Treasury swap facility with the Deutsche

Bundesbank. In addition, the U.S. Treasury was to issue foreign-currency-denominated securities of $10 billion and the amount of gold sold in monthly Treasury gold sales was to increase from 300,000 ounces to at least 1.5 million ounces, beginning in December. And there were to be two new domestic monetary measures. The New York Federal Reserve Bank's discount rate was increased immediately from 8.5 to 9.5 percent. A supplementary reserve requirement equal to 2 percent of time deposits in denominations of $100,000 or more was established, in addition to the existing reserve requirements.

Drawing on the Fund

Because reserve tranche drawings are automatic, the U.S. drawing on the Fund was a simple transaction. The drawing was for SDR 2.3 billion, equivalent to $3 billion. The Executive Board made the equivalent of $2 billion available on November 6, and the balance, equivalent to $1 billion, was drawn after the Fund raised the needed amounts of deutsche mark and yen under the General Arrangements to Borrow. The Managing Director requested U.S. officials to hold a special consultation with the Fund under the provisions of Article IV.

The staff discussions persuant to that consultation, held in December 1978, revealed different interpretations of the U.S. action. To many, mobilization by U.S. officials of large amounts of funds for purposes of intervention suggested a departure from past U.S. policy, signaling the end of benign neglect. In the special consultation with the Fund, U.S. officials admitted that their actions were inspired by international considerations, and in this sense, represented a departure from past practice. At the same time, however, they insisted that they had not changed their policy and were merely intervening in foreign exchange markets to counter disorderly conditions. They continued to believe that exchange rates had to move freely so as to reflect underlying economic conditions and that these conditions were currently such as to enable the dollar to strengthen. The U.S. current account was improving, and prospects for continuing improvement had been enhanced by the anti-inflationary program, by passage of the energy legislation, and by the adoption of an export promotion policy. The expansionary measures taken by the Federal Republic of Germany and Japan were also likely to stimulate economic growth in these countries and to reduce their current account surpluses, thereby bringing about greater balance in international accounts. All these developments would help to restore more stable exchange markets and to avoid the large and unwarranted shifts that the U.S. dollar had experienced from September 1977 through October 1978.

The Fund staff explained the decline in the dollar not in terms of irrational markets but rather in terms of fundamental economic factors. Since the recession of 1974–75, the U.S. economy had grown faster than those of most other industrial countries, and, furthermore, in the early part of the recovery period, U.S. price performance was as good or better than most of its trading partners. In 1977 and

1978, however, inflation rates in a number of countries, notably in the Federal Republic of Germany and Japan, came down substantially while they increased in the United States. Moreover, the U.S. merchandise trade balance shifted sharply from a recession-induced surplus of $9 billion in 1975 to a deficit of $31 billion in 1977 and of nearly $36 billion (annual rate) in the first three quarters of 1978. This deterioration resulted mainly from faster economic growth in the United States than in its trading partners. Consequently more imports were pulled into the United States, including imports from developing countries, and demand for U.S. exports abroad was low. The growth in the volume of oil imports by the United States was especially high in 1976–77 as domestic production of energy failed to increase during the period. All these factors made the U.S. balance of payments worse than it had been, and with continuing bad prospects, speculation against the dollar developed.

The management and staff also took the position that large-scale, one-way intervention could not—and should not—provide a basis for exchange rate stability. Long-lasting stability inevitably depended on the progress industrial countries made in bringing down inflation rates, in reducing differences in their rates of utilization of labor and capital resources, and in moving to current and capital account positions that seemed "sustainable." (The latter was a term coming into greater use within the Fund to characterize a payments situation that might not be balanced but that could be maintained more or less indefinitely.) In all these respects, the situation of the dollar could be expected to improve for the reasons that the Managing Director had noted at the Annual Meeting some months earlier.

Discussion of the U.S. Measures in the Executive Board

By the time the U.S. actions were taken up in the Executive Board on December 13, 1978, rates for the dollar had already been sharply reversed. Intervention and anticipation of greater intervention in exchange markets and of improvement in economic fundamentals restored confidence in the dollar almost overnight. As was customary, the Executive Director from the member with which the consultation was being held made a statement first. Mr. Cross's statement on this occasion brought out the context in which U.S. officials had, after years of resistance, decided to put together large-scale resources to support the dollar. They regarded the situation in exchange markets as dangerous. Disorderly exchange markets were threatening U.S. efforts to control domestic inflation and were adversely affecting the global climate for investment and economic growth. The extreme depreciation of the dollar in 1978 was not justified by underlying economic conditions in the United States. On the contrary, basic economic conditions in the United States were getting better since economic growth rates were going up, energy legislation had been enacted, and the price competitiveness of the United States in foreign markets was improving. Moreover, U.S. authorities believed that they had to put to rest any doubts about their determination to deal with the country's economic problems. The November 1 measures, moreover, were only one part of an integrated array of policies designed to combat inflation, correct the balance of payments deficit, and deal with exchange market difficulties. Finally, these exchange market operations were not to be undertaken by the United States in isolation but rather in a coordinated intervention policy with officials of the Federal Republic of Germany, Japan, and Switzerland.

The U.S. authorities had certainly not changed their minds about flexible exchange rates nor their attitudes toward managing the dollar. They remained opposed to any notions of target rates of exchange or to "floors" or "caps" for movements of the dollar. They had decided only that they needed to correct a situation in which rates for the dollar and market psychology had been excessively affected by false expectations and speculation and in which rates did not reflect the economic fundamentals. They did not want rates for the dollar to be pushed beyond levels consonant with underlying economic conditions and wanted to restore a climate in which rates for the dollar could, and would, respond to fundamental economic circumstances.

Defending the long-standing U.S. policy of letting rates for the dollar float, Mr. Cross stressed that in comparing the changes in the effective rate for the dollar with those for other major currencies, it was evident that longer-term changes in the rates for the dollar were quite moderate. (By December 1978 the effective exchange rate of the dollar as calculated by the Fund staff was about 13 percent below its previous peak in December 1976 and only 7 percent below the level that prevailed when generalized floating began in March 1973. The 13 percent decline in the effective rate for the dollar in the two years from December 1976 to December 1978 was caused mainly by appreciations of the yen, the Swiss franc, and the deutsche mark. These three currencies had appreciated 51, 42, and 24 percent, respectively, in relation to the dollar in that two-year period. The currencies of most other industrial members had also appreciated against the dollar, although by not as much; the pound sterling had appreciated against the dollar by 16 percent, the French franc by 13 percent, and the Italian lira by 2 percent. On the other hand, the U.S. dollar had appreciated vis-à-vis the Canadian dollar and the Swedish krona.)

Most members of the Executive Board welcomed what they construed as a shift in U.S. policy. U.S. officials at last recognized that what happened to the dollar in exchange markets impinged on their ability to carry out domestic programs and they were at last accepting responsibility for market rates for the dollar, even by intervening in large amounts to support the dollar, if necessary. But the range of views expressed by the Executive Directors showed how difficult and complex the issue of exchange rate policy was. All Executive Directors were concerned by the seemingly irrational way in which exchange markets evolved on a day-to-day basis. Mr. Pieske, Mr. Ruding, and Denis Samuel-Lajeunesse (France) stressed that periods of extreme exchange rate instability, such as had been experienced in 1978, could occur again. Such periods definitely had to be avoided in the interest of encouraging private investment so as to stimulate growth, as even U.S. officials were now conceding. Mr. Drabble explained that the Canadian dollar also often underwent gyrations not linked to Canada's underlying economic fundamentals. Mr. Matsunaga confirmed that Japanese experience revealed that the rate instability of 1978 was due largely to speculation. Mr. Samuel-Lajeunesse characterized exchange markets as "having a life of their own," with movements in exchange rates determined more by psychological and political factors than by changes in basic economic phenomena. Messrs. Dini and Jalal pressed again for some kind of target zones for exchange rates. Otherwise exchange markets could become disoriented for prolonged periods before monetary authorities took action.

A possible danger for the world economy if U.S. officials deflated the U.S. economy in order to stabilize the dollar was raised by Messrs. Matti Vanhala (Finland), Jalal, Kharmawan, and Nana-Sinkam. They worried that, with attention centered on the need to defend the dollar, U.S. authorities might take such severe domestic measures as to slow down the U.S. economy excessively, which would depress the trade of other members. In their view, in order to avoid a "crude deflationary overkill" in the United States, industrial countries should take concerted action to help world economic recovery and to correct the persistent and growing current account imbalances among the industrial countries.

Mr. Ruding queried whether the real effective changes in the exchange rate wrought after all these fluctuations were actually likely to have sizable consequences for improving the balance of payments disequilibria among industrial members, as the management and staff were saying. Was the resulting depreciation of the dollar likely to reduce the trade and current account deficit of the United States, and were the corresponding appreciations of the deutsche mark and the yen likely to lessen the current account surpluses of the Federal Republic of Germany and Japan?

The U.S. measures had an immediate impact, and as this Executive Board discussion was going on, the rates for the dollar were already rapidly recovering, marking the end of the exchange crisis of 1978.

THE EUROPEAN MONETARY SYSTEM

While the dollar crisis of 1978 was temporary, it was partly responsible for a fallout with profound long-run consequences for the international monetary system and the International Monetary Fund: the establishment of the European Monetary System (EMS). Upset by the renewed instability of exchange rates, concerned that this instability might endanger even the limited European integration already achieved, and fearful of what they regarded as weak surveillance by the Fund, European officials were propelled to put their own long-planned separate organization into operation.

Although the Werner report of 1970 had originally envisaged the achievement in stages by 1980 of economic and monetary union among European countries, so far the snake had been the only visible result.[15] In 1978, European officials took more concrete action.

---

[15]For some background on the Werner report, see Chap. 1, p. 21, above.

The European Council, composed of the heads of state or government of the EC countries, issued a communiqué at Bremen, after a meeting on July 6 and 7, 1978, in which they declared that they had agreed on a common approach to the economic problems of the European Community. They would move toward closer monetary cooperation, "leading to a zone of monetary stability in Europe."[16] The annex to the communiqué set forth, in five paragraphs, an outline of some elements of the EMS that would create this zone of monetary stability. Finance ministers were instructed to formulate the "necessary guidelines" for the appropriate EC bodies to evolve and the provisions required for operation of the scheme. Intensive negotiations by European finance ministers on detailed arrangements took place in September, October, and November. Then, at a conference in Brussels, on December 4 and 5, 1978, the heads of state or government adopted the resolution establishing a European Monetary System. Belgium, Denmark, France, the Federal Republic of Germany, Ireland, Italy, Luxembourg, the Netherlands, and the United Kingdom thus set up an EMS arrangement, and all except the United Kingdom declared that they would participate in the exchange rate and intervention system. The United Kingdom stated that it might decide to adhere to the intervention system at a later date.

The EMS was designed ultimately to consist of three main elements: an EC exchange rate regime, a European Monetary Fund, and a new currency unit, the European Currency Unit (ECU). Under the exchange rate regime, each participant establishes a central rate for its currency in terms of the ECU. As a result, bilateral parities are created between each pair of currencies of the participants. Participants are to intervene, as in the snake arrangements, to prevent movement greater than 2.25 percent above and below these parities, and there is a presumption that a participating country will change its parity when it needs such alteration. The original margins may exceed these margins, up to a maximum of 6 percent, for currencies that are not in the snake, but the wider margins must be reduced gradually "as soon as economic conditions permit."

The European Monetary Cooperation Fund (EMCF) issues short-term credits as before under the snake arrangement, but new, substantially enlarged credit facilities have also been created, and ultimately all credit facilities are to be consolidated into a European Monetary Fund. ECUs have been issued, composed of a basket of all nine currencies of the EC countries, that is, the Belgian franc, the Danish krone, the deutsche mark, the french franc, the Irish pound, the Italian lira, the Luxembourg franc, the Netherlands guilder, and the pound sterling. An initial supply of ECUs was issued by the EMCF against deposits of 20 percent of both gold and dollar reserves of participating countries.

In short, the EMS, which took effect on March 13, 1979, has all the features associated with the International Monetary Fund—a code of behavior for exchange rates, a fund of credits to be drawn upon for balance of payments purposes, and a new reserve asset. In two respects, the EMS goes significantly further than the Fund:

---

[16]This meeting was described in *IMF Survey*, Vol. 7 (July 17, 1978), pp. 209 and 221.

countries in the EMS agree to try to coordinate their economic and monetary policies and to pool a part of their foreign exchange reserves.[17]

The Resolution of December 5, 1978 declared that the EMS "is, and will remain, fully compatible" with the Articles of Agreement of the Fund. As of the end of 1978, officials were well aware that the EMS, operating independently of the Fund, even if in harmony with its objectives, would have important consequences for the Fund. Would the procedures of the EMS be consistent with those prescribed in the Fund's Articles? Would the EMS assist the Fund in achieving its own objectives? Would the EMS weaken the Fund's authority by becoming a separate, strong organization of a few large industrial countries, supplanting the Fund in its primary exchange rate endeavors? Was the Fund thereby in danger of becoming an organization dealing mainly with developing members? In these circumstances the Fund took a cautious approach. The management and staff merely kept closely in touch with developments in the EMS and informed the Executive Directors of these developments. Basically Fund officials were receptive to the new organization.

The attitude of Fund officials toward the EMS in 1978 and their cautious approach contrasted with their attitude when the European Payments Union (EPU) was formed in the 1940s. At that time Fund officials, worried about the arrival on the scene of a competitor organization, were less than cooperative with arrangements to assist the EPU[18]. In 1978, however, Fund officials generally sought ways to cooperate with the EMS. What the implications of the EMS for the Fund would be in the future only time would tell.

---

[17]A summary of the features of the EMS written by the Fund staff can be found in Horst Ungerer, "European Monetary System Has as Objectives Greater Economic Stability, Policy Convergence," *IMF Survey*, Supplement, Vol. 8 (March 19, 1979), pp. 97–100. See also Horst Ungerer, Owen Evans, and Peter Nyberg, *The Euorpean Monetary System: The Experience, 1979–82*, Occasional Paper 19, The International Monetary Fund (Washington 1983). A discussion of the legal aspects of the EMS, including its relation to the Articles of Agreement of the Fund, can be found in Joseph Gold, "Developments in the International Monetary System, the International Monetary Fund, and International Monetary Law Since 1971," in Hague Academy of International Law, *Recueil des Cours* (The Hague), Vol. 174 (1982), pp. 107–366; and *SDRs, Currencies, and Gold: Fourth Survey of New Legal Developments*, IMF Pamphlet Series, No. 33 (Washington, 1980), pp. 46–64. An evaluation of the EMS by an Alternate Executive Director of the Fund can be found in Tom de Vries, *On the Meaning and Future of the European Monetary System*, Essays in International Finance, No. 138, Princeton University (Princeton, New Jersey: Princeton University Press, 1980).

[18]See *History, 1945–65*, Vol. II, pp. 317–31.

PART ELEVEN

Resurgence of the SDR in 1978

"... Rationality and foresight are essential in development strategy. And also in international cooperation. The movements gestating in the developing world are of vast dimensions and historic importance."

—RAUL PREBISCH, *Change and Development—Latin America's Great Task* (1971)

CHAPTER 45

Allocating More SDRs

*T*IME WAS RIGHT IN 1978 for the SDR to move closer to center stage. The management and staff were concerned that the prolonged decline of the dollar in an environment of floating rates, of closely interconnected intercountry banking transactions, of virtually unrestricted movements of capital, and of large payments imbalances could be dangerous. If private and even official holders of foreign exchange suddenly elected to alter the currency composition of their portfolios, the resulting shifts in currency balances could be destabilizing. This risk, resulting from excessive use of reserve currencies, could make financial officials of member governments more receptive to improving the SDR as an alternative reserve asset. Second, Fund officials had for years been developing specific ideas of how to advance the SDR and were ready to make proposals. Third, the amended Articles of Agreement, which legally permitted the realization of many of these ideas, were now in place.

The management and staff decided to try to get simultaneous action in 1978 on two fronts: resuming allocations of the SDR and altering its features so as to make it more competitive with gold, the U.S. dollar, and other national currencies in international transactions. How the decision to allocate more SDRs came about is discussed in this chapter. Discussion of the measures taken to improve the characteristics and extend the uses of the SDR is deferred to Chapter 46.

NO ALLOCATIONS IN THE SECOND BASIC PERIOD

The decision reached in 1978 to resume allocations of SDRs came after six years in which no SDRs had been allocated. The last allocation of SDRs for the first basic period of three years had been made on January 1, 1972 when SDR 2,951 million was distributed to 112 participants in the Special Drawing Account (equivalent to 10.6 percent of their quotas in the Fund). This allocation ended the allocation of SDRs for the first basic period that had been agreed in 1969. SDRs in the amounts of SDR 3,414 million and SDR 2,949 million had already been allocated on January 1, 1970 and January 1, 1971, respectively.

The amount of SDR 3–3.5 billion a year that had been agreed for the three years of the first basic period was expected to be approximately equal to the gap between the anticipated growth of reserve needs (SDR 4–5 billion a year) and the predicted increase in the supply of reserves other than SDRs (some SDR 1–5 billion a year).[1] But immediately afterwards there had been an unexpected explosion in world reserves. While in the three years 1967–69 members' reserves rose by about SDR 6 billion, in the subsequent three years 1970–72 they rose by more than ten times that amount, about SDR 68 billion. With such huge increases in reserves, many queried in retrospect the need for the SDR allocations of 1969. Where was the predicted shortage of world reserves? It was certainly unlikely that officials would agree to any further allocations of SDRs for the second basic period, to commence on January 1, 1973. Nonetheless, as he was obliged to do under the Articles, Mr. Schweitzer made an effort. The procedure for arriving at a decision on allocations of SDRs, which was precisely defined in the Articles after the First Amendment, required that the Managing Director first determine whether there was broad support for a proposal to allocate SDRs. He was then to make a proposal. If he concluded that no proposal commanded broad support, he was required to make a report instead of a proposal.

As Mr. Schweitzer sought the views of officials in late 1971 and early 1972, he quickly concluded that the swelling supply of other reserve assets precluded agreement on any further allocation of SDRs for some time to come. While some officials favored continuing allocations in the second basic period in roughly the same annual amounts as those of the first basic period and others were prepared to accept annual amounts approximately half this size, officials of the large industrial members wanted no additional allocations. On June 26, 1972, after explaining the results of his talks to the Executive Directors, Mr. Schweitzer formally reported to the Board of Governors that there was insufficient basis for him to submit a proposal.

As obliged to do by the Articles, Mr. Schweitzer again took up with officials in late 1972 and early 1973 allocation of SDRs during the rest of the second basic period. But not surprisingly, he could not gather enough support for a proposal and ceased discussions altogether after an increase in foreign exchange reserves of about $20 billion took place in the first quarter of 1973.

The possibility of an SDR allocation was not considered for the next several years. The second basic period remained an "empty" one. The total of SDRs in existence continued to be SDR 9,315 million.

CONSIDERING ALLOCATIONS OF SDRs
FOR THE THIRD BASIC PERIOD

Against a background of continuing concern about managing international liquidity and the failure of officials to agree in 1975 on establishment of a gold

---

[1]The considerations governing the amount of allocations of SDRs for the first basic period were explained in *History, 1966–71*, Vol. I, pp. 209–16.

substitution account, as described in Chapter 32, the management and staff in 1976 approached the question of allocating more SDRs. The second basic five-year period of SDR allocations started on January 1, 1973 and was to end on December 31, 1977. The Managing Director was required to report to the Board of Governors on a possible allocation by June 30, 1977.

More than a year before this report was due, Mr. Witteveen started to seek agreement on allocations of SDRs for the third basic period. In conversations with financial officials in 1976, Mr. Witteveen inquired about their reactions to allocating more SDRs. Officials from developing members immediately reacted favorably. When the Group of Twenty-Four met in Manila, they formally endorsed his efforts by asking explicitly for another allocation.[2] Officials from other members took a guarded stance. They were considering the possibility of expanding world liquidity through an increase in Fund quotas in the course of the Seventh General Review, but the size of the increase was controversial, and they were unsure about SDR allocations as well. They were not ready to say no, however, either to the Managing Director or to officials from developing members. Hence, the Interim Committee, also meeting in Manila, merely requested the Executive Directors "to keep all aspects of international liquidity under review and to report to it at a later meeting."[3]

The Economic Counsellor and other staff, who had been studying many facets of the SDR and of international liquidity, in line with the directives of the Interim Committee's communiqué, started to send to the Executive Board early in 1977 papers examining the existing adequacy of international liquidity. The Executive Board's consideration of a possible allocation of SDRs was consequently taken up in a broad context. Increasing Fund quotas under the Seventh General Review, the need for a supplementary financing facility that Mr. Witteveen had also meanwhile proposed, and a possible allocation of SDRs were considered simultaneously.

Changing Criteria for the Adequacy of Global Reserves

The staff papers were based on the premise that the criteria for deciding on SDR allocations could not be the same as those used in 1969 when allocations had been justified on the grounds that a shortage of global reserves could be anticipated. After 1969 the Executive Directors regularly reviewed and assessed the adequacy of world reserves as required under Section 10 of the By-Laws enacted after the First Amendment. These reviews were included in the Annual Reports.

These reviews reveal that judgments as to the ease or stringency of global reserves became much more difficult after 1973. Since the SDR came into effect the Fund had used two methods to assess the adequacy of global reserves.[4] The first

---

[2]Communiqué of Group of Twenty-Four, October 2, 1976, par. 5; Vol. III below, p. 648.

[3]Communiqué of Interim Committee, October 2, 1976, par. 4; Vol. III below, p. 229.

[4]The Fund had been assessing reserve adequacy since 1953. For descriptions of these earlier assessments, see *History, 1945–65*, Vol. I, pp. 334–35 and pp. 447–48 and *History, 1966–71*, Vol. I, pp. 25–27, 86–88, and 139–41.

method was based on quantitative indicators. Ratios developed by the staff during the 1960s when they were studying the need to create a new reserve unit were used. The most commonly used ratio was that of aggregate world reserves to aggregate world imports, although this ratio was supplemented with ratios between reserves and imports for a number of individual countries. This first method of judging the adequacy of global reserves also involved use of additional statistical procedures that compared actual reserves with estimated reserve holdings judged appropriate on the basis of past relations between members' reserve holdings and other economic variables.

The second method involved an examination of the policies that members used when they encountered payments imbalances. Answers to a number of questions about recent developments in members' policies with regard to their restrictions, exchange rates, and international borrowing were used as guides to whether members were willing to let their reserves fall or whether they wanted to accumulate more reserves. Were members easing or tightening their restrictions on imports and payments? Were members imposing restrictions on capital flows? How likely were members to devalue or to revalue their currencies when they had prolonged balance of payments deficits or surpluses? Were members reducing or increasing their reliance on credits and borrowings for financing their balance of payments deficits?

The first method of assessing the need for global reserves had the advantage of providing a quantitative figure for reserve excess or inadequacy; it had the disadvantage of being mechanical. The second method had the advantage of allowing for a more careful analysis, but had two drawbacks. It did not provide a concrete figure for reserve excess or inadequacy. It was impossible to judge countries' precise needs for reserves as revealed by their policies on restrictions, exchange rates, and borrowing, since these policies were also influenced by factors other than the size of their reserve holdings. Despite the disadvantages of these methods, Fund officials considered them, used together, as good as any other methods.

After 1973 many developments necessitated altering how the Fund assessed the adequacy of global reserves. First, floating exchange rates meant that reserves were no longer needed to the extent that they had been to defend fixed exchange rates and agreed par values. Because exchange depreciation would take place when payments deficits developed, the need to hold reserves for the eventuality of payments deficits was reduced. On the other hand, despite the greater flexibility of exchange rates, there were still substantial payments imbalances, and how liquidity was provided to finance these imbalances remained of central concern to the Fund. Moreover, even among members whose currencies were floating, management of rates was quite widespread. The substantial intervention in exchange markets that took place did not in practice allow countries to hold less reserves than had initially been expected. In addition, many currencies were pegged to other currencies, to baskets of currencies, or to the SDR. As a result of the management of floating rates and the pegging of currencies, Fund members were still making considerable use of both credit and reserves to deal with payments imbalances. Several members in fact seemed to hold almost as many reserves as before.

Second, soaring prices for gold in private markets meant that members' official holdings of gold were much more valuable. Many members therefore had gold reserves that, at least on paper (since very few transactions in gold had occurred since 1971), were very large. How should these increased gold reserves be assessed?

Third, relative prices of other major reserve assets were also continuously changing by substantial margins, making difficult comparisons in their value over time. For example, from the end of 1970 to the end of 1976, the pound sterling had depreciated against the U.S. dollar by almost 30 percent and the U.S. dollar had depreciated against the SDR (and against reserve positions in the Fund whose value was maintained in terms of SDRs) by 14 percent. Because of the changing value of individual reserve assets, the purchasing power of a given collection of reserve assets depended on its composition.

Fourth, the greatest change that took place after 1973 affecting judgment on the adequacy of reserves was on the supply side of the market. There had been a massive increase in international borrowing. Members had ready access to vastly expanded international capital markets, including borrowing from commercial banks and other private institutions, and their inclination to borrow huge sums to finance their balance of payments deficits greatly reduced their reliance on reserves. The relation between this development and the need for reserves also was not easy to assess, however. On the surface, access to borrowing seemed to reduce the need for reserves. But the increased resort to international borrowing also influenced members' reserve policy in the opposite way, giving to reserves the new function of contributing to the confidence of foreign lenders and of adding to a country's creditworthiness. Many members engaged in borrowing to increase their reserves so as to improve their borrowing capacity.

This development on the supply side of reserves was especially significant. Earlier, particularly in the few years before 1971, the major increase in international reserves took the form of official claims on the United States. But there had been concern about how long the United States could continue to let such claims increase. Now, the change in the elasticity of supply of international liquidity in the 1970s amounted almost to a difference in kind. In most years after 1973, the aggregate addition to official world reserves that reserve center countries such as the United States and the United Kingdom were making was small in comparison with capital market transactions in these and other large industrial countries. By making medium-term loans and by accepting placement of some of the counterpart funds at shorter term, capital markets had in effect become major suppliers of reserves. Thus, Fund members that had access to international capital markets faced within their borrowing capabilities a highly elastic supply of reserves, both individually and in the aggregate. Individually, they could, if they wished, use external borrowing to move toward a particular reserve position. Collectively, the system could generate reserves through intermediation provided by banks and other private financial institutions.

A fifth development affecting the Fund's assessment of reserve adequacy was the growth in the volume of capital flows. For many large industrial members but also for some developing members, capital flows increased more than trade. Increased capital flows meant that imports were a less adequate measure of the size of total international transactions and hence of the need for reserves.

Because of these developments, the Economic Counsellor and other staff came to believe that concepts such as the long-term need for global reserves and the adequacy of reserves were no longer precise nor subject to measurement. No longer was the function of a member's reserves as simple as it had been under the par value system—to finance prospective temporary balance of payments deficits that might arise at a given exchange rate rather than resort to exchange devaluation or to restrictions on trade or payments. The discussions of reserve adequacy contained in the Annual Reports after 1973 were broadened, going beyond the initial comparisons of the actual global volume of reserves and estimated needs for reserves to include consideration of many other factors. Among these factors were the effects on reserve adequacy of the distribution of reserves among countries, the different kinds of reserve assets making up world reserves, the availability of public and private liquid resources other than reserves for financing balance of payments deficits, and the adaptability of the supply of reserves to the existing demand. But even with all this analysis it was difficult, if not impossible, to come to judgments about the need for reserves or, more specifically, for the need for further allocations of SDRs. The topic continued to be intensely studied in the Fund.[5]

RATIONALE FOR ANOTHER ALLOCATION OF SDRs

Against this background the Managing Director and staff undertook in 1977 to present a rationale for allocation of SDRs for the third basic period. They took a very different position from that put forward in 1969 at the time of the first allocation of SDRs.

In 1969, the Managing Director's report had taken the position that the reserve situation then prevailing was tight. Attention was directed to the decline in reserves by over 50 percent relative to world trade since the early 1950s. Reserves, particularly in the traditional forms of gold, of claims on the United States payable in dollars, and of official holdings of pounds sterling, had been declining. An even greater shortage of world reserves appeared to be in the offing. At the time, too, the Fund was the principal source of balance of payments credit for most members. Similarly, it seemed evident that if the desire of members to increase their reserves was to be met, increases in reserves would have to be supplied largely by the Fund. Gold was not expected to be a major source of new reserves, and it was widely felt that the

---

[5]See, for example, Andrew Crockett and William H. White, "The Lessons of the Early-1800s: Controversy Between the British Banking and Currency Schools for Judging the Adequacy of the World's Foreign-Exchange Reserves," *Revue Internationale d'Histoire de la Banque* (Geneva), Vol. 16 (1978), pp. 208–17.

U.S. balance of payments deficit, which had been a major source of past increases in official reserves, would and should be reduced or eliminated. Only two possible sources for reserve increases thus remained—reserve positions in the Fund and SDRs. The first source was dependent on an increase in members' quotas in the Fund and on use of the Fund's resources; the second source depended on approval of SDR allocations.

The first decision to allocate SDRs had therefore been taken in the expectation that demand for reserves would rise and that the supply of reserve assets, other than the SDR, would be inelastic and likely to increase slowly. By tailoring the allocation of SDRs to its best estimate of this excess of demand over supply of reserves from other sources, the Fund was seeking to meet the long-term global need as it arose to supplement existing reserve assets (Article XXIV). It was also widely expected that SDR creation would continue thereafter to account for the bulk of reserve increases.

In 1977, as they considered another allocation of SDRs, the Managing Director and staff were cognizant of the sharply changed demand for, and the supply of, official world reserves, described in the foregoing section. They were well aware, too, that following the decision of 1969 to allocate SDRs, there had been a rapid and unexpected increase in official reserves. Hence, any arguments in support of another allocation of SDRs would have to be along different lines. At the same time, Article XXIV, Section 1(*a*) of the Articles (Article XVIII, Section 1(*a*) of the Articles after the Second Amendment) directed the Fund to "seek to meet the long-term global need, as and when it arises, to supplement existing reserve assets in such manner as will promote the attainment of its purposes and will avoid economic stagnation and deflation as well as excess demand and inflation in the world."

In 1977 the Managing Director and staff, in considering how to apply this provision of the Articles, reviewed the way in which international reserves were being supplied. They argued primarily that an allocation of SDRs was desirable because it would help to improve the composition of the *increases* in reserves that were occurring. As world reserves grew in the form of national currencies, SDRs would become a smaller proportion of world reserves unless more allocations were made. It was essential, they contended, that the proportion of SDRs in total reserves not only not become smaller, but even that it become larger. International management of liquidity would be facilitated. Although it was difficult to judge the ideal size of any annual allocation, the Managing Director and staff suggested a range of SDR 5–8 billion. They left open the period of time over which annual allocations would take place.

When they considered this matter early in 1977, the Executive Directors expressed a range of views that made it clear that no easy agreement would be forthcoming. A number of Executive Directors from developing members supported the management-staff position. Some of them argued that SDR allocations could be justified simply on the basis of an existing need for more global reserves. The Executive Directors from Canada, from some of the smaller European members, and from the United Kingdom wanted allocations of SDRs to be tied to improvements in the characteristics and uses of the SDR. In this way the SDR would be made a more attractive reserve asset by enhancing both its quantity and its quality. These Executive Directors also favored a short period for allocating SDRs, or smaller amounts of allocations than had been suggested by the management and staff. Mr. Cross and Mr. Pieske, however, opposed further allocations of SDRs, at least for the time being. They argued that there was no need to supplement existing reserve assets.

Unable to make a recommendation, the Executive Directors left resolution of the issue up to the Interim Committee. When that Committee met in April 1977, its members were also not ready to agree, so it took an "on-hold" position. In its communiqué, the Committee stated only that it had considered whether a further allocation of SDRs would be desirable, noted that the Executive Directors had been discussing this question, and agreed to request them to give further consideration to all aspects of the matter and to report to the Committee at its first meeting in 1978.[6] Little progress had thus been made since the Annual Meeting seven months before. In June 1977, after consulting with the Executive Directors, Mr. Witteveen reported to the Board of Governors that he could not propose a new allocation of SDRs. In his report he pressed, however, for further consideration of the possibility.[7]

At the 1977 Annual Meeting, several Governors pressed for a new allocation of SDRs. Momčilo Cemović, for example, pointed out the absence of adequate solutions for the transfer of real resources to developing countries, the absence of an increase in "reserves to hold," and the resulting increase in the burden of indebtedness of developing countries. He called a new allocation of SDRs "indispensable."[8]

NO AGREEMENT IN EARLY 1978

SDR allocations were again considered in the Executive Board in early 1978. As part of their preparation for the Interim Committee meeting scheduled for April, the Executive Directors discussed the possibility of allocating SDRs in the context of their discussions of several other subjects—possible changes in the characteristics and uses of the SDR, quota increases under the Seventh General Review, and the need for a supplementary financing facility.

When they discussed SDR allocations, they took up a number of general topics relating to the need for global reserves, with certain points being emphasized. Many members with ready access to international capital markets could borrow not only to meet their current balance of payments financing needs but also to add to their reserves. On the other hand, members that did engage in such borrowing had a problem of needing periodically to refinance their indebtedness. Although most

---

[6]Communiqué of Interim Committee, April 29, 1977, par. 5; Vol. III below, p. 232.
[7]The Managing Director's report is in Vol. III below, pp. 273–74.
[8]Statement by the Governor of the World Bank for Yugoslavia, *Summary Proceedings, 1977*, p. 145.

members had ready access to international capital markets, some members could not borrow so readily in those markets and consequently had need for reserves in the form of SDR allocations. Most members in both groups followed a long-term policy of adding to their reserves as their international transactions grew. Therefore, although world reserves were rapidly rising, members' needs for reserves also seemed to be rising. The main question relevant to SDR allocations in this situation was whether the global need for reserves should continue to be met mainly through increases in holdings of reserve currencies or whether part of the need for additional reserves could and should be met by allocations of SDRs.

The Executive Directors could not agree on the answer. Some argued that no problem arose with respect to world liquidity if increases in reserves continued to take the form of national currencies. No allocations of SDRs were necessary. Others took the position that any further increases in world liquidity through the Fund should be conditional, that is, in the form of larger Fund quotas rather than of SDR allocations. These Executive Directors argued that, were members to receive more SDRs, some might postpone needed balance of payments adjustment. Recourse to conditional liquidity, that is, to use of the Fund's resources, would require them to take measures to reduce their balance of payments deficits.

As of April 1978 there was still not enough support for an allocation of SDRs to enable the Managing Director to make a proposal. The Executive Directors could still make no recommendation to the Interim Committee, and at the Interim Committee meeting at the end of April, officials' views remained far apart. Mr. Matthöfer took the position that, in the absence of a "patent global need for reserves," an increase in the volume of SDRs would not contribute toward making the SDR the principal reserve asset of the international monetary system. On the contrary, a decision to increase SDRs would "weaken confidence in the SDR and in the institution responsible for it." Mr. Monory revealed that French officials were not particularly in favor of a new allocation of SDRs on the grounds that there was no need to add to global liquidity; financial assistance should increasingly be provided by official and conditional facilities as a means of bringing about greater balance of payments equilibrium. Officials of other EC countries, such as Mr. Geens, however, believed that a reasonable increase in the volume of SDRs in circulation would help to maintain the viability of the SDR. Mr. Ghissassi, like other officials from developing members, stressed that the proportion of SDRs in total reserves had decreased over the years and that if the SDR was not to become "totally obsolete," a further substantial allocation was imperative. Mr. Al-Gosaibi argued that the SDR was "still embryonic" and that if it was to fulfill its functions, a continuing increase in its volume as well as progressive improvements in its valuation and characteristics was essential. Other officials, such as Mr. Muldoon, were more concerned with improving the characteristics and uses of SDRs, especially in raising its interest rate, than they were with obtaining further allocations. U.S. officials seemed to be slowly coming around to considering allocations of SDRs, provided members were allowed to use them to pay increases in quotas under the Seventh General Review. This use of SDRs would reduce the impact on world liquidity of a new allocation and would minimize discussion about the reserve assets to be used for quota payments.

In view of these diverse positions, the Interim Committee, in its communiqué, again took an on-hold stance. The Committee noted the report of the Executive Board on improving the characteristics and broadening the uses of the SDR and on the question of an allocation of SDRs. It also noted that a large number of members supported an allocation of SDRs, but that some of these believed that the present state of world liquidity was not such as to justify more than a modest allocation. It agreed to request the Executive Board to pursue work on all these aspects of an allocation of SDRs and to submit appropriate proposals together with draft recommendations for consideration by the Committee at its next meeting, scheduled for the end of September.[9]

AGREEMENT IN SEPTEMBER 1978

Within weeks of his taking office in June 1978, Mr. de Larosière, picking up where Mr. Witteveen had left off, gave added push to the subject of SDR allocations. He met informally with all members of the Executive Board, in small groups or individually, and described "a proposed SDR package" and a procedure by which he hoped to obtain agreement when the Governors assembled for the Annual Meeting. The package consisted of a 50 percent general increase in Fund quotas; SDR allocations of SDR 4 billion annually for three years, starting in 1979; improvement in the characteristics and uses of the SDR, including raising its interest rate; a slight differentiation in the rate of interest on the SDR from the rate of remuneration; and use of SDRs to pay for part of the increases in subscriptions resulting from the increase in quotas under the Seventh General Review. The Executive Directors from developing members were pleased with the package as "fair and reasonable." Executive Directors from industrial members and from relatively more developed members regarded it as a "good compromise" and as "an appropriate basis for further discussion." Since German and U.S. officials were not yet ready to agree to an SDR allocation, however, the Executive Directors again left the decision up to the Interim Committee for its meeting in September 1978.

The Executive Directors' report to the Interim Committee noted the facts and the arguments with respect to SDR allocations. The reserves of most Fund members showed a long-term rising trend. Additional reserves were being accumulated to deal with growing potential payments imbalances arising from the scale of international transactions. Analysis of current circumstances stressed that freedom of access to international capital markets meant that creditworthy countries, operating within their borrowing limits, could satisfy their needs for reserves. Countries following this course of adding to their reserves would, however, be faced with the problem of the periodic refinancing of their borrowings. Moreover, a number of countries were not in fact able to borrow readily in capital markets, a

---

[9]Communiqué of Interim Committee, April 30, 1978, par. 5; Vol. III below, p. 237.

difficulty reflected in the uneven distribution of reserves. These countries under-standably considered sole reliance on this method for obtaining reserves as being inequitable. In addition, in the absence of an SDR allocation, reserve increases would go on taking the form of currency balances. The share of SDRs in total reserves would thus continue to decline, a development in conflict with the objective of the Articles of making the SDR the principal reserve asset in the international monetary system. (The share of SDRs in world reserves, excluding gold, had already declined from 16 percent in 1972 to about 4 percent.) These considerations suggested that an allocation of SDRs was warranted, and that there was in fact a "long-term global need...to supplement existing reserve assets," the condition required by the Articles for an allocation of SDRs. Indeed, a long-term global need could exist even if there was no current shortage of reserves. Furthermore, it was not necessary to prove that SDR allocations were the only way this global need could be met.

The size of the allocation, the report stated, should be decided in the light of the existing magnitude and expected growth of official reserves. The volume of official gold holdings was not expected to grow significantly in the near future, although their exchange value might change. Liquid reserves—SDRs, reserve positions in the Fund, and foreign exchange—amounted to over SDR 230 billion and on conservative assumptions about the growth of the world economy were projected by the staff to increase over the next five years by some SDR 100-200 billion. Although an increase of that size appeared large, the projected rate of growth was in fact significantly lower than in the previous two five-year periods: from 1968 to 1973 total reserves doubled, and from 1973 to 1978 holdings of liquid reserves again doubled. Although figures of this kind did not, of course, provide precise guidance to the appropriate level and timing of SDR allocations, they did offer some point of reference for determining whether a proposed allocation was modest or substantial when compared with plausible estimates for the increase in the demand for reserves.

The report then stated that most Executive Directors believed that these considerations indicated the desirability of a substantial allocation of SDRs. It also explained that much of the analysis put forward in previous discussions of this question suggested little reason to fear any significant expansionary effects from an SDR allocation. But the report added that it was nonetheless understandable that in an inflationary world there was concern not only about the real effects of any international monetary measure of this nature, but also about the appearance. This consideration suggested that at this time any SDR allocation should be modest and its period of distribution short. The Executive Directors recommended an annual allocation for three years in the range of SDR 4–6 billion. But the report also pointed out that some Executive Directors favored smaller or larger amounts and that two Executive Directors still opposed any allocations.

Interim Committee Agrees to Allocations

The Interim Committee, meeting on Sunday, September 24, 1978, surprisingly agreed not only to the increases in quotas for individual industrial members under the Seventh General Review but also to an allocation of SDRs. In essence, officials of the Federal Republic of Germany and the United States had finally agreed to SDR allocations as part of the package arrangement, and their agreement brought about a consensus. Although most officials had reservations on one or another part of the total package, all felt they could accept it as a whole. This agreement came about at approximately the same time as the Fund was advocating a coordinated scenario of world economic growth, as officials of the Federal Republic of Germany agreed at the Bonn summit to expand domestic demand in their country to help the sluggish world economy and as U.S. officials were under pressure to defend the continuously declining dollar. In these world economic troubles, officials were making a deliberate effort to agree on coordinated actions.

As Chairman of the Interim Committee, Mr. Healey pointed out to its members that their agreement on quotas and SDRs would have a positive effect on the world economic environment. They were demonstrating that the Fund was the main organization in the international financial and monetary field, and that it was capable of shouldering the responsibilities facing it during a difficult and turbulent period. Mr. Healey also emphasized that Committee members deserved great credit for being prepared to accept something other than they would have wished in order to achieve an "impressive" consensus.

Mr. Healey also explained that, while the consensus could be announced publicly, the correct procedure was to ask the Executive Board to reach a final decision and then have the Board of Governors adopt a resolution. To implement this procedure, the Interim Committee agreed "to recommend" to the Executive Board that a decision to allocate SDRs on the basis of a proposal to be made by the Managing Director, concurred in by the Executive Board by November 1, 1978, should be acted on by the Board of Governors before the end of the year.[10]

THE PROPOSAL CARRIED OUT

In October 1978 the Managing Director submitted to the Executive Board a proposal for allocations of SDR 4 billion in each of the three years 1979–81, which would bring the total of SDRs in existence to SDR 21.3 billion. The Executive Board concurred, and on October 25 approved forwarding the relevant draft resolution to the Board of Governors. The Board of Governors adopted the resolution, effective December 11, 1978.

The Managing Director's proposal contained the same rationale for allocating SDRs to fill a long-term global need to supplement existing reserve assets that had been given to the Interim Committee in the Executive Directors' report of September. His proposal also explained the considerations governing the size of the allocations. First, members' holdings of official reserves might increase by an estimated SDR 20 billion a year or more over the next five years, taking into account the

---

[10]Communiqué of Interim Committee, September 24, 1978, par. 4; Vol. III below, pp. 240–41.

expected growth in the value of world trade over this period. Second, with a highly elastic supply of reserves from international capital markets, a substantial part of an allocation of SDRs could be expected to substitute for increases in official holdings of foreign exchange that would otherwise take place. Because of this substitution, the inflationary effects of SDR allocations would be limited. However, since SDR allocations might give rise to expectations of further inflation, SDR allocations should be modest with regard to annual size and to the length of the period over which they were allocated.[11]

Obviously these considerations were very general, serving mainly to rationalize a politically agreed figure. But those officials, including three successive Managing Directors who wanted more SDRs to be allocated, had achieved a victory.

TOTAL ASSISTANCE FROM THE FUND

By the end of 1978, the Fund had become a financial institution making money available to its members in a variety of forms. In the traditional way, members could purchase currencies of other members from the Fund in exchange for their own currency. In addition, the Fund was making direct distributions of gold from the Fund's gold holdings and distributing profits from sales of the Fund's gold through the Trust Fund. Loans to some members from the Trust Fund were also being made, and all members were receiving allocations of SDRs. In the seven financial years 1972–78, the amounts from all these sources totaled SDR 21.8 billion, excluding drawings in the gold tranche of another SDR 5.5 billion. Details for each year are given in Table 33.

Net drawings—gross drawings minus repurchases—were about SDR 5.7 billion smaller than gross drawings; they amounted to SDR 12.2 billion in the seven financial years 1972–78. Table 34 lists for these seven years the net drawings plus SDR allocations of each member, grouped by economic category.

---

[11]The Managing Director's proposal and Board of Governors' Resolution No. 34-3 are in Vol. III below, pp. 275–79.

Table 33. Amounts Made Available by the Fund, by Type of Activity,
Financial Years 1972–78

(In millions of SDRs)

	1972	1973	1974	1975	1976	1977	1978	Total 1972–78
Gross drawings[1]	452.0	534.4	450.2	4,121.3	5,267.4	4,749.7	2,367.3	17,941.9
Trust Fund loans	—	—	—	—	—	31.7	268.2	299.9
Gold distribution[2]	—	—	—	—	—	209.7	212.6	422.3
Profits of gold sales distributed to developing members[3]	—	—	—	—	—	—	222.6	222.6
SDR allocations	2,951.4	—	—	—	—	—	—	2,951.4
TOTAL	3,403.4	534.4	450.2	4,121.3	5,267.4	4,991.1	3,070.7	21,838.5
Undrawn balances under stand-by and extended arrangements as of April 30	209.6	143.05	1,231.8	156.0	1,085.8	3,581.1	3,638.8	

[1]Excluding drawings in the gold tranche.
[2]Valued at SDR 35 a fine ounce.
[3]Distribution in U.S. dollars converted into SDRs at prevailing rate.

Table 34. Net Drawings Plus SDR Allocations, by Members, Financial Years 1972–78

(In millions of SDRs)

	Net Drawings (Total Drawings Minus Repurchases)	SDR Allocations[1]	Total[2]
Industrial Members			
Austria	—	28.6	28.6
Belgium	—	68.9	68.9
Canada	—	116.6	116.6
Denmark	42.6	27.6	70.2
France	−767.5	159.0	−608.5
Germany, Federal Republic of	222.9	169.6	392.5
Italy	1,504.4	106.0	1,610.4
Japan	—	127.2	127.2
Luxembourg	−0.7	2.1	1.4
Netherlands	280.4	74.2	354.6
Norway	—	25.4	25.4
Sweden	—	34.4	34.4
United Kingdom	1,962.9	296.8	2,259.7
United States	1,201.9	710.2	1,912.1
Total	4,446.9	1,946.6	6,393.5
More Developed Primary Producing Members			
Australia	246.9	70.5	317.4
Finland	250.1	20.1	270.2
Greece	205.2	14.6	63.6
Iceland	61.2	2.4	63.6
Ireland	—	12.8	12.8
Malta	—	1.7	1.7
New Zealand	422.4	21.4	443.8
Portugal	274.2	—	274.2
Romania	302.5	—	302.5
South Africa	483.2	33.9	517.1
Spain	788.3	41.9	402.1
Turkey	386.1	16.0	830.2
Yugoslavia	199.2	21.9	402.1
Total	3,619.3	257.2	3,876.5
Major Oil Exporting Members			
Algeria	—	13.8	13.8
Indonesia	−188.5	27.6	−160.9
Iran	−47.9	20.4	−27.5
Iraq	−27.2	11.6	−15.6
Nigeria	−22.4	14.3	−8.1
Oman	—	0.7	0.7
Venezuela	—	35.0	35.0
Total	−286.0	123.4	−162.6

Table 34 (continued). Net Drawings Plus SDR Allocations, by Members, Financial Years, 1972–78

(In millions of SDRs)

	Net Drawings (Total Drawings Minus Repurchases)	SDR Allocations[1]	Total[2]
Non-Oil Developing Members			
Africa			
Benin	—	1.4	1.4
Botswana	−0.6	0.5	−0.1
Burundi	−10.5	2.0	−8.5
Cameroon	38.5	3.7	42.2
Central African Republic	9.4	1.4	10.8
Chad	5.6	1.4	7.0
Congo, People's Republic of	12.7	1.4	14.1
Equatorial Guinea	1.0	0.8	1.8
Gabon	—	1.6	1.6
Gambia, The	3.6	0.7	4.3
Ghana	2.5	9.2	11.7
Guinea	11.1	2.5	13.6
Guinea-Bissau	−0.8	—	−0.8
Ivory Coast	24.1	5.5	29.6
Kenya	60.0	5.1	65.1
Lesotho	−1.2	0.5	−0.7
Liberia	−3.7	3.1	−0.6
Madagascar	20.0	2.8	22.8
Malawi	10.7	1.6	12.3
Mali	−0.3	2.3	2.0
Mauritania	17.2	1.4	18.6
Mauritius	12.9	2.3	15.2
Morocco	88.0	12.0	100.0
Niger	—	1.4	1.4
Rwanda	−5.0	2.0	−3.0
São Tomé and Principe	−0.4	—	−0.4
Senegal	27.7	3.6	31.3
Seychelles	−0.1	—	−0.1
Sierra Leone	32.1	2.6	34.7
Somalia	4.0	2.0	6.0
Sudan	70.3	7.6	77.9
Swaziland	−2.1	0.8	−1.3
Tanzania	71.2	4.5	75.7
Togo	7.5	1.6	9.1
Tunisia	4.9	5.1	10.0
Uganda	39.2	4.2	43.4
Upper Volta	−1.8	1.4	−0.4
Zaïre	236.5	12.0	248.5
Zambia	114.2	8.1	122.3
Total	898.4	120.1	1,018.5

Table 34 (*continued*). Net Drawings Plus SDR Allocations, by Members, Financial Years, 1972–78

(*In millions of SDRs*)

	Net Drawings (Total Drawings Minus Repurchases)	SDR Allocations[1]	Total[2]
Non-Oil Developing Members (*continued*)			
Asia			
Afghanistan	−21.8	3.9	−17.9
Bangladesh	190.5	—	190.5
Burma	42.5	6.4	48.9
China	59.8	—	59.8
Fiji	7.4	1.4	8.8
India	201.3	99.6	300.9
Kampuchea, Democratic	18.8	2.6	21.4
Korea	294.1	8.5	302.6
Lao People's Dem. Rep.	9.4	1.4	10.8
Malaysia	11.8	19.7	31.5
Nepal	4.5	1.1	5.6
Pakistan	398.8	24.9	423.7
Papua New Guinea	19.8	—	19.8
Philippines	332.7	16.4	349.1
Sri Lanka	73.4	10.4	83.8
Thailand	67.1	14.2	81.3
Viet Nam	46.5	6.6	53.1
Western Samoa	1.6	0.2	1.8
Total	1,758.2	217.3	1,975.5
Latin America and the Caribbean			
Argentina	265.7	46.6	312.3
Bahamas	−5.0	—	−5.0
Barbados	5.3	1.4	6.7
Bolivia	−14.3	3.9	−10.4
Brazil	—	46.6	46.6
Chile	271.6	16.7	288.3
Colombia	−89.8	16.6	−73.2
Costa Rica	34.0	3.4	37.4
Dominican Republic	24.1	4.6	28.7
Ecuador[3]	−4.3	3.5	−0.8
El Salvador	−22.0	3.7	−18.3
Grenada	1.2	—	1.2
Guatemala	−9.0	3.8	−5.2
Guyana	19.2	2.1	21.3
Haiti	7.3	2.0	9.3
Honduras	4.3	2.6	6.9
Jamaica	97.7	5.6	103.3
Mexico[3]	424.4	39.2	463.6
Nicaragua	−9.0	2.9	−6.1
Panama	41.1	3.8	44.9

Table 34 (*concluded*). Net Drawings Plus SDR Allocations, by Members, Financial Years, 1972–78

(In millions of SDRs)

	Net Drawings (Total Drawings Minus Repurchases)	SDR Allocations[1]	Total[2]
Non-Oil Developing Members (*concluded*)			
Latin America and the Caribbean (*concluded*)			
Paraguay	—	2.0	2.0
Peru	142.9	13.0	155.9
Trinidad and Tobago	−9.1	6.7	−2.4
Uruguay	91.4	7.3	98.7
Total	1,267.7	238.0	1,505.7
Middle East			
Bahrain[3]	5.0	—	5.0
Cyprus	42.6	2.8	45.4
Egypt	194.2	19.9	214.1
Israel	225.7	13.8	239.5
Jordan	—	2.4	2.4
Syrian Arab Republic	−7.3	5.3	−2.0
Yemen Arab Republic	−1.0	1.1	0.1
Yemen, People's Dem. Rep. of	39.1	3.1	42.2
Total	498.3	48.4	546.7
GRAND TOTAL[4]	12,202.4	2,951.4	15,153.8

[1]Countries that did not receive SDR allocations in this period (indicated by a dash (—)) were either not members of the Fund on January 1, 1972, when the only allocations included here were made, or had opted out of the allocation for the first basic period. Some countries that were Fund members at the time, such as Kuwait, Lebanon, Libya, and Saudi Arabia, were not then participants in the Special Drawing Account. Other countries, such as Cape Verde, Comoros, Djibouti, Dominica, Qatar, Suriname, and the United Arab Emirates, joined the Fund after the allocation was made. Since these members also did not draw on the Fund in the period 1972–78, they are not listed in this table.

[2]All members received distributions of gold from the Fund, and developing members also received loans from the Trust Fund and a direct distribution of profits from the Fund's gold sales. The aggregate amounts received by all members from these three activities are given in Table 33 above.

[3]These members and a few other members were actually net oil exporters, but they did not satisfy the criteria used by the Fund to classify them as major oil exporting countries.

[4]Components may not add to totals because of rounding of figures for individual members.

CHAPTER

46

The SDR Improved Further

BECAUSE THE DECISION in September 1978 to allocate more SDRs was part of a package that included the further improvement of the SDR as a reserve asset, discussions and decisions on improvement proceeded simultaneously with those on allocations.

NEED FOR FURTHER IMPROVEMENTS

The Fund continued to nurture the SDR. It had taken many steps to promote its use and, in general, to make it a more attractive reserve asset, better able to compete in international settlements and in reserve holdings with national currencies and gold. As noted in earlier chapters, in 1972 the Fund started to use the SDR rather than the U.S. dollar as its unit of account. In 1973 officials agreed in principle to aim at making the SDR the principal reserve asset of the international monetary system. In the same year, pending agreement on a method for valuing the SDR other than in terms of gold, temporary arrangements were made to enable European countries to use SDRs in settling their accounts under the European snake. In July 1974 a method of valuing the SDR in terms of a basket of 16 currencies was put into operation. Also in 1974 a higher rate of interest was assigned to the SDR and the method of calculating this interest rate was subsequently changed so that it could move more closely in line with market rates on main money instruments. In 1976, as the Fund piled up large amounts of SDRs in its own General Account since members used their SDRs primarily to repurchase their currencies from the Fund and to pay the Fund for charges on their drawings, the Fund decided to provide members drawing from the Fund with SDRs as well as currencies. In a short time members drawing from the Fund received many more SDRs than they did currencies. In 1976 the Fund also widened the use of SDRs in transactions by agreement among participants by allowing participants to effect transactions to promote reconstitution or to bring their holdings of SDRs closer to their net cumulative allocations without subjecting such transactions to the requirement of need; previously all transactions in SDRs had been subject to the requirement of need. A participant could also use its

SDRs to obtain balances of its currency from another participant, but these transactions remained subject to the requirement of need. In April 1978 the Second Amendment made possible the relaxation of many rules and regulations previously restraining use of the SDR.

These developments all represented important improvements in the SDR's features and uses that officials were unwilling to permit when the SDR was negotiated a decade earlier. The SDR, nevertheless, remained in the backwater of international finance. Members continued to rely on the principal national currencies for the bulk of their international settlements and their reserve holdings. International financial organizations other than the Fund also dealt wholly in national currencies, not in SDRs. In addition, the vast expansion of the recycling operations of private banks meant much less use of the SDR than of national currencies in international payments since the SDR could be used only for official and not for private transactions.

To help increase use of the SDR, the management and staff pressed in 1978 to update and possibly simplify the method used for its valuation, to raise its rate of interest, and to reduce members' obligation to reconstitute their holdings. In addition, shortly before he left the Fund, Mr. Witteveen proposed giving consideration to establishing in the Fund a substitution account by which members might exchange a portion of their holdings of reserve currencies for SDRs.

UPDATING THE METHOD OF VALUATION

Agreement in 1974 on a standard basket of 16 currencies as the method of valuing the SDR had come about with reservations. A number of restrictive phrases in the communiqué of the Committee of Twenty, such as "in the present circumstances," "for an interim period," and "without prejudice to the method of valuation to be adopted in the reformed system," suggested that officials were less than completely committed to this method of valuing the SDR. The standard basket was adopted because at the time there seemed to be no alternative. In the standard basket each currency was assigned a fixed amount, which permitted the inclusion of currencies with floating rates as well as of currencies with pegged rates. Other methods of valuing the SDR that were discussed—the asymmetrical basket, the adjustable basket, and the par value technique—could not work under conditions of generalized floating.

Once the standard basket was adopted, it was hard to change. When the Executive Board reviewed the way of valuing the SDR in 1976, it decided to retain the same basket with the same 16 currencies and their same weights. The main reason for this decision was a desire for continuity in the way the SDR was valued. A number of developing members were starting to peg their currencies to the SDR. Many regional and international organizations were also beginning to use the SDR in their accounts, and the SDR was gaining acceptance as the unit of account in international treaties and statutes and in contracts between private parties.[1] A prompt change in its valuation might impede these increasing uses.

Another reason why the mode of valuation was left unchanged in 1976 was that use of a standard basket for valuing the SDR was gradually accepted. Officials came to realize that the standard basket technique was the best method for valuing any composite currency unit and would be so even in an international monetary system with fixed exchange rates.[2] The ECU, the currency unit to be used in the European Monetary System that was based on fixed exchange rates, was also valued by the standard basket technique. The standard basket technique was sufficiently accepted by 1976–78 that, after the Second Amendment, adoption of a different method of valuation was possible only by an 85 percent majority of the total voting power of the Fund.

While the Executive Board's decision of 1976 was to retain the same currency basket, the management and staff and several Executive Directors favored a reduced basket if it could be agreed. They favored a basket with the currencies of the five members with the largest quotas, the deutsche mark, the dollar, the French franc, the pound sterling, and the yen. This reduction would make the basket of currencies used for valuing the SDR symmetrical with the basket of five currencies used for determining the interest rate on the SDR. The concepts of valuation and the operation of the SDR would both be made simpler. But reducing the currencies in the basket was controversial as U.S. officials were opposed to the reduction. This opposition to what other officials regarded as a considerable contribution to making the SDR a more attractive asset was widely interpreted as an inclination on the part of U.S. officials to avoid strengthening the SDR that would make it more competitive against the dollar.

The controversy over changing the method of valuing the SDR kept the Executive Board from agreeing in 1976 to set a date for re-examining the valuation of the SDR. But it was understood that a re-examination would take place sometime before the amended Articles went into force.

A Revised Basket of 16 Currencies Agreed in 1978

The staff circulated papers to the Executive Board relating to a review of the valuation of the SDR in the middle of 1977, while the amended Articles were before members for approval. Interest among officials in the mode of valuation was intense. The Executive Directors debated for months whether or not the currency basket should continue to contain 16 currencies or whether the number of currencies should

---

[1]These developments in the use of the SDR are periodically described by Joseph Gold in the Fund's Pamphlet Series. See, for example, *Floating Currencies, Gold, and SDRs: Some Recent Legal Developments*, IMF Pamphlet Series, No. 19 (Washington, 1976), pp. 51–66, and *Floating Currencies, SDRs, and Gold: Further Legal Developments*, IMF Pamphlet Series, No. 22 (Washington, 1977), pp. 24–49.

[2]J.J. Polak, "The SDR as a Basket of Currencies," *Staff Papers*, International Monetary Fund (Washington), Vol. 26 (December 1979), pp. 627–53.

be decreased. The staff again set forth the arguments in favor of a basket of 5 currencies. The Belgian authorities submitted to the EC Monetary Committee their own proposal, which, as Mr. de Groote explained, changed the role of the U.S. dollar in the valuation of the SDR and in the way the interest rate on the SDR was determined so as to produce a higher yield on the SDR.

As the discussion continued, U.S. opposition to reducing the number of currencies in the basket prevailed. On March 31, the day before the Second Amendment was to enter into force, the Executive Board took a decision, which was not to go into effect until July 1.[3] There would be another basket of 16 currencies, but the currencies of Iran and Saudi Arabia would be included while those of Denmark and South Africa would be dropped. The basis for choosing the 16 members whose currencies were included was the same as that used in 1974. Each member had a share in world exports of goods and services in excess of 1 percent on average over a five-year period. But in 1978 the five-year period used was 1972–76, instead of 1968–72 as in the 1974 basket. The weights for the Austrian schilling, the Belgian franc, and the Netherlands guilder, which were becoming increasingly strong currencies, were increased, while the weights for the Canadian dollar, the pound sterling, and the Swedish krona, which were becoming relatively weaker currencies, were reduced.

The amounts of each of the 16 currencies which were summed to determine the value of one SDR and the weights are listed in Table 35.

The changes in the 1978 basket were thus relatively minor. The preceding debate in the Executive Board was, nonetheless, reflected in the decision that provided for further adjustment of the valuation of the SDR at five-year intervals, beginning on July 1, 1983, unless the Executive Board was to decide otherwise at each quinquennial interval.[4]

RAISING THE INTEREST RATE

From July 1974 until June 1976, the rate of interest on the SDR and the rate of remuneration were determined by a formula based on a weighted average of the rates of interest on five market instruments quoted in the United States, the Federal Republic of Germany, the United Kingdom, France, and Japan. Although the rate of interest on the SDR started at 5 percent a year in July 1974, as a result of semiannual reviews by the Executive Directors and in the light of a generally declining trend in market rates, it was lowered to 3.75 percent in July 1975 and to 3.50 percent in January 1976. As noted in Chapter 30, in June 1976 the Executive Directors reviewed the formula and decided to make the rate of interest on the SDR and the rate of remuneration yet more responsive to variations in market rates of interest. For each

---

[3]E.B. Decision No. 5718-(78/46) G/S, March 31, 1978; Vol. III below, pp. 556–57.

[4]After extensive discussions, the Executive Board decided in September 1980 to adopt the five-currency basket for determining both the value of and the interest rate on the SDR. The new basket came into effect on January 1, 1981.

Table 35. Composition of SDR Currency Basket, July 1978

Currency	Weight (In percent)	Amount (In units of each currency)
U.S. dollar	33	0.40
Deutsche mark	12.5	0.32
Japanese yen	7.5	21
French franc	7.5	0.42
Pound sterling	7.5	0.050
Italian lira	5	52
Netherlands guilder	5	0.14
Canadian dollar	5	0.070
Belgian franc	4	1.6
Saudi Arabian riyal	3	0.13
Swedish krona	2	0.11
Iranian rial	2	1.7
Australian dollar	1.5	0.017
Spanish peseta	1.5	1.5
Norwegian krone	1.5	0.10
Austrian schilling	1.5	0.28

calendar year, these two rates were to be three fifths (60 percent) of the weighted average of short-term market interest rates, rounded to the nearest ¼ of 1 percent, in the five countries, with a formula specifying just which market rates were to be used.

While the rate of interest on the SDR was geared to market rates, the formula itself put the rate at three fifths of market rates. The rationale for a lower interest rate on the SDR than on money market instruments was partly that the SDR, as a basket of currencies, had a more stable capital value and less exchange risk than money market instruments denominated in one national currency. The rate of interest on the SDR was also low because of the relationship between the rate of interest on the SDR and the rate of remuneration required by the Articles of Agreement before the Second Amendment. The level of the rate of remuneration had vital implications for the Fund's financial position and the level of the Fund's charges on use of its resources. Should the rate of remuneration be raised, the Fund might have to increase its charges. The rate of interest on the SDR and the rate of remuneration were also both kept relatively low on the grounds that members should be willing to provide the Fund, a public agency, with some resources with less remuneration than they might command from commercial interest rates, especially since members using those resources were subject to conditions.

Despite these well-accepted reasons, the Managing Director and staff and many Executive Directors were inclined to favor an interest rate on the SDR that was closer to market rates as being essential to promoting the SDR. As interest rates in money markets rose, Fund officials worried that some members might be taking advantage of those rates by decreasing the amounts of SDRs in their reserves even though their total reserves were increasing. Raising the interest rate on the SDR was even more controversial than changing its valuation. European officials who were increasingly holding larger amounts of SDRs as a result of intra-European payments settlements wanted a higher yield on the SDR as well as a higher rate of remuneration on their creditor positions in the Fund. U.S. officials, pursuing in 1977–78 a monetary policy with relatively low interest rates, opposed a higher rate of interest on the SDR. They feared that a higher rate than that prevailing on the dollar might induce shifts of funds from the dollar into SDRs. Officials of developing members worried that higher returns on the SDR and on creditor positions in the Fund would necessitate higher charges by the Fund on use of its resources.

Throughout the first nine months of 1978 the Executive Directors discussed several questions relating to the interest rate on the SDR. There were technical questions. How should an interest rate basket for the SDR be determined? What alternative market rates of interest were most appropriate? How many interest rates should be included? What weighting should be used? How did the existing five-currency basket measure up against these standards? There were questions about the relation between the interest rate on the SDR and interest rates in money markets. At what level of market rates should the interest rate on the SDR be fixed? Most difficult of all were questions about the relation between the rate of interest on the SDR and the rate of remuneration. While the amended Articles permitted the rate of remuneration to be lower than the rate of interest on the SDR, provided it did not fall below 80 percent of the rate of interest on the SDR, several Executive Directors were reluctant to have much, if any, divergence between the two rates.

The management and staff proposed an 80/80 formula, that is, the interest rate on the SDR would be set at 80 percent of market rates, instead of the existing 60 percent, and the rate of remuneration would be set at 80 percent of the interest rate on the SDR. While most Executive Directors were prepared to support this compromise formula, it did not command the majority of the voting power (70 percent) required for the change. Some Executive Directors who were willing to accept the 80/80 formula, moreover, were prepared to do so only if there were a prior agreement to resume allocations of SDRs. Opposition to the 80/80 formula was based on two arguments. The first was that, as a matter of principle, the interest rate on the SDR and the rate of remuneration, as yields on two Fund-related reserve assets, should be the same. The second was that the interest rate on the SDR could not be as high as 80 percent of the market rate if the rate of remuneration were also to be at that level and that the Fund's charges were not to be raised.

To resolve the deadlock, in August 1978 Mr. de Larosière, who had become Managing Director in June, proposed a compromise. The interest rate on the SDR would be set at 80 percent of the combined market rate, and the rate of remuneration would be set at 90 percent of the interest rate on the SDR, that is, an 80/90 formula. This formula gave a rate of remuneration of 72 percent of the market rate, and, on the basis of the then prevailing market rates, a rate that was somewhat above the initial rate of the Fund's charges on its drawings.

This proposal was accepted by the Executive Directors subject to the further proviso that, shortly before the end of each financial year, the Fund would consider whether the estimated net income of the Fund for that year was sufficiently large to permit raising the average annual rate of remuneration applicable for that year above 90 percent of the average annual rate of interest on the SDR. In considering whether to establish a higher rate of remuneration for a particular year, the Fund would also consider the possibility of lowering charges for the future.

In September, the Interim Committee agreed to this solution.[5]

REDUCING THE OBLIGATION
TO RECONSTITUTE HOLDINGS OF SDRs

Because the obligation of members to reconstitute their SDR holdings was considered a major detraction of the SDR as a reserve asset and a legal obligation atypical of other reserve assets, the amended Articles provided for the abolition of this obligation. The obligation had not been altered since it was first introduced in 1969. In 1972 the Executive Directors, obliged to review the rules for reconstitution before the end of the first basic period, had recommended to the Board of Governors that no change be made in the existing rules. Their report to the Governors indicated their conviction that the abrogation of the requirement that participants maintain their SDR holdings at an average of 30 percent of their daily net cumulative allocations over a five-year period would enhance the character of the SDR as a reserve asset. However, because the Committee of Twenty was just starting its deliberations and uncertainty prevailed about the reform of the international monetary system and the role of alternative reserves, the Executive Directors recommended postponing the decision on reconstitution. The Board of Governors approved this recommendation.[6]

The Fund staff continued to make monthly calculations to determine the extent to which each participant needed SDRs to meet its reconstitution obligation. The necessary amounts of SDRs could be obtained either from another participant with a balance of payments need to use SDRs, or from the Fund's General Account against currencies acceptable to the Fund, or as part of a purchase from the General Account in accordance with the Fund's policy on the use of its resources. In the first years of the SDR, SDRs obtained to promote reconstitution were all acquired from the General Account, but after 1976 increasing amounts were acquired from other participants. As participants used more of their SDR holdings to pay charges to the Fund, the need to reconstitute their holdings also increased.

---

[5]Communiqué of Interim Committee, September 24, 1978, par. 5; Vol. III below, p. 241. On January 1, 1979, the 80/90 arrangement went into effect. As a result of the arrangement and the general rise in money market rates, the interest rate on the SDR rose from 4 percent a year in the fourth quarter of 1978 to 6 percent in the first quarter of 1979, and 6.5 percent in the second quarter. The rate of interest on the SDR was raised to 100 percent of the combined market interest rate on May 1, 1981. This completed the process of raising the rate of interest on the SDR in steps from its original 1½ percent a year to a full market-related interest rate.

[6]The report of the Executive Directors of November 15, 1972 and Board of Governors' Resolution No. 28-2, adopted effective December 18, 1972, are in Vol. III below, pp. 267–69.

Just before the end of the second basic period, on December 31, 1977, the Executive Directors reviewed the rules for reconstitution and again recommended to the Board of Governors that no change be made. On this occasion the Executive Directors were in the midst of examining all the characteristics and uses of the SDR, including its valuation and yield, the principles of designation, and the greater freedom to use SDRs under the amended Articles. Since the outcome of this review would affect their review of the rules of reconstitution, they proposed to review reconstitution again. The Board of Governors approved this recommendation in the first week of January 1978.[7]

In August 1978, as part of its continuing broad review of the SDR, the Executive Board recommended to the Interim Committee that participants maintain only 15 percent (rather than 30 percent) of their net cumulative allocations of SDRs over a five-year period. The Executive Directors reasoned that it was no longer necessary to require participants legally to hold a given amount of SDRs, as it was when the SDR was first introduced. The SDR was no longer an unfamiliar asset and its yield was much closer to market yields than before. These and other changes in the features of the SDR could be expected to make participants generally more willing to hold SDRs so that an obligatory reconstitution to prevent an undesirable distribution of SDR holdings among participants was no longer needed. The Executive Directors also explained that, in moving from 30 percent to 15 percent, they were proceeding gradually and would review experience with the reduction later. In September 1978 the Interim Committee agreed to this recommendation.[8] In October the Executive Board took the necessary decision.[9]

INCREASING USE OF THE SDR

While it had remained little used compared with other reserve assets, the SDR, still in its infancy, was nonetheless increasingly used after 1971.[10] The main use that participants continued to make of their SDRs was to pay charges on their drawings from the Fund and to repurchase balances of their currencies held by the Fund. The Fund in turn provided more SDRs from its General Account to members using the Fund's resources and included the SDR in its quarterly currency budgets. Members receiving SDRs when they drew from the Fund could either retain them or use them immediately in a transaction with designation to obtain foreign exchange. Most of

---

[7]The report of the Executive Directors of December 5, 1977 and Board of Governors' Resolution No. 33-1, adopted effective January 4, 1978, are in Vol. III below, pp. 270–71.

[8]Communiqué of Interim Committee, September 24, 1978, par. 5(c); Vol. III below, p. 241.

[9]E.B. Decision No. 5936-(78/168) S, October 25, 1978; Vol. III below, pp. 557. The reconstitution obligation was eliminated altogether on April 30, 1981.

[10]The first two years of experience with SDRs, 1970 and 1971, were described in *History, 1966–71*, Vol. I, pp. 232–47. Experiences in the first three years were described in Walter O. Habermeier, *Operations and Transactions in SDRs: The First Basic Period*, IMF Pamphlet Series, No. 17 (Washington, 1973).

them did the latter. Hence, what the Fund called transactions with designation increased steadily.

Transactions with Designation

In order to ensure that a participant would always be able to use its SDRs to acquire needed foreign exchange, the Fund was required by its Articles after the First Amendment to have a mechanism for designating participants to provide foreign exchange in return for SDRs. The general principles to be used for designation and the rules for the first basic period were specified in the Articles. Briefly, a participant was to be subject to designation if its balance of payments and reserve position was sufficiently strong. Designations of participants were also to aim over time at a balanced or equitable distribution of SDRs among participants. In accordance with the Rules and Regulations, the Executive Board was to adopt at quarterly intervals a designation plan listing the participants subject to designation during that quarter and the amounts for which they could be designated.[11]

As required by the Articles, the rules for designation were reviewed by the Executive Board in 1972, before the end of the first basic period on December 31, 1972, and again at the end of 1977, before the end of the second basic period on December 31, 1977. On both occasions the Executive Board decided to make no change.

To implement the designation rules and procedures, the staff continued in the years 1972–78 to draw up designation plans for each calendar quarter, and the Executive Directors approved each plan. In practice, designation was concentrated to a large extent on France, the United Kingdom, and the United States, and to a lesser extent on Argentina, India, Indonesia, Iran, Italy, South Africa, Venezuela, and Yugoslavia. In general, most of these members had previously used their SDRs, and their low holdings were mainly responsible for their being designated. Belgium, the Federal Republic of Germany, and the Netherlands were receiving large amounts of SDRs in transactions by agreement in settlements of accounts under the European snake. Hence, their holdings of SDRs were relatively large, and they were less designated in the Fund's plans.

In September 1978, the Executive Directors reported to the Interim Committee that they were in broad agreement that experience since 1970 with designation plans was generally satisfactory, but that they were nonetheless planning to review the rules and procedures for designation.

Transactions by Agreement Among Participants

In the years 1972–78, participants in the Special Drawing Account also became freer to use SDRs by agreement among themselves. After August 1976 participants

---

[11]The rules and procedures for designation, the first designation plans, and debates over how to designate participants so as to achieve a balanced or equitable distribution of SDRs among participants were described in *History, 1966–71*, Vol. I, pp. 184–85, 226–29, and 237–42.

could transfer SDRs for certain purposes without filling a requirement of need, and transactions among participants increased. But the big change was to come with the Second Amendment. Until the Second Amendment came into effect, transactions by agreement fell into two categories: (i) those subject to the requirement of need in which a participant used SDRs to obtain balances of its own currency from another participant, and (ii) those (exempt from the requirement of need) that promoted reconstitution or brought the holdings of both participants closer to their net cumulative allocations.

Under the amended Articles, participants were free to use their SDRs to obtain currency in transactions by agreement with other participants without regard to the requirement of need and without the necessity for specific authorization by the Fund. A further provision of the amended Articles enabled the Fund to "prescribe" (permit) operations in which participants might use SDRs by agreement without exchanging them for currency. Toward the end of 1978, the Executive Board took decisions that permitted participants to use SDRs to settle financial obligations, other than to make donations, without first changing them into currencies, to make loans at interest rates and maturities agreed between the parties, and to repay loans and interest.[12] The Executive Directors were also considering their use as security for a loan by another central bank or government, and in donations, swaps, and forward operations.[13]

Another noteworthy development in the SDR in 1978 was that seven members not previously participants in the SDR Department—Ethiopia, Lebanon, Libya, Qatar, Saudi Arabia, Singapore, and the United Arab Emirates—became participants. All but one of the 138 members were thus participants at the end of 1978.[14]

Other Holders

By a decision of the Executive Board on November 26, 1973, approved by a resolution of the Board of Governors on January 21, 1974, by a majority in excess of the required 85 percent of the total voting power of participants, the Fund prescribed the BIS as a holder of SDRs. The BIS adhered to this resolution by a letter to the Fund dated January 30, 1974. Under the resolution, a participant in the Special Drawing Account might use SDRs to obtain currency from the BIS with the assurance that the BIS would use the same amount of SDRs to obtain currency from the participant within a period not exceeding six months.[15]

In 1978 the Executive Directors discussed, and the Interim Committee endorsed, increasing the number of official institutions that might, as "other holders" of SDRs, be authorized to acquire, hold, and use SDRs on terms and

---

[12]E.B. Decision Nos. 6000-(79/1) S, and 6001-(79/1) S, December 28, 1978; Vol. III below, pp. 558–59.

[13]These further uses for SDRs were agreed early in 1979.

[14]With the participation of Kuwait in 1980, all members of the Fund were also participants in the Special Drawing Rights Department.

[15]Board of Governors' Resolution No. 29-1 is in Vol. III below, pp. 281–83.

conditions agreed by the Fund. As 1978 closed, the number of other holders of SDRs was thus about to be expanded considerably.[16]

A SUBSTITUTION ACCOUNT PROPOSED

Deliberations of yet another topic concerning the SDR began late in 1978. The topic was that of establishing a substitution account in the Fund. Such an account had been discussed at the time of the negotiations for reforming the international monetary system and when the amendments to the Articles were being drafted, but because of lack of agreement the idea had been dropped on both occasions.

In April 1978, Mr. Witteveen, who continued to be concerned about the need for management of international liquidity, proposed to the Interim Committee that fresh consideration be given to establishment in the Fund of a substitution account. In suggesting a substitution account in 1978, he had in mind that the expansion of international liquidity that would result from allocating additional SDRs would be partly offset by absorbing some reserve currencies into the substitution account. New allocations of SDRs would then not add equivalent amounts to the aggregate supply of reserves in the world. By tying together proposals for allocating SDRs and creating a substitution account, officials might be more willing to agree to both proposals.

The Executive Board discussed a substitution account intensely in 1978. But it was apparent that these deliberations would go on for many months beyond the end of 1978, and that the topic would be one to which Mr. de Larosière, as Mr. Witteveen's successor, would devote much effort.

■ ■ ■ ■ ■ ■

As 1978 closed, the SDR was beginning to enjoy a resurgence. Participants were using their SDRs more widely. More Fund members were becoming participants in the SDR arrangements. More members were pegging their currencies to the SDR. SDR-denominated currency deposits were being accepted by the BIS and several major commercial banks. Bonds denominated in SDRs were being issued. While some regional organizations had adopted a unit of account composed of regional currencies, the use of the SDR as a unit of account by other international and regional organizations was being increased. The Economic Counsellor was writing about the implications of putting the Fund fully on an SDR basis, that is, of

---

[16]In 1980 seven additional institutions were prescribed as "other holders." These other holders had the same degree of freedom as Fund members to buy and sell SDRs both spot and forward, to borrow, lend, or pledge SDRs, to use SDRs in swaps, or to use or receive SDRs in donations (grants). They could not, however, receive allocations of SDRs nor use SDRs in transactions with designation.

keeping the main assets of the Fund in SDRs and conducting all the Fund's operations and transactions entirely in SDRs.[17] A substitution account was being considered. And the Treasurer was enthusiastic about the prospects for use of the SDR in private markets.[18] All these developments were additional to the new allocations that were to start on January 1, 1979. The SDR seemed to be on the verge of coming into its own.

---

[17]J.J. Polak, *Thoughts on an International Monetary Fund Based Fully on the SDR*, IMF Pamphlet Series, No. 28 (Washington, 1979).

[18]Walter O. Habermeier, "The SDR as an International Unit of Account," *Finance & Development*, Vol. 16 (March 1979), pp. 11–13.

PART TWELVE

Continued Evolution of the Fund as an International Institution (1972-1978)

"The main explanation of the
fact that the intergovernmental
organizations generally survive,
even through the most disappointing
periods, is undoubtedly that people,
at bottom, behind the facade of
nationalistic attitudes, do believe
in, and do desire, international
cooperation."

—GUNNAR MYRDAL, *Beyond the Welfare State,*
Economic Planning and Its International Implications
(1960)

CHAPTER
47

Intensification of Regular Activities

R*EFORMING THE INTERNATIONAL MONETARY SYSTEM*, forecasting the world economic outlook, handling an accelerated use of resources and arranging its financing, holding gold auctions, amending the Articles, preparing for exchange rate surveillance, and improving the SDR all brought an exciting, though hectic and often frustrating, atmosphere to the Fund's activities after 1972. The tempo of work of the Managing Director and staff and of the Executive Directors was greatly stepped up. These activities, however, were by no means all the Fund's endeavors. By 1972 the Fund had established a number of activities that had become routine: preparing for new members, conducting annual consultations, providing technical assistance, training officials from member governments, gathering and dispensing a wide range of economic and financial information to members and to the public, putting out a range of publications, and collaborating with an expanding number of international and regional organizations.

These activities continued to be the main work of the staff. The Fund estimated, for instance, that about one half of the time of the staff in the five Area Departments in the mid-1970s was spent on annual consultations alone. These activities also took up a great deal of the time and effort of the Managing Director and of the Deputy Managing Director, who supervised the briefing and debriefing that were part of the consultations process, the assignment of technical assistance personnel, and other activities involving personal contact between the staff and officials in member governments.

The Fund's regular activities also consumed a considerable part of the time of the Executive Directors. Staff visits to members were discussed in advance with the Executive Director concerned. For the members in his constituency, the Executive Director served as observer in that part of the consultations involving exchanges of views between the staff and officials of members in home capitals. In addition, annual consultations with every member were completed by discussions in the Executive Board, which were usually comprehensive, sometimes lasting several hours. The Executive Board devoted about one fourth to one third of its time in 1972–78 to annual consultations. The Executive Board was also notified of all requests for technical assistance and of the proposals by management to answer the requests. Each year the Executive Board evaluated technical assistance activities as a whole and made decisions on policies governing the Fund's publications, on other information activities, and on the details of its relations with other organizations.

Although these activities involved considerable time and effort by all Fund officials, they were vital for the Fund's success as an international organization. Hence, despite the pressure of other work they were intensified in the 1970s.

This chapter describes the main developments in membership, annual consultations, technical assistance, and training of officials from member governments. Other regular activities are described in Chapters 48 and 49.

MEMBERSHIP

At the end of the 1971 further increases in membership seemed unlikely because few countries, other than Switzerland and the Eastern European nations, were not already Fund members. Nevertheless, the formation of more small, politically independent nation states led to an increase from 120 members at the end of 1971 to 138 members at the end of 1978. The 18 members joining the Fund from 1972 to 1978 and the dates on which they became members, along with their initial quotas, are listed in Table 16 in Chapter 27. The list of the 138 members as of the end of 1978 and the dates on which they became members are given below in Table. 36.

Table 36. Membership on December 31, 1978

	Effective Date of Membership
Afghanistan	July 14, 1955
Algeria	Sept. 26, 1963
Argentina	Sept. 20, 1956
Australia	Aug. 5, 1947
Austria	Aug. 27, 1948
Bahamas	Aug. 21, 1973
Bahrain	Sept. 7, 1972
Bangladesh	Aug. 17, 1972
Barbados	Dec. 29, 1970
Belgium	Dec. 27, 1945
Benin	July 10, 1963
Bolivia	Dec. 27, 1945
Botswana	July 24, 1968
Brazil	Jan. 14, 1946
Burma	Jan. 3, 1952
Burundi	Sept. 28, 1963
Cameroon	July 10, 1963
Canada	Dec. 27, 1945
Cape Verde	Nov. 20, 1978
Central African Republic	July 10, 1963

Table 36 *(continued)*. Membership on December 31, 1978

	Effective Date of Membership
Chad	July 10, 1963
Chile	Dec. 31, 1945
China	Dec. 26, 1945
Colombia	Dec. 27, 1945
Comoros	Sept. 21, 1976
Congo, People's Republic of the	July 10, 1963
Costa Rica	Jan. 8, 1946
(Cuba)[1]	(Mar. 14, 1946)
Cyprus	Dec. 21, 1961
(Czechoslovakia)[2]	(Dec. 26, 1945)
Denmark	Mar. 30, 1946
Djibouti	Dec. 29, 1978
Dominica	Dec. 12, 1978
Dominican Republic	Dec. 28, 1945
Ecuador	Dec. 28, 1945
Egypt	Dec. 26, 1945
El Salvador	Mar. 14, 1946
Equatorial Guinea	Dec. 22, 1969
Ethiopia	Dec. 12, 1945
Fiji	May 28, 1971
Finland	Jan. 14, 1948
France	Dec. 27, 1945
Gabon	Sept. 10, 1963
Gambia, The	Sept. 21, 1967
Germany, Federal Republic of	Aug. 14, 1952
Ghana	Sept. 20, 1957
Greece	Dec. 26, 1945
Grenada	Aug. 27, 1975
Guatemala	Dec. 28, 1945
Guinea	Sept. 28, 1963
Guinea-Bissau	Mar. 24, 1977
Guyana	Sept. 26, 1966
Haiti	Sept. 8, 1953
Honduras	Dec. 26, 1945
Iceland	Dec. 27, 1945
India	Dec. 27, 1945
Indonesia[3]	Feb. 21, 1967
Iran	Dec. 29, 1945
Iraq	Dec. 26, 1945
Ireland	Aug. 8, 1957
Israel	July 12, 1954
Italy	Mar. 27, 1947
Ivory Coast	Mar. 11, 1963
Jamaica	Feb. 21, 1963
Japan	Aug. 13, 1952

905

Table 36 (continued). Membership on December 31, 1978

	Effective Date of Membership
Jordan	Aug. 29, 1952
Kampuchea, Democratic	Dec. 31, 1969
Kenya	Feb. 3, 1964
Korea	Aug. 26, 1955
Kuwait	Sept. 13, 1962
Lao People's Dem. Rep.	July 5, 1961
Lebanon	Apr. 11, 1947
Lesotho	July 25, 1968
Liberia	Mar. 28, 1962
Libya	Sept. 17, 1958
Luxembourg	Dec. 26, 1945
Madagascar	Sept. 25, 1963
Malawi	July 19, 1965
Malaysia	Mar. 7, 1958
Maldives	Jan. 13, 1978
Mali	Sept. 27, 1963
Malta	Sept. 11, 1968
Mauritania	Sept. 10, 1963
Mauritius	Sept. 23, 1968
Mexico	Dec. 31, 1945
Morocco	Apr. 25, 1958
Nepal	Sept. 6, 1961
Netherlands	Dec. 26, 1945
New Zealand	Aug. 31, 1961
Nicaragua	Mar. 14, 1946
Niger	Apr. 24, 1963
Nigeria	Mar. 30, 1961
Norway	Dec. 27, 1945
Oman	Dec. 23, 1971
Pakistan	July 11, 1950
Panama	Mar. 14, 1946
Papua New Guinea	Oct. 9, 1975
Paraguay	Dec. 28, 1945
Peru	Dec. 31, 1945
Philippines	Dec. 21, 1945
(Poland)[4]	(Jan. 10, 1946)
Portugal	Mar. 29, 1961
Qatar	Sept. 8, 1972
Romania	Dec. 15, 1972
Rwanda	Sept. 30, 1963
São Tomé and Principe	Sept. 30, 1977
Saudi Arabia	Aug. 26, 1957
Senegal	Aug. 31, 1962
Seychelles	June 30, 1977
Sierra Leone	Sept. 10, 1962

Table 36 (*concluded*). Membership on December 31, 1978

	Effective Date of Membership
Singapore	Aug. 3, 1966
Solomon Islands	Sept. 22, 1978
Somalia	Aug. 31, 1962
South Africa	Dec. 26, 1945
Spain	Sept. 15, 1958
Sri Lanka	Aug. 29, 1950
Sudan	Sept. 5, 1957
Suriname	Apr. 27, 1978
Swaziland	Sept. 22, 1969
Sweden	Aug. 31, 1951
Syrian Arab Republic	Apr. 10, 1947
Tanzania	Sept. 10, 1962
Thailand	May 3, 1949
Togo	Aug. 1, 1962
Trinidad and Tobago	Sept. 16, 1963
Tunisia	Apr. 14, 1958
Turkey	Mar. 11, 1947
Uganda	Sept. 27, 1963
United Arab Emirates	Sept. 22, 1972
United Kingdom	Dec. 27, 1945
United States	Dec. 20, 1945
Upper Volta	May 2, 1963
Uruguay	Mar. 11, 1946
Venezuela	Dec. 30, 1946
Viet Nam	Sept. 21, 1956
Western Samoa	Dec. 28, 1971
Yemen Arab Republic	May 22, 1970
Yemen, People's Dem. Rep. of	Sept. 29, 1969
Yugoslavia	Dec. 26, 1945
Zaïre	Sept. 28, 1963
Zambia	Sept. 23, 1965

[1]Cuba withdrew from the Fund on April 2, 1964
[2]Czechoslovakia ceased to be a member on December 31, 1954.
[3]Indonesia became a member of the Fund on April 15, 1954 and withdrew from membership on August 17, 1965; Indonesia was readmitted as a member on February 21, 1967.
[4]Poland withdrew from the Fund on March 14, 1950.

Impact on Fund's Work

The increased number of members was a crucial factor enlarging the Fund's regular work. Even before a country became a member, several topics had to be discussed and negotiated: the obligations and prerogatives of membership, an initial quota, the payment of a subscription to the Fund, participation in the Special Drawing Rights Department, the country's eligibility for the various financial facilities of the Fund, the possibility of technical assistance and training of the country's officials, and procedures for electing an Executive Director and for participating in the Interim Committee, the Development Committee, and Annual Meetings. Some of these topics were at times controversial. A prerequisite for the Fund's assessment of an appropriate quota was a comprehensive analysis by the staff of the country's domestic economy and its external payments. Thus, an application for membership set off a complicated process. To smooth a country's entry into the organization, the Fund customarily sent a sizable mission to a prospective member and the Executive Directors set up a Committee on Membership.

Once membership was attained, more work developed. Statistical and factual information had to be gathered from the member and analyzed. Information had to be supplied to the member. The Fund's procedures and policies, and often their past history, had to be explained. Contacts and channels of communication had to be developed. Annual consultations had to be held. Moreover, in the circumstances of 1973 and after, almost immediate requests for use of the Fund's resources usually had to be negotiated.

Time spent by Fund officials on relations with a small new member was often as great as time spent with a long-standing large member. The new member might well involve more time and effort. Since most members joining in the 1960s and 1970s lacked the instruments needed to conduct modern monetary, fiscal, and exchange policies, they usually requested technical assistance and frequently asked for a resident representative from the Fund staff.

The Fund's other work also grew correspondingly with increases in membership. Consistent with its aim of treating all members uniformly, the Fund tried to include as many members as possible in its overall reports, such as the world economic outlook paper, the Annual Reports of the Executive Directors, the Annual Reports on Exchange Restrictions, in its statistical publications, and in its internal papers. General support services also were extended to a growing number of members.

The countries that joined the Fund in the seven years ended in 1978 had three noteworthy characteristics. First, the number and influence of oil exporting countries rapidly expanded as Bahrain, Qatar, and the United Arab Emirates joined the Fund. Second, Romania became the first country that was also a member of the Council for Mutual Economic Assistance (CMEA) to join the Fund.[1] With its admission in 1972 and the Fund's decision on September 15, 1976 to allow the Socialist Republic of Viet Nam to succeed to the earlier membership of South Viet Nam, the Fund was adding members regarded as socialist or as having a centrally planned economy. Third, and most important, with the exception of Bangladesh and Romania, the new members were small countries and, with the exception of Romania, developing countries. The

---

[1]Countries belonging to the CMEA are Bulgaria, Cuba, Czechoslovakia, the German Democratic Republic, Hungary, Mongolia, Poland, Romania, the U.S.S.R., and Viet Nam. Because the CMEA was established in 1949, Czechoslovakia and Poland were not members when they joined the Fund in 1945 and 1946, respectively. Since both countries left the Fund in 1954 and 1950, respectively, neither was a Fund member when Romania joined.

Fund placed Romania in the category of a more developed primary producing country along with Greece, Portugal, Spain, Turkey, Yugoslavia, and a few other members. Romanian officials, however, continued to refer to Romania as a developing country.[2]

Since 1965, Fund membership was increasingly composed of small developing countries, several of them of a size referred to in the United Nations as ministates or microstates.

CONSIDERATION OF MEMBERSHIP OF SMALL STATES

The applications of ministates for membership raised the question in the mid-1960s whether a nation had to be of a certain size in order to be admitted to international organizations. The Secretary-General of the United Nations and the U.S. representative to the United Nations first broached this question in 1965 in relation to memberhship in the United Nations. The subject was studied for a few years by a committee of experts (Ministate Committee), but because of its important legal and political ramifications, it was allowed by the United Nations after 1971 to become dormant.

In the meantime, in 1966 the management of the Fund, recognizing the significance of Fund membership to small countries, settled on the proposition that the Fund should consider the application of any independent country, regardless of size, but this proposition was subject to review should the United Nations refuse membership to a ministate on grounds of size.

In February 1977 in meetings of the Executive Directors at which applications for membership were being considered, some Executive Directors, noting the marked trend of membership applications from ever smaller states, raised the question of the continued admission to the Fund of such states. In preparation for Executive Board discussion of the question, the Legal Department circulated a paper in March 1977 dealing with the two basic legal questions: Can the Fund withhold membership from small states? Can the Fund establish a special status for small states? The paper came to a number of conclusions. The Articles of Agreement contain four criteria for membership in the Fund that are to be applied to each applicant: the applicant is a country, the country is in formal control of its external relations, the country is willing to perform the obligations imposed by the Articles, and the country is able to perform the obligations. Special criteria do not exist for applications classified as small, however "small" may be defined. The Fund applied liberally the criterion of ability to perform the obligations imposed by the Articles. The criterion could not be interpreted to mean that a member will be able to observe the optimal obligations immediately on entering the Fund. If an applicant meets the four criteria, membership is open to it. The Fund's authority to prescribe the time of

---

[2]See statement by the Governor of the Fund and the World Bank for Romania, *Summary Proceedings, 1978*, p. 178.

and terms for membership cannot be exercised so as to postpone indefinitely membership for an applicant that meets the criteria. The Fund cannot create a special class of members by prescribing terms that would establish permanent rights and duties for this class that would distinguish it from all other members.

In April 1977, the Treasurer's Department also circulated a paper on the same subject. While this paper contained no conclusions, it assisted the Executive Board in its discussion by providing background on the implications for the Fund of membership of small states. To help the Executive Board assess the number of potential requests for membership from small states, the paper provided a list of small states and territories that were either independent or, based on reviews of the United Nations, had the potential for independence. There were 97 such states and territories, of which 65 were not members of the Fund, 27 were already Fund members, and 5 were pending applicants. The paper also briefly examined the impact of a number of new small members on use of the Fund's resources, on the Fund's administrative budget, on aggregate quotas, and on voting arrangements. It also examined in a general way the ability of some small states to undertake the full obligations of membership, using the Fund's experience with small states that were already members. It pointed out that some small states had difficulty in fulfilling these obligations, most notably in providing information and undertaking regular consultations with the Fund but also in managing their foreign exchange systems. Because small country applicants particularly often suffered initially from an absence of economic data and of appropriate financial and economic institutions, they often required considerable technical assistance from the Fund and from other international organizations, including the World Bank. Under Article II, Section 1, of the World Bank's Articles, membership in the World Bank was open only to members of the Fund, a requirement that influenced some countries to join the Fund.

In June 1977, with these two staff papers at hand, the Executive Directors addressed the question of Fund membership of small states. Their discussion revealed that the issues involved were by no means simple. Although they did not want formally to endorse the legal staff's position, most members of the Executive Board believed that the Fund could not legally refuse membership to an applicant country on the grounds that it was too small. Most believed that it would also be undesirable politically for the Fund to refuse membership to a country for this reason. The main exception to this view was that of Mr. Amuzegar, who took the position that since each member received a basic 250 votes (augmented by 1 vote for each portion of its quota equivalent to SDR 100,000), each member should be able to support a certain minimum quota. Most members of the Executive Board considered any criteria of smallness arbitrary, and Messrs. Al-Eyd and Guarnieri expressed strong opposition to setting up any requirement, such as a minimum quota, for entry into the Fund.

While they were not opposed to the Fund continuing to accept virtually all small country applicants into membership, Messrs. Cross, Kafka, Kent, and Pieske emphasized the serious problems the Fund would encounter if many small members joined the Fund in a short time. Small members added considerably to the Fund's administrative costs and to the staff's workload. They required more than average technical assistance. Holding annual consultations with each member, in accordance with the Fund's policy, would be a burden not only on the staff but also on the Executive Board. These burdens were significant, especially since it was desirable to keep the staff relatively small and since the Executive Board's agenda was crowded. In addition, there were potential political problems. Other international agencies, especially the United Nations, had found that a large increase in the number of small members had weakened the credibility of their decisions. Voting power in the Fund could be diffused. Under the proposed Second Amendment, amendments to the Articles had to be accepted by 60 percent of the members having 85 percent of the total voting power before they entered into force. With an increasing number of small members, this requirement could become an obstacle in the future to the prompt entry into force of amendments to the Articles of Agreement.

These Executive Directors suggested possible solutions to these problems. The Fund might, for instance, provide technical assistance to an applicant country before it became a member in return for the payment of fees. While the Fund did not charge members for technical assistance, it was clear that the Fund could charge nonmembers for this assistance and so recoup some of its costs. Perhaps the Fund did not need to treat all members "uniformly." For example, the Fund might not have to hold consultations every year with every small member. Perhaps the Executive Board could approve some consultations on a lapse-of-time basis rather than hold a formal meeting. Perhaps the Fund did not have to have every member covered by an economist or did not have to supply resident representatives to every member that requested one. Since countries were often more interested in seeking membership in the World Bank than in the Fund, possibly the World Bank's Articles could be amended to end the prerequisite of membership in the Fund for a country to join the World Bank.

Mr. Drabble and Mr. Whitelaw, who had small states in their constituencies, pointed out the benefits to small states of Fund membership. They received assistance in starting to manage their own economies instead of struggling on their own. They became more readily integrated into the international community. The Fund, moreover, was particularly well suited to dealing with the problems of small states. The Fund's weighted voting and constituency system gave it a great advantage over other institutions where "one member, one vote" seemed to impede decision making and operations. Furthermore, it was imperative that the Fund retain its image and function as a truly world organization, and not an exclusive one.

Toward the end of the discussion, Mr. Kharmawan suggested that the Executive Directors not try to reach a conclusion. To him, whether examined from a legal, political, administrative, or humanitarian standpoint, the question of Fund membership of small states clearly gave rise to problems that had not yet been adequately considered and, in these circumstances, it was premature for the Executive Board to take a decision. The Chairman, Mr. Witteveen, then put forward a proposal to this effect and the Executive Directors accepted it.

The intention of the Executive Directors, as interpreted by management and staff, was to consider later the general question of the acceptance of new applications for Fund membership by very small states and meanwhile not to preclude the consideration of new applications in accordance with existing rules. In other words, the Fund would continue to act on this question as it had been doing.

ANNUAL CONSULTATIONS

Until consultations under the amended Article IV were started in April 1978, the Fund held consultations with members under the provisions of Article VIII and Article XIV. As in the years since 1952 when consultations under Article XIV began, the target was to hold a consultation annually with each member. While this target was not fully met, consultations were usually held annually with most members.

For members retaining restrictions on current international payments and transfers under Article XIV, annual consultations were mandatory. The great majority of members remained under that Article. As of the end of 1978, of a total membership of 138, only 46 had assumed the obligations of Article VIII. Eleven of these (Bahamas, Bahrain, Chile, Fiji, Oman, Papua New Guinea, Qatar, Seychelles, South Africa, the United Arab Emirates, and Venezuela) did so after 1971.[3]

Annual consultations with members that had accepted the obligations of Article VIII, similar in scope to consultations under Article XIV, although not required by the Articles, were first held in 1960. They continued for the next 18 years, until consultations under the amended Article IV were begun in early 1978. Article IV consultations "comprehended," that is, encompassed, the consultations previously held under Articles XIV and VIII. Between April 1, 1978 and the end of 1978, Article IV consultations were initiated with 70 members, of which 35 were completed by Executive Board discussions.

Adaptation of the Process

As the workload of the staff grew heavier, especially with the negotiation of many more stand-by and extended arrangements, as national officials were faced with frequent staff missions in connection with these arrangements, as the staff held special consultations twice a year with a number of members in connection with the world economic outlook exercise, as the Executive Board regularly reviewed the economic condition of the large industrial members in the context of their

---

[3]El Salvador, Guatemala, Mexico, Panama, and the United States assumed the obligations of Article VIII, Sections 2, 3, and 4 shortly after the Fund came into existence, and Canada, the Dominican Republic, Haiti, and Honduras did so in the early 1950s. In 1961–62, a few years after external convertibility of the major currencies was achieved, Austria, Belgium, France, the Federal Republic of Germany, Ireland, Italy, Luxembourg, the Netherlands, Peru, Saudi Arabia, Sweden, and the United Kingdom assumed the obligations of Article VIII. These members were followed in 1963–71 by Argentina, Australia, Bolivia, Costa Rica, Denmark, Ecuador, Guyana, Jamaica, Japan, Kuwait, Malaysia, Nicaragua, Norway, and Singapore.

consideration of the world economic outlook, and as the agenda of the Executive Board became exceedingly crowded, it was inevitable that the annual consultations process would undergo further streamlining. Mainly at the urging of Mr. Palamenghi-Crispi, the process was adapted further along the lines of modifications made earlier. Staff reports on the discussions with officials of members were altered to eliminate the dialogue form of presentation in which the staff faithfully summarized the exchange of views that had taken place. Staff reports could, therefore, be made still shorter, often less than 15 pages, and could deal entirely with the broad policy issues raised by the member's situation. All factual material was relegated to the background report, the recent economic developments (RED) report. Still greater use was made of tables, charts, and other visual aids, often as appendices to the staff reports on the discussions with officials, to afford a quick picture of the changes in the member's economy. To ease the workload of the Executive Directors, consultations and requests for stand-by or extended arrangements for several members were taken up simultaneously in the Executive Board.

On the whole, however, the conduct of consultations was left basically unchanged. As Fund officials had long been aware, the Fund's consultations, in which the Executive Board held regular, thoroughgoing reviews of the economic policies of each Fund member, based on broad-gauged discussions of the staff with officials of that member, were unique among international organizations. Consultations were the essence of the Fund's activities vis-à-vis its members. Through regular consultations the Fund could most effectively influence the economic policies of its members, particularly of the large industrial members that rarely, or never, came to the Fund for a stand-by arrangement. Consultations were also the means by which the Managing Director and staff and Executive Directors stayed up to date on members' situations so that they could handle urgent requests for financial assistance, if necessary. Information gained through periodic consultations, moreover, enriched the Fund's general assessment of the world economy and payments situation and enabled the Fund better to evaluate the structure of members' exchange rates. The new special consultations were considered supplementary, not a substitute.

The usefulness of the Fund's consultations for the period in which floating rates were expected to prevail was noted by Jelle Zijlstra at the 1975 Annual Meeting. Explicitly complimenting the Fund on the excellent work done under difficult circumstances, Mr. Zijlstra noted that, in the Netherlands, individual consultations often initiated reconsideration of certain policies or policy instruments.[4] After 1975, when it was becoming clear that consultations under the amended Article IV would be the chief means of implementing exchange rate surveillance by the Fund, nearly all officials stressed the need for "full and effective consultations." Earlier concerns of some Executive Directors with the need to simplify or reduce the process of annual consultations were diminished. The long-established and accepted process of

---

[4]Statement by the Governor of the Fund for the Netherlands, *Summary Proceedings, 1975*, p. 193.

annual consultations under Article VIII and Article XIV became the basis for the consultations to be held under the new Article IV.

Adaptation of the Topics

The topics covered in the Fund's annual consultations in the years 1972–78 were adapted to the rapidly changing economic problems confronting members. As in the past, the Fund concentrated on assessing a member's macroeconomic policies, especially its monetary and fiscal policies, and the effects of those policies on the member's own balance of payments position and, where relevant, on the world payments situation. In the circumstances of 1974 and thereafter, discussions of the internal economy in the consultations with industrial members dealt primarily with how best to control inflation, the need to stimulate economic recovery and growth without worsening inflation, and possible coordination of actions by the large industrial members to stimulate economic growth. Discussions of the external economies of industrial members, especially after 1976, dealt heavily with balance of payments adjustment. Consultation discussions with industrial members also included the need for them to help alleviate the acute payments problems of developing members. Also after 1976, at the request of the Development Committee, the consultations with a number of capital-exporting members, such as Belgium, France, the Federal Republic of Germany, Japan, the Netherlands, the United Kingdom, and the United States, included discussion of access of developing members to industrial members' capital markets. The Fund's consultations with developing members concentrated heavily on such topics as the financing of their balance of payments deficits, the prospects for their exports, the management of their internal economies, and their mounting levels of external indebtedness.

More changes in coverage were made after Article IV consultations were introduced. Special attention was devoted to factors influencing a member's exchange rate. The use of restrictions on trade and payments to lessen exchange rate pressures, the use of controls to restrain inward or outward flows of capital, recourse to official borrowing to finance payments deficits, which effectively lightened pressures on the exchange rate, and the extent of official intervention in exchange markets were examined. Article IV consultations also began regularly to include an appraisal of a member's competitive position in world markets, and in the instance of the largest members, an assessment of the impact of their financial and exchange rate policies on the economies and on the adjustment of the balance of payments positions of other members.

ILLUSTRATIVE CONSULTATIONS: SIX COUNTRY VIGNETTES

Illustrative of the range of the Fund's concerns covered in annual consultations are the subjects discussed in the 1978 consultations with three large industrial members—the United States, Japan, and the Federal Republic of Germany—and with three very different, developing members, Korea, Brazil, and Bangladesh.

The 1978 Article IV consultations with the United States put emphasis on measures to combat inflation and to stimulate greater economic growth without worsening inflation. On the external side, the continued large trade and balance of payments deficits of the United States were emphasized. As far as inflation was concerned, the use of incomes policy, in addition to monetary and fiscal policy, was explored. With regard to promoting faster economic growth, the possibility of encouraging greater private investment was discussed. The emphasis on private investment reflected the concerns of Mr. Witteveen, who, in thinking about the need to encourage greater private investment, proved to be a few years ahead of political leaders in the United Kingdom and in the United States. Early in 1977 he was already pointing to the need of industrial members to take measures to revive lagging private investment as a prerequisite for once again achieving more rapid rates of growth.[5] Hence, in the 1978 consultations with the United States, Fund officials raised questions about the degree of profitability of U.S. industry and the relation between profitability and the prospects for greater private investment.

With regard to the prolonged and sizable U.S. trade and payments deficits, discussions dealt heavily with U.S. efforts to conserve energy and reduce imports of oil. U.S. policies with regard to the dollar and official attitudes toward intervention in exchange markets were also discussed. With regard to policies affecting developing members, several questions were taken up: What were U.S. officials doing to keep open U.S. markets to manufactured products from developing members? How were U.S. officials countering the rising trend toward protectionism? What were the prospects for foreign economic assistance? How much access did developing members have to U.S. capital markets, and how might that access be increased?

In the 1978 Article IV consultation with Japan, most of the discussion both between the staff and Japanese officials and in the Executive Board was about how Japan's persistent trade surplus might be reduced in the interest of a better structure of world payments. Exchanges of views took place on questions such as the following: What were the prospects for speeding up the growth of Japan's domestic economy so as to help attract more imports into Japan? How effective were the measures that had already been taken which aimed at increasing imports and at restraining exports? What were the prospects for reducing Japan's reliance on exports to achieve growth in the domestic economy? What were the effects on Japan's exports and imports of the appreciation of the yen in exchange markets? What was the extent of official intervention in exchange markets which tended to prevent appreciation of the yen? What were the trends in Japan's capital account? What measures were being taken to ensure that developing members had adequate access to Japan's capital markets?

---

[5]Mr. Witteveen's address, "The Current Economic Situation in the Industrial Countries," delivered before the National Federation of Banks, July 28, 1977, in Manaus, Brazil; reprinted in *IMF Survey* (Washington), Vol. 6 (August 1, 1977), pp. 247–51.

The 1978 Article IV consultation with the Federal Republic of Germany concentrated heavily on why the strategy of the German authorities after the recession of 1975 had gone wrong. This strategy had aimed at increasing domestic demand and re-establishing a high level of employment while further reducing the rate of inflation. Although progress had been made in reducing inflation, the failure of the German economy to grow at anything like the rate hoped for raised a number of questions. In line with Mr. Witteveen's thinking at the time that greater economic growth in the large industrial members would require special action to encourage greater private investment, much of the discussion centered on the prospects for private investment and the factors that were impeding it. How profitable were industrial enterprises? What was the relation between their profitability and the disappointing investment performance of the German economy? To what extent were governmental regulations an impediment to the recovery of private investment? There was discussion, too, of the rising levels of unemployment, particularly among young people. A number of questions dealt with the German trade and payments surpluses. What was the strategy of German officials for achieving lower surpluses? Why did the German economy remain so export oriented? What exchange market policies were being pursued? As in the instance of other industrial members, rising protectionism and access of developing members to German capital markets were also taken up.

Developing Members

In the consultations with developing members, the exchanges of views between Fund staff and members' officials and the issues considered by the Executive Directors necessarily involved an entirely different set of topics that varied with the individual member.

In the 1978 Article IV consultation with Korea, most attention was devoted to the reasons for the remarkable success of the Korean economy. Korea continued to have rates of growth of real gross national product of over 10 percent a year and a continuously expanding volume of exports that was making Korea, a relatively small country, an important trading nation. The specific topics taken up can be summarized in the following questions. What were the prospects for continued rapid industrialization? To what extent were shortages of skilled labor and pressures for wage increases likely to hamper the growth of Korean exports? How could Korean authorities best deal with new threats from inflation coming from increases in money supply as a result of rising foreign exchange reserves? To what extent could import restrictions and exchange controls be relaxed without unduly upsetting Korea's balance of payments? Relaxation of restrictions would, Fund officials stressed, help mitigate international resentment against the rapid expansion of Korean exports and the growing tendency abroad of restricting imports of Korean goods. What were the implications of Korea's growth for the internal distribution of income?

Like Korea, Brazil was industrializing rapidly and becoming what was being referred to as one of the newly industrialized countries. Hence, in the 1978 Article IV consultation with Brazil, attention centered on the factors that explained high real growth. Less attention was devoted to the temporary circumstances of 1978, such as the drought in the southern part of the country, which had been something of an economic setback. In Brazil's case, the incongruity of high rates of growth for over a decade with persistently high rates of inflation was of special interest. Did not Brazil's experience cast doubt on traditional economic policies, including the doctrines advocated by the Fund? How were monetary indicators that suggested an overheated economy compatible with indicators that suggested rapid growth in real terms? Recognizing that Brazil's "economic miracle" was not a miracle, but rather the result of good economic management and entrepreneurial expertise, Fund officials looked into Brazil's experience with the uses made of foreign capital. How had funds borrowed abroad been so successfully channeled into income-generating investments, particularly into industries producing import substitutes and competitive exports? Since balance of payments deficits seemed to have been contained to some extent by import restrictions, export incentives, and continuous depreciation of the exchange rate, Fund officials also pressed to see whether Brazil's usually strong payments and reserve position would permit a reduction in import restrictions and export subsidies. Fund officials believed that it was likely, too, that some of Brazil's inflation was attributable to tight restrictions on imports and to continuous exchange depreciation. Hence, among the topics discussed was the possibility of shifting the emphasis in exchange rate policy from improving the competitiveness of Brazil's exports to overcoming domestic inflation.

The 1978 Article XIV consultation with Bangladesh raised other issues. Bangladesh had a very low per capita income. Agriculture was the main sector of the economy so that economic development through earnings from the two main exports, jute and tea, was dependent on weather conditions. The Government was trying hard to obtain more food, by production and by importation, to feed a rapidly growing population. The Fund's consultations were concerned with both production and finance. The topics discussed can be summarized in the following questions. What policies would most encourage greater domestic production of foodgrains? What kind of domestic pricing policy should be followed for foodgrains? Specifically, what kind of pricing policy would best reconcile keeping food prices down in the interest of consumers with the need to maintain appropriately high prices so as to encourage producers to enlarge their output? What policies could be used to achieve a more rapid growth of exports and a more diversified pattern? Were exports sufficiently profitable? What exchange rate policy would best help promote greater exports? What kind of taxation policy should be pursued in an economy like that of Bangladesh? To what extent should taxes be placed on exports and imports? What financial policies would help the authorities mobilize domestic resources? What were the most appropriate roles for the national government, including state enterprises, and for the private sector? To what extent should foreign private investment be encouraged, and how?

The foregoing descriptions of the topics considered in the 1978 consultations with these six members exemplify the far-ranging discussions of current economic issues covered in the Fund's annual consultations.

TECHNICAL ASSISTANCE

Since its earliest days, the Fund had provided technical assistance to its members. After 1965 this assistance evolved into a large program, and in the years 1972–78 it continued as one of the Fund's most absorbing activities.[6] Much of the Fund's assistance was in central banking, fiscal affairs, statistics, and legal matters, but the Fund was also called upon frequently to provide assistance in other fields. Assistance was provided through staff missions, field assignments by staff or by outside experts, and studies and recommendations prepared in Washington.

Central Banking

Technical assistance in central banking, provided by the Central Banking Service, gradually changed in character in the period reviewed here. Initially this assistance mainly took the form of helping newly independent nations create national currencies and establish central banks to issue and regulate these currencies and providing managers for these new central banks. By 1972 most of these needs had been met, as virtually all members already had central banks. Most could, and wanted to, appoint their own heads for their central banks. The Fund no longer needed to set up central banks and needed to provide fewer and fewer managers.

Requests for technical assistance in central banking persisted, but they were now for very specialized types of assistance. Members asked for help, for instance, to extend supervision by the central bank over commercial banks; to develop bank inspection units; to help develop local capital markets; to improve the management of their foreign exchange operations, including their new exchange rate arrangements; to set up forward exchange markets; to strengthen research services; to develop training and recruiting facilities; and to apply computer technology to central banking operations. Some long-established central banks also sought the Fund's assistance to reorganize their central banking operations or to update the provisions of the central bank statutes.

By 1978 about 800 man-years had been provided by outside experts to 88 central monetary institutions, and 74 members had received assistance from headquarters by staff advisory missions since the Central Banking Service was established 15 years before. Typically, at any one time, some 70 experts were on assignment in about 40 members, while about 6 advisory projects were in preparation at headquarters.

---

[6]A description of the evolution of the Fund's technical assistance program can be found in *History, 1966–71,* Vol. I, pp. 578–88.

Fiscal Affairs

Technical assistance in fiscal affairs provided by the Fiscal Affairs Department also became broader after 1971. Assistance was given in tax policy, tax and customs administration (including training of local personnel), budget preparation and expenditure control, government accounting, and general financial administration. Examples of specific types of technical assistance in fiscal affairs included setting up sales, corporation, or property taxes; reviewing the rate structures of income taxes; improving procedures for the assessment and collection of taxes; and helping with revisions of customs tariffs. This assistance continued to be provided through staff missions, through staff assignments in the field, and through use of outside experts.

In the financial year ended April 30, 1978, 41 members utilized all three forms of technical assistance in fiscal affairs—staff missions, staff assignments in the field, and outside experts—compared with 33 in the previous financial year. Seventy individual field assignments were carried out, of which 41 were long term and 29 short term; 358 man-months were spent in the field. Furthermore, as in previous years, the staff visited several members in order to inspect the progress made and to review requests for further assistance. Staff at headquarters also continued to be deeply involved in work tosupport and monitor the activities of experts in the field.

Statistics

The Bureau of Statistics continued in the years covered here to provide technical assistance to members mainly to help them improve their central bank bulletins. This assistance involved discussions with national officials and technicians of the statistical concepts and classification standards used in assembling and presenting statistics. Emphasis was on statistics covering international reserves, money and banking, interest rates, prices, production, external trade, government finance, balance of payments, and, where available, national accounts. The intent was to promote the use of similar statistical definitions and methods in all members so as to facilitate intercountry comparisons.

In addition to its work on central bank bulletins, the Bureau of Statistics continued to provide members with other assistance in statistics, mainly in balance of payments statistics and, after 1974/75, in government finance statistics. Fund staff explained to members the concepts and classification standards set out in the Fund's *Balance of Payments Manual* and in the *Draft Manual on Government Finance Statistics*, which was distributed in 1974/75. In 1978 the distribution of the fourth edition of the *Balance of Payments Manual* led to assistance to apply the concepts and classification standards used in that manual.

Legal Affairs

The Legal Department also provided substantial technical assistance to members. The occasion of the Second Amendment meant that many members requested and received technical assistance from the Fund's legal staff. The Fund's lawyers, for instance, helped many members to develop the procedures needed to accept the Second Amendment and to modify their laws because of the Second Amendment. Furthermore, members constantly requested explanations of particular legal aspects of the Articles before and after the Second Amendment.

In addition, a great many of the requests for technical assistance coming into the staff in the Central Banking Service or in the Fiscal Affairs Department involved requests for the drafting of legislation or other legal documents. This technical assistance was provided by the Legal Department. In the years reviewed here, lawyers on the Fund staff helped members with central banking matters by drafting legislation or developing negotiable instruments concerned with central banking, other banking, currency, and exchange. They provided assistance in respect to fiscal affairs by drafting tax legislation, such as legislation for individual and corporation income taxes, and indirect taxes (such as customs, excises, and sales taxes, including value-added sales taxes) and legislation for capital gains taxes, property taxes, and land taxes.

Staff of the Legal Department also provided technical assistance to members on matters related to membership in the Fund. For example, they assisted prospective members in drafting legislation that permitted them to join the Fund, to accept and carry out the provisions of the Articles of Agreement, to accept quota increases and to pay increases in subscriptions, and to participate in allocations of SDRs. They also often provided advice to officials of other international organizations in the drafting of legislation or other texts relating to the SDR.

Other Forms

In the years 1972–78 substantial technical assistance was provided by staff in other departments, particularly in the Area Departments, the Exchange and Trade Relations Department, and the Treasurer's Department. But all departments of the Fund occasionally provided some technical assistance of one kind or another. Some technical assistance was short term and some was provided in the course of staff missions concentrating on consultations or negotiations for stand-by or extended arrangements. Some took the form of stationing resident representatives in members. As of the end of 1978 there were 19 resident representatives, of whom, for the first time in the Fund's history, one was female. A resident representative served primarily as policy advisor to the member, but also explained the Fund's policies to the officials of the member government and gave Fund officials a greater under-standing of the economic and financial policies pursued by the member. Another responsibility of a resident representative was to serve as liaison between the Fund and the member in carrying out other details of the Fund's business, such as helping the member with the mechanics of drawings, repurchases, and SDR reconstitutions, reconciling differences in the data used by the member and by the Fund staff, and assisting with the selection of participants for the Fund's training programs. In these ways, the resident representative acted as a troubleshooter or expediter. In addition, a resident representative helped to collect, maintain, and improve the series of key economic and financial data on the member to which he was assigned and sometimes helped to train junior and middle-level technicians in central banks and ministries of finance. The earlier major role of a resident representative as a monitor of stabilization programs associated with stand-by arrangements was greatly reduced in the 1970s.

In 1976 some Executive Directors were concerned that the number of resident representatives (then 30) was proliferating and that some posts had been occupied for over a decade. They were concerned both with costs and with the possible encroachment of resident representatives on the functions of Executive Directors. Starting in 1976, a ceiling on the number of resident representative posts for any given year was set as part of the administrative budget. Thereafter, the number of resident representatives declined.

Members also asked for assistance in administering and reforming their exchange systems, in developing macroeconomic models for their economies, in learning electronic data processing, and in setting up accounts to keep track of their transactions and operations vis-à-vis the Fund, in both the General Resources Account and the Special Drawing Rights Department. Prospective members asked for assistance in collecting data appropriate for the calculation of quotas and in putting together other financial material associated with achieving membership.

Fund staff also frequently gave technical assistance to other international or regional agencies. Some illustrations are: drafting an agreement for the Arab Monetary Fund; helping establish the Islamic Development Bank; helping the African Development Bank assess the balance of payments problems of African countries resulting from the rise in the cost of oil imports; advising the Special Fund of the OPEC on criteria for balance of payments support to the most seriously affected (MSA) countries, as defined by the United Nations; advising the West African Economic Community on how to implement the monetary and trading provisions specified in its treaty of establishment; advising the West African Monetary Union on the reform of the monetary institutions of its members and their common central bank; advising the European Space Agency on how to make allowances in its accounts for fluctuations in countries' exchange rates and for continuous rises in general price levels; advising the Central African Customs and Economic Union on tariff and tax matters; and helping the East Caribbean Currency Authority with central bank legislation.

Technical assistance was indeed an absorbing activity for the Fund. By the end of the 1970s Fund officials felt obliged to put out a special pamphlet explaining the extent of the Fund's technical assistance program.[7]

---

[7]*Technical Assistance Services of the International Monetary Fund*, IMF Pamphlet Series, No. 30 (Washington, 1979). This pamphlet was updated and extended as *Technical Assistance and Training Services of the International Monetary Fund*, IMF Pamphlet Series, No. 43 (Washington, 1985).

TRAINING BY THE IMF INSTITUTE

Training of officials by the IMF Institute continued to be an important part of the Fund's assistance to its members in the years 1972–78.[8] The objective continued to be enabling participants to discharge their responsibilities more effectively after they returned to their home countries. Although the great majority of participants were from developing members, some participants also came from industrial members.

As of 1978 the Institute's principal course was a 10-week course on financial analysis and policy, conducted in English, French, and Spanish. This course presented an exposition of the Fund's procedures and policies, examined the tools of modern economic analysis, and provided a study of the monetary, fiscal, and balance of payments policy instruments used to affect the performance of a national economy. Case studies and workshops were heavily relied on as teaching devices.[9]

The IMF Institute also provided on a regular basis two other courses, given in English, French, or Spanish, as required. An 8-week course on balance of payments methodology was given in collaboration with the Balance of Payments Division of the Bureau of Statistics. This course explained the balance of payments concepts and definitions that the Fund used. The intent was to assist members to collect and present balance of payments statistics on a basis comparable with that of other members. A 20-week course in public finance, given in conjunction with the Fiscal Affairs Department, dealt with the planning and management of public expenditures, taxes and tax administration, and the relation between fiscal policy and economic stability and economic development.

In addition, for the first time in 1977, a 4-week pilot course (in English) on government finance statistics was conducted in conjunction with the Government Finance Statistics Division of the Bureau of Statistics. This course undertook to explain the concepts, definitions, and procedures set out in the *Draft Manual on Government Finance Statistics*, the manual to be used for compiling statistics relating to government accounts.

By the end of the 1977/78 financial year, 2,127 officials from 130 members had been trained at the Institute since its inception in 1964.

---

[8]The growth of the IMF Institute in earlier years has been described in *History, 1966–71*, Vol. I, pp. 588–90.

[9]In 1981 for the first time the IMF Institute published an illustration of the material used, *Financial Policy Workshops: The Case of Kenya* (Washington, 1981).

CHAPTER

48

Added Responsibilities

*E*XTERNAL INDEBTEDNESS, international capital markets, especially the Eurocurrency market and the access of developing countries to the world's capital markets, relations with commercial banks, and trade policy were of increasing concern to members after 1971. The Fund therefore took on more responsibility for following these subjects, for assisting members in their regard, and for trying, where possible, to oversee or monitor developments.

EXTERNAL INDEBTEDNESS

When the Fund first became more involved with the problems of members' external indebtedness in the mid-1960s, it concerned itself mainly with the servicing of debt, that is, with the ability of members regularly to meet their interest payments and amortization schedules.[1] It continued this emphasis after 1971. As an item in a country's balance of payments, debt servicing was a natural topic of interest to the Fund. Moreover, problems relating to external indebtedness usually showed up initially in the form of payments arrears, that is, a member engaged in restrictions or other practices that delayed paying interest on its indebtedness. The emergence of arrears involved the Fund because the member had a balance of payments problem. More important, under the policies of the Fund after 1970, payments arrears were regarded as restrictions subject to the Fund's approval.[2] Reasons for giving priority to the avoidance of debt-servicing difficulties, however, went beyond those for keeping the balance of payments situation and payments restrictions under control. Experience demonstrated that when members started to accumulate payments arrears and were unable to meet their current debt-servicing obligations, their relations with all possible financiers, governmental as well as private, were immediately threatened. Acute debt-servicing difficulties also had a profoundly

---

[1]The Fund's activities with regard to members' external indebtedness until 1971 were summarized in *History, 1966–71,* Vol. I, pp. 593–601.

[2]A definition of payments arrears and a discussion of the Fund's decision to regard them as restrictions is in *History, 1966–71,* Vol. I, pp. 591–93.

detrimental impact on the inflows of capital into a country, which in turn undermined whatever trade, employment, and development objectives the country might have.

The Fund used a number of techniques to head off problems with debt servicing. The staff and the Executive Directors continued, as they had for many years, to review during annual consultations the external debt of each member that had any sizable debt outstanding. The management of external debt, including the procedures and policies that a member used to control borrowing abroad by its public sector agencies, was discussed. For members in which the external debt of the private sector was part of the balance of payments problem, policies used to limit foreign borrowing by the private sector were also reviewed.

A second review of external debt problems took place in the context of the review of the world economic outlook. As the external debt of developing countries started to grow larger after 1974–75 because of the higher payments for oil imports, the staff and the Executive Directors, in discussing the world economy, regularly examined the problems of rising external indebtedness and the prospects for debt servicing.

These techniques notwithstanding, the most effective leverage the Fund had in dealing with the debt-servicing problems of its members was through its policies on use of its resources. As seen in Chapter 25, by 1978 nearly all the stabilization programs that accompanied stand-by arrangements included, as performance criteria or as statements of policy, quantitative limits on new medium-term external borrowing. Some stabilization programs also included ways to strengthen the government's procedures for controlling the outstanding amounts of external debt.

Participation in Multilateral Debt Renegotiation Meetings

As it had since the late 1950s, in 1972–78 the Fund, at the request of both debtor and creditor nations, also had staff participate in all official multilateral debt renegotiation meetings between government officials of creditor and of debtor countries to rearrange the terms of repayment for certain categories of external debt, that is, the "Paris Club" negotiations. Intergovernmental debt was involved as well as debts owed by a government to private entities if these private lenders had obtained a guarantee from an agency of the government of the creditor country. Debt owed by a borrowing government to private banks or to international financial agencies, such as the Fund and the World Bank, and debt owed by a private debtor to a private creditor without a government guarantee in the creditor country were not involved.

In earlier years debt renegotiation meetings were held at The Hague and in London under the auspices of ad hoc groupings. By the 1970s multilateral debt renegotiation meetings were usually held in Paris, customarily at the Kléber Center, and were usually chaired by a senior official of the French Treasury. It was for this reason that they were referred to as Paris Club negotiations. They were the major forum for rescheduling official debt, with meetings usually initiated at the request of the country seeking to reschedule its external debt. Although Paris Club negotiations were still informal, the groupings were by the 1970s no longer ad hoc. A fairly steady composition of creditor countries attended the meetings and negotiations also took place under more defined rules and structure than in the past.

Generally, Paris Club meetings were attended by observers from the Fund, the World Bank, the OECD, and the UNCTAD. For its part, the Fund staff played the role of a neutral middleman, "an honest broker," between the creditor countries and the debtor. The debtor country usually had to begin the meeting with a detailed report on its economic condition and an assessment of the amount and nature of debt relief that it regarded as necessary. Prior to the meeting, Fund staff often provided technical assistance to the debtor member by assisting in the preparation of this report and of other necessary statistical and analytical documentation. For the creditor members, the Fund staff usually provided an assessment of the debtor member's economic condition and prospects, especially regarding its balance of payments. At the negotiations themselves, staff representatives, if requested, provided further details to creditors. The staff often gave assessments of the balance of payments implications of alternative proposals for debt relief made by the creditors. Staff of the Fund usually concentrated on the short-term situation, leaving the provision of information and views on the debtor member's long-term needs and capabilities to staff of the World Bank. But the particular involvement of the Fund staff varied considerably from one debt renegotiation to another. For its part, the Fund's interest was to help create conditions that would improve the medium-term balance of payments prospects of the debtor member, thereby providing for continued debt servicing and for continued flows of capital to the member.[3]

As described in Chapter 49, the Fund staff also participated in the consortia arranged by the World Bank for a number of countries. In some of these consortia, debt rescheduling was a prime subject.

In 1974 the staff prepared a study of the experience of the four members— Chile, Ghana, India, and Pakistan—which together had gone through several multilateral debt renegotiations in the period 1971–74. This study updated a 1971 study reviewing the experiences of eight members (Argentina, Brazil, Chile, Ghana, India, Indonesia, Peru, and Turkey) which had recourse to multilateral debt renegotiations in the period 1961–70.[4] While the new study was intended primarily to give the Executive Directors an overall view of the developments of the previous three years in the handling by the international community of external debt problems of developing countries, it had a secondary purpose as well. Just as the timing of the 1971 study was geared to a request by the Inter-American Committee on the Alliance for Progress, so the timing of the 1974 study was geared to a request of the ad hoc group of Governmental Experts on Debt Problems of Developing

---

[3]Further information on how debt rescheduling works can be found in "Debt Rescheduling: What Does It Mean?" *Finance & Development*, Vol. 20 (September 1983), pp. 26–30.

[4]*History, 1966–71*, Vol. I, pp. 596–97.

Countries that the UNCTAD had established in July 1973 for a more recent evaluation of countries' experiences with multilateral debt renegotiations.

The study was devoted mainly to a detailed review of the experiences of the four members, with the staff emphasizing the considerable variation in their external debt problems and in the underlying balance of payments problems that led to the need to renegotiate. It was given to the UNCTAD for its exclusive use in November 1974. In addition, Fund staff participated, as observers, in the meetings of the UNCTAD on debt for which the study had been prepared.

In the years 1975–78 Fund staff continued to participate in multilateral debt renegotiation meetings. Gabon, Peru, Sierra Leone, Turkey, and Zaïre, among other members, had recourse to such negotiations. In the 1970s creditor members frequently made the rescheduling of debt subject to the conclusion by the debtor member of a stand-by arrangement with the Fund in the upper credit tranches, that is, a stand-by arrangement that had stricter conditionality than a stand-by arrangement confined to the first credit tranche.

As time went on, there were proposals from the UNCTAD and from several other quarters to have the Fund assume a more active role in Paris Club negotiations including chairing the meetings. The position of the management and staff, supported by most Executive Directors, however, was that the close and continuing collaboration between the Fund and all its members, both creditors and debtors, and the advisory role that the Fund had at debt renegotiation meetings could be jeopardized if the Fund was also to chair the meetings.

Further Work with Regard to External Debt

After 1971 the Fund stepped up its work on external debt in other ways too. The staff kept much closer track of the magnitude of members' indebtedness. They supplemented the data obtained by the Fund with the periodically updated information on external public and publicly guaranteed debt collected through the World Bank's Debtor Reporting System. The staffs of the Fund and of the World Bank also had informal debriefing sessions following staff visits to members to ensure consistency in the data used by the two institutions.

In addition to keeping track of the size of members' external debt, the staff began by the late 1970s to develop tools for analyzing external debt and to assess the concepts customarily used to evaluate it. The staff developed, for example, a theoretical model that related foreign borrowing to a country's rate of growth, to its financial flows, and to its balance of payments.[5] In a major effort, the staff began also to try to answer such questions as the following: What was the impact of inflation on debt? In other words, how burdensome were the rapid increases in debt if allowance was made for inflation and figures for debt converted into constant prices? Was debt

---

[5]Claudio M. Loser, "External Debt Management and Balance of Payments Policies," *Staff Papers*, International Monetary Fund (Washington), Vol. 24 (March 1977), pp. 168–92.

"in real terms" a serious problem? How useful were the various indicators used to measure the burden of external debt service, such as the ratio between total external debt and annual gross national product and the ratio between annual debt service and yearly export earnings?

The staff began to study, too, the particular economic and financial characteristics of members with serious difficulties in servicing their debts and examined the experiences of members that had restructured their debts. The staff, moreover, began to extrapolate members' debt for a year or so in the future to help determine whether additional indebtedness could be accommodated without undue concern. They started to undertake these studies to improve the advice that they and the Executive Directors gave to members on managing external debt and to assess better members' balance of payments positions so that the Fund could formulate viable stabilization programs.[6]

In addition to these studies, staff participated in meetings of experts assembled by international agencies from time to time to consider how debt-servicing problems of developing members might best be handled by the international financial community. As problems of debt became a prime concern of financial officials, in addition to the meetings of the UNCTAD, other organizations, such as the OECD and its Development Assistance Committee (DAC), and the commissions of the Conference on International Economic Cooperation (CIEC)—the North-South dialogue—also held meetings, in which Fund staff participated, to discuss external debt problems.

Fund staff also continued regularly to attend as observers the semiannual meetings of the Union d'Assureurs des Crédits Internationaux (the Berne Union), comprising a large group of governmental and related public agencies, including some from developing countries, which guaranteed or insured export credits, including short-term trade credits. At these meetings, the agencies represented exchanged information on their operations and reviewed attitudes toward specific countries. This information gave the Fund staff more insight into member's situations.

Beginning in 1976, moreover, debtor members, notably Zaïre, requested the Fund staff to provide technical assistance or attend as observers meetings in which the debtor was negotiating with private commercial banks for a restructuring of its debts. These requests were becoming more frequent as the period reviewed here was coming to an end.

EXTERNAL DEBT BECOMES WORRISOME

By 1977 the external indebtedness of developing members was becoming worrisome. The outstanding public and publicly guaranteed medium-term and long-

---

[6]The Fund published in 1981, in a newly inaugurated Occasional Papers series, its first major study on external debt. *External Indebtedness of Developing Countries*, by a Staff Team Headed by Bahram Nowzad and Richard C. Williams, Occasional Paper No. 3 (Washington, 1981).

term external debt of developing countries, according to staff estimates, had jumped from $91 billion at the end of 1972 to $244 billion at the end of 1977 to $310 billion at the end of 1978, an increase of three and a half times in six years. Service on this debt leapt even higher, from $12 billion in 1972 to $36 billion in 1977 to $49 billion in 1978, a more than fourfold increase. Over a dozen members had accumulated large debts: Algeria, Argentina, Brazil, Egypt, India, Indonesia, Iran, Israel, Korea, Mexico, Pakistan, Peru, the Philippines, Turkey, Venezuela, and Yugoslavia. More than another dozen relatively small members had accumulated debt that was large relative to their gross national product or their total export earnings: Bangladesh, Chile, Colombia, Ecuador, Greece, Ivory Coast, Malaysia, Morocco, Nigeria, Portugal, Sudan, Syrian Arab Republic, Thailand, Tunisia, and Zaïre. Indebtedness was not due solely to the oil problem. Some borrowing countries were themselves major oil exporters, but because they had relatively low per capita incomes, they could be expected to be net capital importers—Algeria, Indonesia, Iran, and Nigeria, for instance.

Another problem about debt was that a substantial proportion was to private banks. Debt owed to private banks usually had higher interest rates and shorter maturities than debt owed to government institutions. Rollover and rescheduling of debt owed to commercial banks presented a still further problem in an era of high and rising interest rates. In the mid-1970s instead of fixed interest rates, many commercial banks began to charge floating interest rates linked to general market rates of interest. Hence, members rescheduling their debts were likely to have to pay higher interest rates than they did prior to the rescheduling.

The size and nature of the debt made for a worrisome situation, to which many Governors from developing and industrial members alike began to refer. At the 1977 Annual Meeting, Abdel Moneim El Kaissouni, for example, drew attention to the serious concerns of all officials as a result of the continued growth in the external debt of the developing countries and the increase in the burden of debt servicing.[7] H.M. Patel stressed the need for a "new bold and imaginative generalized approach" to the solution of the chronic debt service problem of developing countries.[8] Marcel Yondo complained that the developed countries had "refused to grant the moratorium requested by the developing nations."[9]

Governors from industrial members tried to allay fears and to suggest possible approaches. W. Michael Blumenthal, for instance, urged that officials approach the management of international indebtedness not as a crisis but as a short-term and medium-term balance of payments problem.[10] Robert Boulin emphasized that the problem of indebtedness could really be solved for some countries only through an

---

[7]Statement by the Governor of the World Bank for Egypt, *Summary Proceedings, 1977*, p. 150.

[8]Statement by the Governor of the Fund and the World Bank for India, *Summary Proceedings, 1977*, pp. 54–55.

[9]Statement by the Governor of the Fund for Cameroon, *Summary Proceedings, 1977*, p. 72.

[10]Statement by the Governor of the Fund and the World Bank for the United States, *Summary Proceedings, 1977*, p. 68.

increase in the transfer of real resources.[11] Xenophon Zolotas suggested the creation of an international loan insurance scheme along the lines of national export guarantee arrangements and the OECD support fund that was being proposed at the time. The bulk of the funds needed by non-oil developing countries would continue to be provided out of the OPEC countries' surpluses through the intermediary of the international banking system. But the industrial nations and the OPEC countries would provide their collective guarantee to loans extended by private banking institutions.[12]

The context of the fears of officials was well expressed by R.D. Muldoon. Predictions of massive payments deficits for the non-oil developing countries were not, he stressed, simply statistics. They represented still further accumulations of debt. He warned of two potentially dangerous circumstances: the increasing difficulty of recirculating the proceeds of continuing surpluses and the diminishing ability of many countries to service accumulating debt. Inevitably not just economic instability, but also political instability would result. Confidence in the international financial system was lower than it had been for some time, and for the first time in many years officials were hearing, instead of "rescheduling," the ominous word "default."[13]

The topic of the external debt of developing countries was paramount again at the 1978 Annual Meeting. In the first plenary session, Mr. de Larosière referred to the "burdensome debt positions" of the non-oil developing countries.[14] Petar Kostić and Hannes Androsch also referred to the same problem.[15] H.M. Patel warned that acute debt-servicing problems might force some non-oil developing countries to adopt deflationary measures or severely restrictive import policies unless adequate debt relief or new credit was made available.[16] Hamed El-Sayeh advocated a greater flow of resources from both advanced countries and international institutions to alleviate the debt service burden of the non-oil developing countries.[17] Tatsuo Murayama explained the new policy measures of the Japanese Government to help with debt relief for poor developing countries.[18]

Its accelerated activities thrust the Fund deeply into the external debt problem. As 1978 closed, the external debt of developing countries was clearly uppermost among financial officials' concerns, and it appeared certain that, in the future, the Fund would have to deal even more with this problem.

---

[11]Statement by the Governor of the Fund for France, *Summary Proceedings, 1977*, p. 86.

[12]Statement by the Governor of the Fund for Greece, *Summary Proceedings, 1977*, p. 34.

[13]Statement by the Governor of the Fund for New Zealand, *Summary Proceedings, 1977*, pp. 97–98.

[14]Opening Address by the Managing Director, *Summary Proceedings, 1978*, p. 19.

[15]Statements by the Governors of the World Bank for Yugoslavia and for Austria, *Summary Proceedings, 1978*, pp. 55–56 and 60–61.

[16]Statement by the Governor of the Fund and the World Bank for India, *Summary Proceedings, 1978*, p. 71.

[17]Statement by the Governor of the World Bank for Egypt, *Summary Proceedings, 1978*, p. 165.

[18]Statement by the Governor of the Fund and the World Bank for Japan, *Summary Proceedings, 1978*, p. 53.

INTERNATIONAL CAPITAL MARKETS

Following and analyzing developments in international capital markets were other responsibilities the Fund took on after 1971. Here, the Fund inevitably gave considerable attention to the Eurocurrency market, an immense, intriguing capital market in which currencies were deposited, borrowed, and lent outside the countries issuing them and in which banks located abroad dealt in third-country currencies. Not only did British banks located in London deal in U.S. dollar deposits but German banks located in London also dealt in U.S. dollar deposits.[19] In earlier years staff had followed the origin, in the late 1950s, of the Eurodollar market and its rapid growth in the 1960s into other currencies to become the Eurocurrency market, or markets. In the 1960s staff attended meetings at the BIS about the Eurocurrency market and in 1971–72 examined the relation between the Eurocurrency market and the need for greater international liquidity, the prime topic of the time. But these staff studies and attendance at BIS meetings mainly kept the Fund abreast of developments in the growing Eurocurrency market and did not reflect any identification of the Fund's interest with developments in that market.

Beginning in 1973, the Fund's interest in the Eurocurrency market greatly accelerated for several reasons. Many of the Fund's members operated in the market, either as a source of funds or as a depository for their reserves, and were therefore vitally concerned with developments in the market. Moreover, the Eurocurrency market was continuing to grow at the astonishing rate of 35 percent a year and easily dominated all other international capital markets. Its sheer size meant that were the flows of funds through the market to become unstable, much of the mechanism for effecting international payments and settlements could be upset and the whole international monetary system put in chaos.

Another spur to the Fund's study of the Eurocurrency market was the sharpened interest of financial officials of industrial members in seeing whether the market could, or should, be controlled. As noted in earlier chapters, controls on capital movements were on the agenda of the Committee of Twenty's initial discussions in 1972. By 1973 financial officials of industrial members were becoming concerned about the limited public surveillance of the Eurocurrency market and their lack of control over it. Knowing that speculative flows of capital had wrecked the par value system and could play havoc with the new floating rate system that had developed earlier in the year, they were increasingly interested to control flows of capital, especially of speculative capital, so as to reduce exchange rate instability. But the flexibility and anonymity of operations in the Eurocurrency market, as well as the fact that the market was not confined within the boundaries of any single country, made flows of short-term capital extremely hard to control. Financial officials were also concerned that the operations of the Eurocurrency market would reduce in the pursuit of national monetary policies the independence that they

---

[19]This territorial aspect of the Eurocurrency market no longer applied after the establishment of interbanking facilities in New York early in the 1980s.

hoped to achieve with the onset of floating rates. They could not effectively conduct national policies with regard to money supplies and interest rates if large amounts of capital could suddenly and easily shift from one currency to another whenever changes in expectations or other developments motivated shifts of short-term capital. Such shifts of capital decreased or enlarged a country's reserves and money supply, negating the effects of monetary policies.

Officials of industrial members were accordingly interested in investigating the introduction of governmental measures to regulate operations in the Eurocurrency market. Because the banks of different countries competed with each other for operations in the market and because governments did not want to put their own banks at a disadvantage compared with the banks of other countries, officials of any given country could not apply regulations unilaterally. Any regulations had to be applied in some parallel or international manner.

In 1974 the Fund's interest in the Eurocurrency market also increased because financial officials became concerned about the ability of the market to handle the massive recycling of petrodollars and because they became nervous about the possibility of widespread bank failures after some heavily publicized bank failures occurred.

Nature of Accelerated Studies

As part of the Fund's growing interest in international capital markets, including the Eurocurrency market, in mid-1973 the staff did an introductory study of the extension of short-term banking credits to developing members, including credits through Eurocurrency markets. To collect information for the study, staff held discussions with officials of several commercial banks, in London, Milan, New York, Paris, and Rome, with officials of central banks and of finance ministries in the countries visited, and with officials of some other financial institutions in those countries.[20]

Following this introductory study, the staff, realizing that for many developing countries extensive use of bank credits was a new experience, decided to attempt an analysis of how selected countries in the developing world might be affected by extensive reliance on international banking credits. To this end, in late 1973, staff visited five Asian members—three developing members, Indonesia, Korea, and the Philippines, and two capital exporting members, Japan and Singapore. The staff examined both banking credits raised in Eurocurrency or "offshore" money markets (where transactions took place in a currency other than the currency of the country where the lending took place) and banking credits in "inshore" markets (where transactions were denominated in the currency of the country from which the lending occurred). They also examined three policy issues arising out of the

---

[20]This study was later published as Azizali F. Mohammed and Fabrizio Saccomanni, "Short-Term Banking and Euro-Currency Credits to Developing Countries," *Staff Papers*, Vol. 20 (November 1973), pp. 612–38.

extensive use of bank credits—the constraints on monetary policy, the management of external debt, and the management of foreign exchange reserves.

In early 1974, at Mr. Witteveen's initiative, an interdepartmental staff committee was set up to plan and direct a major study of the Eurocurrency market. The study was planned as broadly based, not simply as a study to find means of evolving international controls over the market. The Managing Director and staff were well aware that officials of developing members were satisfied with their freedom to operate in the Eurocurrency market and were dubious about the appropriateness of any action that might impede the flow of resources to them or raise their costs of borrowing.

In September 1974, after several months of work, the staff circulated three papers for consideration by the Executive Directors. One paper contained detailed statistics on the market, pointed out the gaps in the statistics on international banking, and made suggestions as to how these statistics could be improved. A second paper traced the origin and growth of the Eurocurrency market and described the ways in which it functioned, such as the lending and borrowing practices and the effects of interest rate differentials on movements of funds. It also analyzed the controversial question of whether the Eurocurrency market was a source of credit expansion additional to that of national money markets, thereby complicating the attempts of national authorities to control the growth of aggregate demand. A third paper, which was to be the basis of the Executive Board's discussion, suggested ways in which the Fund could make a contribution. The conclusion of this paper was guarded. Financial officials and commercial bankers needed more complete and detailed information on the Eurocurrency market, and the Fund might be able to assist in providing this information. The staff would investigate the possibility of publishing more statistics on international banking in *International Financial Statistics* (IFS), the Fund's monthly statistical publication, and would expand its work with members to improve the reporting of international banking credits. A supplementary paper issued in October 1974 described the banking regulations of four members, the Federal Republic of Germany, Japan, the United Kingdom, and the United States, to illustrate the diversity of approach of national authorities in regard to the government standards required for private banking operations.

The Executive Directors welcomed the initiative of the Managing Director and staff in opening discussions in the Executive Board of the Eurocurrency market. They made suggestions for further study of international capital markets, including not only the market for currencies, such as the Eurocurrency market, but also the markets for bonds.

After 1974 the staff prepared annual reports on international capital markets. These reports described recent developments in international credit and capital markets and assessed the near-term prospects for international lending through banks and through bond placements. These reports were based partly on data collected by national monetary authorities, and by the BIS, the OECD, and the World

Bank, as these organizations gradually began to collect and publish more data on international banking, and partly on discussions that the staff held with officials of government agencies, particularly agencies responsible for supervision of banks, with officers of many leading private commercial banks, and with staff of the BIS, the EC, and the OECD. Initially, these studies were for use only within the Fund but later parts were published in the *IMF Survey*.[21]

The creation of credit through the Eurocurrency market and possible controls on the market continued to interest Fund officials, as well as economists generally, and were often studied by the staff.[22] When Mr. Witteveen again became concerned about the inflationary potential of the Eurocurrency market, toward the end of his term in mid-1978, as described in Chapter 46, another staff working group was set up to study the macroeconomic effects of the Eurocurrency market. In January and February 1978, this working group made visits within the United States and to several European countries to hold discussions on this topic with government officials, with officers of private commercial banks, and with the staffs of the BIS and the OECD.

Financial officials had interest, too, in the subject of controls on flows of capital, especially of short-term capital, under the rules of the Fund. The General Counsel undertook to describe at some length the status of international movements of capital under the law of the Fund from the time that the Articles of Agreement were originally negotiated in the 1940s through the provisions planned in the Second Amendment.[23] The Fund's work with regard to international capital movements was thus continuously increasing. As 1978 ended, plans were being made to create an International Capital Markets Division in the Exchange and Trade Relations Department.

Access of Developing Countries to Bond Markets

Another topic in the field of international capital markets to which the Fund began to devote attention in 1976 was that of the access of developing countries to international bond markets. This work was done in conjunction with the Development Committee.

---

[21] See *IMF Survey*, Supplement on International Lending (June 6, 1977), pp. 177–88 and *IMF Survey*, Report on International Lending (July 31, 1978), pp. 225–36. In 1980 and 1981, in the new Occasional Papers series, the Fund published these reports: *International Capital Markets: Recent Developments and Short-Term Prospects*, by a Staff Team Headed by R.C. Williams, Exchange and Trade Relations Department, Occasional Paper No. 1 (Washington, 1980) and *International Capital Markets: Recent Developments and Short-Term Prospects, 1981*, by a Staff Team Headed by Richard C. Williams, with G.G. Johnson, Occasional Paper No. 7 (Washington, 1981).

[22] Among studies by the staff were those by John Hewson and Eisuke Sakakibara, "The Euro-Dollar Deposit Multiplier: A Portfolio Approach," *Staff Papers*, Vol. 21 (July 1974), pp. 307–28, and by Andrew D. Crockett, "The Euro-Currency Market: An Attempt to Clarify Some Basic Issues," *Staff Papers*, Vol. 23 (July 1976), pp. 375–86. In addition, Manfred Willms, temporarily in the Fund in 1975, did a study entitled "Money Creation in the Euro-Currency Market" (unpublished, International Monetary Fund, December 17, 1975).

[23] Joseph Gold, *International Capital Movements Under the Law of the International Monetary Fund*, IMF Pamphlet Series, No. 21 (Washington, 1977).

At its third meeting, in June 1975, the Development Committee set up a special Working Group on Access to Capital Markets instructed to review the regulatory and other constraints that hindered access of developing countries to private capital markets and to make proposals to help them gain greater access to these markets.[24] Fund staff regularly attended meetings of this Working Group until it completed its work in 1978.

In the course of its work, the Development Committee's Working Group on Access to Capital Markets studied several relevant topics. They examined regulations, restrictions, and other practices in capital exporting countries that impeded access to their capital markets by developing countries. They examined possible measures to improve market perceptions of the creditworthiness of developing country borrowers. They looked into the usefulness of technical assistance to familiarize potential borrowers with the requirements of, and the potential for, various bond markets. They studied possible financial mechanisms, such as official guarantees, cofinancing between development banks and private financial institutions, and establishment of an international investment fund, to assist potential borrowers.[25]

At its sixth meeting, in Manila, in October 1976, on the basis of a report from this Working Group, the Development Committee adopted a set of recommendations. Capital exporting countries would endeavor, as far as their balance of payments situations permitted, to move progressively toward greater liberalization of capital movements, particularly of capital outflows. In the meantime, when regulations governing capital outflows were maintained for unavoidable reasons, capital exporting countries would afford favorable treatment, among foreign borrowers, to developing country borrowers with regard to permission to make an issue or placement. Other favorable treatment for the bond issues of developing countries was also agreed.[26]

As a follow-up to these recommendations of the Development Committee, the Fund's Executive Board agreed in 1976 that in the Fund's annual consultations with the main capital exporting members, the staff would inquire about the implementation of the Committee's recommendations and report their findings in the staff paper on the policy discussions with the member. As noted in Chapter 47, the staff did include the topic of developing countries' access to capital markets in their consultations with a member with financial markets. As time went on, the information obtained through regular consultations was heavily supplemented by staff discussions with authorities in the members with large financial markets in the course of periodic informal and fact-finding missions. The question of access by

---

[24]Communiqué of Development Committee, June 13, 1975; Vol. III below, pp. 581–84.

[25]Further information on the activities of this Working Group can be found in the annual reports of the Development Committee for the years July 1975–June 1976 and July 1976–June 1977, Vol. III, pp. 597–603 and 604–10. A report on regulations and practices affecting access to capital markets was also summarized in *IMF Survey*, Vol. 5 (December 6, 1976), pp. 354–57.

[26]Communiqué of Development Committee, October 3, 1976, par. 6; Vol. III below, p. 588.

developing countries to capital markets was also discussed by the CIEC in 1976 and 1977, and in the text agreed in May 1977 participants in the CIEC pledged to support efforts to expand this access. The CIEC also endorsed a role for the Fund in reviewing progress toward implementation of the Development Committee's recommendations.

In early 1978 Fund staff prepared an overall report on their discussions with the large capital exporting members. The main conclusions were that little progress had been made in implementing the Development Committee's recommendations and that few steps had been taken to give preferential treatment to the bond placements of developing countries. When the Development Committee met in Mexico at the end of April 1978, the group of senior officials from national capitals that had become allied with the Development Committee discussed the report. The senior officials welcomed it and expressed the view that it would be useful for the Fund to continue to report regularly on changes in developing countries' access to capital markets. They also noted that insufficient progress had been made since the Development Committee's recommendations of October 1976, although they offered few explanations other than lack of action by capital exporting countries for the difficulties that developing countries were experiencing in floating their bond issues in foreign and international markets. These explanations included high interest rates and lack of knowledge in capital exporting countries of the credit standings of potential borrowers.[27] When the Executive Board considered the staff's report in May 1978, it took a decision asking the staff to continue its inquiry into the implementation of the Development Committee's recommendations when it held further consultation discussions with capital exporting members and to report its findings before the middle of 1979.

As the amount of official financial aid available to developing countries was relatively small and was increasingly earmarked for very poor developing countries without access to international credit and capital markets and unable to afford market rates of interest, more attention was given to access to capital markets by middle-income level developing countries that were considered creditworthy and could borrow on commercial nonconcessional terms. Access to capital markets was referred to, for instance, for the first time by the Interim Committee in its communiqué after its meeting in September 1978 and in the report that Mr. Healey as its Chairman gave to the Governors at the 1978 Annual Meeting.[28] At that Annual Meeting, Governors from industrial as well as developing members also brought up the topic. Mr. Blumenthal, stressing that developing countries, particularly middle-income countries, had to have access to a growing flow of nonconcessional capital from abroad, suggested action by both industrial and borrowing countries.[29] Mr. Murayama, noting that it was vitally important for developing countries to start

---

[27]Development Committee Report (July 1977–June 1978), par. 26; Vol. III below, p. 615.

[28]Communiqué of Interim Committee, September 24, 1978, par. 2; Vol. III below, pp. 239–40.

[29]Statement by the Governor of the Fund and the World Bank for the United States, *Summary Proceedings, 1978*, p. 95.

raising funds by themselves in the world capital markets, drew attention to the "remarkable" contributions of Tokyo's markets. Yen-denominated bond issues floated by developing countries were rapidly increasing in 1978 and were already about $1.1 billion, more than twice the figure of 1977.[30]

RELATIONS WITH COMMERCIAL BANKS

As the Fund's work on members' external indebtedness and international capital markets increased, it was inevitable that its relations with commercial banks would also increase, particularly as commercial banks were increasingly involved in the financing of the balance of payments deficits of many of the Fund's non-oil developing members. The Managing Director and staff began to hold informal talks with officers of commercial banks about debts owed to banks and about capital markets. The number of subjects talked about informally necessarily grew, especially since by the late 1970s it not infrequently happened that a member was negotiating concurrently with the Fund and with private banks. The Fund and commercial banks thus came to have a common interest in the financial positions of some members. Bankers needed to base their judgments about lending on a realistic assessment of the economic outlook of the country and wanted to have assurances that the authorities of the country were making a reasonable effort to adjust the country's balance of payments. The member and the Fund staff needed an accurate assessment of the potential debt relief that the member might expect from commercial banks so as to be able to agree on an appropriate stabilization program.

In 1976 Mr. Witteveen devoted a speech entirely to the Fund's relations with commercial banks. Emphasizing the complementary roles of the Fund and the international banking community, Mr. Witteveen pointed out that they both had been playing central roles in meeting the unprecedented challenge of financing the large payments imbalances of the previous two years and that they shared a deep common involvement in international finance. He spelled out a number of questions that arose in the minds of financial officials and of leading commercial bankers because of the trend toward balance of payments financing by private banks, and offered tentative answers. Was the participation of the banking system in balance of payments financing excessive, either in general or in specific instances? Had competitive enlargement of the role of private banks fostered a climate of all too easy borrowing by deficit countries, thus facilitating inflationary financing and delaying the adoption of needed policies of balance of payments adjustment? How much further could indebtedness be pushed before the mounting debt burden became hazardous?[31]

---

[30]Statement by the Governor of the Fund and the World Bank for Japan, *Summary Proceedings, 1978*, p. 54.

[31]"The IMF and the International Banking Community," address before a conference sponsored by the *Financial Times of London*, April 29, 1976, in New York, reprinted in *IMF Survey*, Vol. 5 (May 3, 1976), pp. 138–40.

Giving Information to Banks

Relations between the Fund, as an official international agency, and private commercial banks were extremely sensitive, however. Many officials were concerned that an excessively close connection might develop between the financial operations of the Fund and those of commercial banks. The independence of the Fund could be compromised were Fund officials to take into account the interests of commercial banks. Some, especially in the U.S. Congress, opposed any operations of the Fund that suggested "a bailing out of the commercial banks" by lending to members to repay commercial banks. Many financial officials, especially Executive Directors from developing members, were concerned simply that the Fund staff might disclose too much information to private bankers.

The question of giving information to bankers became important. Many financial officials, including Arthur F. Burns, Chairman of the Board of Governors of the Federal Reserve System in the period 1970–78, believed that the Fund might assist commercial bank decisions to lend by providing more information on debtor countries. In this way the Fund could help avoid bank losses or failures and might help assure continued bank financing of members' deficits.

The management and staff suggested to the Executive Directors that members be authorized to make available, outside official channels, the recent economic developments (RED) reports on their own economies. These reports could be appropriately modified by deleting confidential material. No member would be forced to make its report available. Some members already provided their RED reports to banks with which they were negotiating but did so in violation of the Fund's rules prohibiting outside circulation of Fund documents. The intent of the proposal of the management and staff was to legalize this practice.

In discussions by the Executive Board in 1977, most Executive Directors were inclined to agree that the Fund's cooperation with commercial banks should take the form of assisting the banks to obtain information. Commercial banks themselves favored this form of cooperation with the Fund. Other forms of cooperation, such as the Fund issuing certificates of creditworthiness to members, of the Fund's sharing its judgments with commercial banks about a member's creditworthiness, or of some joint lending arrangements between the Fund and commercial banks, had distinct drawbacks.

Messrs. Cross, de Vries, Laske, Ryrie, and Wahl were in favor of the proposal by management and staff. But, while agreeing that the Fund's best form of cooperation was to improve the flow of information to banks, Messrs. Al-Eyd, de Groote, Kafka, Kharmawan, Lynch, Mung'omba, Rasaputram, and Whitelaw pointed out major objections to the method proposed by the management and staff. One objection was that as an intergovernmental institution, owing loyalty only to member governments, the Fund should not single out any particular private sector to receive special information. Any information that the Fund made available should be for the public at large.

A second objection was that, if the Fund authorized members to make their reports available to commercial banks, a member's refusal to do so would be interpreted as an admission of a lack of creditworthiness. Even the deletion of confidential material would become known so that eventually the debtor member would be forced to release the full report.

Still a third objection, which was most serious, was the threat to the confidential relations between the Fund and its members that the Fund had painstakingly been developing for several decades. These Executive Directors pointed out that the Fund had always zealously guarded all reports on its members as confidential. Distribution of staff reports even to other international organizations was restricted, requiring the approval both of the individual Executive Director concerned and of the Executive Board. Publicizing Fund documents could only damage the relations between the Fund and its members and affect the quality and content of the Fund's reports.

Therefore, they concluded, nothing resembling the reports on recent economic developments in their existing format could be safely released. Commercial banks could have the benefit of the statistical and other factual data that the Fund published in IFS, in the *Balance of Payments Yearbook*, in other statistical publications, in the *Annual Reports on Exchange Restrictions*, in its *Annual Reports*, and in its occasional publications, but not of any other material.

Taking a decision was postponed until after the 1977 Annual Meeting at which differing views on the subject were again expressed. Some Governors from industrial members cautiously suggested that the Fund could somehow make available more information to private bankers. Mr. Blumenthal noted that while commercial banks received help in their lending policies through the Fund's stand-by arrangements since the latter strengthened the creditworthiness of borrowing countries, a greater availability of information might also prove "useful and feasible."[32] Mr. Duisenberg was "very reluctant about more formal cooperation between the Fund and private banks in the form, for example, of joint credit-granting" but believed that an exchange of information on the economic situation of debtor countries—with the concurrence of the country concerned—might be useful.[33] Mr. Simonsen, however, further advanced the position that Mr. Kafka had taken earlier in the Executive Board. He categorically rejected any role for the Fund in providing to nonofficial bodies anything except published statistical and institutional facts. No confidential information such as judgments, forecasts, or analyses regarding the economic performance of countries should be provided.[34] Overand R.

---

[32]Statement by the Governor of the Fund and the World Bank for the United States, *Summary Proceedings, 1977*, p. 66.

[33]Statement by the Governor of the World Bank for the Netherlands, *Summary Proceedings, 1977*, p. 46.

[34]Statement by the Governor of the Fund and the World Bank for Brazil, *Summary Proceedings, 1977*, p. 90.

Padmore explicitly opposed the Fund's providing private commercial banks with any judgments or opinions except those which were published.[35]

Because of these divergent views, any proposal for having members give to commercial banks Fund reports on their economies was dropped. To satisfy Executive Directors concerned about possible divulgence of confidential information, the staff continued to maintain a detailed record of all informal contacts between staff and officials of commercial banks.

But it was obvious that with large indebtedness to commercial banks by the governments of several Fund members, with some of this indebtedness likely to be renegotiated and rescheduled, with continued lending by commercial banks to the governments of members, and with growing amounts of "lending" to its members by the Fund itself, the topic of relations between the Fund and commercial banks was likely to recur, and indeed, could well be a key topic in the 1980s.

TRADE POLICY

Trade policy was another area in which the Fund, within the constraints of its limited jurisdiction, took on more responsibility after 1971.[36] The Fund's increasing responsibility in this field in 1972–78 took the form of a voluntary declaration on trade measures that members were induced to sign in 1974 and the form of an undertaking to avoid restrictions on imports that the Fund attached as a condition to use of the oil facility in 1974 and 1975.

In addition, the Fund continued to follow developments in restrictions and payments policies and, as it had since 1952, reported on them in the *Annual Reports on Exchange Restrictions*. As the Fund followed these developments, it was clear that after years of liberalization of trade and payments restrictions, a marked reversal began in 1975. In that year both developed and developing countries started to reintroduce restrictive import policies. This reversal was brought about by the enlarged balance of payments deficits that emerged in 1974, after the first round of oil price increases, compounded by the deep recession of 1974–75. The new or intensified restrictions of 1975 were applied selectively, however, rather than generally, as after World War II. This selective use of restrictions indicated a desire by countries to protect specific industries from increased import competition in the conditions of weak demand and not, as after World War II, a desire to use import restrictions as an instrument of balance of payments policy.

During 1976 and early 1977, the drift toward restrictions on imports grew more pronounced. Continuing high levels of unemployment, especially in labor-intensive industries in the industrial countries, gave rise to pressure for increased protection

---

[35]Statement by the Governor of the Fund and the World Bank for Trinidad and Tobago, *Summary Proceedings, 1977*, pp. 192–93.

[36]Background on the constraints on the Fund's jurisdiction in the field of international trade can be found in *History, 1945–65*, Vol. I, pp. 171–75, 290–92; Vol. II, pp. 221–23, 235–40, 332–46, and 553–55; and in *History, 1966–71*, Vol. I, pp. 284–85 and 607–608.

from comparable imported products. A larger number of members resorted to more restrictive policies, especially to nontariff barriers on selected imports. In addition, many countries were negotiating export restraint agreements with their trading partners as a way to reduce imports. By early 1977, import restrictions for protective purposes in the industrial countries, as well as in the more developed primary producing countries and in developing countries, were noticeably greater than they had been before 1975. The liberal trading policies that had been pursued by Canada and the United States for three decades and by the industrial countries in Western Europe for two decades were in jeopardy.

Concern About Rising Protectionism

By early 1977, protectionism was becoming a serious concern. Increased restrictions on imports would reduce the access of developing countries to the markets of industrial countries at a time when developing countries desperately needed to expand markets for their exports. Rising protectionism would also reduce levels of world trade generally, worsening inflation, unemployment, and real income in industrial countries as well.

In its communiqué after its meeting in April 1977, the Interim Committee stated that special efforts should be made to improve market access for the exports of the developing countries and that any tendencies toward protectionist trade policies could not be considered acceptable from an international point of view.[37] The leaders of Canada, France, the Federal Republic of Germany, Italy, Japan, the United Kingdom, and the United States, meeting in London in May 1977 for their third economic summit, declared, "We reject protectionism..."[38]

In their Annual Report for 1977, issued just before the Annual Meeting, the Executive Directors stated that if the forces of protectionism were not resisted "the resort to restrictions on trade would harm the open international trading system" and "could have effects destructive of prosperity in the world economy."[39] At the 1977 Annual Meeting, President Jimmy Carter, welcoming financial officials to Washington, and George Colley and H. Johannes Witteveen, in their opening addresses, all referred to problems of increasing trade restrictions and the threat of rising protectionism.[40] Warnings of protectionist pressures and pleas to resist them were given also by numerous Governors.[41]

---

[37]Communiqué of Interim Committee, April 29, 1977, par. 2, I(b); Vol. III below, p. 230.

[38]*IMF Survey*, Vol. 6 (May 16, 1977), p. 152.

[39]*Annual Report, 1977*, p. 2.

[40]Statements by the President of the United States, by the Chairman of the Boards of Governors of the Fund and the World Bank, and by the Managing Director, *Summary Proceedings, 1977*, pp. 3, 7, and 13.

[41]See the statements by the Governor of the World Bank for Belgium, the Governor of the Fund and the World Bank for Japan, the Governor of the World Bank for Sweden, the Governors of the Fund for Indonesia and for the United Kingdom, the Governors of the Fund and the World Bank for the United States and for Brazil, the Governor of the World Bank for the Federal Republic of

Deteriorating Situation and Special Fund Study

The situation grew worse. Throughout the rest of 1977 and early 1978, the EC countries, as well as the United States, Canada, and several other developed countries, made still more frequent use of protective trade measures. They used quantitative import controls, including licensing and quotas, import surcharges and taxes, advance deposit requirements and other regulations affecting payments for imports, anti-dumping and countervailing duties, and bilateral arrangements which placed quantitative limits on trade. The *Twenty-Ninth Annual Report on Exchange Restrictions* that the Fund issued in the middle of 1978 concluded that "the trade-impeding effect of these measures, as well as some measures by a number of developing countries, has been detrimental to balanced growth of international trade" and "particularly harmful to those developing countries that have sought to sustain the growth of their economies, in part through the expansion of nontraditional exports."[42]

Moreover, since the pressures for protectionism were coming from disappointingly slow recovery of the world economy, with the concomitant problem of continuing high unemployment, there seemed little hope for an early respite. In addition, pressures for protectionism in industrial members were being brought about by long-term structural problems in industries such as steel, textiles and clothing, and footwear. These structural problems were due to low rates of growth of productivity in these industries, combined with limited mobility of the factors of production so that resources could not readily be shifted to industries with higher productivity. Many of the industries of the industrial countries were also experiencing keener competition from the products of developing countries that had become much more industrialized. These structural problems were not likely to be solved soon.

Under these circumstances the Fund examined trade policy in greater depth in its consultations with members, as described in Chapter 47, and the staff undertook the large special study of protectionism referred to in Chapter 40. In order to make the special study of protectionism more manageable, the staff concentrated on the measures taken by Canada, the EC, Japan, and the United States. These industrial members represented about 60 percent of total world imports, and although the major portion of these imports was effected *within* this group, many smaller members—especially developing members—were also highly dependent on exports to them. In general, the staff surveyed the restrictive trade actions taken by these members since 1971, but most emphasis was given to the restrictions which they took from 1974 to 1977. Attention was given to a number of individual industries. As part of this study, a sizable staff team held discussions with officials of Canada,

---

Germany, the Governors of the Fund for South Africa and Italy, the Governor of the World Bank for Algeria, and the Governors of the Fund and the World Bank for Luxembourg, Barbados, and Mexico, *Summary Proceedings, 1977*, pp. 25, 27, 42, 51, 59, 65, 89, 93, 101, 109, 121, 129, 164, and 169.

[42]The portion quoted is on p. 6.

Japan, and the United States and of several developing members, including China, Colombia, Korea, Mexico, the Philippines, Tunisia, and Uruguay, as well as with officials of the EC in Brussels, of the OECD in Paris, and with the secretariat of the GATT in Geneva. The study included not only a review of the restrictions taken but also of the factors inducing protectionist measures and an assessment of the significance of the rise in protectionism.

This study was discussed by the Executive Board as part of the review of the world economic outlook and was to be the start of annual reports on trade policy prepared by the staff for discussion by the Executive Board.

In short, protectionism grew to be a constant concern of the Fund. To help prevent the erosion of a liberal trade and payments system, the Fund, though continuing also to collaborate closely with the GATT, was itself getting more into the area of international trade policy.[43]

---

[43]The topic of the Fund's relations with the GATT is covered in Chapter 49.

CHAPTER

49

Expansion of
Informational Activities and of
Relations with Other Organizations

M OUNTING WORLD ECONOMIC PROBLEMS and marked changes in
    the Fund's functions after 1971 led to an expansion of the Fund's
informational activities and of its relations with other international, regional, and
subregional organizations.

THE FUND AS A CENTER FOR CONFIDENTIAL INFORMATION

From its beginning the Fund has acted as a center for the collection and
exchange of information on monetary and financial problems. Its original Articles
(Article VIII, Section 5(*a*)) required members to furnish the Fund with such
information as it deemed necessary for its operations. As a minimum, members were
to provide data on official and private holdings of gold and foreign exchange, gold
production and trade, merchandise trade, items in the balance of payments,
international investment, national income, price indices, exchange rates, exchange
controls, and details on payments arrears. This provision was retained intact when
the Articles were amended in 1969 and in 1978, continuing as Article VIII,
Section 5(*a*). The Fund has fully implemented this "furnishing of information"
provision of its Articles and consequently regularly receives from all members a great
deal of statistical and other information.

In addition, under other provisions of the Articles, members are obliged to
notify the Fund whenever they make any changes in their exchange rate arrangements and in their exchange restrictions and controls. Considerably more information is obtained in regular consultations with members, in discussions with members
when they seek the Fund's approval for changes in their exchange rates or in their
restrictions, and in negotiations with members seeking to use Fund resources. On
such occasions, the staff obtains detailed information pertaining not only to
members' external economies but also to their domestic economies and policies,

such as budget and fiscal policies, money supply and credit, employment, wages and costs, plans for economic growth and development, near-term prospects for these economic phenomena, and the views of members about their economic situations.

The Fund staff also independently assesses the position of and prospects for a member's internal and external economy. This assessment, together with the information collected by the Fund, is valuable. Executive Directors require this material to take necessary decisions, and officials in home capitals want an outside expert appraisal of their own country's economic situation and policies as well as information and appraisals in regard to other member countries. Officials seek these papers especially because they are prepared by a number of staff, often from several departments, and are approved by the Managing Director before being circulated to the Executive Board. They therefore present a joint staff position, supported by the management. In fact, some countries join the Fund specifically to receive the inside information that the Fund collects and the Fund's analyses of countries' economic situations. While this motive applies especially to the relatively small developing countries lacking alternative sources of economic and financial intelligence and the means with which to appraise it, the desire to obtain information through the Fund applies to all members.

By the 1970s, advances in communication technology, in jet travel, and in the use of computers produced an explosion of information elsewhere, and in the Fund as well. The Fund's documentation also increased because the Fund was unusually active in changing its functions and dealing with rapidly evolving economic issues. Officials in member governments were asked to take action on, for instance, reform of the international monetary system and, in the absence of a reformed system, on policies that the Fund could introduce on floating exchange rates and gold. They also had to take a stand on the Fund's policies for borrowing from members to augment resources available from quota subscriptions, the terms of stand-by and extended arrangements in general or for a particular member, the provisions of revised amendments to the Articles of Agreement, and increases in quotas under the Sixth and Seventh General Reviews. The international monetary system and the Fund's policies and operations, in general and with regard to individual countries, were discussed not only in the Fund but also in the United Nations General Assembly, in special sessions of the United Nations, in the UNCTAD, the OECD, the BIS, the EC, the GATT, the Group of Ten and the Group of Twenty-Four, and at economic summit meetings. Heads of state and government, finance ministers, foreign ministers, governors of central banks, undersecretaries, and their advisors and technical staff had a vital need for full and frank information and analyses. They often called upon their Executive Directors in the Fund, who quickly responded to this need.

The staff prepared detailed papers for internal use on the general topics described in this History, as well as reports on their discussions with officials of each member as part of the annual consultations and accompanying detailed recent economic developments (RED) reports. There were reports, too, on stand-by and extended arrangements with individual members and on all other uses of Fund resources. In addition, there were extensive minutes of the Executive Board meetings and papers stating the decisions finally taken by the Executive Board, and, in many instances, reports of the Managing Director or of the Executive Directors to the Interim Committee.

Staff papers that require action by the Executive Board are designated by the initials SM (Staff Memorandum). In addition to papers requiring action by the Executive Board, the staff occasionally prepares papers in the SM series presenting a joint staff position approved by management on general topics of relevance to the Fund's policies and operations that do not necessarily require Executive Board action, but which are sent to the Executive Directors for information. In the years 1972–78, for instance, there were staff papers on such topics as the relation between exchange rates and interest rates, the adequacy of international liquidity, developments in the trade and payments restrictions of members, trends in and prospects for international banking, oil conservation, and the development of alternative sources of energy by users of the Fund's oil facility. Because of rapidly changing exchange rates and exchange rate arrangements, there were also periodic staff papers describing the exchange rate regimes maintained by members. Moreover, staff representing the Fund at meetings of other organizations, such as the UN General Assembly, special sessions of the United Nations or of its regional economic commissions, or of the UNCTAD and its committees, of the GATT Council of Representatives or of GATT committees, or of regional development banks, always prepared reports on them for the information of the Executive Directors.

In addition to Staff Memoranda, the staff prepares papers that set out the results of the research or analysis of a particular department or division of a department, or of an individual staff member. Designated by the initials DM (Departmental Memorandum), these papers circulate within the Fund. In 1977 and 1978 there were nearly 250 DM papers describing or analyzing such topics as money markets in individual members or in a group of members, the monetary or fiscal policies of a member or group of members, exchange rates, inflation, balance of payments analysis, as well as monthly reports on developments in foreign exchange markets, in members' balances of payments, and on the prices for gold in world markets.

All this enormous wealth of information is confidential. A few documents, particularly RED reports on individual members and in some circumstances staff reports on consultation discussions, are provided to a selected number of other international organizations, but only with agreement of the Executive Board, following the consent of the Executive Director for the member concerned, who can request the deletion of any sensitive material. While a few DM studies of broad academic interest are published in *Staff Papers* or occasionally in other journals, most remain internal documents.

Every working day, the *Morning Press*, known internally as "the blue sheet," is also distributed within the Fund. This legal-size sheet, printed on both sides on blue paper, gives a digest of financial news around the world, gathered by the staff from the main newspapers and news services. Copies are made available to staff of the World Bank and to officials of member governments represented in Washington.

PUBLISHED INFORMATION

From its earliest years, the Fund has published a considerable amount of the information collected from its members. Publication of material produced in the course of the Fund's work is a convenient way to supply members, as well as the public, with nonconfidential data and other information. As it has from the beginning, the Fund acts as its own publisher, selecting and preparing material for publication, executing the graphics, dealing with vendors of typesetting and printing (and in some instances using in-house printing facilities), proofreading and checking the composition, and undertaking sales and distribution.

Like its internal documents, the Fund's publications expanded, in length and in number, in the years 1972–78. Officials, bankers, monetary specialists, and the general public developed a widening interest in the Fund's activities. As commercial bankers, for example, increased their lending to governments, they inevitably became more interested in the Fund's concurrent financial operations. Since the subject of international monetary economics was relatively new, economists in academic and research institutions were devoting more effort to its study and were often making suggestions on reform of the international monetary system, or of the Fund itself. They increasingly looked to the Fund for reports and decisions on the world monetary system and for information on the Fund's reasoning in taking these decisions. The general public in many countries, moreover, became more aware of the Fund. Rates for the dollar and for other currencies, rises and falls in the prices of gold, the size of countries' external payments deficits and surpluses, new loans by the Fund and the conditions associated with them, and other international financial and monetary developments were reported daily in the press, and broadcast on radio and television.

Press Releases, Reports, and Basic Documents

To satisfy this widening interest, as well as to acquaint the public with its policies, operations, and decisions, the Fund expanded further its output of material. The number of press releases issued following the Fund's transactions and other important decisions of the Executive Board grew considerably. By 1976–78, for example, the Fund was issuing about 100 press releases a year. A monthly newsletter, the *IMF Memorandum*, continued to be distributed in English, French, German, and Spanish to financial writers in all members. It was chiefly devoted to highlighting economic developments reflected in the regular statistical publications, especially *International Financial Statistics.*

As required by the Articles, just before each Annual Meeting the Fund publishes the *Annual Report of the Executive Directors.*[1] As it has from its first publication in 1946, the Fund's Annual Report represents a major effort both for the staff in its drafting and for the Executive Directors in its approval. Chapter 1 presents a broad survey of the main developments in the world economy in the year reviewed and the officially agreed views of the Executive Directors with regard to these developments. Chapter 2 reviews the main developments in exchange rates and in reserves and, as required by the Fund's By-Laws after SDRs came into being in 1969, presents the Fund annual assessment of the adequacy of global reserves. Chapter 3 summarizes the Fund's activities during the year, describing the main decisions of the Executive Board and what took place in respect to drawings and repurchases, operations in SDRs and in the Trust Fund, gold sales, charges, the payment of remuneration, and the Fund's budget. Appendices contain statistical tables relating to the Fund's operations and transactions, the principal policy decisions and reports of the Executive Board, the press communiqués of the Interim Committee, lists of the Executive Directors and their voting powers and changes in membership of the Executive Board during the year, and, as required by the Articles, the financial statements relevant to the Fund.

As the Annual Report grew, it was redesigned in the 1970s to present the broad economic survey more concisely. A shorter version expedited agreement by the Executive Directors on the detailed content of the Report. Hence, in the years reviewed in this History, the Annual Report, while still relatively lengthy, was shorter than before.

Since 1950, the Fund has also published an *Annual Report on Exchange Restrictions* (renamed the *Annual Report on Exchange Arrangements and Exchange Restrictions* after the Second Amendment), the other report legally required by the Articles of Agreement. This report is voluminous, demanding considerable staff effort. The 1978 report, for instance, ran to nearly 500 oversized pages. The bulk of the report comprises detailed surveys of the exchange systems of each member (and sometimes of nonmembers as well, notably Switzerland). Restrictive systems are described in their entirety (except for the tariff structure and for direct taxes on exports and imports) and are not limited to exchange restrictions and exchange controls under the Fund's jurisdiction. The main trends in restrictive practices during the year reviewed are summarized in a report of some twenty-five pages which forms Part I, introducing the country-by-country description of Part II.

The Fund also publishes each year *Summary Proceedings* of the Annual Meetings. These *Summary Proceedings* reproduce the speeches of the Chairman of the Board of Governors and the Managing Director, and the statements, or portions of statements, related to the work of the Fund presented by Governors during the Annual Meeting, resolutions of the Board of Governors, and reports and communi-

---

[1]Beginning with the Annual Report for 1978, the Report was called the *Annual Report of the Executive Board,* following the introduction of the term "Executive Board" into the Articles of Agreement after the Second Amendment.

qués of committees of the Board of Governors issued at the time of the Annual Meeting. A volume containing *Selected Decisions of the International Monetary Fund and Selected Documents* is also put out from time to time. Similarly, several basic documents, such as the Articles of Agreement, the By-Laws, and the Rules and Regulations are published periodically. From time to time, the Fund publishes special reports of the Executive Directors, such as some of those reproduced in Volume III below. Occasionally, the Fund puts out a brochure describing its organization and functions.

Pamphlets, Books, and Periodicals

In 1972–78 the Fund published 9 more pamphlets in its series, started in 1964, on special topics relating to the Fund, bringing the total to 25 by the end of 1978. The 9 new pamphlets, all cited in footnotes in earlier chapters, covered such topics as operations in SDRs and issues involved in their valuation, legal developments with respect to floating currencies, SDRs, and gold, the Second Amendment of the Articles of Agreement, the rise in protectionism, and the status of international capital movements under the Fund's rules.

In the years 1972–78 the Fund also published a number of books, of which most have been cited in footnotes in earlier chapters. In 1976 the Fund published a two-volume History of the Fund covering the six-year period 1966–71. These two volumes were a sequel to the three-volume History published in 1970, describing the Fund's origin and its activities from 1945 to 1965. The 1966–71 volumes were researched and written by a Historian, Margaret Garritsen de Vries, especially appointed in 1973 to write Histories of the Fund on a continuing basis.

The Fund, in the period reviewed here, published two books written by its then General Counsel, Joseph Gold. *Voting and Decisions in the International Monetary Fund: An Essay on the Law and Practice of the Fund*, put out in 1972, described the process by which the Fund took decisions. *Membership and Nonmembership in the International Monetary Fund: A Study in International Law and Organization*, put out in 1974, took up several subjects relating to countries' membership in the Fund and described some problems raised for the Fund and for its members because some countries were not Fund members.

In 1973 the Fund published *Instruments of Monetary Policy in the United States: The Role of the Federal Reserve System*, which explained the organization and operations of the central bank of the United States and its role in implementing national monetary policy. This book, written by Ralph A. Young while he was serving as consultant to the Fund's Central Banking Service after his retirement from a long career in the Board of Governors of the Federal Reserve System, grew out of a series of internal studies on the instruments of monetary policy in various countries that was being written in the Fund at the time.

In 1977 the Fund issued *The Monetary Approach to the Balance of Payments: A Collection of Research Papers by Members of the Staff of the International Monetary Fund*, which brought together the most important research papers on this subject that had been published by the Fund staff (all except one in *Staff Papers*) from 1957 to 1973. The monetary approach to balance of payments analysis had come to be widely accepted by economists and policymakers and the book recorded the contribution made by the Fund staff to the early development of this approach.

In 1972–78 the Fund also published, in English, Volumes 5, 6, and 7 in its series, *Surveys of African Economies*. The three new volumes together covered 15 African members: Algeria, Botswana, Burundi, Equatorial Guinea, The Gambia, Ghana, Lesotho, Liberia, Mali, Morocco, Nigeria, Rwanda, Sierra Leone, Swaziland, and Tunisia. In these years, too, Volumes 5, 6, and 7 were published in French.

In addition to press releases, reports, proceedings, basic documents, pamphlets, and books, the Fund continues to issue a number of periodical publications. The monthly *International Financial Statistics (IFS)* which had long before established itself throughout the world as the standard source of comparable data for all domestic and international finance, contains thousands of time series for international trade, prices, reserves, banking, and money supply supplied to the Fund by its members, and marked three decades of publication in December 1977. Beginning with the issue for May 1975, IFS was published in separate English, French and Spanish editions, which replaced the trilingual edition that had been published since 1966. In a pioneering effort, the three editions were produced by photocomposition directly from the IMF Data Fund, a computer system for the storage and continuous maintenance of data, for the calculation of derivatives and transformations, for the assembly of tables, and for the updating of notes. This process also made it possible to produce *IFS* on tape for subscription. To accompany the Fund's other statistical yearbooks, a separate *IFS Yearbook* was also started containing the annual data previously incorporated in the May issue, that issue giving yearly data because it followed the end of the Fund's financial year on April 30.

The *Balance of Payments Yearbook* (renamed *Balance of Payments Statistics* in 1981) continues to be published, as it has been since 1949. The Yearbook presents balance of payments data for many countries, using mainly the material sent to the Fund by its members. The monthly *Direction of Trade* and a companion *Direction of Trade Yearbook* (renamed *Direction of Trade Statistics* in 1982), which presents detailed data on the exports and imports of 150 countries, are also regular statistical periodicals.

Staff Papers continues as it has since 1950 to give scholars in the outside world the benefit of selected research studies by individuals on the Fund staff. These papers, usually taken from the DM series described above, are on topics of direct interest to the Fund but are generally treated in a broad, analytical way, without discussing the Fund's policies or activities. Studies in *Staff Papers* in the years 1972–78 included, for example, analyses of inflation and of the demand for, and supply of, money, analyses of international capital markets, theoretical and empirical examinations of the effects of changes in prices and in exchange rates on exports, imports, and payments balances, economic models for studying exchange rates, changes in reserves, the market for gold, and the markets for primary commodities, analyses of monetary instruments, theoretical and empirical examination of countries' experiences with monetary and fiscal policies, and macroeconomic models of a number of countries. In addition, *Staff Papers* from time to time publishes studies by the legal staff relating to jurisprudence throughout the world involving the Fund's Articles. In 1978, the number of issues of *Staff Papers* published each year was increased from three to four.

Finance & Development, started in 1964 as a joint publication with the World Bank to explain in short articles in nontechnical terms the policies and activities of the Bretton Woods institutions and topics related to their interests, is published four times each year in English, French, and Spanish, and since September 1970, in German.[2] From 1966 to 1979, selected articles were published once a year in Portuguese and from 1975 to 1978 in Arabic.[3] In the years 1972–78, the articles relating to the Fund explained, for instance, issues involved in reforming the international monetary system, policy issues involved in floating exchange rates and in surveillance by the Fund, the Fund's policies on use of its resources, its borrowing policies, the operation of the Trust Fund, the Second Amendment to the Articles of Agreement, developments in gold markets and in international banking, the resurgence of protectionism, and the issues involved in the Tokyo Round of Multilateral Trade Negotiations. Some of the articles are summaries in nontechnical terms of more technical papers published in *Staff Papers*. In addition, the December issue surveys statements by Governors at the Annual Meetings, emphasizing important areas of consensus or disagreement. *Finance & Development*, distributed without charge, continues to have one of the largest circulations of economic periodicals. It circulates especially among professors and students all over the world.

In the years 1972–78, the Fund also inaugurated two new publications, the *IMF Survey* and the *Government Finance Statistics Yearbook*, and published a fourth edition of the *Balance of Payments Manual*.

The *IMF Survey*, cited in several footnotes in earlier chapters, was started in August 1972, appearing twice each month, except in December, when a single issue is published. The periodical began being published in English, and French and Spanish editions were added in 1974. This periodical is intended to inform the public of the Fund's activities on an up-to-date basis, reporting them in the broader context of developments in the international economy and with emphasis on individual economies on the basis of Fund staff analysis. It regularly reproduces the texts of all the Fund's press releases, key decisions of the Executive Board, communiqués (first of the Committee of Twenty and then of the Interim Committee and the Development Committee), actions of the Board of Governors, and many of the public addresses of the Managing Director. It also often contains material giving background to these actions by the Fund, written by the staff. In addition, it contains summaries of the Annual Report, the Annual Report on Exchange Restrictions, the contents of Fund pamphlets, and, at times, of articles in *Staff Papers* and tables

---

[2]The origin of *Finance & Development* was described in *History, 1945–65*, Vol. I, pp. 556–57.
[3]These annual editions were later replaced by quarterly editions.

giving data for recent drawings on the Fund, changes in exchange rates, and the current values of the SDR in various currencies. Through this publication the Fund released some of the results of its internal studies on international banking, on the world economic outlook, and on members' external indebtedness. Surveys of national economies are usually included, so that by the end of 1978 surveys of nearly 100 of the Fund's members had been published, several of them more than once. Summaries are included of reports by other organizations dealing with topics of interest to the Fund, such as reports of the BIS, the GATT, the OECD, and the UNCTAD, and there are brief notes on the major financial developments throughout the world. The *IMF Survey* quickly developed a large circulation, both free and paid, mainly among government officials, university economists, bankers, and business executives.

Complexities in International Publishing

From the 1940s onward, the Fund has often encountered special problems in publishing material on an international basis. In the years reviewed here, publishing the *Government Finance Statistics Yearbook (GFS Yearbook)* and the fourth edition of the *Balance of Payments Manual* illustrate these problems.

In the instance of the *Government Finance Statistics Yearbook*, the Fund was entering a new field, and prior to the first Yearbook on this subject, staff members went through five years of effort. They began by preparing a draft manual explaining the concepts and procedures to be used for developing, standardizing, collecting, and publishing statistics on government finance, that is, on the revenues, grants, expenditures, lending, and debt of central governments, and what might be available with respect to local governments. Beginning in 1973 the staff also made arrangements with the OECD for working out these concepts jointly and for compiling the necessary statistics for countries that were members both of the Fund and of the OECD. Close contact was also kept with the UN Statistical Commission. When the manual was prepared, it was sent to members. The next step was holding seminars abroad, including two seminars in Africa and another in Latin America, to help explain the manual to members' technicians. It was then time to begin assembling data for the first Yearbook, through questionnaires distributed to members. The series was started in 1977 and continued with a second Yearbook in 1978. Also, as was mentioned in Chapter 47, a course on Government Finance Statistics was introduced in the IMF Institute to help technicians from members understand and prepare the data needed by the Fund for the Yearbook.

Publication of the fourth edition of the *Balance of Payments Manual* also occurred only after several years of preparation, discussion, and revision. As in the instance of the three earlier editions of the Fund's balance of payments manuals, the concepts and methods to be used were subjected to considerable discussion by officials and technicians in member governments, who frequently held differing views on how best to define and measure the elements comprising a country's balance of payments. The concepts and methods used to characterize a country's balance of payments situation, moreover, were by no means of only academic interest. The nature and size of a country's balance of payments position was important for a government's policies and basic to all the Fund's policies and operations. A member's balance of payments position determined, for instance, the member's need and ability to draw on the Fund, whether its currency would be included in the Fund's currency (operational) budget for drawings and repurchases, whether the member would be designated to encash SDRs, and possibly the size of its quota in the Fund.

Developments in the U.S. Government with regard to balance of payments statistics indicate some of the problems presented for the Fund staff as they set out early in the 1970s to revise the Fund's *Balance of Payments Manual*, whose third edition had been published in 1961. From 1965 to 1976, the U.S. Government used the "official settlements balance" to measure the size of a deficit or surplus in the U.S. balance of payments accounts.[4] With the advent of flexible exchange rates, users of U.S. balance of payments statistics, both inside the U.S. Government and outside, questioned the relevance of the official settlements balance, arguing that changes in official reserve assets and liabilities, the basis of the official settlements approach, could no longer be taken to reflect mandatory intervention in exchange markets as under the par value system. Changes in reserve assets and liabilities thus were no longer a measure of market pressure on exchange rates nor an appropriate indicator of the size of a country's balance of payments deficit or surplus. In effect, they contended, variations in exchange rates under floating rates, at least in theory, equilibrated a country's balance of payments, eliminating any deficit or surplus. Under floating rates, a surplus or deficit simply could not arise.

The U.S. Government in effect concluded that, under floating rates, the concepts of a balance of payments surplus or deficit no longer applied and, starting in 1976, abolished these concepts and no longer published figures for an overall balance in the U.S. balance of payments position. This decision influenced the attitudes of U.S. technicians toward the concepts used in the planned fourth edition of the Fund's *Balance of Payments Manual*, raising problems for the Fund staff. Obviously the Fund could not apply the concepts of the U.S. Government to all Fund members since most Fund members continued to have fixed exchange rates.

Not only did the onset of floating exchange rates necessitate a thoroughgoing re-examination of balance of payments concepts and measurements, but the onset of chronic balance of payments deficits and surpluses for which adjustment in the short term was not feasible also altered the meaning of the terms balance of payments "surplus" and "deficit." Thus, all the technical questions involved in balance of payments compilation had to be reopened for consideration and a fresh look had to be taken at the underlying analysis, or philosophy, involved in presenting balance of payments statements. The initial draft manual prepared by the staff in 1972 was

---

[4]The official settlements balance used by the U.S. Government and the alternative concept of basic balance developed by the staff of the Fund were explained in *History, 1966–71*, Vol. I, pp. 211 and 489.

criticized. To help secure an agreed draft, a small group of consultants, made up of official experts from seven countries, Australia, France, the Federal Republic of Germany, Ghana, the United Kingdom, the United States, and Venezuela, was asked to work with the Fund staff. The five large industrial members included were those whose experts had been the main critics of the first draft, while consultants from Ghana and Venezuela provided the perspective of the developing members. By the time a new manual was ready, experts from 25 members and international organizations participated in one series of meetings or another. Members were also asked to reply to a survey about their practices and preferences regarding difficult technical questions, such as the recording of merchandise trade and direct investment. Eventually a draft of the completed manual was sent to all members for comment, and the fourth edition of the *Balance of Payments Manual* was finally published in 1977.

This lengthy and often frustrating process had both advantages and disadvantages. The wide variety of views expressed by officials and technicians in members and the controversial nature of many of the issues complicated the explanations of the methods that were eventually worked out for use in balance of payments accounting. On the other hand, the methods finally agreed for Fund use for collecting and presenting the balance of payments were generally accepted by the officials and technicians who were responsible for compiling this data.[5]

PUBLIC APPEARANCES

Mr. Schweitzer, Mr. Witteveen, and Mr. de Larosière became familiar figures as they traveled extensively, representing the Fund at financial meetings and giving addresses. The Managing Directors also maintained communication with the press through off-the-record interviews and general press conferences. Mr. Dale, Executive Directors, and other staff, likewise undertook speaking engagements and represented the Fund at international meetings. As the Fund became less shy of publicity, staff, as well as some Executive Directors, began to publish articles in periodicals and to contribute to volumes published outside the Fund.

RELATIONS WITH INTERNATIONAL AND REGIONAL ORGANIZATIONS

Because of the severity and the pervasiveness of world economic problems during the 1970s and the worsening of the financial position of many countries, international or regional organizations with economic and financial responsibilities accelerated their activities. In the mutual quest for solutions and action, the Fund necessarily worked even more closely than before with these organizations.

---

[5]Longer descriptions of the process of producing the fourth edition of the *Balance of Payments Manual* and summaries of the contents of the *Manual* are to be found in John S. Smith, "The Fund's New Balance of Payments Manual," *Finance & Development* (March 1978), p. 41.

In addition, as newly emerging countries began to find a closer mutual identity, they established regional or subregional organizations aimed at focusing on their own economic or financial problems. Among the organizations that came into being in the 1970s were the African Centre for Monetary Studies, the Bank of Central African States (BEAC), the West African Economic Community (WAEC), and the Arab Bank for Economic Development in Africa (BADEA). In Asia, the Middle East, and the Pacific, the Arab Monetary Fund (AMF), the Asian Clearing Union (ACU), the Islamic Development Bank (ISDB), the South-East Asian Central Banks (SEACEN) Research and Training Centre, and the South Pacific Bureau for Economic Cooperation (SPEC) were set up. In Europe, the Nordic Investment Bank was established, and in the Western Hemisphere, the Andean Reserve Fund (ARF).

To accompany its other regional economic commissions, in 1973 the United Nations established an Economic Commission for Western Asia (ECWA), composed of 14 members (Bahrain, Egypt, Iran, Jordan, Kuwait, Lebanon, Oman, Palestine Liberation Organization, Qatar, Saudi Arabia, Syrian Arab Republic, United Arab Emirates, Yemen Arab Republic, and People's Democratic Republic of Yemen). As noted in previous chapters, in 1976 a special Conference on International Economic Cooperation (CIEC)—a North-South dialogue—was also called. The Fund's relations with other organizations inevitably had to increase.

Article X obligated the Fund to cooperate, within the terms of its overall Articles, with any general international organization and with public international organizations having specific responsibilities in related fields. In carrying out this obligation, the Fund was guided by its own special areas of concern and its emphasis on protecting the confidentiality of its relations with its members. The Fund dealt with organizations dealing with general international economic problems, the economies of individual countries, international finance, banking, capital flows, international trade, and primary commodities, more closely than with organizations dealing with industrial development or with energy. In the interests of confidentiality, Fund staff did not, however, discuss with officials of other organizations the Fund's current negotiations with its members.

The Fund collaborated with other organizations in providing technical assistance and exchanging documents on a restricted basis. Moreover, representatives of the Fund, including the Managing Director, regularly attended meetings of many other organizations, and Fund staff participated in their working groups and seminars. In turn, representatives of other organizations were observers at the Joint Annual Meetings of the Boards of Governors of the Fund and the World Bank, meetings of the Committee of Twenty, at both ministerial level and at deputy level, and meetings of the Interim Committee. From its earliest days, the Fund appointed a staff member as Special Representative to the United Nations to maintain liaison with that body. Shortly after its establishment, the Fund set up a European Office in Paris and by the 1970s the primary function of this office was to carry on the Fund's relations with the OECD, the EC, the BIS, and other groups meeting in Europe. In the 1960s, the Fund also set up an office in Geneva to have primary responsibility for the

Fund's relations with the GATT, with the UNCTAD and its various bodies, and with other UN agencies meeting in Geneva. The Fund's Special Representative to the United Nations and the staff of the Paris and Geneva offices were often joined at meetings of other organizations by staff from headquarters.

Cooperation with the World Bank

The Fund's closest relationship by far is with the World Bank, its sister organization from their joint creation at Bretton Woods, and its near neighbor in Washington, where both have their headquarters. After years of working together, the two organizations reached a fresh understanding to strengthen their collaboration in 1970.[6] There were to be exchanges of information and views between the Fund and the World Bank before missions went out to talk with member governments. A similar exchange was to take place following the return of country missions to learn of the most recent economic developments in the country concerned, subject to the need to maintain confidential relations with that member. The two institutions were to make increased efforts to use the same basic data and the same statistical definitions and time series. Final reports, as well as drafts, were to be regularly exchanged. Material prepared by one institution could at times be used in the reports of the other. Although joint staff missions were ruled out by both the Fund and the World Bank, serious efforts were to be made to coordinate the field operations of the two organizations. This cooperation became standard practice after 1970.

Admittedly, cooperation between the two institutions did not always proceed smoothly. Disagreements among economists about the effectiveness of alternative economic policies were unavoidable and took place even among Fund staff. Differences of view continued on the emphasis to be given to the Fund's primary objectives for a member—achievement of internal financial stability and a stronger external payments position in the relatively short term, usually through tighter monetary and credit policies—and the World Bank's primary goals—achievement of economic growth over a longer period by fostering investment and larger productive capacity. At times, these points of view came into conflict, especially in instances where the Fund's conditionality involved curtailment of current consumption and investment. Fund staff saw such adjustment as the essential foundation for growth and development, but they were sometimes seen by World Bank staff as countering the Bank's development aims. These conflicts became sharper as the World Bank's management and staff oriented themselves increasingly to satisfying the basic needs of poverty-stricken populations, to increasing current employment, and to redistributing domestic income.

---

[6]The Fund's cooperation with the World Bank before 1970 and the new understanding reached in 1970 were described in *History, 1966–71*, Vol. I, pp. 610–15. A brief discussion of the areas of responsibility of the two organizations and of the structural relation between them can be found in Joseph Gold, "The Relationship Between the International Monetary Fund and the World Bank," *Creighton Law Review*, Vol. 15 (Omaha, Nebraska, 1981–82), pp. 499–521.

Despite these difficulties, cooperation was closer than it had been in the past and the specific guidelines of the understanding of 1970 gave management and staff of both institutions guidance on how to proceed. In addition—although still avoiding joint missions—the two institutions undertook more often to have staff of one institution participate in missions arranged by the other. Resident representatives of the two institutions stationed in the same member country also tried to keep in close contact.

The continued participation of Fund staff in consortia and consultative groups sponsored by the World Bank was another important part of their collaboration after 1970. In the years 1972–78, staff participated in the consortia for India and Pakistan, in consultative groups for aid coordination for Bangladesh, Colombia, Ethiopia, Kenya, Korea, the Lao People's Democratic Republic, Morocco, Peru, the Philippines, Sudan, Tanzania, Thailand, Tunisia, and Zaïre, in World Bank-sponsored aid groups for Bangladesh and for Sri Lanka, and in meetings sponsored jointly by the World Bank and the Asian Development Bank to consider aid for reconstruction and economic development in Indo-China.

Collaboration with the World Bank, moreover, was frequently reviewed by the Fund's management and staff to develop ways for the two institutions to cooperate more fruitfully in economic work on individual members. Much of the motivation of the Fund's management and staff for greater association with the World Bank came from a desire to reduce the staff's workload and the burden on members' officials by avoiding duplication of effort by the two institutions. The Fund's increasing attention to the external indebtedness of its members strengthened its contacts with the World Bank. The Fund relied on data from the World Bank for necessary debt statistics to supplement those of the BIS. The Fund also relied on data from the World Bank for the per capita income of members when the Fund undertook to identify "developing countries" for purposes of its Trust Fund. The implementation of the extended facility that the Fund introduced in 1974 also meant that the Fund was moving into activities that lay in the expertise of the World Bank, such as shifts in a country's resources over a period longer than one year in the Fund's customary stand-by arrangement. As 1978 ended, it was clear that Fund-Bank collaboration would have to grow still closer in the future.

Relations with the United Nations and the GATT

As a specialized agency of the United Nations, the Fund from its inception has had especially close relations with that body. In the years of this History, the Managing Director continued to make an annual address to the Economic and Social Council (ECOSOC), and either he or the Deputy Managing Director participated with heads of other UN agencies in meetings of the Administrative Committee on Coordination and its joint meeting with the Committee for Program and Coordination. Staff representatives also attended the sessions of the UN General Assembly and any special sessions, meetings of the Council of the UN Development Program (UNDP), and regular meetings of the various UN regional economic commissions, such as the Economic Commission for Africa (ECA), the Economic Commission for Europe (ECE), the Economic Commission for Latin America (ECLA), the Economic and Social Commission for Asia and the Pacific (ESCAP) (previously the Economic Commission for Asia and the Far East—ECAFE), and the Economic Commission for Western Asia (ECWA).

In the years 1972–78 Fund staff representatives also participated in the Commission on International Trade Law, in the ILO's International Labor Conference and its interagency conference to assess the value of comprehensive missions to various countries aimed at increasing employment, and in many ad hoc meetings of UN bodies. Enhanced attention by the Fund to the problems of primary commodities also brought Fund staff into closer working relations with various intergovernmental commodity groups under the auspices of the Food and Agriculture Organization (FAO).

The Fund also continued to have close relationships with the UNCTAD. Mr. Schweitzer addressed the third UNCTAD Conference (UNCTAD III) in Santiago, in April 1972, and Mr. Dale the fourth UNCTAD Conference (UNCTAD IV) in Nairobi, in May 1976. Other staff represented the Fund at other sessions of these UNCTAD Conferences. Fund staff also generally attended meetings of the committees of the UNCTAD dealing with topics of interest to the Fund. For example, from 1973 Fund staff participated in meetings of UNCTAD's Committee on Invisibles and Financing Related to Trade. Similarly, Fund staff attended meetings and worked closely with the UNCTAD Committee on Commodities when it was considering the Integrated Program for Commodities—the common fund—referred to in Chapter 21, and with the international expert group set up by the UNCTAD to study external debt, referred to in Chapter 48. Because of its compensatory financing and buffer stock facilities, the Fund was very much interested in developments in commodities, especially in international commodity agreements.

Increasing attention was focused in 1972–78 on the difference in the decision-making process in the United Nations and many UN-related bodies and the decision-making process in the Fund. In the United Nations and in many UN-related bodies, each member has a single vote. Hence, as an increasing number of developing countries have become members of the United Nations, their total votes have considerably exceeded those of the industrial and relatively more developed members. With their organization of the Group of Seventy-Seven as a means of formulating and presenting a common position, the developing countries have increasingly been able to muster the votes needed to pass resolutions in the United Nations. In the Fund's area of monetary and exchange matters, it is the "financial arm" of the Group of Seventy-Seven, the Group of Twenty-Four, that has considerable influence in the decision-making process of the United Nations.[7]

---

[7]The Group of Seventy-Seven and the Group of Twenty-Four are described in Chapter 50.

In the Fund, on the other hand, voting continues to be based on weighted voting, that is, each member's voting power reflects its quota in the Fund. As seen in Chapter 27, in 1972–78 relative quotas were much discussed in the Fund, and developing members began to press for increasing their relative share. At times they also suggested that the Fund's weighted voting process be altered to the one-member one-vote process of the United Nations or that some power for decisions on financial topics be transferred from the Fund to the United Nations.

Since the beginning of the GATT, the Fund has always had a special relationship with it, partly reflecting the provision in the Articles of the GATT explicitly specifying a role for the Fund.[8] The CONTRACTING PARTIES to the GATT are to seek cooperation with the Fund so that the GATT and the Fund might pursue a coordinated policy on the exchange questions within the jurisdiction of the Fund and the questions of quantitative restrictions and other trade measures within the jurisdiction of the GATT. Furthermore, whenever the GATT holds consultations on import restrictions imposed by a country for balance of payments purposes, or deals with problems concerning monetary reserves, balance of payments, or foreign exchange arrangements, the GATT is to consult fully with the Fund and in these consultations has to accept the Fund's findings on whether the restrictions imposed or maintained by the contracting party in question exceeds those necessary to forestall an imminent threat to a country's monetary reserves, or to stop a serious decline in them, or in the instance of a country with low reserves, to achieve a reasonable rate of increase in reserves. The Fund is thus directly involved in consultations held by the GATT.

The working arrangements giving effect to the formal provisions for cooperation and consultation between the Fund and the GATT were established in 1948–51 and continued to be followed in the 1970s. A short document setting forth the Fund's findings on the need for restrictions is transmitted to the GATT's Committee on Balance of Payments Restrictions, together with the RED reports on the country, or a specially prepared paper, if a recent RED report is not available. The Fund's findings are approved by its Executive Board after discussion, and documents for the GATT are transmitted by the Executive Board's Committee on Liaison with the GATT. During the course of the GATT consultations, Fund staff are present and often give additional comments in reply to queries from members of the GATT's Committee on Balance of Payments Restrictions. In providing such comments, the staff is instructed to confine itself to correcting any distortion or false impression that a contracting party consulting with the GATT may give, and to adhere strictly to the findings approved by the Executive Directors. Fund staff usually provide informal assistance in the drafting of the report of the GATT's Balance of Payments Committee.

In 1976, at the initiative of Olivier Long, Director-General of the GATT, a number of proposals for closer collaboration between the Fund staff and the GATT Secretariat within the context of the existing formal arrangements were discussed. As a result, some changes were made to improve the two-way flow of information

---

[8]Descriptions of the Fund's relations with the CONTRACTING PARTIES to the GATT in earlier years can be found in *History, 1945–65*, Vol. II, pp. 332–46 and *History, 1966–71*, Vol. I, pp. 607–608.

on trade policy of common members, to provide an opportunity for informal discussions in Geneva before scheduled GATT consultations, and to enable senior officials of the two organizations, including the Managing Director of the Fund and the Director-General of the GATT, to exchange views on matters of mutual concern, especially trade policy measures that might have broad implications. The idea was to develop a sustained informal dialogue between the GATT and the Fund. This procedure exemplified the Fund's long-standing policy of trying to avoid formalizing its relations with the GATT in favor of evolving relations in an informal, pragmatic way.

In the years 1972–78, Fund staff also attended the annual sessions of the GATT, meetings of the Council of Representatives, the Consultative Group of Eighteen, and other GATT bodies. The GATT had set up the Consultative Group of Eighteen, a group of senior civil servants, in order to have a smaller body, similar to the Fund's Executive Board, in which to deliberate and take decisions.

A major development in trade from 1973 onward was the multilateral trade negotiations (MTN), and the Fund followed the developments closely. Fund staff attended the preparatory meeting in Geneva as well as the ministerial meeting in Tokyo, on September 12–14, 1973, when it was officially agreed that there would be held the first world trade talks since the end of the Kennedy Round in 1967. These talks were to be the most ambitious and complex since the GATT was formed in 1948. While the Kennedy Round achieved its objective of an overall reduction in tariffs, the Tokyo Round aimed at a progressive dismantling of tariff and nontariff obstacles to trade, improving the framework for the conduct of world trade, and obtaining greater benefits for the trade of developing countries. Shortly after the Tokyo meeting, Mr. Witteveen, addressing the Governors at the Annual Meeting in Nairobi on September 24, 1973, welcomed the fact that many nations represented in Nairobi had just met in Tokyo and had agreed to enter into comprehensive multilateral trade negotiations. Mr. Witteveen underscored the importance of this undertaking for furthering the economic progress of all nations, including a contribution to the more effective functioning of the international monetary system, and promised that "we shall do our best to be of assistance in this endeavor."[9]

The negotiations that began in Geneva in February 1975 involved 99 countries, including all the major industrial members of the Fund and a considerable number of developing members, plus many socialist countries of Eastern Europe. Of the 99 countries participating in the negotiations, 26 were not CONTRACTING PARTIES to the GATT and only 3 acceded to the GATT provisionally, but all agreed to negotiate under the auspices of the GATT.[10] The Fund staff closely followed the progress of the negotiations that went on in seven technical negotiating committees. Since these negotiations were confidential, Fund staff initially attended them as observers on an ad hoc basis, but gradually their attendance became more regular.

---

[9]Opening Address by the Managing Director, *Summary Proceedings*, *1973*, p. 23.
[10]For a summary of the issues involved in the negotiations, see *IMF Survey*, Vol. 4 (March 10, 1975), pp. 65–77.

These negotiations proceeded even more slowly than had the Kennedy Round, which had lasted from 1964 to 1967. Serious negotiations were held up until the middle of 1977 because of a procedural dispute between the EC and the United States on the treatment of agricultural trade. Thereafter, the negotiations made substantial progress, especially in the intensive bargaining session which took place in the first two weeks of July 1978. In July 1978, a framework of understanding was issued by the delegations of Canada, the EC, Japan, New Zealand, the Nordic countries, Switzerland, and the United States.[11]

The multilateral trade negotiations, starting while the Committee of Twenty was considering reform of the international monetary system, reflected a broad development influencing Fund-GATT relations in the 1970s: trade issues and finance or monetary issues became more intertwined. The Committee of Twenty was not limited to a discussion of monetary issues but was explicitly directed to discuss trade issues as well. It recommended that Fund members subscribe to a voluntary declaration on trade restrictions. In the same way, the idea of the meeting in Tokyo in 1973 to inaugurate trade negotiations was that international discussions of trade issues would proceed parallel with the discussions on reform of the international monetary system. Similarly, the terms of reference of the Consultative Group of Eighteen of the GATT stipulated that the trade measures of countries which were CONTRACTING PARTIES to the GATT had to take into account their balance of payments positions. In the work of both the Fund and the GATT, it was becoming increasingly apparent that issues of exchange rate policy and of balance of payments policy generally could not be discussed without reference to issues of trade policy, and vice versa.

Working relationships with both the UNCTAD and the GATT are conducted through the Fund's office in Geneva.

Relations with the OECD

In 1972–78, the Fund continued to have close relations with the OECD. The Managing Director was invited to attend the meetings of the OECD Council at ministerial level, of the Development Assistance Committee (DAC) at high level, and of the Executive Committee in Special Session. The Director of the Fund's European Office in Paris was also invited to attend the regular meetings of the OECD Council and the Executive Committee when matters of special interest to the Fund were being discussed. Fund staff either from Washington or from the European Office in Paris attending OECD meetings had the status of observers and were designated as representatives of the Managing Director rather than of the Fund, which meant that they reported to the Managing Director rather than to the Executive Board.

The OECD meetings regularly attended by Fund staff included those of the Economic Policy Committee and its Working Parties, such as Working Party No. 3

---

[11]Major agreements were announced in April 1979, after five years of intensive negotiations. A summary of the main points of agreement can be found in Mark Allen, "The Multilateral Trade Negotiations—A Background Note," *Finance & Development* (September 1979), pp. 21–23.

(Policies for the Promotion of Better International Payments Equilibrium), the Economic and Development Review Committee, the Committee on Capital Movements and Invisible Transactions, the Development Assistance Committee (DAC) and its Working Parties, the Committee on Fiscal Affairs, and the Committee on Financial Markets. Staff attendance at these meetings kept the Fund management and staff closely informed on economic conditions in countries belonging to the OECD, on the views of government officials with respect to these conditions, on economic developments in Europe of direct interest to the Fund (inflation, monetary policies, harmonization of monetary policies, trade, foreign exchange policy, external indebtedness, foreign assistance, including the tying of aid, export credits to developing countries, international investment, and multinational enterprises), and on any debates going on in the European Community.

The Fund staff and the OECD Secretariat also had close contact on a number of technical subjects, on balance of payments statistics, on government finance statistics, and on short-term forecasts for the economic situations of countries belonging both to the OECD and to the Fund.

Associations with Other Organizations

In the years 1972–78 the Fund strengthened its relations with both the Commission of the European Communities (CEC) and the BIS. In 1972 arrangements were made for the exchange of documents between the Fund and the CEC, with the Fund agreeing to supply copies of its Article XIV and Article VIII consultations reports on the same basis as it supplied these reports to the OECD. The EC was able to receive these consultations reports on countries that were members of the EC. Fund staff, mainly from the European Office in Paris, covered the activities of the Commission. As in the past, Fund relations with the EC were informal and there was no specified role for Fund participation in the meetings or sessions of the EC.

With the BIS, the special monitoring role of the Managing Director with regard to balances of pounds sterling in a facility provided to the United Kingdom by the BIS with the support of participating central banks, for instance, was discussed in Chapter 24. The Managing Director usually attended the Annual Meetings of the BIS, frequently attended the monthly meetings of governors of the central banks of the major industrial countries, and participated in meetings of the central bank governors of the countries adhering to the arrangements on gold, composed of the countries in the Group of Ten, Switzerland, and Portugal. If the Managing Director himself did not go to one of these monthly meetings, a staff member designated as his representative, usually the Director of the European Office in Paris, attended. The frequent informal discussions between the Managing Director and BIS officials also continued as did the close contacts of the Fund staff with the staff of the BIS. Fund staff also maintained contacts with the European Investment Bank (EIB) in Luxembourg and the Council of Europe in Strasbourg.

Among the organizations composed of Caribbean and Latin American countries, the Fund's relations with the Organization of American States (OAS) and the Inter-American Development Bank (IDB) were the most continuous, and the Fund traditionally sent representatives to their meetings. In 1974 the Inter-American Committee on the Alliance for Progress (CIAP), a committee of the OAS, was reorganized and its name changed to Permanent Executive Committee of the Inter-American Economic and Social Council (CEPCIES). There were contacts as well between Fund staff and a number of other Latin American organizations, such as the Central American Monetary Council, the Central Banking Experts of the American Continent, the Center for Latin American Monetary Studies (CEMLA), and the Andean Subregional Integration Agreement (Cartagena Agreement).

Staff regularly attended the annual meetings of the Boards of Governors of the regional development banks, such as the African Development Bank (AfDB), the Asian Development Bank (AsDB), and the Islamic Development Bank (IsDB), as well as the Caribbean Development Bank (CDB) and the Inter-American Development Bank (IDB). In Africa and Asia, too, Fund staff attended many special ad hoc meetings, conferences, and seminars.

In the field of commodities, Fund staff maintained contact with several intergovernmental commodity agencies in addition to those of the FAO and the UNCTAD, particularly because of the need of the Fund staff to operate the Fund's own compensatory financing and buffer stock facilities. These commodity groups included the International Tin Council and the International Coffee Organization, for which the Fund supplied information on exchange rates in connection with the Coffee Diversification Fund. In the years 1972–78 Fund staff also attended several seminars to discuss problems of primary commodities.

CHAPTER
50

Changes in Policymaking

F *ROM ITS ESTABLISHMENT* until late 1972, the Fund formed policies through the Board of Governors, the Executive Board, and the Managing Director and staff. Member governments were the ultimate authority, with the line of formal authority extending down from the Board of Governors, the highest formal authority, through the Executive Directors, to the Managing Director and staff.[1] Beginning in 1972, however, the establishment of committees of the Board of Governors and the provision in the amended Articles of Agreement for a permanent Council meant the introduction of new elements into the Fund's policymaking machinery, the first substantive change in Fund policymaking since 1944. In 1972–78 developments of considerable importance took place, moreover, in the influence of the groups outside the Fund into which some members had organized themselves, such as the Group of Ten and the Group of Twenty-Four. Although these groups were not in any sense instruments of the Fund, they played a role in shaping its policies.

This chapter describes the Fund's policymaking at the level of the Board of Governors in the period 1972–78, concentrating especially on changes. The Board of Governors met intermittently, most often in Washington. In this respect, it differed from the Executive Board and the Managing Director and staff, who were in continuous session at headquarters. Discussion of policymaking at headquarters is described in Chapters 51 and 52.

FUND POLICYMAKING: AN IN-HOUSE PROCESS

Policymaking in the Fund can be thought of largely as an "in-house" process. With few exceptions initiatives for new policies and for changes in existing ones almost always come, at least formally, from financial officials acting in their capacities within the Fund. Initiatives commonly come from a Governor at an Annual Meeting. At times Governors of several members, having coordinated their

---

[1] A description of these five instruments and of their interrelations at the end of 1965 can be found in *History, 1945–65*, Vol. II, pp. 4–19. A detailed description of the changes in these instruments can be found in *History, 1966–71*, Vol. II, pp. 616–49.

positions in advance in a group outside the Fund, all suggest the same initiative. Initiatives for policy changes are also often made by Executive Directors, who at times also make a common proposal. More often, especially as the Fund has matured, initiatives are made by the Managing Director, acting either on his own or on ideas generated within the staff.

There have, of course, been exceptions to these in-house initiatives. For example, in the early 1960s, the Group of Ten took the initiative on measures to increase international liquidity. The United Nations played a role in the compensatory financing facility that the Fund introduced in 1963, and the UNCTAD suggested the liberalization of the facility that came about in 1966. Financial officials are sometimes influenced by the academic community, as, for instance, in the 1960s when they suggested remedies for defects in how liquidity was being injected into the international monetary system and again in the early 1970s when they considered making exchange rates more flexible. The early and continued advocacy of floating exchange rates by Professors Milton Friedman and Gottfried Haberler and their impact on official thinking in the United States, especially by 1972, and the successful efforts of academic economists in the Federal Republic of Germany in persuading German officials to introduce a floating rate for the deutsche mark in 1971 have already been noted in Chapter 6.

A participant in forming the U.S. proposals to the Committee of Twenty maintains that Professor Friedman was the inventor of the U.S. proposal for reserve indicators, suggesting it to Mr. Shultz when he was Director of the Office of Management and Budget. After Mr. Shultz became Secretary of the Treasury, he made Professor Friedman's proposal the basis of U.S. planning, and Professor Friedman played a role in drafting the speech to the 1972 Annual Meeting in which Mr. Shultz put forward the U.S. proposals for reform described in Chapter 9. Professor Friedman, a leading advocate of floating rates, was politically realistic enough to appreciate that the world was not then prepared to accept a floating rate system. But a system involving margins around a reserve norm—which seemed to Professor Friedman analogous to the Bretton Woods system involving margins around exchange rate parities—and requiring exchange rate changes whenever the reserve margins were exceeded, would, he believed, engender more frequent changes in exchange rates than under the system based on par values.[2]

Initiatives by a Governor usually reflect ideas discussed within his own government or within a group of governments. An Executive Director is often following up on an idea presented by a Governor at an Annual Meeting or is the channel through which officials of a government in his constituency are operating. The Managing Director, too, is often trying to advance a suggestion made by a Governor at an Annual Meeting or an action contemplated in one or more national

---

[2]Kenneth W. Dam, *The Rules of the Game: Reform and Evolution in the International Monetary System* (Chicago and London: University of Chicago Press, 1982), pp. 223–24.

governments. In following up on proposals of a Governor or of other public officials, an Executive Director or the Managing Director may be seizing the opportunity to gain support for changes in policy already advocated within the Fund. Thus, initiatives by high-level financial officials frequently affect the timing of the introduction of a new or changed policy in the Fund as much as they do the substance of the policy.

Once ideas for policies are introduced, their substance and details are developed through a process in an inverse order to that of the formal line of authority. The work starts with the staff, under the Managing Director, and proceeds upward to the Executive Directors, to the Board of Governors, and finally to member governments. Papers drafted by the staff and supported by the Managing Director are discussed by the Executive Directors, usually formally but occasionally informally to enable them to exchange ideas without taking official positions. As Executive Directors iron out disagreements, negotiation among governments is in effect taking place. To help the negotiating process, the Managing Director, aided by the staff, often puts forward concrete suggestions for compromise.

Discussion and negotiation within the Executive Board is also often influenced by discussions in other forums. Positions taken by the Group of Ten, the Group of Twenty-Four, or the EC often have a direct bearing on the positions taken by Executive Directors. Discussions in the UNCTAD or resolutions passed by the United Nations also at times influence Executive Directors' positions.

Because the Executive Directors keep in daily contact with officials in the member governments that have appointed or elected them, the decisions that are finally taken by the Executive Board are usually supported by member governments, at least by their executive branches. Discussions usually go on until Executive Directors can agree on a decision. Similarly, on those relatively few occasions when the Executive Directors send to the Board of Governors a draft resolution for formal approval, this approval is always virtually assured. Policies requiring action by legislatures in member governments are not necessarily so assured, at least not quickly.

In this process of discussion and decision by the Executive Board and of action by the Board of Governors, member governments in the end determine the Fund's policies. The Fund can go only as far in fulfilling the objectives and deciding what policies it will pursue as its members will allow. For many member governments, actions relating to their participation in the Fund—for example, amending the Articles, consenting to increased quotas, and lending to the Fund—require the explicit approval of their legislative bodies. (The need for legislative action is established by a member's law, not by the Fund's Articles.) In many member governments, too, as officials in the executive branch take actions involving the Fund, such as negotiating a stand-by arrangement or altering an exchange rate arrangement, they are necessarily responsive to reactions by officials in their legislative branches.

ROLE OF THE BOARD OF GOVERNORS
AND OF GOVERNORS' COMMITTEES

The highest level of formal authority rests with the Board of Governors. Every member appoints a Governor (usually the minister of finance or the governor of the central bank) and an Alternate Governor. It is through the Governors that the Fund customarily deals formally with members. Hence, as described in Chapter 8, Governors are the political figures in the Fund's policymaking. Under the Articles after the Second Amendment, certain powers are conferred directly on the Board of Governors and cannot be delegated to the Executive Board.

Powers that are exercisable only by the Board of Governors have increased over the years. Under the original Articles, the most common powers reserved to the Board of Governors pertained primarily to authorizing the admission of new members, determining the conditions of their membership, and approving proposed changes in members' quotas. The First Amendment of the Articles of Agreement instigated a notable increase in the powers exercisable only by the Board of Governors. Only the Governors could, for example, allocate or cancel SDRs, alter the duration of a basic period for allocation, change the rates of allocation, or modify the rules for reconstitution. Ensuring that decisions on SDRs could be taken only by the Board of Governors was a technique used by those members mainly belonging to the EC that wanted to make these decisions harder to take. In addition, power was given to the Governors alone to decide on mitigating the effects of payment of increases in quotas following a general review of quotas, to revise the provisions on repurchases, and to make transfers to the Fund's General Reserve from any special reserve.[3]

Decisions by the Board of Governors take the form of resolutions on which each Governor is asked to vote. Governors are frequently polled by mail or cable to enable resolutions to be adopted between Annual Meetings, assuring ready access to the Board of Governors. It is normal practice for the Executive Board to make recommendations on taking decisions to the Board of Governors and to send draft resolutions to the Board of Governors.

Committees

The introduction of new committees of the Board of Governors beginning in 1972 profoundly changed the Fund's policymaking. Various facets relating to the Committee of Twenty—the reasons for its creation, its organization, its relation to the other policymaking bodies of the Fund, the reasons it was only an ad hoc (temporary) committee, its usefulness as an instrument of policymaking, and how it paved the way for establishment of the Interim Committee and of the Development Committee and for provision in the amended Articles for a Council—have been

---

[3]For a fuller description of the powers of the Board of Governors, see Joseph Gold, *Voting and Decisions in the International Monetary Fund* (Washington: International Monetary Fund, 1972), pp. 9–15.

examined in earlier chapters. The nature of the Interim Committee and of the Development Committee, the reasons they were established, and their terms of reference have been explained in Chapter 16. This chapter looks at the subsequent work of the Interim and Development Committees.

THE INTERIM COMMITTEE

The Interim Committee, formally the Interim Committee of the Board of Governors on the International Monetary System, to repeat briefly, was set up pending approval of amendments to the Articles of Agreement, which were to include provision for a permanent Council of Governors, and is to continue only until that Council is established. It is therefore designated the "Interim" Committee. The establishment of this Committee meant the creation, after nearly 30 years, of a body of senior financial officials to meet several times a year to consider Fund business, as originally proposed by Lord Keynes and supported by several delegations at Bretton Woods as the way in which the Board of Executive Directors should function. U.S. officials at Bretton Woods felt this proposal would make for a relatively inactive Board of Executive Directors. Hence, when the Fund was created, U.S. officials successfully pushed for Executive Directors in continuous session in Washington, engaged full time on the Fund's business.[4] In 1974 the Fund's policymaking machinery was altered to include both groups. As before, Executive Directors were to be in full-time residence and to meet several times each week, particularly to take decisions involving the Fund's relations with individual members, and always to be on call to handle the Fund's daily business. In addition, there is now a group of high-ranking financial officials with major functions and responsibilities in their home governments. They meet a few times each year to discuss and reach understandings on policy issues that affect all members and the international monetary system as a whole. Executive Directors prepare issues to be put to the higher-ranking group. The Fund's policymaking machinery has thus become a blend of positions taken by the United Kingdom and the United States three decades earlier. In this way, the establishment of the Interim Committee represents a significant strengthening of the Fund's policymaking machinery.

The Interim Committee was set up so as to differ in three ways from its predecessor, the Committee of Twenty. First, the way in which the Interim Committee functions recognizes more fully the role of the Executive Directors. After helping resolve issues of a political nature, as distinct from those of a technical nature, put to them by the Executive Directors, the members of the Interim Committee refer matters back to the Executive Directors, who work out the details and take final decisions. Several examples of resolutions of political issues by the Interim Committee and referrals back to the Executive Directors for further work

---

[4]See *History, 1945–65*, Vol. I, pp. 106–107 and 130–35.

were described in earlier chapters. This procedure of the Interim Committee means that the Committee does not undermine the authority of the Executive Board.

The second difference from the Committee of Twenty is that the Interim Committee has no deputies. Instead the Executive Directors are explicitly given the role equivalent to deputies. The deputies of the Committee of Twenty who did the preparatory work for the ministers on the Committee had been regarded as being in direct competition with the Executive Directors. Hence, when the Interim Committee was established, it was decided that the Executive Board should perform for that Committee, and for the later permanent Council, the function that the deputies had performed for the Committee of Twenty. It seemed logical for the Executive Board to perform the function of undertaking the preparatory work for the Interim Committee, or for the Council, for another reason as well. Although the task of the Committee of Twenty had been the negotiation, within a specific period of time, of a reformed international monetary system, the major task of the Interim Committee, and of the Council, is to supervise the system. Such supervision may go on indefinitely and requires the help of a technically knowledgeable body. The Executive Directors, assisted by the staff, are the best body to provide this help on an indefinite basis. Thus, both the first and second differences in the working methods of the Interim Committee are designed to avoid undermining the authority of the Executive Board.

The third difference is that the Interim Committee is to supervise the management and adaptation of an evolving international monetary system, while the Committee of Twenty had the temporary and limited assignment of negotiating a reformed system. The Interim Committee could go on indefinitely, although it was not initially so intended; as was intended, the Committee of Twenty went out of existence once the *Outline of Reform* was completed.

Under its terms of reference, the Interim Committee is to advise and report to the Board of Governors on the responsibilities of the Board of Governors in three areas. One is in "supervising the management and adaptation of the international monetary system, including the continuing operation of the adjustment process, and in this connection reviewing developments in global liquidity and the transfer of real resources to developing countries." A second area is "considering proposals by the Executive Directors to amend the Articles of Agreement." The third is "dealing with sudden disturbances that might threaten the system." In addition, the Interim Committee is to advise and report to the Board of Governors on any other matters on which the Board of Governors seek the advice of the Committee.[5]

These terms of reference were worked out as a compromise so that the functions specified for the Committee satisfied the disparate views of all Fund members. The first broad area, concerning the evolution of the system, means that the Interim Committee is to advise and report to the Board of Governors on all the

---

[5]Resolution No. 29-8, adopted by the Board of Governors, effective October 2, 1974; Vol. III below, pp. 213–15. The quoted portions are in par. 3.

elements of the international monetary system which officials had been debating in the Committee of Twenty. The Interim Committee is thus to make recommendations on such difficult questions as how the need for balance of payments adjustment should be determined, what rules should govern exchange rates, how international liquidity should be managed, what actions should be taken with respect to SDRs and gold, and to what extent and how the international monetary system should be used so as to help transfer resources in real terms from industrial to developing countries. These issues concern officials from different groups of members. Officials of developing members are deeply concerned with the last issue. Officials of the major industrial members have concentrated attention on exchange rates. In fact, part of their motivation in setting up the Interim Committee was to create a high-level body that would be available to help apply pressure on member governments to take actions recommended by the Executive Directors. In the minds of these officials, the decisions of the Executive Board would have more force if they were backed up by a higher-level political group. At the time that the Interim Committee was established it was expected that the decisions that might particularly need such pressure would pertain to members' exchange rates.

The Interim Committee was also to consider proposals worked out by the Executive Board for amending the Articles inasmuch as it was known in 1974, when the Committee was established, that the Executive Board would be undertaking the drafting of the Second Amendment. The Interim Committee's third function of considering the responses to be made to sudden disturbances to the international monetary system was included at the insistence of the 100 or so Fund members that did not belong to the Group of Ten. These members wanted to institute a broader forum than the Group of Ten to consider crises in the international monetary system. (The function of considering responses to crises in the international monetary system was omitted in the tasks provided for the permanent Council so as to avoid the impression that emergencies were expected once the Second Amendment went into effect.)

Proceedings and Achievements

As seen in Chapter 16, the Interim Committee was set up along the same lines as the Committee of Twenty. Each member that appointed or each group of members that elected an Executive Director appointed a member of the Committee, who had to be a Governor of the Fund, a minister, or someone of comparable rank. This last expression was intended to include governors of central banks but it was deliberately meant to be vague and broad. Each constituency could determine freely whom it appointed and by what procedures.

Until November 1978, there were 20 members of the Executive Board and therefore 20 members of the Interim Committee. But, like the meetings of the Committee of Twenty, each meeting of the Interim Committee was attended by nearly 200 people, as up to 7 associates for each member of the Committee, plus Executive Directors, the Managing Director, and a limited number of observers also attended. The Managing Director was accompanied by the Deputy Managing Director and a few senior staff. Although the resolution establishing the Interim Committee declared that it would ordinarily meet three or four times a year, it was not found convenient or necessary to meet so often. The Committee met for the first time in October 1974. It met three times in 1975, three times in 1976, twice in 1977, and twice in 1978. Most meetings, which normally lasted one or two days, were held in Washington, but one was held in Paris, one in Kingston, Jamaica, two in Manila, and one in Mexico City.

For each meeting of the Interim Committee a draft agenda is prepared by the Managing Director and discussed by the Executive Board. The agenda is then agreed with the Chairman of the Committee and dispatched on his behalf to members of the Committee as his proposal. At first there was a tendency to submit numerous technical questions to the Committee. If various solutions to a technical issue were possible, the Executive Directors were tempted to look to the Committee for guidance. This practice ceased after the Committee sent these issues back to the Executive Board for solution. The first Chairman of the Committee, in fact, advised that the agenda of the Interim Committee not be crowded with a long list of technical issues. Since the Committee was intended to be composed of people with political responsibility, the issues referred to it should be issues that involve political considerations.

For each substantive item on the agenda there is a report of either the Executive Directors or the Managing Director. At the meetings, the Managing Director usually introduces each substantive item on the agenda, shares the rostrum with the Chairman at all times, and takes an active role in the proceedings. All members of the Committee tend to speak in turn on important items, and active interchanges often occur. The proceedings, according to one Chairman of the Committee, are "frank, pertinent, and instructive." Another Chairman has said that members of the Committee "have spoken with a degree of frankness that is not characteristic of many international discussions." When matters of unusual sensitivity are discussed or when impasses are reached after discussion, meetings of members of the Committee and the Managing Director are held in restricted session. The friendly interchanges in these sessions contribute to consensus. Sometimes solutions are found at a similarly restricted dinner or luncheon. The communiqués that have always been issued at the end of the meetings record the understandings reached and, on the whole, express the Committee's views effectively, sometimes because of what they contain and sometimes because of what they omit.[6]

In the four years from October 1974 to December 1978, John N. Turner, Minister of Finance of Canada, Willy De Clercq, Minister of Finance of Belgium, and Denis W. Healey, Chancellor of the Exchequer of the United Kingdom, served as Chairmen. Turnover in the chairmanship resulted because Mr. Turner and then Mr. De Clercq, each while serving a two-year term as Chairman, ceased to hold their

---

[6]The communiqués issued by the Interim Committee after the first 11 meetings (all the meetings held through the end of 1978) are in Vol. III below, pp. 217–42.

posts as ministers of finance in their own countries, and it was the practice of the Committee that the Chairman would be a sitting minister of finance. Each year at the Annual Meeting, the Chairman of the Interim Committee presented to the Board of Governors a report on the Committee's activities.[7]

From the actions of the Interim Committee described in previous chapters, it can readily be inferred that the Committee quickly became an effective and integral part of the Fund's policymaking process. It demonstrated not only that it could arrive at conclusions but also that these conclusions could have prompt and practical consequences. From 1975 to 1978, the Committee reached understandings on a number of contentious issues relating to the Second Amendment, on the size of increases in Fund quotas, on policies relating to the use of the Fund's resources, on a coordinated strategy for world economic growth, on the resumption of allocations of SDRs, on an increase in the rate of interest on holdings of SDRs, on an increase in the rate of remuneration paid in the General Resources Account, and on a reduction in the obligation to reconstitute holdings of SDRs.

Reaching understandings on these issues by the Interim Committee enabled the Executive Directors to proceed with their work on these topics. The Interim Committee also served to indicate whether officials of members were ready to compromise and reach consensus on an issue or whether no consensus was yet possible. The usefulness of the Interim Committee was demonstrated by the gearing up of much of the work of the Executive Board, and of the management and staff, to the meetings of the Interim Committee.

Postponement of Council

It had been assumed in the early stages of drafting of the amendments that the Council would spring into life the moment the Second Amendment became effective. Later, when the amendments were being worked out it was agreed that the Council would come into being only when the Board of Governors decided, by an 85 percent majority of the total voting power of members, to establish the Council. This compromise put off the event indefinitely.

There were a number of objections to the Council. Some long-time Executive Directors were concerned about a possible loss of power by the Executive Board. Some of the Executive Directors elected by developing members holding this view regarded themselves as more experienced than their finance ministers, who tended to be in office only for short periods, and they therefore tended to downplay the need for setting up a permanent Council. Officials of developing members also preferred the Interim Committee to the Council because ad hoc groups, such as the Interim Committee, can make only recommendations and not decisions. Although such recommendations are obviously powerful and likely to be respected, they are not binding. Moreover, officials of developing members were concerned that the Council would also take power away from the Board of Governors, in part because of

---

[7]The four reports presented at the Annual Meetings for 1975, 1976, 1977, and 1978 were included in *Summary Proceedings*.

a provision of the amended Articles that an Annual Meeting of the Board of Governors was no longer required. If Governors no longer met annually they feared that the Governors of the smaller members would lose their best opportunity to express their views on a world stage and to meet as regional groups of Governors with the Managing Director. In the meetings of the ad hoc committees of the Board of Governors, Governors of the smaller members felt overshadowed by Governors from the large members.

As the Second Amendment was being drafted in 1975, it also became possible for officials of the industrial and more developed members to accept an indefinite postponement of the establishment of the Council because the Interim Committee had by that time already shown much vitality. The Interim Committee seemed a satisfactory de facto alternative to the Council. It also provided the opponents of the Council with the argument that more experience with the Committee would be helpful before a decision was taken on the Council. Thus, while ad hoc committees were accepted, the fight about a high-level group of Governors centered on the Council.[8]

THE DEVELOPMENT COMMITTEE

The reasons a Joint Ministerial Committee of the Boards of Governors of the Bank and the Fund on the Transfer of Real Resources to Developing Countries (the Development Committee) was set up at the same time as the Interim Committee, in October 1974, were discussed in Chapter 16. To repeat briefly, a technical group of the Committee of Twenty had done some work on the broad question of the transfer of real resources to developing countries and officials of many countries felt the need for a ministerial forum to continue this work and give specific attention to the problems of economic development in developing countries. Developments in the world economic situation during 1973 and 1974 had left most developing countries facing trade and current account deficits in 1974 that were several times larger than in 1973. This situation greatly increased the need of developing countries for concessional financing at a time when the international climate for an increased flow of concessional funds was not favorable. This formidable combination of adverse factors was seen as a threat to the economies and the development prospects of the adversely affected developing countries.

When the Development Committee was established, it was with the expectation that it could make progress in these areas by serving as a forum at a high political level for a comprehensive overview of international development activities and for orderly and constructive exchanges among officials of industrial members and relatively more developed members, of oil exporting developing members, and

---

[8]Further discussion of the Interim and Development Committees and of the Council can be found in Joseph Gold, "The Fund's Interim Committee—an Assessment," *Finance & Development* (September 1979), pp. 32–35, and in Joseph Gold, "Political Bodies in the Fund," Essay No. 6 in his *Legal and Institutional Aspects* (cited in fn. 1 of Chap. 8 above), pp. 261–86.

of non-oil developing members on issues related to development and to the transfer of real resources.

The terms of reference given to the Development Committee were broad. It was to "maintain an overview of the development process," to "advise and report" to the Boards of Governors of both institutions "on all aspects of the broad question of the transfer of real resources to developing countries," to "make suggestions for consideration by those concerned regarding the implementation of its conclusions," and to "review, on a continuing basis, the progress made in fulfillment of its suggestions."[9]

The Development Committee met when the Interim Committee met. Henri Konan Bédié, Minister of Economy and Finance for Ivory Coast, served as Chairman from October 1974 until October 1976 when he was succeeded by Cesar E.A. Virata, Secretary of Finance of the Philippines. Mr. Virata was re-elected in September 1978 to serve for another two years. Communiqués were issued after the first six meetings, that is, through October 3, 1976, with announcements issued to cover the next five meetings. Each year at the Annual Meeting, the Chairman presented a report to the Boards of Governors of the Fund and the Bank on the Committee's activities for the year.[10]

Proceedings and Achievements

The Development Committee did not become an integral part of the policy-making process of either the World Bank or the Fund. In fact, the Development Committee, in contrast to the Interim Committee, was intended by its proponents to remain at arm's length from the World Bank and the Fund. Placing the Development Committee in the two organizations was merely a convenient device to house it somewhere and to have it financed.

Furthermore, although the Development Committee was a joint committee of the Boards of Governors of the Fund and of the World Bank, the Fund regarded it as mainly in the line of business of the World Bank. Until after 1978, Fund officials, accordingly, took much less interest in, and responsibility for, the Development Committee than they did in the Interim Committee. At the same time, from the perspective of the Fund, it appeared that the President of the World Bank at the time, Robert S. McNamara, and other World Bank officials were also inclined to take relatively little interest in the Development Committee, treating it as the outside group that its proponents had intended. Hence the Development Committee was not integrated into the policymaking processes of the World Bank either.

Because of its nature, the Development Committee, moreover, had a different relationship with the Executive Board of the World Bank (and with the Executive

---

[9]Resolution No. 29-9 adopted by the Boards of Governors of the World Bank and the Fund, effective October 2, 1974; Vol. III below, pp. 575–78. The quoted portions are in par. 4(a).

[10]The communiqués issued by the Development Committee after its first six meetings and the annual reports presented by the Chairman of the Development Committee from 1975 through 1978 are in Vol. III below, pp. 579–617.

Board of the Fund) than the Interim Committee had with the Executive Board of the Fund. Rather than having the preparatory work done by the Executive Board, assisted by the staff, as was done in the Fund for the Interim Committee, the preparatory work for the Development Committee was done by a small secretariat that the members of the Development Committee appointed especially for this purpose. This procedure meant that, unlike the situation with respect to the Interim Committee, the Development Committee did not receive reports and recommendations that were endorsed by the Executive Boards either of the World Bank or of the Fund. The documents the Development Committee received thus did not have the same force as documents going to the Interim Committee.

The annual reports of the Development Committee mentioned above describe what the Committee did in the four years until 1978. In brief, the Committee, with the assistance of its secretariat, had a role in promoting the opening of a "third window" for intermediate-term lending by the World Bank, made studies of the capital requirements of developing countries, worked intensively on the problems of developing countries' access to international bond markets (as was described in Chapter 48), and studied a number of problems related to official development assistance and to the transfer of resources to developing countries. As 1978 was ending, the Committee was undertaking special work on the problem of stabilization of export earnings. Probably the most substantive accomplishment of the Committee through 1978 was its work on the access of developing countries to the world's capital markets.

While the Interim Committee was scheduled to come to an end when the permanent Council was voted into existence, the resolution establishing the Development Committee did not provide a date for ending that Committee, but required that the work of the Committee be reviewed at the end of two years, in October 1976. In 1976 the Executive Directors of the World Bank and the Fund prepared a report reviewing the performance of the Development Committee, which it sent to the Committee in July. This report noted that, while work was in progress on a number of subjects, it had not reached the stage where it was ready to be put before the Committee for discussion and that, therefore, it was premature to assess the Committee's progress. The report recommended that the Boards of Governors review the performance of the Development Committee at the end of four years, on October 2, 1978, thereby giving the Development Committee another two years on its existing basis. Mr. Witteveen, as Managing Director of the Fund, transmitted this report to the Chairman of the Boards of Governors for the 1976 Annual Meeting, together with a proposed resolution to implement this recommendation. Mr. Bédié, as Chairman of the Committee, presented the Committee's concurrence with this recommendation, and the Boards of Governors agreed.[11]

In September 1978, Mr. Virata, as Chairman of the Development Committee,

---

[11]The report of the Executive Directors of the World Bank and the Fund and the resolution adopted by the Fund's Board of Governors on October 5, 1976 (Resolution No. 31-9) are in Vol. III below, pp. 619–22.

presented another report to the Boards of Governors of the two institutions again reviewing the Development Committee's performance. The report was frank in stating that the results achieved by the Development Committee had been disappointing. Not only had the Committee been unable to produce concrete results relating to the transfer of resources, but there had also been some concern that the Committee pursued technical issues and that its work lacked focus. In a candid assessment, the report also offered several reasons why the Committee had not been more successful and discussed whether it should be restructured as "a Bank-only Committee, rather than a joint Bank/Fund Committee" and how its method of work could be improved.

The report concluded that retention of the Development Committee was essential. It was the only forum where finance ministers from developing members could discuss broad problems of development and resource transfers with their counterparts from developed members in the presence of the multilateral organizations concerned with North-South development issues. The Group of Twenty-Four also pointedly urged that the Development Committee be continued. Its methods of work should be reorganized, however, and to accomplish this the President of the World Bank and the Managing Director of the Fund should consult with the Chairman of the Development Committee. The Development Committee would be reorganized so as to operate in a way more comparable to that of the Interim Committee. The Development Committee's separate secretariat would be eliminated. The position of Executive Secretary would continue to exist, but the function would be more limited. Preparatory work would be done by the staffs of the World Bank and of the Fund, and the Executive Boards of the two institutions would discuss in advance the items on the agenda and make recommendations to the Committee. On this basis, the Development Committee should be continued and its performance reviewed again not later than June 30, 1980.

The Boards of Governors of the two organizations agreed to this recommendation effective September 27, 1978.[12]

MEMBERS: INFLUENCE OF GROUPS

The descriptions in this narrative and in the History for 1966–71 of how the Fund's policies originated and were developed demonstrate that after about 1963 groups of members began to influence the Fund's policies by concerted action. The groups outside the Fund into which the financial officials of member governments had organized themselves to discuss and to coordinate their positions on issues being considered in the Fund and on other questions affecting the international monetary system had substantial consequences for the Fund's policies.

---

[12]The report of 1978 on the review of performance of the Development Committee and Resolution No. 33-10 of the Board of Governors are in Vol. III below, pp. 623–26.

Three Groups in 1972

By the beginning of 1972 the three outside groups that were the most prominent in international monetary concerns were the Group of Ten, the Group of Twenty-Four, and the European Economic Community. These three groups are not, of course, of the same character. The European Economic Community is part of the European Communities, a legal entity with an elaborate structure and functions governed by treaty. The Group of Ten and the Group of Twenty-Four are groups of high-ranking financial and monetary officials of specified countries who meet periodically.

The Group of Ten was extremely influential from early 1963 until the end of 1971. But, as noted in Chapter 8, by the end of 1971, financial officials of the United States had become disenchanted with the Group of Ten, which was one of the main reasons the Committee of Twenty was formed. By the mid-1960s, the European Economic Community also began to have a more potent influence on the policies of the Fund than it previously had. By working in unison, the six countries that then comprised the European Economic Community—Belgium, France, the Federal Republic of Germany, Italy, Luxembourg, and the Netherlands—succeeded in forcing changes in several rules and practices of the Fund on the use of its general resources as a condition for their agreement on an SDR facility and in obtaining an effective joint veto over allocations of SDRs.[13] Because these six members also met separately in advance of meetings of the Group of Ten to reach agreement on the common positions that they would take, they also had a substantial impact on the decisions of the Group of Ten, as described in Chapter 8.

The Group of Twenty-Four, more formally the Inter-Governmental Group of Twenty-Four on International Monetary Affairs, was set up in November 1971 by the Group of Seventy-Seven to be its "financial arm" because the developing countries wanted to have their own body comparable to the Group of Ten.[14] Officials of developing countries openly expressed their resentment at the exclusiveness and the influence of the Group of Ten and decided that their best defense lay in coordinating their own positions on international monetary issues. The formation of the Group of Twenty-Four in November 1971 was timed to the start of negotiations to reform the international monetary system.

The Group of Twenty-Four consisted of 24 finance ministers or senior monetary or financial authorities, 8 appointed by each of the African, Asian, and Latin American contingents of the Group of Seventy-Seven. Any member of the Group of Seventy-Seven could, however, participate in all meetings and deliberations, and just as the Group of Seventy-Seven gradually increased to well over 100 members by the end of 1978, nearly all of which were represented at meetings, so the meetings of the Group of Twenty-Four were usually attended by representatives from many more than 24 countries. The Group of Twenty-Four was to some extent

---

[13]See *History, 1966–71*, Vol. I, pp. 127, 131–33, and 155–56.

[14]The Group of Seventy-Seven was established by the developing countries in 1964 when the Unctad was being formed and planning to hold its first session.

modeled on the Group of Ten. There were, for example, deputies to each of the finance ministers or other high-level officials in the Group and Executive Directors from members of the Group were entitled to sit in on the meetings of the deputies, and in some instances Fund Executive Directors served as deputies. These arrangements made for an unusual closeness of officials from developing members serving in the Fund and officials serving on the Group of Twenty-Four.

Still another grouping of officials that influenced the Fund's policies was the "G-9 caucus" within the Fund, a caucus of the 9 Executive Directors elected exclusively by developing members. These Executive Directors started to meet, informally, usually monthly, in 1966 to consider questions coming up in the Executive Board. Their number increased to 10 in November 1978 when Saudi Arabia appointed an Executive Director.

Another group of officials that met to consider topics in the Fund's area of concern and interest was the Commonwealth finance ministers. The finance ministers of Commonwealth countries regularly met in the capital city of one of these countries during the week preceding the Annual Meetings to discuss international monetary questions.[15] They usually issued a communiqué following their meeting putting forth their positions. From time to time the Commonwealth heads of government also met to discuss economic issues.

Developments in the Group of Ten and the EC After 1972

The direct influence of the Group of Ten on decisions taken in the Fund was less in 1972–78 than it had been earlier. After 1971 the Group of Ten met less often than in the 1960s and broad decisions relating to the international monetary system did not await prior action by the Group of Ten nearly to the same extent. The decline in activity by, and in the visibility of, the Group of Ten was, of course, related to the establishment first of the Committee of Twenty and then of the Interim Committee. Officials of the ten largest industrial members tended to dominate the proceedings of these Committees, and for them the continuing Interim Committee was a politically more acceptable forum than the Group of Ten in which to take key international monetary decisions.

Other factors also help explain the change in the influence of the Group of Ten. One was the fact that the major industrial members were often divided on international monetary questions, as has been amply revealed in previous chapters, and a second was the emergence of the "Group of Five." This informal group began when the finance ministers of the five largest industrial countries—France, the Federal Republic of Germany, Japan, the United Kingdom, and the United States—in November 1975 took the occasion of the first economic summit in Rambouillet to

---

[15]The Commonwealth countries included Australia, Bahamas, Barbados, Botswana, Canada, Cyprus, Fiji, The Gambia, Ghana, Guyana, India, Jamaica, Kenya, Lesotho, Malawi, Malaysia, Malta, Mauritius, New Zealand, Nigeria, Pakistan, Sierra Leone, Singapore, Sri Lanka, Swaziland, Tanzania, Tonga, Trinidad and Tobago, Uganda, the United Kingdom, Western Samoa, and Zambia.

meet separately. Although this economic summit meeting also included Italy and subsequent economic summit meetings included Canada as well, the finance ministers of the five largest industrial countries continued subsequently to meet on an ad hoc basis from time to time, very much behind the scenes.

The Group of Ten, nevertheless, remained a force in international monetary affairs and in many of the Fund's decisions in 1972–78. Decisions of the Group of Ten, meeting jointly with the European Economic Community, in March 1973 ushered in the new era of floating rates for the main currencies. In September 1974, the Group of Ten agreed once again to renew the General Arrangements to Borrow, enabling the Fund to continue to have access to this prime source of borrowed funds. The Group of Ten was also responsible for decisions basic to the resolution of the gold problem in 1975 and for decisions in 1975 on how increases in the quotas for their own countries could be worked out in the Sixth General Review of Quotas. In 1975, too, the Group of Ten brought pressure on officials of France and of the United States to work out their differences on an amended Article IV of the Fund's Articles, on exchange rate arrangements, and after French and U.S. officials had agreed on an amended version, the Group of Ten approved the result before it was considered in the Executive Board and in the Interim Committee.

At times, moreover, the Group of Ten met as they gathered for an Interim Committee meeting to give the financial officials of the ten largest industrial members an opportunity to express their positions and to reach agreement on issues in a smaller setting prior to confronting officials of other Fund members. These meetings took place especially when the issues had political repercussions. For example, the Group of Ten—sometimes limiting themselves only to the ten ministers of finance—met when changes in the quotas in the Fund of the ten big industrial members were being considered. The Group of Ten continued to meet either at the level of ministers or at the level of deputies and sometimes in working parties whenever they felt the need. Some of the meetings were formal; some were informal "working dinners." After some, but not all, of the formal meetings, communiqués were issued.[16]

As in the past, the chairmanship of the Group of Ten rotated each year, as ministers of finance of the ten countries took turns. Changes also occurred at the level of Deputies. Rinaldo Ossola (Italy), who had served as Chairman of the Deputies of the Group of Ten since 1967, following Robert V. Roosa (United States) and Otmar Emminger (Federal Republic of Germany), resigned during the 1976 Annual Meeting in Manila. He was succeeded by Jacques de Larosière (France). When Mr. de Larosière became Managing Director of the Fund in 1978, Karl-Otto Pöhl (Federal Republic of Germany) was elected Chairman of the Deputies of the Group of Ten.

Countries belonging to the EC grew to nine on January 1, 1973 when Denmark, Ireland, and the United Kingdom joined the other six. As a group these countries

---

[16]Four of the most substantive communiqués issued by the Group of Ten from 1972 to 1978 are reproduced in Vol. III below, pp. 629–33.

had an impact on many Fund policies, especially on exchange rates. Their activities with regard to the European narrow margins arrangements (the snake) were of vital importance in several of the Fund's decisions. The problem for the Fund as 1978 ended, however, was not so much that these members would exert undue influence on Fund policies as it was that they might go their own independent way, in the European Monetary System.

Developments in the Group of Twenty-Four

One of the most notable developments in the groups of members outside the Fund after 1972 was the emergence of the Group of Twenty-Four as an effective force. While the Group of Ten can be regarded as a steering committee, the Group of Twenty-Four can be likened more to a pressure or lobbying group. From the time of the first meeting of the Group of Twenty-Four in April 1972, officials both at the ministerial level and at the level of deputies met regularly before each meeting of the Committee of Twenty and later before each meeting of the Interim Committee and the Development Committee. Occasionally they also met in between these meetings.

At their meetings, the Group of Twenty-Four could take positions on the currently outstanding international monetary questions and issue communiqués announcing these positions.[17] Officials of developing countries often exhibited a unity and solidarity not originally expected. During the negotiations of the Committee of Twenty in 1973 and 1974, for example, they took a strong stand favoring a link between SDR allocations and development finance, complained about how floating exchange rates had come into being by decisions taken entirely by officials from industrial countries, expressed their preference for a system of stable exchange rates based on adjustable par values, urged that an extended facility be established in the Fund, stated that developing members ought to have a substantially higher share of quotas and voting power in the Fund, and, when the Committee of Twenty was to come to an end, insisted on the establishment of a Development Committee. The Group of Twenty-Four had special influence at the time of the Committee of Twenty because amendment of the Fund's Articles of Agreement was not possible without the concurrence of the Fund's developing members.

After negotiations for the reformed system were abandoned, the Group of Twenty-Four took further effective positions. Their positions helped achieve a subsidy account for the oil facility, the floating in the gold tranche of the buffer stock facility, a substantial liberalization of the compensatory financing facility, the distribution to developing members of part of the profits realized by sale of some of the Fund's gold and establishment of a Trust Fund in the International Monetary Fund, retention of the share of non-oil developing members in Fund quotas when the share in those quotas of oil exporting members was doubled, and a review of conditionality that the Fund attached to use of its resources. It was a time when officials of industrial and developed members wanted to satisfy the officials of

---

[17]Nine of these communiqués are reproduced in Vol. III below, pp. 635–57.

developing members as much as they felt they could without seriously jeopardizing their own immediate interests. The positions taken by the Group of Twenty-Four made clear what actions were favored by developing countries and made it more awkward for officials of other countries to reject their requests.

Moreover, officials participating in other bodies and forums, such as in the UNCTAD, in the General Assemblies of the United Nations, and in some of the special sessions of the United Nations, frequently looked to the Group of Twenty-Four for guidance. As the Group of Seventy-Seven came to dominate the General Assembly of the United Nations, including the UNCTAD, many resolutions passed in these other bodies were based directly on work of the Group of Twenty-Four. Resolutions of the United Nations tended to give added support to whatever pressures were being generated directly within the Fund by the Group of Twenty-Four.

By the end of the period reviewed here the Group of Twenty-Four was to some extent less unified, and differing viewpoints were being put forward in its meetings and by officials from developing members in the meetings of the Interim Committee. As a result, communiqués of the Group of Twenty-Four were beginning to include proposals favored by one group of developing countries or another, and officials of other countries were more inclined to view these proposals—or demands—as impracticable.

In the seven years 1972–78, several officials served as Chairman of the Group of Twenty-Four as the position was rotated among its geographical constituencies. Serving as Chairman successively were Pedro R. Tinoco, Alfredo Lafee, and Luis E. Oberto G., of Venezuela; Ismail Mahroug, of Algeria; N.M. Perera and H.E. Tennekoon, of Sri Lanka; Luis Barua Castaneda, of Peru; R.K.A. Gardiner, of Ghana; and S. Osman Ali and A.G.N. Kazi, of Pakistan. The Chairman of the deputies was from the same country as the Chairman at the ministerial level. Serving concurrently with the ministers from their countries were Carlos Rafael Silva, of Venezuela; Rachid Bouraoui, of Algeria; Lal Jayawardena, of Sri Lanka; Manuel Moreyra Laredo and Winston Temple-Seminario, of Peru; Kwaku Gyasi-Twum, of Ghana; and Ziauddin Ahmad, of Pakistan.

The Fund staff provides services to the Group of Twenty-Four, which has its own Bureau to prepare position papers.

CHANGES IN ANNUAL MEETINGS

Separate committees of the Board of Governors were established because Annual Meetings of the Board of Governors were an inefficient forum for negotiation. However, rather than detracting from the significance of Annual Meetings, these committees made the Annual Meetings more important occasions. The Committee of Twenty, the Interim Committee, and the Development Committee always planned meetings at the time of the Annual Meetings, usually a day or two preceding the opening plenary session. In addition, Governors from individual members, as well as from geographic regions, especially of Africa and of Latin America, used the occasion to meet separately with the Managing Director. These Governors and the Managing Director both regarded separate caucuses with the Managing Director as important opportunities to explain their positions. The formal groups outside the Fund also took advantage of the presence of relevant financial officials to call meetings. The Group of Ten and the Group of Twenty-Four usually met both at the level of ministers and at the level of deputies in preparation for the Annual Meetings.

Holding these ancillary meetings had several consequences for Annual Meetings, which became even more massive affairs, as they attracted the highest-ranking financial officials of all members. Virtually all officials concerned with international economics and finance gathered to meet formally or informally with their counterparts from other countries. Current finance ministers and governors of central banks of 130 or more members, plus their alternates and advisors and the Executive Directors and their Alternates and Advisors were, of course, present. Many members of legislatures and other government officials responsible for action on international monetary questions also served on members' delegations. Several former finance ministers and governors of central banks and other former governmental financial officers continued to attend, in one capacity or another. As the number of international monetary institutions multiplied, these former officials came in new roles or were included as advisors in members' delegations. Some members had as many as 50 in their delegations. The directors and other top officers from the BIS, the EC, the GATT, the OECD, the OPEC, and the UNCTAD, and from the Swiss National Bank came as observers. Some monetary specialists and economists from universities and research institutions came as special guests. As commercial banks increased their lending to governments after 1973, the number of private bankers who came as special guests or as visitors also swelled, as both bankers and officials of countries wanted to take the opportunity to talk over their private transactions. Some of the large delegations included bankers so as to give bankers a more official status. Finally, hundreds of financial and economic reporters from all over the world came to cover the proceedings.

Holding ancillary meetings simultaneously made Annual Meetings the highlight of the Fund's calendar year. As in the past, the Annual Report had to be published for presentation to the Governors before the Annual Meetings, and its preparation was a major effort for the staff and for the Executive Directors. The review of the world economic outlook, too, was timed not only for the Annual Report but also for the meeting of the Interim Committee where it had become a regular item on the Committee's agenda. Resolution of outstanding issues, such as decisions on quotas or on allocations of SDRs, frequently awaited the Interim Committee at Annual Meeting time. The Executive Board resumed discussion of outstanding issues promptly after the Annual Meeting, after receiving the views or decisions of the Board of Governors and the advice of the Interim Committee.

Although Annual Meetings were becoming more important, high-ranking financial officials were assembling two or three days ahead of the opening plenary session of the full Board of Governors to attend meetings of various committees and groups. Since many could not be away from their home capitals for seven or eight days, some left before the closing session of the Annual Meeting. This situation was embarrassing. Governors especially from the largest members pressed to be allowed to give their speeches in the first day or two, while Governors from smaller members, giving their speeches later in the week, often spoke to a greatly reduced audience. Starting in 1978, the regular Annual Meeting was therefore shortened from five to four days.

CHAPTER
51

Policymaking at Headquarters:
The Executive Board

*A*T THE FUND'S HEADQUARTERS two groups are in full-time residence: the Board of Executive Directors, their Alternates, Advisors, and Technical Assistants, and the Managing Director, the Deputy Managing Director, and the staff. The Executive Board does the preparatory work for the Board of Governors, takes general policy decisions without referring to the Board of Governors, and takes almost all the decisions relating to individual members. In short, the Executive Board does the bulk of the Fund's decision making.

The Executive Board, in turn, depends on the Managing Director in his capacity as Chairman of the Executive Board for information, proposals, direction, and assistance in reaching decisions. How the Managing Director performs these tasks is pivotal in the Fund's decision-making process.

The Managing Director is assisted by an international staff, which obtains, analyzes, and evaluates the information needed for determining policies, helps to formulate and to draft whatever proposals the Managing Director wants to put forward to the Executive Board, and implements the decisions taken by the Executive Board.

In the years 1972–78 as the Fund's activities and responsibilities changed, as changes took place in the relative economic and political power of different countries, and as new personalities came on the scene, important developments took place in the relations among the Executive Board and the Managing Director and staff. This chapter describes the functions and working methods of the Executive Board, noting especially the changes taking place in 1972–78. Chapter 52 provides the same type of coverage with regard to the Managing Director, the Deputy Managing Director, and the staff.

IMPORTANCE OF THE BOARD OF EXECUTIVE DIRECTORS

As it always had, so in 1972–78 the Executive Board continued as principal policymaking body at Fund headquarters. Pierre-Paul Schweitzer in his farewell

983

remarks to the Executive Board in August 1973 noted that when he addressed new staff members at the end of their orientation program, he usually reminded them that "the Fund is comprised of three parts: the Executive Directors, the staff, and the management. Then I tell them what the order of importance of these three parts is, and I tell them: First comes the Executive Directors; secondly comes the Executive Directors; thirdly comes the Executive Directors."

It is through the Executive Directors that member governments run the Fund. All general policies of the Fund and all actions with respect to individual members are discussed at length and decided by the Executive Board. Policies are called "Fund" policies only after they have been agreed by the Executive Board; Fund decisions are decisions of the Executive Board. The Executive Board, moreover, discusses and decides on the Fund's administrative budget in detail and takes decisions relating to the Fund's day-to-day work, including the review of changes in the senior staff. The approval of the Executive Directors, either by the Executive Board as a whole or by the Executive Director appointed or elected by the member concerned, is required even for matters that seem on the surface relatively minor, such as filling a member's request for technical assistance by the staff, filling a request of an international organization for a copy of a Fund report on a given member, and official travel by the staff to a member. None of these decisions is pro forma or to be taken for granted.

EXECUTIVE BOARD MEETINGS

The importance of the Executive Board is demonstrated most concretely by the activity within the Fund that centers around meetings of the Executive Board. The Executive Board meets regularly on Monday and Wednesday mornings, to allow those Executive Directors who serve on both Executive Boards to attend World Bank meetings on Tuesdays and Thursdays. When necessary—and it was often necessary in the years reviewed here—additional meetings of the Executive Board are held in the afternoons and on Fridays, often both in the morning and afternoon, and occasionally on Tuesdays and Thursdays. When business demands it, Executive Board meetings are also held on holidays, on weekends, and in the evenings. Because the Executive Board is required by the Articles (Article XII, Section 3(g)) to be in continuous session, it is always on call.

Statistics of the number of Executive Board meetings held and the hours involved in these meetings are a simple although incomplete measure of the workload. In 1975, for example, the Executive Board, faced with many new tasks including drafting the Second Amendment, met more times than ever before. There were 208 formal Executive Board meetings. There were also 11 informal sessions and meetings of the Committee of the Whole and 4 consultations on currency budgets in which the entire Executive Board participated. The accumulated time involved was 495.5 hours, an average of about 10 hours a week. Some 175 hours were devoted only to the draft Second Amendment. Another 40 hours were devoted to the Trust

Fund and related topics, 29 hours to the oil facility, over 20 hours to the Sixth General Review of Quotas, 15 hours to the buffer stock and compensatory financing facilities, and 14 hours to the world economic outlook exercise. Another 100 hours were devoted to regular consultations or considering requests for use of the Fund's resources.

Again in 1978, when the Executive Board was especially busy taking the decisions needed to retool the Fund after the Second Amendment went into effect, the Executive Directors held over 200 formal meetings (an average of 4 a week) and the accumulated time involved was nearly 500 hours for the year (again an average of 10 hours a week).

How Conducted

The formal meetings of the Executive Board are always conducted according to a specific agenda known to the Executive Directors in advance so that they can prepare for the meetings. Their willingness to discuss items on the agenda at the meeting is ascertained in advance. Not infrequently discussion of an item is postponed at the request of an Executive Director. Executive Directors also have the power to request a topic to be placed on the agenda.

After 1977, when the Executive Board's agenda became particularly crowded, systematic work programming was initiated. Three or four times a year forecasts of the Executive Board's schedule of work, together with a tentative schedule of Executive Board meetings are prepared by the staff and discussed by the Executive Board. Periodic review by the Executive Directors of their future work load facilitates the determination of topics to be given priority and the completion of Executive Board discussions of these topics within an appropriate time. Despite the preparation and review of these work programs, the heavy work load of the Executive Board makes occasional bunching of major items on the agenda unavoidable and repeatedly forces postponement of discussion of less urgent items. While Executive Board activity is particularly intense just before meetings of the Interim Committee and the Annual Meeting and when deadlines have to be met, periods of relatively low activity are infrequent and brief.

For each item on the agenda, papers analyzing the subject and usually containing recommendations are prepared by the staff, approved by the Managing Director, and circulated to the Executive Directors. Papers are generally submitted to the Executive Board as staff memoranda (designated by the initials SM) rather than as memoranda from the Managing Director, even though in many instances they contain specific policy proposals or draft decisions for adoption by the Executive Board. The rationale for this procedure is that it gives the Managing Director, in his capacity as Chairman of the Executive Board, more freedom and flexibility to search with the Executive Board for acceptable compromises.

Papers are usually circulated well in advance of the Executive Board meeting so as to give Executive Directors sufficient time to study the documentation as well as an opportunity to seek comments or instructions from officials of the members in their constituencies and to exchange views informally with other Executive Directors, the Managing Director, and staff. In fact, the insistent urging by Executive Directors that they have staff papers "well" in advance of the Executive Board meeting has gradually led to rigid rules governing the time prior to the Board meeting that the staff paper has to be circulated. For many years, the management's practice was to send papers to the Executive Directors on a flexible basis, doing its best to give the Executive Directors as much time as possible. By 1978, it had become an informal maxim that papers on all general Fund policies, on all substantive issues, and on all major members be distributed at least two weeks prior to the scheduled Executive Board meeting. But as topics were becoming more complex, as interest in decisions on international monetary subjects was increasing, as the length of staff papers was expanding, as the number of members in Executive Directors' constituencies was growing, and as the postal system in many countries was too slow, Executive Directors were complaining that even two weeks were insufficient.

Executive Directors want extra time mainly to ascertain the positions of officials of the members in their constituencies. After they have learned these positions, they also want time to consult informally with each other and with the Fund management. Informal consultation among Executive Directors before Executive Board meetings has gradually become an intrinsic part of the Fund's working methods. At times Executive Directors of certain groups of members, such as the Executive Directors of the countries in the EC or of the G-9 caucus, get together informally in advance of an Executive Board meeting.

The Managing Director and senior staff are also available for informal talks with Executive Directors prior to the consideration of an item. The Managing Director frequently meets informally with Executive Directors to seek their views on confidential or sensitive matters. That the members of the Executive Board meet informally in each other's offices and also have opportunities to talk with each other, with the Managing Director and the Deputy Managing Director, and with the senior staff in the corridors and in the dining room, makes for a great deal of informal exchange prior to the formal Executive Board meeting.

Since about 1968 an Executive Director often circulates a written statement a day or two in advance of the Executive Board meeting, particularly when a member in his constituency is being discussed. When the budget or the Executive Board's work program or other topics of general interest are being discussed, the Managing Director also circulates a prepared statement in advance. These statements enable Executive Directors to prepare their own remarks in advance of the meeting. The prepared statement is incorporated in the record without the need for the Executive Director or the Managing Director to repeat it at the Board meeting, thereby shortening discussion at the Executive Board meeting.

As noted earlier, the Managing Director is both Managing Director and Chairman of the Executive Board. He, or in his absence, the Deputy Managing Director, chairs Executive Board meetings. The Managing Director usually makes certain that either he or the Deputy Managing Director is available to serve as Chairman of the Executive Board. In exceptional circumstances when someone else must act as Chairman, the Executive Directors choose an Executive Director. The Managing Director or Deputy Managing Director chooses a senior member of the staff as their *locum tenens* for all other purposes.

An Executive Director usually ensures that either he, or his Alternate, or a person designated well in advance as a certified Temporary Alternate Executive Director, is available to attend every Executive Board meeting. No seats around the Executive Board table are vacant. Executive Directors are seated according to the alphabetical order of their surnames. Seating is changed on November 1 of even-numbered calendar years, following the biennial election of Executive Directors, when a new Executive Board takes office.

In addition to the Executive Directors and their Alternates, the Advisors and Technical Assistants who are part of the office of each Executive Director usually attend Executive Board meetings. However, only those around the table, one for each constituency, speak. An Executive Director can speak only for himself, never for a group of Executive Directors. As Chairman, the Managing Director or Acting Managing Director sits at the head of the table. He is flanked on one side by the Deputy Managing Director, who also normally attends Executive Board meetings, and on the other side by the Secretary, who is responsible for coordinating the work program of the staff and of the Executive Board. One or two staff members responsible for the work on a particular country item or on a general topic also sit at the table. They usually explain or defend the staff position and answer specific questions raised by the Executive Directors. Senior staff from the Exchange and Trade Relations Department, the Legal Department, the Research Department, the Treasurer's Department, and from some of the other departments are also customarily present in the Executive Board room in order to answer any questions relating to Fund policy, law, financial operations, or research that might come up and to learn of the positions being expressed by the Executive Directors. Attendance by staff at Executive Board meetings is controlled, however. Usually, the Executive Directors speak first as they are called upon by the Chairman, and the staff answers questions and explains the staff's position toward the end of the discussion of an item.

To emphasize the distinct responsibilities of the staff and the Executive Board, Executive Directors are not entitled to correct, or to request redrafting of, the text of staff papers on country matters, even if the text or draft paper applies to a member whose Executive Director has a different view. Executive Directors can—and often do—express their agreement or disagreement with staff papers in whole or in part at Board meetings, and their comments and views are fully reflected in the minutes of the meetings. Frequently, the Executive Board requests the staff to redraft general policy papers and to put forward revised proposals.

At Executive Board meetings there are comprehensive discussions of the details and mechanics of all the Fund's policies and activities as well as of the major issues involved, many of which are complicated and technical. The Executive Directors take an active part in working out the complications of the Fund's policies; it is not only the management and staff that are involved in the details.

Extraordinarily full, but deliberately not verbatim, minutes of Executive Board meetings are prepared by the staff. The Rules and Regulations (Rules C-14 and C-15 as adopted on September 25, 1946 and amended on April 1, 1978) provide for the preparation of a "summary record" of the proceedings of the Executive Board and for the keeping of verbatim records in the archives of the Fund only if the Chairman or an Executive Director so requests. Verbatim records may also be kept to assist the Secretary to prepare the summary record of a meeting of the Executive Board, provided that these verbatim records are destroyed after a reasonable time.[1] The purpose of not normally having verbatim minutes is to give Executive Directors some flexibility later to clarify what are called their interventions.

Minutes of Executive Board meetings are comprehensive, often 40 or more pages of single-spaced typescript. Once the minutes are prepared, a "preliminary draft minute" is circulated for comment, and those members of the Executive Board who spoke at the meeting are given an opportunity to refine or amend their recorded statement. The completed "draft minute" is distributed to Executive Directors and approved on a lapse-of-time basis, a procedure by which an item is deemed approved unless an Executive Director objects within a specified time. This lapse-of-time procedure is used frequently for routine items requiring Executive Board approval if the Fund management and staff are reasonably certain that no Executive Director is likely to be opposed. The minutes of Executive Board meetings receive very limited distribution even within the Fund and remain confidential indefinitely. These minutes are a major source of information, used, for example, in the preparation of these Histories of the Fund and in the development of the Fund's policies and of its law and practice.

Decision by Consensus

The cardinal rule governing the Executive Board's work methods, written into the Fund's Rules and Regulations as Rule C-10, is that the Chairman is ordinarily to ascertain the "sense of the meeting" rather than to call for a formal vote. Although each Executive Director has the right to call for a vote on any issue, formal votes are rarely taken. In the years 1972–78, for instance, formal votes were taken on only three occasions, all in October 1978 and all to do with staff salaries. In all the years from the beginning of the Fund's operations in 1946 to the end of 1978, there were only 34 formal votes taken (apart from voting on the Fund's schedule of charges required by the Articles). Avoidance of formal voting in the Executive Board has become a policy to which all Fund officials subscribe. By the 1970s it had become almost impolite for an Executive Director to call for a formal vote.

The sense of the meeting is defined as "a position supported by Executive

---

[1]The Rules are reproduced in Vol. III below, pp. 457–81.

Directors having sufficient votes to carry the question were a vote to be taken." In other words, as he determines the sense of the meeting, the Chairman, without commenting, informally notes the voting power of the Executive Directors holding differing positions.

In their desire to reach decisions by virtually full agreement, a broader concept than sense of the meeting, the Executive Directors make a painstaking effort to find common ground. They are not limited in time in expressing their positions, reservations, and questions, and the Chairman normally defers ascertaining the sense of the meeting until all who wish to speak have had a chance to do so. Often Executive Directors speak a second or third time in response to the arguments or positions of other Executive Directors. In practice, this procedure means that all the Executive Directors around the table usually speak. Decision making by consensus thus tends to enlarge the number of speakers and to increase the length and frequency of interventions.

In the years reviewed here, at the end of the Executive Board's discussion of an item on the agenda, the Chairman began to present a summing up, which is a statement of the consensus as seen by the Chairman. Initially, in 1974 and 1975, this summing up was a very brief statement, but after Mr. de Larosière became Managing Director, it gradually became a fuller and more detailed statement on the sense of the meeting. Executive Directors have an opportunity to comment on the oral summing up, and their comments are reflected in the written summing up and incorporated in the minutes of the Executive Board meetings. Summing up received an even more formal role in 1978, after the Second Amendment was introduced. The Executive Board decided that its conclusions to the consultations with members under Article IV would take the form of a summing up by the Chairman.

Another work method of the Executive Board that facilitates the attainment of consensus is the use in decisions of the review clause started in the 1970s. In the instances of the oil facility, the liberalization of the compensatory financing facility, and the extended facility, the Executive Board included in its decision a clause to the effect that the decision was to be reviewed at a later date. Such clauses are included in decisions in which the Executive Directors are breaking new ground and wish to examine their actions after gaining some experience. On many occasions, including in decisions a clause for a later review is an important element in getting Executive Directors to agree. The Executive Board can, in addition, at any time initiate a review of any aspect of existing Fund policy, whether or not the particular decision contains a mandatory review clause. In fact, in the years 1972–78 the Executive Board did review certain broad policy decisions of the Fund, particularly with respect to use of the Fund's resources.

Other Working Methods

Final decisions of the Executive Board are drafted with great care. Words that might adversely affect the prestige or domestic affairs of a member are avoided. Recommendations for action are couched in phrases that carefully reflect the limits of the Fund's authority. Efforts are made to incorporate the points of view of as many Executive Directors as possible, consistent with a meaningful decision. Once the decision is taken, it becomes the decision of the Executive Board as a whole. No publicity is given to the dissenting view of individual Executive Directors.

A procedure of informal sessions of the Executive Board and seminars of the Executive Directors has been developed in the belief that the Executive Board can have a more useful and stimulating exchange of view on topics in a preliminary stage or in need of exploring if the Executive Directors meet in a setting more relaxed than formal Executive Board meetings. In informal sessions or seminars, Executive Directors are more likely to exchange views that they have gained from their own professional knowledge and experience and less likely to advance the positions of member governments. At the same time, because Executive Directors understand and usually sympathize with the positions of the members' governments in their constituencies, the differing views of member governments do come out in the course of the discussion. Informal sessions of the Executive Directors thus serve to acquaint the Executive Directors with the range of views held by their colleagues on the subject at hand. In addition, informal sessions of the Executive Directors provide the management and staff with a way to learn informally of the views of Executive Directors on the subject. The management and staff can then decide how to proceed in drafting a policy proposal for the Executive Board to consider formally. Records of informal sessions are prepared but do not receive formal Executive Board approval.

Decision making by the Executive Board is also aided by the use of a few standing committees. There is, for example, a committee on Executive Board administrative matters, and ad hoc Executive Board committees, such as on the terms of membership for applicant countries or on regulations for the conduct of the biennial election of Executive Directors, are established whenever the need arises. The function of these ad hoc committees is to consider specific matters and to make reports and recommendations to the Executive Board as a whole. The Chairman selects the membership of all committees, but because Executive Directors do not want positions on important issues to be developed in a body in which they have no opportunity to express a view, all Executive Directors are permitted to attend committee meetings and to participate in the discussions.

EXECUTIVE DIRECTORS' ACCESS TO CONFIDENTIAL INFORMATION

A salient advance in the Fund's policymaking after the mid-1950s has been the Executive Board's willingness to have the Managing Director be the main or sole recipient of special confidential information from a member, if the member so wishes. It had gradually become accepted that officials of member governments might informally raise Fund-related topics with the Managing Director, directly or indirectly (by, for example, raising topics with the staff when a staff mission is in the country concerned), and that these subjects could be treated confidentially, that is, without the need for the Managing Director to divulge the details to Executive Directors, either in written reports or orally, unless the member itself gives a waiver permitting release of the information. In the same way, it had gradually become accepted that the Managing Director—or staff acting on his behalf—could take the initiative in raising Fund-related matters with officials of members. By the 1970s, in fact, the Managing Director was at times explicitly directed by the Executive Board to get in touch personally with officials of members.

Acceptance of the fact that officials of members might reveal to the Managing Director information that they did not want to have revealed to governments around the world through the Fund's Executive Board was a significant evolution in the relations between the Executive Board and the Managing Director. Nothing had been mentioned in the original Articles of Agreement or in the Rules and Regulations about the provision of information by members on a confidential basis.

Inevitably, the question of access of the Executive Directors to such information would arise, and it did very soon, in March 1947, the second year in which the Fund was operating. At that time the position of Executive Directors on confidential information, including the position of an Executive Director appointed or elected by the member itself that had supplied the information, was clarified. The interpretation of the Articles of Agreement was that an Executive Director had no special legal privileges in relation to the members in his constituency; all Executive Directors had the same rights in relation to all members of the Fund. Specifically, nothing in the Articles of Agreement bound an Executive Director to act on the instructions given to him by a member in his constituency or even to take the guidance of the members that had elected him. In this sense, an Executive Director was not a representative of the members in his constituency and therefore he was not necessarily entitled to have copies of all documents relating to the members in his constituency. By the same interpretation, once he had been elected as an Executive Director by a member, the Executive Director could not be removed from office by the member, as might be desired when the member underwent a change in government. The decision taken in March 1947 by the Executive Board, while in effect giving no special rights to an Executive Director appointed or elected by the member supplying confidential information, nonetheless specified that every member of the Executive Board was entitled to request and receive all the information in the possession of the Fund. An exception was made for information on par values communicated by a member to the Managing Director under a request for secrecy.

Subsequently, if it was necessary for the Managing Director or staff to disclose confidential information to the Executive Directors, in general, or to an individual Executive Director, or group of Executive Directors, it became the Fund's usual practice to seek the consent of the member concerned. As time went on, the Executive Board adopted several decisions recognizing the confidential character of certain information. In 1970, for instance, the Executive Board adopted a decision about information to be given to the Executive Directors regarding transactions in SDRs. At the time, these transactions were just beginning and there was some objection to revealing what transactions were taking place. In essence, the Executive Directors agreed not to receive information that would reveal to other participants using SDRs the particular participants designated in each transaction to provide currency.[2] In November 1973, the Managing Director was directed by the Executive Board to initiate special consultations with several members that had floating rates, and Executive Directors chose not to receive confidential information obtained in the course of these consultations. In the decision of June 1974 on the guidelines for the management of floating exchange rates, Executive Directors agreed that there could be confidential interchange between the member and "the Fund," that is, without the information being given to the Executive Board. A similar statement about confidentiality with the member was included in the decision on exchange rate surveillance of April 1977.

The major theme running through these Executive Board decisions was that such treatment of confidential information would enable the Fund to promote its purposes and exercise its powers more effectively. A minor theme was that the information, or conclusions based upon it, would often be provided to the Executive Board in some circumspect form.

In sum, Executive Directors had over the years come to accept a method of working in the Fund in which officials of member governments gave special information to the Managing Director, or to the staff, on the assurance that this information would not be passed along to the full membership through the Executive Board. Executive Directors themselves recognized that members did not want all information that they might provide to the Fund distributed to other member governments. They recognized also that there had been occasional embarrassing leaks to the press of confidential information that could have come from members of the Executive Board themselves. Thus, through experience, Executive Directors had come to realize that confining certain information to the management and staff made officials of members less reluctant to speak frankly with the Managing Director and staff and enabled the Fund to work more closely and effectively with individual members.

The Managing Directors and many of the senior staff were personally acquainted with many of the financial officials of member governments and had developed considerable experience and expertise. Hence, confidential discussions between officials and Fund management and staff were not unusual, especially in negotiations for use of the Fund's resources. To an increasing extent, officials sought the advice of the Managing Director and the staff not only on matters directly related to the Fund, but also on their national monetary and financial policies. Occasionally officials even sought the views of the Fund's management and staff as a way to strengthen their own domestic political positions. In order to head off foreseeable problems in individual members, the Managing Director and the staff often took the initiative in proposing to members the holding of informal and confidential talks with the general knowledge and implicit consent of the Executive Directors. In fact,

---

[2]See *History, 1966–71,* Vol. I, p. 233.

by 1978 the Managing Director was being asked by the Executive Board to suggest informally to officials of members with potential balance of payments difficulties that they come to the Fund for financial assistance before their difficulties became unmanageable.

Procedures Questioned

The issue of the treatment of confidential information came to the fore again in 1976 and 1977, for the first time in 30 years. The issue was raised by Muhammad Al-Atrash (Syria) in 1977 and 1978, on two occasions, each concerning a request of a member in his constituency for technical assistance by the Fund staff. In the first case, Mr. Al-Atrash asked that any information transmitted by the staff in the course of technical assistance be subject to the same procedure followed for transmitting recent economic developments (RED) reports on members to other international organizations. Under that procedure, the Executive Director elected or appointed by the member was first consulted so as to ensure that the member concerned had no objection to release of the report.

In the opinion of the Managing Director, Mr. Al-Atrash's proposal raised an important question of principle. The proposal would make technical assistance supplied by the staff to members subject to the same restricted procedure used for transmitting staff-prepared RED reports to other international agencies. Mr. Witteveen held that there was a critical difference between the release of RED reports to other international agencies and the technical assistance provided by the staff pursuant to specific requests by members or, on occasion, pursuant to requests by organizations to which some of the members of the Fund belonged. Once the request for technical assistance had been approved by the Executive Directors, it had not been the management's practice to clear with individual Executive Directors the information or advice given by the staff to the members or organizations that had requested the technical assistance. Moreover, the views expressed by the staff in providing technical assistance to a member were not normally presented as the views of the Fund as an organization; rather, they were presented as the expert views of the staff member who rendered the assistance or, on occasion, of the outside specialist recruited and retained by the Fund for the assignment.

In the light of these considerations, the Managing Director advised the Executive Board not to accept Mr. Al-Atrash's proposal. In his view, to agree to Mr. Al-Atrash's request for formal clearance would substantially alter the Fund's existing procedures. However, he pointed out that he would have no difficulty with an understanding that the Executive Director elected by the member requesting the technical assistance should receive the information and advice given by the staff before they were transmitted and that he would have an opportunity to offer comments to the staff.

When the Executive Directors discussed this topic, the majority preferred a solution that left the Fund's existing procedures intact. They believed that it would be an unfortunate precedent if the Executive Board were to decide that the staff could express only views cleared by the Executive Director appointed or elected by the member concerned. Hence, a solution was worked out in which Mr. Al-Atrash would have an opportunity to express views on the staff's information before it was transmitted, but in which he would not be able to delay or block unduly the transmittal of the information.

The second occasion arose in 1978 when another member in Mr. Al-Atrash's constituency requested technical assistance. The issue of whether the technical assistance provided by the staff should first be cleared with the Executive Director was of prime importance to the Managing Director and the staff. They felt strongly that the confidentiality of relations between member governments and the Fund management and staff, so fundamental to the successful operations of the Fund, could be impaired. They feared that were a member government to believe that any information provided to the Fund would be made available to governments around the world, there would be a devastating effect on the future of the Fund. If Executive Directors were to direct the Managing Director in conducting the ordinary business of the Fund, the Fund could become a minor institution, with no effective relations with member governments. Ivar Rooth, the second Managing Director, had pointed out in his closing address to the Executive Board in 1956 that the failure of the Fund to achieve as much as it might have in its first decade lay in the difficult area of the respective responsibilities of Executive Directors and staff. Mr. Rooth had emphasized, as had Camille Gutt, his predecessor, the desirability of entrusting to the management and staff the application of the Fund's policies and the day-to-day administration of its activities.[3] In the subsequent 22 years the Fund had made much progress in giving the Managing Director more authority.

After deliberation, the Executive Board reached a consensus to the effect that the previous Executive Board decisions on this subject, including the decision of March 1947, and the long-standing practices of the Executive Board would continue to prevail. In short, the Executive Board decided that the Managing Director and the staff would continue to have considerable freedom with respect to confidential information.

At the same time, measures were taken to correct shortcomings that might develop as a result of existing practices. Reports prepared by the staff, including reports prepared by technical assistance missions, would be made available to the Executive Director unless the government in his constituency specifically requested that such reports be withheld. Staff members were asked to make certain that they understood the intentions of a government that requested confidentiality and to indicate to those governments that it was not desirable to withhold information from an Executive Director unless doing so was absolutely essential. The Managing Director was to hold informal discussions with all the Executive Directors more regularly than in the past to keep them apprised as far as possible of the progress of negotiations with member governments. Since Mr. Witteveen was leaving the Fund,

---

[3]*History, 1945–65*, Vol. I, pp. 297–98 and 423–25.

he agreed to urge his successor to keep Executive Directors regularly informed. In addition, as a kind of court of higher appeal, a committee was to be established to settle any ad hoc conflicts concerning access to information that the Managing Director was unable to resolve. The committee was to consist of the Managing Director as Chairman, the dean of the Executive Board (the one with the longest service on the Board), and one other Executive Director.

As of the end of 1978, there had been no occasion to use this committee.

PROCEDURES OF EXECUTIVE BOARD MEETINGS REAFFIRMED

During the years 1972–78, the Executive Directors also discussed the procedures to be followed at their meetings, particularly the precise order in which amendments and motions of Executive Directors should be considered. In the past, the Executive Directors had avoided making their procedures too formal so that all could express their views fully and frankly and be more able to reach a consensus.

In the period reviewed here, Jahangir Amuzegar (Iran) as well as Mr. Al-Atrash raised questions concerning the long-standing way in which Executive Board meetings were conducted and requested that the Executive Board discuss its procedures. As a result of this discussion, the Executive Board, in 1975, decided on certain guidelines. These guidelines stated that questions of procedure had priority over discussion of substantive matters and that if there was more than one proposal before the Executive Board, proposals were to be considered one at a time and in the order in which they were submitted. The guidelines also defined an amendment to a proposal and specified the order in which amendments were to be considered.

In 1977 another discussion of procedures centered around Rule C-10 of the Fund's Rules and Regulations that stated that the Chairman should ordinarily try to ascertain the sense of the meeting instead of submitting the item to a formal vote but that any Executive Director might require a formal vote. The question raised concerned the procedure to be followed if an Executive Director called for a vote *after* the Chairman had presented his understanding of the sense of the meeting on an item on the agenda.

Nearly all Executive Directors took the position that the Executive Board should continue to operate informally and with the assurance that Executive Directors would continue to treat each other fairly and reasonably. No special procedure for voting in these circumstances was necessary or desirable. While no Executive Director should be deprived of his right to request a formal vote, the Fund's success had rested in part on the ability of the Executive Board to reach a consensus on most issues. The Executive Board's tradition of conducting its business with the maximum informality consistent with orderly procedures and with the minimum of formal voting should be preserved.

These discussions revealed that the Executive Directors were clearly unwilling to formalize their procedures. This became particularly evident in late 1978 when the staff was drafting the revised Rules and Regulations to implement the amended

Articles of Agreement. At that time, the staff drafted into the proposed rules regarding the Executive Board's procedure some of the details of the procedural guidelines and the procedures to be followed for voting in relation to the sense of the meeting that had come out of the Executive Board discussions in 1976 and 1977. Inasmuch as the Executive Board had agreed on these procedural matters, the staff thought that it would be desirable to incorporate these rules into the formal Rules and Regulations. The Executive Directors did not do so, however. They preferred to leave their procedures flexible as they had traditionally been.

AN EFFECTIVE BODY

A number of factors explain why the Fund's Executive Board has become an effective body in Fund policymaking. The working methods and procedures described earlier in this chapter have surely helped. In addition, even in the context of a frequently changing composition of the Executive Board, Executive Directors have learned how to work together. They usually respect each other's points of view and the instructions each receives from the members in his constituency and realize that, in the interest of continuing to be able to work together, it is often preferable to retreat from positions that other Directors consider to be extreme.

The Executive Directors consider carefully the subjects on which they are asked to take decisions and try hard to find compromises, adapting both the substance and the language of their decisions to obtain a decision that all can support, or at least not object to. As might be expected, decisions are often weaker than officials of some members or the Managing Director might wish. Any compromises made usually show. Some decisions contain only the minimal features that can be agreed upon. Often the Managing Director has to wait to advance a proposal until it seems likely that the Executive Directors can reach a decision. These procedures are, however, unavoidable in deciding on topics in which member governments have strong and possibly conflicting vested interests.

Probably the overriding factor explaining the effectiveness of the Fund's Executive Board is that the Executive Directors confine their efforts to the specialized area of the Fund's limited jurisdiction. In their discussions and decisions, they continuously regard themselves as guided by the six purposes stated in the Fund's Articles. They concentrate on ways to promote international monetary cooperation, to facilitate the expansion and balanced growth of international trade, to promote exchange stability, to eliminate restrictions on payments, to help members in balance of payments difficulties by providing some of the Fund's financial resources, and to shorten the duration and lessen the degree of balance of payments disequilibrium. More particularly, Executive Directors are guided by judging whether the proposals at hand best enable the Fund's members to obtain sustainable external payments positions that are also compatible with full employment, economic growth, and the most productive use of resources and with exchange stability and freedom from restrictions on payments. This specialized area of concern gives their discussions a very specific focus and provides clear direction for their decisions.

Moreover, in recent years, Executive Directors have had to be careful guardians of the Fund's resources and monitors of members' exchange and payments policies. A common responsibility for disposal of the Fund's money and for ensuring that any member's exchange and payments policies do not damage the interests of any other member or of the membership at large has provided a great inducement to work together.

THE EXECUTIVE BOARD OF THE MID-1970s

The Executive Board is a continuously changing body that nevertheless has the advantage of some continuity of individual Executive Directors. From March 1949 to December 1978, the United States appointed only three Executive Directors, and the first two, Frank A. Southard, Jr. and William B. Dale, left office only because they were elevated to the position of Deputy Managing Director; the third, Sam Y. Cross, who joined the Board in April 1974, was still Executive Director as 1978 ended. Several Executive Directors are also re-elected time and again, so that they, too, have many years of continuous service.

Two elected Executive Directors who retired in the 1970s had each served for about two decades. André van Campenhout (Belgium), who retired from the Board at the end of October 1973, had been an elected Executive Director for nearly 19 years. Pieter Lieftinck (Netherlands), who retired at the end of 1976, had been on the Board for over 21 years. Both were regarded as elder statesmen of the Executive Board, and each in turn was "dean." On the dean of the Executive Board falls certain functions, such as addressing the Board when a formal occasion calls for a spokesman of the Executive Board. (The dean never speaks for the Executive Directors on policy matters.)

As of the end of 1978, other elected Executive Directors, and some of the Alternate Executive Directors, also had many years of continuous service. Two of the Executive Directors had been on the Board for 10 years or longer—Alexandre Kafka (Brazil), who joined the Board in November 1966, and Byanti Kharmawan (Indonesia), who joined in November 1968. Mr. Kafka became dean of the Executive Board when Mr. Lieftinck retired. Three Alternate Executive Directors as of the end of 1978 had served in that capacity for 8 years or more—Costa P. Caranicas (Greece), who was first appointed as Alternate Executive Director in 1952, Tom de Vries (Netherlands), who became an Alternate Executive Director in January 1969, and Heinrich G. Schneider (Austria), who became an Alternate Executive Director in December 1970. In addition to Sam Y. Cross (United States), already mentioned, another four Executive Directors had by the end of 1978 served for 4 or more of the 7 years covered in this History: Jahangir Amuzegar (Iran), who joined the Board in August 1973, Jacques de Groote (Belgium), who joined in November 1973, succeeding Mr. van Campenhout, Bernard J. Drabble (Canada), who joined in November 1974, and Eckard Pieske (Federal Republic of Germany), who joined in January 1975. Two other Executive Directors at the end of 1978 had served for more than 3 of the 7 years covered here—R.J. Whitelaw (Australia), who joined the Board in April 1975, and William S. Ryrie (United Kingdom), who joined in October 1975.

Several Executive Directors who had left the Board prior to the end of 1978 also served for from 3 to 5 of the 7 years reviewed here: Jacques Wahl (France) was Executive Director from July 1973 to September 1978, thus serving more than 5 of the 7 years from 1972 to 1978. Antoine W. Yaméogo (Upper Volta), who had come to the Executive Board in November 1966, remained until October 1976, and Nazih Deif (Egypt), who became Executive Director in November 1970, remained until October 1976, so that they both served almost 5 of the 7 years from 1972 to 1978. Francesco Palamenghi-Crispi (Italy), who had come to the Board in December 1967, remained until July 1976, and Kaichi Kawaguchi (Japan) was Executive Director from November 1972 to October 1976, so that they both were Executive Directors for more than 4 years of this 7-year period. Lindsay B. Brand (Australia) was on the Board from December 1970 to April 1975, and P.S.N. Prasad (India) from June 1971 to May 1975, so that their periods of service both spanned more than 3 of the 7 years from 1972 to 1978.

Occasionally, too, Alternate Executive Directors later become Executive Directors, another way in which there is continuity on the Executive Board. In the period 1972–78, Samuel Nana-Sinkam (Cameroon), who became Executive Director in November 1976, had been Alternate Executive Director since October 1972; Mohamed Finaish (Libya), who became Executive Director in November 1978, had been Alternate Executive Director since August 1973. H.R. Monday, Jr. (The Gambia) was first an Alternate Executive Director from November 1972 to October 1974, and then Executive Director from November 1974 to October 1976. Muhammad Al-Atrash (Syria) also served as Alternate Executive Director from December 1970 until January 1973 and then as Executive Director from November 1976 to October 1978.

Several Alternate Executive Directors also spanned at least 3 years of the 1972–78 period. They were Peter J. Bull (United Kingdom), Lore Fuenfgelt (Federal Republic of Germany), Charles R. Harley (United States), Donal Lynch (Ireland), George Reynolds (Ireland), W.M. Tilakaratna (Sri Lanka), and Mikio Wakatsuki (Japan).[4]

The Executive Board also changes in the sense that member countries making up the various constituencies change. An earlier chapter mentioned the addition on November 1, 1978 of an Executive Director appointed by Saudi Arabia. More commonly, changes in constituencies are to accommodate new Fund members in the Executive Board.

The number of "mixed" constituencies has been growing. Several new developing members have become part of the constituencies headed by Executive Directors from industrial members or more developed primary producing members.

---

[4]Appendix A contains a listing of all of the members of the Executive Board for the years 1972–78 and the dates of their service.

For example, at the end of 1978, Mr. Drabble had not only Canada and Ireland in his constituency but also the Bahamas, Barbados, Grenada, and Jamaica. Mr. Whitelaw included in his constituency not only Australia and New Zealand, but also Korea, Papua New Guinea, the Philippines, Seychelles, Solomon Islands, and Western Samoa. As CMEA countries joined the Fund, they were added to existing constituencies. At the end of 1978, H.O. Ruding (Netherlands) not only had Cyprus, Israel, the Netherlands, and Yugoslavia in his constituency, but also Romania.

Countries themselves get together to make their own constituencies in the Fund and to elect Executive Directors. A type of bargaining often goes on in the process. In one of the Latin American groupings, for example, there is an agreement regularly to rotate the country from which the Executive Director comes. In the constituency headed by Australia and in the constituency headed by Indonesia, there is a system of rotation of the Alternate Executive Directors. In the constituencies headed by Belgium and by Canada, it is agreed that the Alternate Executive Director will come from one of the other members in the constituency. The Advisors and Technical Assistants attached to the offices of Executive Directors also often come from members different from the member country of the Executive Director and the Alternate Executive Director.

The development of larger and more mixed constituencies on the Executive Board itself has had the effect of helping Executive Directors achieve a meeting of minds and the taking of decisions that reflect the possibly conflicting interests of the diversified membership of the Fund. By canvassing their own constituencies, the Executive Directors from Australia or from Canada, for example, become well aware of the positions of developing members before they ever reach the Executive Board room to discuss an item on the agenda, and to satisfy their own constituencies, they might have to modify or temper the positions of the countries from which they themselves come.

In the years 1972–78, there were also other changes in members' constituencies. China did not participate in the regular elections of Executive Directors after 1970.[5] Because of political considerations, Egypt did not participate in the regular election of Executive Directors in 1978, when Mr. Finaish of Libya was elected by other members in the Middle East. India had had an appointed Executive Director from the time of the first Executive Board in 1946 until 1972, but on November 1, 1970, Japan replaced India as one of the five members having the largest quotas and therefore qualified to appoint an Executive Director. India, however, was permitted to appoint an Executive Director until the next regular election of Executive Directors in 1972. After November 1, 1972, India formed an elected constituency with Bangladesh and Sri Lanka.

A Strong Board

The Executive Board of the mid-1970s can be regarded as a strong Board. On many occasions the Executive Board took decisions that advanced the Fund into

---

[5]See fn. 6 of Chap. 2.

hitherto uncharted directions. Such decisions as those that introduced new facilities for use of the Fund's resources, such as the oil facility and the extended facility, liberalized the compensatory financing facility, changed the method in which the SDR was valued, provided for auctions of the Fund's gold, and enlarged the Fund's resources by means of two increases in quotas and by borrowing arrangements, all enabled the Fund to adapt to an international monetary system that was rapidly changing, often in wholly unexpected ways. Without such decisions, the Fund would have been left out of current international financial affairs. With such decisions, it played an active role. In addition, the Executive Board of the mid-1970s bore the major responsibility for drafting the comprehensive Second Amendment to the Articles of Agreement. Not only was the precise language worked out in the Executive Board but so were most of the compromises that enabled agreement to be reached. As noted in earlier chapters, Executive Directors themselves put forward concrete proposals. Moreover, in the period reviewed here, the Executive Board assumed considerable responsibility for administrative matters within the Fund, including the controversial subject of staff salaries.

One of the reasons for the Executive Board's powerful role is that the Fund's activities have become ever more complex. The Executive Directors are unique among financial officials in being well versed in the reasoning underlying the Fund's policies and in the intricacies of the Fund's transactions and operations. Officials in home governments cannot possibly take the time to familiarize themselves with the details of the topics considered in the Fund. Executive Directors are in the best position to help find solutions for disputed points.

The meetings of the Interim Committee have added to the work load and functions of the Executive Board. For weeks in advance, Executive Directors hold discussions of the questions at hand and prepare for the members of the Interim Committee brief reports summarizing the main issues yet to be settled. In the interest of leaving to the Interim Committee only questions of a political nature that cannot be resolved in the Executive Board, such as how to redistribute members' relative quotas in the Fund, the Executive Directors often undertake to resolve in the Executive Board differences in the positions of various member governments. The Executive Board is thus the forum in which arduous debate takes place, in which alternative solutions to issues are proposed, discussed, rejected, or accepted, and in which many elements of compromise are worked out. On several occasions in the latter part of the 1970s members of the Interim Committee, unable to reach agreement, referred a controversial issue back to the Executive Board.

CHAPTER

52

Policymaking at Headquarters: The Managing Director and Staff

*L*ONG BEFORE 1972 it had become established that the Managing Director acts as head of the Fund, and is the only spokesman for the institution. Executive Directors cannot speak for the Fund because their positions are usually influenced by the particular interests or positions of the members that have appointed or elected them. Executive Directors owe their allegiance both to the Fund and to the members that appoint or elect them. The Managing Director, as Chairman of the Executive Board, in contrast, has responsibility to the entire Fund membership. Staff members are not permitted to speak on Fund matters or to publish material relating to the Fund except with the express authorization of the Managing Director.

The Managing Director addresses the Board of Governors at Annual Meetings and meets with separate groups of Governors on the occasion of Annual Meetings. The Managing Director attends meetings of financial officials at ministerial level, such as the Group of Ten, or meetings of the governors of central banks at the Bank for International Settlements, Basle. The Managing Director calls press conferences. These functions of the Managing Director are additional to those he performs as Chairman of the Executive Board, as described in Chapter 51.

In filling his role as head of the Fund and as the Fund's spokesman, the Managing Director is responsible to, as well as responsive to, the Executive Board. The views that he expresses on the outside and the public positions that he takes on behalf of the Fund would have already been discussed formally in the Executive Board or informally with the Executive Director or Directors immediately concerned. The Rules and Regulations specify that he is to inform the Executive Board of all official travel by the staff and of any action to appoint or dismiss any person at or above the rank of division chief. Under the terms of his contract, he is to inform the Executive Board of his own official travel.

The Managing Director is in charge of the international staff and closely supervises its work. As a starting point, the Managing Director or the Deputy Managing Director directs the staff on the kinds and extent of information it is to collect and to evaluate. He often helps the staff assess the information. Beyond that the Managing Director or the Deputy Managing Director clears in advance all contacts by the staff with officials of members and the points of view to be expressed by the staff to officials of members. Staff discussions related to consultations with members and staff missions negotiating stand-by arrangements are conducted on the basis of detailed briefing papers that the Managing Director has cleared in advance. Upon return from abroad, staff members report immediately to the Managing Director. The Managing Director or the Deputy Managing Director, acting on his behalf, likewise clears in advance the views to be expressed by staff attending international conferences or meetings of other international organizations. Consequently, staff of the Fund are always acting as representatives of the Fund, under the supervision of the management, and rarely, if ever, act or speak in their own personal capacities.

The centralization of power over the staff's activities in the Office of the Managing Director, combined with the responsibility of the Managing Director to the Executive Board and the existence of a strong Executive Board, enables the Fund to carry out its functions more effectively than under a more decentralized and less controlled arrangement. Officials of member governments are more willing to discuss their vital economic policies with members of the Fund staff and to negotiate changes in these policies precisely because these officials know that the staff is speaking on behalf of the Managing Director and is acting within the directives established by the Executive Board. A side benefit of this method of work is that the Managing Director and the Deputy Managing Director are familiar with many individuals on the staff and with their work. At the same time that there is centralization, the frequent and frank exchanges of views between the management and the staff give a great deal of scope for initiative.

The precise ways in which a Managing Director carries out these responsibilities differ from one Managing Director to another, depending on his style of management. The period covered by this History is very unusual in that in a span of only seven years three persons served as Managing Director.

PIERRE-PAUL SCHWEITZER LEAVES THE FUND

As of January 1, 1972, Pierre-Paul Schweitzer, who had become Managing Director on September 1, 1963, was serving his second five-year term. Prior to August 15, 1971 when the U.S. authorities suspended official convertibility of the dollar, Mr. Schweitzer had behind him eight years of remarkable successes as Managing Director. By greatly widening the Fund's programs for technical assistance and training and by presiding over adaptations of the Fund's policies on use of its resources, he had integrated into the Fund's work and policies the growing number of developing members. The apogee of Mr. Schweitzer's achievements, however, was the creation of the SDR in the Fund. Demonstrating exceptional personal courage and dedicated internationalism, he persuaded financial officials of the ten large industrial members to resolve what they then perceived as a world shortage of liquidity by establishing a truly international reserve asset. This solution had not at all been among their original inclinations.[1]

As the par value system started to disintegrate in the first years of the 1970s, Mr. Schweitzer believed that the Fund's responsibilities made it imperative for the Managing Director to express some public position. Inasmuch as the United States was running large balance of payments deficits and there was great concern about the U.S. dollar, he focused his attention on these deficits and on the dollar. At the Annual Meeting in 1970, in a first reference to asset settlement, a form of convertibility, he spoke about the need for the United States to settle its balance of payments with primary reserve assets. In September 1971, after the U.S. authorities had closed the gold window, he made a television appearance, which was in itself an uncommon event for a Managing Director. In that appearance, a reporter managed to elicit from him a statement to the effect that the United States "ought to make a contribution toward a general realignment of currencies." In effect, Mr. Schweitzer was suggesting that the dollar be devalued. Since both asset settlement and devaluation of the dollar were hotly debated at the time, U.S. officials believed that their negotiating positions with European and Japanese officials had been compromised and reacted adversely to these statements.

Subsequently, early in 1972, when officials began to consider whom they might support for the position of Managing Director of the Fund on the expiration of Mr. Schweitzer's second term in 1973, President Richard M. Nixon, as well as his two successive Secretaries of the Treasury, John B. Connally and George P. Shultz, informally expressed opposition to a reappointment for Mr. Schweitzer. Other factors were also relevant to the decision of financial officials not to support a third term for Mr. Schweitzer. Discussions about reforming the system were just getting under way early in 1972, and financial officials, not only from the United States but from other members as well, were inclined to believe that the timing was appropriate for new leadership in the Fund. The Committee of Twenty was being formed as a new type of policymaking body, reflecting the desire of officials for change in the inner workings of the Fund. Financial officials of several members wanted change in the Fund, including a new Managing Director, partly because they were concerned that under Mr. Schweitzer, the Fund staff, on whom Mr. Schweitzer depended heavily for advice, would dominate the negotiations on international monetary reform. In addition, Mr. Schweitzer had already served for two full five-year terms, the only Managing Director to have done so. Neither Mr. Gutt nor Mr. Rooth was reappointed to a second term. Mr. Jacobsson's first term was extended to his seventieth birthday, but he died in May 1963 before reaching that age. Several financial officials believed that ten years as Managing Director was long enough for anyone.

---

[1] An appreciation of Mr. Schweitzer's achievements through the end of 1971 can be found in *History, 1966–71*, Vol. I, pp. 632–35 and in Margaret G. de Vries, "The Fund under Pierre-Paul Schweitzer," *IMF Survey*, Vol. 2 (June 11, 1973), pp. 161 and 168–71.

To express their esteem for Mr. Schweitzer, the Governors and the other financial officials making up the delegations to the Annual Meeting in September 1972 gave him an unusually prolonged ovation when he stepped to the podium to address them. But shortly thereafter it was apparent that Mr. Schweitzer did not have sufficient support to remain as Managing Director, and in March 1973 he told the Executive Board that his tenure of office would end when his contract expired on August 31, 1973.

Mr. Schweitzer was a man of unusual warmth and charm, well liked by financial officials and by Executive Directors, and held in deep affection by the staff. When he left the Fund building at the end of his last day as Managing Director, on Friday, August 31, 1973, nearly all the staff gathered in the Fund's inner court to say goodbye. In 1983 the French Government awarded him the Grand Cross in the French Legion of Honor, the highest rank in this national order, which was instituted in 1802, to recognize outstanding public service.

H. JOHANNES WITTEVEEN'S YEARS

H. Johannes Witteveen, of the Netherlands, became the Fund's fifth Managing Director on September 1, 1973. Mr. Witteveen, who was then 52 years old, had already had a distinguished career. From 1948 to 1963, he had been a professor of economics at the Rotterdam School of Economics. From 1963 to 1965, he had been Minister of Finance. From 1965 to 1967, he had been in the Dutch Parliament. From 1967 to 1971, he had been both Deputy Prime Minister and Finance Minister. He was to be Managing Director until June 1978. Five of the seven years covered in this History are thus "Witteveen years."[2]

He became Managing Director only three weeks before the Annual Meeting was held in Nairobi and was immediately plunged into the midst of difficult international monetary problems. He was likewise plunged into a situation in which relations between the Fund and the United States, the largest member and one of the two members responsible for creation of the Fund, were seriously disturbed for the first time since the Fund was formed. Mr. Witteveen had not been an active candidate for the position of Managing Director. But Mr. Witteveen was passionately and completely devoted to the causes that he decided to serve, and it was immediately apparent that he was ready to serve the Fund. Thus, from his opening address to the Board of Governors at the Annual Meeting in 1973 to his concluding remarks a few days later, it was clear that Mr. Witteveen was quick to spot troubles in the world economy, eager to find solutions, and prepared to speak out forcefully and candidly to persuade officials to adopt suggested policies. For example, he addressed the then new problem of accelerating inflation. He urged members to make a vigorous cooperative effort to bring inflation under control through national

---

[2]An evaluation of Mr. Witteveen's years in the Fund can be found also in Margaret Garritsen de Vries, "IMF Under H.J. Witteveen: World Economic Cooperation Sustained in Years of Crisis," *IMF Survey*, Vol. 7 (June 19, 1978), pp. 178–83.

economic policies, even suggesting that incomes policy, which was considered controversial, might be used to supplement monetary and fiscal policies. He expressed his preference for management of floating exchange rates, which had come into being only six months before, and for surveillance by the Fund of exchange rate policies under internationally agreed rules and procedures, positions contrary to those favored by U.S. officials at the time.

He soon went further and suggested specific new forms of consultations between the Fund and members to consider their exchange rate policies. Mr. Witteveen's original thinking and activist approach were displayed still more dramatically in January 1974, when, right after the first big jump in oil prices, he initiated and gained support for his proposal for an oil facility in the Fund. He was later to regard the January 1974 meeting of the Committee of Twenty, in Rome, the first which he attended as Managing Director, and the support his ideas received there as giving him one of the happiest, most satisfying moments of his life.

This approach of Mr. Witteveen was to continue for the next four years. The foregoing chapters are replete with examples of his initiatives and innovations—the introduction of special consultations in the context of the review of the world economic outlook, the establishment of an Interim Committee of the Board of Governors, a first and then a second oil facility based on funds borrowed from member governments, a Subsidy Account to accompany the second oil facility so as to reduce the cost of using the facility for specified low-income countries, a three-pronged solution to the heretofore unresolvable gold problem, which included selling some of the Fund's gold at auctions, a supplementary financing facility also based on funds borrowed from member governments, and a strategy for coordinated economic growth to help pull the world economy out of a marked slowdown.

Mr. Witteveen's understanding of the needs of the international monetary system and his initiatives to meet those needs gave the Fund vitality and dynamism at a critical time in its history. Prior to his arrival in September 1973, the Fund had gone through a very discouraging two years. It seemed that the Fund, having lost its functions in regard to exchange rates and the management of international liquidity and, with no agreed new rules for international monetary arrangements in sight, might well recede into the background. There was even some talk that the Fund was no longer needed. However, under Mr. Witteveen's leadership, the Fund quickly developed new functions. By creating new facilities, he greatly increased members' use of the Fund. By introducing new borrowing arrangements, he converted the Fund into a major intermediary in world financial markets. By coming forward with new analyses and statements of world economic problems, he made the Fund a principal forum for deliberations on these problems. By stating his views on the world economy, he helped officials of members, whose views necessarily reflected their national interests, gain a wider perspective and a better understanding of what was in the best interests of the international community. And in putting forward workable proposals to help officials of different members resolve their conflicting positions, he advanced the cause of international monetary cooperation.

His skill as an analyst was matched by his skill as a negotiator. He was an experienced politician and was thus able to negotiate considerable additional money for the Fund. He helped conclude stand-by arrangements with two of the Fund's largest industrial members, Italy and the United Kingdom. He helped bring about many of the compromises needed to complete the Second Amendment. In the interest of the Fund and of the international community generally, he frequently took stands that the financial officials of members were reluctant to hear. For instance, in 1974 and 1975, when officials of European members pressed to be able to buy gold from the Fund in the Fund's gold auctions at prices above the official price—an act that was contrary to the Fund's Articles as they then existed—Mr. Witteveen pointed out that it was unwise for them to set an unfortunate precedent by violating international rules to which they had agreed. European officials, accordingly, had a greater interest in working to amend the Fund's Articles so as to help resolve their own problems about gold.

Intellectually challenged by the pressing problems facing the Fund and the world economy generally, Mr. Witteveen, himself a professional economist, originated many of his own proposals. He was also aware of criticisms being made at the time by some financial officials of the power of the Fund staff. As has been related, the oil facility, for instance, was Mr. Witteveen's own idea, and he was prepared to proceed despite the staff's misgivings. At other times, too, his thinking about economic problems differed from that of the staff. For example, his persistent view that the Eurocurrency market was an important source of international inflation was not accepted by the Research Department.

In order to obtain funds for his proposals for new facilities in the Fund and to gain support for these proposals and for his other suggestions, Mr. Witteveen was away from headquarters, and from meetings of the Executive Board, considerably more often than previous Managing Directors had been. His frequent absences from Headquarters meant that more duties fell to Mr. Dale, the Deputy Managing Director. Some Executive Directors became unhappy about his frequent absences from Executive Board meetings. Particularly awkward was the episode of late in 1976, described in Chapter 24, when Mr. Witteveen went secretly to London in connection with the negotiations with officials of the United Kingdom for a stand-by arrangement. There were also other activities, such as the negotiations with Italian officials for a stand-by arrangement and his efforts to obtain funds for the supplementary financing facility, that Mr. Witteveen felt were best carried out quietly and independently by the Managing Director. Yet some of these negotiations went on for considerable periods, and despite efforts of the Managing Director and the staff to maintain secrecy, press speculation was rampant. The Executive Directors inevitably felt excluded. Mr. Witteveen tried to deal with this problem vis-à-vis the Executive Directors by keeping them informally apprised of the status of the negotiations in which he was involved.

There is no question, however, that Mr. Witteveen's initiatives and his successes in carrying them to fruition enormously increased the Fund's involvement in international monetary affairs. As a consequence, the staff and the Executive Board in the years 1973–78 were busier and more actively concerned with the problems of members and of the world economy generally than they would have been without his initiatives.

Mr. Witteveen left the Fund in 1978 by his own decision. In September 1977, a year before his term expired, to the surprise of financial officials and the Fund staff, he announced that he would not be available for a second five-year term. Certainly he could have received support for another term, particularly as he had greatly improved the Fund's relations with the officials of the United States. Here, of course, Mr. Witteveen was aided by the fact that, after August 1974, there were new Administrations in the United States. Mr. Witteveen undertook some functions at the request of President Ford, and at the 1977 Annual Meeting, President Carter asked Mr. Witteveen whether he would not like to change his mind and remain as Managing Director. But Mr. Witteveen had done what he thought he could to offer solutions to the most pressing problems of the Fund and of the world economy, and his thinking did not run in terms of managerial position or institutional matters. Also, for personal reasons, he wanted to return to the Netherlands.

Because he himself had found it a disadvantage to take up the post of Managing Director just before an Annual Meeting, Mr. Witteveen relinquished his post in June 1978, about two and a half months before the end of his term, to enable his successor to settle in before the 1978 Annual Meeting. One of his main regrets was that he was not able to get a substitution account for gold established in 1975 when the Second Amendment was being drafted. Because he continued to be concerned about the need to control the expansion of international liquidity, he proposed renewed consideration of a substitution account in April 1978. His other main regret was that he was unable to obtain higher salaries for the staff and higher remuneration for the Executive Directors.

After Mr. Witteveen said goodbye to the Executive Board, it unanimously adopted a resolution which referred to his "acumen, devotion and imagination," to the "new courses" he had charted, and to "his intellectual dynamism and tireless search for solutions to the critical problems of his time."

J. DE LAROSIÈRE ARRIVES

J. de Larosière, of France, was unanimously appointed sixth Managing Director and Chairman of the Board of Executive Directors. He took up his duties on June 17, 1978. Mr. de Larosière, then 48 years old, had already had a distinguished career in the French civil service. He had been Director of the French Treasury since 1974. He had been Personal Assistant and Director of the Cabinet Office of Valéry Giscard d'Estaing for a time when the latter was Minister of Economy and Finance. He was well known among financial officials. He had participated in meetings of the Committee of Twenty, of the Interim Committee, and of the Development Committee. He had served on the Economic Policy Committee and the Development

Assistance Committee of the OECD. It was Mr. de Larosière who had worked with Edwin H. Yeo III, when the latter was U.S. Treasury Under Secretary for Monetary Affairs, to obtain an agreed version of an amended Article IV of the Fund's Articles, as noted in Chapter 37. At the time he became Managing Director, Mr. de Larosière was also serving as Chairman of the Deputies of the Group of Ten.

Mr. de Larosière came to the Fund with a mission. Some financial officials, especially in the ten largest industrial countries, were inclined to regard the Fund as a relatively unimportant institution in international monetary affairs. They were inclined to feel that the most crucial decisions were being made by smaller groups of key officials, such as the "Big Five" contacting each other informally, or heads of the seven largest nations at economic summit meetings, or even the private banking community. Mr. de Larosière wanted to change this view of the Fund. He aimed to make the Fund the real centerpiece of international monetary relations and decision making.

At the end of 1978, the cutoff date of this History, Mr. de Larosière had been Managing Director for only six months. Discussion of his period as Managing Director thus has to await later Histories of the Fund. However, even in the first six months in which he held office, Mr. de Larosière proceeded remarkably quickly with the business in progress. Within three months, he had led the Seventh General Review of Quotas and the allocation of SDRs for the third basic period to successful conclusions, and he had prompted a renewed consideration of a substitution account. By the end of 1978, it was also becoming clear that the Fund was entering yet another new era and that Mr. de Larosière would steer the Fund firmly in whatever new directions that might develop.

FRANK A. SOUTHARD, JR. LEAVES THE FUND

Frank A. Southard, Jr., who had been Deputy Managing Director since November 1, 1962, continued in the post until March 1, 1974. (After the expiration of his second five-year term, he had been appointed, effective November 1, 1972, for a four-year term.) Until Mr. Schweitzer left the Fund on August 31, 1973, Mr. Southard continued to be an integral part of a closely knit "Schweitzer-Southard" management team, and early in 1973, after it was known that Mr. Schweitzer would be leaving the Fund, Mr. Southard notified the Executive Board that he wished to retire after the appointment of a new Managing Director, but he stayed on for six months into the term of Mr. Witteveen to help smooth the transition.[3]

---

[3]An appreciation of Mr. Southard's contributions to the Fund as Deputy Managing Director can be found in *History, 1966–71*, Vol. I, pp. 635–36.

WILLIAM B. DALE BECOMES DEPUTY MANAGING DIRECTOR

William B. Dale, who had been the Executive Director appointed by the United States since November 1, 1962, when Mr. Southard became Deputy Managing Director, also succeeded Mr. Southard as Deputy Managing Director. Appointed for a five-year term starting on March 1, 1974, Mr. Dale was still in his first term as Deputy Managing Director at the end of 1978.

Mr. Dale brought to the position of Deputy Managing Director considerable experience. He had served with the U.S. Government in the Department of Commerce and in the Department of the Treasury, and he had worked with a private research corporation. Most important, he had more than a decade of experience on the Executive Board, and was intimately familiar with the Fund's policies, including the controversies and the compromises that had gone into their making. He was well acquainted with the complexities of the Fund's transactions and operations, and knew well the members of the Executive Board and most of the staff.

After 11 years of consultation discussions in the Executive Board, he was well grounded, too, in the economic problems of virtually all of the Fund's members. He had attended, or participated in, many meetings of the highest-ranking financial officials of the Fund's members—most recently meetings of the Committee of Twenty—so that he knew personally the financial officials of most members. All this experience was particularly pertinent to being Deputy Managing Director. Mr. Dale was consequently unusually qualified to assist and advise Mr. Witteveen, a relatively new Managing Director when Mr. Dale was appointed early in 1974, and later to assist and advise Mr. de Larosière when the latter became Managing Director in June 1978. Thus, Mr. Dale, like Mr. Southard before him, provided continuity from one Managing Director to another.

The Deputy Managing Director usually attends all Executive Board meetings even when the Managing Director is in the chair. When the Managing Director is away, the Deputy Managing Director serves as Acting Chairman. In Mr. Witteveen's years as Managing Director, Mr. Dale formed a vital backstop by frequently serving as Acting Chairman of the Executive Board. From March 1, 1974, when he first became Deputy Managing Director, until the end of 1974, Mr. Dale chaired 55 of the 147 meetings of the Executive Board. Subsequently, in the three and a half years from January 1975 until June 16, 1978, when Mr. Witteveen left the Fund, Mr. Dale regularly chaired about one third of the meetings of the Executive Board.

The Deputy Managing Director also assists in the administration of the staff. He plays a major role in planning, with the senior staff, the Fund's administrative budget, the assignments given and the composition of missions sent to member countries, and in seeing final reports through to completion. He usually attends the informal meetings of the Managing Director with members of the staff and with individual Executive Directors and meetings held at headquarters with officials of member governments. Mr. Dale's personal qualities made him unusually valuable in all these capacities, especially in an international organization. He was easily approachable and well liked by both Executive Directors and staff. His helpful role in 1972, as U.S. Executive Director, in enabling the Fund to get out a report on reform at a time when the position of the U.S. Administration was not yet formed has already been noted in Chapter 7.[4]

STAFF: SLOW GROWTH AND INCREASING WORK LOAD

While the staff had numbered about 500 in 1962, there were 1,175 staff members on April 30, 1972. This growth came about in the "Schweitzer-Southard" years. After they took office in 1962 and 1963, Messrs. Schweitzer and Southard substantially reorganized the staff. Following the creation of a new African Department in 1961, they created a number of new departments to provide technical assistance and training primarily to African members—the Central Banking Service, the Fiscal Affairs Department, and the IMF Institute. They also set up a new Bureau of Language Services. They opened a new Fund Office in Geneva. To increase public knowledge of the Fund, they started the publication of *Finance & Development*, Fund Histories, and the *IMF Survey*. Moreover, they gave many new responsibilities to the Treasurer's Department, which had hitherto been a small controller's type of department. They converted the Exchange Restrictions Department into the Exchange and Trade Relations Department and broadened its responsibilities. They asked the staff, particularly the Bureau of Statistics, to engage in more technical assistance. As a result of these new departments and new functions, there was need to add a good deal more staff, especially in the years until 1972.

When Mr. Witteveen and Mr. Dale took over, following the rapid expansion of the previous decade, they made a determined effort to avoid further increases in the staff. Moreover, they did not want to go through another staff reorganization, which might be required if the staff were further increased. In addition, the Fund management has always emphasized the desirability of having "a short chain of

---

[4]Mr. Dale retired at the end of May 1984 after completing his second term as Deputy Managing Director, on which occasion the Executive Board paid him warm tribute for his long and distinguished service and unanimously adopted the following resolution of appreciation:

WHEREAS on May 31, 1984, Mr. William B. Dale is to retire from the International Monetary Fund which he served as Deputy Managing Director since March 1, 1974, after having been Executive Director from November 1, 1962, thus completing more than two decades of service totally dedicated to the Fund; and

WHEREAS Mr. Dale has contributed decisively to the development of Fund policies and practices that permitted the Fund to respond successfully to rapidly changing circumstances in a demanding period that was critical for the maintenance of the goals for which the Fund exists; and

WHEREAS Mr. Dale in carrying the administrative burden of the Deputy Managing Director brought to his dealings with Executive Directors and staff alike invariable helpfulness, innate courtesy, and unequaled experience; and

WHEREAS all of his colleagues during his years in the Fund were fortunate in having had ready recourse to his friendship and wise counsel;

NOW THEREFORE IT IS RESOLVED: That the members of the Executive Board place on record their deep appreciation of Mr. Dale's intellectual and personal qualities, their gratitude for his long and distinguished service, their feeling of loss at his retirement from the Fund and their best wishes for his future.

command." The Managing Director and the Deputy Managing Director can best supervise the staff and yet still encourage staff initiative if they deal directly not only with Directors of Departments and Deputy Directors and Senior Advisors but also with Division Chiefs and with the desk economists who handle the Fund's business with particular member governments. Mr. Witteveen and Mr. Dale firmly believed that keeping the chain of command short required keeping the number of staff relatively small. Still a fourth reason was that they wanted to preserve the Fund as an organization of a relatively small group of specialists. Last, there was the budgetary constraint that developed after the Fund started to run budget deficits in 1971. From 1974 onward budgetary deficits were a factor in the Executive Board's, as well as the management's, desire to avoid staff increases.

In the financial year ended April 30, 1976, in presenting the budget to the Executive Board, the management proposed the smallest annual increase in the staff ceiling since financial year 1961—an increase of only 20 over the previous year. A total of 1,379 staff positions was allowed for, of which 65 were shared with the World Bank in joint activities, such as the Joint Library, the Joint Computer Center, the Annual Meetings Office, and *Finance & Development*. In financial year 1978, mainly to show that there could even be a reduction, the management proposed a net *reduction* of 2 staff positions; the staff ceiling was set at just under 1,400. Thus, there was only a 10 percent increase in the Fund staff in the whole seven-year period from April 30, 1972 to April 30, 1978.

The staff continued to be organized into 14 departments, 2 bureaus, and certain other units in the Office of the Managing Director. The departments were the Administration Department, the African Department, the Asian Department, the Central Banking Service, the European Department, the Exchange and Trade Relations Department, the Fiscal Affairs Department, the IMF Institute, the Legal Department, the Middle Eastern Department, the Research Department, the Secretary's Department, the Treasurer's Department, and the Western Hemisphere Department. The two bureaus were the Bureau of Language Services and the Bureau of Statistics. The units that were part of the Office of the Managing Director in the organizational structure were the European Office in Paris, the Office in Geneva, the Special Representative to the United Nations, the Information Office, the Internal Auditor, and the editor and staff of *Finance & Development*.

Increasing Work Load

The small growth in the size of the staff, combined with the expansion of the Fund's activities, gradually made for a much heavier work load. The activities and responsibilities that the Fund took on in the middle 1970s were superimposed on the traditional ones. Moreover, as the Fund took on additional activities, it made a much greater attempt than it had in the past to include all members, the smallest as well as the largest. The inclusion of as many members as possible is illustrated by the increasing coverage of the world economic outlook exercise. Trying to include all members in any broad activities and reports of the Fund stemmed partly from pressure from the Executive Directors elected by developing members to make sure that the staff paid sufficient attention to the problems of the members in their own constituencies. The trend toward covering as many members as possible in any broad group of activities and reports also added to the staff's work load.

Even in the absence of specific measures of productivity, it was obvious that the work load of virtually every staff member was increasing substantially. Staff members of all five area departments, for example, were covering more member countries and dealing with more requests for use of the Fund's resources, first under the oil facility and then under the compensatory financing facility. They were undertaking more missions for consultation discussions and for negotiations on stand-by arrangements and were providing more technical assistance.

The faster tempo of the use of the Fund's resources also fell heavily on the staff of the Treasurer's Department. These staff members were not only arranging for numerous transfers of currencies to members using the Fund's resources but they were also working on increases in members' quotas and on borrowing arrangements to enlarge the Fund's resources. Staff members of the Treasurer's Department also had the main responsibilities for conducting gold auctions, for handling the new Trust Fund, for operating the new Subsidy Account, and for operating the Fund's SDR mechanism. Indeed, as increased lending and arranging the money for this lending became a much more important part of the Fund's activities, the Treasurer's Department gradually became one of the biggest and most influential departments.

Since the research done in the Fund has always been related to the Fund's policies and operations, the Research Department likewise found itself with additional duties. It was the Research Department, for example, that formed the general policies used in the compensatory financing facility and the buffer stock financing facility. In order to propose these policies, as well as to understand members' payments positions, the Research Department staff was following the developments taking place in the markets for primary commodities, especially for oil and foods. Research Department staff also undertook more studies of inflation and monetary policy and carried out the research needed with regard to the management of international liquidity by, for example, examining developments in world reserves with a view toward ascertaining the need for possible new allocations of SDRs and for the possible establishment of a substitution account in the Fund. Furthermore, the Research Department had primary responsibility for preparing the regular surveys of the world economic outlook and for drafting the economic chapters of the Annual Report.

The additional responsibilities that the Fund took on with regard to members' external indebtedness, international capital markets, the access of developing members to capital markets, and international trade policy much increased the work load of the Exchange and Trade Relations Department. This department also had to handle the Fund's growing informal relations with private commercial banks. Meanwhile, responsibilities of the Exchange and Trade Relations Department with regard to the conduct of consultations, including designing new Article IV consultations, with regard to stand-by arrangements and related stabilization and adjustment programs, including the conditionality associated with use of the Fund's resources, and with regard to members' exchange rate arrangements had also become much more difficult and time consuming.

The Secretary's Department also had increased responsibility. Planning the work program of the Executive Board and coordinating the related work of the staff so that the Executive Board could accomplish its expanding volume of business became a challenging task by itself. The Secretary's Department also had to help conduct and keep records of the much greater number of Executive Board meetings and had to handle the growing amount of work associated with the Annual Meetings and the ancillary meetings, including the new series of meetings of the Interim and Development Committees, and it took on the task of assisting in the meetings of the Group of Twenty-Four. In addition, the Secretary's Department had to send and receive a much greater flow of communications between the Fund and member governments and in more languages. These and other functions vis-à-vis the Executive Board and the Board of Governors had to be conducted in an especially sensitive manner. In effect, the Secretary's Department was having an increasing responsibility for the Fund's relations with the highest financial officials of member governments.

The Legal Department at the end of 1978, after having completed the intensive drafting of the Second Amendment, was unusually busy explaining to colleagues and to officials of member governments the provisions of the amended Articles and implementing the new provisions. It was also providing an impressive amount of technical assistance to help member governments in accepting the Second Amendment and in revising their banking legislation. The Central Banking Service and the Fiscal Affairs Department were likewise called upon to furnish more technical assistance and to undertake new kinds of research as many member governments updated and revised their instruments of monetary policy and their fiscal techniques.

The European Office in Paris continued to serve as a listening post for the Fund in its relations with members in Europe. As the activities of the EC, the OECD, and the BIS increased, this Office had considerably more work. As in the past, the staff members in this Office served as representatives of the Managing Director and their increased work load was reflected in the sharp increase in the number of their reports, formal and informal, to him and in the frequency with which they were called upon to advise him. Because some staff in this Office had been there for many years, they had developed many contacts based on mutual respect and trust. They were thus able to report to and advise the Managing Director on sensitive subjects.

In the years reviewed in this History, the European Office in Paris also had additional work because some meetings of the Committee of Twenty and of the Interim Committee were held at the Fund's quarters in Paris. They also had a large responsibility in connection with the Conference on International Economic Cooperation (CIEC), for which work began in July 1975, well ahead of the opening of the

Conference in December 1975, and continued through June 1977, when it ended. In order to follow the work of the four commissions of the CIEC—on energy, raw materials, development, and financial affairs—the Fund staff in Paris had to deal with many unfamiliar issues. They also had to help determine the topics to be put on the agenda of the Development Committee as a result of the proceedings of the Conference. In addition, one member of the Paris Office continued to serve as part of the three-person secretariat covering the meetings of the Group of Ten, which also often met there.

Staff of the Office in Geneva likewise were much busier than in the past as the GATT and the UNCTAD greatly stepped up their activities, especially those closely allied to the Fund's concerns and interests. The staff in Geneva, supplemented at times by staff from headquarters, had to follow many more consultations held by the GATT, the multilateral trade negotiations that were discussed in Chapter 49, and the increased number of meetings of the UNCTAD. They were frequently called upon to advise the Managing Director on positions and actions that he should take.

Similarly the Special Representative to the United Nations was busier than in the past. Not only did the agencies of the United Nations, as well as the United Nations itself, hold more meetings and sessions but more of these meetings and sessions were concerned with economic, financial, and monetary subjects in which the Fund had a direct interest. Furthermore, more resolutions were passed by the United Nations and by UN-related agencies that recommended or urged action by the Fund.

Staff of the Joint Fund-Bank Library were collecting and circulating to the rest of the staff and the Executive Directors many more books, periodicals, newspapers, and other material from even more countries than in the past and were beginning to undertake a full-scale automation of the Library's collection. Staff of the Bureau of Statistics were covering more members with more statistics, rendering more technical assistance, compiling government finance statistics for the first time, and giving courses and seminars on these new types of statistics. Staff of the IMF Institute were giving more courses to more participants. Staff of the Bureau of Language Services were translating many more documents and Fund publications into a greater number of languages. Staff members in the Office of Information were putting out considerably more information about the Fund to satisfy a widening public interest and dealing with a rapidly growing number of informal inquiries about the Fund. Staff preparing and editing the Fund's publications were not only putting out more periodicals, pamphlets, and books, but most of these publications were also getting longer.

The Administration Department entered into its most difficult period since the early 1950s when the Fund was developing its functions amid budget deficits. After a 16-year period of surpluses, the Fund was again running deficits, so that planning and executing the Fund's administrative budget was much harder. In the changed environment of the 1970s, young professional people were generally more prone, in the quest for a variety of experiences, to change jobs more frequently than were previous generations. Recruiting adequately qualified personnel and trying to widen the geographic distribution of the staff became a demanding activity. Existing staff became restless as work loads increased and as opportunities for promotion became scarce in an institution that was not expanding. Staff dissatisfaction and turnover became problems for the Fund for the first time in at least 20 years. The issues coming up about staff compensation, discussed in the following section, exacerbated staff discontent. Many of these problems were very time-consuming for the Administration Department. These problems, moreover, took place when both the Managing Director and the Deputy Managing Director were also new to their posts. In these circumstances, the Administration Department began to take on additional responsibilities for designing new policies for career mobility within the Fund, for effective utilization of existing staff, for recruitment and training, and for examining the prospects for promotion within the Fund as some of the older staff reached retirement age. Inevitably staff in the Administration Department were absorbed in difficult and often frustrating problems.

As the Fund's operations and staff grew, the activities of the Internal Auditor, who reviews and reports to the Managing Director on the soundness, adequacy, and application of financial and operating controls and procedures, also increased. Even the Health Room, initially a very small facility which the Fund and the World Bank had operated since 1947 to provide their staffs with routine injections needed for travel and with similar conveniences, had to provide more services, expand its facilities, and add to its personnel.

The staff handled the greater work burden mainly by expending considerably additional effort. Simply put, everybody worked harder. For some staff, working harder meant working on weekends or in the evenings and losing vacations. Many staff members had to travel abroad considerably more than in the past. Virtually all staff members became intensely absorbed in current operations and activities requiring immediate attention. Greater productivity was made possible also by an increase in the number of staff members who provided a variety of supporting services to help the work of economists and other staff responsible for the Fund's relations with members and for the Fund's operations and research. Staff members supplying supporting services included, for example, persons specializing in translating documents into a number of languages, in electronic data processing, in designing and operating computer systems, and in arranging international meetings. Often it was the efforts of these staff members that made the work of the staff who were out front look good. More than one third of the growth in the number of staff from 1972 to 1978 took the form of staff supplying supporting services, especially computer specialists and language translators. Also, to enable the staff to work more efficiently, the Fund made increasing use of more advanced typewriters, word processors, dictating machines, copiers, and of the new Joint Computer Center, in which the Fund shared a large in-house computer with the World Bank.

Despite the greater use of specialized staff and of labor-saving devices, however, as of the end of 1978 the work load of the staff had increased to such a degree that the prospect of an overload on at least some of the staff could be envisaged.

Issue of Staff Compensation

After the devaluation of the U.S. dollar in 1971, some of the Fund staff began to feel that their salaries and other payments, which were specified and paid in U.S. dollars, had been effectively reduced. Since a sizable number of Fund staff spent money in their homelands or sent some of their income back home, the devaluation of the dollar reduced their receipts in terms of other currencies. Moreover, the need for highly qualified personnel in other parts of the world, in both the public and private sectors, was rapidly increasing. In order to recruit qualified economists and other specialists, other agencies began to pay salaries markedly higher than those paid by the Fund. The Fund itself was beginning to have a harder time recruiting staff and was experiencing a higher turnover.

At the same time, officials of some member governments were of the view that the salaries paid to Fund staff were already relatively high. Officials of the U.S. Government, both in the executive branch and in the Congress, were especially inclined to view Fund staff salaries as high compared with those of officials in the U.S. Government, where salaries of higher-ranking employees were held below a ceiling fixed by the wage income of members of the U.S. Congress. When the supplementary financing facility was being considered in the Congress, some members commented on what they considered to be the relatively high salaries of the Fund and World Bank staffs.

As the question of cost of living increases came up in the first years of the 1970s, U.S. officials, through their Executive Director, explained their view that Fund salaries were already high. Each year there was a debate about the size of the cost of living increase. As time went on, allowances for cost of living increases, especially for the senior staff, fell below the actual increases in the cost of living and the real incomes of the Fund staff began to decline. In the course of time, too, the Fund's Staff Association, which had been formed in the 1940s but which had long been inactive, became strong and more vocal.

Against this background, the scene was set for confrontation. It took place in April 1976. While the issue of the size of the allowance as a cost of living increase to be granted to the Fund staff was before the Executive Board, U.S. Treasury Secretary, William E. Simon, as Governor of the Fund, sought the support of other Governors to reduce the allowance. Mainly to protest the interference of Mr. Simon with the Fund's normal procedures for handling salary questions, the Staff Association, on April 28, 1976, called for a one-day work stoppage. Virtually all the Fund staff heeded the call. In effect, for the first time ever, the Fund staff was on strike.

The issue of 1976 was resolved, but the salary issue was to continue in the next year too. Accordingly, in July 1977, the Executive Boards of the Fund and the World Bank set up a Joint Committee on Staff Compensation Issues. It was to examine the principles that should be adopted in establishing appropriate compensation levels for the two organizations. Since Alexandre Kafka was Chairman, the Committee was referred to internally as the Kafka Committee. The Committee issued a comprehensive report in January 1979. In brief, the report suggested the use of a system of "comparators" in determining the "correct" level for salaries of Fund and World Bank staff. Thereafter, the two organizations were to use the system of comparators.

The salary issue was not yet at rest, however. U.S. officials persisted in trying to find ways to reduce salaries of Fund staff.

STAFF PORTRAITS

The teamwork and general anonymity that had characterized the work of the staff since the Fund's inception continued. Regardless of nationality, the staff works together as a body of international civil servants in the interests of the Fund. They do not try to represent, or lobby for, the national interests of particular member governments; indeed, under the rules applying to the staff, they are forbidden to do so. The end product of virtually all the work done by the staff is the result of the combined efforts of many people. While there are divisions of responsibility, in carrying out their responsibilities staff from the various departments pool and share their information and ideas and their specialized knowledge and experience. This collaboration greatly strengthens the work of the staff. Also, at times there are diverse views among the staff, just as officials and economists outside the Fund hold varying views on economic questions. The staff thus has a chance to learn of diverse opinions within the institution.

Collaboration, nevertheless, means that it is seldom possible to separate from the final product the contribution of any individual. Furthermore, much of the work of the Fund involves confidential information and discussions that cannot be revealed. Hence, while the work of individual staff members is well known within the organization and among colleagues, and often among the monetary and financial officials of member countries, most members of the staff, like civil servants throughout the world, remain anonymous to all but a very limited number of people.

Low visibility, relative obscurity, and lack of freedom to express opinions publicly were distinct drawbacks from a professional point of view for many Fund staff, especially in the period reviewed in this History. It was a time when international monetary topics were of widespread interest. Topics relating to the international monetary system, to the monetary problems of individual countries, and to the monetary problems of various economic categories of countries were regularly commented upon in newspapers, in weekly news magazines, in the rapidly growing number of periodicals that were devoted to the subject of money, and on radio and television. There were frequent informal talks and speeches and numerous more formal meetings and conferences on these topics. There was advice to be given informally to candidates for public office and to members of legislatures in many of the Fund's member countries. In these circumstances, economists working in the private sector—in universities, research institutions, commercial banks, and the like—and even many who were associated with national governments had unprecedented opportunities to write and speak publicly, enhancing their professional reputations and prestige. These opportunities were much less available to members of the Fund staff. Staff of the Fund, moreover, like the staff of other international organizations, did not usually receive the recognition and awards that national governments customarily bestow on senior civil servants to recognize their public service.

The Fund management and the staff itself recognized that the Fund staff had the professional advantages associated with helping to determine the Fund's policies on critical issues, with being in the midst of important discussions with high-level officials of member governments on vital economic policies, and with being given an opportunity possibly to have some influence on decisions taken by member governments. Because of these opportunities, Fund staff generally considered that experience gained in the Fund was its own reward. Nevertheless, to the extent possible, given the Fund's need to protect the confidentiality of its relations with members and the need for the Fund to form and announce its policies as the policies of an institution and not as the views of any individual, the Fund management tried to a greater degree than in the past to reduce the anonymity of members of the Fund staff. Names of staff appeared in more internal documents and in more of the Fund's publications. On occasion, staff members were permitted to publish signed articles in professional journals. And more staff members began to speak to outside groups and to participate in professional conferences.

Because of the teamwork involved in all the Fund's activities and the difficulty in separating from the whole the contribution of any individual, there has been a marked absence of staff names in this History, although the names of many Governors and virtually all members of the Executive Board have been mentioned. Only a very few staff members closely identified with particular events are mentioned in the text, and a few staff members whose articles were published by the Fund have been cited in footnotes. To give identity to the often-used term "the Fund staff," an appendix lists several staff names, and a number of staff members are mentioned here. Strict selection among 1,400 staff members must inevitably be made, nonetheless. Appendix B lists the names of staff members who held the position of Division Chief or above at the end of 1978. By virtue of their rank, these senior staff members can be regarded as being in a special category. Several of them, moreover, had by the end of 1978 given long years of service to the Fund and so by virtue of rank and lengthy service are mentioned here.

By the second half of the 1970s many senior staff members who had been with the Fund for years began to reach retirement age. A comparison of Appendix B in *History, 1966–71* with Appendix B in this History shows that of the 18 Directors of departments, offices, and bureaus at the end of 1971 (those listed in the first column), 12 had retired, died, or otherwise left the Fund by the end of 1978.

Similarly, many of the staff who were Deputy Directors, Senior Advisors, Assistant Directors, Advisors, and Division Chiefs at the end of 1971 had retired by the end of 1978. Specifically, nearly 50 of the 135 listed in the second column of Appendix B of *History, 1966–71* had retired or otherwise left the Fund by the end of 1978.[5]

Since many of the departing staff had held key posts for several years, this change in the senior staff represents a substantial changing of the guard. The veterans who had come to the Fund staff when they were young, who had served for a quarter of a century or more, and who had made most, if not all of their careers, in the Fund, were leaving and a new generation was taking over.

A brief description follows of those who were Directors of the 14 departments, 2 offices, and 2 bureaus at the end of 1978, and then of those Deputy Directors and Senior Advisors who by the end of 1978 had been on the staff for 20 years or more. Of the latter, within each department, those who were still on the staff in late 1984 are listed first. While this treatment helps to limit the number of names, it means that senior staff who retired before the end of 1978, many of whom contributed to the events described in this History, are not mentioned. However, most of these staff members were cited in *History, 1966–71*.

As of the end of 1978, the General Counsel and Director of the Legal Department, Joseph Gold, and the Economic Counsellor and Director of the Research Department, J.J. Polak, had had more than three decades of service to the Fund and had made outstanding contributions. Within a little more than another year, both were to retire. Since 1966, when the Fund especially created the positions of General Counsel and Economic Counsellor, these two staff members had held a rank above other Directors of Departments. Mr. Gold and Mr. Polak also customarily served as representatives of the Managing Director at the meetings of the Deputies of the Group of Ten and thus accompanied the Managing Director to the ministerial meetings of the Group of Ten. They both also served as informal advisors to the Managing Director on a host of topics.

Joseph Gold came to the Fund in October 1946. He continued as General Counsel and Director of the Legal Department until July 1979. In an earlier chapter, Mr. Gold's work on the Second Amendment has been described. But Mr. Gold's contributions to the Fund go well beyond his work on the Second Amendment. He was also responsible for the First Amendment. Equally impressive are the ways in which Mr. Gold enabled the Fund to change without amending its Articles of Agreement. It is to his ingeniousness in interpreting the Articles of Agreement and in implementing their provisions over the whole 30-year period that the Fund owes much of its ability to adapt and adjust to changing circumstances and to introduce new policies. Under his guidance, the Fund always found its Articles to be a broad constitution. The Fund was never bound by a legal straitjacket. Yet at the same time,

---

[5]Appendix B of *History, 1966–71* is in Vol. I, pp. 663–66; Appendix B of this History is in Vol. II, pp. 1056–59. By late 1984, only 2 staff members who were Department Heads at the end of 1971 remained, and more than 60 percent of the other 135 senior staff members at the end of 1971 had left the Fund.

Mr. Gold always provided the Fund with the protection it needed to operate within an agreed legal framework. In the years 1972–78, he found ways to enable the Fund to establish a Committee of the Board of Governors, to institute higher charges on its oil facility so as to be able to pay lenders the interest rates they required, to sell some of its gold, and to establish a Trust Fund, even under the pre-amended Articles.

In undertaking his work in the Fund, Mr. Gold also consciously sought to develop and advance international monetary law generally. In addition, his many writings about the Fund have served to enlighten specialists and the public about the Fund. His ability to be so prolific while carrying on his duties as General Counsel and Director of the Legal Department has been a source of inspiration to his colleagues.[6]

J.J. Polak, came to the Fund in January 1947. He continued as Economic Counsellor and Director of the Research Department until December 1979. Earlier chapters detail many of Mr. Polak's contributions to the Fund in the 1972–78 period. But Mr. Polak's contributions extend well beyond his work in these seven years. In the 1940s, when quantitative research was yet in its infancy, it was Mr. Polak who introduced the new methodologies into the Fund. Thereafter, he continued to lead the Fund staff into complex model building. Mr. Polak's main contribution, however, was to the development of the Fund's policies. After he became Director of the Research Department in 1958, he continued to follow in the tradition of that department of having the Fund's economic research serve the Fund's policy and operational needs. Moreover, he had a talent unusual among economists of knowing how to use the theoretical and analytical tools of economics to help derive usable policies. Mr. Polak was thus one of the founders of the monetary approach to balance of payments analyses, and hence of the Fund's conditionality. He was also responsible for much of the Fund's work on exchange rates and international liquidity. Here, Mr. Polak's most significant contribution to the Fund is the SDR. He was largely responsible for helping to develop most of the economic features of the SDR that gradually emerged in the 1960s and were specified in the outline that was agreed in Rio de Janeiro in 1967. His personal efforts in nurturing this infant reserve asset of the Fund also helped ensure that the SDR was quickly integrated into the international monetary system.

In addition, Mr. Polak was principal advisor to the Managing Director on all economic policy topics, playing an especially active role in the ten years from 1963 to 1973 when Mr. Schweitzer was Managing Director. For some years Mr. Polak also led the staff team in consultation discussions with the United States. In 1968 he played a role in getting the officials of the United Kingdom to take stricter monetary and fiscal measures to make the devaluation of the pound sterling of November 1967 more effective.[7]

---

[6]Since his retirement, Mr. Gold has held the position of Senior Consultant, and as a national of the United Kingdom, following his leaving the Fund staff, he was knighted by Queen Elizabeth II.

[7]See *History, 1966–71*, Vol. I, pp. 443 and 445. After his retirement from the staff at the end of 1979, Mr. Polak served briefly as Advisor to the Managing Director, and then in January 1981 he

The three other staff members who were Directors of Departments as of the end of 1978 who were also to retire within the next few years are Kenneth N. Clark, Richard Goode, and Ernest Sturc.

Kenneth N. Clark, Director of the Administration Department, joined the staff in 1947 and served in the Administration Department in various capacities, including Deputy Director, until December 1976 when he became Director. In his long service with the Fund, Mr. Clark was well liked and noted particularly for his fairness and consideration in dealing with the staff on personnel and other administrative matters. He retired at the end of 1979.

Richard Goode, Director of the Fiscal Affairs Department, had left the Fund in 1959 after being Assistant Division Chief in the Research Department and Assistant Director in the Asian Department. In 1965 he returned as the first Director of the newly established Fiscal Affairs Department. It was thus Mr. Goode who built up the staff of the department and developed the department's functions. Under his direction, the department was developed as a major vehicle of the Fund's technical assistance to member countries and of research on fiscal subjects. But technical assistance and research were only part of the functions of the Fiscal Affairs Department. The department also provided economists for missions and reviewed the fiscal contents of the stabilization and adjustment programs associated with stand-by arrangements. Mr. Goode was himself highly regarded as a general economist and as a specialist in public finance. He retired in July 1981.

Ernest Sturc, Director of the Exchange and Trade Relations Department, joined the Fund staff in 1946 after having been at the Bretton Woods Conference as an advisor to the Czechoslovak delegation. Before becoming Director of the Exchange and Trade Relations Department in 1965, Mr. Sturc had a long career in the European Department. Mr. Sturc had a broad concept of his work in the Fund. For him, assessment of a member's economic problems and policies had to go well beyond what might be learned from the use of formal methodologies. He usually looked into the problems of businessmen, bankers, and labor, and he was acutely conscious of the political factors underlying economic policies. Within the constraints required of a member of the Fund staff, he was at times willing to try to help officials of member governments persuade some of their political opposition of the desirability of changing their economic policies. While he was Director of the Exchange and Trade Relations Department, the functions of the department were broadened and changed in accordance with the Fund's changing responsibilities. Throughout his Fund career, Mr. Sturc also remained interested in, and knowledgeable about, the countries in Eastern Europe, and was often helpful to his colleagues in providing insight into the economic problems of these nonmember countries of the Fund. Mr. Sturc retired in January 1980. He died shortly thereafter, in October 1980.

---

was elected as the Executive Director for the constituency of Cyprus, Israel, the Netherlands, Romania, and Yugoslavia. As a national of the Netherlands, after his retirement from the Fund staff, he received a special award, the Netherlands form of knighthood, from Queen Juliana.

Two long-standing senior staff members—one of whom had been Director of the Bureau of Statistics since 1968 and one of whom had been a Deputy Director of the Research Department since 1964—who died before the end of 1978, also deserve mention at this point.

Earl Hicks was one of the Fund's first staff members, having joined the staff in July 1946. For many years, Mr. Hicks was Chief of the Statistics Division. In 1968, at least partly in recognition of Mr. Hicks's outstanding contributions to the Fund's work in statistics, the Fund established a Bureau of Statistics and made Mr. Hicks the Director. He held this position until he took early retirement just before his death in January 1978. Mr. Hicks, too, was unusually creative and hard working. And he was wholly devoted to making the Fund's statistical work of first quality, appropriate to answer the unique needs of the international community. His efforts were very successful. Mr. Hicks put the Fund far in the forefront in the gathering and publishing of international financial statistics. *International Financial Statistics*, the Fund's monthly publication, is the source to which officials and scholars around the world look for data of this type. Moreover, by keeping up with changing times in the field of electronic data processing and setting up a data fund, Mr. Hicks left the Fund a legacy in which the statistics that the Fund gathered were to become even more available and useful.

J. Marcus Fleming, who joined the staff of the Research Department in 1954 and who had been Deputy Director of that department since 1964, died in February 1976. Mr. Fleming was unusually creative, hard working, and dedicated to what he was doing in the Fund. His analytical work greatly advanced economists' understanding of balance of payments phenomena and of the consequences of the alternative policies that might be used to correct disequilibria. In addition, Mr. Fleming made numerous contributions to the shaping of international monetary arrangements. The Fund's compensatory financing facility, several of the features of the SDR, and the schemes for multicurrency and SDR intervention considered in the discussions for reforming the international monetary system, for instance, all owe much to Mr. Fleming's ideas. He also had an uncanny ability to translate many of his ideas into policies and to get them accepted by the Executive Board. In an unusual tribute to a staff member, the conference on the New International Monetary System held at the Fund's headquarters in 1976, described in Chapter 32, derived its impetus partly from the desire for a suitable memorial to Mr. Fleming.

The two Directors of Departments who were already Directors as of the end of 1971 and who continue to be Directors are Walter O. Habermeier and L. Alan Whittome.

Mr. Habermeier joined the staff as Deputy Treasurer in 1966. He was appointed Treasurer in February 1969. In accordance with the deliberate decision of the management, Mr. Habermeier greatly enlarged the responsibilities of the Treasurer's Department for the formation of the Fund's financial policies, such as policies in regard to general reviews of quotas, the formula for calculating quotas, the operational budgets used to determine the currencies and SDRs used in drawings and repurchases, and the charges levied on use of the Fund's resources. The Treasurer's Department took on several new areas of operation and policy, as has been described in this History, and under Mr. Habermeier's direction, it grew to be one of the Fund's largest and most active departments. One of Mr. Habermeier's special contributions was his insistence that the Fund itself undertake to auction its holdings of gold. On January 1, 1980 Mr. Habermeier was appointed Counsellor as well as Treasurer. In that capacity, he was to serve as one of the Managing Director's principal advisors.

Mr. Whittome joined the staff as Director of the European Department in August 1964. Chapters 23 and 24 describe his successful negotiations in concluding stand-by arrangements with Italy and with the United Kingdom in 1974 to 1977. As head of the European Department, Mr. Whittome, in the period 1972–78, also directed the staff work on and was the principal advisor to the Managing Director on the economies and economic policies of more than 20 members, including 4 non-European members. The European Department is also responsible for following economic developments in Switzerland and the nonmember countries in Eastern Europe. Mr. Whittome directed the Fund's relations with many members in an unusually difficult time. Many members for which the European Department was responsible came to the Fund for financial assistance for the first time in many years. New special consultations and consultations under Article IV also had to be introduced and developed. The European Department works with other departments in the review of general policy papers and Mr. Whittome himself is one of the Managing Director's advisors on problems of general Fund policy. In addition, the European Department supplements the work of the Office in Europe (Paris) in maintaining contact with the EC and the OECD. In January 1980 Mr. Whittome became Counsellor as well as Director of the European Department.

The Directors of the other seven departments, two offices, two bureaus, and the units in the Office of the Managing Director were all new to their positions as of the end of 1978, although most of them were not new to the Fund staff.

In the African Department, J.B. Zulu was Director. He had been appointed in November 1976. Earlier, Mr. Zulu had been an Alternate Executive Director. In the period reviewed here, the African Department was responsible for the Fund's relations with more than 40 members, the largest number of members in any of the Fund's Area Departments.

In the Asian Department, Tun Thin was Director. Appointed in 1972, Mr. Tun Thin had been on the staff of the Asian Department since September 1959, and had been Deputy Director for several years. Earlier he had been an Alternate Executive Director. In the period reviewed here, Mr. Tun Thin directed the Fund's relations with more than 20 members and played a special role in negotiations resulting in the relatively heavy use of the Fund's resources by several Asian members.

In the Central Banking Service, Roland Tenconi had become Director in February 1978. Mr. Tenconi had joined the Central Banking Service as Advisor in June 1965, shortly after it had been created, and had assisted the previous Director in developing the functions of the Central Banking Service. He had also spent considerable time advising many members, especially in Africa, with regard to their central banking problems. In January 1980 Mr. Tenconi was to be appointed Director of the Administration Department.

In the IMF Institute, Gérard M. Teyssier became Director in December 1972. After being an Alternate Executive Director from 1964 to 1967, Mr. Teyssier joined the staff as Deputy Director of the Institute in 1967, where he had helped develop the courses and programs of this relatively new Institute. In the period reviewed here, Mr. Teyssier broadened the work of the Institute to include new courses and seminars and workshops.

In the Middle Eastern Department, A. Shakour Shaalan had become Director on May 1, 1977. He was thus to direct the Fund's relations with 18 members. By 1977, Mr. Shaalan had already been on the Fund staff for over 16 years, and in the Middle Eastern Department since 1963. He had been a Senior Advisor since 1975. In the period reviewed here, one of Mr. Shaalan's principal activities was to assist the Managing Director in his efforts to borrow money from the oil exporting countries in the Middle East.

In the Secretary's Department, Leo Van Houtven had become Secretary on August 1, 1977. He came into the position as the Secretary was assigned increased responsibilities for coordinating the work program of the staff and of the Executive Board. The new Secretary was long experienced in the Fund, having been on the staff of the European Department since November 1958. He became an Assistant Director in 1973. He had been Director of the European Office in Paris since June 1974. In the period covered here, Mr. Van Houtven, among other activities, assisted the Managing Director in the conduct of Executive Board meetings and served as an informal advisor to the Managing Director on a number of troublesome, or potentially troublesome, problems involving institutional arrangements.

In the Western Hemisphere Department, E. Walter Robichek, who had joined the staff in February 1947, had become Director in early 1977, having served earlier as Assistant Chief, Division Chief, and Deputy Director of that department. In this capacity, Mr. Robichek directed the Fund's relations with over 30 members in an unusually busy period. Since Mr. Robichek had been Deputy Director of the Western Hemisphere Department since 1961, he had long experience in helping the previous Director administer the department and in shaping the Fund's policies vis-à-vis members in the Western Hemisphere. In earlier years in his work with Latin American members, Mr. Robichek had also helped initiate the Fund's monetary approach to balance of payments analysis. Late in 1982, Mr. Robichek was appointed Advisor to the Managing Director. He retired in mid-1984.

In the Bureau of Language Services, Bernardo T. Rutgers had become Director late in 1977. Mr. Rutgers had joined the staff of the Bureau in May 1975. Mr. Rutgers was thus in charge of a large and growing staff which provided translations, interpretations, and related services to the rest of the staff and to Executive Directors. Mr. Rutgers left the Fund in late 1981.

In the Bureau of Statistics, Werner Dannemann had become Director in June 1978. He had been Acting Director since January 1978, following the retirement due to illness of the Director. Mr. Dannemann had joined the staff of the Bureau of Statistics as Assistant Director in September 1969.

In the European Office in Paris, Aldo Guetta had become Director in late 1977. Mr. Guetta had been with the Fund since 1956, and with the European Office in Paris since September 1958. Mr. Guetta had been Assistant Director of that Office since 1968.

In the European Office in Geneva, Fernando Vera had become Director in 1978. Mr. Vera was another staff member who was long experienced in the Fund, having joined in 1948. He spent most of his career working with the Latin American members, and had been Deputy Director of the Western Hemisphere Department since 1966. Mr. Vera retired late in 1982.

In the Office of Information, Jay H. Reid had been Director since May 1972. Mr. Reid had joined the staff in 1948 to be in charge of the Fund's information and public relations activities. In the period of this History, he was thus in charge of the rapidly expanding activities of this type in which the Fund was engaging. Mr. Reid retired in 1980.

In the African Department, Messrs. Rattan J. Bhatia, Senior Advisor, and Edwin L. Bornemann, Senior Advisor, had both joined the staff in 1958 and both joined the African Department in 1961 when it was first formed. In the period 1972 to 1978 these two men worked intensively with several African members, often leading missions pursuant to consultations and requests for use of the Fund's resources.

In the Asian Department, P.R. Narvekar, joined the staff in June 1953. He continued thereafter to work with the Asian members. He was appointed Deputy Director in 1972. In the period reviewed here, Mr. Narvekar not only shared the responsibility with the Director for administering the department and planning the work of the staff, but he himself was also closely identified with the work on certain Asian members, especially Indonesia, and led staff missions to several Asian members. Andreas Abadjis and Albert A. Mattera, Senior Advisors, and W. John R. Woodley, Deputy Director, were to retire within a few years after 1978. In the period covered here, these three men were closely identified with the Fund's relations with the Philippines, with Burma and Korea, and with Japan, respectively.

In the European Department, Brian Rose, Deputy Director, had been on the staff since 1947. In his more than 30 years with the Fund, Mr. Rose had dealt continuously with virtually all of the members for which the European Department was responsible. Mr. Rose often served as advisor to the Director of the European Department on the Fund's relations with European members and frequently led missions to some of the members with the most complex problems. In the period 1972–78, as a recognition of his unusual service, Mr. Rose was promoted from Senior Advisor in the European Department to Deputy Director. Rolf Evensen, Senior Advisor, closely associated with the Fund's relations with a number of European countries, and Albin Pfeifer, Deputy Director, who also helped shape policy in the European Department, retired shortly after the period covered here.

In the Exchange and Trade Relations Department, C. David Finch, a Deputy Director, was a member of the senior staff who also had been with the Fund for nearly 30 years by the end of 1978. Mr. Finch first joined the staff of the Research Department in 1950. He transferred to the Western Hemisphere Department in 1957 where he became Assistant Director in 1964. He then rejoined the Research Department and in 1965 became Assistant Director of the Exchange and Trade Relations Department. He was appointed Deputy Director in that department in 1966. In the period reviewed here, Mr. Finch was especially associated with helping to evolve the Fund's policies for dealing with the external indebtedness problems of developing members and helping to develop the Fund's growing informal relations with commercial banks. In January 1980, Mr. Finch was appointed Director of the Exchange and Trade Relations Department. Subimal Mookerjee, Senior Advisor, first joined the staff in June 1951. Then after a hiatus from 1956 to 1960, he returned to the Fund. These 23 years of service were all with the Exchange and Trade Relations Department. In the period reviewed here, Mr. Mookerjee was identified with helping to develop a number of general Fund policies, including the extended facility, and he also worked with several members in the Middle East. Following Mr. Finch's promotion to Director, Mr. Mookerjee was appointed a Deputy Director of the Exchange and Trade Relations Department. He retired at the end of 1984.

In the IMF Institute, Ciro Tognetti was Senior Advisor and U Tun Wai was Deputy Director. Mr. Tognetti had joined the staff of the Asian Department in 1958. He had been with the Institute since 1964 when the Institute first started. Mr. Tun Wai had been on the staff since 1955, first in the Research Department and then in the African Department, before joining the Institute. In the period reviewed here, both of these men helped plan the content of courses given by the Institute and were part of the teaching staff.

In the Legal Department, other than the General Counsel already mentioned, the Associate General Counsel and the Deputy General Counsel were both long-standing members of the staff. George Nicoletopoulos was appointed Associate General Counsel in 1977. Mr. Nicoletopoulos had come to the legal staff in 1949 and been appointed Deputy General Counsel in 1964. Among other duties, Mr. Nicoletopoulos at times attended meetings of the Deputies of the Group of Ten. He was also the principal assistant to Mr. Gold in the drafting of the Second Amendment. In 1979 Mr. Nicoletopoulos was appointed Director of the Legal Department. James G. Evans, Jr., Deputy General Counsel, had joined the staff of the Fund's Legal Department in May 1953. In the period reviewed here, among Mr. Evans's responsibilities was regular attendance at meetings of the Executive Board in order to be on hand should legal questions arise. He also assisted with legal issues involved in the oil facility and the Trust Fund.

In the Middle Eastern Department, the two Deputy Directors, A.S. Ray and A.K. El Selehdar, both had many years of experience on the staff dealing with the Middle Eastern members. They had both been on the staff of the Middle Eastern Department since 1951. In the period reviewed in this History, Mr. Ray and Mr. El Selehdar had to handle the Fund's relations with an increasing number of Middle Eastern countries which had joined the Fund. Moreover, as the importance of oil exporting countries in the world economy grew and as Middle Eastern members began lending to the Fund, the Fund's relations with these members also became more complicated.

In the Secretary's Department, D.E. Brantley, Deputy Secretary, who was responsible for arranging the Annual Meetings, retired after the 1979 Annual Meeting, held in Belgrade, Yugoslavia.

In the Western Hemisphere Department, in addition to the Director, a Deputy Director and a Senior Advisor had been with the Fund for at least two decades. Carlos E. Sansón, who had come to the Fund in 1952, became Senior Advisor in 1970 and Deputy Director in 1977. He left the staff in October 1962 temporarily to take up the duties of Alternate Executive Director but rejoined the staff of the Western Hemisphere Department in November 1964. Edison V. Zayas joined the staff of the Research Department in 1946. In 1953 he moved to the Western Hemisphere Department and was appointed Assistant Director in 1970 and Senior Advisor in 1977. In the period 1972–78 these men often led missions to Latin American members pursuant to consultations, to technical assistance, and to the requests of Latin American members for use of the Fund's resources. In early 1983 Mr. Sansón took up the position of Director of the Office in Geneva. Mr. Zayas retired in June 1983.

Other staff members with less than 20 years of service by the end of 1978 also had a major role in the formulation and implementation of the policies described in this History, or in the research underlying those policies. With the retirement of so many staff members who had come to the Fund no later than the end of 1958 (that is, those listed above who had had 20 years of service by the end of 1978), it was the staff who had come to the Fund in 1959 and the first few years of the 1960s that made up the bulk of the senior staff. As can be seen from Appendix B, there were more than 100 members of the staff not cited above who by 1978 had attained Division Chief status or higher. Thirteen had become Deputy Directors and 5 had become Senior Advisors. Eight among them had already become either a Senior Advisor or a Deputy Director by May 1974 so that they were at these ranks for most of the years of this History and those who were Senior Advisors all later became Deputy Directors, or Directors. All of these 8, except one, had had at least 10 years of service in the Fund by the end of 1978, and 4 were continuing to serve the Fund in late 1984. An additional 4 staff members, 3 of whom had been with the Fund for several years, also had become Deputy Directors in 1977 or 1978 and were still on the staff in late 1984. These 12 staff members are listed in alphabetical order.

W.A. Beveridge, Deputy Director of the Fiscal Affairs Department, joined the staff of the European Department in July 1959. He transferred to the Fiscal Affairs Department as Senior Advisor in September 1970 and became Deputy Director in May 1975. In the period reviewed here, Mr. Beveridge was thus closely associated with all activities of the Fiscal Affairs Department. After the period reviewed here, Mr. Beveridge became a Deputy Director in the Exchange and Trade Relations Department. Sterie T. Beza, Deputy Director in the Western Hemisphere Department, came to the staff of that department in 1961. Subsequently, Mr. Beza worked continuously on the Fund's relations with members for which the Western Hemisphere Department is responsible. He became a Senior Advisor in 1970 and a Deputy Director in 1977. In the period 1972–78, Mr. Beza is closely associated most of all with the Fund's work on the two large industrial members, Canada and the United States. In addition, he led staff missions to several of the member countries in Latin America. In January 1983, Mr. Beza was appointed Associate Director of the Western Hemisphere Department. Robert J. Familton, Deputy Treasurer, joined the staff of the European Department in 1962. He moved to the Exchange and Trade Relations Department in 1966 and from there to the Treasurer's Department in 1969. He was appointed Deputy Treasurer in 1970. In the period covered here, Mr. Familton was thus closely associated with many of the activities undertaken by the Treasurer's Department that have been described in earlier chapters. While still on the staff, Mr. Familton died at the end of 1982. P.N. Kaul, Deputy Director in the Administration Department, joined the staff in August 1963. He became Deputy Director in May 1973. In the years 1972–78, Mr. Kaul was therefore, along with the two who served as Directors of the Administration Department in this period, responsible for the various activities of the Administration Department that have been described earlier in this chapter. In mid-1980, the Central Banking Service was made into a department and Mr. Kaul became the Director. Mr. Kaul retired in late 1984.

Rasheed O. Khalid became Deputy Director in the Fiscal Affairs Department in May 1977. Mr. Khalid had first joined the staff of the Fiscal Affairs Department in September 1965. He was thus closely associated with many of the activities undertaken by the Fiscal Affairs Department in the 1972–78 period. Joseph W. Lang, Jr., was appointed Deputy Secretary in 1977. Mr. Lang joined the staff of the Legal Department in 1960. He moved to the Secretary's Department in 1962 and became Assistant Secretary in 1967. Except for the period 1974–76 when he served as Advisor in the European Office in Paris, Mr. Lang was thus involved in all the activities of the Secretary's Department in the period reviewed here. Oumar Barou Makalou joined the staff of the African Department in June 1977, as Deputy Director. Azizali F. Mohammed, Senior Advisor in the European Department, came to the staff of the Research Department in November 1960. He became Assistant Division Chief in the Middle Eastern Department in 1962, Division Chief in the Exchange and Trade Relations Department in 1966, and Assistant Director of that department in 1970. He was promoted to Senior Advisor in the European Department in May 1974. In the period covered by this History, Mr. Mohammed was thus associated from 1972 to early 1974 with a number of activities performed by the Exchange and Trade Relations Department, and from May 1974 to the end of 1978 with handling the Fund's relations with several European members. In August 1980, following a period of a year and a half in which he served as advisor to the Saudi Arabian Monetary

Agency, Mr. Mohammed became Director of a newly created Office of External Relations, which a year later became the External Relations Department.

Donald K. Palmer, Deputy Director of the Exchange and Trade Relations Department, joined the staff of that department in January 1969. He was promoted to Deputy Director in May 1970. In the period reviewed here, Mr. Palmer was closely associated with helping the Director of the Exchange and Trade Relations Department plan and supervise the work of the department, including the staffing of missions, and with assisting in the evolution and implementation of the Fund's policies for which the department was responsible. In mid-1983, Mr. Palmer was promoted to be Associate Director of the Exchange and Trade Relations Department. He retired in mid-1984. Rudolf R. Rhomberg joined the staff of the Research Department in 1959. He was promoted to Senior Advisor in May 1974. In the years reviewed here, Mr. Rhomberg was thus associated with much of the economic research and economic policy work of the Research Department, including, for example, work on the multilateral exchange rate model, on "Project Link," analyzing world trade, and on the SDR. After the end of the period reviewed here, Mr. Rhomberg was appointed Deputy Director. Charles F. Schwartz, Deputy Director of the Research Department, came to the staff in 1959 as Chief of the North American Division in the Western Hemisphere Department. In that capacity he worked primarily on the Fund's relations with Canada and the United States. He was appointed Deputy Director of the Research Department in 1966. Mr. Schwartz is identified closely with the world economic outlook project. It was primarily he who made this the comprehensive project that has merited a separate chapter earlier in this volume. In early 1979 Mr. Schwartz was appointed Associate Director of the Research Department and Director of Adjustment Studies. He retired in 1983. David Williams was appointed Deputy Treasurer in May 1978. Mr. Williams joined the staff of the European Department in 1963 and later moved to the Research Department and then to the Treasurer's Department. He became a Senior Advisor in 1976. Thus in the years 1972–78, Mr. Williams was involved in a senior capacity in virtually all of the events and policies for which the Treasurer's Department was responsible.

Two additional staff members should also be mentioned.

Lamberto Dini, who had been on the staff for 16 years and had attained the rank of Senior Advisor in the African Department in 1970 and of Deputy Director in 1975, moved from the staff to the Executive Board in 1976 and was still on the Executive Board as of the end of 1978. Mr. Dini came to the staff in 1959 and joined the African Department when it was first formed in 1961. He took on the duties of Executive Director elected by the constituency comprising Italy, Malta, Portugal, and Spain in July 1976. Mr. Dini remained on the Executive Board until November 1980.

William H. White, Senior Economist in the Financial Studies Division of the Research Department, joined the staff of the Research Department in May 1948 and was an economist in that department for more than 35 years, still serving the Fund at the time of his death in October 1983. Mr. White was the author of numerous pieces of theoretical and analytical research on the major topics of concern to the Fund, inflation, monetary theory and policy, interest rates, stabilization policy, and exchange rates. His work was known for its scholarliness, rigor, and insight. Several of his pieces were published in *Staff Papers*, some of which have been cited in footnotes above. Other pieces were published in the professional journals of the academic community, where Mr. White was widely respected. Also exceptionally well acquainted with the theoretical literature, Mr. White was an economist's economist, unusually sought after by his colleagues for discussions of economic ideas and for comments on their own work. Mr. White died in October 1983, while still on the staff.

As the Fund celebrated its thirty-third anniversary in December 1978, many other individuals both among the professional and supporting staff had served the Fund for over two decades, or even longer. Many of these individuals, too, however, were on the verge of retirement.

As the posts left vacant were filled, especially in the senior slots, the Fund management tried hard to get as wide a geographic distribution of senior staff as was possible, consistent with the Fund's need for particularly well-qualified specialists. As time has gone on, considerably fewer of the senior staff have been nationals of the United States, and many more have been nationals of European and developing members. Special efforts were being made to recruit nationals of developing members. It was difficult, however, to recruit highly trained staff from many of the developing members, especially from members in Africa and in Latin America. There were shortages of qualified persons from these geographic areas and many preferred to remain in their own countries where they could attain very high posts.

There were notably few women among the senior staff. As of the end of 1978, no woman had yet attained the rank of a Director of a department, bureau, or office—what was known within the Fund as "M" level status—although there were 19 such positions. Nor had any woman yet attained the rank of Deputy Director or Senior Advisor—the "L" level—although there were 36 such positions. This situation meant that when the Fund management, as was the regular custom, held meetings of Department Directors, which Deputy Directors and Senior Advisors also attended, there was not one woman among the 57 staff members present. Only 11 women were Assistant Directors, Advisors, or Division Chiefs—the "K" and "J" levels—despite the existence of 164 such positions. Five of these 11 women had been with the Fund for over 30 years, and one for over 20 years. These 6 long-standing women staff members as of 1978 are the following. Anne Romanis Braun, appointed Advisor in the Research Department in 1975, first joined that department in December 1957. In the period of this History, Mrs. Braun worked on a wide range of economic topics but became especially expert on the balance of payments adjustment policies and the incomes policies of industrial members. Several of her articles have been cited in footnotes in foregoing chapters. Margaret Garritsen de Vries, Historian, first joined the staff as an economist in the Research Department in August 1946. Later she served as Senior Economist and Assistant Division Chief in the Exchange Restrictions Department, where, among other responsibilities, she helped to evolve the Fund's policies on multiple exchange rates. In 1957 she became Chief of the Far Eastern Division in the Asian Department, the first woman to become a Chief of a Division. In 1963 Mrs. de Vries became a consultant to the Fund especially to assist in the writing of Fund Histories. She was appointed Historian in May 1973, and promoted to Assistant Director level in May 1978. Philine R. Lachman, appointed Assistant General Counsel in May 1974, joined the Legal Department staff in 1947. In the period under review, Ms. Lachman worked on the legal aspects of many of the Fund's regulatory and financial functions and on the difficult undertaking of adapting them to the changing circumstances within the constraints of the Articles of Agreement prior to the Second Amendment. She was also part of the small team of lawyers that prepared and drafted the Second Amendment of the Fund's Articles and the accompanying explanatory materials. Katherine F. Magurn, gifted with an unusual skill in languages, had been in charge of language services since September 1946, pioneering that field from the Fund's early days. She was appointed Assistant Secretary in 1970. Rose S. Porras, a Senior Counsellor, was another long-standing lawyer on the Fund's staff. Mrs. Porras joined the Legal Department staff in November 1946. Her main area of specialization was to advise the Fund on administrative legal problems. Marie C. Stark joined the Fund in 1947, was appointed Archivist in 1951, and was gradually promoted to the Assistant Director level. The structure and content of the Fund's Archives remain as her achievement. Mrs. Braun, Mrs. Magurn, and Miss Stark retired in the early 1980s.

The absence of women among the senior staff of the Fund persisted despite the fact that two of the Executive Directors called to the management's attention the absence of women in the Fund's upper echelons and despite the legal requirement imposed on the U.S. Executive Director that he report to the Congress on the status of women in the Fund. But it is also to be noted that as of the end of 1978 no woman had yet been appointed or elected by member governments as an Executive Director and only one had been an Alternate Executive Director. None had been an Advisor in the office of an Executive Director and only a very few had been Technical Assistants.

The situation in the Fund was similar to that in most governments and private financial institutions. Although women were beginning to make inroads into many professions and positions hitherto occupied entirely by men, they were not yet being admitted into the powerful ranks of those who made decisions on money and finance. The absence of women in the world of finance was increasingly and abundantly evident at the Annual Meetings of the Fund and the World Bank. Among the many thousands of men in attendance, there was at most a handful of women.

The hopeful prospect, however, was that the situation, at least in the Fund, as an international organization, was likely to change soon. There was an increasing number of young women economists among the ranks of the Fund staff and they were being given opportunities to do the Fund's main lines of business. It was evident that they would eventually advance into senior positions.

CHAPTER
53

Thirty-Three Years
of Experience

*B*Y THE END OF 1978 it had been 33 years since 29 members, in a ceremonial signing on December 27, 1945, in Washington, had accepted the Articles of Agreement. The International Monetary Fund had been in existence sufficiently long for some conclusions to be drawn from its experience.

Much has been learned since 1945 and the world has become much more complicated. The desirability of fixed exchange rates and of a gold exchange standard as essential preconditions for expanding world trade and investment, and hence for fostering full employment and economic growth, that dominated economic thinking in the 1940s and underlay the creation of the Fund is much too easy and simple for the world of today. Similarly, the concepts of avoiding competitive depreciation and of changing exchange rates only to correct fundamental disequilibrium that were embedded in the Fund's original framework, although still relevant for exchange rate policy, now are incomplete guidelines for the policies to achieve and maintain a smoothly functioning international monetary system.

The development of a close economic interdependence among virtually all countries and between private banks and financial institutions in many countries has vastly altered the requirements of international monetary arrangements. The Bretton Woods system was based on the premise that individual countries are independent economic as well as political entities. Nations were assumed to have control over their own economic policies, including exchange rates. What had been newly learned from the interwar experience is that these policies have repercussions on other nations. Hence, in order to live together, they need to follow a code of conduct with regard to their currencies that will not damage each other's trade and investment. In the world of the 1970s, however, nations were clearly no longer independent economic entities, but had become interdependent. How differences in interest rates between nations affect capital flows is one illustration of this interdependence. It has accordingly been common for some years to speak of the need for harmonization of monetary policies if exchange rates are to be stable. Whether the largest industrial countries are in the same or opposite stages of cyclical swings has important consequences for the global economy, and the need for concerted economic policies is often mentioned. If world recovery from recession is to be stimulated, many countries must pursue expansionary macroeconomic policies simultaneously, and if world inflation is to be checked, countries must pursue contractionary macroeconomic policies together. Interdependence among nations has since 1975 also brought about the annual economic summit meeting at which leaders of the major industrial nations gather to consider issues of mutual interest.

Much has also been learned since 1945 about the injection of liquidity into the international monetary system. It is now almost universally recognized that the amounts by which international liquidity is expanded, the form in which increases in reserve assets occur, the extent to which increases in liquidity are effected through the extension of international credit rather than through increases in reserve assets, and the extent to which international credit is extended by official agencies or by private banks all need to be taken into account in assessing the adequacy of international liquidity. What is under dispute is whether international liquidity needs to be managed and, if so, how. In the meantime, too, an instrument for possible international management of liquidity—the SDR—has been introduced.

Fund officials have learned a great deal about how the Fund might best use its financial resources. They have, for instance, developed new ideas about how long the Fund might usefully commit resources to a member. They are continuously learning about the circumstances that might justify use of the Fund's resources, about conditionality and about its relationship to the adjustment of balance of payments deficits, and about how to augment the Fund's resources by borrowing.

The Fund's experience of 33 years thus leads to the conclusion that the international monetary arrangements appropriate for the 1970s and 1980s are much more complex than those deemed appropriate for the circumstances immediately after World War II. In the 1940s the Fund could be conceived of as a monitoring organization to enforce a relatively simple code of conduct, with a small pool of resources available as an aid to enforcement. Now, much broader functions for the Fund are at times proposed, including the possibility of its becoming a supranational or world central bank.

Foregoing chapters contain important generalizations about the Fund's experience with international monetary arrangements. In addition, they contain several observations about the functioning of the Fund as an international organization and about how it takes actions and reaches decisions in an international setting. They also include material that reveals how the Executive Board came to various decisions during 1972–78. In addition, specific information has been included to show how the Fund's policymaking machinery worked in the 1972–78 period. In the discussion of "the gold problem," for example, a commentary on how the problem was resolved illustrates the general process of international decision making in monetary affairs in the 1970s. Other chapters contain an overview of the process by which the Fund's policies are generated, developed, and implemented, explanations of how the Executive Board works and of some of the issues that came up in the 1970s pertaining to relations between the Executive Board and the Managing Director and staff, and suggestions as to the factors that have made the Executive Board a relatively effective body.

These earlier generalizations notwithstanding, specialists in foreign affairs and international relations, political scientists, experts in international organizations, and the public, as well as economists, economic historians, specialists in international monetary law, and government officials study the International Monetary Fund's experiences for the insight they might gain about international organizations, especially international economic organizations, and about multinational cooperation. The development of the Fund sheds light also on the economic history of the world since World War II. For it has been primarily since World War II that international economic organizations, such as the Fund, have been an important part of the scene. The earlier precedent, the League of Nations' Economic Section, located in Geneva, was almost entirely a research unit. Thus it seems worthwhile to present a few additional generalizations about the Fund's development.

CHANGE AND FLEXIBILITY

Throughout its three decades the Fund has been characterized by change and flexibility. From 1946 onward, the means by which the Fund has tried to achieve its purposes, the general policies that it has formulated, and the ways in which these policies have been implemented have all been subject to frequent change. New institutional arrangements, such as the General Arrangements to Borrow, the Committee of Twenty, the Interim Committee, and the Development Committee, have been created. The Articles of Agreement themselves have been twice amended. The Fund, moreover, has applied flexibly whatever general policies have existed at any given time. In applying its general policies, the Fund has usually taken into account the circumstances of the individual member. The concept of a case-by-case approach in which the circumstances of the individual member are considered was already well developed by 1950. Thus the Fund has shown a capacity to adapt that was not anticipated by its founders.

The Histories of the Fund abound with examples of the Fund's changing policies and techniques. The theme of change and flexibility as characterizing the Fund's evolution is often stressed by the Fund's former General Counsel in his writings. In a previous History, in a section entitled "Constitutional Development and Change," Mr. Gold traced the Fund's evolution in its first 20 years as seen from a legal point of view.[1] In a subsequent essay, Mr. Gold explored how further changes in the Fund's policymaking machinery came about in a legal way, that is, how continuously evolving international monetary arrangements and instruments of policy were also continuously regulated by international law.[2] Flexibility in applying the Fund's policies and procedures is likewise a subject that Mr. Gold has frequently

---

[1] *History, 1945–65*, Vol. II, pp. 513–605.

[2] See his "International Monetary System and Change: Relations Between Mode of Negotiation and Legal Technique," in his *Legal and Institutional Aspects*, pp. 217–37.

addressed.[3] By the mid-1970s, the concept of change was so ingrained in the Fund that in drafting provisions of the Second Amendment, as noted in earlier chapters, great emphasis was placed on the Fund's having sufficient authority to adapt the international monetary system to changing conditions.

Changes in the Fund, it needs to be stressed, have not been made merely for the sake of change. Nor are the changes symptomatic of unstable policy. Rather, they can be regarded as creative developments. Building on what it had learned from its past policies and procedures but at the same time ensuring that it was not entrapped or imprisoned in its past, the Fund has deliberately tried to find new policies geared to the present or looking to the future. The changes introduced have been aimed at trying to make the Fund a dynamic force in a world economy that has been changing at an exponential rate and in a world in which the willingness of members to work through an international organization on an issue at hand has varied.

If any conclusion can be drawn about economic events since World War II, it is that they can change incredibly fast. The world dollar shortage became a world dollar glut within a little more than 15 years. The balance of payments positions of large industrial, and seemingly relatively stable, countries and the related effects on their currencies are subject to quick turnarounds. Changes in attitudes toward, or expectations for, a currency can suddenly affect the capital inflows and outflows into those currencies, threatening the international monetary system. In December 1973 the jump in oil prices altered the pattern of world payments overnight. In the same vein, the balance of payments positions of many developing countries, individually and collectively, have suddenly deteriorated or suddenly improved.

The advances in economic analysis since World War II have also induced change in the Fund's policies. From its earliest days, the Fund has been confronted with problems that were relatively new to economists. Hence, the problems that are continuously arising for the Fund in shaping its policies have been a spur to the thinking of economists both in and out of the Fund. Fund staff have themselves over the years contributed a great deal to the advances in understanding of such topics as the causes of balance of payments disequilibrium, the factors involved in determining an appropriate exchange rate, the effectiveness of changes in exchange rates, the relation between monetary phenomena and monetary policy and a country's balance of payments position, the dynamics of the inflationary process, and the factors to be taken into account in judging the adequacy of world reserves. In more recent years, Fund staff have also contributed to the understanding of such topics as the simultaneous determination of a number of exchange rates, the relation between interest rates and exchange rates, the factors involved in controlling inflation in an interdependent world also characterized by recession, and the ways in which balance of payments adjustment can best be achieved. Fund staff have played an

---

[3]See, for example, his "Law, Change, and Adaptation in the International Monetary System," in his *Legal and Institutional Aspects*, pp. 25–73.

unusually important part in the evolution of the Fund especially because, as described in Chapter 50, the Fund's policies and procedures are nearly always generated internally.

That the Fund would have to adapt to existing circumstances and to advances in knowledge was obvious at the time that the Fund was created. As early as 1946, the Fund, confronted by economic circumstances in many member countries and with political attitudes toward working through an international organization that were different from what had been expected after World War II, had to shape its policies and its immediate objectives to prevailing economic circumstances and to the functions and policies that member governments were prepared to accept. Faced with a world in which the Fund could not carry out its longer-term objectives for some years and in which its authority was under severe attack, the Fund started to seek a role for itself. Thereafter, Fund officials continuously undertook to examine prevailing circumstances to seek the best role that the Fund could play. The Fund's Annual Reports, for example, have almost always commented about the role of the Fund in existing circumstances. Speeches by the Managing Director often refer to the specific role the Fund is playing in a given situation. To some critics, the Fund's persistent search for a role suggests that the Fund has, at least to some extent, been uncertain or unsure just what to do. But by continuously seeking to understand and to fulfill a relevant role, the Fund has had frequently to adapt, modify, and transform its policies, its ways of working, its emphasis, and its institutional features.

Changes in Accord with Given Objectives

Another way in which one might look at the Fund's experiences is that the rules applied to international monetary arrangements, in the sense of the rules of the game or the code of conduct for international monetary relations, have to be applied flexibly and changed substantially from time to time. It has not been possible to apply uniformly and consistently to international monetary arrangements any rules or code of conduct that are not continuously subject to interpretation and to flexible application.

In fact, critics of the Fund complain that the Fund has changed excessively. Their complaint is that in changing its policies, the Fund has not adhered sufficiently strictly to its originally intended purposes. Often, these critics have in mind, however, not the Fund's six broad purposes as stated in Article I, but rather *particular* international monetary arrangements. Some critics, for instance, object that the Fund no longer enforces the original Bretton Woods system, based on par values and convertibility of currencies. Hence, rather than see virtue in the changes that the Fund has undergone, they fault the Fund for inconstancy.

Creative change has two aspects. The first is the need for change as circumstances change, the change that prevents institutions from becoming obsolete. The second is that change must take place within some set of guidelines or some framework. Otherwise, frequent pragmatic changes do not necessarily lead to progress. There has to be some plan, some grand design, in accordance with which changes are made.

In this regard, in undergoing a virtual transformation in its policies, its methods, and its policymaking machinery, the Fund has kept its focus on its main objectives. The primary objective has been to secure the cooperation of its members and to obtain the fullest and frankest consultation possible between the Fund and its members. Collaboration, cooperation, and consultation on international monetary problems, stated as the Fund's first purpose in Article I, have been given priority.

Fund officials have, furthermore, kept in mind the Fund's five other purposes. The purpose of facilitating the expansion and balanced growth of international trade, as a means of contributing to the promotion and maintenance of high levels of employment and real income and to the development of the productive resources of all members, has underlain the Fund's framework. In this respect, the Fund has continued to consider as one of its main objectives helping members attain sustainable balance of payments positions by trying to develop policies that seem most appropriate to alleviate the balance of payments adjustment constraint on their economic growth and on the most productive use of their resources. Similarly, the Fund has tried to develop those policies that at the time seemed most likely to enable members to avoid use of restrictions on payments. In short, the Fund has tried to foster "a liberal trade and payments regime." It has continued to insist on whatever was defined at the time as "good conduct" in international monetary relations.

Moreover, recognizing its limited authority, the Fund has worked within that authority. It has not tried to enter what is understood to be the province of other international economic organizations, however closely related to the Fund's endeavors. Nor has the Fund tried to go into areas clearly defined as the internal responsibilities of its members.

In sum, in undergoing a metamorphosis, the Fund has often altered its policies, procedures, and policymaking machinery, and twice amended its Articles in ways that seemed suited at the time to attain international monetary cooperation and to achieve the six purposes acceptable to member governments and within the Fund's area of competence.

The result has not, of course, always been entirely satisfactory. Member governments do not surrender sovereignty without struggle. Nearly always compromises have had to be made. There have been monetary functions over which the Fund has no authority. At times the Fund could exercise its powers only in a perfunctory way. Some critics, therefore, have complained that the Fund has, at times, been timid. They say that the Fund has shied away from taking on certain functions essential for a well-working international monetary system. There have been times, too, when some of the functions that are, or could be, the responsibility of the Fund have been performed by other groups of financial officials. All of these developments, however, seem to be a necessary part of the Fund's evolution.

The Fund's six purposes as stated in Article I of its Articles of Agreement are very broad. Moreover, the boundaries of the Fund's authority have, from the Fund's earliest days, been expanding. Consequently it is essential for Fund officials and for monetary authorities to have a vision of the desirable international monetary system and of a desirable Fund toward which evolution is taking place. The vision, moreover, and the means to achieve it must be fairly concrete. Only in this way can Fund officials and monetary authorities adapt and modify the activities, responsibilities, and functions of the Fund in line with the agreed vision. Developing such a concrete agreed vision was, of course, the purpose of the Bretton Woods Conference. It was also the purpose of the *Outline of Reform*. But because circumstances change so rapidly, Fund officials and monetary authorities need from time to time to review the overall direction in which they are proceeding.

ADDITIONAL OBSERVATIONS ON THE FUND'S EVOLUTION

Another generalization, in addition to that of change and flexibility, that can be drawn from the Fund's experience is perhaps obvious. Mediation or initiation by an international organization is needed, or at least accepted, whenever officials of governments are unable to agree among themselves. On a number of occasions, when the principal parties involved in designing an international monetary policy or arrangement were unable to agree among themselves, they brought the problem into the Fund, or at least they welcomed initiatives from Fund officials. In the years covered in this History, there are, for example, several illustrations of how Fund officials acted as an intermediary or took the initiative to facilitate agreement on an international monetary arrangement or policy.

A related observation is that monetary and financial issues usually inflame passions and emotions. Where money or finance is concerned, critical vested interests are at stake, and it becomes exceedingly difficult for monetary authorities to compromise. Hence, monetary authorities of various countries often agree on an international solution to a question only after a crisis has arisen or threatens to arise. The leading example, of course, is the creation of the Fund itself. It took the catastrophe of World War II to get monetary authorities to agree to establish the Fund. Not infrequently, observers have wondered whether the Fund would subsequently ever have been created. In the period covered in this History, there are several examples of agreement coming about because a crisis was at hand. The people, the hour, and a proposed solution all have to coalesce.

A fourth observation is that Fund officials have frequently relied on technical solutions. Rather than try to establish broad policies and broad principles with which the authorities of so many member governments might not be able to agree, Fund officials have often come up with solutions that are relatively technical. Perhaps the best illustration of a successful resolution of a much disputed arrangement by use of technical devices is the SDR. Agreement came about on the SDR as Fund officials devised features of the SDR that combined the various features of a reserve asset on which the monetary authorities of various member governments could agree. As a result of the Fund's reliance on technical solutions, many of the Fund's techniques and policies and much of its jargon seem unduly complicated to the outsider. But these complications, technicalities, involved procedures, and abstruse language have formed the nucleus by which compromise and agreement could be obtained.

As time has gone on, solutions have become more complicated and intricate, also because the interests of more individual members and of more groups of members have had to be accommodated. Furthermore, the monetary authorities of more members and of more groups of members have become increasingly sophisticated in suggesting ways in which these interests can be accommodated.

A fifth observation is that the Fund's most important dealings with individual members usually take place in an atmosphere of crisis. In effect, the Fund is asked to respond to an emergency. In the days of the par value system, a member's proposal to change its par value, or otherwise to alter its exchange rate, and its request for the Fund's approval customarily took place after confidence in the member's currency had been badly shaken and after the member had lost substantial foreign exchange reserves. Proposals for exchange rate changes had to be handled immediately and secretly, usually after business hours or over a weekend, when exchange markets were closed. For this reason, from its inception, the Fund arranged to be open around-the-clock. Even now, a member's request for use of Fund resources usually occurs only when the member is facing an immediate financial crisis.

Because of the emergency circumstances in which the Fund often has to take action, Fund officials, in conjunction with officials of the member concerned, concentrate on appropriate short-term measures to cope with the crisis at hand. In so doing, the aim is to help the member resolve the immediate crisis in ways that are compatible with satisfactory medium-term or longer-term solutions. Because of the crisis situation, Fund officials also have to take into account the impact of these solutions on other members. As a result, Fund officials have often thought of the Fund as an agency to extinguish in one member the fire that might spread to other members.

A sixth and last observation about the Fund's 33 years of experience is that in the Fund's internal way of working the Managing Director and staff can fairly readily propose new policies and fairly readily obtain guidelines for implementing policies. The Executive Board and, in recent years, the Interim Committee have operated so as to expedite action. A related point also needs emphasis. From its inception, the Fund has had dedicated officials. Over the years, many persons on the Executive Board, among the Managing Directors, and on the staff have been immersed in the Fund as an instrument of world government and have been determined to see that the instrument is successful. They have conceived of the Fund as an instrument for waging world peace, as a mechanism for developing international cooperation which, using the terminology of economic theory, is "a scarce good." To bring about a solution to a controversial issue that would be in the interest of the Fund as an international organization and in the interest of the international community, numerous individuals have been willing to operate out of the limelight, behind the scenes. Some have proposed imaginative solutions. A few have taken courageous and unpopular stands. This dedication of Fund officials is perhaps the most important observation to be drawn from the Fund's experience.

Until about 1970 international monetary cooperation usually meant that the monetary authorities of the members of the Fund were willing to talk over their mutual problems and to try to come to decisions about the agreed rules, procedures, and policies with which they would conduct their international monetary arrangements. Usually such discussions took place in the Executive Board. However, after 1970 cooperation could no longer be regarded merely as consulting or holding meetings. Conferring was easy. Talking, discussing, and meeting went on frequently in many forums. Holding international conferences became a way of life for many officials and individuals. Often both participants and observers concluded that nothing happened as a result of talks or meetings. Moreover, by the 1970s, there were difficult problems that needed resolution. International cooperation, therefore, had to take the form of governments reaching agreed solutions for these problems. The criterion of success became the outcome of the conference or of the meeting, not merely holding it.

By this criterion, the international monetary cooperation achieved through the Fund in the years 1972 to 1978 was certainly good. It was an unusually difficult environment in which international monetary cooperation in these years had to take place. On the economic side, as seen throughout this narrative, the Fund and its members were faced with the most serious world economic problems in several decades. High rates of inflation, deep recession, slow economic growth, widespread large payments disequilibria, and unstable currency relationships persisted. Moreover, all the concepts and guideposts for judging the evolution of international monetary arrangements and of the Fund's activities, and even of economic affairs generally, were no longer applicable. As the accepted economic theories and conventional wisdom were challenged and disputed, there was little agreement on the new directions to be taken or the new guideposts to be used.

There were also political problems. More than ever officials who came to the negotiating table had different backgrounds, different cultures, different expectations, and different negotiating experiences and skills. While these differences had existed since the Fund's establishment, there were now more officials at the negotiating table with more diverse backgrounds than before, and they all were more vocal. In addition, the authorities of the industrial members of the Fund held differing views on many issues, and in a multipolar situation in which economic power was diffused, they were conducting a power struggle over which views were to be dominant. Developing members also were by no means homogeneous, economically or politically. But the authorities of developing members, nonetheless, wanted to be regarded as working together in a common cause. Moreover, as nationalism became a dominant theme in the Third World, the common interest of officials of developing members often seemed to be to develop positions that so emphasized their demands that North-South confrontation was inevitable.

1041

Given this environment, the cooperation that was actually attained in the Fund from 1972 to 1978, achieved partly by habit and partly by the urgency of the circumstances, has to be regarded as remarkable.

If the Fund "came into being as a result of a supreme act of faith," by 1978 experience had amply demonstrated that the faith of those who more than 30 years before had dared to create the Fund had decidedly been justified.[4] The experiment in international monetary cooperation had proved to be successful, even through the extremely difficult years of the 1970s.

As 1978 came to an end, some of the problems in international monetary arrangements and for the Fund that had emerged in the previous seven years seemed to be subsiding. The first oil crisis was over. The industrial countries had been able to finance the large payments deficits that had suddenly confronted them in 1974. While many developing countries still had huge oil-related payments deficits, for the most part they were finding necessary financing, much of it through private channels. Indeed, the economies of some developing countries were growing even more rapidly than those of many industrial countries. After some years of resistance, the industrial countries had agreed to pursue a coordinated strategy for economic growth. The U.S. authorities were starting to take steps to stabilize the dollar and, after some years of weakness, the pound sterling and the Italian lira were stronger than they had been. New Articles of Agreement were in force, and the Fund, under a new Managing Director, was looking forward to enlarged quotas under the Seventh General Review, to a supplementary financing facility, to new allocations of SDRs, to improving the SDR, to fresh consideration of a substitution account, and to other arrangements that would help the international monetary system evolve further.

This relatively brighter outlook as of the end of 1978 was to be reversed when severe new problems erupted in 1979, including a second round of oil price increases. But the new problems starting in 1979 begin yet another era of Fund history.

---

[4]*History, 1945–65*, Vol. I, p. 1.

Appendices

Appendix A. Executive Directors and their Alternates, 1972–78

In the three tables of Appendix A, the various constituencies are listed, in descending order, by the size of the voting power of their Executive Director on December 31, 1978. An exception is made in Table A–2 where the constituency headed by China, formed in 1960 and ended in 1972, is listed first. (See footnote 6 of Chapter 2, page 35.) In Tables A–2 and A–3, members of a constituency are listed in the chronological order in which they joined the constituency.

Table A–1. Appointed Executive Directors and Their Alternates, 1972–78

| Member | | Appointed Director | | Executive Director and Alternate[2] | | |
| | | | | | Service[3] | |
Name	Became Member[3]	From	To	Name	From	To
United States	12/27/45	1946		William B. Dale	11/1/62	2/28/74
				Charles R. Harley	*9/17/70*	
				Sam Y. Cross	5/3/74	
				Charles R. Harley		*11/4/75*
				Thomas Leddy	*11/5/75*	
United Kingdom	12/27/45	1946		Derek Mitchell	11/7/69	12/17/72
				Ronald H. Gilchrist	*7/20/70*	
				Peter J. Bull	*7/9/72*	*7/8/72*
				Anthony K. Rawlinson	12/18/72	10/15/75
				Peter J. Bull		
				William S. Ryrie	10/17/75	
				Peter J. Bull	*5/3/76*	
				Pendarell Kent		*5/2/76*
Germany, Federal Republic of	8/14/52	1960		Günther Schleiminger	5/1/68	12/13/74
				Lore Fuenfgelt	*8/26/68*	*12/31/74*
				Eckard Pieske	1/1/75	
				Gerhard Laske	*1/1/75*	

Table A-1 (*concluded*). Appointed Executive Directors and Their Alternates, 1972-78

Member[1]		Appointed Director		Executive Director and Alternate[2]		
					Service[3]	
Name	Became Member[3]	From	To	Name	From	To
France	12/27/45	1946		Marc Viénot	11/1/70	6/30/73
				Claude Beaurain	*1/1/71*	
				Jacques Henri Wahl	7/1/73	9/4/78
				Claude Beaurain		*7/31/74*
				Gérard de Margerie	*8/1/74*	*6/30/75*
				Jean Foglizzo	*8/1/75*	*8/31/77*
				Denis Samuel-Lajeunesse	*9/1/77*	
				Paul Mentré de Loye	9/5/78	
				Denis Samuel-Lajeunesse		
Japan	8/13/52	1970		Hideo Suzuki	11/1/70	10/31/72
				Koichi Satow	*11/1/70*	
				Kaichi Kawaguchi	11/1/72	10/31/76
				Koichi Satow		*6/14/73*
				Mikio Wakatsuki	*6/15/73*	*7/19/76*
				Rei Masunaga	*7/20/76*	
				Masanao Matsunaga	11/1/76	
				Rei Masunaga		
Saudi Arabia[4]	8/26/57	1978		Mahsoun B. Jalal	11/1/78	

[1] Article XII, Section 3(b)(i) provides for the appointment of Executive Directors by the five members having the largest quotas.
[2] Alternate Executive Directors, always appointed by the Executive Director, are indicated by italic type.
[3] Dates are given in the following order: month/day/year.
[4] Saudi Arabia appointed an Executive Director under the terms of Article XII, Section 3(c) of the Articles of Agreement as amended on April 1, 1978. An Alternate Executive Director, Yusuf A. Nimatallah, was appointed effective January 15, 1979.

Table A–2. Elected Executive Directors and Their Alternates, 1972–78

	Members of Constituency[1]			Executive Director and Alternate[2]	Service[3]	
		In Constituency				
Name	Became Member[3]	From	To	Name	From	To
China[4]	12/27/45	1960	1972	Peh Yuan Hsu (China)	11/1/70	6/15/72
Korea	8/26/55	1966	1972	*Nguyên Huu Hanh (Viet Nam)*	*11/1/68*	
Viet Nam	9/21/56	1966	1972	Placido L. Mapa, Jr. (Philippines)	6/16/72	10/31/72
Philippines	12/27/45	1970	1972	*Nguyên Huu Hanh (Viet Nam)*	*6/16/72*	*10/31/72*[5]
Netherlands	12/27/45	1946		Pieter Lieftinck (Netherlands)	10/1/55	12/31/76
Israel	7/12/54	1954		*Tom de Vries (Netherlands)*	*1/15/69*	
Yugoslavia	12/27/45	1954		H.O. Ruding (Netherlands)	1/1/77	
Cyprus	12/21/61	1962				
Romania[6]	12/15/72	1974		*Tom de Vries (Netherlands)*		
Canada	12/27/45	1946		Robert Bryce (Canada)	10/1/71	10/31/74
Ireland	8/8/57	1960		*Donald Owen Mills (Jamaica)*	*1/1/71*	*10/31/72*
Jamaica	2/21/63	1964		George Reynolds (Ireland)	11/1/72	
Barbados[7]	12/29/70	1972		Bernard J. Drabble (Canada)	11/1/74	
Bahamas[6]	8/21/73	1974		*George Reynolds (Ireland)*	*11/1/75*	*10/31/75*
Grenada[8]	8/27/75	1976		Donal Lynch (Ireland)		
Italy	3/27/47	1947[9]		Francesco Palamenghi-Crispi (Italy)	12/1/67	7/5/76
Spain	9/15/58	1958	1978	Carlos Bustelo (Spain)	11/1/68	11/16/73
Portugal	3/29/61	1962		*Jose Luis Mora (Spain)*	*12/17/73*	*1/31/76*
Malta	9/11/68	1970		*Eduardo O. de Toledo (Spain)*	*2/1/76*	
Greece	12/27/45	1978		Lamberto Dini (Italy)	7/6/76	
				Eduardo O. de Toledo (Spain)	*11/1/78*[10]	*10/31/78*
				Costa P. Caranicas (Greece)		

Table A-2 (continued). Elected Executive Directors and Their Alternates, 1972–78

Members of Constituency[1]				Executive Director and Alternate[2]		
		In Constituency			Service[3]	
Name	Became Member[3]	From	To	Name	From	To
Australia	8/5/47	1948[9]		Lindsay B. Brand (Australia)	12/24/70	4/13/75
South Africa	12/27/45	1948	1974	Robert van S. Smit (South Africa)	6/5/71	10/31/74
Viet Nam	9/21/56	1956	1966	R. S. Deane (New Zealand)	11/1/74	
New Zealand	8/31/61	1962		R. J. Whitelaw (Australia)	4/14/75	
Lesotho	7/25/68	1968	1972	R. S. Deane (New Zealand)		10/31/76
Swaziland	9/22/69	1970	1974	Ernest Leung (Philippines)	11/1/76	10/31/78
Western Samoa[7]	12/28/71	1972		Richard John Lang (New Zealand)	11/1/78	
Philippines	12/27/45	1974				
Papua New Guinea[8]	10/9/75	1976				
Korea	8/26/55	1978				
Seychelles[11]	6/30/77	1978				
Solomon Islands	9/22/78	1978				
Egypt[12]	12/27/45	1946		Nazih Deif (Egypt)	11/1/70	10/31/76
Iran	12/29/45	1946	1972	Muhammad Al-Atrash (Syrian Arab Republic)	12/1/70	1/5/73
Iraq	12/27/45	1946				
Lebanon	4/14/47	1948		M. M. Ahmad (Pakistan)	6/8/73	8/28/73
Syrian Arab Republic	4/10/47	1948		Mohamed Finaish (Libya)	8/29/73	
Pakistan	7/11/50	1950		Muhammad Al-Atrash (Syrian Arab Republic)	11/1/76	10/31/78
Jordan	8/29/52	1952				
Afghanistan	7/14/55	1956		Mohamed Finaish (Libya)		
Saudi Arabia	8/26/57	1958	1974	Kadhim A. Al-Eyd (Iraq)	5/24/77	5/23/77
Kuwait	9/13/62	1962	1978	Mohamed Finaish (Libya)	11/1/78	
Somalia	8/31/62	1964		Kadhim A. Al-Eyd (Iraq)		
Yemen Arab Republic	5/22/70	1970				
Yemen, People's Democratic Republic of	9/29/69	1970	1972			
Oman[7]	12/23/71	1972	1974			
Bahrain	9/7/72	1972				
Libyan Arab Jamahiriya[13]	9/17/58	1972				
Qatar	9/8/72	1972				
United Arab Emirates	9/22/72	1972				
Maldives[11]	1/13/78	1978				

Country				Executive Directors and Alternates		
Belgium	12/27/45	1946		André van Campenhout (Belgium)	12/1/54	10/31/73
Luxembourg	12/27/45	1946		*Heinrich G. Schneider (Austria)*	*12/1/70*	
Austria	8/27/48	1954		Jacques de Groote (Belgium)	11/1/73	
Turkey	3/11/47	1954		*Heinrich G. Schneider (Austria)*	*11/1/73*	
Algeria	9/26/63	1972		Mohammed Yeganeh (Iran)	11/1/72	8/7/73
Ghana	9/20/57	1972		*Costa P. Caranicas (Greece)*	*11/1/72*	
Greece	12/27/45	1972		Jahangir Amuzegar (Iran)	8/8/73	
Iran	12/29/45	1972	1978	Costa P. Caranicas (Greece)		*10/31/78*[10]
Morocco	4/25/58	1972		*Mohammed Yeganeh (Iran)*	*12/19/78*	
Tunisia	4/14/58	1972				
Yemen, People's Democratic Republic of	9/29/69	1972	1978			
Afghanistan	7/14/55	1974				
Oman	12/23/71	1974				
India[14]	12/27/45	1972		P.S.N. Prasad (India)	6/5/71	5/31/75
Bangladesh	8/17/72	1972		*Sharad S. Maranthe (India)*	*2/1/69*	*10/31/72*
Sri Lanka[15]	8/29/50	1972		*W. M. Tilakaratna (Sri Lanka)*	*11/1/72*	
				S. Jagannathan (India)	6/1/75	10/31/76
				W. M. Tilakaratna (Sri Lanka)		*6/30/76*
				Warnasena Rasaputram (Sri Lanka)	*7/1/76*	
				M. G. Kaul (India)	11/1/76	3/14/77
				Warnasena Rasaputram (Sri Lanka)		
				S. D. Deshmukh (India)	6/3/77	
				Warnasena Rasaputram (Sri Lanka)		

Table A-2 (continued). Elected Executive Directors and Their Alternates, 1972–78

| Members of Constituency[1] | | | | Executive Director and Alternate[2] | | |
Name	Became Member[3]	In Constituency From	In Constituency To	Name	Service[3] From	Service[3] To
Denmark	3/30/46	1952		Erik Brofoss (Norway)	11/1/70	10/31/73
Finland	1/14/48	1952		*Sigurgeir Jónsson (Iceland)*	12/31/68	10/31/72
Iceland	12/27/45	1952		*Sven Lampe (Sweden)*	11/1/72	
Norway	12/27/45	1952		Per Åsbrink (Sweden)	11/1/73	10/31/76
Sweden	8/31/51	1952		*Sven Lampe (Sweden)*	2/1/74	1/31/74
				Knut J. M. Andreassen (Norway)	3/1/75	2/28/75
				Jørn H. Kjaer (Denmark)		
				Frede Hollensen (Denmark)	11/1/76	10/31/78
				Jørn H. Kjaer (Denmark)		2/28/77
				Matti Vanhala (Finland)	3/1/77	
				Matti Vanhala (Finland)	11/1/78	10/31/78
				Gisli Blöndal (Iceland)	11/1/78	
Ghana	9/20/57	1958	1972	Byanti Kharmawan (Indonesia)	11/1/68	
Libyan Arab Jamahiriya[13]	9/17/58	1958	1972	*Costa P. Caranicas (Greece)*	11/1/70	10/31/72[10]
Malaysia[15]	3/7/58	1958	1970	Nguyên Huu Hanh (Viet Nam)	11/1/72	10/31/74[5]
		1972		*Maung Shein (Burma)*	11/1/74	1/19/76
Morocco	4/25/58	1958	1972	*Sein Maung (Burma)*	1/20/76	10/31/76
Tunisia	4/14/58	1958	1972	*Kiat Chong Ng (Singapore)*	11/1/76	10/31/76
Lao People's Democratic Republic[15]	7/5/61	1962	1970	*Savenaca Siwatibau (Fiji)*	11/1/78	
		1972				
Algeria	9/26/63	1964	1972			
Singapore[15]	8/3/66	1966	1970			
		1972				
Indonesia[16]	2/21/67	1968				
Democratic Kampuchea[17]						
Greece	12/27/45	1970	1972			
Burma[15]	1/3/52	1972				
Fiji[7]	5/28/71	1972	1978			
Korea	8/26/55	1972				

Country				Director / Alternate		
Nepal[15]	9/6/61	1972				
Philippines[15]	12/27/45	1972				
Thailand[15]	5/3/49	1972				
Viet Nam	9/21/56	1972	1974			
Burundi	9/28/63	1964		Maurice P. Omwony (Kenya)	11/1/70	10/31/72
Guinea	9/28/63	1964		*S. B. Nicol-Cole (Sierra Leone)*	*11/1/70*	*10/31/72*
Kenya	2/3/64	1964		S. B. Nicol-Cole (Sierra Leone)	11/1/72	10/31/74
Liberia	3/28/62	1964		*H. R. Monday, Jr. (The Gambia)*	*11/1/72*	*10/31/74*
Nigeria	3/30/61	1964		H. R. Monday, Jr. (The Gambia)	11/1/74	10/31/76
Sierra Leone	9/10/62	1964		*J. B. Zulu (Zambia)*	*11/1/74*	*7/5/76*
Sudan	9/5/57	1964		*Wila D. Mung'omba (Zambia)*	*10/4/76*	*10/31/76*
Tanzania	9/10/62	1964		Wila D. Mung'omba (Zambia)	11/1/76	10/31/78
Trinidad and Tobago	9/16/63	1964	1976	*Festus G. Mogae (Botswana)*	*11/1/76*	
Uganda	9/27/63	1964		Festus G. Mogae (Botswana)	11/1/78	
Malawi	7/19/65	1966		*Semyano Kiingi (Uganda)*	*11/1/78*	
Zambia	9/23/65	1966				
Botswana	7/24/68	1968				
Gambia, The	9/21/67	1968				
Ethiopia	12/27/45	1970				
Lesotho	7/25/68	1972				
Swaziland	9/22/69	1974				
Benin	7/10/63	1963[9]		Antoine W. Yaméogo (Upper Volta)	11/1/66	10/31/76
Cameroon	7/10/63	1963[9]		*Léon M. Rajaobelina*	*11/1/66*	*8/15/72*
Central African Republic	7/10/63	1963[9]		*(Madagascar)*		
Chad	7/10/63	1963[9]		*Samuel Nana-Sinkam*	*10/15/72*	*10/31/76*
Congo	7/10/63	1963[9]		*(Cameroon)*		
Gabon	9/10/63	1963[9]		Samuel Nana-Sinkam (Cameroon)	11/1/76	
Ivory Coast	3/11/63	1963[9]		*Victor Alipui (Togo)*	*1/19/77*	*10/31/77*
Madagascar	9/25/63	1963[9]		*Abderrahmane Alfidja (Niger)*	*1/3/78*	
Mauritania	9/10/63	1963[9]				
Niger	4/24/63	1963[9]				
Rwanda	9/30/63	1963[9]				
Senegal	8/31/62	1963[9]				

1051

Table A-2 (concluded). Elected Executive Directors and Their Alternates, 1972–78

| Members of Constituency[1] | | | | Executive Director and Alternate[2] | | |
| Name | In Constituency | | | Name | Service[3] | |
	Became Member[3]	From	To		From	To
Togo	8/1/62	1963[9]				
Upper Volta	5/2/63	1963[9]				
Zaïre	9/28/63	1966				
Mauritius	9/23/68	1968				
Equatorial Guinea	12/22/69	1970				
Mali	9/27/63	1970				
Comoros	9/21/76	1978				
Guinea-Bissau[11]	3/24/77	1978				
São Tomé and Principe[11]	9/30/77	1978				
Cape Verde[18]	11/20/78	—				
Djibouti[18]	12/29/78	—				

[1] Article XII, Section 3(b)(iii) of the Articles of Agreement was applicable until the 1978 regular election of Executive Directors. Executive Directors who took office on November 1, 1978 were elected in accordance with the amended provision of Article XII, Section 3(b)(iii) introduced by the Second Amendment.

[2] Alternate Executive Directors, always appointed by the Executive Director, are indicated by italic type.

[3] Dates are given in the following order: month/day/year.

[4] See fn. 6 of Chap. 2, p. 35.

[5] Effective November 1, 1972, Nguyên Huu Hanh (Viet Nam) became Alternate to Byanti Kharmawan (Indonesia).

[6] The Bahamas and Romania joined the Fund after the 1972 regular election of Executive Directors. The Bahamas designated Robert Bryce (Canada) to look after its interests in the Fund until the next regular election of Executive Directors in 1974; Romania designated Pieter Lieftinck (Netherlands).

[7] Barbados, Fiji, Oman, and Western Samoa joined the Fund after the 1970 regular election of Executive Directors. Barbados designated Robert Bryce (Canada) to look after its interests in the Fund until the next regular election of Executive Directors in 1972; Fiji designated Byanti Kharmawan (Indonesia); Oman designated Nazih Deif (Egypt); Western Samoa designated Lindsay B. Brand (Australia).

[8] Grenada and Papua New Guinea joined the Fund after the 1974 regular election of Executive Directors. Grenada designated Bernard J.Drabble (Canada) to look after its interests in the Fund until the next regular election of Executive Directors in 1976; Papua New Guinea designated R. J. Whitelaw (Australia).

[9] Interim elections, pursuant to Board of Governors Resolutions Nos. IM–10, 2–8, and 17–5, as amended by Resolution No. 18–7, respectively.

[10] Effective November 1, 1972, Costa P. Caranicas (Greece) became Alternate to Mohammed Yeganeh (Iran), and effective November 1, 1978, Alternate to Lamberto Dini (Italy).

[11] Guinea-Bissau, Maldives, São Tomé and Principe, and Seychelles joined the Fund after the 1976 regular election of Executive Directors. Guinea-Bissau and São Tomé and Principe designated Samuel Nana-Sinkam (Cameroon) to look after their interests in the Fund until the next regular election of Executive Directors in 1978; Maldives designated Muhammad Al-Atrash (Syrian Arab Republic); Seychelles designated R. J. Whitelaw (Australia).

[12] Egypt did not participate in the regular election of Executive Directors in 1978.

[13] The full formal name, the Socialist People's Libyan Arab Jamahiriya, became effective on March 2, 1977.

[14]India had an appointed Executive Director from 1946 until 1972. On November 1, 1970, Japan replaced India as one of the five members having the largest quotas and therefore qualified to appoint an Executive Director in accordance with Article XII, Section 3(b)(i). India continued, however, to be entitled to appoint an Executive Director until the next regular election of Executive Directors in 1972, pursuant to Board of Governors Resolution No. IM–7. After November 1, 1972, India formed an elected constituency with Bangladesh and Sri Lanka.

[15]Burma, Lao People's Democratic Republic, Malaysia, Nepal, Singapore, Sri Lanka, and Thailand, whose votes were not cast for any of the Executive Directors elected in the 1970 regular election of Executive Directors, designated Hideo Suzuki (Japan) to look after their interests in the Fund until the next regular election of Executive Directors in 1972.

[16]Indonesia became a member of the Fund on April 15, 1954, withdrew effective August 17, 1965, and rejoined on February 21, 1967.

[17]In June 1978 the Fund, as was done in the United Nations, began to use the name Democratic Kampuchea to refer to what was previously called Cambodia or the Khmer Republic.

[18]Cape Verde and Djibouti joined the Fund after the 1978 regular election of Executive Directors. They designated Samuel Nana-Sinkam (Cameroon) to look after their interests in the Fund until the next regular election of Executive Directors in 1980.

Table A–3. Elected Executive Directors and Their Alternates (Latin America and Caribbean), 1972–78

Members of Constituency				Executive Director and Alternate[2]		
		In Constituency			Service[3]	
Name	Became Member[3]	From	To	Name	From	To
Costa Rica	1/8/46	1946		Luis Ugueto (Venezuela)	11/1/70	10/31/72
El Salvador	3/14/46	1946		Guillermo González (Costa Rica)	11/25/70	10/31/72
Guatemala	12/28/45	1946		Guillermo Bueso (Honduras)	11/1/72	10/31/74
Mexico	12/31/45	1946		Alfredo Phillips O. (Mexico)	11/13/72	5/19/73
Venezuela	12/30/46	1948		Francisco Suárez (Mexico)	5/20/73	10/31/74
Honduras	12/27/45	1952		Francisco Suárez (Mexico)	11/1/74	10/31/76
Nicaragua	3/14/46	1952		Roberto Guarnieri (Venezuela)	11/1/74	10/31/76
Spain	9/15/58	1978		Roberto Guarnieri (Venezuela)	11/1/76	10/31/77
				Néstor O. Caldera (Nicaragua)	11/1/76	
				Eduardo Mayobre (Venezuela)	11/1/77	10/31/78
				Néstor O. Caldera (Nicaragua)		10/31/78
				Joaquín Muns (Spain)	11/1/78	
				Ariel Buira (Mexico)	11/1/78	
Brazil	1/14/46	1946		Alexandre Kafka (Brazil)	11/1/66	
Peru	12/31/45	1946		Basilio Martins (Brazil)	10/2/71	11/6/74
Dominican Republic	12/28/45	1948		Clovis L. A. Albuquerque (Brazil)	11/11/74	10/31/75
Panama	3/14/46	1952		Winston Temple-Seminario (Peru)	11/1/75	12/31/77
Haiti	9/8/53	1954				
Colombia	12/27/45	1956		T. Ainsworth Harewood (Trinidad and Tobago)	1/1/78	
Guyana	9/26/66	1970				
Trinidad and Tobago	9/16/63	1976				
Suriname	4/27/78	1978				

1054

Member	Date	Year	Executive Director / Alternate	From	To
Argentina	9/20/56	1956	Carlos Massad A. (Chile)	11/1/70	10/31/74
Bolivia	12/27/45	1956	*Ricardo H. Arriazu (Argentina)*	*11/1/68*	*10/31/74*
Chile	12/31/45	1956	Roberto Gavaldá (Argentina)	11/1/74	7/15/76
Ecuador	12/28/45	1956	*José Luis Zabala (Chile)*	*11/1/74*	*10/31/75*
Paraguay	12/28/45	1956	*Santiago Sevilla (Ecuador)*	*11/1/75*	
Uruguay	3/11/46	1956	Dante Simone (Argentina)	7/20/76	10/31/78
			Santiago Sevilla (Ecuador)		*12/31/76*
			Alfredo Crespo (Ecuador)	*1/21/77*	*10/31/78*
			Francisco Garcés (Chile)	*11/1/77*	*10/31/78*
			Francisco Garcés (Chile)	11/1/78	
			Julio C. Gutierréz (Paraguay)	*11/1/78*	

[1] Article XII, Section 3(b)(iv) of the Articles of Agreement governing election of Executive Directors from Latin American and Caribbean members was applied until the 1978 regular election of Executive Directors. Executive Directors who took office on November 1, 1978 were elected in accordance with the amended provision of Article XII, Section 3(b)(ii) introduced by the Second Amendment. After the 1978 election of the Executive Directors, the constituency made up mostly of the Central American Republics had the largest voting power because Spain joined the constituency; hence this constituency is listed first in the table.

[2] Alternate Executive Directors, always appointed by the Executive Director, are indicated by italic type.

[3] Dates are given in the following order: month/day/year.

APPENDICES

Appendix B. Management and Senior Staff
as of December 31, 1978

The Managing Director   Jacques de Larosière
The Deputy Managing Director   William B. Dale

The General Counsel   Joseph Gold
The Economic Counsellor   J. J. Polak

Department or Office	Head of Department or Office	Other Senior Staff[1]
Administration	Kenneth N. Clark	P.N. Kaul
		William M. Avery
		Timothy Cole
		John D. Huddleston
		Henri H.P. King
		Charles O. Olsen
		Ronald J. Powell
		Chaiha K. Rhee
African	J.B. Zulu	R.J. Bhatia
		Edwin L. Bornemann
		Jack D. Guenther
		Kwame Kwateng
		Oumar Barou Makalou
		D. Boushehri
		Evangelos A. Calamitsis
		Francis d'A. Collings
		Alberto S. Foz
		Christian A. Francois
		Bo Karlstroem
		Joseph G. Keyes
		Joachim W. Kratz
		Massimo Russo
		Grant B. Taplin
Asian	Tun Thin	Andreas Abadjis
		Albert A. Mattera
		P.R. Narvekar
		W. John R. Woodley
		Joachim Ahrensdorf
		Paul Chabrier
		Hubert Neiss
		Kunio Saito
		Douglas A. Scott
		Kemal Siber
		Bruce J. Smith
		Gunnar Tomasson
Central Banking Service	Roland Tenconi	San Lin
		N.H. Hanh
		D.R. Khatkhate
		Richard H. Miller
		James K. Nettles

Department or Office	Head of Department or Office	Other Senior Staff[1]
European Department	L.A. Whittome	Rolf Evensen Azizali Mohammed Albin Pfeifer Brian Rose Ekhard O.C. Brehmer Patrick B. de Fontenay Hans O. Schmitt Geoffrey Tyler Horst Ungerer Harilaos Vittas A. Charles Woodward
Exchange and Trade Relations	Ernest Sturc	C. David Finch S. Kanesa-Thasan Subimal Mookerjee Donald K. Palmer Eduard H. Brau Michael Dakolias Erik Elmholt Hans W. Gerhard Manuel Guitián W.F. Hughes John B. McLenaghan Bahram Nowzad Richard C. Williams
Fiscal Affairs	Richard Goode	W.A. Beveridge Rasheed O. Khalid Leif Muten A.M. Abdel-Rahman Carlos A. Aguirre E.A. Conrad Jean-Francois Garnier Richard S. Latham A. Premchand Richard A. Radford Alan A. Tait Vito Tanzi David C. Treffry
IMF Institute	Gerard M. Teyssier	Ciro Tognetti U Tun Wai Andrew H. Gantt M. Haris Jafri Orlando H. Lobo Jean-Marie Parmentier Arthur H. Whitfield
Legal Department	Joseph Gold	George Nicoletopoulos[2] James G. Evans, Jr. Robert C. Effros William E. Holder

APPENDICES

Department or Office	Head of Department or Office	Other Senior Staff[1]
		Philine R. Lachman Rose S. Porras Stephen A. Silard Olav C.A. Snellingen John V. Surr
Middle Eastern	A.S. Shaalan	A.K. El Selehdar A.S. Ray
		Andrew Crockett F. Drees A.S. Gerakis S.H. Hitti B.A. Karamali S. von Post Muhammad Yaqub
Research	J.J. Polak	Rudolf R. Rhomberg Charles F. Schwartz John H. Young
		Jacques Artus Carl P. Blackwell Anne W.R. Braun Louis M. Goreux Anthony Lanyi John S. Smith George von Furstenberg
Secretary's	Leo Van Houtven	D.E. Brantley Joseph W. Lang, Jr.
		Margaret G. de Vries Norman K. Humphreys Katherine F. Magurn Marie C. Stark Alan Wright
Treasurer's	Walter O. Habermeier	Robert J. Familton David Williams
		Muhammad N. Bhuiyan Duane H. Brown A.G. Chandavarkar David Cutler Dhruba Gupta Willard A. Hawxhurst Walter T. Powers Anna Watkins Gunter Wittich
Western Hemisphere	E. Walter Robichek	Sterie T. Beza Carlos E. Sanson Edison V. Zayas
		Omar Albertelli

Department or Office	Head of Department or Office	Other Senior Staff[1]
		Marcello Caiola
		Joseph Chatelain
		Joaquin Ferran
		Julio E. Gonzalez
		Linda M. Koenig
		Horst J.O. Struckmeyer
		Jose D. Teigeiro
		Frits van Beek
Bureau of Language Services	Bernardo T. Rutgers	Antonio Medrano
		Jean E. Merry
Bureau of Statistics	Werner Dannemann	Arie C. Bouter
		Jai B. Gupta
		Robert L. Kline
		Jonathan V. Levin
		Akira P. Nose
		Anne F. Oesterlen
		Chandrakant A. Patel
		Dan R. Silling
		Muthuswami Swaminathan
Office in Europe	Aldo Guetta	Andrew J. Beith
		Julius K. Rosenblatt
Office in Geneva	Fernando Vera	Jack P. Barnouin
Finance & Development		Samuel I. Katz
Information Office	Jay H. Reid	Charles S. Gardner
Internal Auditor		J. William Lowe
Special Representative to the United Nations		Jan-Maarten Zegers

[1]In each department or office the first grouping lists, in alphabetical order, Deputy Directors and Senior Advisors or the equivalent; the second grouping lists, in alphabetical order, all other senior staff.
[2]Associate General Counsel.

Appendix C. Chronology, 1972–78

1972

January 1 — The third and final allocation of SDRs (SDR 2.95 billion) for the first basic period was made, bringing the total of SDRs allocated since January 1970 to a little over SDR 9.3 billion.

January 4 — The Executive Board took a decision specifying the exchange rates to be used in lieu of par values for computations in the Fund's transactions and operations and for adjustments of the Fund's holdings of currencies, thereby enabling the Fund to resume temporarily its financial operations disrupted since the United States suspended official convertibility of the dollar on August 15, 1971.

February 25 — The Executive Board recommended to the Board of Governors that the Fund express its financial accounts in terms of SDRs instead of U.S. dollars. The Board of Governors approved the recommendation, effective March 20, 1972.

April 3–7 — The Group of Twenty-Four held inaugural meetings at the level of both deputies and ministers in Caracas, Venezuela. The Managing Director addressed the first ministerial meeting.

April 24 — The narrow margins agreement of the European Community (EC), "the snake in the tunnel," entered into force as the central bank governors of the six members agreed that the margins of fluctuation between their currencies would not be permitted to exceed 2¼ percent, half the margin permitted under the Fund's temporary regime of central rates and wider margins.

April 26 — Agreement was reached on arrangements for the United Kingdom to effect a large repurchase of pounds sterling from the Fund. Agreement had been difficult because the United Kingdom wanted to repurchase with U.S. dollars, but the Fund could not accept that currency in repurchase.

May 8 — The new par value for the U.S. dollar, devaluing the dollar by 7.89 percent in terms of gold, became effective. Several other members also changed the par values of their currencies. The Executive Board specified the exchange rates to be used for computations in the Fund's transactions and operations and for adjustments of the Fund's holdings of currencies. The decision of January 4, 1972 was terminated.

June 23
U.K. officials informed the Fund that the pound sterling would be allowed to float temporarily. This was the first break in the exchange rates agreed in December 1971. The six countries of the EC resolved to keep stable the rates of their own currencies.

June 26
The Executive Board agreed on a draft resolution to the Board of Governors recommending that an ad hoc Committee of Governors on Reform of the International Monetary System and Related Issues, referred to as the Committee of Twenty, be set up. This resolution was adopted by the Board of Governors, effective July 26, 1972.

August 17
Bangladesh, with a quota of SDR 125 million, became the 121st Fund member and a participant in the Special Drawing Account.

August 18
The Executive Board submitted to the Board of Governors a report entitled *Reform of the International Monetary System.*

August 31
The Board of Governors adopted a resolution taking note of a report of the Executive Directors recommending that the size of the Executive Board should remain at 20 and that the African members should continue to be entitled to elect 2 Executive Directors.

September 7
Bahrain, with a quota of SDR 10 million, became the 122nd Fund member and a participant in the Special Drawing Account.

September 8
Qatar, with a quota of SDR 20 million, became the 123rd Fund member, but not a participant in the Special Drawing Account.

September 22
The United Arab Emirates, with a quota of SDR 15 million, became the 124th Fund member, but not a participant in the Special Drawing Account.

September 28
The Committee of Twenty held its inaugural meeting (at the ministerial level) in Washington and selected Ali Wardhana, Finance Minister of Indonesia, as Chairman.

September 29
The deputies of the Committee of Twenty held their first meeting in Washington and selected C. Jeremy Morse of the United Kingdom as Chairman.

November 1
The term of Frank A. Southard, Jr. as Deputy Managing Director of the Fund was extended for another four years. He had been Deputy Managing Director since November 1962.

November 27–29   The deputies of the Committee of Twenty held their second meeting, in Washington, the first at which substantive issues were discussed. Attention centered on a U.S. proposal for signaling the need for balance of payments adjustment by use of reserve indicators.

December 15   Romania, with a quota of SDR 190 million, became the 125th Fund member and a participant in the Special Drawing Account.

December 15–20   After reviewing the rules for reconstitution of SDRs, the Executive Board recommended that the same rules be continued, and a few days later, the Board of Governors adopted a resolution to this effect. The Executive Board also decided not to adopt any new rules or procedures for designation of SDRs.

1973

January 1   A second SDR period, an empty period in which no SDRs were allocated, began. Denmark, Ireland, and the United Kingdom joined the European Community, enlarging its membership to nine.

January 21–22   The deputies of the Group of Twenty-Four met in Paris to discuss international monetary questions and reiterated the aspiration that a link be established between allocations of SDRs and the provision of development finance.

January 22   To stem large capital outflows and heavy loss of reserves, Italy introduced a free market for capital transactions, the second break in the exchange rates agreed in December 1971.

January 23   The Swiss franc was permitted to float.

January 23–25   The deputies of the Committee of Twenty, at their third meeting, held in Paris, turned their attention to the role of reserve assets and to methods for achieving "asset settlement," a new form of currency convertibility.

February 12   George P. Shultz, Secretary of the U.S. Treasury, announced late at night that President Nixon was requesting the U.S. Congress to authorize a proposal to the Fund that there be a devaluation of the U.S. dollar of 10 percent in terms of SDRs, the second devaluation of the dollar in 14 months. The Executive Board, meeting later, discussed the U.S. action and supported it.

February 13	Italian authorities informed the Fund that for the time being the rate for the lira in the official exchange market (for current transactions) would float. Japan also informed the Fund that, as a temporary measure, the Japanese yen would float.
February 16	The Executive Board put the new par value of the U.S. dollar into effect for purposes of the Fund's transactions and operations. The new rate of US$1 = SDR 0.828 948 was to be in use for the Fund's purposes prior to the formal establishment of this par value with the Fund by the U.S. authorities, which occurred on October 18, 1973.
March 2	Turbulence in exchange markets again led to the closing of markets around the world. The Executive Directors held a discussion of this further crisis.
March 9	The finance ministers and central bank governors of the Group of Ten met in Paris, under the chairmanship of Valéry Giscard d'Estaing, together with representatives of the countries of the EC, to discuss the exchange crisis. Pierre-Paul Schweitzer and Ali Wardhana also participated.
March 11	The finance ministers of six countries of the EC decided to introduce a joint float against the U.S. dollar. They were to maintain a maximum margin of 2¼ percent in the rates between their own currencies. Sweden and Norway joined the arrangements shortly thereafter. Ireland, Italy, and the United Kingdom continued to float their currencies independently of the joint arrangements.
March 16	The finance ministers and central bank governors of the Group of Ten and officials of the EC countries met in Paris and reached agreement on the new joint float arrangements. Mr. Schweitzer attended the meeting.
March 19	Major foreign exchange markets, closed on March 2, reopened. The par value system agreed in 1944 thus came to an end as a new regime of floating rates for most major currencies came into being.
March 22–23	The deputies of the Committee of Twenty met for the fourth time, in Washington, and decided to proceed urgently with the drafting of an Outline of the reformed system. They set up a Technical Group on Indicators and one on Disequilibrating Capital Flows.
March 26–27	The Committee of Twenty held its second meeting, in Washington. The ministers supported the decision of their deputies to prepare a draft Outline of Reform.

March 30	Mr. Schweitzer officially informed the Executive Directors that he expected his service with the Fund to terminate on August 31, 1973 when his second five-year term expired.
April 23	The Executive Board adopted a decision permitting the buffer stock facility to be used by members in connection with their loans to the International Cocoa Council to build up cocoa stocks.
May 21–25	The deputies of the Committee of Twenty, meeting for the fifth time, in Washington, considered a preliminary draft Outline of a reformed system. A Technical Group on the SDR/Aid Link and Related Proposals was set up to study the possibility of a link between allocations of SDRs and development finance.
July 11–13	The deputies of the Committee of Twenty held their sixth meeting, in Washington, to consider a revised Outline of a reformed system.
July 30–31	The Committee of Twenty held its third meeting, in Washington. Optimism increased that agreement on the reformed system might be reached.
August 21	The Bahamas, with a quota of SDR 20 million, became the 126th Fund member and a participant in the Special Drawing Account. The Board of Governors' resolution on membership for the Bahamas provided for the subscription to be paid wholly in Bahamian dollars (rather than partly in gold), at least for the time being, the first time such payment in gold had been formally waived by membership resolution.
August 31	Pierre-Paul Schweitzer's second five-year term as the fourth Managing Director ended.
September 1	H. Johannes Witteveen, of the Netherlands, became the fifth Managing Director.
September 5–7	The deputies of the Committee of Twenty, at their seventh meeting, in Paris, considered compromise arrangements for balance of payments adjustment and for currency convertibility, but failed to agree.
September 12–14	At a ministerial meeting in Tokyo, decisions were taken on the scope and timing of the Tokyo Round of Multilateral Trade Negotiations, to be conducted in Geneva, thereby inaugurating the most important international trade negotiations since the establishment of the GATT.
September 23–24	The Committee of Twenty held its fourth meeting, in Nairobi, but ministers continued to disagree. The Committee set July 31, 1974 as the deadline to complete its work.

Meanwhile, it issued an interim report to the Board of Governors, attaching a First Outline of Reform, which was written in very general terms and regarded as a document agreed by technicians only and not by officials at the political level.

September 27   The deputies of the Committee of Twenty, at their eighth meeting, in Nairobi, set up four more Technical Groups—on Intervention and Settlement, on Adjustment, on Global Liquidity and Consolidation, and on the Transfer of Real Resources.

October 10–17   Six members of OPEC, for the first time, unilaterally set new posted prices for crude oil. Prices were raised for Saudi Arabian crude oil, for example, from $3.01 to $5.12 a barrel, a 70 percent rise.

October 18   The new par value for the U.S. dollar was established with the Fund, formally instituting the dollar devaluation of February 1973.

October 31   The Executive Board agreed to special consultations by the Fund with members whose external policies were of major international importance, to be held in conjunction with the world economic outlook exercise. Mr. Witteveen had proposed these consultations as a way for the Fund to monitor the exchange rates of members with floating rates.

November 5   The Executive Board suspended for 120 days the provision of the Articles of Agreement which applied the equal value principle to transactions and operations in SDRs. This decision temporarily enabled settlements in SDRs to be made among the EC countries participating in the snake arrangements, until a new method for valuing the SDR was worked out.

November 7   The Executive Board revised its decision of December 18, 1971 temporarily permitting central rates and wider margins. A member could now fix a central rate for its currency if its rate was maintained in relation to a currency that was itself floating under the decision.

November 12   The governors of the central banks of the seven countries that had at one time actively participated in the Gold Pool, meeting at the Bank for International Settlements (BIS) in Basle, decided to terminate their agreement of March 1968 that prevented them from selling gold on the free market. Central banks could now sell gold at market prices.

November 26	The Executive Board requested the Board of Governors to prescribe the BIS as a holder of SDRs. On January 21, 1974, the BIS became the first agency other than a member government of the Fund to be permitted to accept, hold, and use SDRs.
December 7	The Executive Board agreed to a request by South Africa to terminate its agreement with the Fund of December 30, 1969 allowing South Africa to sell gold to the Fund under certain circumstances when prices for gold in free markets were relatively low.
December 23	Six oil exporting countries once more raised prices of crude oil, this time to an average of about $11 per barrel, thus nearly quadrupling the prices for crude oil since the beginning of October.

1974

January 3	Mr. Witteveen cabled Mr. Wardhana to suggest that the Committee of Twenty, planning to meet two weeks later, urgently consider the problems raised by the large rise in oil prices. Mr. Witteveen also proposed that an oil facility be created in the Fund, thereby initiating a technique that was to become known as recycling petrodollars.
January 14–15	The deputies of the Committee of Twenty held their ninth meeting, in Rome. Most deputies agreed that because of the new serious disequilibria in world payments, floating rates for the major currencies were likely to continue for some time and that prospects for a reformed international monetary system were seriously dimmed.
January 15	In a speech in London, Mr. Witteveen urged officials of members to accept oil deficits rather than curb them by deflation and restrictions, thereby possibly throwing the world economy into recession.
January 17–18	The Committee of Twenty, meeting for the fifth time, in Rome, in effect abandoned its efforts at full-scale reform of the international monetary system and decided to let a new system evolve out of existing arrangements.
January 21	France informed the Fund that the franc was being withdrawn from the EC snake to float freely for six months. The Fund welcomed the intention of the French authorities to be guided by the Fund's decision of November 1973 providing for consultations with members on external policies.

January 23	The Executive Board took a decision stating that in its consultations with members the Fund would pay special attention to the restrictions on trade and payments imposed by members.
March 1	William B. Dale, U.S. Executive Director since 1962, was appointed the Fund's fourth Deputy Managing Director, following the retirement of Mr. Southard, who had been with the Fund for 25 years, including 13 years as Executive Director for the United States.
March 4	The Board of Governors adopted a resolution extending the suspension of the equal value principle of the Articles of Agreement for an additional period of 240 days, until October 31, 1974.
March 21	Because floating of the franc made a dual market unnecessary, France abolished the separate market for financial transactions established in August 1971. The next day Italy also eliminated the dual market it had established in January 1973.
March 27–29	The deputies of the Committee of Twenty, at their tenth meeting, in Washington, received the reports of three of the Technical Groups set up in Nairobi and worked on a Final Outline of Reform.
April 5–18	After having gone to Iran in February, Mr. Witteveen went to Algeria, Kuwait, Libya, Saudi Arabia, and the United Arab Emirates to explore possibilities of Fund borrowing for the proposed oil facility. At the end of April, Mr. Dale went to Nigeria for the same purpose.
April 9–May 2	At the insistence of officials of developing countries, the Sixth Special Session of the General Assembly of the United Nations was held in New York to discuss problems of raw materials and economic development. A resolution was adopted calling for the establishment of a "new international economic order."
April 10	The Fund approved a one-year stand-by arrangement for SDR 1,000 million, in the upper credit tranches, for Italy. This stand-by arrangement was the first for Italy and the largest since that approved for France in 1969.
April 22–23	The EC finance ministers, meeting in Zeist, Netherlands, agreed that central banks should be free to buy and sell gold among themselves at prices related to prices for gold in private markets and to purchase in the market at least limited amounts of gold at prices other than the official price.

April 30	The report of the Technical Group on the Transfer of Real Resources, sent to the deputies of the Committee of Twenty, recommended the establishment of a joint committee of Governors of the Fund and of the World Bank to study the transfer of real resources to developing countries. This recommendation was the origin of the Development Committee.
May 7–9	The deputies of the Committee of Twenty, at their eleventh meeting, in Paris, completed the draft of the revised Outline of Reform and discussed the immediate steps needed to help an "unreformed" system evolve.
June 10–11	The deputies of the Committee of Twenty held their twelfth, and final meeting, in Washington, completing their work.
June 11	The finance ministers and central bank governors of the Group of Ten, meeting in Washington, agreed that central banks might value their official gold stocks at free market prices when they used such gold as collateral for loans from other central banks. The decision was expected to help Italy use its gold stocks as a basis for borrowing from the Federal Republic of Germany.
June 12–13	At its sixth and final meeting, in Washington, the Committee of Twenty agreed on several immediate steps: establishment of an Interim Committee, with advisory powers, adoption of a method of valuation of the SDR based on a basket of 16 currencies and of an initial interest rate on the SDR of 5 percent, establishment of guidelines for the management of floating exchange rates, establishment of an oil facility in the Fund, provision for countries to pledge themselves on a voluntary basis not to introduce or intensify restrictions, early adoption of an extended Fund facility, and establishment of the Development Committee. The Committee agreed also on an Outline of Reform.
June 13	The Executive Board adopted several decisions implementing the immediate steps agreed on by the Committee of Twenty.
June 14	The Chairman of the Committee of Twenty submitted to the Board of Governors the final report of the Committee of Twenty, accompanied by an *Outline of Reform*, endorsed by the Committee of Twenty.
June 26	The Executive Board took a decision associating the Fund with the Committee of Twenty's invitation to members to subscribe voluntarily to a declaration on trade aimed at avoiding an escalation of restrictions.

July 1   The Fund put into operation a method of valuing the SDR, based on a basket of the 16 currencies most used in world trade.

July 9   The Fund circulated to the Executive Directors the first draft amendments to the Articles, heralding the start of preparing the Second Amendment of the Articles of Agreement.

August 7   The Executive Board established a procedure for calls to be made on lenders in connection with purchases under the oil facility and approved borrowing agreements with seven members.

August 22   The Fund announced that, having completed borrowing agreements with seven lenders for SDR 2.8 billion for the period ending December 1975, it was now in a position to begin processing members' requests for purchases under the 1974 oil facility. Requests for purchases started to come in immediately.

September 13   The Fund established an extended facility to give medium-term assistance to developing members.

September 30   In his opening address at the Annual Meeting, Mr. Witteveen urged that another and larger oil facility for 1975 be established in the Fund.

October 2   The Committee of Twenty formally ceased to exist and the Interim Committee of the Board of Governors on the International Monetary System was established. On the following day the Interim Committee held its inaugural meeting, in Washington, and John N. Turner, Minister of Finance of Canada, was selected Chairman for two years.

October 2   The Joint Ministerial Committee of the Boards of Governors of the World Bank and the Fund on the Transfer of Real Resources to Developing Countries (the Development Committee) was established. It held its inaugural meeting, in Washington, and Henri Konan Bédié, Minister of Finance and Economy of the Ivory Coast, was selected Chairman. The immediate focus of the Committee's work would be to consider problems of the developing countries "most seriously affected" by higher oil prices and sharply higher prices for food.

October 23   After agreement in September by the Group of Ten to renew the General Arrangements to Borrow (GAB) for five more years, beginning on October 24, 1975, the Executive Directors adopted a decision agreeing to renewal of the Arrangements. This was the third renewal of the GAB.

November 14	U.S. officials were not receptive to another oil facility in the Fund. Secretary of State Henry A. Kissinger proposed instead that a "common loan and guarantee facility" (a "safety net") be created through the Organization for Economic Cooperation and Development (OECD) to redistribute up to $25 billion of petrofunds for industrial countries in 1975. In order to offer a facility to developing countries, he also proposed that a Trust Fund, managed by the International Monetary Fund, be set up to offer concessional balance of payments assistance to the poorest developing members.
December 6	In its second review of the 1974 oil facility, the Executive Board decided that members might draw up to the maximum amount of their calculated access and that a member could still draw under the oil facility if the Fund received from the member, before February 28, 1975, a statement of its intention to draw.
December 15–16	President Valéry Giscard d'Estaing of France and President Gerald R. Ford of the United States, meeting in Martinique, agreed that a government could revalue its official gold holdings on the basis of current market prices, an accord hailed as a breakthrough on the impasse between France and the United States on international monetary arrangements.
December 23	The Executive Board agreed to recommend to the Interim Committee, which was to meet in a few weeks, that the Fund have an oil facility for 1975.
December 31	U.S. citizens were permitted to buy, sell, and own gold for the first time since 1933.

1975

January 6	The U.S. Treasury held its first auction to dispose of a portion of its gold holdings.
January 9	France revalued its gold reserves on the basis of free market prices. Revisions in the revaluation were to be made every six months.
January 15–16	The Interim Committee, meeting for a second time, in Washington, agreed on an oil facility for 1975 that was larger than the one for 1974 and on establishment of a Subsidy Account to help the most seriously affected developing members defray the interest costs of using the 1975 facility. The Committee also agreed that under the Sixth General

Review total quotas should be increased by 32.5 percent from SDR 29.2 billion to SDR 39 billion, with the quotas of oil exporting members as a group being doubled. The Committee also agreed on the general scope of provisions for draft amendments to the Articles and that, when the Articles of Agreement were amended, the official price of gold would be abolished and that obligatory payments of gold by members to the Fund would be eliminated.

January 17 The Development Committee, at its second meeting, in Washington, agreed on a program of work and welcomed the larger oil facility, the prospective Subsidy Account, and the possibility of a special Trust Fund.

January 27 The Managing Director, accompanied by senior staff, began an extensive trip to Iran, Iraq, Lebanon, Qatar, Saudi Arabia, and the United Arab Emirates, and to the Federal Republic of Germany, the Netherlands, and Switzerland to try to arrange borrowing by the Fund for a 1975 oil facility.

January 31 After a year of discussion, the Executive Directors were unable to agree on how increases in quotas under the Sixth General Review should be distributed among various groups of members. Since under the Articles of Agreement the review of quotas was to be completed before February 9, 1975, the Executive Directors asked the Board of Governors to adopt a resolution noting that the required review was in progress. The Board of Governors adopted the resolution effective March 4.

February 11–13 The Tokyo Round of Multilateral Trade Negotiations by some 80 industrial and developing countries began in Geneva under the auspices of the CONTRACTING PARTIES to the General Agreement on Tariffs and Trade (the GATT).

March 14 The staff circulated to the Executive Directors a Comprehensive Draft Amendment that proposed pervasive modification of the Articles of Agreement. The Executive Directors' consideration of amending the Articles of Agreement, which resumed at the end of March, thereby reached a new stage.

April 4 The Executive Board took the necessary decisions to establish an oil facility for 1975, to continue until March 31, 1976. Use of the facility was subject to greater conditionality than the 1974 facility.

May 28 The Executive Board agreed on a report to the Interim Committee concerning possible improvements in the Fund's buffer stock facility, including an amendment that would

	permit drawings under that facility to float in the reserve tranche as did drawings under the compensatory financing facility.
June 8–9	The Group of Twenty-Four, meeting at ministerial level for the tenth time, in Paris, expressed their grave concern at the adverse effects of inflation and recession in industrial countries on balances of payments positions of developing countries and urged the Fund to liberalize its compensatory financing facility.
June 10–11	At its third meeting, in Paris, the Interim Committee held a detailed discussion about gold, but was able to agree only on the principles of a solution, not on specific arrangements. It failed to agree also on the disputed issue of the relative size of the quotas of industrial members under the Sixth General Review of Quotas.
June 12–13	The Development Committee, at its third meeting, in Paris, welcomed the request of the Interim Committee to the Executive Directors to consider modifications in the Fund's compensatory and buffer stock facilities.
July 7	Kenya became the first member to use the Fund's new extended facility.
July 28	In its first review of the 1975 oil facility, the Executive Board liberalized access to the facility by permitting a member to request up to 50 percent of its "calculated maximum access" rather than 30 percent.
August 1	The Executive Board established a Subsidy Account to assist the Fund's most seriously affected members to meet the cost of using the 1975 oil facility. The decision was to be reviewed annually.
August 24	The finance ministers of the EC countries, meeting in Venice, agreed on a common position to be taken at the forthcoming Interim Committee meeting regarding the disposition of the Fund's gold holdings, gold trading by EC countries, and Fund quotas under the Sixth General Review.
August 27	Grenada, with a quota of SDR 2 million, became the 127th Fund member and a participant in the Special Drawing Account.
August 30	The Group of Twenty-Four asked the Fund to review the conditionality on use of its resources and to liberalize its compensatory financing and buffer stock facilities. The Group also asked that industrial members agree soon on quotas under the Sixth General Review and stressed that in

future reviews of Fund quotas the share of developing members should progressively increase. The Group also stated that no arrangements for gold were satisfactory unless they substantially raised the flow of financial resources to developing countries and did not accentuate the already inequitable distribution of international liquidity and urged study of a gold substitution account.

August 31   The Interim Committee, at its fourth meeting, in Washington, reached a consensus on arrangements for gold. The Committee agreed also upon the sale of one sixth of the Fund's gold (25 million ounces) for the benefit of developing members, the establishment of a Trust Fund, and the restitution (the return at the official price) of one sixth of the Fund's gold to all members. Agreement was reached also on the size of quotas for large industrial members under the Sixth General Review.

September 1–16   The Seventh Special Session of the UN General Assembly called for early establishment of a Trust Fund in the International Monetary Fund for the benefit of developing countries, and planned that UNCTAD IV, to be held in Nairobi in mid-1976, consider an integrated program for commodities and a "Common Fund" for commodity price support.

September 3–4   The Development Committee, at its fourth meeting, in Washington, gave support to a Trust Fund. The Committee also gave special attention to commodity price fluctuations and their consequences on developing countries' export earnings.

October 9   Papua New Guinea, with a quota of SDR 20 million, became the 128th Fund member and a participant in the Special Drawing Account.

October 13   The central bank governors of the countries of the Group of Ten, meeting at the BIS in Basle, held their first discussion to set up arrangements to oversee their gold trading, as had been agreed by the Interim Committee in August. The Fund's Managing Director and the Governor of the Swiss National Bank were present.

November 5   The agreement by which Switzerland, not a member of the Fund, was associated with the General Arrangements to Borrow was extended until October 23, 1980. This was the third extension of the association of Switzerland with the GAB.

November 15–17   The leaders of six major industrial countries met in the Chateau de Rambouillet, in France, the first summit on economic topics. They issued a declaration on the need jointly to assure the recovery of their economies from the 1974–75 recession and to reduce "the waste of human resources involved in unemployment." Following agreement between U.S. and French monetary officials settling their differences on the nature of exchange rates acceptable in amending the Fund's Articles, the Presidents of the United States and France also reached rapprochement on exchange rates, removing the last obstacle to agreement on amended Articles of Agreement for the Fund.

December 16–19   The Conference on International Economic Cooperation (CIEC) met in Paris at the ministerial level. The Conference had been proposed by the President of France for a "dialogue" between industrial countries and developing countries (commonly called the North-South dialogue) on energy, raw materials, and the problems of development.

December 19   The ministers of finance and central bank governors of the Group of Ten, meeting in Paris, agreed on proposals of the United States and France for amendments to Article IV of the Fund's Articles of Agreement regarding a new exchange rate regime. They agreed also on arrangements to coordinate the sale and purchase of gold by their central banks.

December 23   In an intensive day of three meetings, the Executive Board agreed to the draft Article IV on exchange rate arrangements proposed jointly by the Executive Directors appointed by France and the United States. The Executive Board had also almost finished its work on the draft comprehensive amendment. The way was now paved for what was soon to be the proposed Second Amendment.

December 24   Having agreed on quotas for all individual members under the Sixth General Review of Quotas, the Executive Board now approved a report listing the proposed quotas for transmittal to the Interim Committee. The Executive Board also invited the staff to send to the Interim Committee a report urging agreement on temporary enlarged access to the Fund's resources under existing quotas, pending the new larger quotas under the Sixth General Review, and on establishment of a Trust Fund. The Executive Board also adopted a decision substantially liberalizing the compensatory financing facility. Moreover, the Board adopted a decision specifying that purchases under the buffer stock financing facility were not to exceed 50 percent of a member's quota.

December 31   The Fund approved a purchase by the United Kingdom for SDR 1,000 million under the 1975 oil facility and a one-year stand-by arrangement for SDR 700 million, in the first credit tranche, for the United Kingdom.

December 31   According to the World Bank's debtor reporting system, the external public debt of 84 developing countries at the end of 1975 reached $174.1 billion, compared with $103 billion at the end of 1970.

January–December   Drawings on the Fund in 1975 totaled SDR 4.7 billion, the largest amount ever registered in a single year.

1976

January 6   The Group of Twenty-Four, meeting in Jamaica, just before meetings of the Interim and Development Committees, expressed their "strong disappointment" that the interests and concerns of developing countries had received so little attention in the negotiations on international monetary reform, and that "decisions affecting all countries continued to be taken in restricted groups of countries." The Group also expressed strong dissatisfaction with the proposed arrangements for gold as grossly distorting the distribution of international liquidity at the expense of developing countries and undermining the position of the SDR.

January 7–8   The Interim Committee, at its fifth meeting, in Jamaica, under the chairmanship of Willy De Clercq, Minister of Finance of Belgium, completed arrangements for an "interim reform" of the international monetary system. In the Jamaica accord, which was regarded as ushering in a new "unre-formed" international monetary system to be legalized in a Second Amendment of the Fund's Articles, agreement was finally reached on the arrangements for exchange rates to be put in the amended Articles (a new Article IV), on the treatment to be given to gold, on a number of other provisions aimed at improving the operation of the General Account and the characteristics and uses of the SDR, on the establishment of a Trust Fund for developing countries, and on increases for individual members' quotas under the Sixth General Review. Because the quota increases could not become effective until the Second Amendment went into effect, the Interim Committee agreed to the temporary enlargement of access to the Fund's resources under existing quotas, described in the entry for January 19.

January 9   The Development Committee, at its fifth meeting, in Jamaica, noted with concern that in 1976 the non-oil developing countries were likely to incur extraordinarily large current account deficits for the third successive year and that the minimum 6 percent growth target of the Second Development Decade was not likely to be met.

January 19   Following agreement by the Interim Committee at its meeting in Jamaica, the Executive Board made arrangements to extend temporarily the size of each credit tranche by 45 percent, that is, to enlarge "lending" by the Fund through its "normal channels" by 45 percent. The action was designed mainly to enable the Fund's developing members to draw more from the Fund's regular resources before the increased quotas under the Sixth General Review went into effect.

February 10   The Group of Seventy-Seven, in which 111 developing countries took part, met in Manila, to prepare for UNCTAD IV to be held in May and agreed on two documents known as the Manila Charter. Proposals included an integrated program of commodity stabilization agreements with a $3 billion common fund to finance buffer stocks in ten basic commodities.

February 19   The Executive Board sent to the Board of Governors a Report on the Sixth General Review of Quotas. The Board of Governors approved the necessary resolution effective March 22.

March 18   In its final review of the 1975 oil facility, the Executive Board increased access to 78.46 percent of the calculated maximum access.

March 24   Having completed its work on the drafting of the Proposed Second Amendment to the Articles of Agreement, the Executive Board submitted the Amendment to the Board of Governors for approval. On April 30 the Board of Governors approved the Proposed Second Amendment, which was then submitted to member countries for acceptance.

April 2   The Philippines became the second member for which an extended arrangement was approved.

April 28	In a new dispute over salaries, the Fund staff held a one-day work stoppage, the first such event since the Fund started to employ staff in April 1946.
May 3–31	At UNCTAD IV, in Nairobi, the principal issues discussed included the stabilization of raw material prices, debt burdens of developing countries, the international transfer of technology, the regulation of multinational corporations, and increased economic cooperation among the developing nations themselves.
May 5	The Executive Directors agreed on the policies and procedures to be used to effect the sale of one third of the Fund's holdings of gold. A program of regular gold auctions for the next two years was announced. The Executive Board also took a decision establishing a Trust Fund.
May 21	In view of the expectation that in the near future drawings under the compensatory financing facility after the December 1975 decision might exceed SDR 1.5 billion, the Fund conducted the review required by that decision when drawings in any 12-month period exceeded SDR 1.5 billion. The Fund decided to make no further changes in the facility.
May 30	The last purchases under the oil facilities took place, bringing total purchases under the 1974 and 1975 oil facilities to over SDR 6.9 billion.
May 31	Total drawings from the Fund of SDR 4.64 billion in the first five months of 1976 alone attained levels near the record amount of SDR 4.66 billion reached in the full year 1975.
June 2	The Fund conducted its first gold auction, awarding 780,000 ounces of gold to successful bidders at a common price of $126 an ounce. Proceeds of the sale were to go to the newly established Trust Fund.
June 8	The Group of Ten, Switzerland, and the BIS granted a $5.3 billion stand-by credit to the United Kingdom to prevent a further decline in the exchange rate of the pound sterling.
June 23	The Executive Board decided that the Fund would meet members' requests for financial assistance up to the full amount of their compulsory contributions to the tin buffer stocks to be established under the new Fifth International Tin Agreement, which was to go into effect on July 11, 1976.
June 27–28	The leaders of seven major industrial countries met at Dorado Beach, Puerto Rico, for a second economic summit. They reviewed progress since the first economic summit at

Rambouillet in November 1975 and resolved to continue to consult and cooperate to coordinate their countries' policies for achieving sustained and orderly economic growth with price stability.

June 30   The Executive Board completed reviews of the valuation of the SDR, the rate at which the Fund paid remuneration on members' super gold tranche positions in the Fund, and the rate of interest on the SDR. The rate of remuneration was to be determined quarterly and was to be three fifths of the weighted average of short-term money market rates in the United States, the Federal Republic of Germany, the United Kingdom, France, and Japan. This decision was to be reviewed in three years. No change was made in the method of valuing the SDR agreed in June 1974.

July 22   The Fund made the first payments under the Subsidy Account to defray interest costs in using the 1975 oil facility to 18 eligible members. Payments amounted to SDR 13.8 million.

August 24   The Fund announced changes in its gold auction procedures. Successful bidders were to pay the prices they bid, rather than a common price, and the names of successful bidders would be published after the auction.

August 25   The Executive Board decided that participants in the Special Drawing Account might engage in transactions by agreement that brought the holdings of both participants closer to their net cumulative allocations, and the users of SDRs in these transactions would be exempt from the requirement of balance of payments need. The users of SDRs in a transaction by agreement to promote reconstitution of their position in SDRs were also exempted from the requirement of balance of payments need.

September 1   Faced with a precarious foreign exchange situation, the Mexican Government decided to sever the 22-year link of 12.50 Mexican pesos per U.S. dollar and, for the first time in modern history, allowed the peso to float.

September 15   The Executive Board decided that the Socialist Republic of Viet Nam, composed both of North Viet Nam, which had not been a member, and of South Viet Nam, which had been a member, was a member of the Fund.

September 20   The Executive Board reviewed the decision setting up the extended facility and decided not to modify the facility, but to review it again in the future and in any event when total drawings under extended arrangements reached SDR 2 billion.

September 21

The Comoros, with a quota of SDR 1.9 million, became the 129th Fund member and a participant in the Special Drawing Account.

October 1–8

The Group of Twenty-Four, at its thirteenth meeting, in Manila, asked for a new allocation of SDRs, less conditionality, and the establishment of an SDR/aid link. At the Thirty-First Annual Meeting, in Manila, Mr. Witteveen told the Governors that the time had come for them to lay more stress on adjustment of oil-related balance of payments deficits and less emphasis on financing. The Interim Committee, at its sixth meeting, shared the Managing Director's view. It also asked the Executive Directors to consider how the Fund should exercise "firm surveillance" over members' exchange rate policies. At its sixth meeting, the Development Committee again urged that more resources be committed to international lending institutions. The Interim Committee, at its seventh meeting, selected Willy De Clercq, Minister of Finance of Belgium, to continue as Chairman for a new term. The Development Committee, at its seventh meeting, selected Cesar E.A. Virata, Secretary of Finance of the Philippines, as Chairman.

November 5

The Executive Board decided, and the ten participants in the General Arrangements to Borrow agreed, on an increase in the amount of Japan's credit arrangement in the GAB from ¥ 90 billion to ¥ 340 billion, thereby for the first time raising the size of the GAB, to approximately SDR 6.2 billion.

December 7

The Executive Board reviewed the Fund's experience with selling its gold holdings and established a new program of auctions designed to enhance the smoothness of the sales. After the fifth and sixth gold auctions on December 8, 1976 and January 26, 1977, again for 780,000 ounces, regular monthly auctions of 525,000 ounces were to start in March 1977 on the first Wednesday of each month.

December 22

The Executive Board approved an agreement with the Swiss National Bank by which the Fund could borrow U.S. dollars equivalent to SDR 300 million to help finance purchases under an anticipated stand-by arrangement with the United Kingdom. Representatives of the Group of Ten meeting in Paris agreed to a proposal by the Managing Director to provide SDR 2,560 million under the General Arrangements to Borrow to help finance a stand-by arrangement with the United Kingdom.

January–December   Drawings on the Fund in 1976 totaled SDR 7 billion, much larger even than the record amount of 1975.

1977

January 3   The Executive Board approved a two-year stand-by arrangement for the United Kingdom for SDR 3,360 million, the largest amount ever approved by the Fund and the first stand-by arrangement to exceed one year.

January 10   The governors of the central banks of Belgium, Canada, the Federal Republic of Germany, Japan, the Netherlands, Sweden, Switzerland, and the United States agreed on arrangements among themselves and the BIS to support a medium-term financing facility for $3 billion under which balances of pounds sterling held by official entities abroad were to be reduced.

January 25   The Executive Board decided that the Fund would make the first interim loan disbursements to 12 members deemed eligible to qualify for loans from the Trust Fund.

February 23   The Fund completed the first of four annual restitutions of gold to its members. Just under 6 million ounces were sold at the official price of SDR 35 an ounce to 112 members in proportion to their quotas.

March 11   The Executive Board again reviewed the compensatory financing facility. No further modifications in the facility were made but another review was to be conducted when drawings in any 12-month period exceeded SDR 1.5 billion, or when outstanding drawings exceeded SDR 4.0 billion, and in any event, not later than May 31, 1979.

March 24   Guinea-Bissau, with a quota of SDR 3.2 million, became the 130th Fund member and a participant in the Special Drawing Account.

March 28   In an important first-time activity in the history of the Fund, the Managing Director was asked to help monitor the arrangement concerning sterling balances made in January between the Bank of England and the central banks of other large industrial countries and the BIS. The Executive Board agreed to the Managing Director's participation.

April 1   The Executive Board increased the Fund's charges to help bring the Fund's income into line with its operating expenses and agreed on a formula to safeguard the Fund's budgetary position whenever the margin between the rate of charges and the rate of remuneration became so narrow as to endanger that position.

April 25   The Executive Board approved a stand-by arrangement for Italy for SDR 450 million, to continue until December 31, 1978 (a 20-month period). The Executive Board also approved an agreement between the Fund and the Swiss National Bank by which the Fund could borrow U.S. dollars equivalent to SDR 37.5 million to help finance purchases under the stand-by arrangement.

April 26   The Group of Twenty-Four, at their fourteenth meeting, in Washington, advocated a second round of SDR allocations, establishment of the temporary supplementary financing facility that Mr. Witteveen had proposed, continuation of the Subsidy Account for low-income developing members, an increase of 100 percent in quotas under the Seventh General Review, a link between SDRs and development finance, and a review of the Fund's conditionality.

April 27   The Development Committee held its eighth meeting, in Washington, and emphasized the need for increased flows of official development assistance.

April 28–29   The Interim Committee, at its eighth meeting, in Washington, considered the main issues relating to the Seventh General Review of Quotas and agreed that there should be an adequate increase. The Committee also supported the temporary supplementary financing facility and the principles agreed by the Executive Board for surveillance of exchange rates by the Fund. In addition, the Interim Committee requested the Executive Directors to consider a further allocation of SDRs and to review the characteristics of the SDR.

April 29   The Executive Board adopted a decision on the exercise of Fund surveillance of the exchange rate policies of members when the new Article IV of the proposed Second Amendment became effective.

May 7–8   The third economic summit took place in London. The conferees pledged cooperation on economic problems and support for the Fund. They stressed that the Fund play a prominent role in balance of payments financing and adjustment and agreed that there was need for a supplementary financing facility in the Fund and for another round of quota increases.

APPENDICES

May 30–June 2	The Conference of International Economic Cooperation (CIEC) held its final meeting in Paris, under the co-chairmanship of Allan J. MacEachen, President of the Privy Council of Canada, and Manuel Perez-Guerrero, Minister of State for International Economic Affairs of Venezuela. Agreement was reached on the principle of establishing a common fund to help stabilize the prices of several commodities simultaneously, negotiations for which were to take place in the UNCTAD. CIEC also asked the Development Committee to review the problem of stabilization of export earnings of developing countries.
June 29	The Managing Director reported to the Executive Board that he was unable to obtain enough support among participants to propose an allocation of SDRs for the third basic period, starting January 1, 1978.
June 30	Seychelles, with a quota of SDR 1 million, became the 131st Fund member and a participant in the Special Drawing Account.
July 25	The Executive Board adopted a decision on a list of members eligible to receive a direct transfer of profits that the Fund received from the sale of gold through the Trust Fund.
August 6	At the invitation of the Managing Director, representatives of 14 potential lenders to the Fund met in Paris to discuss amounts that they would lend for the supplementary financing facility and the terms and conditions on which they would make these loans to the Fund.
August 29	The Executive Board adopted a decision establishing a supplementary financing facility in the Fund to go into effect when loan agreements totaling not less than SDR 7.75 billion were completed. The Managing Director aimed at a facility of $10 billion (SDR 8.6 billion), and SDR 8.4 billion had been pledged.
September 21	Mr. Witteveen announced that when his first term expired on August 31, 1978, he would not be available for a second term as Managing Director.
September 24	At its ninth meeting, in Washington, under the chairmanship of Denis Healey, Chancellor of the Exchequer, who was selected Chairman to finish the term of Mr. De Clercq, the Interim Committee reviewed the world economic outlook, expressed concern about the faltering of economic activity in several industrial countries, agreed on a series of policies for economic recovery, and welcomed the supplementary

financing facility. Agreement was not yet reached on the Seventh General Review of Quotas.

September 25

The Development Committee held its ninth meeting, in Washington. This meeting was preceded by a first meeting of deputies of the Development Committee, held in Paris, September 15–16, also under the chairmanship of Cesar E.A. Virata. The Development Committee requested a study by the staffs of the Fund and the World Bank on the stabilization of export earnings.

September 30

At the closing session of the Thirty-Second Annual Meeting, the Managing Director summed up the consensus of officials to the effect that the world needed "to restore a satisfactory rate of recovery and expansion while continuing to make progress in reducing inflation." During the Annual Meeting it was announced that Willy Brandt, former Chancellor of the Federal Republic of Germany, would chair a new commission on international development issues.

September 30

São Tomé and Principe, with a quota of SDR 1.6 million, became the 132nd Fund member and a participant in the Special Drawing Account.

October 28

The Executive Board agreed on a list of members eligible to receive loans from the Trust Fund for the second period.

December 16

The Fund decided that its buffer stock facility might be used by members in connection with their financing of special stocks of sugar to be established under the 1977 International Sugar Agreement.

January–December

Drawings on the Fund's resources during 1977 totaled just over SDR 3.4 billion, a little less than half the amount of 1976. Since there was also a record volume of repurchases, total net drawings for 1977 were only SDR 488 million.

1978

January 4–5

The rates for the U.S. dollar had been steadily declining since September 1977. The U.S. Treasury and the Federal Reserve Board issued a joint statement on U.S. intervention policy. The Exchange Stabilization Fund of the U.S. Treasury ($4.7 billion) was to be used together with the $20.2 billion of reciprocal currency arrangements. The Deutsche Bundesbank also issued a statement announcing extension of a new credit line to the Treasury's Exchange Stabilization Fund, which could be drawn on for intervention in the dollar market. Intervention in the markets was aimed at "checking speculation and re-establishing order in foreign exchange markets." It was explicitly "not to peg rates for the dollar."

January 13   Maldives, with a quota of SDR 700,000, became the 133rd Fund member and a participant in the Special Drawing Account.

January 31   The transitional arrangements governing gold trading among the countries of the Group of Ten and Switzerland, to which Portugal also adhered, were allowed to expire after two years of life.

March 13   The rates for the dollar against the deutsche mark continued to depreciate, and in a joint statement, Hans Matthöfer, Finance Minister of the Federal Republic of Germany, and W. Michael Blumenthal, Secretary of the U.S. Treasury, outlined cooperative measures "to counter disorderly conditions in exchange markets." The measures included a doubling—to $4 billion—of the amount of the reciprocal currency arrangements (swap arrangements) between the Deutsche Bundesbank and the U.S. Federal Reserve System. The total of the swap lines between the Federal Reserve System and 14 central banks abroad and the BIS now came to $22,160 million. U.S. officials agreed also to draw on the U.S. reserve tranche position in the Fund up to $5 billion, if necessary, to support the dollar.

March 22   Under the amended Articles of Agreement, shortly to go into effect, members were to make early repurchases of their drawings in certain circumstances. The Executive Board adopted a series of guidelines to clarify these circumstances.

March 31   Under the Sixth General Review, 85 members, representing 78.52 percent of total Fund quotas as of February 19, 1976, finally consented to quota increases agreed by the Board of Governors in March 1976. The increases thus went into effect.

March 31   The Executive Board adopted a decision changing the valuation of the SDR, effective July 1, 1978. A basket of 16 currencies was to be retained, with some changes in the currencies included.

April 1   After a process lasting nearly two years, the necessary three fifths of the members representing four fifths of the total voting power finally accepted the Second Amendment of the Articles of Agreement. The new Articles entered into force, applicable to all members.

April 24   The Executive Board agreed to a schedule of higher charges to be applicable to balances of a member's currency acquired by the Fund under the regular credit tranches that raised the Fund's holdings of the currency above 200 percent of the member's quota, not counting the holdings acquired under certain special facilities. The separate schedule of higher charges was considered appropriate for such exceptional use of the Fund's resources and to maintain equity with the schedule of charges adopted in September 1977 for use of the Fund's resources under the supplementary financing facility.

April 27   Suriname, with a quota of SDR 25 million, became the 134th Fund member and a participant in the Special Drawing Rights Department. (The term Special Drawing Right Department was substituted for the term Special Drawing Account following entry into force of the amended Articles of Agreement.)

April 28   The Development Committee had a meeting of "senior officials," rather than a full meeting, in Mexico City. The senior officials discussed, among other topics, the status of the study by the staffs of the Fund and the World Bank on the stabilization of export earnings.

April 29–30   At its tenth meeting, in Mexico City, the Interim Committee reached a consensus on the general outlines of a coordinated strategy designed to promote noninflationary growth in the world economy in the medium term through 1980. The Interim Committee's discussion was facilitated by a report submitted by the Managing Director on the "World Economic Outlook and Working of the Adjustment Process." This was also the first time that even a summary version of the world economic outlook report was made public. The Interim Committee noted with approval the Fund's implementation of the new provisions of the Articles on exchange rate surveillance. The Interim Committee failed to reach agreement on quotas under the Seventh General Review, however. An allocation of SDRs, establishment of a substitution account in the Fund, and the Fund's conditionality were to be reviewed.

May 8   In a speech in London, Mr. Witteveen explained and defended the Fund's conditionality, which was coming under increasing criticism.

May 19   As the Fund completed the second year of its four-year gold sales program, the Executive Board reviewed the policies and procedures for the Fund's sales of gold and decided on the terms and conditions for the auctions to be held during the next 12 months.

June 2   The Executive Board started a review of the conditions associated with use of the Fund's resources in the upper credit tranches.

June 2   The Executive Board took a decision amending the General Arrangements to Borrow to make them conform to the provisions of the Fund's amended Articles of Agreement.

June 14–15   At the ministerial level annual meeting of the Council of the 24-member OECD, agreement was reached on the major components of a broad program of an internationally coordinated action to stimulate growth in the world economy without rekindling inflation.

June 16   The Executive Board decided that the receipts from gold sales temporarily held in the Trust Fund could be placed in deposits with the BIS. Thus, for the first time, investments by the Fund could be in a form other than U.S. Government securities.

June 16–17   Mr. Witteveen ended his term as Managing Director, and J. de Larosière, of France, took office as the sixth Managing Director.

June 26   The Executive Directors reviewed the study on the stabilization of export earnings prepared by the staffs of the Fund and the World Bank in response to the request by the Development Committee. A major section of the study was devoted to the Fund's compensatory financing facility. The Executive Directors agreed that the study should be transmitted to the Development Committee as a staff study not endorsed by the Executive Board.

July 1   The revised basket of 16 currencies used for determining the value of the SDR, agreed in March, went into effect.

July 6 and 7   The European Council, composed of the heads of state or of government of the nine EC countries, meeting in Bremen under the chairmanship of Helmut Schmidt, Chancellor of the Federal Republic of Germany, decided on a common approach to the economic problems facing the European Community and firmed up arrangements for a European Monetary System (EMS).

July 13   A framework of understanding on the Tokyo Round of Multilateral Trade Negotiations, taking place since 1973 under the auspices of the GATT, was issued in Geneva. The framework expressed hope that the Tokyo Round would see a major liberalization of trade, new rules for the GATT, new mechanisms for international consultations and the settlement of disputes in international trade, and additional benefits for developing countries.

July 16–17   An economic summit meeting was held in Bonn. The leaders of the seven major industrial nations agreed on a comprehensive strategy of mutually reinforcing action to promote world economic recovery similar to that recommended by the Interim Committee in April and the OECD in June. U.S. officials emphasized that exchange rate stability depended on solving world economic problems first but promised to intervene to the extent necessary to counter disorderly conditions in exchange markets.

September 22   Solomon Islands, with a quota of SDR 2.1 million, became the 135th Fund member and a participant in the Special Drawing Rights Department.

September 23 and 27   The Development Committee held two meetings, in Washington, mainly to consider the study on stabilization of export earnings prepared by the staffs of the Fund and the World Bank. Its members expressed a strong desire for further liberalization of the Fund's compensatory financing facility.

September 24   The Interim Committee at its eleventh meeting, in Washington, agreed to a 50 percent increase in the overall size of members' quotas in the Fund under the Seventh General Review. This increase would raise total quotas from SDR 39 billion to SDR 58.6 billion. The Interim Committee agreed to support greater use for the SDR and other changes that the Executive Directors were considering. Discussion of a possible substitution account was also getting under way. The Interim Committee also agreed to an allocation of SDRs— SDR 4 billion in each of the three years, 1979, 1980, and 1981—for the third basic period.

September 25   Addressing the Board of Governors as Managing Director for the first time, Mr. de Larosière stressed the seriousness of the problems of the world economy and instability in exchange markets.

October 25   The Executive Board took a decision reducing the minimum average holdings of SDRs that members had to maintain from 30 percent to 15 percent of their net cumulative allocations. The Executive Board also agreed on a report containing proposals for increases in individual members' quotas under the Seventh General Review. The Managing Director made a proposal, in which the Executive Board concurred, to make allocations of SDRs in accordance with the Interim Committee agreement in September. These actions were forwarded to the Board of Governors for approval.

November 1   In accordance with the provision of the Articles of Agreement that a member lending certain amounts to the Fund could appoint an Executive Director, an Executive Director appointed by Saudi Arabia took a seat on the Executive Board. The number of appointed Directors rose from 5 to 6, and the Executive Board was temporarily enlarged from 20 to 21.

November 1   President Jimmy Carter undertook measures to strengthen the dollar in foreign exchange markets. The measures included a drawing from the Fund of $3 billion (a reserve tranche drawing), the sale of $2 billion in SDRs, and the expansion of reciprocal currency arrangements (swap lines) with the Federal Republic of Germany, Japan, and Switzerland from a total of $7.4 billion to $15 billion. Measures were taken also to counter inflationary pressures in the domestic economy with the intent also of helping support the dollar abroad.

November 14   In a speech in Chicago, Mr. de Larosière described the procedures that the Fund expected to follow to exercise surveillance of members' exchange rate policies under the new Article IV of the amended Articles of Agreement.

November 20   Cape Verde, with a quota of SDR 2 million, became the 136th Fund member and a participant in the Special Drawing Rights Department.

December 4–5   Meeting in Brussels, the European Council reached agreement to launch the European Monetary System on January 1, 1979.

December 4   The Executive Board took a decision considerably broadening the authority of the Trust Fund to make investments other than in U.S. government securities or deposits in the BIS.

December 11   The Board of Governors adopted resolutions agreeing to increases in members' quotas, thereby completing the Seventh General Review of Quotas, and agreeing to allocations of SDRs for 1979, 1980, and 1981.

December 12	Dominica, with a quota of SDR 1.9 million, became the 137th Fund member and a participant in the Special Drawing Rights Department.
December 17	Officials of OPEC, meeting in Abu Dhabi, decided to raise oil prices by 14.5 percent by the end of 1979, thus starting a second round of oil price increases.
December 29	Djibouti, with a quota of SDR 3.8 million, became the 138th Fund member and a participant in the Special Drawing Rights Department.
January–December	During the year 1978 there was a net contraction of Fund credit as repurchases of SDR 4.9 billion exceeded total drawings of SDR 3.8 billion. By the end of 1978, Ethiopia, Lebanon, Libya, Qatar, Saudi Arabia, Singapore, and the United Arab Emirates, which had not previously been participants in the Special Drawing Rights Department, became participants. (The only member that was still not a participant was Kuwait.)

Indexes

Index

References are to pages; page numbers marked with an asterisk (*) refer to tables in the text, and those marked with the letter n refer to footnotes. The appendices have not been included in this index.

INDEX

Economic situation and policies, 439
Exchange arrangements, 804*, 806; policies, views on, 816, 818
Intermediary in gold restitution, 659
Membership in Fund, 538, 904*
Quota in Fund, 525, 537n, 538, 540*
Schilling: central rate, 58; rate for, 811; use in Fund transactions, 32, 33–34, 576, 580*; use in SDR currency basket, 293*, 892, 893*
Signatory of voluntary declaration on trade, 349
SDR allocations, 885*
Subsidy Account contribution, 354*
Trust Fund, exclusion from, 674

B

BADEA. *See* ARAB BANK FOR ECONOMIC DEVELOPMENT IN AFRICA

BAFFI, PAOLO, 453

BAHAMAS
Art. VIII, acceptance of obligations under, 912
Drawings (purchases) from Fund (net), 887*; repurchases, 572*
Exchange arrangements, 804*
Gold sales, profits received from, 679*
Membership in Fund, 536*, 904*; gold subscription payment, 611
Per capita income, 676
Quota in Fund, 536*, 539, 542*; subscription payments, 611–12
Trust Fund eligibility, 675–76

BAHRAIN
Acceptance of Second Amendment, 769
Art. VIII, acceptance of obligations under, 912
Classification by Fund, 42n, 526n, 888n
Dinar: use in Fund transactions, 321, 577, 580*
Drawings (purchases) from Fund, 438*, (net), 888*
Exchange arrangements, 804*
Gold sales, profits received from, 679*
Membership in Fund, 536*, 904*, 908
Quota in Fund, 524, 536*, 539, 543*

BALANCE OF PAYMENTS
Definitions: basic balance, 174–75, 952n; official settlements balance, 952; "surplus" and "deficit" changed with floating rates, 952; "sustainable," 864
Effects of oil price increases on, 305–306, 308–10, 313, 315–16, 359–60, 642
Massive disequilibria: as problem for world economy, 387; as reason for oil facility, 791
Need test required for: buffer stock drawings, 419; compensatory drawings, 406; oil facility drawings, 321–22, 324; Trust Fund loans, 671; use of Fund resources, 700, 715; use of SDRs, 706, 731, 889–90, 898
Positions: developing members, 308–309; European countries, 109
See also TRADE, INTERNATIONAL *and* individual countries

BALANCE OF PAYMENTS ADJUSTMENT
As problem of Bretton Woods system, 103–105; aggravated by capital mobility, 66, 106; given less priority than liquidity in, 107, 108, 109–111
By industrial members, 98; by developing members, 99
Changed nature of, following oil price increases, 313–14

Emphasis on instead of deficit financing, 392, 490, 495–96, 497, 499, 529, 831–32
In *Outline of Reform*, 257
Model of Bureau of Committee of Twenty on, 232, 235; opposing views of European officials, 234–35, 238; U.S. officials, 234, 238–39; views of developing members, 236; views of Mr. Morse, 237
Policies for dealing with: in consultations, 94; under par value system, 96–97, 108
Pressures for. *See* PRESSURES
Relation to: exchange rate policy treated in Second Amendment, 755; resource transfer to developing members, 251–52
U.S. proposal for compared with Keynes's plan, 169
See also COMMITTEE OF TWENTY—DELIBERATIONS; EXCHANGE RATES: Role in adjustment; INDICATORS; STABILIZATION PROGRAMS; *and* WORLD ECONOMIC OUTLOOK

BALANCE OF PAYMENTS MANUAL, 919, 950
Problems of publishing, 951–53

BALANCE OF PAYMENTS YEARBOOK, 949

BALOGH, THOMAS, 89

BANGLADESH
Acceptance of Second Amendment, 769
Art. XIV consultations, 917
Drawings (purchases) and repurchases from Fund: purchases, 436*, (net), 887*; under compensatory financing facility, 400, 411, 412*, 425*; under oil facility, 331, 347*; repurchases, 568, 571*
Exchange arrangements, 804*
Gold sales, profits received from, 679*
Membership in Fund, 55n, 535, 536*, 904*, 908
Quota in Fund, 526, 532, 535, 536*, 542*
Stand-by arrangements with Fund, 426*
Subsidy Account payments received, 355*
Taka floating, 55
Trust Fund: eligibility, 670n; loan from, 672, 673*

BANK FOR INTERNATIONAL SETTLEMENTS (BIS)
As bidder in Fund's gold auctions, 633–34, 635, 649, 650, 652
As other holder of SDRs, 898, 899
Attendance by Managing Director and staff at meetings of, 630, 631, 635
Credits to U.K., 467
Depository of Fund instrument, 681
Exchange rate policy discussions, 850
Fund relations with, 954, 961, 981; on capital markets, 932–33; on Eurocurrency markets, 930
Involvement in safety net proposal, 339
Role in Group of Ten gold arrangements, 626, 630–31, 634, 635; views on role of gold, 630
Sterling agreement: role in, 475; Managing Director's special role in, 475–76, 478
World economy surveyed, 394

BANK OF CENTRAL AFRICAN STATES (BEAC), 954

BANKS, COMMERCIAL
Access to related to reserve adequacy, 875
Fear of failure of, 334, 336, 555, 931
Fund relations with, 931, 933; on external debt, 936; transmittal of information to discussed, 937, 939
Lending by: controls on, views of developing members on, 642; effects of Fund's conditionality on, 493–94; effects of oil price increases on,

357; increase in related to international liquidity, 637–38; preferred over use of Fund resources, 507, 547–48, 555; U.S. views on, 341; related to Fund quota increases, 530; to developing members, Fund studies and implications of, 931–32; to developing members increased, 333–34, 382

Oil facility's impact on, 359

Trend toward financing developing countries' deficits, 936

See also DEBT, EXTERNAL, OF DEVELOPING MEMBERS

BARBADOS
Dollar floating, 55
Drawings (purchases) and repurchases from Fund: purchases, 437*, (net), 887*; under compensatory financing facility, 44, 413*; repurchases, 572*
Exchange arrangements, 804*
Gold sales, profits received from, 679*
Membership in Fund, 904*
Quota in Fund, 542*
SDR allocations, 887*

BARDEPOT. See CAPITAL MOVEMENTS: Measures to control

BARBER, ANTHONY, 240, 254, 290
Comments and views on: aspects of reformed system, 130–31, 164, 167, 193; balance of payments adjustment, 48, 228; floating of pound, 50; par values, 191; U.K. repurchase, 34

BARRATTIERI, VITTORIO, 248, 252

BASLE AGREEMENT. *See* BANK FOR INTERNATIONAL SETTLEMENTS: Sterling agreement

BEAC. *See* BANK OF CENTRAL AFRICAN STATES

BEAURAIN, CLAUDE, 248, 277, 299
Comments and views on: gold, 31, 136; special consultations, 277; staff sketch on reform, 132

BELGIUM
Art. VIII, acceptance of obligations of, 912*n*
Borrowing by Fund for: oil facility, 345, 346*; supplementary financing facility, 557*n*
Classification by Fund, 42*n*, 789
Consultations, special, 278
Economic situation and policies, 439
Exchange arrangements, 805*, 806; dual market, 64, 192, 215; policies, 816; views on fixed versus floating rates, 169, 172
Franc: central rate, 39, 58; convertible in fact, 764; floating jointly with EC, 23, 79, 80; *see also* Participation in snake, *below*; use in Fund transactions, 33–34, 576, 580*, 581; use in SDR currency basket, 293*, 892, 893*
Intermediary in gold restitution, 659
"Link," views on, 205, 224
Membership in: Fund, 904*; Group of Ten, 11
Participation in snake, 802–803, 811, 812, 813
Proposals on: gold substitution account, 616, 639–40; SDR valuation and interest rate, 892
Quota in Fund, 525, 537*n*, 538, 540*
Reserve currencies, views on, 179, 217
Signatory of voluntary declaration on trade, 349
SDRs: allocations, 885*; holdings, 897
Stand-by arrangements with Fund, 426*
Subsidy Account contribution, 354*
Trust Fund, exclusion from, 675

BENIN
Exchange arrangements, 804*
Gold sales, profits received from, 679*
Loan from Trust Fund, 673*

Membership in Fund, 904*
Quota in Fund, 541*
SDR allocations, 886*

BENNETT, JACK F., 662, 814–15

BENSLIMANE, ABDEL-KADER, 254

BERGSTEN, C. FRED, 111

BERNE UNION. *See* UNION D'ASSUREURS DES CREDITS INTERNATIONAUX

BERNSTEIN, EDWARD M., 85, 87, 93, 102, 760

BEVERIDGE, W.A., 1027

BEZA, STERIE F., 1028

BHATIA, RATTAN J., 1025

"BIG FIVE." *See* GROUP OF FIVE

BIS. *See* BANK FOR INTERNATIONAL SETTLEMENTS

BLUMENTHAL, W. MICHAEL, 554, 858, 938
Comments and views on: access to capital markets by developing members, 935; balance of payments adjustment and conditionality, 495; exchange rates, 818; international debt, 928; international monetary cooperation, 853–54; supplementary financing facility, 556; transmittal of information to commercial banks, 938; U.S. economic situation and policies, 855–56, 861

BOARD OF GOVERNORS
Annual Meetings: new significance of, 980–82; not required under Second Amendment, 971–72; role in, 142
By-Laws of. *See* BY-LAWS, FUND
Committees: as new elements in Fund policymaking, 963, 966–67, 980; efforts to establish before 1972, 145–48; *see also* COMMITTEE OF TWENTY; DEVELOPMENT COMMITTEE; *and* INTERIM COMMITTEE; on interpretation, 145–47; not established, 147, 774; to study reserve creation (1966), 145
Policymaking process, role in, 963, 964–66
"Political" organ of Fund, 142
Powers of, 693, 721, 966
Resolutions: as decision-making tool, 966; on Committee of Twenty establishment and termination, 155, 303; on Development Committee's work, 974, 975; on Interim and Development Committees' establishment, 303; on quotas, 526–27, 535, 708; on reform of monetary system, 242; on SDR as Fund's unit of account, 31; on Second Amendment, 768
Voting, 692

BOH, HIDEO, 818

BOHMAN, GÖSTA, 635, 855

BOLIVIA
Acceptance of Second Amendment, 769
Art. VIII, acceptance of obligations of, 912*n*
Drawings (purchases) and repurchases from Fund: purchases, 437*, (net), 887*; under buffer stock facility, 427; repurchases, 572*
Exchange arrangements, 804*
Gold sales, profits received from, 679*
Membership in Fund, 904*
Par value and currency unit change, 57
Quota in Fund, 527, 542*
SDR allocations, 887*
Stand-by arrangements with Fund, 426*
Trust Fund: eligibility, 671*n*; loan from, 673*

BORNEMANN, EDWIN L., 1025

Quota in Fund, 541*
SDR allocations, 886*
Subsidy Account payments received, 355*

CENTRAL AMERICAN CLEARING HOUSE (CACH), 245

CENTRAL AMERICAN COMMON MARKET
Participants in, 245

CENTRAL AMERICAN MONETARY COUNCIL, 962

CENTRAL BANKING EXPERTS OF THE AMERICAN CONTINENT, 962

CENTRAL BANKING, TECHNICAL ASSISTANCE IN. *See* TECHNICAL ASSISTANCE

CENTRAL BANKS
Currency swap arrangements among, 107, 467, 820, 853, 862
Eligibility of to bid in Fund gold auctions, 650, 651, 656
Establishment of in developing members, 918
Fund technical assistance to, 918, 919, 920, 921
Loans to U.K., 467, 475
See also EXCHANGE MARKETS: Intervention *and* GOLD TRANSACTIONS OF CENTRAL BANKS

CENTRALLY PLANNED ECONOMIES
Fund members with increased, 908

CENTRAL RATES
As factor in creation of snake, 280
Temporary regime: established, 29, 279; revised, 280–81
Use of, 39–40, 58, 64, 72, 280, 812; in Fund's computations, 29; proposed in Second Amendment draft, 738, 740
Views on: of France, 132, 280–81; of Italy, 39, 40
Wider margins, 280

CEPCIES. *See* PERMANENT EXECUTIVE COMMITTEE OF THE INTER-AMERICAN ECONOMIC AND SOCIAL COUNCIL

CHAD
Acceptance of Second Amendment, 769
Drawings (purchases) and repurchases from Fund: purchases, 434*, (net), 886*; under compensatory financing facility, 412*; under oil facility, 347*; repurchases, 570*
Exchange arrangements, 804*
Gold sales, profits received from, 679*
Loan from Trust Fund, 673*
Membership in Fund, 905*
Quota in Fund, 541*
SDR allocations, 886*

CHARGES ON USE OF FUND'S RESOURCES
As factor in establishing Subsidy Account, 351, 352, 353–54
Calculation of currency holdings, 563–64
Concessionality of, 566
Conditionality related to low rates of, 327
Developments: before 1974, 559–60; increased (1974), 560–61; (1977), 561–62
For: extended arrangements, 369, 562, 565, 565*; oil facilities, 295–96, 327–28, 329*, 344–45, 345*, 561, 562, 564; payments for gold, 659; reserve (gold) tranche drawings, 589; stand-by arrangements, 564–65, 565*; supplementary financing, 546, 548, 552, 553*, 553–54, 565; Trust Fund loans discussed, 669
Income from, 562–63, 564, 599–601, 603*
Linked to remuneration, 560, 561, 562–63, 564, 566, 600
Media of payment of: gold, 560; SDRs, 778

Need for uniformity of, 296, 327–28; views of developing members, 327, 560; industrial members, 327, 328, 560
Penalty rates, 560
Related to: Fund borrowing for oil facility, 317, 326–28; Fund's budgetary position, 295, 327, 560, 561, 562–63, 564, 566, 600, 601, 602; market interest rates, 560, 561, 566
Schedules: changes in, 295–96, 296*, 560; new, 561, 562, 562*, 565, 565*, 566; original, 559
Second Amendment. *See* ARTICLES . . . SECOND AMENDMENT—DRAFT AMENDMENTS: General Account *and* . . . FINAL PROVISIONS
Service charges, 559, 561, 562, 562*, 565*; on reserve (gold) tranche drawings, 559, 561, 563; eliminated, 561, 600

CHAVAN, Y.B., 190, 228, 254

CHILE
Art. VIII, acceptance of obligations under, 912
Debt, external, 925, 928
Drawings (purchases) and repurchases from Fund: purchases, 437*, (net), 887*; under compensatory financing facility, 400, 411, 413*; under oil facility, 331, 347*; repurchases, 568, 572*, 612
Exchange arrangements, 805*, 806
Gold sales, profits received from, 679*
Membership in Fund, 905*
Quota in Fund, 539, 542*; views on, 525
SDR allocations, 887*
Stand-by arrangements with Fund, 426*

CHINA
Arrangements for gold restitution, 659
Drawings (purchases) and repurchases from Fund: purchases, 436*, (net), 887*; repurchases, 571*
Exchange arrangements, 804*
Executive Board representation, 767n, 999
Fund study on protectionism discussed with, 942
Membership in Fund, 905*
Par value change, 35, 36*
Quota in Fund, 513, 521, 523, 527, 534, 538n, 542*
Representation in Fund, 35n
Trust Fund, exclusion from, 675

CHOI SIEW HONG, 245

CHONG HON NYAN, 404, 418

CHRETIEN, JEAN, 856, 859

CLAPPIER, BERNARD, 654, 746, 817, 829

CLARK, KENNETH N., 1021

COLLEY, GEORGE, 859, 940

COLOMBIA
Capital inflows, 43
Debt, external, 928
Drawings (purchases) and repurchases from Fund: purchases, 318, 437*, (net), 887*; repurchases, 318, 572*, 612
Exchange arrangements, 805*, 806
Fund study on protectionism discussed, 942
Gold sales, profits received from, 679*
Membership in Fund, 905*
Participant in gold auctions, 657
Peso: use in Fund transactions, 577, 578, 580*
Quota in Fund, 526, 542*; views on, 525
SDR allocations, 887*
Stand-by arrangements with Fund, 362, 427*

COLOMBO, EMILIO, 335, 404, 446, 448, 449

COMMONWEALTH FINANCE MINISTERS' MEETINGS, 977

COMOROS

Drawings (purchases) and repurchases from Fund, 434*, 570*

Exchange arrangements, 804*

Membership in Fund, 536*, 905*

Quota in Fund, 536*, 541*

COMPENSATORY FINANCING FACILITY

Access to by developing members: easing of, 209; limited, 407, 408; views on, 223

Calculation of export shortfalls, 406–407, 408, 409–10, 414, 415–16

Decision on: new, 409–10; reviewed, 411, 416

Established, 200

Extension to: export earnings in real terms, 401, 408; invisible earnings suggested, 404, 408, 414, 415, 416n

Floating alongside tranches, 406, 417n, 418, 419

Liberalization of: called for before 1975, 399–400, 414, 415–16; called for by Group of Twenty-Four, 401, 414; called for by Interim and Development Committees, 401–402; discussed in Executive Board and Board of Governors, 403–404, 407–409; proposals on, by U.S., 404–405, 407; by UNCTAD, 400

Joint ceiling with buffer stock financing facility, 406, 407, 409, 410, 420

Limits on purchases, 406, 407, 416; abolished, 416n; increased, 409

Operation of prior to 1975, 405–407; terms of, 406–407

Relation to concern with commodity prices, 401–402, 413

Relation to proposal for liberalization of with Trust Fund establishment, 405, 408, 668, 669–70

Use: as ratio of total Fund credit, 585*; drawings (purchases), 383, 400, 410, 411, 545, 584*; total (1972–78), 412*, 425*; reclassification of, 425*; repurchase provisions, 407, 410, 414

CONDITIONALITY

As factor in reduced use of Fund resources alleged, 382, 383, 501, 504, 507

Automaticity: for gold tranche drawings instituted, 483; versus conditionality, 482, 483, 485

Criticized, 441, 489–93; as compromising economic growth, 493; as having political effects, 491; as monetarist, 491–92; as "too strict" and "unduly severe," 491; by developing members, 489, 490, 491, 492, 493; by World Bank, 492, 955; Fund staff's style of operation, 493

Defended, 494, 495–96, 498–500; by Managing Director, 496–98

Incorporated into: Articles of Agreement, 482, 485; stand-by arrangements as performance criteria, 483–85, 486

Multiplier effects of, 493–94

New guidelines established for, 506–507

Origin and evolution, 482–85

Positions of: Executive Directors from developing members on, 446, 485–86, 501–503, 507; developing members on, 457, 490–91, 493; industrial and more developed primary producing members on, 482, 503–506

Provisions for under: compensatory financing facility, 406, 408; extended arrangements, 362–65, 369; first credit tranche, 528, 529; oil facility, 320, 322, 343–44, 349; stand-by arrangements, 446; supplementary financing facility, 546; Trust Fund discussed, 669

Related to adequacy of Fund quotas, 530, 531

Review of: called for, 490–91; (1978), 500–506

Uniformity of treatment questioned, 493, 501, 502; uniformity becomes "nondiscriminatory," 506

See also STABILIZATION PROGRAMS and STAND-BY ARRANGEMENTS

CONFERENCE ON INTERNATIONAL ECONOMIC COOPERATION (CIEC), 746, 954

Commodities, views on, 399, 414

Fund relations with, 1013–14; on capital markets, 935; on debt problems, 927

Representation at, 414n

CONGO, PEOPLE'S REPUBLIC OF THE

Drawings (purchases) and repurchases from Fund: purchases, 434*, (net), 886*; under compensatory financing facility, 412*; repurchases, 570*

Exchange arrangements, 804*

Gold sales, profits received from, 679*

Loan from Trust Fund, 673*

Membership in Fund, 905*

Quota in Fund, 541*

SDR allocations, 886*

Stand-by arrangements with Fund, 427*

CONNALLY, JOHN B., 24

Comments and views on: Group of Ten, 149; new par value for U.S. dollar, 19, 34, 35; reappointment of Mr. Schweitzer, 1003

CONSOLIDATION ARRANGEMENTS

Committee of Twenty: model of Bureau on, 234; opposing views of in, 217

Defined, 126, 181

Proposals for: by Germany, Fed. Rep., 182–83; by Italy, 183–84; by U.K., 183; by U.S., 182; in staff sketch, 126–27, 131, 132, 133

See also COMMITTEE OF TWENTY—DELIBERATIONS; . . . TECHNICAL GROUPS; and SUBSTITUTION ACCOUNT

CONSULTATIONS

Adaptation of: process, 912–13; topics covered, 914

Committee of Twenty discussions on, 194

Developing countries' access to capital markets included in, 914, 915, 916

Examples of: Bangladesh, 917; Brazil, 917; Germany, Fed. Rep., 916; Japan, 915; Korea, 916; U.S., 915

In connection with oil facility, 322

Reports made available to EC and OECD, 961

Special: for countries with floating rates, 51, 52, 53, 276–78, 301, 302; inaugurated on external policies, 278–79; introduced for world economic outlook exercise, 278, 279, 791, 797, 848, 912–13; suggested for balance of payments adjustment, 213–14, 257; supplementary not substitute for regular, 913; under Art. IV discussed, 857

Staff time involved in, 903

Under Art. IV, 841, 845–46, 848, 849–50; begun, 912, 913–14; changes in coverage, 914; conduct of Managing Director in intervals between, 848–49; number of, 912

Under Art. VIII, 13–15, 15–16, 46, 276, 841, 849–50, 912

Under Art. XIV: 276, 279, 841, 849–50, 912; procedures for similar to gold auction procedures, 653–54

Usefulness of, 913

With developing members, 914, 916–17; with EC as a group suggested, 80; with industrial members, 915–16; *see also* individual countries

CONVERTIBILITY
Committee of Twenty discussions, 226–27, 227–28; views of: European countries, 180, 183–84; U.S., 180–81
Dealt with in *Outline of Reform*, 257, 259
Definitions: "on demand," 128, 181; "primary asset holding limits," 168, 259
Fund staff study on, 185–86
Mandatory or voluntary debated, 180, 181, 184, 246–47
Model of Bureau of Committee of Twenty, 232–34, 235–36, 237; opposing views on: of European officials, 233, 234–35, 238; of U.S. officials, 233, 234, 235, 238–39; views of: developing members, 236; Mr. Morse, 237
Of U.S. dollar: calls for by EC, 20, 38, 124; debated, 39–40; U.S. views, 38–39, 112; significance of, 111; suspension of, 83; suspension of related to collapse of par value system, 83–84, 111–12
Proposals for by: Germany, Fed. Rep., 182–83; Italy, 183–84; U.K., 183; U.S., 4, 168, 182; compared, 184–85
See also ASSET SETTLEMENT

COOPER, RICHARD N., 760

COORE, DAVID H., 43, 254

COSTA RICA
Art. VIII, acceptance of obligations of, 912n
Drawings (purchases) and repurchases from Fund: purchases, 437*, (net), 887*; under oil facility, 331, 347*; repurchases, 572*
Gold sales, profits received from, 679*
Par value change, 37
Quota in Fund, 542*
SDR allocations, 887*
Stand-by arrangements with Fund, 427*

COUNCIL, FUND
As successor to Interim Committee, 303–304
Considered by Committee of Twenty, 157
Developing members' views on, 243
Establishment of proposed in connection with surveillance, 857
In *Outline of Reform*, 261
Modeled on Committee of Twenty, 141–42, 145
Opposition to, reasons for, 971–72
See also ARTICLES OF AGREEMENT: SECOND AMENDMENT—DRAFT AMENDMENTS *and* . . . FINAL PROVISIONS

COUNCIL FOR MUTUAL ECONOMIC ASSISTANCE (CMEA/COMECON), 908, 999

CRAWFORD, MALCOLM, 470

CREAN, F.D., 229

CREDIT CONTROLS. *See* DOMESTIC CREDIT EXPANSION *and* STABILIZATION PROGRAMS

CREDIT TRANCHES
Application in connection with: oil facility, 464; supplementary financing facility, 546, 548, 551–52
Policy on established in 1952, 483
Temporary enlargement of, 527–29, 530, 795
See also RESOURCES OF FUND—USE *and* STABILIZATION PROGRAMS

CROMER, LORD, 470

CROSS, SAM Y., 910, 937
Comments and views on: Art. IV, 737, 738, 748, 749, 754, 755; commodities, 419; compensatory financing, 408; conditionality, 504; floating rates and surveillance, 300, 302, 703; Fund's jurisdiction in trade matters, 705; gold auctions, 650; gold, role of, 615, 640–41; indicators, 212; membership of small states, 910; oil facility, 340–41; quotas, 518–19, 528, 530, 533, 534; repurchase provisions, 698; SDR allocations, 878; SDR reconstitution, 722; stand-by arrangements, 504; supplementary financing facility, 547; transmittal of information to commercial banks, 937; Trust Fund proposal, 662–63, 669; eligibility for, 675, 677; U.S. economic measures (1978), 864–65; U.S. policy on intervention, 815, 838
Service, 997

CUBA
Stand-by arrangements with Fund, 427*

CURRENCIES. *See* CURRENCY HOLDINGS OF FUND; SELECTION OF CURRENCIES IN FUND TRANSACTIONS; RESOURCES OF FUND—USE; RESERVE CURRENCIES; *and* individual countries

CURRENCY BUDGET, FUND. *See* SELECTION OF CURRENCIES IN FUND TRANSACTIONS

CURRENCY CONVERTIBLE IN FACT
Defined, 589n, 706
Interconvertibility abolished, 764
Related to equal value principle, 281

CURRENCY HOLDINGS OF FUND
Arrangements for use in Fund transactions in sixth quota review, 527, 577
Magnitudes, 578, 579, 582, 584, 584*
Opposition to use of for oil facility, 319–20
Rates used in Fund computations, 37, 777–78
Replenishment of by sales of gold, 647, 663; *see also* GOLD AUCTIONS
Significance of in Fund's liquidity, 582
U.S. dollars, 578, 580, 583, 584*
Value of, 69, 287, 292; maintenance of, 596–98, 777–78; temporary arrangements for, 28–29
See also ARTICLES OF AGREEMENT: SECOND AMENDMENT—DRAFT AMENDMENTS: General Account *and* REMUNERATION ON NET CREDITOR POSITIONS

CURRENCY SWAP ARRANGEMENTS. *See* CENTRAL BANKS

CYPRUS
Drawings (purchases) and repurchases from Fund: purchases, 438*, (net), 888*; under compensatory financing facility, 413*; under oil facility, 347*; repurchases, 573*
Exchange arrangements, 804*
Gold sales, profits received from, 679*
Membership in Fund, 905*
Participant in gold auctions, 657
Pound: use in Fund transactions, 576
Quota in Fund, 543*
SDR allocations, 888*

CZECHOSLOVAKIA
Membership in Fund, withdrawal from, 93, 908n

D

DAANE, J. DEWEY, 166, 168
DAHOMEY. *See* BENIN

Powers of, 721
Reports. *See* specific subjects
Representation on, 520
Role: in Committee of Twenty, 153, 154, 156, 158, 196, 243; in Fund policymaking, 964–65, 983–84; in Interim Committee, 967–68, 1000; powerful in mid-1970s, 999–1000
Size and structure of: changes in, 765; changes in discussed and studied, 765; provisions in original Articles on, 764; report on (1972), 765–66; under Second Amendment, 766–67
Time spent on Fund's regular activities, 903–904
Treatment of in History, 15*n*
Voting, 294*n*, 677, 692; bloc versus split, 692–93; by "sense of the meeting" defined, 988–89; formal, 988, 995; procedures for discussed, 995–96
See also Appendices A-1, A-2, A-3 (pp. 1045–55 of this volume) *and* individual members of Executive Board

EXPORTS
By developing members, 42, 43, 200, 201, 209
See also BUFFER STOCK FINANCING FACILITY; COMPENSATORY FINANCING FACILITY; *and* TRADE, INTERNATIONAL

EXTENDED FUND FACILITY (EXTENDED ARRANGEMENTS)
Arguments for, 361–65
Arrangements with: Egypt, 380–81; Haiti, 381–82; Jamaica, 380–81; Kenya, 370–73; Mexico, 377–80; Philippines, 373–77
Augmentation rights, elimination of, 780–81
Conceived during "link" discussions, 206, 255
Developing members' concept of, 209, 223, 366–67
External factors decisive in success of, 376–77, 380, 383
Nature of discussed, 365–66; Executive Board consideration and decision, 366–68; terms of, 368–70
Overlap with World Bank caused by, 956
Relation to: stand-by arrangements, 362, 364, 365; supplementary financing, 551–52, 554
Revised forms for, 776–77
Stabilization programs for, 363, 364–65, 365–66, 369
Undrawn balances under (1972–78), 884*
Use: drawings (purchases) by: Kenya, 372; Mexico, 379; Philippines, 376; total, 425*;less than anticipated, 382–83
Views of: developing members, 382–83; industrial and more developed primary producing members, 383

F

FAMILTON, ROBERT J., 1028
FAO. *See* FOOD AND AGRICULTURE ORGANIZATION
FELDT, KJELL-OLOF, 191, 228, 254
FERNANDEZ HURTADO, ERNESTO, 180
FIJI
Art. VIII, acceptance of obligations under, 912
Dollar: floating, 55; use in Fund transactions, 580*
Drawings (purchases) and repurchases from Fund: purchases, 435*, (net), 887*; under compensatory financing facility, 411, 412*; under oil facility, 331, 347*; repurchases, 571*

Exchange arrangements, 804*
Gold sales, profits received from, 679*
Membership in Fund, 905*
Quota in Fund, 542*
SDR allocations, 887*
Stand-by arrangements with Fund, 424, 427*, 431

FINAISH, MOHAMED, 367, 766, 998, 999
FINANCIAL POSITION OF FUND. *See* BUDGET OF FUND
FINANCIAL PROGRAMS. *See* STABILIZATION PROGRAMS
FINANCE & DEVELOPMENT, 950, 1010
FINCH, C. DAVID, 1026
FINLAND
Classification by Fund, 42*n*, 789
Drawings (purchases) from Fund, 423, 433*, (net), 885*; under oil facility, 347*
Exchange arrangements, 804*, 806
Membership in Fund, 905*
Quota in Fund, 540*
SDR allocations, 885*
Stand-by arrangements with Fund, 424, 427*
Subsidy Account contribution, 354*
Trust Fund, exclusion from, 675

FISCAL POLICY
Cyclically neutral budget concept used in world economic outlook, 792–93
For combating inflation, 816
In stabilization programs, 363, 455, 486–87
See also MONETARY POLICY *and* individual countries

FLEMING, J. MARCUS, 1022
FOGLIZZO, JEAN, 248, 677
FOOD AND AGRICULTURE ORGANIZATION (FAO), 87, 957
FORD, GERALD R., 335, 453, 470, 744, 746, 747, 818, 1007
Meeting in Martinique and agreement on gold, 617, 618, 619, 627
Proposal on Trust Fund, 405
Role in Mr. Witteveen's U.K. visit, 471–72

FOURCADE, JEAN-PIERRE, 254
Comments and views on: compensatory financing, 404; Council, 720; floating rates, 701, 736; gold arrangements and quotas, 627; gold holdings of Fund, 619; gold reserves, valuation of, 617; gold subscription payments, 614–15; gold substitution account, 641; oil facility, 335; par values, 742
Role in Art. IV negotiations, 740–41, 746, 747, 749, 754, 755

FRANCE
Art. VIII, acceptance of obligations of, 912*n*
Asset settlement, consolidation, and convertibility: proposal on, 248, 249; views on, 216, 217, 222, 227, 235, 238
Balance of payments, 391; adjustment, proposal for pressures for, 224–25, 228; views on U.S. deficits, 171, 172
Consultations, special, 278, 279
Credits to U.K., 467
Capital movements, measures to control, 18
Central rates, views on, 280
Classification by Fund, 42*n*, 789
Drawings (purchases) and repurchases from Fund: purchases, 423, 433*, (net), 885*; repurchases, 568, 569*
Economic situation and policies, 440, 816

G

GOLD SUBSTITUTION ACCOUNT
Discussed in: Executive Board, 640–41; Interim Committee, 641–42
Proposed by Mr. de Groote, 616, 639–40
Rejection, reasons for, 642–43
Staff draft of, 639, 641
Views of: developing members, 624, 640; industrial and more developed members, 616, 640–41; Interim Committee, 625, 627; Managing Director, 638–39
See also ARTICLES OF AGREEMENT: SECOND AMENDMENT—DRAFT AMENDMENTS

GOLD TRANCHE
Defined, 283, 582*n*; super, 283, 593
Valuation, 582*n*
Use of, 423–24, 425*, 431, 883, 884*; elimination of service charge on, 590
See also RESERVE TRANCHE

GOLD TRANSACTIONS OF CENTRAL BANKS
Arrangements on: debated, 608–609, 613, 615–16, 618–20; for Group of Ten proposed by Managing Director, 621–22; discussed by EC, 625; discussed by Group of Ten, 622; endorsed, 626, 731; expired, 635–36; Group of Ten technical group on, 631; implemented, 634–35
Pressures on to deal at premium prices, 637
Provisions of Articles on, at premium prices, 609, 619–20, 630–31, 632, 633, 649
Simultaneity of with disposition of Fund's gold discussed, 630–31, 633
See also GROUP OF TEN: Gold arrangements of

GOLD TRANSACTIONS AND OPERATIONS OF FUND
Purchases from members discussed in staff sketch, 127; from South Africa, 127*n*; terminated, 610–11
Repurchases, 581*; postponed, 611–12
Sales for currency replenishment, 647, 663; *see also* GOLD HOLDINGS OF FUND: Sales of
Sales in connection with GAB activities, 647
Subscriptions, payments of, 518, 524, 614, 615–16; by new members, 611–12
See also ARTICLES OF AGREEMENT: SECOND AMENDMENT—FINAL PROVISIONS *and* GOLD HOLDINGS OF FUND

GOMEZ MORALES, ALFREDO, 228

GOODE, RICHARD, 1021

GOVERNMENT FINANCE STATISTICS YEARBOOK, 919, 950, 951

GOVERNORS OF FUND. *See* BOARD OF GOVERNORS

GONZALEZ DEL VALLE, JORGE, 245

GREECE
Classification by Fund, 42*n*, 789, 909
External debt, 928
Drawings (purchases) and repurchases from Fund, 433*, (net), 885*; under compensatory financing facility, 412*; under oil facility, 331, 347*; repurchases, 569*
Exchange arrangements, 805*, 806
Membership in Fund, 905*
Par value change, 35, 36*
Quota in Fund, 540*
SDR allocations, 885*
Subsidy Account contribution, 354*
Trust Fund: contribution, 676; proposed exclusion from, 674–75, 676, 678

GRENADA
Drawings (purchases) and repurchases from Fund: purchases, 437*, (net), 887*; under oil facility, 347*; repurchases, 572*
Exchange arrangements, 804*
Gold sales, profits received from, 679*
Membership in Fund, 536*, 674, 905*
Quota in Fund, 536*, 543*
Stand-by arrangements with Fund, 424, 427*
Subsidy Account payments received, 353
Trust Fund: eligibility, 671*n*, 674; loan from, 673*

GROSS NATIONAL PRODUCT (GNP)
Declines in 1975, 387, 389; *see also* INDUSTRIAL MEMBERS: Output and gross national product *and* WORLD ECONOMY

GROUP OF FIVE ("BIG FIVE")
Exchange arrangements and gold discussed, 743, 850
Informal meetings of, 977–78
Position in Committee of Twenty, 240
Views of developing members on, 68

GROUP OF NINE ("G-9 Caucus"), 977, 986

GROUP OF SEVENTY-SEVEN
Adoption of Algiers Charter, 325
Common fund on buffer stocks proposal, 414
Formation of, 957
Position on commodities, 402, 414
Relation: to Group of Twenty-Four, 957, 976; to UN, 980

GROUP OF TEN
As factor in formation of Committee of Twenty, 143, 148–49
Chairmanship of deputies, 978
Communiqués, 188, 344*n*, 588*n*, 749
Composition, 11, 143
Criticized by U.S., 148–49
Fund relations with, 977–78
Gold arrangements of: agreed, 634–35; expired, 635–36; objections to, 635; supervisor of suggested, 619; technical group established on, 631; valuation of gold reserves used as collateral for loans, 614
Influence on Fund policymaking, 144, 964, 976, 977–78
Meetings: deputies, 154, 342–43, 548, 591–92, 622, 632, 748; joint with EC, 77, 78–79, 189, 978; joint with Executive Directors, 143–44; ministers, 11, 147, 344, 525, 589, 591, 626, 632–34, 746, 749; representation by Fund staff at, 1014
Model for Group of Twenty-Four, 976
Origin and functions, 143, 588, 978
Participation in Fund's gold sales discussed, 633, 635
Role in: amended Art. IV negotiations, 978; reserve creation, 143
Views on: floating rates, 188; gold sales and restitution, 632; oil facility and OECD safety net, 344
Working group on proposal for financing oil deficits, 343

GROUP OF TWENTY. *See* COMMITTEE OF TWENTY—CREATION AND ORGANIZATION

GROUP OF TWENTY-FOUR (INTERGOVERNMENTAL GROUP OF TWENTY-FOUR ON INTERNATIONAL MONETARY AFFAIRS)
Communiqués, 623, 645, 739, 754–55, 859, 980
Formation and composition, 43, 144, 976–77
Influence of: increased, 979–80; in establishing Development Committee, 979; on Fund policy-

H

I

IBRD. *See* WORLD BANK

ICELAND

Classification by Fund, 42*n*, 789

Drawings (purchases) and repurchases from Fund: purchases, 433*, (net), 885*; under compensatory financing facility, 410, 412*; under oil facility, 331, 347*; repurchases, 569*

Economic situation and policies, 57–58

Króna: pegged to U.S. dollar, 55

Membership in Fund, 905*

Par value change, 35, 36*, 57

Quota in Fund, 540*

SDR allocations, 885*

Stand-by arrangements with Fund, 428*

Trust Fund, exclusion from, 675

IDA. *See* INTERNATIONAL DEVELOPMENT ASSOCIATION

IDB. *See* INTER-AMERICAN DEVELOPMENT BANK

ILO. *See* INTERNATIONAL LABOR ORGANIZATION

IMF MEMORANDUM, 946

IMF SURVEY, 933, 950–51

IMPORTS

By developing countries, 351; concern about, 642

Fund study on, 942

Need for continuation of after oil price increases, 350

Oil, 356

Restrictions: avoidance of as condition for oil facility use, 939; avoidance of included in stabilization programs, 487; in individual countries, 939; Canada, 941; EC countries, 941; U.S., 941; selective, increased, 939–40, 941

Substitution, as development strategy, 92, 370, 373–74

See also TRADE, INTERNATIONAL

INAMURA, KOICHI, 173, 189, 208, 235–36

INCOME AND EXPENDITURE OF FUND, 599–603*

Developments, 295

Distribution of net income, 599

Investment income, 599

INCOME DISTRIBUTION

Related to: extended arrangements, 378, 379; stabilization programs, 492

Policies on: in Mexico, 378, 379; in U.K. discussed, 474

INCOMES POLICY

Significance of in stand-by arrangements, 479

Use: by Italy, 455, 456–57; by U.K., 462, 465, 467, 473, 787

INDIA

Consultations, special, 279

Debt, external, 928; renegotiation, staff study on, 925

Drawings (purchases) and repurchases from Fund: purchases, 436*, (net), 887*; under compensatory financing facility, 400, 412*; under oil facility, 331, 348*; repurchases, 568, 571*

Economic situation and policies, 331

Exchange arrangements, 804*, 807

Executive Board representation, 999

Gold sales, profits received from, 679*

Membership in Fund, 905*

Participant in gold auctions, 657

Quota in Fund, 526, 532, 542*, 672

Rupee: floating, 55; rates for, changes in, 51–52

SDR: allocations, 887; holdings, 897

Stand-by arrangements with Fund, 428*

Subsidy Account payments received, 355

Trust Fund eligibility, 670*n*

INDICATORS

Basic balance: defined, 174–75; discussed in Committee of Twenty Technical Group, 212; proposed by Italy, 174–75, 189

Composite, 212

For use in surveillance, 842

Fund staff study on, 175–76

Objective, 212, 213

Proposals for: by Germany, Fed. Rep., 175, 247; by Italy, 174–75, 189; by U.S., 168–69, 212, 247; objections to U.S. proposal, 173–74, 176

Reserve: discussed in Committee of Twenty, 226; discussed in guidelines for floating rates, 298, 299; German proposals for, 175, 247; U.S. proposal for, 168–69, 212, 247; used to assess global reserve needs, 874

Technical Group of Committee of Twenty on, 212–13, 247

See also BALANCE OF PAYMENTS ADJUSTMENT

INDONESIA

Acceptance of Second Amendment, 769

As major oil exporter, 308

Balance of payments, 318

Classification by Fund, 42*n*

Consultations, special, 279

Credits from banks, Fund study on, 931

Debt, external, 928; renegotiation, 925

Drawings (purchases) and repurchases from Fund: purchases, 434*, (net), 885*; under buffer stock financing facility, 417; repurchases, 569*

Gold sales, profits received from, 679*

Membership: in Fund, 905*; in OPEC, 306

Quota in Fund, 540*, 672

Rupiah: use in Fund transactions, 321, 577, 578, 580*

SDR: allocations, 885*; holdings, 897

Stand-by arrangements with Fund, 362, 428*, 431

Trust Fund eligibility, 670*n*, 674

INDUSTRIAL MEMBERS

Balance of payments positions, 65, 115–16, 308, 309, 357, 390, 391, 395, 832

Borrowing by Fund from, 315, 326, 546

Capacity utilization, 387, 389, 391

Classification of by Fund, 42*n*, 789

Coverage in world economic outlook, 786–90, 792–94

Decision making by, 610, 644

Effect of oil price increases on, 313

Output and gross national product, 312, 387, 389, 390, 391, 787, 788

Price increases, 311

Quotas in Fund, 525, 526, 537, 537*, 538

SDR allocations, 885*

Use of Fund resources, 72–78, 424, 431, 432*, 433*, 569*, 885*

Views on: conditionality, 495, 503–506; Council, 972; exchange rate policies, 839; gold arrangements, 644–45; quotas, 511, 512, 519, 520

See also individual countries

INFLATION

As major economic problem of postwar years, 92

Causes of, contrasting views of, 829–30

Coexisting with: high growth rate, 917; unemployment, 49, 390, 823

for, 441, 451–53; performance of, 446–49, 458–59; programs for, 443–44, 454–56, 486; proposed by officials, 452–53; purchase provisions, 456; significance of for Fund, 478–79

Subsidy Account contribution, 354*

Transactions with Fund: drawings (purchases), 423, 433*, (net), 885*; in gold tranche, 441; under oil facility, 331, 347, 347*, 349, 448–49, 450; under stand-by arrangements, 349, 431, 457, 458, 590, 592, 816; repurchases, 457, 458, 568, 569*

Trust Fund, exclusion from, 674

Unemployment and inflation, 12, 449

Views on: consolidation, 217; global need for reserves, 179; "link," 205, 224; oil facility, 339; par value changes, 170; valuation of gold, 608

Wage indexation system. *See* Incomes policy, *above*

IVORY COAST

Consultations, special, 279

Debt, external, 928

Drawings (purchases) and repurchases from Fund: purchases, 435*, (net), 886*; under compensatory financing facility, 410, 412*; under oil facility, 331, 348*; repurchases, 570*

Exchange arrangements, 804*

Gold sales, profits received from, 679*

Loan from Trust Fund, 673*

Membership in Fund, 905*

Quota in Fund, 539, 541*

SDR allocations, 886*

Subsidy Account payments received, 355*

J

J-CURVE. *See* EXCHANGE RATES: Changes in, effects of

JACOBSSON, PER. *See* MANAGING DIRECTOR

JAGANNATHAN, S., 331, 640, 651, 668, 722, 754

JALAL, MAHSOUN B., 767, 866

JAMAICA

Art. VIII, acceptance of obligations of, 912*n*

Dollar floating, 55

Drawings (purchases) and repurchases from Fund: purchases, 437*, (net), 887*; under compensatory financing facility, 400, 411, 413*; under oil facility, 348*; repurchases, 573*

Economic situation and policies, 381

Exchange arrangements, 805*

Extended arrangement with Fund, 380–81

Gold sales, profits received from, 679*

Membership in Fund, 905*

Par value change, 56

Quota in Fund, 539, 543*

SDR allocations, 887*

Stand-by arrangements with Fund, 428*, 431

JAMAICA AGREEMENT

Assessed, 760–62; criticized, 759; hailed, 758

Compared with *Outline of Reform*, 759–60

Elements of, 757–58

JAMAL, A.H., 415

JANSON, GEORGES, 172, 208

JAPAN

Acceptance of Second Amendment, 769

Art. VIII, acceptance of obligations of, 912*n*

Balance of payments surpluses, 15, 16, 73, 308, 391, 855, 861; oil deficit, 390

Banking regulations, Fund study on, 932

Borrowing by Fund for supplementary financing facility, 557*n*

Capital markets, Fund study on, 931

Capital movements and measures to control, 73, 215, 854

Central rate used, 39, 58, 72, 280

Classification by Fund, 42*n*, 789

Consultations: Art. IV, 915; Art. VIII, 16; special, 75, 278, 279

Economic situation and policies: discount rate reduced, 854; expansionary (1978), 857, 858, 861, 863; measures needed to stabilize world economy, 393, 394, 855; reluctance to resolve by revaluation, 71, 72; views on, 73–74; restrained, 818

Exchange arrangements, 805*; policies discussed by Executive Directors, 838; views on floating, 73, 173, 188–89; views on intervention, 816, 818

Exchange market intervention, 72, 75, 818; criticism of, 74–75; policy on coordinated with U.S., 865

Executive Board representation, 999

General Arrangements to Borrow: borrowing under, 590; commitment enlarged, 590

Gross national product, 24–25, 389, 391

Import restrictions, Fund study on, 942

Intermediary in gold restitution, 659

Membership in: Fund, 71, 538, 905*; in Group of Ten, 11

Participation in: Big Five meetings, 743, 977–78; Committee of Twenty, 156; summit meetings, 745–46, 746–47, 940

Par value, 71

Proposal for MCI system, 245

Quota in Fund, 513, 525, 530, 532, 533, 540*; views on quotas, 512, 519–20, 530, 532, 533, 539

SDR allocations, 885*

Stand-by arrangements with Fund, 428*

Subsidy Account contribution, 354*

Swap arrangements with U.S., 862

Trade: negotiations with U.S., 72, 960; restrictions on, 72–73; signatory of voluntary declaration on, 349; surpluses, 16, 71, 73; U.S. views on Japan's restrictions, 74; views on Fund's role in, 221

Trust Fund, exclusion from, 675

Unemployment and inflation, 12, 864

Yen: currency convertible in fact, 589*n*; floating, 69–70, 71–72, 276; freely usable currency, 776; rates for, 70–71, 72, 75, 809, 811, 853, 860, 861, 862, 865; reserve currency, 637; revaluation, 15; use in computations for remuneration and SDR interest rate, 594, 596, 891, 892; use in Fund transactions, 32, 33–34, 539, 576, 577, 580*; use in SDR currency basket, 293, 293*, 893*

Views on: asset settlement and convertibility, 226–27, 235–36; balance of payments adjustment and pressures, 188–89, 235–36; gold, 618; "link," 224; reform group, 152; SDR valuation and interest rate, 179, 229, 285–86

JAYAWARDENA, LAL, 207, 980

JIMENEZ M., BERNAL, 415, 654

JOHNSON, LYNDON B., 147

JOINT MINISTERIAL COMMITTEE OF THE BOARDS OF GOVERNORS OF THE BANK AND THE FUND ON THE TRANSFER OF REAL RESOURCES TO DEVELOPING COUNTRIES. *See* DEVELOPMENT COMMITTEE

N

of developing members, 323; views of industrial members, 324

See also SUBSIDY ACCOUNT

OIL PRICE

As factor in Committee of Twenty deliberations, 270

Increases, 306, 307, 356–57, 359; effects on balance of payments positions, 289, 305, 308–10, 315, 337, 387; impact of first round of, 355–57; impact of second round of, 359–60; implications of for economic growth, 264, 305; implications of for inflation and recession, 289, 310–12, 313, 315, 358, 387; reasons for, 307

U.S. views on, 337–38

See also OIL FACILITY and ORGANIZATION OF PETROLEUM EXPORTING COUNTRIES

OMAN

Art. VIII, acceptance of obligations of, 912n

Borrowing by Fund for oil facility, 330, 345, 346*

Classification by Fund, 42n

Exchange arrangements, 804*

Gold sales, profits received from, 680*

Membership in Fund, 906*

Quota in Fund, 532, 534, 540*

Rial: use in Fund transactions, 321, 577, 581*

SDR allocations, 885*

Signatory of voluntary declaration on trade, 349

Trust Fund, exclusion from, 674

OMWONY, MAURICE P., 765

OORT, C.J., 172, 175, 179, 234–35

OPEC. See ORGANIZATION OF PETROLEUM EXPORTING COUNTRIES

ORGANIZATION FOR ECONOMIC COOPERATION AND DEVELOPMENT (OECD)

Commodities, views on, 402

Declaration on trade restrictions adopted, 91, 350

Fund relations with, 954, 960–61, 981; on capital markets, 932–33; on compiling statistics, 951; on debt problems, 925, 927; on trade policy, 942

Membership, 344n

Participation in Committee of Twenty, 220

Role in: exchange rate realignment, 126; Fund's world economic outlook, 785–86, 795

Safety net proposal, 314–15, 344, 548, 549, 664; by Secretary-General, 339, 343; by U.S., 338–39, 343; not established, 357, 549

Working Party 3, 110, 850

World economic outlook strategy, 394

ORGANIZATION OF AMERICAN STATES (OAS), 962

ORGANIZATION OF PETROLEUM EXPORTING COUNTRIES (OPEC)

As source of financing balance of payments deficits, 382

Decision to raise oil prices, 306, 359

Establishment and membership in, 306

Fund relations with, 981

Meetings, 306

Oil embargo, 306

Participation in supplementary financing facility discussed, 548, 550, 555

Reserves, estimates of, 310

Special Fund, technical assistance by Fund staff, 921

Terms of trade, 356–57

OSSOLA, RINALDO, 78, 158, 188, 452, 622, 978

Comments and views on: indicators, 234; "link," 208

Proposal on: asset settlement, 183; global liquidity related to world trade, 179; indicators, 174–75, 212; substitution, 217

Role in Committee of Twenty, 158–59

OUTLINE OF REFORM

Annexes, 256, 259–60, 262

Approved by Committee of Twenty, 255

As basis for draft amendments, 271, 686–87, 688, 690, 702, 736–37, 741

Compared with Jamaica agreement, 759–60

Contents, 256–61, 262–63

Declaration on trade and other current account measures, 349

Disagreement about need for, 253

Discontent of developing members with, 255

Drafting, 211, 223, 253; Committee of Twenty decision on, 193, 194; difficulties of, 194–95; Mr. Morse's reasons for, 193–94; optimism about, 195–96

Fund's role defined in, 256–57

Main features of, 257

Provisions on: adjustment, 257–59; capital controls, 257, 258–59; consultations, 257–58; convertibility, 257, 259–60; Council, 261; developing members, special position of, 258–59, 261; exchange rates, 257, 258; gold, role of, 257, 260; SDR as numeraire, 260; SDR as principal reserve asset, 257, 260; SDR "link," 261; SDR valuation and interest rate, 260, 294; substitution account, 260; trade measures, 302–303; transfer of real resources, 257, 261

Reformed system characterized by Mr. Morse, 261–62

OVERBY, ANDREW N., 88

OVERSEAS STERLING AREA, 50

P

PADMORE, OVERAND, 938–39

PAKISTAN

Consultations, special, 279

Debt, external, 925, 928

Drawings (purchases) and repurchases from Fund: purchases, 436*, (net), 887*; under compensatory financing facility, 411, 412*, 425*; under oil facility, 331, 348*; repurchases, 568, 572*

Exchange arrangements, 804*; multiple rates eliminated, 37

Gold sales, profits received from, 680*

Membership in Fund, 906*

Par value change, 35, 36*, 37

Quota in Fund, 526, 532, 542*

Rupee pegged to U.S. dollar, 55

SDR allocations, 887*

Stand-by arrangements with Fund, 426, 429*, 431

Subsidy Account payments received, 355*

Trust Fund: eligibility, 670n; loan from, 672, 673*

PALAMENGHI-CRISPI, FRANCESCO, 452, 913

Comments and views on: asset settlement, 248; central rates, 39, 40; extended Fund facility, 319, 367; guidelines for floating rates, 299, 302; "link," 205; oil deficit financing, 252; oil facility, 319, 324, 328, 339; quotas, 522; SDR allocations, 248; SDR reconstitution, 722

Role in Italian stand-by arrangement, 441, 446, 447, 451

Service, 998

General reviews of, 511; prior to sixth, 512–14

Implications for composition of Executive Board, 539

Increases, general: not taken, 520; prior to sixth, 513; proposed in sixth, 517, 518, 521; proposed in seventh, 529–30; proposed for eighth, 880; *see also* Selective increases, *below*

Minimum for membership considered, 910

Of new members, 514, 515, 521, 535, 536*

Relation to world liquidity, 873

Relative distribution among economic groups, 511–12, 517, 518, 519, 520–21, 521–22, 523, 525–26, 530–31, 536–39

Role of, 511; examination of called for, 520

Selective increases, 511, 513, 515, 523, 526, 530–31, 533, 534, 538

Seventh General Review, 529–33; agreed, 533–35, 881–82; debated, 529–32; delay in, 556

Sixth General Review, 517–26; concluded, 524–25; debated, 518–21, 522–24; delay in taking effect, 526–27, 546; problems in amending Articles, 708

Small quota policy, 515

Subscriptions, media of payment of: in currencies, 518, 522, 524, 526–27, 533, 535, 579; in gold, 512, 514, 517–18, 522, 611, 614–15, 687, 688; *see also* ARTICLES OF AGREEMENT: SECOND AMENDMENT—DRAFT AMENDMENTS: Gold *and* . . . FINAL PROVISIONS; in SDRs, 522, 524, 526–27, 533, 535, 579

Total, 512, 513, 521, 527, 530, 531, 535, 540*–43*, 584*; percentages by economic group (1945–78), 537*

Voting majorities for changes in, 514

R

RAFAEL SILVA, CARLOS, 250

RAMBOUILLET MEETING. *See* SUMMIT MEETINGS

RASAPUTRAM, WARNASENA, 937

RAWLINSON, ANTHONY K., 75, 302, 328, 339, 419, 616, 665

RAY, A.S., 1026–27

RAZALEIGH HAMZAH, TENGKU, 416

REAGAN, RONALD, 646

RECESSION

Effects on nonindustrial members, 389

In industrial members, 12, 62–63, 389, 391

Of: 1969–71, 12; 1974–75, 333, 389, 395, 642, 666

Relation to oil price increases, 311–12, 315

See also UNEMPLOYMENT *and* individual countries

RECENT ECONOMIC DEVELOPMENTS (RED) REPORTS, 944, 958

Transmittal to other organizations, 937, 993

See also CONSULTATIONS: Adaptation of

RECONSTITUTION. *See* SDR—RECONSTITUTION

REFORM OF INTERNATIONAL MONETARY SYSTEM

Based on par values, 124–26, 134, 137

Board of Governors' resolution, 123

Concept changed after August 1971, 124

Considered after Smithsonian, 12, 16, 17, 264

Effects of floating rates on, 51

Executive Directors' report on (1972), 123, 202; contents, 137–40; problems in drafting, 134–37; significance of, 140; U.S. views, 135, 136

Failure of, 140

Fund's role in discussed, 131

Fund staff sketch on, 123–30; Executive Directors' reactions to, 130–34; U.S. views, 133–34, 150

Need for shown by U.S. dollar devaluation, 68

Proposals on: by U.K., 130–31; by U.S., 24, 134, 166–69

See also COMMITTEE OF TWENTY *and* OUTLINE OF REFORM

REID, JAY H., 1025

REMUNERATION ON NET CREDITOR POSITIONS

Changes in, 593–96; raised in 1974, 594; reviewed, June 1974–1976, 595–96

Formulas for determining, 594, 595, 596, 894–95

Magnitudes, 600, 603*

Rates of (1969–78), 597*

Relation to: Fund's budgetary position, 599, 600, 601, 602; Fund's charges, 563, 564, 600; interest rates, 892–93; SDR interest rate, 294–95, 593–94, 595, 596, 893, 894–95

Split rate, 295, 593–95; eliminated, 595, 597*

REPRESENTATIVE RATE. *See* EXCHANGE RATES

REPURCHASES

Attribution, 567, 779, 780

By individual countries, 568, 569*–73*, 575

Currencies used in, 31, 32, 33, 34, 576, 577–78, 580*–81*, 581; rules for, 574–75, 575–76, 577

Definition, 566

Early, guidelines for, 778–79

Magnitudes, 567–68, 568*, 576; by economic category, 569*–73*

Media for effecting: gold, 566, 581*; SDRs, 566–67, 575, 581, 581*, 612, 778, 889

Obligations, extension of, 567

Of extended Fund facility and oil facility drawings, 567

Problems of U.S. dollar inconvertibility, 28, 31, 32, 575

Special arrangements: after August 1971, 31–32, 566, 575–76; for U.K., 32–34, 575–76

Under Second Amendment. *See* ARTICLES OF AGREEMENT: SECOND AMENDMENT—DRAFT AMENDMENTS: General Account *and* . . . FINAL PROVISIONS

Waivers, 566

See also individual countries

REQUIREMENT OF NEED

For use of: buffer stock financing facility, 419; compensatory financing facility, 406; oil facility, 321–22, 324, 341; SDRs, 706, 731, 889–90, 898; Trust Fund loans, 671

Linked to reserve position, 700, 715, 724

RESERVE ASSETS

Committee of Twenty discussions, 176–80

In: *Outline of Reform*, 259–60; report on reform, 139

SDR as principal agreed, 178, 217–18, 260, 889

See also GOLD RESERVES; RESERVE CURRENCIES; SDR—ROLE IN INTERNATIONAL MONETARY SYSTEM

RESERVE CURRENCIES

Control of suggested: by Managing Director, 638–39; in staff draft of gold substitution account, 641

Proposals to reduce use of national currencies as, 51–52, 179; cooperation clause, 633; in report on

Gold sales, profits received from, 680*
Membership in Fund, 906*
Quota in Fund, 541*
SDR allocations, 886*
Stand-by arrangements with Fund, 429*

RYAN, RICHIE, 624

RYRIE, WILLIAM S., 937
Comments and views on: Art. IV, 754; credit tranche enlargement, 528; quotas, 533; stand-by arrangements (Italy), 456; (United Kingdom), 465–66, 477; surveillance, 843
Service, 998

S

SAAD, AHMED ZAKI, 325
Comments and views on: Fund's authority, 143–44; reserve indicators, 173–74

SAID NABULSI, MOHAMMAD, 858

SAMBWA PIDA NBAGUI, 43, 190

SAMUEL-LAJEUNESSE, DENIS, 865, 866

SANDBURG, CARL, 4

SANSON, CARLOS E., 1027

SAO TOME AND PRINCIPE
Drawings (purchases) from Fund (net), 886*; repurchases, 571*
Exchange arrangements, 804*
Membership in Fund, 536*, 906*
Quota in Fund, 536*, 541*

SAUDI ARABIA
Acceptance of Second Amendment, 769
Art. VIII, acceptance of obligations of, 912n
As major oil exporter, 306, 308
Borrowing by Fund: for oil facility, 325, 326, 330, 345, 346*; for supplementary financing facility, 546–47, 556, 557n
Classification by Fund, 42n
Consultations, special, 279
Exchange arrangements, 805*
Executive Director appointed, 766, 767, 977
Gold sales, profits received from, 680*
Imports, 356
Membership: in Fund, 906*; in OPEC, 306
Participant in Special Drawing Rights Department, 898
Proposal for concessionary aid, 314
Quota in Fund, 527, 532, 534, 540*
Riyal: use in Fund transactions, 577, 581*; use in SDR basket, 892, 893*
Subsidy Account contribution, 354*
Trust Fund: contribution to, 677, 678; exclusion from, 675, 764

SCHILLER, KARL, 24, 113, 813

SCHLEIMINGER, GÜNTHER, 212, 299, 612, 698, 705
Comments and views on: asset settlement, 131; dollar inconvertibility, 39; extended arrangements, 365, 366; gold substitution account, 616; "link," 203–204; oil facility, 316; quotas, 518–19, 520; SDR as Fund's unit of account, 31; SDR as primary reserve asset, 204; transfer of official resources, 250–51; world economic outlook, 786

SCHMIDT, HELMUT, 24, 240, 254, 469, 746, 796
Comments and views on: convertibility and asset settlement, 227; floating rates, 191; "link," 230;

oil facility, 316; reformed international monetary system, 164, 326

SCHNEIDER, HEINRICH G., 248, 698
Comments and views on: buffer stock financing, 419; conditionality, 505; dollar inconvertibility, 39; gold substitution account, 616; guidelines for floating rates, 299; SDR reconstitution, 722
Service, 997

SCHUMAN, ROBERT, 171

SCHWARTZ, CHARLES F., 1029

SCHWEITZER, PIERRE-PAUL. See MANAGING DIRECTOR

SDR—ALLOCATIONS
First basic period, 671–72; amounts, 872, 884*, 885*–88*
Importance of for developing members, 248
Managing Director's "package" proposal, 880, 882–83; Executive Directors' report on, 880–81
Procedures for, 872, 882
Related to global need for reserves, 178, 204, 248, 753–54, 873–76, 877, 878–80
Relation to proposal for substitution account, 899
Second basic period, report on, 872–73
Third basic period: agreement for explored, 873; agreement reached, 881–82; rationale for discussed, 877–78, 878–80; report on, 878
Tie-in to improvements in characteristics and uses suggested, 878, 879; Managing Director's proposal for, 880
Views of: developing members, 873, 877, 878, 879, 880; Group of Twenty-Four, 873; industrial members, 872, 879, 880
See also LINK . . . DEVELOPMENT FINANCE

SDR—CHARACTERISTICS AND USES
As unit of account for international organizations, treaties, and contracts, 890–91, 899
Improvements in: before Second Amendment, 889–90; Committee of Twenty discussions on, 176–78; necessary after Second Amendment, 890; proposal by Managing Director as part of SDR "package," 880; see also SDR—INTEREST RATE; SDR—RECONSTITUTION; SDR—ROLE IN INTERNATIONAL MONETARY SYSTEM; and SDR—VALUATION
Increased use to: pay charges, 895, 896; repurchase, 895
Other holders prescribed, 898–99
Tie-in to allocations suggested, 877–78
Transactions by agreement: under First Amendment, 897–98; under Second Amendment, 898; use as security for loans, in donations, swaps, 898
Use in intra-European settlements, 275, 286–87, 889, 894, 897
See also ARTICLES OF AGREEMENT: SECOND AMENDMENT—DRAFT AMENDMENTS: SDRs and . . . FINAL PROVISIONS; and COMMITTEE OF TWENTY—DELIBERATIONS

SDR—INTEREST RATE
Committee of Twenty discussions, 227, 229
Formulas for, 293–94, 594, 595, 892n, 894–95
Increased (1974), 293–94, 593–94, 889, 892; (1976), 596, 892–93; proposed as part of SDR allocation package, 880
Low rate, reasons for, 282–83, 285, 893
Relation to Fund's charges, 283
Significance of after August 1971, 284
Tied to: remuneration rate, 283, 294–95, 593–94, 595, 596, 893; SDR valuation, 284–85

U

V

W

Index to Publications Cited

Numbers refer to pages. The publication is usually cited in a footnote. The list is also intended to serve as a guide to the short titles that have been used in this History for publications frequently cited. For a description of the publications issued by the Fund in the years 1972–78, see Chapter 49, pages 946–53, of this History.

A

Alexander, Sidney S. "Effects of a Devaluation on a Trade Balance," *Staff Papers*, Vol. 2 (April 1952), pp. 263–78: 93

Allen, Mark. "The Multilateral Trade Negotiations—A Background Note," *Finance & Development* (Washington), Vol. 16 (September 1979), pp. 21–23: 960

Amuzegar, Jahangir. "The North-South Dialogue: From Conflict to Compromise," *Foreign Affairs* (New York), Vol. 54 (April 1976), pp. 547–62: 760

Andreotti, Giulio. *Diari, 1976–1979: gli anni della solidarietà* (Milan: Rizzoli, 1981): 453, 454, 456

Annual Report, 19—: see International Monetary Fund, *Annual Report of the Executive Directors . . .*

Argy, Victor, and Zoran Hodjera. "Financial Integration and Interest Rate Linkages in the Industrial Countries," *Staff Papers*, Vol. 20 (March 1973), pp. 1–77: 824

Artus, Jacques R. "Exchange Rate Stability and Managed Floating: The Experience of the Federal Republic of Germany," *Staff Papers*, Vol. 23 (July 1976), pp. 312–33: 825

———, and Andrew D. Crockett. *Floating Exchange Rates and the Need for Surveillance*, Essays in International Finance, No. 127, Princeton University (Princeton, New Jersey: Princeton University Press, 1978): 845

———, and Anne Kenny McGuirk. "A Revised Version of the Multilateral Exchange Rate Model," *Staff Papers*, Vol. 28 (June 1981), pp. 275–309: 810

———, and Rudolf R. Rhomberg. "A Multilateral Exchange Rate Model," *Staff Papers*, Vol. 20 (November 1973), pp. 591–611: 810

———, and John H. Young. "Fixed and Flexible Exchange Rates: A Renewal of the Debate," *Staff Papers*, Vol. 26 (December 1979), pp. 654–98: 835

B

The Balance of Payments Adjustment Process in Developing Countries: Report to the Group of Twenty-Four, UNDP/UNCTAD Project INT/75/015 (New York, January 1979): 491

Balogh, Thomas. "The International Aspects of Full Employment," in his *The Economics of Full Employment* (Oxford: Basil Blackwell, 1946): 90

———. "The United States and International Economic Equilibrium," in Seymour E. Harris, ed., *Foreign Economic Policy for the United States* (Cambridge, Mass.: Harvard University Press, 1948), pp. 446–80: 90

Bank for International Settlements. *Forty-Second Annual Report, April 1, 1971–March 31, 1972* (Basle, 1972): 108

Behrens, William W. III. *See* Meadows, Donella, Dennis L. Meadows, Jørgen Randers, and William W. Behrens III

Bell, Philip W. *The Sterling Area in the Postwar World: Internal Mechanism and Cohesian, 1946–1952* (Oxford: Clarendon Press, 1956): 54

Bennett, Jack F. Remarks before National Economists Club, Washington, D.C., December 17, 1974, in U.S. Treasury Department, *News* (WS-185), December 17, 1974, p. 8: 663

Bergsten, C. Fred. *The Dilemmas of the Dollar: The Economics and Politics of United States International Monetary Policy* (New York: New York University Press, 1975): 111

———. "The New Economics and U.S. Foreign Policy," *Foreign Affairs* (New York), Vol. 50 (January 1972), pp. 199–222: 111

Bernstein, Edward M. "The History of the International Monetary Fund, 1966–71," *Finance & Development* (Washington), Vol. 14 (December 1977), p. 17: 87

———. "The New International Monetary System," in Edward M. Bernstein et al., *Reflections on Jamaica*, Essays in International Finance, No. 115, Princeton University (Princeton, New Jersey: Princeton University Press, 1976), pp. 1–8: 760

———. "Strategic Factors in Balance of Payments Adjustment," *Staff Papers*, Vol. 5 (August 1956), pp. 151–69: 93

Beveridge, W.A., and Margaret R. Kelly. "Fiscal Content of Financial Programs Supported by Stand-By Arrangements in the Upper Credit Tranches, 1969–78," *Staff Papers*, Vol. 27 (June 1980), pp. 205–49: 486

Bhagwati, Jagdish N., ed. *The New International Economic Order: The North-South Debate* (Cambridge, Mass.: MIT Press, 1977): 201

Bilson, John F.O. "The Monetary Approach to the Exchange Rate: Some Empirical Evidence," *Staff Papers*, Vol. 25 (March 1978), pp. 48–75: 825

———. "Rational Expectations and the Exchange Rate," in Jacob A. Frenkel and Harry G. Johnson,

Goldstein, Morris. *Have Flexible Exchange Rates Handicapped Macroeconomic Policy?* Special Papers in International Economics, No. 14 (Princeton, New Jersey: Princeton University Press, 1980): 835

———. "Whither the Exchange Rate System?" *Finance & Development* (Washington), Vol. 21 (June 1984), pp. 2–6: 835

———, and John H. Young. "Exchange Rate Policy: Some Current Issues," *Finance & Development* (Washington), Vol. 16 (March 1979), pp. 7–10: 828

Goreaux, Louis M. *Compensatory Financing Facility*, IMF Pamphlet Series, No. 34 (Washington: International Monetary Fund, 1980): 414

———. "Compensatory Financing: The Cyclical Pattern of Export Shortfalls," *Staff Papers*, Vol. 24 (November 1977), pp. 613–41: 413

———. "Recovery of Commodity Prices Is Expected to Slow Compensatory Drawings This Year," *IMF Survey* (Washington), Vol. 6 (March 7, 1977), pp. 66–69: 413–14

———. "The Use of Compensatory Financing," *Finance & Development* (Washington), Vol. 14 (September 1977), pp. 20–24: 413

Group of Ten. Communiqué of the Ministers and Governors, December 18, 1971, *International Financial News Survey* (Washington: International Monetary Fund), Vol. 23 (December 22–30, 1971), p. 418: 19.

———. Communiqué of the Ministers and Central Bank Governors, *IMF Survey* (Washington), Vol. 4 (January 20, 1975), p. 19: 344

———, and European Economic Community. Joint communiqués, March 9 and 16, 1973: 188

Guindey, Guillaume. *The International Monetary Tangle: Myths and Realities*, trans. by Michael L. Hoffman (White Plains, New York: M.E. Sharpe, Inc., 1977): 171

Guitian, Manuel. *Fund Conditionality: Evolution of Principles and Practices*, IMF Pamphlet Series, No. 38 (Washington: International Monetary Fund, 1981): 485

———, and Carl-Johan Lindgren. "Mexico's Adjustment Program Shows Success in Reducing Inflation Rate, Payments' Deficit," *IMF Survey* (Washington), Vol. 7 (April 17, 1978), pp. 119–21: 380

Gupta, Dhruba. *See* Cutler, David S., and Dhruba Gupta

H

Haberler, Gottfried. *Currency Convertibility* (Washington: American Enterprise Association, Inc., 1954): 101

———. "The International Monetary System after Jamaica and Manila," *Weltwirtschaftliches Archiv: Review of World Economics* (Kiel), Vol. 113 (No. 1, 1977), pp. 1–30: 760

———. *Money in the International Economy* (London: Institute of Economic Affairs, 2nd ed., 1969): 115

———. *The Theory of International Trade with Its Applications to Commercial Policy* (New York: Macmillan, 1937): 830

———. *The World Economy, Money, and the Great Depression, 1919–1939*, Foreign Affairs Study, 30 (Washington: American Enterprise Institute for Public Policy Research, 1976): 102

———. *See also* Dreyer, Jacob S., Gottfried Haberler, and Thomas D. Willett, eds.

Habermeier, Walter O. *Operations and Transactions in SDRs: The First Basic Period*, IMF Pamphlet Series, No. 17 (Washington: International Monetary Fund, 1973): 896

———. "The SDR as an International Unit of Account, *Finance & Development* (Washington), Vol. 16 (March 1979), pp. 11–13: 900

Halm, George N., ed. *Approaches to Greater Flexibility of Exchange Rates: The Bürgenstock Papers* (Princeton, New Jersey: Princeton University Press, 1970): 102

———. *Jamaica and the Par-Value System*, Essays in International Finance, No. 120, Princeton University (Princeton, New Jersey: Princeton University Press, 1977): 760

Hansard. House of Lords (London), 5th Series, Vol. 131, Cols. 838–49: 86

Heller, H. Robert. "International Reserves and World-Wide Inflation," *Staff Papers*, Vol. 23 (March 1976), pp. 61–87: 393

Hewson, John, and Eisuke Sakakibara. "The Euro-Dollar Deposit Multiplier: A Portfolio Approach," *Staff Papers*, Vol. 21 (July 1974), pp. 307–28: 933

———. "The Impact of U.S. Controls on Capital Outflows on the U.S. Balance of Payments: An Exploratory Study," *Staff Papers*, Vol. 22 (March 1975), pp. 37–60: 215

Higgins, Ilse. *See* Hirsch, Fred, and Ilse Higgins

Hillman, John R. "The Mutual Influence of Italian Domestic Politics and the International Monetary Fund," *Fletcher Forum* (Medford, Mass., Winter 1980), pp. 1–22: 459

Hirsch, Fred. "The Exchange Rate Regime: An Analysis and a Possible Scheme," *Staff Papers*, Vol. 19 (July 1972), pp. 259–85: 125

———. "SDRs and the Working of the Gold Exchange Standard," *Staff Papers*, Vol. 18 (July 1971), pp. 221–53: 117

———, and Ilse Higgins. "An Indicator of Effective Exchange Rates," *Staff Papers*, Vol. 17 (November 1970), pp. 453–84: 810

History, 1945–65
The International Monetary Fund, 1945–1965: Twenty Years of International Monetary Cooperation (Washington: International Monetary Fund, 1969). **Vol. I,** *Chronicle*, by J. Keith Horsefield: 3, 15, 27, 37, 52, 54, 85, 86, 88, 92, 358, 482, 483, 513, 514, 515, 526, 560, 587, 607, 647, 724, 765, 873, 939, 950, 967, 994, 1042; **Vol. II,** *Analysis*, by Margaret G. de Vries and J. Keith Horsefield with the collaboration of Joseph Gold, Mary H. Gumbert, Gertrud Lovasy, and Emil G. Spitzer and edited by J. Keith Horsefield: 3, 27, 52, 54, 57, 88, 92, 146, 200, 327, 358, 399, 406, 482, 483, 484, 485, 513, 514, 560, 575, 587, 598, 599, 607, 647, 654, 697, 704, 762, 835, 837, 841, 868, 958, 963, 1035; **Vol. III,** *Documents*, edited by J. Keith Horsefield: 3, 89, 145, 200, 292, 482, 483, 568

T

U

V

W

Y